MICHIGAN
Law and Practice

Encyclopedia

SECOND EDITION

Based on Michigan Statutes; Case Law,
State and Federal; Law Reviews

VOLUME 26

REAL PROPERTY §§ 401 to end

CITE AS
M.L.P.2d Real Property § 401

Editorial Offices
121 Chanlon Rd., New Providence, NJ 07974 (908) 464-6800
201 Mission St., San Francisco, CA 94105-1831 (415) 908-3200
www.lexisnexis.com

MATTHEW◆BENDER

MICHIGAN LAW AND PRACTICE ENCYCLOPEDIA, SECOND EDITION is designed to enable Michigan judges, lawyers, and other legal professionals to conduct their research with maximum efficiency and minimal effort.

Michigan Law and Practice Encyclopedia, Second Edition (cited M.L.P.2d) gives the Bench and Bar of Michigan quick access to the law in a useful text-and-footnote format. The text explains the law concisely while reservations, exceptions to, and illustrations of the leading principles are footnoted. Citations and cross-references point out secondary authorities that can be consulted for further research.

Prepared by Experienced Editors. The value of any such work depends primarily on the care and skill with which information is condensed and arranged so as to provide a complete, intuitive research tool. M.L.P.2d represents the combined efforts of expert legal analysts and editors on the staff of LexisNexis, a company at the forefront of the legal information industry with over 150 years of editorial tradition.

Based on Michigan Statutes and Cases. M.L.P.2d sets forth the law of Michigan, compiled from the reported cases and statutes of Michigan, as well as United States Supreme Court cases and opinions of federal courts construing Michigan law. It presents the rules of Michigan law and their exceptions, qualifications, limitations, and extensions, in concise but comprehensive text.

Factual Applications of the Law. M.L.P.2d presents the "black-letter" law that practitioners and other researchers need, but it is not a mere statement of the fundamental rules. The work also consists of the application of legal rules to the varying facts of litigated cases. These factual illustrations of the law are presented in the text itself, where relevant, as well as in the footnotes.

Scope of Title. As an aid in finding the desired section of text, a complete section analysis is provided at the head of each title.

Library References to other useful LexisNexis, Matthew Bender, and Shepard's publications are found at the beginning of each topic and chapter.

Law Reviews. This listing, at the beginning of each topic and chapter, contains topically-relevant law review articles to assist the researcher in identifying pertinent secondary material.

Concise Text Summaries, set out in distinctive type as an introduction to each section, are of great convenience and value in legal research.

An Up-To-Date Index. The freestanding General Index contains the index material for the M.L.P.2d volumes. The Index is revised and expanded annually.

Supplemental Service. M.L.P.2d will be kept current by means of annual cumulative pocket parts, as well as an annual Interim Supplement. These supplements will keep subscribers abreast of recent cases and other new developments in Michigan law.

ABBREVIATIONS

Ave Maria L. Rev.	Ave Maria Law Review
Black	Black's Reports, U.S.
B.R.	United States Bankruptcy Court
C.C.A.	United States Circuit Court of Appeals Reports
Cranch	Cranch's Reports, U.S.
Dall.	Dallas' Reports, U.S.
Det. B.Q.	Detroit Bar Quarterly
Det. C.L. Rev.	Detroit College of Law Review (1975 -1998)
F	Federal Reporter
F.2d	Federal Reporter, Second Series
F.3d	Federal Reporter, Third Series
Fed. Cas. No.	Federal Cases
F.R.D.	Federal Rules Decisions
F. Supp.	Federal Supplement
F. Supp. 2d	Federal Supplement, Second Series
How.	Howard's Reports, U.S.
L. Ed. 2d	U.S. Supreme Court Cases, Lawyers' Edition
L. Rev M.S.U.-D.C.L.	Law Review of Michigan State University Detroit College of Law (1999 -2003)
MCLS	Michigan Compiled Laws Service
MCR	Michigan Court Rules
Mich.	Michigan Reports
Mich. App	Michigan Appeals Reports
Mich. B.J.	Michigan Bar Journal
Mich. J. Gender & L.	Michigan Journal of Gender & Law
Mich. J. Race & L.	Michigan Journal of Race & Law
Mich. L. Rev.	Michigan Law Review
Mich. St. DCL L. Rev.	Michigan State DCL Law Review (2003)
Mich. St. L. Rev.	Michigan State Law Review (2003 -Present)
MRE	Michigan Rules of Evidence
N.W.	North Western Reporter
N.W.2d	North Western Reporter, Second Series
Op. Atty. Gen	Attorney General Opinions
Pet	Peter's Reports, U.S.
S. Ct.	Supreme Court Reporter
T.M. Cooley L. Rev.	Thomas M. Cooley Law Review
U. Det. L.J.	University of Detroit Law Journal

TITLES IN VOLUME

REAL PROPERTY

CHAPTER 19. RIGHTS AND LIABILITIES OF PARTIES.

CHAPTER 22. EXCHANGE OF PROPERTY.

CHAPTER 23. NATURE AND VALIDITY OF MORTGAGES.

A. THE NATURE OF MORTGAGES.

B. THE VALIDITY OF MORTGAGES.

CHAPTER 31. FORECLOSURE BY EXERCISE OF POWER OF SALE.

CHAPTER 32. FORECLOSURE OF MORTGAGES AND LAND CONTRACTS BY SUIT.

A. IN GENERAL.

Chapter 13

NATURE AND INCIDENTS OF SALE OF REAL PROPERTY

A.   THE NATURE OF SALES OF REAL PROPERTY

§ 401.   Definitions

A vendor is the seller in a sale or contract of sale of real property. A vendee is the buyer in a sale or contract of sale of real property. A sale, as the term is used with respect to land, is a parting with one's interest in the land for a valuable consideration.

Library References

> Michigan Digest
> John G. Cameron, Jr., Michigan Real Estate Forms
> LexisNexis® Automated Michigan SCAO Forms
> Thompson on Real Property, Thomas Edition (David A. Thomas, ed.)
> Powell on Real Property® (Michael Allan Wolf, ed.)
> Purchase and Sale of Real Property (Karl B. Holtzschue, ed.)

Law Reviews

> John A. Taylor, Commercial and Contract Law, 54 Wayne L. Rev. 85 (2008); Kelli P. Murphy, Michigan Business Tax Apportionment and Sales Sourcing Provisions, 53 Wayne L. Rev. 1395 (2007); Gregg A. Nathanson, What's New in Residential Transactions, 86 MI Bar Jnl. 16 (2007); Michael A. Luberto, Title Insurance for the General Practitioner: Some Insider Tips, 86 MI Bar Jnl. 28 (2007); Jeffrey A. Cojocar, "As Is" Clauses: The Law Behind "As Is" Clauses in Residential Real Estate Transactions, 84 Mich. B.J. 35 (2005); Michael Hauser, The Tax Treatment of Intangibles in Acquisitions of Residential Rental Real Estate, 49 Wayne L. Rev. 1051 (2004).

A "sale" is applied to a "transaction under a land contract as well as to a conveyance by deed for a consideration."[1]

In Michigan, a "sale" in connection with real property is a parting with one's interest in the real property for a valuable consideration.[2] There may be a transfer or change of title without a sale.[3] But in every sale there is a transfer or change of title from the vendor to the vendee.[4]

A "vendor" is the "seller in a sale or contract of sale of real property."[5] A "vendee" is the "buyer in a sale or contract of sale of real property."[6] The term "purchaser" as employed in the statute relative to conveyances of real property, "embraces every person to whom any estate or interest in real estate, shall be conveyed for a valuable consideration, and also every assignee of a mortgage, or

---

1. Ballentine's Law Dictionary at 1133 (3d ed. 1969).

2. Steadman v. Clemens, 321 Mich. 54, 32 N.W.2d 45 (1948).

3. Western Massachusetts Ins. Co. v. Riker, 10 Mich. 279 (1862).

4. Steadman v. Clemens, 321 Mich. 54, 32 N.W.2d 45 (1948).

Essence of sale

A transfer of title for a consideration is the essence of a sale.—Berry v. Kavanagh, 137 F.2d 574 (6th Cir. Mich. 1943).

5. Ballentine's Law Dictionary at 1335 (3d ed. 1969).

6. Ballentine's Law Dictionary at 1335 (3d ed. 1969).

lease, or other conditional estate."[7]

§ 402. Distinctions

The relationship of vendor and vendee has been distinguished from other relationships, such as those arising from agency or assignment, or landlord and tenant.

The relationship of vendor and vendee has been distinguished from that arising from an agency[8] or assignment.[9] It has also been distinguished from the relationship of landlord and tenant.[10]

On the other hand, where the essentials of a sale are present, and the relationship of the parties is clearly that of vendor and vendee, the transaction will be construed as a sale.[11]

B.   POWERS OF APPOINTMENT

§ 411. Powers of Appointment

A power of appointment is an authority enabling one person to dispose of an interest that is vested in another person.

A power of appointment is an authority enabling one person to dispose of an interest that is vested in another person.[12]

The Powers of Appointment Act of 1967[13] applies to powers whether created before or after its adoption.[14] The act preserves the common law that is not in conflict with the act or with another statute.[15]

Powers of sale in real estate mortgages, land contract mortgages, and trust

---

7. MCLS § 565.34.

Mortgage

Defendant's mortgage constitutes a "conveyance" under MCLS § 565.29 because under the statute, that term is construed to encompass "every instrument in writing, by which any estate or interest in real estate is created, aliened, mortgaged or assigned.—Bank of N.Y. v. Fifth Third Bank, 2009 Mich. App. LEXIS 1049 (Mich. Ct. App. May 14, 2009).

8. Berry v. Kavanagh, 137 F.2d 574 (6th Cir. Mich. 1943) (essence of "agency to sell" is delivery of property to agent as property of principal who remains owner and has right to control such sale, fix prices and terms, and receive proceeds less agent's commission upon sales made).

Greenough v. Willcox, 238 Mich. 52, 213 N.W. 175 (1927) (option will be construed as creating agency relation, if circumstances show an intent to do so).

9. Turney v. Combination Brick Co., 184 Mich. 439, 151 N.W. 590 (1915) (writing was held to be

assignment of contract to convey, and not absolute assignment of vendor's title and interest in land sufficient to pass title to party designated by purchaser).

10. Smith v. Detroit Loan & Bldg. Ass'n, 121 Mich. 104, 79 N.W. 1097 (1899).

Unambiguous agreement

Agreement was held to be unambiguous, merely providing for stipulated rental and not contract of sale and purchase.—Hickey v. Lundy, 168 Mich. 336, 134 N.W. 4 (1912).

11. Garvey v. Parkhurst, 127 Mich. 368, 86 N.W. 802 (1901) (correspondence constituted contract of sale, and not mere license).

12. Ballentine's Law Dictionary at 971 (3rd ed. 1969).

13. MCLS §§ 556.111 et seq.

14. MCLS § 556.132.

15. MCLS § 556.129.

deeds are discussed elsewhere.[16] Powers in trusts,[17] powers granted to mere agents or attorneys by letters of attorney or otherwise,[18] and the validity and construction of particular instruments reserving or granting powers,[19] are also covered elsewhere.

§ 412.   Creation of Powers

A power may be a power of appointment over any legal or equitable interest in real or personal property, including choses in action.

A power may be a power of appointment over any legal or equitable interest in real or personal property, including choses in action.[20] The rules that apply to powers affecting realty also apply to powers concerning personalty.[21] A power may be created by deed, will, trust agreement, or other writing or document that creates or reserves the power.[22] However, the instrument must be executed in the manner required by law for that instrument.[23]

Powers are classified as general or special. A "general power" is one exercisable in favor of the recipient of the power or the estate, creditors, or creditors of the estate of the recipient, whether or not it is exercisable in favor of others. A power to appoint to any person or a power that is not expressly restricted concerning the person to whom the exercise of the power transfers the interest in property is general.[24] On the other hand, a "special power" is one exercisable only in favor of one or more persons, not including the recipient or the estate, creditors, or creditors of the estate of the recipient.[25] A power may be general as to some property and special as to other property.[26]

The creator of a power must be a person capable of transferring the interest in property to which the power relates and having a transferable interest in that property.[27]

§ 413.   Revocation and Release

Generally, the creation of a power is irrevocable, unless the creating instrument reserves the power to revoke it.

The creation of a power is irrevocable unless the creating instrument reserves

16. See infra Chapters 31, 32.

17. *See* M.L.P.2d Trusts.

18. *See* M.L.P.2d Agency.

19. *See* M.L.P.2d Deeds, M.L.P.2d Trusts, and M.L.P.2d Wills and Estate Administration.

20. MCLS § 556.112.

Annual Survey of Michigan Law; June 1, 2004 - May 31, 2005: Trusts And Estates, 52 Wayne L. Rev. 1019 (2006).

21. Townsend v. Gordon, 308 Mich. 438, 14 N.W.2d 57 (1944).

Smith v. Cigar Makers' International Union, 203 Mich. 249, 168 N.W. 954 (1918).

Holmes v. Hall, 8 Mich. 66 (1860).

22. MCLS § 556.112.

23. MCLS § 556.113.

24. MCLS § 556.112.

Paine v. Kaufman (In re Estate of Reisman), 266 Mich. App. 522, 702 N.W.2d 658 (2005).

25. MCLS § 556.112.

Paine v. Kaufman (In re Estate of Reisman), 266 Mich. App. 522, 702 N.W.2d 658 (2005).

26. MCLS § 556.112.

27. MCLS § 556.113.

the power to revoke it.[28] There is a distinction between powers generally and powers coupled with an interest, and the latter have been deemed irrevocable[29] and to survive the donor.[30]

Generally, any power may be released. But the creating instrument may expressly provide that a power cannot be released or expressly restrict the time, manner or scope of release. Furthermore, a power that is not presently exercisable or is exercisable by a trustee or other fiduciary in a fiduciary capacity that requires the exercise of the power cannot be released.[31]

A release may limit in any respect the extent or manner in which the power may be exercised. If releasable, it may be released in whole or in part, and a release may be effected with or without consideration by a written instrument signed by the recipient of the power and delivered by one of the enumerated methods.[32]

A release of any part of a power may not be revoked unless the release instrument provides for the revocation of the release.[33]

§ 414. Rights of Third Persons

A purchaser without actual notice of the power who pays valuable consideration for any legal or equitable interest in the property takes the interest free of any rights that the donee's estate or a creditor of the donee might have under the power.

A purchaser without actual notice of the power who pays valuable consideration for any legal or equitable interest in the property takes the interest free of any rights that the donee's estate or a creditor of the donee might have under the power.[34]

If the recipient of a power has a general power, any interest that the recipient has power to appoint or has appointed is to be treated as the recipient's property for satisfying the claims of his or her creditors. If the power is unexercised, it may be reached to the extent that the donee's individual assets are insufficient to satisfy the claim. But if the power has been exercised, it can be reached to the same extent that under the law relating to fraudulent conveyances, the creditor could reach property that the recipient has owned and transferred. A general assignee for the benefit of creditors has the standing of a creditor.[35] If the donee, at the time of death, has a general power, exercised or not, his or her legal representatives may reach on behalf of creditors any interest that the donee could have appointed to the extent that the claim of a creditor has been filed and allowed in the recipient's estate but not paid because the assets of the estate are insufficient.[36]

If more than one person is a donee, it is presumed that the interest subject to

28. MCLS § 556.119.

29. Ecclestone v. Indialantic, Inc., 319 Mich. 248, 29 N.W.2d 679 (1947).

30. Kimmel v. Hammond, 352 Mich. 625, 90 N.W.2d 681 (1958).

31. MCLS § 556.118.

32. MCLS § 556.118.

33. MCLS § 556.119.

34. MCLS § 556.123.

35. MCLS § 556.123.

36. MCLS § 556.123.

the power is equally owned among them unless the creating instrument indicates otherwise.[37]

When the grantor in a conveyance reserves an unqualified power of revocation, the grantor is thereafter still the absolute owner of the estate conveyed, so far as the rights of his or her creditors and purchasers are concerned. If that grantor dies without exercising the power, the estate of the power remains part of the deceased grantor's estate in respect to the rights of his or her creditors.[38]

§ 415.   Execution

Generally, a power must be exercised by a written instrument executed by a donee with the power to transfer the right or interest in real property.

Any donee capable of transferring the interest in property to which the power relates may exercise a power. The exercise of a power requires the execution of a written instrument necessary for the owner of the property to transfer the interest to be transferred.[39] The exercise of a power of appointment is controlled by the law in effect at the time of exercise rather than the law in effect at the creation of the power.[40]

Unless otherwise contemplated in the creating instrument, a power may be exercised only by a written instrument that complies with any requirements of the creating instrument. However, a power exercisable only by deed is always exercisable by a proper written will.[41] If the donor has authorized the power to be exercised by an instrument not sufficient to pass the interest, the power is not void, but may be exercised by an instrument that conforms to the donor's direction and is also sufficient to transfer the interest under the law.[42]

When a power is vested in two or more persons, all must unite in its

---

37. MCLS § 556.123.

38. MCLS § 556.128.

39. MCLS § 556.115.

Proper exercise of special power through trust

Where a wife's revocable living trust created a marital trust at her death, which in turn granted her husband a "limited power of appointment" over the assets in the marital trust, with the limitations that (1) the husband could only distribute the assets to the wife's children and descendants, (2) the power could only be exercised in the husband's will, and (3) the exercise of the power must specifically refer to the grant of power, the husband's exercise of the power in a codicil to his will so as to transfer the assets to the trustee of his revocable trust with instructions to distribute the assets to the wife's children and descendants was a valid exercise of the power; the husband's exercise of his power effectively stripped the trustee of any authority to use the assets for anything other than distribution to the wife's children and descendants, and meant that the husband's exercise of his power through his trust did not benefit his estate or creditors and that the assets were not available to pay trust expenses.—Paine v. Kaufman (In re Estate of Reisman), 266 Mich. App. 522, 702 N.W.2d 658 (2005).

40. Hund v. Holmes, 395 Mich. 188, 235 N.W.2d 331 (1975).

41. MCLS § 556.115.

Execution by will

Testator's statement of purpose in will of making disposition of entire estate and any estate that she might have power to dispose of, and residuary bequest giving "any estate which I may have the power to dispose of," demonstrated, unequivocally intention to exercise power of appointment left to testator by her husband and no issue was presented for jury as to whether testator intended to exercise power of appointment.—In re Estate of Willey, 9 Mich. App. 245, 156 N.W.2d 631 (1967).

42. MCLS § 556.115.

exercise.[43] If one or more donee dies, becomes incapable of exercising the power, or releases the power, the power may be exercised by the others, unless the creating instrument manifests the contrary intent.[44]

Unless otherwise provided in the creating instrument, an instrument manifests an intent to exercise the power if it purports to transfer an interest in the appointed property that the recipient has no power to transfer except by virtue of the power, even though the power is not recited or referred to in the instrument. The instrument may also manifest that intent either expressly or by necessary implication from its wording interpreted in light of the circumstances surrounding its drafting and execution. Subject to the foregoing, a residuary clause or other general language in the donee's will purporting to dispose of all the donee's estate of property is sufficient to exercise the power only if it is a general power exercisable by will with no express gift in default specified in the instrument creating the power.[45]

The exercise of a power is irrevocable unless the instrument exercising the power reserves the right to revoke the exercise.[46]

Consent requirement. The donor or other person whose consent is specified for the exercise of a power must execute an instrument to that effect. Unless the instrument creating the power manifests intent otherwise, the power may be exercised with the express intent of a deceased person whose consent is required under the instrument creating the power.[47] The exercise of a power without satisfying the requirement of consent upon which exercise is conditioned is void.[48]

Contract to appoint. Generally, the recipient of a power presently exercisable can contract to appoint if neither the contract nor the promised appointment confers a benefit upon anyone who is not a permissible appointee. The donee of a power not presently exercisable cannot make this type of contract. The promisee of a recipient who contracts to appoint a power not presently exercisable is limited to damages equal to the value given for the promise.[49]

Failure to appoint. In case of a lack of effective exercise, or total release, the interest involved passes according to the direction of the creating instrument, if any.[50] If the creating instrument contains no express gift in default and does not clearly indicate that the permissible appointees are to take only if the donee

43. MCLS § 556.115.

Shaw v. Canfield, 86 Mich. 1, 48 N.W. 873 (1891).

Rock River Paper Co. v. Fisk, 47 Mich. 212, 10 N.W. 344 (1881).

44. MCLS § 556.115.

45. MCLS § 556.114.

Intent of will

Statutory rules of construction in effect at time of her death rather than at time of execution of her will control determination of whether or not general language of residuary clause in will manifested intent by testator to exercise power of appointment conferred upon her by donor who provided for express gift in default of exercise of

power.—Hund v. Holmes, 395 Mich. 188, 235 N.W.2d 331 (1975).

46. MCLS § 556.119.

47. MCLS § 556.115.

48. Limitation of power

Where testator devised land to his wife for life, with power, "under the direction of the judge of probate," to sell so much as would be sufficient to support her for life, sale by wife without approval of the judge was void, since provision of approval was not merely nominal condition, but was limitation of power to sell, and a special guard for protection of remainderpersons.—Bates v. Leonard, 99 Mich. 296, 58 N.W. 311 (1894).

49. MCLS § 556.120.

50. MCLS § 556.122.

exercises the power, the property passes equally to the permissible appointees living at the time of termination or release of the power. If the power is to appoint among a class, then it passes to those persons with the closest degree of kinship by way of representation who would take under an express appointment to the described class effective as of the termination or release.[51]

If the creating instrument contains no express gift in default and clearly indicates that the permissible appointees are to take only if the recipient exercises the power, the property passes by reversion to the creator of the power or his or her estate. But if the creating instrument expressly states that there is no reversion, any language in the creating instrument indicating or stating that the permissible appointees are to take only if the donee exercises the powers is to be disregarded, and the interest passes to permissible donees.[52]

C.   ABSTRACTS OF TITLE

§ 421.   Definition

An abstract of title is a short account of the state of the title to real estate, or a synopsis of the instruments which show title—an epitome of the record evidence of title.

An "abstract of title" is a "short account of the state of the title to real estate, or a synopsis of the instruments which show title—an epitome of the record evidence of title."[53]

The registration and recording of titles to land are discussed elsewhere,[54] as are aspects of title insurance[55] and the admissibility in evidence of abstracts of title.[56]

Proceedings to recreate public records of lands are also treated elsewhere.[57]

§ 422.   Who May Make Abstracts

A county board of supervisors may provide for an abstractor. The business of abstracting may also be carried on by private persons and corporations.

The Legislature has made it possible for certain individual counties[58] to establish and maintain a system of abstracts of title to all lands within their boundaries.[59] The board of supervisors of an eligible county "may provide that the register of deeds shall be the abstractor, or may provide for the appointment or employment of a superintendent or abstractor who shall perform his duties under the supervision of such officer or officers of the county as shall be designated in such ordinance or resolution. The compensation for exercising the functions and

51. MCLS § 556.122.

52. MCLS § 556.122.

53. Ballentine's Law Dictionary at 8 (3d ed. 1969).

54. M.L.P.2d Deeds.

55. M.L.P.2d Insurance.

56. M.L.P.2d Evidence.

57. M.L.P.2d Records.

58. MCLS § 53.151.

59. MCLS § 53.141.

performing the duties aforesaid shall be fixed in advance of the election, appointment or employment."[60]

The business of abstracting titles may also be carried on by private persons and corporations.[61] The right of a maker of abstracts of title to have access to files and records pertaining to real estate in the county clerk's office, to enable him or her to make abstracts to use in the business, does not depend on the privileges that the register may choose to permit others to enjoy, but is measured by the law. It cannot be diminished for the benefit of others, nor increased by reason of indulgence to others. A person whose business requires much examination has no greater rights than one whose interests require but little.[62]

A county register of deeds must "furnish proper and reasonable facilities for the inspection and examination of the records and files in his or her office, and for making memorandums or transcripts from the records and files during the usual business hours, to an individual having a lawful purpose to examine the records and files."[63] The register may regulate access to the records to protect them and to prevent interference with the duties of the register. But upon receiving a request for the reproduction of a document, the register of deeds must either reproduce it in accordance with the Records Reproduction Act[64] at cost or at a fee provided by law, provide equipment for the individual to use to reproduce the document, or allow the individual to reproduce the document on his or her own equipment in the register's office.[65] A register of deeds may prohibit the reproduction of an instrument

60. MCLS § 53.144.

61. Beckovsky v. Burton Abstract & Title Co., 208 Mich. 224, 175 N.W. 235 (1919).

Day v. Button, 96 Mich. 600, 56 N.W. 3 (1893).

Burton v. Tuite, 78 Mich. 363, 44 N.W. 282 (1889).

Alpena Title, Inc. v. Alpena County, 84 Mich. App. 308, 269 N.W.2d 578 (1978).

62. Burton v. Reynolds, 102 Mich. 55, 60 N.W. 452 (1894).

Alpena Title, Inc. v. Alpena County, 84 Mich. App. 308, 269 N.W.2d 578 (1978) (register may set wholesale prices for abstractors).

63. MCLS § 565.551.

64. MCLS §§ 24.401 et seq.

No right to microfilmed records

The Freedom of Information Act (FOIA) does not require a county register of deeds to provide copies of records in a microfilm format rather than in the form of a paper copy, and even if there was such a requirement under FOIA, it would be overridden by the provision of the Inspection of Records Act granting the register of deeds authority to reproduce records "using a medium selected by the register of deeds" (MCLS §§ 15.233(1), 565.551(2)(a)).—Lapeer County Abstract & Title Co. v. Lapeer County Register of Deeds, 264 Mich. App. 167, 691 N.W.2d 11 (2004).

Annual Survey of Michigan Law; June 1, 2004 - May 31, 2005: Administrative Law, 52 Wayne L. Rev. 305 (2006).

65. MCLS § 565.551.

See, also, MCLS § 15.233 (Freedom of Information Act).

Alpena Title, Inc. v. Alpena County, 84 Mich. App. 308, 269 N.W.2d 578 (1978) (register may set wholesale prices for abstractors).

Abstractor's fee is not required

Under this section, whether the register of deeds charges abstractors a fee for photocopying records is discretionary and there is no clear legal duty to collect fees.—Burton Abstract & Title Co. v. Martin, 38 Mich. App. 178, 196 N.W.2d 23 (1972).

Amendment of statute in 1992

Whether plaintiff may recover statutory copying fees for copies made before the effective date of the 1992 amendment to MCLS § 565.551. Plaintiffs argue on appeal that the 1992 amendment should be applied retroactively because it was remedial in nature and affected no substantive rights. Plaintiffs further argue that the sole effect of the 1992 amendment was the addition of different acceptable technologies beyond photography for use in creating copies. Plaintiffs sought recovery of statutory copy fees for copies made between August 19, 1991, the date of the trial court

temporarily left with the register of deeds to be recorded in the register of deeds' office.[66]

Under the Freedom of Information Act, a person may subscribe to receive copies of new public records as they are created, issued, or disseminated.[67]

§ 423.   Form and Contents

An abstract of title should contain a full summary of all grants, conveyances, wills and all records and judicial proceedings whereby the title is in any way affected, and all encumbrances and liens of record, showing whether they have been released or not.

An abstract of title "should contain a full summary of all grants, conveyances, wills and all records and judicial proceedings whereby the title is in any way

decision allowing defendant to keep its photocopier in the registrar's office, and June 26, 1992, the effective date of 1992 PA 112. The court's reading of the plain statutory language convinced it that the only change achieved by the 1992 amendment was the permitted use of technologies other than photography for reproduction of records. Both before and after 1992, MCLS § 565.551 required the register of deeds to permit some type of reproduction of files and records. Yet, both versions of the statute are silent regarding who may reproduce the records and whether a fee can be charged for the copy. Nevertheless, the issue of fees is governed by MCLS § 600.2567. At all relevant times, that statute allowed the register of deeds to charge $ 1 per page for copies of records or papers.—Tuscola County Bd. of Comm'rs & Tuscola County Register of Deeds v. Tuscola County Abstract Co., 2001 Mich. App. Lexis 260 (Mich. Ct. App. Dec. 11, 2001).

Conditioned sales in bulk or of microfilmed records

In light of the constitutional provision that statutes concerning counties must be liberally construed in the counties' favor, a county register of deeds had authority to condition the bulk sale of copies of records at a reduced rate or the sale of microfilmed copies on a party agreeing to a contract that included a restriction against the party's providing copies of the records to third parties; statutes providing the register of deeds with such authority included (1) the Inspection of Records Act, which does not preclude such a contract, (2) the Revised Judicature Act, which provides that a register of deeds "is entitled" to a fee of "$1.00 per page" for "copies of any records or papers," and (3) the statute granting counties the authority "to make all necessary contracts" (Mich. Const., art. VII, § 34; MCLS §§ 565.551, 600.2567(1)(b), 45.3).—Lapeer County Abstract & Title Co. v. Lapeer County Register of Deeds, 264 Mich. App. 167, 691 N.W.2d 11 (2004).

Copy fee not a tax

A payment made to obtain a copy of a record from a register of deeds office does not constitute a tax, but is essentially a voluntary payment in return for provision of a tangible service; thus, the fee cannot constitute an illegal tax in violation of the requirement of the Headlee Amendment for voter approval (Mich. Const., art. IX, § 31; MCLS §§ 565.551, 600.2567(1)(b)).—Lapeer County Abstract & Title Co. v. Lapeer County Register of Deeds, 264 Mich. App. 167, 691 N.W.2d 11 (2004).

Discretion of register what to charge

Registers of deeds have the discretion to permit parties seeking copies of records maintained in the office of the register of deeds to make their own copies of the records or, in the alternative, to supply those copies for those parties for a fee; because the choice of the matter in which the copies are supplied is left to the discretion of the register of deeds, mandamus does not lie to require a register of deeds to permit a party to make its own copies.—Tuscola County Abstract Co. v. Tuscola County Register of Deeds, 206 Mich. App. 508, 522 N.W.2d 686 (1994).

Register decides options for reproduction of documents by abstractors

It is the function of the registers of deeds, reviewable only by the courts, and not by the county boards of supervisors, to determine what are reasonable and proper facilities for inspection and copying of office records, whether they include the privilege of keeping the abstractors' equipment in the registers' offices while not actually in use for copying records, and to determine the reasonableness of rules relating to the use of such facilities.—Washtenaw Abstract Co. v. Mayer, 347 Mich. 228, 79 N.W.2d 480 (1956).

66. MCLS § 565.551.

67. MCLS § 15.233.

See M.L.P.2d Records.

affected, and all encumbrances and liens of record, showing whether they have been released or not."[68]

Generally, the abstract consists simply of a copy or duplicate of the tract index page or pages. Unless there is some special provision in a particular recorded instrument, a copy of the index entry would in itself make a complete abstract of the documents. Those indices, under appropriate headings, may give the following information as to each conveyance under a section in which the particular parcel of land is described:

Name of grantor;

Name of grantee;

Kind of instrument;

Consideration;

Date of instrument;

Date of recording of instrument;

Liber and page on which instrument is recorded;

Whether or not there is a building restriction; and

Other remarks.[69] In the column for remarks, all unusual provisions and omissions or defects in execution of the instruments are inserted.[70]

It is for the court, and not the jury, to construe an abstract of title.[71]

Purchasers at an executor's sale who are furnished an abstract showing only a life estate in the testator cannot claim a greater title as against the remainderpersons.[72]

§ 424.   Duties and Liabilities of Abstractors

Except as enlarged or restricted by agreement, an abstractor's duty is to make a proper search and examination of the public records, and to set forth in an abstract all the material facts of record that relate to, or may affect, the title under investigation.

Except as enlarged or restricted by agreement, an abstractor's duty is to make a proper search and examination of the public records, and to set forth in an abstract all the material facts of record that relate to, or may affect, the title under investigation.[73]

The undertaking implied by law from engaging in the business of searching

68. Ballentine's Law Dictionary at 8 (3d ed. 1969).

69. Thomas v. Bd. of Supervisors, 214 Mich. 72, 182 N.W. 417, 1921 Mich. LEXIS 852 (1921).

70. Thomas v. Bd. of Supervisors, 214 Mich. 72, 182 N.W. 417, 1921 Mich. LEXIS 852 (1921).

71. Frederick v. Hillebrand, 199 Mich. 333, 165 N.W. 810 (1917).

72. Sprunger v. Ensley, 211 Mich. 103, 178 N.W. 714 (1920).

73. Constructive fraud
Certification of abstract that makes no mention

the public records, examining titles to real estate, and making abstracts of them, is that a person engaged in that business possesses the requisite knowledge and skill, and that he or she will use due and ordinary care and skill in the performance of those duties.[74]

The general rule is that an abstractor is only liable to one with whom he or she contracts.[75] The cause of action arising from the breach of an abstractor's contractual duty is an action in negligent misrepresentation.[76]

However, an abstractor may owe a duty to subsequent purchasers or mortgagees even though they are not in privity to the contract.[77] An exception arises if the abstractor knew that the party would rely on the abstract.[78] The key factor in finding liability outside contractual privity is a party's reliance upon the abstract. The abstractor owes a duty to any party he or she could reasonably foresee as relying on the abstract.[79]

On the other hand, while an action in negligent misrepresentation brought against an abstractor is premised on negligence in title search, the abstractor is not a title insurer. The abstractor is not responsible for the legal conclusion regarding

---

of properly recorded conveyance is constructive fraud.—Williams v. Polgar, 43 Mich. App. 95, 204 N.W.2d 57 (1972), aff'd, 391 Mich. 6, 215 N.W.2d 149 (1974).

74. Smith v. Holmes, 54 Mich. 104, 19 N.W. 767 (1884).

Measure of duty

Measure of duty required to be exercised by abstractor is whether duty was performed in diligent and reasonably skillful, workmanlike manner.—Williams v. Polgar, 391 Mich. 6, 215 N.W.2d 149 (1974).

75. Bonner v. Chicago Title Ins. Co., 194 Mich. App. 462, 487 N.W.2d 807 (1992) (no duty to owners of neighboring property, and could not be held liable in negligence to owners of neighboring property).

Appraisal not performed

While the Michigan courts have not directly addressed whether there is a duty of care to parties for whom an appraisal was not performed, in Michigan there can be a general duty of care to third parties based on a contract.—Willecke v. Kozel, 395 Fed. Appx. 160, 2010 U.S. App. LEXIS 17700, 2010 FED App. 538N (6th Cir.) (6th Cir. Mich. 2010).

Proof of contract

Liability to a purchaser was based on fact that the purchaser testified that he said to defendant: "I want you to certify the abstracts, and I want you to charge the bill to [the vendor]"; defendant's claim that the plaintiff was not the party who suffered the damage was not well taken, where property was taken in name of plaintiff's wife, but the declaration charged that plaintiff was the one purchasing

the property, and to make the record clear, had taken a quitclaim from his wife, and the proof showed that the entire consideration passed from the plaintiff to his vendor.—Beckovsky v. Burton Abstract & Title Co., 208 Mich. 224, 175 N.W. 235 (1919).

76. Bake v. Wolverine Title Co., 1999 Mich. App. LEXIS 1372 (Mich. Ct. App. Mar. 26, 1999).

Bonner v. Chicago Title Ins. Co., 194 Mich. App. 462, 487 N.W.2d 807 (1992).

Williams v. Polgar, 391 Mich. 6, 215 N.W.2d 149 (1974).

77. Williams v. Polgar, 43 Mich. App. 95, 204 N.W.2d 57 (1972), aff'd, 391 Mich. 6, 215 N.W.2d 149 (1974).

78. Buyer of property

Buyer of property who has relied on faulty abstract to his detriment may recover from abstractor, though there is no clear contractual privity between them, if abstractor in fact knew that buyer would rely on abstract.—Williams v. Polgar, 391 Mich. 6, 215 N.W.2d 149 (1974).

79. Bonner v. Chicago Title Ins. Co., 194 Mich. App. 462, 487 N.W.2d 807 (1992) (owners of alleged servient estate in illegal easement not entitled to damages against abstractor or title insurance company of claimant of easement).

Reasonable reliance

Defendant cannot claim that he reasonably relied on the legal description since he admitted that he has always known that the easement is only thirty-three feet wide and that he did not read the description. No duty could have been owed absent this reliance.—Austin v. McGuirk, 1999 Mich. App. LEXIS 367 (Mich. Ct. App. Feb. 23, 1999).

whether good title exists on the basis of his or her abstract. An abstractor is therefore not liable for the failure to record items not contained in the public record nor part of a contract of employment.[80]

Compensation. Even where a customer ordering or requesting the preparation of an abstract does not expressly agree to pay the abstractor for his or her services in preparing or certifying it, the law will imply an undertaking on the customer's part to make reasonable payments.[81]

---

80. Williams v. Polgar, 391 Mich. 6, 215 N.W.2d 149 (1974).

81. Value of certificates

Certificates by an abstractor that certain printed papers are correct copies of an abstract involve something more valuable than the mere clerical work in making them, and, in the absence of an express agreement as to the price to be paid therefor, he is allowed to recover their reasonable value.—Kenyon v. Charlevoix Imp. Co., 135 Mich. 103, 97 N.W. 407 (1903).

Chapter 14

OPTIONS

§ 431. Options to Purchase

An option is a contract by which an owner of realty agrees that another has the right to buy the owner's property at a fixed price within a specified time. It binds the optionor to sell but does not bind the optionee to purchase.

Library References

Michigan Digest
John G. Cameron, Jr., Michigan Real Estate Forms
LexisNexis® Automated Michigan SCAO Forms
Thompson on Real Property, Thomas Edition (David A. Thomas, ed.)
Powell on Real Property® (Michael Allan Wolf, ed.)
Purchase and Sale of Real Property (Karl B. Holtzschue, ed.)

Law Review

Lenin Lopez, A Matter Of Semantics: Should Tenancies-In-Common Be Treated as Securities or Real Estate Interests?, 8 J. Bus. & Sec. L. 1 (2007).

An option is a contract by which an owner agrees that another person has the right to buy the owner's property at a fixed price within a specified time.[82] An option is a preliminary contract for the privilege of purchase, and is not a contract of purchase.[83]

But as with a contract for sale, the statute of frauds applies to options.[84] An

---

82. Phillips v. Homer (In re Smith Trust), 480 Mich. 19, 745 N.W.2d 754, 2008 Mich. LEXIS 466 (2008) (an option is an enforceable promise not to revoke an offer for a specified time).

Le Baron Homes, Inc. v. Pontiac Housing Fund, Inc., 319 Mich. 310, 29 N.W.2d 704 (1947).

Bailey v. Grover, 237 Mich. 548, 213 N.W. 137 (1927).

Cameron v. Shumway, 149 Mich. 634, 113 N.W. 287 (1907).

Miranda & Assoc v. George Abro & Johnny Enters., 2009 Mich. App. LEXIS 2719 (Mich. Ct. App. Dec. 29, 2009).

Board of Control of Eastern Mich. Univ. v. Burgess, 45 Mich. App. 183, 206 N.W.2d 256 (1973).

Agreement was option

Preliminary agreement providing that plaintiffs would purchase a motel and restaurant and acknowledging receipt of $2,000 as a binder was an "option."—Duiven v. Brakesman, 356 Mich. 1, 95 N.W.2d 868 (1959).

Right of first refusal

A right of first refusal must contain a definite term for performance; an agreement providing that covenants including a right of first refusal would continue until January 1, 1960, at which time they would be automatically extended for successive periods of 10 years unless a majority of the then owners agreed to change the covenants, was for a definite duration and the renewal provision did not transform the agreement into an agreement of indefinite duration.—Randolph v. Reisig, 272 Mich. App. 331, 727 N.W.2d 388 (2006).

A right of first refusal, or preemptive right, is a conditional option to purchase dependent on the landowner's desire to sell.—Randolph v. Reisig, 272 Mich. App. 331, 727 N.W.2d 388 (2006).

83. Oshtemo Twp. v. Kalamazoo, 77 Mich. App. 33, 257 N.W.2d 260 (1977).

Greenwald v. Veurink, 37 Mich. App. 700, 195 N.W.2d 305 (1972).

84. Caughey v. Ames, 315 Mich. 643, 24 N.W.2d 521 (1946).

option satisfies the statute of frauds[85] if it names parties, property, price, and times and terms of payment, thereby leaving no essential element to be determined by parol.[86]

An option is binding on the optionor, but not on the optionee.[87]

Instead of being an absolute option, an option may cause the right to purchase to arise only on various conditions precedent.[88] A preemptive option with a fixed price is not void.[89]

The use of the term "option" is not essential to the creation of an option contract, although it is a factor for consideration.[90]

False representations. An option will be set aside if it is induced by false representations by the purchaser of the option.[91] Neither speculative or other statements not amounting to false representations,[92] nor the alleged concealment of certain facts[93] constitute remediable fraud invalidating an option contract.

85. M.L.P.2d Frauds, Statute of.
MCLS § 566.106.

86. Caughey v. Ames, 315 Mich. 643, 24 N.W.2d 521 (1946) (must be signed by optionor).

87. Le Baron Homes, Inc. v. Pontiac Housing Fund, Inc., 319 Mich. 310, 29 N.W.2d 704 (1947).

No obligation to buy

Where agreement to sell land referred to escrow agreement that provided that, if titles were not acceptable, money and deeds were to be returned to respective parties, prospective purchaser was not bound to buy property because total agreement was in effect an option.—Deane v. Rex Oil & Gas Co., 325 Mich. 625, 39 N.W.2d 204 (1949).

88. Lantis v. Cook, 342 Mich. 347, 69 N.W.2d 849 (1955).

Conditional option

"First option to purchase" was conditional option or right of first refusal, rather than absolute option to purchase property, even though language in will which bequeathed option indicated that alleged option holder was to purchase property at fair market value at time of exercising option.—Czapp v. Cox, 179 Mich. App. 216, 445 N.W.2d 218 (1989).

Right of first refusal

A right of first refusal, or preemptive right, is a conditional option to purchase dependent upon the landowner's desire to sell. Rights of first refusal must contain a definite time for performance. Such agreements are not void, however, merely because they lack a specific time for performance. Rather, in the absence of a specific time period, courts will construe agreements to be for a reasonable period of time, and thus, such agreements are valid only for a reasonable period of time. There is a strong tendency to construe an option of preemption to be limited to the lives of the parties unless there is

clear evidence of a contrary intent.—Randolph v. Reisig, 272 Mich. App. 331, 727 N.W.2d 388, 2006 Mich. App. LEXIS 2850 (2006).

Real Property, 54 Wayne L. Rev. 387 (2008).

89. Lantis v. Cook, 342 Mich. 347, 69 N.W.2d 849 (1955).

90. Muirhead v. Freimann, 270 Mich. 181, 258 N.W. 238 (1935).

91. Evidence sufficient to set aside option

Evidence sustained order setting aside an option to purchase on ground that option was given on defendant's false representation to plaintiffs that a third party was willing to pay $17,500 for the property but no more and that land values were declining.—Peters v. Brooks, 370 Mich. 363, 121 N.W.2d 856 (1963).

92. Evidence insufficient

Evidence was insufficient to establish fraud in procuring option for sale of real estate.—Stout v. Hallsted, 239 Mich. 81, 214 N.W. 160 (1927).

Promises or predictions

Even if in procuring option to purchase realty statements were made to effect that apartments would be constructed on the property or in the area and road might be constructed through the property and future special assessments might be levied, such statements did not constitute such actionable fraud as would invalidate the option.—Roy Annett, Inc. v. Kerezsy, 336 Mich. 169, 57 N.W.2d 483 (1953).

93. Concealing name of real purchaser

Concealment when obtaining option to purchase of name of corporation for which option was being procured related to possible future contingency and did not constitute such actionable fraud as would invalidate the option.—Roy Annett, Inc. v. Kerezsy, 336 Mich. 169, 57 N.W.2d 483 (1953).

Form and requisites. The option contract must be complete.[94] While it must contain a description of the land covered, the description is sufficiently definite if it enables the optionee to go to the premises and recognize them without other aid.[95] It is not essential that the optionee sign the contract.[96]

Seller Disclosure Act. The disclosure requirements of the Seller Disclosure Act apply to the transfer of any interest in real estate consisting of not less than one or more than four residential units whether by sale, exchange, installment land contract, lease with an option to purchase, any other option to purchase, or ground lease coupled with proposed improvements by the purchaser or tenant, or a transfer of stock or an interest in a residential cooperative.[97]

§ 432.   Option Distinguished From Sale

A contract for the sale of land differs from an option in that the former obligates the vendor to sell and the vendee to buy, whereas an option constitutes a mere offer to sell.

An option to purchase land may ripen into a binding bilateral contract of purchase and sale.[98] But while a contract for the sale of land obligates the seller to sell and the purchaser to buy,[99] an option is a mere offer, acceptance of which must be in compliance with the proposed terms as to both the thing offered and the time specified.[100]

An instrument obligating the vendor to sell and the vendee to buy for a stated price and stated terms is a contract for the purchase and sale of real estate and not

---

94. Amounts of payments uncertain

An option for purchase of land, providing that "balance to be in reasonable quarterly payments after first year," thus contemplating agreement on some reasonable amount to be paid quarterly, was incomplete, and tender by optionee of mortgage in terms satisfactory to himself did not make complete contract, or place on optionor an enforceable obligation to convey.—Pfent v. Michaux, 231 Mich. 500, 204 N.W. 86 (1925).

"Fair market value" is sufficient in conditional option

"First option to purchase" was conditional option or right of first refusal, rather than absolute option to purchase property, even though language in will which bequeathed option indicated that alleged option holder was to purchase property at fair market value at time of exercising option.—Czapp v. Cox, 179 Mich. App. 216, 445 N.W.2d 218 (1989).

95. Sulzberger v. Steinhauer, 235 Mich. 253, 209 N.W. 68 (1926) (holding description of land as about 20 acres on "S.E." corner of named roads in named township sufficiently definite, irrespective of existence of another township by that name in or out of state).

96. Sulzberger v. Steinhauer, 235 Mich. 253, 209 N.W. 68 (1926).

97. Seller disclosure act, *infra*, Chapter 15.

MCLS §§ 565.951 et seq.

Annual Survey of Michigan Law; June 1, 2004 - May 31, 2005: Real Property, 52 Wayne L. Rev. 941 (2006).

Stigmatized Property Law: To Disclose or Not To Disclose, That is the Question for Michigan Residential Sellers, 85 MI Bar Jnl. 34 (2006).

"As Is" Clauses: The Law Behind "As Is" Clauses in Residential Real Estate Transactions, 84 Mi Bar Jnl. 35 (2005).

98. Le Baron Homes, Inc. v. Pontiac Housing Fund, Inc., 319 Mich. 310, 29 N.W.2d 704 (1947).

99. Le Baron Homes, Inc. v. Pontiac Housing Fund, Inc., 319 Mich. 310, 29 N.W.2d 704 (1947).

Muirhead v. Freimann, 270 Mich. 181, 258 N.W. 238 (1935).

Greater Bloomfield Real Estate Co. v. Braun, 64 Mich. App. 128, 235 N.W.2d 168 (1975).

100. Le Baron Homes, Inc. v. Pontiac Housing Fund, Inc., 319 Mich. 310, 29 N.W.2d 704 (1947).

Grasman v. Jelsema, 70 Mich. App. 745, 246 N.W.2d 322 (1976).

a mere "option."[101]

§ 433.   Consideration

An option contract must be supported by a consideration, but a nominal consideration is sufficient.

An option to purchase land given without consideration is unenforceable.[102] A contract purporting to give the right to purchase real estate at a specified price and within a certain time, and providing for the payment of specified sums for failure to comply, not based upon a consideration, is a nullity and of no effect prior to acceptance of the offer to sell.[103]

A merely nominal consideration, however, is sufficient to support an option contract.[104] Indeed, even a payment of $1 is a sufficient consideration for an option to purchase land.[105] However, the time and money spent by the holders of an option for the purchase of land, in trying to find a purchaser to whom to sell it, cannot be construed as a consideration to the parties granting the option so as to make it binding upon them as an option for the time and according to the terms specified.[106]

§ 434.   Exercise of Option

To be effective, the exercise of an option must be made in compliance with its terms and within the time stipulated.

An option must be exercised or accepted in compliance with its terms.[107] The evidence must sufficiently show the intent to accept and delivery.[108] If it complies with the terms of the option agreement, acceptance may be made in the form of a

---

101. McIntosh v. Hopkins, 255 Mich. 493, 238 N.W. 198 (1931).

Range v. Davison, 242 Mich. 73, 218 N.W. 789 (1928).

Solomon v. Shewitz, 185 Mich. 620, 152 N.W. 196 (1915).

Name as not changing character

Character of instrument as land contract cannot be altered by calling it option.—Range v. Davison, 242 Mich. 73, 218 N.W. 789 (1928).

Option in substance

Contract requiring purchaser to make deposit, and payments at specified times, and providing for vendor's retention of payments and improvements on vendee's default, was not mere option for purchase.—Hedrick v. Firke, 169 Mich. 549, 135 N.W. 319 (1912).

102. Bailey v. Grover, 237 Mich. 548, 213 N.W. 137 (1927).

Board of Control of Eastern Mich. Univ. v. Burgess, 45 Mich. App. 183, 206 N.W.2d 256 (1973).

103. Axe v. Tolbert, 179 Mich. 556, 146 N.W. 418 (1914).

104. Windiate v. Lorman, 236 Mich. 531, 211 N.W. 62 (1926).

Sulzberger v. Steinhauer, 235 Mich. 253, 209 N.W. 68 (1926).

George v. Schuman, 202 Mich. 241, 168 N.W. 486 (1918) (nominal sum of money sufficient).

Board of Control of Eastern Mich. Univ. v. Burgess, 45 Mich. App. 183, 206 N.W.2d 256 (1973).

105. Wayne Woods Land Co. v. Beeman, 211 Mich. 360, 178 N.W. 696 (1920) (three-month option to purchase land at a price of $11,500).

106. Axe v. Tolbert, 179 Mich. 556, 146 N.W. 418 (1914).

107. Le Baron Homes, Inc. v. Pontiac Housing Fund, Inc., 319 Mich. 310, 29 N.W.2d 704 (1947).

Beardslee v. Grindley, 236 Mich. 453, 210 N.W. 486 (1926).

Cleaves v. Walsh, 125 Mich. 638, 84 N.W. 1108 (1901).

108. Acceptance shown

Goldberg v. Drake, 145 Mich. 50, 108 N.W. 367 (1906).

letter.[109]

The optionee must comply strictly with its terms, not merely substantially.[110] The acceptance or exercise of an option must be unconditional.[111] A purported acceptance incorporating a new condition or proposal or a modification of the terms of the option does not constitute an acceptance of its remaining terms.[112]

When an option to purchase land is accepted in compliance with its terms, it becomes an executory land contract.[113] However, the optionee's failure to accept or exercise the option relieves the optionor of all obligation in the matter, even if the parties negotiate subsequently.[114]

The refusal of the vendor or optionor to perform the option contract does not relieve the optionee or vendee from accepting the option in compliance with its terms.[115] However, the refusal of the optionor to accept a properly tendered letter of acceptance does not deprive the letter of its effect as an exercise of the option.[116]

Acceptance of an option contract may be signified by filing a complaint for specific performance within the option period.[117] But the complaint cannot be

Curran v. Rogers, 35 Mich. 221 (1876).

Oshtemo Twp. v. Kalamazoo, 77 Mich. App. 33, 257 N.W.2d 260 (1977).

Rapanos v. Plumer, 41 Mich. App. 586, 200 N.W.2d 462 (1972).

109. Letter sufficient

Letter would not constitute a defective exercise of option merely because party employed the plural "we" and "our" rather than the singular "I" therein.—Catsman v. Eister, 8 Mich. App. 563, 155 N.W.2d 203 (1967).

110. Bergman v. Dykhouse, 316 Mich. 315, 25 N.W.2d 210 (1946).

Beecher v. Morse, 286 Mich. 513 (1938).

Bailey v. Grover, 237 Mich. 548, 213 N.W. 137 (1927).

Olson v. Sash, 217 Mich. 604, 187 N.W. 346 (1922).

111. Thomas v. Ledger, 274 Mich. 16, 263 N.W. 783 (1936).

112. Weadock v. Champe, 193 Mich. 553, 160 N.W. 564 (1916).

Rashken v. Smith, 236 Mich. 440, 210 N.W. 485 (1926) (acceptance within stipulated time but imposing condition contrary to terms of option creates no contract).

New requirement as to abstract of title

Bergman v. Dykhouse, 316 Mich. 315, 25 N.W.2d 210 (1946).

Thomas v. Ledger, 274 Mich. 16, 263 N.W. 783 (1936).

Time and terms not accepted

A completed contract for the purchase of land cannot be said to have been made by an acceptance in writing of a refusal of the land at a stated price, but without agreeing as to the time and terms of payment, or upon other matters subsequently incorporated in a written agreement.—Wylie v. Gamble, 95 Mich. 564, 55 N.W. 377 (1893).

113. Ludwig v. Hall, 234 Mich. 478, 208 N.W. 436 (1926).

Agar v. Streeter, 183 Mich. 600, 150 N.W. 160 (1914).

Sieradzki Inv. Co. v. Texas Twp., 15 Mich. App. 430, 166 N.W.2d 669 (1968).

114. No waiver of defects in acceptance

Where option to purchase realty expired without having been effectively exercised, defects in purported exercise of option were not waived by subsequent dealings between optionor and optionee with respect to purchase of the realty, because expiration of option relieved optionor of any obligation he may have owed optionee.— Mathieu v. Wubbe, 330 Mich. 408, 47 N.W.2d 670 (1951).

115. Clark v. Muirhead, 245 Mich. 49, 222 N.W. 79 (1928).

116. Roy Annett, Inc. v. Kerezsy, 336 Mich. 169, 57 N.W.2d 483 (1953).

117. Rashken v. Smith, 236 Mich. 440, 210 N.W. 485 (1926).

Shiller v. Lange, 217 Mich. 121, 185 N.W. 699 (1921).

maintained if it rests on a demand contrary to the terms of the option.[118]

Assignment or resale. The assignee of an option contract acquires only the rights of the assignor.[119] An optionee who agrees to sell the land to a third person may not, in derogation of the purchaser's rights, take a conveyance to others.[120]

Tender or payment of purchase price. Under an option contract providing for payment of all or a portion of the purchase price in order to exercise the option, as a rule the optionee must not only accept the offer but also make the stipulated payment or tender within the prescribed time in order to protect his or her rights under the option.[121] The payment or tender must be made in precisely the form prescribed by the terms of the option contract.[122] No payment or tender need be made where it is not called for by the terms of the option.[123]

Time of acceptance. The acceptance or exercise of an option must be made within the time stipulated in order to be effective.[124] The optionor may not deprive the optionee of his or her rights by avoiding the optionee until expiration of the time for exercise of the option.[125] The optionee's right to exercise the option at the end of a fixed period does not authorize the optionee to exercise it prior to the time

---

118. Rashken v. Smith, 236 Mich. 440, 210 N.W. 485 (1926).

119. Cameron v. Shumway, 149 Mich. 634, 113 N.W. 287 (1907) (assignee obtained only right to pay price according to option, on or before time as extended, and on his failure so to do his rights terminated).

120. Solomon v. Shewitz, 185 Mich. 620, 152 N.W. 196 (1915).

121. Bergman v. Dykhouse, 316 Mich. 315, 25 N.W.2d 210 (1946).

Beecher v. Morse, 286 Mich. 513 (1938).

Bailey v. Grover, 237 Mich. 548, 213 N.W. 137 (1927).

122. "Cashier's check" not "certified check"

A tender of a "cashier's check" was an insufficient acceptance of offer in option requiring optionee to tender agreed amount either in cash or by certified check prior to expiration of time specified, notwithstanding bank on which cashier's check was drawn was a going concern at time check was issued and tendered, and continued to conduct business afterward, given that "cashier's check" and "certified check" were not identical.—Beecher v. Morse, 286 Mich. 513 (1938).

123. Catsman v. Eister, 8 Mich. App. 563, 155 N.W.2d 203 (1967).

No sum stated

Purchaser need not accompany acceptance of option by payment, where contract provided for payment "stated below" and no sum was there stated.—Jefferson v. Brix, 244 Mich. 688, 222 N.W. 80 (1928).

Release and discharge of mortgage

Under option for purchase of land requiring first payment on exercising of option to consist of release and discharge of mortgage, timely notice of election to exercise option without tender of payment constituted binding contract.—Beardslee v. Grindley, 236 Mich. 453, 210 N.W. 486 (1926).

124. Mathieu v. Wubbe, 330 Mich. 408, 47 N.W.2d 670 (1951).

Le Baron Homes, Inc. v. Pontiac Housing Fund, Inc., 319 Mich. 310, 29 N.W.2d 704 (1947).

Bergman v. Dykhouse, 316 Mich. 315, 25 N.W.2d 210 (1946).

Beecher v. Morse, 286 Mich. 513 (1938).

Olson v. Sash, 217 Mich. 604, 187 N.W. 346 (1922).

Oshtemo Twp. v. Kalamazoo, 77 Mich. App. 33, 257 N.W.2d 260 (1977).

Evidence of time

Where real estate option provided that all parties would make diligent effort to zone property for use of ultimate purchaser and in case of emergency option would be extended to allow that zoning, testimony of vendor that provision was inserted to allow reasonable time for zoning was sufficient to permit court to find that purchaser who exercised option some six days prior to official approval of zoning had done so timely notwithstanding claim that option had expired by its other specific terms.—Catsman v. Eister, 8 Mich. App. 563, 155 N.W.2d 203 (1967).

125. O'Toole & Nedeau Co. v. Boelkins, 254 Mich. 44, 235 N.W. 820 (1931).

designated in the option contract.[126]

§ 435.   Construction and Operation

An option contract conveys no interest in the land prior to its exercise, and the construction and operation of such a contract will be determined in light of the intention of the parties as revealed by a consideration of the contract as a whole and the surrounding circumstances.

Prior to its exercise, an option to purchase land does not have the effect of conveying any interest in the land to the optionee.[127] Generally speaking, the operation and effect of option contracts or clauses depend upon the intention of the parties and the circumstances of the particular case.[128]

An option contract must be construed as a whole and so as to effectuate the intention of the parties.[129] A party may seek a court's determination of whether an option is a right of first refusal or an option with a condition precedent,[130] what affirmative acts the optionor must take upon the exercise of the option,[131] whether an option is exercisable at the death of one of the parties,[132] or whether a condition precedent has been met.[133] A court strictly construes the terms of an option.[134]

126. Nu-Way Service Stations v. Vandenberg Bros. Oil Co., 283 Mich. 551, 278 N.W. 683 (1938).

127. Windiate v. Leland, 246 Mich. 659, 225 N.W. 620 (1929).

Cameron v. Shumway, 149 Mich. 634, 113 N.W. 287 (1907).

Oshtemo Twp. v. Kalamazoo, 77 Mich. App. 33, 257 N.W.2d 260 (1977).

128. Standard Oil Co. v. Murray, 214 Mich. 299, 183 N.W. 55 (1921).

Contract for sale with liquidated damages clause

Contract for sale of realty providing that, if offer was accepted by vendor, purchaser agreed to complete purchase of realty within time indicated or to forfeit to vendor deposit made by purchaser as liquidated damages did not give purchaser option either to forfeit deposit and be released from liability thereon, or to complete purchase.—Randall v. Douglass, 321 Mich. 492, 32 N.W.2d 721 (1948).

Riders

An option contract offer would be inconsistent with the language directing plaintiffs to match the terms and conditions of the offer by purchasing the land. If plaintiffs bound themselves to the same terms and conditions as an offer to enter into an option contract, plaintiffs would not inform defendants of an intent to purchase as the rider contemplates; rather plaintiffs would merely have to inform defendants of an intent to retain the right to purchase at a later date.—A & E Holding, Inc. v.

Consumers Petroleum, 2001 Mich. App. LEXIS 1487 (Mich. Ct. App. June 8, 2001).

129. Weadock v. Champe, 193 Mich. 553, 160 N.W. 564 (1916).

Tattan v. Bryant, 198 Mich. 515, 165 N.W. 778 (1917).

Gary Boat Club, Inc. v. Oselka, 31 Mich. App. 465, 188 N.W.2d 127 (1971).

130. Not preemptive option

Option clause in a warranty deed, reciting that if the grantees did not wish at any time to use the property as a home the grantors had the first privilege to purchase at any future time at a price stated in the deed was not preemptive option but an ordinary option to arise on a condition precedent.—Lantis v. Cook, 342 Mich. 347, 69 N.W.2d 849 (1955).

131. Obtainment of title

Where vendees' interest under contract to purchase realty was assigned and assignment contract was accompanied by written agreement granting to assignors option to purchase property from assignees, option agreement placed on assignees obligation of acquiring legal title to property in event assignors exercised their rights.—Porritt v. Stone, 340 Mich. 645, 66 N.W.2d 244 (1954).

132. Lantis v. Cook, 342 Mich. 347, 69 N.W.2d 849 (1955).

133. Condemnation not a sale

Under option agreement providing that if property owners sold property other than to optionee for more than a certain price they would evenly

§ 436.   Termination

An option may terminate by lapse of the set time. An option unsupported by a consideration may be withdrawn by the optionor at any time prior to acceptance by the optionee.

An option to purchase is of such a nature that it is nearly always intended to be of limited duration.[135] An option expires when it is not exercised within any time limit specified.[136] On such expiration of the option, the optionor is relieved of whatever obligation he or she may previously have owed to the optionee.[137] Thus, after the expiration, the optionor may sell the property at any price that he or she chooses and to anyone, including the optionee, or to no one.[138]

One holding an option to repurchase land may release and abandon the option. Thereafter, it cannot be enforced by the optionee's successors in title.[139]

An option may become ineffective if a change of conditions makes it impossible to fulfill.[140]

Death of optionee. An option does not lapse by reason of the death of the optionee but passes to the latter's personal representative.[141]

A preemptive clause giving a vendor the option to repurchase may be so

split any sale price over the specified price with optionee, land condemned by city was not "sold" by property owners, and optionee had no interest in proceeds nor standing to question right of court to amend jury verdict by striking names of optionee and his wife as parties in interest.—In re Petition of Harper Woods, 353 Mich. 166, 91 N.W.2d 277 (1958).

Reasonable time

Where option giving right to purchase property including transfer of liquor license provided that down payment must be returned if license is not approved by the authorities, optionee's attempt to exercise the right to purchase within three days after license was renewed was within reasonable time contemplated by the option.—Caughey v. Ames, 315 Mich. 643, 24 N.W.2d 521 (1946).

Transfer by gift not a sale

Evidence, in action to set aside a transfer of realty by decedent, sustained finding that property was transferred by decedent to her two brothers for and in consideration of love and affection, and was not a sale in violation of an agreement which provided plaintiffs would have first opportunity to purchase the property if decedent desired to sell it.—Ridinger v. Ryskamp, 369 Mich. 15, 118 N.W.2d 689 (1963).

134. Bennett v. Eisen, 64 Mich. App. 241, 235 N.W.2d 749 (1975).

135. Glocksine v. Malleck, 372 Mich. 115, 125 N.W.2d 298 (1963).

136. Thomas v. Ledger, 274 Mich. 16, 263 N.W. 783 (1936).

Grasman v. Jelsema, 70 Mich. App. 745, 246 N.W.2d 322 (1976).

137. Mathieu v. Wubbe, 330 Mich. 408, 47 N.W.2d 670 (1951).

McWilliams v. Urban American Land Development Co., 37 Mich. App. 587, 194 N.W.2d 920 (1972).

138. Mathieu v. Wubbe, 330 Mich. 408, 47 N.W.2d 670 (1951).

139. Stoney Pointe Peninsula Ass'n v. Broderick, 321 Mich. 124, 32 N.W.2d 363 (1948).

140. Preemptive option

Where option agreement stated that purchaser would have first option if vendor decided to "sell" land, but in fact vendor gave land to her sons, and option had not been exercised for 20 years, option was ineffective.—Bennett v. Eisen, 64 Mich. App. 241, 235 N.W.2d 749 (1975).

141. Gustin v. Union School Dist. of Bay City, 94 Mich. 502, 54 N.W. 156 (1893).

Required personal volitional act

Option to repurchase terminated on the death of the grantee because it required a personal volitional act in her lifetime.—Waterstradt v. Snyder, 37 Mich. App. 400, 194 N.W.2d 389, 1971 Mich. App. LEXIS 1241 (1971).

drafted as to be either personal or descendible.[142] But the general rule is to construe an option or preemption as limited to the lives of the parties, unless there is clear evidence of a contrary intent.[143]

Revocation. An option that is not supported by a consideration may be revoked or withdrawn by the optionor at any time prior to its acceptance. The optionor is not obligated to submit any other terms to the optionee.[144] On the other hand, an option supported by a consideration may not be revoked or withdrawn by the optionor during the period that it specifies, even though the consideration for the option is only nominal.[145]

An option for the purchase of land is not revoked by the giving of a second option to another party that does not bind the vendor to make a conveyance, except on expiration of "any option, if such option exists on some part of such land."[146]

The modification of an option by agreement of the parties so as to reserve a

---

142. Personal right extinguished by death

Preemption clause in conveyance to school district giving "said grantors" right to purchase before all others created personal right in grantors that was extinguished by their deaths.—Old Mission Peninsula School Dist. v. French, 362 Mich. 546, 107 N.W.2d 758 (1961).

Where deed provided that "The grantee agrees that if she ever desires to sell the aforementioned property, the grantors herein are to have the right and option to buy the same for $9,000" and there was no mention of personal representatives, successors, or assigns, the option to repurchase required the personal volitional act of the grantee in her lifetime, and it terminated on her death, absent clear evidence of contrary intent.—Waterstradt v. Snyder, 37 Mich. App. 400, 194 N.W.2d 389 (1971).

143. Waterstradt v. Snyder, 37 Mich. App. 400, 194 N.W.2d 389 (1971).

144. Cancellation

Optionor's letter to optionee containing a clear import in writing that optionor was no longer willing to let option stand on its original terms, option being without consideration, amounted to withdrawal and cancellation of option in terms as originally drafted, so that, in absence of subsequent agreement of parties concerning new terms, optionee, not having accepted continuing offer under option before its withdrawal, was not entitled to enforce conveyance under terms of original option.—Michigan v. Owen, 312 Mich. 73, 19 N.W.2d 491 (1945).

145. George v. Schuman, 202 Mich. 241, 168 N.W. 486 (1918).

Right of first refusal created an option to purchase

A lease agreement granting the tenant a right of first refusal to purchase the property once the tenant received notice of a third party offer created an option to purchase the leased premises in the event the owner decided to sell the land (as evidenced by language in the lease referring to an "option to purchase") and, as such, the option was enforceable for the 30-day period set out in the lease and could not be revoked by the owner; once the tenant was notified by the owner of a third party's offer to purchase the property, the option in the lease agreement became operative and the owner could not revoke the offer to sell the property during the option period set out in the lease agreement.—In re Smith Trust, 480 Mich. 19, 745 N.W.2d 754, 2008 Mich. LEXIS 466 (2008).

Right of first refusal "transmuted" into option

When a lessor notified its lessee, who held a right of first refusal under the lease agreement, of a bona fide offer to purchase the property, the right of first refusal "transmuted" into an option, and the option was not revocable for the period specified in the option; the lease provided that the option would terminate if the lessee failed to exercise the option within 30 days, but did not permit the lessor to revoke the offer during the 30-day period.—Phillips v. Homer (In re Smith Trust), 274 Mich. App. 283, 731 N.W.2d 810, 2007 Mich. App. LEXIS 396 (2007).

146. Ward v. Davis, 154 Mich. 413, 117 N.W. 897 (1908).

portion of the land to the optionor does not constitute an annulment of the option.[147] A grantor's refusal to perform before any exercise by the optionee does not constitute a renunciation of the contract sufficient to terminate the optionee's rights if the option is based on a valuable consideration.[148]

147. Sulzberger v. Steinhauer, 235 Mich. 253, 209 N.W. 68 (1926).

148. Solomon Mier Co. v. Hadden, 148 Mich. 488, 111 N.W. 1040 (1907).

Chapter 15

REQUISITES AND VALIDITY OF CONTRACT FOR SALE OF LAND

§ 451.   Contracts for Sale of Real Property

The essentials of a contract between vendor and vendee are the same as those of contracts generally. All of the essential elements of a contract for the sale of real property must be put down in a writing executed by the parties in order for the agreement to be enforceable.

Library References

Michigan Digest
John G. Cameron, Jr., Michigan Real Estate Forms
LexisNexis® Automated Michigan SCAO Forms
Thompson on Real Property, Thomas Edition (David A. Thomas, ed.)
Powell on Real Property® (Michael Allan Wolf, ed.)
Purchase and Sale of Real Property (Karl B. Holtzschue, ed.)

Law Reviews

Jason C. Long, This Time It's Personal(?) Property Classification And Recent Amendments to Michigan's Property Tax Laws, 25 T.M. Cooley L. Rev. 303 (2008); Jeffrey A. Cojocar, "As Is" Clauses: The Law Behind "As Is" Clauses in Residential Real Estate Transactions, 84 Mich. B.J. 35 (2005); Ronald S. Melamed & Edward S. Gusky, Preparing a Commercial Real Estate Purchase Agreement: The Ins and Outs for the Seller and Purchaser, 84 MI Bar Jnl. 32 (2005); Patrick J. Ennis, Annual Survey of Michigan Law: June 1, 2001 - May 31, 2002: Real Property, 49 Wayne L. Rev. 593 (2003); Lawrence R. Shoffner, Real Property Law: Real Evidence: Special Rules For Real Estate Disputes, 80 Mich. B.J. 28 (2001); Carl W. Herstein, Annual Survey Of Michigan Law: June 1, 1999–May 31, 2000: Real Property, 47 Wayne L. Rev. 669 (2001).

A "contract for the sale of land" is, quite simply, a purchase contract for real property.[149] By contrast, a "land contract" is an agreement for the sale of an interest in real property under which the purchase price is to be paid in installments, other than an earnest money deposit and a lump-sum payment at closing, and no promissory note or mortgage is involved between the seller and the buyer.[150] Either or both the vendor's and the vendee's interests in a land contract may be mortgaged by the holder of that interest.[151]

The elements of a contract between a vendor and a vendee are substantially those of contracts in general. If the essential elements are present, the contract will not be invalidated by the fact that it is inequitable or a bad bargain for one of the parties to it.[152]

149. Zurcher v. Herveat, 238 Mich. App. 267, 605 N.W.2d 329, 1999 Mich. App. LEXIS 325 (1999).

150. McMahon Helicopter Servs., And Brian McMahon, Plaintiffs/Counter-Defendants-Appellants v. Mid-West Dev., 2007 Mich. App. LEXIS 1685 (Mich. Ct. App. June 26, 2007).

Hall v. Independence Twp., 2001 Mich. App. LEXIS 1251 (Mich. Ct. App. Aug. 14, 2001).

Zurcher v. Herveat, 238 Mich. App. 267, 605 N.W.2d 329, 1999 Mich. App. LEXIS 325 (1999).

151. Mortgages, *see, infra,* Chapters 23 et seq. MCLS §§ 565.356 et seq.

152. Burlingame v. B.E. Taylor Realty Co., 247 Mich. 109, 225 N.W. 562 (1929).

Vincent v. McIntyre, 244 Mich. 112, 221 N.W. 136 (1928) (that owner contracting for sale of land

All of the essential elements of a contract for the sale of real property must be put down in a writing executed by the parties in order for the agreement to be enforceable.[153] A valid contract for sale of land is bilateral and mutually enforceable.[154]

Where restrictions against alienation are not involved, the subject matter of a sale of real estate may include a vendee's interest or property owned by the vendor,[155] or any portion of the interest or property.[156] It may include any equitable estate or interest that the vendor may own.[157]

A contract to convey land may be valid even though the vendor does not own the premises, in which case the proper remedy against the vendor is an action for damages.[158]

A later agreement supersedes and rescinds an earlier agreement for the sale of land if the parties to the earlier agreement enter into a subsequent agreement that completely covers the same subject but that contains terms inconsistent with those of the prior agreement and if the two agreements cannot stand together.[159]

Parties. An essential term of a land sale contract is the identification of the parties. A contract meets this requirement by designating the names of the buyer and the seller with sufficient certainty so as to identify them.[160]

dealt unwisely affords no ground for equitable relief).

Tucson v. Farrington, 396 Mich. 169, 240 N.W.2d 464 (1976) (as a general rule, term of credit is essential term of contract for sale of land, and it must be stated with substantial certainty in written memorandum).

153. In re Estate of Trainor, 2009 Mich. App. LEXIS 2591 (Mich. Ct. App. Dec. 17, 2009).

Schneider v. Touhy, 2001 Mich. App. LEXIS 914 (Mich. Ct. App. May 29, 2001).

Zurcher v. Herveat, 238 Mich. App. 267, 605 N.W.2d 329, 1999 Mich. App. LEXIS 325 (1999).

154. Western Michigan University Board of Trustees v. Slavin, 381 Mich. 23, 158 N.W.2d 884 (1968).

155. Owner under deed from court

Lumber company that held a deed of property from circuit court commissioner on foreclosure of a mechanic's lien with an order for possession and a warranty deed from defendant was owner of the property, and entitled to its possession, so that it could lawfully sell it to defendant for whatever price to which defendant might agree.—City Lumber Co. v. Hollands, 181 Mich. 531, 148 N.W. 361 (1914).

156. Any portion desired

One owning a tract of land, or two or more adjoining lots, when no public or private rights are interposed, may sell any portion he or she wishes, and terms of grant as they appear from language of deed legally construed will measure rights of

grantee.—Burling v. Leiter, 272 Mich. 448, 262 N.W. 388 (1935).

157. Miner v. O'Harrow, 60 Mich. 91, 26 N.W. 843 (1886) (sale of equitable interest is as good foundation for legal contract as any other consideration).

158. Stolberg v. Oakman, 233 Mich. 92, 206 N.W. 488 (1925).

Brin v. Michalski, 188 Mich. 400, 154 N.W. 110 (1915).

Homestead does not invalidate contract for sale

Although part of the premises that defendant agreed to convey constituted the homestead, which he could not convey alone, yet the contract was valid as to him, and value of the land may be recovered for its breach.—Dikeman v. Arnold, 78 Mich. 455, 44 N.W. 407 (1889).

159. Lawyers Title Ins. Corp. v. First Federal Sav. Bank & Trust, 744 F. Supp. 778, 1990 U.S. Dist. LEXIS 10310 (E.D. Mich. 1990).

Lewis v. First Alliance Mortgage Co., 2004 Mich. App. LEXIS 1623 (Mich. Ct. App. June 17, 2004).

Omnicom of Michigan v. Giannetti Inv.Co., 221 Mich. App. 341, 561 N.W.2d 138, 1997 Mich. App. LEXIS 31 (1997).

Culver v. Castro, 126 Mich. App. 824, 338 N.W.2d 232 (1983).

160. Miranda & Assoc v. George Abro & Johnny Enters., 2009 Mich. App. LEXIS 2719 (Mich. Ct. App. Dec. 29, 2009).

A contract for the sale of land is not binding on one who is neither party nor privy to it.[161] Payment on a contract does not necessarily make the payor privy to the contract.[162]

§ 452.   Offer and Acceptance

As in the case of contracts generally, there can be no valid contract for the sale of land without an offer and acceptance. For a response to an offer to be deemed an acceptance as opposed to a counteroffer, the material terms of the agreement cannot be altered.

As in the case of contracts generally, there can be no valid contract for the sale of land without an offer and acceptance.[163] But where offer and acceptance are shown, a contract may be effected.[164]

The substance of a binding contract for the sale of land is governed by the general contract law concept that there must be a meeting of the minds regarding the "essential particulars" of the transaction.[165]

For a response to an offer to be deemed an acceptance as opposed to a counteroffer, the material terms of the agreement cannot be altered.[166]

To change an acceptance into a counteroffer, the changes to a material term must themselves be material.[167]

Offer to sell. An offer to sell real estate becomes a binding contract if it is

---

Zurcher v. Herveat, 238 Mich. App. 267, 605 N.W.2d 329 (1999).

161. Briggs v. Colgrove, 267 Mich. 504, 255 N.W. 416 (1934).

Compare Rossman v. Marsh, 287 Mich. 580, 283 N.W. 696 (1939).

Ignorance of transaction

A person cannot become a purchaser by a transaction of which he or she is wholly ignorant.—Weare v. Linnell, 29 Mich. 224 (1874).

162. Payment as not admission

Where two certain persons were not named in a land contract taken in the name of a third, and contract did not purport to bind them in any way, the mere fact that subsequently each paid a third of interest on price did not amount to admission that they were bound by the contract.—Ferris v. Snow, 130 Mich. 254, 90 N.W. 850 (1902).

163. M.L.P.2d Contracts.

Seymour v. Canfield, 122 Mich. 212, 80 N.W. 1096 (1899).

Wilhelm v. Fagan, 90 Mich. 6, 50 N.W. 1072 (1892).

Seelye v. Broad, 2 Mich. App. 177, 139 N.W.2d 126 (1966), rev'd on other grounds, 379 Mich. 289, 150 N.W.2d 785 (1967).

164. Walsh v. Oakman, 199 Mich. 688, 165 N.W. 737 (1917).

165. McMahon Helicopter Servs., And Brian McMahon, Plaintiffs/Counter-Defendants-Appellants v. Mid-West Dev., 2007 Mich. App. LEXIS 1685 (Mich. Ct. App. June 26, 2007).

Churchill v. Swarthout, 2006 Mich. App. LEXIS 1119 (Mich. Ct. App. Apr. 11, 2006).

Malburg v. Wayne J. Lennard & Sons, 2003 Mich. App. LEXIS 2090 (Mich. Ct. App. Aug. 28, 2003).

Zurcher v. Herveat, 238 Mich. App. 267, 605 N.W.2d 329 (1999).

166. Foster v. Berrien Hills Country Club, 2009 Mich. App. LEXIS 346 (Mich. Ct. App. Feb. 17, 2009).

EJS Props. LLC v. Ferguson, 2004 Mich. App. LEXIS 438 (Mich. Ct. App. Feb. 12, 2004).

Zurcher v. Herveat, 238 Mich. App. 267, 605 N.W.2d 329 (1999).

167. Boyd v. Burke, 2007 Mich. App. LEXIS 1418 (Mich. Ct. App. May 17, 2007).

Zurcher v. Herveat, 238 Mich. App. 267, 605 N.W.2d 329 (1999).

accepted before its withdrawal.[168] But the offer cannot become a contract prior to its acceptance.[169] Where the so-called offer is incomplete and looks to further negotiations, it is not susceptible of acceptance.[170]

The offer of a vendor must be accepted by the vendee in compliance with its terms.[171] The failure to comply with the conditions of an offer is fatal to acceptance.[172] If the vendee interjects different terms in trying to accept the offer, this does not constitute an acceptance.[173]

A vendor's offer must be accepted within the time fixed for acceptance in the offer,[174] or, if no time is set, within a reasonable time.[175]

Offer to purchase. Where a vendor accepts the vendee's offer to purchase his or her property, a contract is created.[176] However, to effect a contract, the vendor's acceptance of the vendee's offer to purchase must be made in compliance with the terms of the offer.[177] If the vendor interjects different terms in trying to accept the offer, this does not constitute an acceptance but is a mere counteroffer on the vendor's part.[178] If one offering to purchase property accepts the vendor's

---

168. Brenner v. Duncan, 318 Mich. 1, 27 N.W.2d 320 (1947).

169. Brenner v. Duncan, 318 Mich. 1, 27 N.W.2d 320 (1947).

Board of Control of Eastern Mich. Univ. v. Burgess, 45 Mich. App. 183, 206 N.W.2d 256 (1973).

170. Wardell v. Williams, 62 Mich. 50, 28 N.W. 796 (1886).

171. Bewick v. Hanika, 142 Mich. 206, 106 N.W. 63 (1905).

De Jonge v. Hunt, 103 Mich. 94, 61 N.W. 341 (1894).

Sands & Maxwell Lumber Co. v. Crosby, 74 Mich. 313, 41 N.W. 899 (1889).

Seelye v. Broad, 2 Mich. App. 177, 139 N.W.2d 126 (1966), rev'd on other grounds, 379 Mich. 289, 150 N.W.2d 785 (1967).

172. Deposit not made

Offer to sell lands at certain price, and send deeds to bank on being informed that price had been deposited, was not accepted by letter directing vendor to send deeds, unaccompanied by evidence of deposit required.—Dunn v. Dunn, 132 Mich. 461, 93 N.W. 1072 (1903).

173. Material variation

There is no acceptance of a proposal to sell real estate when the proposal involves executory proceedings on each side and the person to whom it is made couples with his acceptance conditions that essentially change the offer or materially vary its effect.—Eggleston v. Wagner, 46 Mich. 610, 10 N.W. 37 (1881).

174. Five days

Offer to sell lands if the price is paid within five days cannot be accepted by tendering the price after five days, and after notice of the withdrawal of the offer.—Dunn v. Dunn, 132 Mich. 461, 93 N.W. 1072 (1903).

175. Hawley v. Jelly, 25 Mich. 94 (1872).

Acceptance after rejection

Where purchaser of land from state for taxes stated orally that he would sell lands to respondent, who claimed to own them, for what purchaser paid, which offer was not accepted, it could not be regarded as remaining open for more than reasonable time.—McFarlane v. Simpson, 153 Mich. 193, 116 N.W. 982 (1908).

176. Glanbin v. Kousin, 249 Mich. 603, 229 N.W. 417 (1930) (offer to buy city lot).

Lansing Co. v. Rogers, 183 Mich. 334, 149 N.W. 1000 (1914).

177. Connor v. Buhl, 115 Mich. 531, 73 N.W. 821 (1898).

178. Kashat v. Prangs, 16 Mich. App. 76, 167 N.W.2d 603 (1969).

Spaulding v. Wyckoff, 320 Mich. 329, 31 N.W.2d 71 (1948) (adding provision to printed form).

Additional condition

Where prospective purchasers' offer to buy store building did not contain any reference to lessee's option right to purchase the building, and vendors' alleged acceptance contained as an additional condition the compliance by vendors with

counteroffer, this will result in the making of a binding contract.[179]

Where the purchaser's offer to buy land is based on fulfillment of specified conditions, these conditions must be fulfilled before the offer and acceptance may ripen into a contract.[180]

Contracts by correspondence. To effect a contract for sale of land by correspondence, the correspondence must show a meeting of the minds of the vendor and vendee, with an acceptance of the offer in compliance with its terms.[181]

§ 453. Form and Execution

The question of requirements as a contract is separate from the requirements of the statute of frauds. The contract need not be in any particular form of words or form of instrument, and the omission of nonessential details does not invalidate it.

To satisfy the statute of frauds, every contract for the sale of lands, or an interest in lands, is void unless the contract, or some note or memorandum to it, is in writing and signed by the party by whom the sale is to be made or by some person whom that party lawfully in writing authorizes to sign it.[182] The question of

the option requirements of the lease, vendors' alleged acceptance amounted only to a counteroffer, and prospective purchasers' acknowledgment of receipt of the purported acceptance did not constitute acceptance of the counteroffer, and, hence, there was no binding agreement to purchase and sell.—Harper Bldg. Co. v. Kaplan, 332 Mich. 651, 52 N.W.2d 536 (1952).

179. Wilkinson v. Lanterman, 314 Mich. 568, 22 N.W.2d 827 (1946).

180. Modern Globe, Inc. v. 1425 Lake Drive Corp., 340 Mich. 663, 66 N.W.2d 92 (1954) (approval by stockholders).

Title insurance

Where offer to purchase property provided that sale was to be consummated within 30 days after delivery of abstract to purchasers, if owners could convey marketable title, but that if objection was made to title, purchasers were required to consummate the sale within 10 days if owners elected to furnish them a policy of title insurance, and where purchasers were supplied abstract showing marketable title but raised objections, and owners did not elect to furnish policy but notified purchasers that offer had lapsed, offer was not ambiguous, and by its terms was terminated.—Cunningham v. Garber, 361 Mich. 90, 104 N.W.2d 746 (1960).

181. Dunn v. Dunn, 132 Mich. 461, 93 N.W. 1072 (1903).

Correspondence held to establish contract

Garvey v. Parkhurst, 127 Mich. 368, 86 N.W. 802 (1901).

Corning v. Loomis, 111 Mich. 23, 69 N.W. 85 (1896).

Place of payment

Where the owner of land wrote a person in a distant city that he would take for the land a certain net sum, and that person answered that he accepted the offer, and requested the owner to send a deed to parties named, in such city, to whom he would pay the money on receipt of the deed, there was no completed contract, the offer implying payment at the owner's residence.—De Jonge v. Hunt, 103 Mich. 94, 61 N.W. 341 (1894).

182. M.L.P.2d Frauds, Statute of.

MCLS § 566.108.

Rathbun v. Herche, 323 Mich. 160, 35 N.W.2d 230 (1948) (essential components include contents identifying the parties, property, consideration, and terms and time of performance).

Partial performance

Plaintiff argued that the doctrine of partial performance should remove this case from the statute of frauds, but the partial performance doctrine has not been applied to contracts that cannot be performed within a year.—Rutila Props. v. Cellular, 2011 Mich. App. LEXIS 252 (Mich. Ct. App. Feb. 10, 2011).

Requirements under statute of frauds

For a memorandum to be sufficient under the statute of frauds, it must be certain and definite as to the parties, property, consideration, premises,

requirements as a contract is separate from the requirements of the statute of frauds.[183] Under contract law, the material terms of the contract that must be clearly established are the identification of the property, the parties, and the consideration.[184]

The contract need not, however, be in any particular form of words or form of instrument, and the omission of nonessential details does not invalidate it.[185]

A party to the contract may obtain enforcement of contracts relating to the sale of land that are sufficiently complete and definite to be enforceable,[186] including provisions with respect to the description of the property,[187] and the sharing of expenses incurred in any joint defense against a suit challenging the resulting title or interest.[188]

The failure to specify the rate of interest or the date of possession does not

and time of performance.—Zurcher v. Herveat, 238 Mich. App. 267, 605 N.W.2d 329 (1999).

Unenforceable contract

When the parties indicate that they intend a credit sale but fail to set forth the terms and times of payments, a court's ability to impose reasonable terms is absent and such a contract is unenforceable.—Hyne v. Pool, 2004 Mich. App. LEXIS 911 (Mich. Ct. App. Apr. 13, 2004).

183. Zurcher v. Herveat, 238 Mich. App. 267, 605 N.W.2d 329 (1999).

184. EJS Props. LLC v. Ferguson, 2004 Mich. App. LEXIS 438 (Mich. Ct. App. Feb. 12, 2004).

Zurcher v. Herveat, 238 Mich. App. 267, 605 N.W.2d 329 (1999).

185. Rathbun v. Herche, 323 Mich. 160, 35 N.W.2d 230 (1948).

Janiszewski v. Shank, 230 Mich. 189, 202 N.W. 949 (1925).

186. Woodliff v. Citizens' Bldg. & Realty Co., 233 Mich. 288, 206 N.W. 542 (1925).

Soloman v. Western Hills Dev. Co., 88 Mich. App. 254, 276 N.W.2d 577 (1979).

MacRitchie v. Plumb, 70 Mich. App. 242, 245 N.W.2d 582 (1976).

Removing encumbrances

Where purchasers were purchasing free and clear of liens and encumbrances, their method of removal by vendors was immaterial and fact that preliminary agreement contained no provision for discharge thereof could not impair its validity.—Emlong Nurseries, Inc. v. Warner, 364 Mich. 462, 110 N.W.2d 713 (1961).

187. Zurcher v. Herveat, 238 Mich. App. 267, 605 N.W.2d 329 (1999).

Description by name

In a contract for the sale of land a description by name is sufficient if it can be identified by extrinsic evidence not contradictory of the contract.—Garvey v. Parkhurst, 127 Mich. 368, 86 N.W. 802 (1901).

Pipeline

Agreement-conveyance of right-of-way for pipeline was not void for uncertainty where grantor saw stakes grantee had set out before he signed agreement, there was no doubt whatsoever between the parties as to where the pipeline would be laid, and while the exact space which might eventually be required was not stated, the area of grantor's property that grantee might ultimately utilize was not undefined.—Johnston v. Michigan Consol. Gas Co., 337 Mich. 572, 60 N.W.2d 464 (1953).

Reference to abstract

The description of the property may be aided by reference to another paper, such as an abstract.—Janiszewski v. Shank, 230 Mich. 189, 202 N.W. 949 (1925).

Surplusage

Where lots were in "Beech Hill subdivision," but described as "Beech Hill Park subdivision" in land contract, word "Park" was mere surplusage because other description was sufficient.—MacLeod v. Hamilton, 254 Mich. 653, 236 N.W. 912 (1931).

Surveyor's map

Deficiency in contractual description asserted by vendors to vitiate contract could be made clear through use of surveyor's map prepared by vendors and given to their agent for purpose of describing property.—Emlong Nurseries, Inc. v. Warner, 364 Mich. 462, 110 N.W.2d 713 (1961).

188. Jones v. Shaw, 56 Mich. 332, 23 N.W. 33 (1885).

necessarily invalidate a contract for sale of land.[189]

Furthermore, the inclusion of optional provisions, such as those concerning defeasance, insurance, repairs, and taxes, does not invalidate a contract for sale of land.[190]

A subsequent agreement may make a contract relative to the sale of land sufficiently certain to be enforceable.[191]

Execution and acknowledgment. Effective March 4, 2002, the execution of contracts for the sale of land or an interest in land no longer have to be witnessed by two people who subscribe their names to it.[192] As of that date, the vendor named in the contract only has to execute it and acknowledge it before any judge or notary in the state. The judge or notary public must sign and endorse on it a certificate of the acknowledgment and the date of its making.[193] There are also statutory provisions relative to contracts for the sale of land executed in another state or in a foreign country.[194]

The signature of a party to the contract may be made by his or her agent.[195]

Delivery. A written contract for the sale of land executed in duplicate is enforceable regardless of whether or not the purchaser received a copy of the contract.[196] On the other hand, a delivery in escrow lacks legal effect until compliance with the conditions under which it is so delivered. The mere fact that the purchaser obtained possession of the contract before compliance does not give it legal effect.[197]

The fact that a contract for the sale of land remains in the custody of one party is unimportant in determining the true date of the contract.[198]

§ 454. Consideration

An executory contract for the sale of land must be supported by a sufficient consideration. The rate of interest that may be charged in a land contract may be subject to Michigan's strict usury laws.

An executory contract for the sale of land supported by a sufficient consideration will be enforced.[199] Good consideration for a contract for sale may

---

189. Janiszewski v. Shank, 230 Mich. 189, 202 N.W. 949 (1925).

190. Permissive

Provisions on insurance, repairs, and taxes may be included in land contract, but are not essential to its validity or to specific performance of it.—Rathbun v. Herche, 323 Mich. 160, 35 N.W.2d 230 (1948).

191. Waites v. Miller, 244 Mich. 267, 221 N.W. 171 (1928) (subsequent agreement concerning selling price).

192. 2002 Pub. Act 20.

193. MCLS § 565.351.

194. MCLS §§ 565.352, 565.353.

Himelson v. Galusz, 309 Mich. 512, 15 N.W.2d 727 (1944).

195. Wexler v. Poe, 245 Mich. 442, 222 N.W. 715 (1929).

196. George v. Smilanski, 238 Mich. 700, 214 N.W. 61, 1927 Mich. LEXIS 706 (1927).

197. Dikeman v. Arnold, 71 Mich. 656, 40 N.W. 42 (1888).

198. White v. Evangelical Lutheran Salem Church, 239 Mich. 216, 214 N.W. 245 (1927).

199. Huff v. Hall, 56 Mich. 456, 23 N.W. 88 (1885).

consist of a check for a nominal amount of money[200] or the transfer of an equitable interest in property.[201]

The consideration for a sale of realty on acceptance of an option to purchase is entirely apart from the consideration of the latter, and must be specified.[202]

The existence of a lease on the land contracted to be sold does not necessarily invalidate the contract on the ground of want or failure of consideration.[203]

The rate of interest that may be charged in a land contract may be subject to Michigan's strict usury laws.[204] A usurious rate of interest is without effect.[205]

§ 455. Validity and Reality of Assent

Mutuality of assent is essential to render a contract for the sale of land enforceable.

Stanley v. Nye, 54 Mich. 277, 20 N.W. 73 (1884).

Greater Bloomfield Real Estate Co. v. Braun, 64 Mich. App. 128, 235 N.W.2d 168 (1975).

Good-faith claim

A contract to purchase the interest in lands of one who, although having no ownership, yet in good faith asserts a claim to one, so that the proposed purchaser, with full knowledge of the extent and validity of that claim, is willing to buy, is not void for want of consideration.—Sheldon v. Estate of Rice, 30 Mich. 296 (1874).

200. Czeizler v. Radke, 309 Mich. 349, 15 N.W.2d 665 (1944) (check for $100 from their agent accepted by sellers, and representing binder payment made by purchasers to agent constituted sufficient consideration for agreement to sell realty).

201. Miner v. O'Harrow, 60 Mich. 91, 26 N.W. 843 (1886).

202. Sulzberger v. Steinhauer, 235 Mich. 253, 209 N.W. 68 (1926).

203. English v. Yore, 119 Mich. 444, 78 N.W. 476 (1899) (land contract is not necessarily void because of lease on land, because it may not prevent performance of contract's terms).

204. M.L.P.2d Interest.

MCLS §§ 438.31 et seq., §§ 438.41 et seq., §§ 438.61 et seq., and §§ 438.101 et seq.

Assignees

As assignees of the original mortgage, bringing an independent action, plaintiffs were not entitled to any remedy flowing from the alleged usurious transaction. The statute requires that all prior interest paid under a usurious contract be applied to extinguish any principal balance due. However a buyer or borrower can only avail themselves of this statute when the seller brings an action to enforce a usurious contract. A buyer or borrower cannot bring an independent action to recover interest paid on a usurious contract.—Fisher v. Rasch, 1997 Mich. App. LEXIS 1232 (Mich. Ct. App. Jan. 10, 1997).

Penalty

A buyer under a usurious land contract may seek the statutory penalty under which interest already paid is applied toward reducing the outstanding principal only where the seller brings an action for enforcement of the land contract.—Olsen v. Porter, 213 Mich. App. 25, 539 N.W.2d 523 (1995).

Right to refinance

Plaintiff argued that trial court erred by dismissing usury claim before discovery was complete, whereas defendants contended that discovery concluded before the trial court dismissed plaintiff's usury claim. Regardless of whether discovery ended before or after the trial court dismissed the usury claim, dismissal was proper because usury is a defense to a cause of action and does not form the basis of an independent action.—Sand v. Borrowers Network, 2010 Mich. App. LEXIS 46 (Mich. Ct. App. Jan. 12, 2010).

205. M.L.P.2d Interest.

MCLS § 438.31.

Penalty applicable

Although plaintiffs were not seeking to make the usurious interest rate effective, they were certainly attempting to compel defendants to abide by the terms of the usurious contract. Therefore, the statutory penalty was applicable.—Washburn v. Michailoff, 240 Mich. App. 669, 613 N.W.2d 405, 2000 Mich. App. LEXIS 94 (2000).

Reformation not possible in mutual mistake

A court may not reform a usurious land contract where the parties, being mutually mistaken about the statutory maximum interest at the time they executed the land contract, agreed to an illegal interest rate.—Olsen v. Porter, 213 Mich. App. 25, 539 N.W.2d 523 (1995).

Mutual assent is essential to the validity of a contract, and there can be no enforceable contract for the sale of real estate unless both parties assent to the contract understandingly and without fraud, mutual mistake, or another factor destroying the reality of their assent.[206] In determining the existence or nonexistence of reality of assent, the courts consider all factors pertinent to the issue.[207]

A sale of land for an exorbitant price may be set aside on grounds of equity even though the purchaser buys with full knowledge of its value, if the vendor compels the sale by taking advantage of the possession of a fictitious claim against the purchaser.[208]

Mistake. A contract for the sale of land is subject to rescission for a mutual mistake concerning a material matter.[209] The remedy is granted only in the sound discretion of the court.[210]

A contract for the sale of land may be rescinded for mutual mistake by the adversely affected party only where the mistake is legally significant unless the

206. M.L.P.2d Contracts.

First Baptist Church v. Solner, 341 Mich. 209, 67 N.W.2d 252 (1954).

Gower v. Wieser, 269 Mich. 6, 256 N.W. 603 (1934).

Shaw v. Joquico, 2001 Mich. App. LEXIS 2647 (Mich. Ct. App. Aug. 28, 2001).

Greater Bloomfield Real Estate Co. v. Braun, 64 Mich. App. 128, 235 N.W.2d 168 (1975) (delay by selling agent in notifying vendor of purchaser's acceptance of vendor's counteroffer for sale of land did not affect contract between vendor and purchaser; vendor used selling agent to transmit offer to purchaser, and, absent contrary indications from vendor, purchaser was able to accept in same manner).

207. Examination by attorney

Fact that vendor would not receive old-age assistance during period when he was able to take care of himself and when he would have a home for life together with upkeep and taxes and sufficient funds to keep him at least for a considerable time did not appeal to court as equitable reason for setting aside real estate contract whereby vendor was to have use of first floor of house for life, and purchaser was to pay upkeep and taxes; and where parties had already agreed to terms of contract, and attorney selected by purchaser to draft contract met with full approval of vendor, and attorney did not influence transaction, fact that attorney had previously served as attorney for purchaser did not affect validity of contract.—Foshee v. Krum, 332 Mich. 636, 52 N.W.2d 358 (1952).

It was error to charge that if, before signing the contract to purchase, defendant said that he wished his attorney to look the papers over, but afterward changed his mind, and executed the contract, it would bind him as though nothing had been said about the attorney looking over the papers.—

Dikeman v. Arnold, 71 Mich. 656, 40 N.W. 42 (1888).

Incompetence

Contract by deceased to sell realty made before deceased was declared insane was, at most, voidable.—Van Horn v. Herndon, 253 Mich. 408, 235 N.W. 201 (1931).

208. Storrs v. Scougale, 48 Mich. 387, 12 N.W. 502 (1882).

209. Lenawee County Bd. of Health v. Messerly, 417 Mich. 17, 331 N.W.2d 203 (1982).

First Baptist Church v. Solner, 341 Mich. 209, 67 N.W.2d 252 (1954) (mutual misunderstanding and mistake as to whether special assessment outstanding as lien on realty must be paid by vendors or vendee justified granting rescission).

Acreage sale

Where acreage sale was intended, but due to mutual mistake, written contract giving option to purchase land described as containing 20 acres more or less actually covered almost 24 acres, optionors were entitled to rescind contract upon repayment of the consideration for option.—Detroit Edison Co. v. Malburg, 148 F. Supp. 361 (D. Mich. 1957).

Party must be blameless

the trial court will not grant rescission unless the party requesting it is blameless. The trial court's finding that the contract was breached the contract negates any such finding of innocence on defendant's part. The trial court properly denied defendants' claim for rescission of the agreements.—Stanton v. Dachille, 186 Mich. App. 247, 463 N.W.2d 479, 1990 Mich. App. LEXIS 452 (1990).

210. Lenawee County Bd. of Health v. Messerly, 417 Mich. 17, 331 N.W.2d 203 (1982).

Stanton v. Dachille, 186 Mich. App. 247, 463 N.W.2d 479, 1990 Mich. App. LEXIS 452 (1990).

adversely affected party bears the risk of the mistake.[211] The mistake must have a material effect on the agreed exchange of performances and relate to a basic assumption of the parties upon which the contract is made.[212]

But a unilateral mistake arising from a lack of understanding by one party to the contract not induced by misrepresentation of the other party, and that might have been avoided by the due examination of the matter, does not invalidate a contract for the sale of land.[213] Likewise, an immaterial mistake does not support rescission of a contract for the sale of land.[214]

The vendor's and purchasers' mutual mistaken belief that property is suitable for human habitation and could be used to generate rental income does not justify rescission of a land contract, in light of a clause in the contract that provides that the purchasers accept the property "in its present condition."[215]

211. Lenawee County Bd. of Health v. Messerly, 417 Mich. 17, 331 N.W.2d 203 (1982).

Garb-Ko, Inc. v. Lansing-Lewis Services, Inc., 167 Mich. App. 779, 423 N.W.2d 355 (1988).

Risk assumed

Niecko v. Emro Mktg. Co., 769 F. Supp. 973 (E.D. Mich. 1991), aff'd, 973 F.2d 1296 (6th Cir. Mich. 1992).

212. Lenawee County Bd. of Health v. Messerly, 417 Mich. 17, 331 N.W.2d 203 (1982).

Bayagich v. Rose Twp., 2007 Mich. App. LEXIS 1289 (Mich. Ct. App. May 15, 2007).

Garb-Ko, Inc. v. Lansing-Lewis Services, Inc., 167 Mich. App. 779, 423 N.W.2d 355 (1988).

213. Standard Oil Co. v. Murray, 214 Mich. 299, 183 N.W. 55 (1921).

Leal v. Terbush, 52 Mich. 100, 17 N.W. 713 (1883).

Beebe v. Birkett, 109 Mich. 663, 67 N.W. 966 (1896) (failure to use ordinary care).

No evidence of mistake

Where purchaser of subdivision containing 91 lots sued vendors for partial rescission of land contract on grounds of fraud, misrepresentation, failure of consideration and mistake after purchaser had constructed 49 residences and thereafter had been refused septic tank permits, but there had been no mistake as to form or substance of the contract or the description of the property constituting the subject matter, purchaser was not entitled to partial rescission on ground of mistake in absence of fraud or reliance on any alleged misrepresentation of material facts, even though subdivision was of less value than purchaser had expected at time of entering into contract.—A & M Land Dev. Co. v. Miller, 354 Mich. 681, 94 N.W.2d 197 (1959).

Sewer facilities

Where prospective purchaser of vacant city lots and vendors had considered specific question of

adequacy of sewers but vendors refused to execute agreement containing a condition that sale was not to be consummated unless a satisfactory agreement could be worked out with city for sewers, and purchasers signed an agreement without such a condition and made payments thereunder, fact that subsequently an engineering report to city advised that sewers were overloaded, did not justify rescission of contract on ground of mutual mistake since there was not any want of mutual assent, or any lack of meeting of minds with respect to effect that inadequacy of sewers was to have on contract obligations of parties.—Friedman v. Grevnin, 360 Mich. 193, 103 N.W.2d 336 (1960).

214. Mistake in description not material

Possibility that vendor was unaware of extent of its property through some form of inadvertence was not "mistake" raising possibility of rescission of contract.—Goodwin, Inc. v. Coe, 392 Mich. 195, 220 N.W.2d 664 (1974) (abrogated on other grounds as stated in Converge, Inc. v. Topy Am., Inc., 316 Fed. Appx. 401, 2009 U.S. App. LEXIS 4917, 2009 FED App. 185N (6th Cir.) (6th Cir. Mich. 2009)).

Misdescription in land contract of property sold was not ground for rescission where purchasers knew boundaries and were not claiming that they had received less property than they had paid for.—Young v. Zavitz, 365 Mich. 354, 112 N.W.2d 493 (1961).

215. Lenawee County Bd. of Health v. Messerly, 417 Mich. 17, 331 N.W.2d 203 (1982) (property was uninhabitable because of inadequate and uncorrectable sewage system).

Additional representations

There were additional representations in the listing agreement and advertising that the land was zoned commercial and defendants furnished plaintiffs with drawings dividing the property for commercial use.—Britton v. Parkin, 176 Mich. App. 395, 438 N.W.2d 919, 1989 Mich. App. LEXIS 142 (1989).

On the other hand, vendors are entitled to rescission of a contract for the sale of commercial real property as a result of a mutual mistake of fact concerning the condition of the property, notwithstanding an "as is" clause where the contract was entered into without any knowledge by either party that the property is contaminated and where the vendors have a continuing obligation and responsibility under environmental protection statutes to control the use of the property in order to contain further cleanup costs and third-party claims arising from use of the contaminated property.[216]

§ 456.   —Vendor's Fraud and False Representations

A contract for the sale of land may be rescinded upon a showing of common-law fraud, innocent misrepresentation, or silent fraud under a duty to disclose.

A contract for the sale of land may be rescinded upon a showing of common-law fraud, innocent misrepresentation, or silent fraud under a duty to disclose.[217] In all cases, the representation must cause injury to the vendee.[218]

While under the common law doctrines outlined above, a vendee who takes on the risk of defects contractually is not entitled to relief for the vendor's misrepresentations, because the vendor has no duty to disclose,[219] the Seller Disclosure Act does not explicitly include instances of the vendee's contractual acceptance of responsibility for the property's condition in its list of transactions excepted from the

216. Garb-Ko, Inc. v. Lansing-Lewis Services, Inc., 167 Mich. App. 779, 423 N.W.2d 355 (1988).

217. Bayagich v. Rose Twp., 2007 Mich. App. LEXIS 1289 (Mich. Ct. App. May 15, 2007).

M & D, Inc. v. McConkey, 231 Mich. App. 22, 585 N.W.2d 33 (1998).

M & D, Inc. v. McConkey, 226 Mich. App. 801, 573 N.W.2d 281, 1997 Mich. App. LEXIS 446 (1997).

Stigmatized Property Law: To Disclose or Not To Disclose, That is the Question for Michigan Residential Sellers, 85 MI Bar Jnl. 34 (2006).

218. Dobson Trust v. S. Mich. Bank & Trust, 2010 Mich. App. LEXIS 96 (Mich. Ct. App. Jan. 19, 2010).

Huhtasaari v. Stockemer, 2005 Mich. App. LEXIS 3210 (Mich. Ct. App. Dec. 20, 2005).

M & D, Inc. v. McConkey, 231 Mich. App. 22, 585 N.W.2d 33 (1998).

M & D, Inc. v. McConkey, 226 Mich. App. 801, 573 N.W.2d 281, 1997 Mich. App. LEXIS 446 (1997).

Meander line unimportant

Where meander line was 277 feet from water's edge on Lake Michigan, purchaser from riparian owner, relying on representation that stake 100 feet from water marked boundary, suffered no damage from misrepresentation of boundary line, meander line not being boundary.—Hilt v. Weber, 252 Mich. 198, 233 N.W. 159 (1930).

219. Ivie v. Diversified Lending Group, Inc., 2011 U.S. Dist. LEXIS 27680 (W.D. Mich. Mar. 17, 2011).

Huhtasaari v. Stockemer, 2005 Mich. App. LEXIS 3210 (Mich. Ct. App. Dec. 20, 2005).

M & D, Inc. v. McConkey, 231 Mich. App. 22, 585 N.W.2d 33 (1998).

Property sold "as is"

Vendor of real property did not commit fraud by failing to disclose to purchasers that underground storage tanks were once located on property but had been removed, and that connecting pipes remained underground at time of sale; vendor had not affirmatively stated that tanks had not been removed or that pipes did not exist, vendor had no actual knowledge of chemical contamination of land, and under circumstances there was no duty to make further disclosure.—Niecko v. Emro Mktg. Co., 769 F. Supp. 973 (E.D. Mich. 1991), aff'd, 973 F.2d 1296 (6th Cir. Mich. 1992).

Termites

Vendors of real property sold "as is" do not have duty to warn purchasers of termite infestation; termite condition was not concealed given fact that competent inspector should reasonably have discovered evidence of active termites in home.—Conahan v. Fisher, 186 Mich. App. 48, 463 N.W.2d 118 (1990).

applicability of the duty it imposes.[220]

Of course, for any fraud, the vendee has to have been deceived by the vendor's false representation.[221]

That the vendee has a right to rely on what the vendor represented may also be required.[222] However, if the vendor's misrepresentation is the procuring cause of the contract, the vendor may not argue that the vendee might have discovered the true facts by the exercise of diligence,[223] especially when the vendor's statement or conduct induces the vendee to rely on the representations without making further inquiry.[224] Even the vendee's exercise of the opportunity to inspect the property does not relieve the vendor from the consequences of purposeful misrepresentations that an inspection cannot reveal.[225]

More clearly, a vendor is not responsible for the vendee's misinterpretation of the vendor's statements to the vendee.[226] Likewise, a vendor is not responsible for a vendee's reliance on the vendor's statement that the vendee can verify, so long as the vendor does not deter the vendee's verification.[227]

A vendor is equally responsible for fraudulent representations inducing the sale whether they were made by him- or herself or by a third person to whom he or she referred the vendee with the expectation that the vendee would be deceived.[228]

If a vendor ratified his or her attorney's claimed modification of a land

220. MCLS § 565.953.

Real Property Law: What's New in Residential Transactions?, 86 MI Bar Jnl. 16 (2007).

"As Is" Clauses: The Law Behind "As Is" Clauses in Residential Real Estate Transactions, 84 MI Bar Jnl. 35 (2005).

221. German Bundesheim Soc'y v. Schmidt, 242 Mich. 139, 218 N.W. 664 (1928).

Whiting v. Hill, 23 Mich. 399 (1871).

222. Hammer v. Martin, 205 Mich. 359, 171 N.W. 419 (1919).

223. Lewis v. Peck, 251 Mich. 501, 232 N.W. 219 (1930) (fact that purchaser had some information and sought more from other sources would not relieve vendor from fraudulent representations, if purchaser relied on them).

224. Webster v. Bailey, 31 Mich. 36 (1875).

225. Water and sewer lines

That officers of corporate purchaser of land went on the land before they executed land contract did not, of itself, prohibit their showing, in their action to rescind the land contract, that they were misled by misrepresentation of the vendors that water and sewage facilities were available.—Le Roy Constr. Co. v. McCann, 356 Mich. 305, 96 N.W.2d 757 (1959).

226. Lack of easement for driveway

Statement in preliminary sales agreement that "driveway on north to be used as long as avail-

able" should have put grantees and anyone seeking to depend on it on notice that there was no easement or joint ownership but rather that use of driveway was temporary and permissive only and might be terminated whenever driveway was no longer available.—Troff v. Boeve, 354 Mich. 593, 93 N.W.2d 311 (1958).

227. Amount of property taxes

Representation that taxes on lot would be only $8 and would not be increased while lot remained unimproved could not be entirely relied on by purchaser seeking cancellation.—Burlingame v. B.E. Taylor Realty Co., 247 Mich. 109, 225 N.W. 562 (1929).

Misrepresentation not shown

Evidence that failed to reveal vendor's earnings from resort property prior to sale, but that revealed purchasers' failure to insist upon inspection of vendors' books and records, failed to establish misrepresentation or fraud sufficient to warrant rescission of contract of purchase in regard to alleged statements of gross rental income.—Young v. Zavitz, 365 Mich. 354, 112 N.W.2d 493 (1961).

228. Graham v. Moffett, 119 Mich. 303, 78 N.W. 132 (1899).

Invalidity of whole contract

A contract for purchase of land and chattels was not severable, with respect to fraud vitiating the whole contract.—Gyles v. Stadel, 252 Mich. 349, 233 N.W. 339 (1930).

contract, and then repudiated the modification, that fact does not constitute fraud relating back to the original contract.[229]

Advertisements. False newspaper advertisements may constitute fraud that will avoid a contract of sale.[230]

Expressions of opinion. Ordinarily the vendor's mere expression of opinion cannot amount to a misrepresentation entitling the vendee to avoid the contract.[231] But this rule is inapplicable where the representation is one of fact rather than of opinion,[232] or where it is a mixed statement of fact and opinion.[233]

Predictions and promises. The vendor's unfulfilled predictions as to what might happen in the future,[234] or vendor's broken promises,[235] as with respect to his or her future conduct,[236] are not ground for avoidance of the contract by the vendee in the absence of fraudulent intent on the part of the vendor. On the other hand, the vendee may be entitled to avoid the contract if the vendee acted in reliance on a promise made by the vendor with no intent to perform it,[237] or where the statement was a mixture of fact and prediction or promise.[238]

§ 457.   —Fraudulent or Innocent Misrepresentation

A vendor's knowingly false representation concerning a material matter, relied on by the vendee, gives the latter the right to avoid the contract.

In addition to the vendee's injury, for common-law fraud to give the vendee

229. Pine Shores Realty Co. v. Parker, 253 Mich. 300, 235 N.W. 163 (1931).

230. Le Roy Constr. Co. v. McCann, 356 Mich. 305, 96 N.W.2d 757 (1959).

231. Burlingame v. B.E. Taylor Realty Co., 247 Mich. 109, 225 N.W. 562 (1929).

Draft v. Hesselsweet, 194 Mich. 604, 161 N.W. 864 (1917).

Cost of repairs

Statement by real estate salesman that cost of repairs to home would not exceed $2,000 was merely opinion and fraud could not be predicated on such statement.—Windham v. Morris, 370 Mich. 188, 121 N.W.2d 479 (1963).

232. Reese v. Elliott, 216 Mich. 620, 185 N.W. 693 (1921).

Kefuss v. Whitley, 220 Mich. 67, 189 N.W. 76 (1922) (vendor's reason for selling).

233. Intermingling

Where representations of one who has been in actual occupation and cultivation of land, and purports to speak from actual results, so far combine matters of fact with matters of opinion that purchaser is justified in placing reliance on them, and if such representations are fraudulent and untrue, it will entitle the purchaser to cancellation.—Wright v. Wright, 37 Mich. 55 (1877).

234. Burlingame v. B.E. Taylor Realty Co., 247 Mich. 109, 225 N.W. 562 (1929) (representation that gas and water systems would be installed within six months).

Future possibility

Where the vendor's agent wrote that fruit on the farm would pay for the farm the first year, that statement was an opinion as to a future possibility, and its falsity afforded no ground to rescind.—Draft v. Hesselsweet, 194 Mich. 604, 161 N.W. 864 (1917).

235. Taylor v. Ward, 264 Mich. 118, 249 N.W. 473 (1933) (in absence of proof that vendee had no intention to keep promise, vendor could not claim rescission for fraud based on promise).

236. Schnitz v. Grand River Ave. Development Co., 271 Mich. 253, 259 N.W. 900 (1935).

Kellam v. Frischkorn Real Estate Co., 242 Mich. 572, 219 N.W. 658 (1928).

237. Promise to employ vendee

Promises of vendor's agent to resell lots at profit to couple and to erect gas station and barbecue stand and hire husband as manager, made to induce couple to enter into contract for purchase of lots and without any intention of performing, were fraudulent.—Gower v. Wieser, 269 Mich. 6, 256 N.W. 603 (1934).

238. Conger v. Thomas & Lane, 258 Mich. 702, 242 N.W. 815 (1932).

the right to repudiate the contract, the vendor must make a material representation,[239] the vendor's representation must be false,[240] the vendor has to have known it was false or recklessly disregarded the possibility that it was false when the vendor made the representation,[241] and the vendee must have relied on the representation.[242] Thus, a vendor's knowingly false representation concerning a material matter, relied on by the vendee, gives the latter the right to avoid the contract.[243]

To be able to recover for innocent misrepresentation,[244] the vendee must show all the elements of common-law fraud except for the vendor's knowledge or reckless disregard of the possibility that the representation is false. The vendee must also prove that the vendor made the unintentionally false representation in connection with the making of the contract and that the benefit from the injury suffered by the vendees inures to the vendor.[245]

§ 458.   —Duty to Disclose

Under common law, to be able to recover for silent fraud in a contract for the sale of land, the vendee must show that the vendor made a representation that was false. The Seller Disclosure Act generally imposes a duty of extensive disclosure on the vendor about the condition of residential real property being sold.

To be able to recover for silent fraud in a contract for the sale of land, the vendee must show that the vendor made a representation that was false. The misrepresentation need not necessarily be words alone, but can be shown where the

---

239. Jackson v. Armstrong, 50 Mich. 65, 14 N.W. 702 (1883) (vendor's false representation of rate of interest on mortgage subject to which he or she sells is material).

M & D, Inc. v. McConkey, 231 Mich. App. 22, 585 N.W.2d 33 (1998) (no material representation made).

M & D, Inc. v. McConkey, 226 Mich. App. 801, 573 N.W.2d 281, 1997 Mich. App. LEXIS 446 (1997) (no material representation made).

240. M & D, Inc. v. McConkey, 231 Mich. App. 22, 585 N.W.2d 33 (1998).

M & D, Inc. v. McConkey, 226 Mich. App. 801, 573 N.W.2d 281, 1997 Mich. App. LEXIS 446 (1997).

241. M & D, Inc. v. McConkey, 231 Mich. App. 22, 585 N.W.2d 33 (1998).

M & D, Inc. v. McConkey, 226 Mich. App. 801, 573 N.W.2d 281, 1997 Mich. App. LEXIS 446 (1997).

Actions designed to deceive

Where plaintiffs were deceived in purchase of realty by means employed by defendant that were designed to cause deception and that he knew did

cause it, court would grant relief from contract.— Match v. Hunt, 38 Mich. 1 (1878).

242. German Bundesheim Soc'y v. Schmidt, 242 Mich. 139, 218 N.W. 664 (1928).

M & D, Inc. v. McConkey, 231 Mich. App. 22, 585 N.W.2d 33 (1998).

M & D, Inc. v. McConkey, 226 Mich. App. 801, 573 N.W.2d 281, 1997 Mich. App. LEXIS 446 (1997).

243. Kroninger v. Anast, 367 Mich. 478, 116 N.W.2d 863 (1962).

Lackovic v. Campbell, 225 Mich. 1, 195 N.W. 798 (1923).

Banski v. Michalski, 204 Mich. 15, 169 N.W. 932 (1918).

244. Houder v. Reynolds, 195 Mich. 256, 161 N.W. 856 (1917).

Britton v. Parkin, 176 Mich. App. 395, 438 N.W.2d 919 (1989).

245. M & D, Inc. v. McConkey, 231 Mich. App. 22, 585 N.W.2d 33 (1998) (no representation).

M & D, Inc. v. McConkey, 226 Mich. App. 801, 573 N.W.2d 281, 1997 Mich. App. LEXIS 446 (1997) (no representation).

party, if duty bound to disclose, intentionally suppresses material facts to create a false impression to the other party. It is not enough that the seller had knowledge of the defect and failed to disclose it.[246] Highly misleading actions on the vendor's part can constitute the silent fraud.[247] A vendee can recover for silent fraud even if the defects did not raise unreasonable danger.[248]

Thus, silent fraud occurs where the vendor has the duty to disclose.[249] In this context, a vendor has a duty to disclose when the vendee has expressed a particular concern or made a direct inquiry regarding a specific issue.[250] If a vendor acquires

246. Roberts v. Saffell, 280 Mich. App. 397, 760 N.W.2d 715, 2008 Mich. App. LEXIS 1756 (2008).

Huhtasaari v. Stockemer, 2005 Mich. App. LEXIS 3210 (Mich. Ct. App. Dec. 20, 2005).

Chesstnutt v. Crist, 1999 Mich. App. LEXIS 2341 (Mich. Ct. App. Sept. 17, 1999).

M & D, Inc. v. McConkey, 231 Mich. App. 22, 585 N.W.2d 33 (1998).

M & D, Inc. v. McConkey, 226 Mich. App. 801, 573 N.W.2d 281, 1997 Mich. App. LEXIS 446 (1997).

Stigmatized Property Law: To Disclose or Not To Disclose, That is the Question For Michigan Residential Sellers, 85 MI Bar Jnl. 34 (2006).

"As Is" Clauses: The Law Behind "As Is" Clauses in Residential Real Estate Transactions, 84 MI Bar Jnl. 35 (2005).

247. Groening v. Opsata, 323 Mich. 73, 34 N.W.2d 560 (1948).

No highly misleading actions

That vendor "cleaned up" property by removing "all outward traces of the flooding" in that the basement was painted and recarpeted was not sufficient evidence that seller intended to create an affirmative impression that there was no flooding problem with the building; sellers will often take steps to improve the property in an effort to get more money from buyer; these actions cannot automatically lead to the conclusion that seller is perpetrating fraud against potential buyers.—M & D, Inc. v. McConkey, 231 Mich. App. 22, 585 N.W.2d 33 (1998).

Provision in purchase agreement

Plaintiff acknowledged that her purchase agreement contained an "as is" clause and that the property listing, contained other statements that specifically disclaimed any representations and warranties about the property. The purchase agreement also contained a provision stating, "Buyers and Sellers acknowledge that they are not relying on any other written or verbal representations by each other or by Listing or Selling Brokers that are not explicitly set forth in this agreement or attached hereto." Contrary to plaintiff's argument, the court disagreed that the "as is" clause in the purchase agreement was without effect concerning the alleged misrepresentations. This was not a case in which the buyer expressed some particularized concern or made a direct inquiry, and the seller concealed material facts or made fraudulent representations to the buyer, on which the buyer relied, such that the "as is" clause is ineffective. Nor was this a case in which "highly misleading actions" could support a claim of silent fraud, absent a buyer's specific inquiry. The court found no error in the grant of a motion for summary disposition.—Seit-Olsen v. Appraisals, 2006 Mich. App. LEXIS 1493 (Mich. Ct. App. Apr. 27, 2006).

248. Elliott v. Therrien, 2010 Mich. App. LEXIS 166 (Mich. Ct. App. Jan. 26, 2010).

Roberts v. Saffell, 280 Mich. App. 397, 760 N.W.2d 715, 2008 Mich. App. LEXIS 1756 (2008).

M & D, Inc. v. McConkey, 231 Mich. App. 22, 585 N.W.2d 33 (1998).

Clemens v. Lesnek, 200 Mich. App. 456, 505 N.W.2d 283 (1993).

249. Beshada v. Millard Realty, Railside Appraisal Servs., 2004 Mich. App. LEXIS 54 (Mich. Ct. App. Jan. 13, 2004).

M & D, Inc. v. McConkey, 231 Mich. App. 22, 585 N.W.2d 33 (1998).

Existence of hidden defect

A plaintiff is required to establish more than just an awareness by the vendor of the existence of a hidden defect. To prove a silent fraud claim, "a plaintiff must show that some type of representation that was false or misleading was made and that there was a legal or equitable duty of disclosure." Specifically, "a claim of silent fraud is established when there is a suppression of material facts and there is a legal or equitable duty of disclosure. . . . There must be some type of misrepresentation, whether by words or action, in order to establish a claim of silent fraud."—Huhtasaari v. Stockemer, 2005 Mich. App. LEXIS 3210 (Mich. Ct. App. Dec. 20, 2005).

250. Groening v. Opsata, 323 Mich. 73, 34 N.W.2d 560 (1948).

Kefuss v. Whitley, 220 Mich. 67, 189 N.W. 76 (1922) (vendor's reason for selling).

new information after responding to a concern of the vendee, the vendor has a duty to convey it to the vendee.[251]

The Seller Disclosure Act generally imposes a duty on the vendor of extensive disclosure of information about the condition of residential real property being sold, such information to be set forth on a form specified by statute.[252]

Seller Disclosure Act. The disclosure requirements of the Seller Disclosure Act apply to the transfer of any interest in real estate consisting of not less than one or more than four residential units whether by sale, exchange, installment land contract, lease with an option to purchase, any other option to purchase, or ground lease coupled with proposed improvements by the purchaser or tenant, or a transfer of stock or an interest in a residential cooperative.[253] The act excepts certain transactions from its reach.[254]

Under the act, the transferor of real property has a duty to deliver to the transferor's agent, the transferee, or the transferee's agent the required written disclosure statement as to the condition of the property.[255] Delivery of the information after the execution of a binding contract for sale of real property allows the purchaser to terminate the agreement by delivering a written notice to that effect to the vendor or the vendor's agent within the specified deadline.[256] The form of the statement is specified by statute.[257] The form must state the condition of the property in good faith[258] based on the best information available and known to the vendor.[259]

If the vendee accepts performance of the contract, his or her right to rescind

Elliott v. Therrien, 2010 Mich. App. LEXIS 166 (Mich. Ct. App. Jan. 26, 2010).

Woodland Harvesting v. Ga. Pac. Corp., 2010 U.S. Dist. LEXIS 70674 (E.D. Mich. July 14, 2010).

Expression of concern

Michigan law provides that a duty of disclosure may arise from an expression of concern by a contracting party. Abstract, generalized, or ambiguous expressions of concern, however, will not suffice; full disclosure is required only in response to "some particularized concern" or "direct inquiry." But while an expression of particularized concern has been said to give rise to a duty to disclose, no silent fraud case in Michigan has found liability based on such facts; rather, in every case, the fraud by nondisclosure was based upon statements that were made in response to a specific inquiry, which statements were in some way incomplete or misleading.—First Presbyterian Church v. H.A. Howell Pipe Organs, Inc., 2010 U.S. Dist. LEXIS 24050 (E.D. Mich. Mar. 16, 2010).

Silent fraud not shown

Vendee did not show duty of vendor to disclose flooding problem, and vendee never made inquiries requiring disclosure of vendor's knowledge of extent of problem with basement in house on real property being sold.—M & D, Inc. v. McConkey, 231 Mich. App. 22, 585 N.W.2d 33 (1998).

251. Hord v. Environmental Research Inst., 463 Mich. 399, 617 N.W.2d 543, 2000 Mich. LEXIS 2064, 16 I.E.R. Cas. (BNA) 1567, 142 Lab. Cas. (CCH) P59068 (2000).

Gadjev v. Anderson, 2004 Mich. App. LEXIS 1796 (Mich. Ct. App. June 29, 2004).

M & D, Inc. v. McConkey, 231 Mich. App. 22, 585 N.W.2d 33 (1998).

252. MCLS §§ 565.951 et seq.

Stigmatized Property Law: To Disclose or not to Disclose, that is the Question for Michigan Residential Sellers, 85 MI Bar Jnl. 34 (2006).

"As Is" Clauses: The Law Behind "As Is" Clauses in Residential Real Estate Transactions, 84 MI Bar Jnl. 35 (2005).

253. MCLS § 565.952.

Westrick v. Jeglic, 2010 Mich. App. LEXIS 1360 (Mich. Ct. App. July 15, 2010).

254. MCLS § 565.953.

255. MCLS § 565.954.

256. MCLS § 565.954.

257. MCLS § 565.957.

258. MCLS § 565.960.

Bad faith failure to disclose

Circumstantial evidence existed to create a genuine issue of material fact as to whether a roof

under the Seller Disclosure Act is extinguished.[260]

A city, town, or county may enact additional requirements concerning the necessary disclosures and the form on which the disclosures are to be made.[261]

Neither the transferor or the transferor's agent is liable for any error, inaccuracy, or omission in information that the transferor discloses if the error, inaccuracy, or omission is not within the personal knowledge of the transferor, or is based entirely on information provided by public agencies or provided by other persons or experts, and ordinary care is exercised in transmitting the information.[262]

Except as the act provides, the failure of the vendor to comply with the Seller

in a room leaked at the time sellers delivered a disclosure statement to the purchasers as required under the Michigan Seller Disclosure Act suggesting that the roof had leaked in the past, that the leak had been fixed, and that there were no existing problems of leakage, and as to whether sellers acted in bad faith and had personal knowledge of leakage or whether they should have had personal knowledge through the exercise of reasonable care; the circumstantial evidence included the considerable extent of the leak and affidavits from contractors suggesting that the leakage was a long-term condition that could be corrected only by a complete overhaul of the room (MCLS §§ 565.952, 565.954(1), 565.955, 565.957, 565.960, 565.961).—Bergen v. Baker, 264 Mich. App. 376, 691 N.W.2d 770 (2004).

Item specified for disclosure

Where an item is specified for disclosure on the SDS, a transferor may be liable for fraud or silent fraud if the elements of those causes of action are proved, including that the transferor possessed personal knowledge about the item but failed to exercise "good faith" by disclosing that knowledge.—Roberts v. Saffell, 280 Mich. App. 397, 760 N.W.2d 715, 2008 Mich. App. LEXIS 1756 (2008).

Reliance on disclosure statement

Purchasers of residential real property created a genuine issue of material fact sufficient to survive summary disposition with regard to whether they reasonably relied on the sellers' disclosure statement delivered as required by the Michigan Seller Disclosure Act, where purchasers' complaint alleged that sellers failed to disclose a leaking roof in a hot tub room, and where the disclosure statement could be read as suggesting that the roof in the hot tub room had leaked in the past, that the leak had been corrected, and that there were no existing or active problems with roof leakage (MCLS §§ 565.952, 565.954(1), 565.955, 565.957, 565.960, 565.961).—Bergen v. Baker, 264 Mich. App. 376, 691 N.W.2d 770 (2004).

259. MCLS § 565.956.

Elliott v. Therrien, 2010 Mich. App. LEXIS 166 (Mich. Ct. App. Jan. 26, 2010).

Roberts v. Saffell, 280 Mich. App. 397, 760 N.W.2d 715, 2008 Mich. App. LEXIS 1756 (2008).

"Error" in disclosure statement

Purchasers of residential real estate established a genuine issue of material fact as to whether sellers' disclosure statement made under the Michigan Seller Disclosure Act was "in error, inaccurate, and reflected a misrepresentation or omission," where the suggestions in the disclosure statement that there had a been a past problem with water leakage, that the problem had been fixed, and there was not a current problem with leakage, would be "in error" if the leakage problem existed when the disclosure statement was made (MCLS §§ 565.952, 565.954(1), 565.955, 565.957, 565.960, 565.961).—Bergen v. Baker, 264 Mich. App. 376, 691 N.W.2d 770 (2004).

260. MCLS § 565.954.

261. MCLS § 565.959.

262. MCLS § 565.955.

Innocent misrepresentation not actionable

In lieu of granting leave to appeal, the Supreme Court affirmed the judgment of the Court of appeals that a claim of innocent misrepresentation is not a viable cause of action under the Seller Disclosure Act (SDA); the SDA provides that a seller is "not liable for any error, inaccuracy, or omission in any information delivered pursuant to this act if the error, inaccuracy, or omission was not within the personal knowledge of the transferor" and a claim for innocent misrepresentation requires that a defendant make a false statement "without knowledge" of its falsity (MCLS § 565.955(1)).—Roberts v. Saffell, 483 Mich. 1089, 766 N.W.2d 288, 2009 Mich. LEXIS 1381 (2009).

Innocent misrepresentation is not a viable theory of liability under the Seller Disclosure Act (MCLS § 565.957).—Roberts v. Saffell, 280 Mich. App. 397, 760 N.W.2d 715, 2008 Mich. App. LEXIS 1756 (2008).

Disclosure Act does not otherwise invalidate a contract for sale of real property.[263]

While under the common law doctrines, including silent fraud, a vendee who takes on the risk of defects contractually is not entitled to relief for the vendor's misrepresentations,[264] the Seller Disclosure Act does not explicitly include instances of the vendee's contractual acceptance of responsibility for the property's condition in its list of transactions excepted from the applicability of the duty it imposes.[265]

§ 459.   —Representations as to Particular Matters

Various acts of fraud or false representations are grounds for avoidance of a contract for the sale of land, such as false representations with respect to future profits, title, or market price.

Where the elements of remediable fraud are present, the vendee is entitled to avoid a contract for the sale of land for false representations of the vendor as to various matters,[266] such as the condition of the land,[267] the principal balance remaining on a mortgage to be assumed,[268] the cost of insurance,[269] the location of the property,[270] the past earnings of business property,[271] the productive capacity of a farm,[272] or the sufficiency of a foundation.[273] The contract may be avoided by the

263. MCLS § 565.964.

264. Huhtasaari v. Stockemer, 2005 Mich. App. LEXIS 3210 (Mich. Ct. App. Dec. 20, 2005).

McGrath v. Webber, 2004 Mich. App. LEXIS 2001 (Mich. Ct. App. July 20, 2004).

M & D, Inc. v. McConkey, 231 Mich. App. 22, 585 N.W.2d 33 (1998).

Property sold "as is"

Vendor of real property did not commit fraud by failing to disclose to purchasers that underground storage tanks were once located on property but had been removed, and that connecting pipes remained underground at time of sale; vendor had not affirmatively stated that tanks had not been removed or that pipes did not exist, vendor had no actual knowledge of chemical contamination of land, and under circumstances there was no duty to make further disclosure.—Niecko v. Emro Mktg. Co., 769 F. Supp. 973 (E.D. Mich. 1991), aff'd, 973 F.2d 1296 (6th Cir. Mich. 1992).

Termites

Vendors of real property sold "as is" do not have duty to warn purchasers of termite infestation; termite condition was not concealed given fact that competent inspector should reasonably have discovered evidence of active termites in home.—Conahan v. Fisher, 186 Mich. App. 48, 463 N.W.2d 118 (1990).

265. MCLS § 565.953.

266. Existence of beach

Where representation that lot had sand bathing beach was material, relied on, and false, rescinding

land contract for fraud was proper.—Clark v. Bingham & Bingham, 259 Mich. 697, 244 N.W. 206 (1932).

267. Cole Lakes, Inc. v. Linder, 99 Mich. App. 496, 297 N.W.2d 918 (1980).

268. Past due

Representation by one exchanging land that there was nothing past due on contract of sale was material, and other party was entitled to rescind, where more than $600 was past due at time.—Banski v. Michalski, 204 Mich. 15, 169 N.W. 932 (1918).

269. Chanler v. Venetian Properties Corp., 254 Mich. 468, 236 N.W. 838 (1931) (annual cost of insurance, fuel, and taxes).

270. Billig v. Goodrich, 199 Mich. 423, 165 N.W. 647 (1917) (incorrect map).

J.B. Millet Co. v. Andrews, 175 Mich. 350, 141 N.W. 578 (1913) (situation of building lot).

271. Miller v. Voorheis, 115 Mich. 356, 73 N.W. 383 (1897).

272. Blampey v. Pike, 155 Mich. 384, 119 N.W. 576 (1909).

273. Caveat emptor inapplicable

Purchasers of cottage could rescind the contract because of vendor's misrepresentations as to sufficiency of foundation under the house on discovery that the foundation was of such shallow depth that, taken in connection with the porous condition of the filled-in land on which the house was built, the house settled, the defect being a latent one, and

vendee for false representations of the vendor regarding the receipt of other offers for the property.[274] The vendee may also avoid a contract for false representations by a person claiming to be agent for another in the sale of land to the effect that the owner would not take less than a specified price for the property.[275]

Future profits. A vendor's expression of an erroneous opinion about the probable future profits to be received from business property is not grounds for avoiding a contract for its sale.[276] But where the vendor makes false representations of fact respecting the conditions on which the purchasers base their estimates of future profits, this may constitute misrepresentation invalidating the contract.[277]

Title. The vendor's false representation concerning his or her title to the property may afford ground for avoiding the contract,[278] provided the misrepresentation of title results in injury.[279] But where the vendors did not have a perfect title to the property sold but were in a position to perfect it and did so within a reasonable time after execution of the contract, the vendor's oral representations of ownership did not authorize a rescission of the contract.[280]

Value. Ordinarily, an expression of opinion as to the value of real estate,[281] or the future increase in its value,[282] does not afford grounds for avoiding the contract on the basis of fraud or false representation. However, an exception may apply if there is a relation of trust and confidence, if the value is peculiarly within the knowledge of the vendor, if the vendee's reliance on the representation is clearly

the doctrine of caveat emptor being inapplicable.—Mulheron v. Henry S. Koppin Co., 221 Mich. 187, 190 N.W. 674 (1922) (overruled in part on other grounds by Witte v. Hobolth, 224 Mich. 286, 195 N.W. 82 (1923)).

274. German Bundesheim Soc'y v. Schmidt, 242 Mich. 139, 218 N.W. 664 (1928).

275. Norris v. Home City Lodge, 203 Mich. 90, 168 N.W. 935 (1918).

276. Sweet v. Martin, 233 Mich. 655, 207 N.W. 845 (1926).

277. Sweet v. Martin, 233 Mich. 655, 207 N.W. 845 (1926).

278. Title in fee

Where defendant represented to plaintiffs that he had title in fee, and he had only a contract for a deed by which he agreed with his vendor to accept a deed subject to overdue mortgages, the misrepresentation was sufficient to warrant a rescission of plaintiff's contract to purchase.—Allen v. Talbot, 170 Mich. 664, 137 N.W. 97 (1912).

279. Walcrath Realty Co. v. Van Dyke, 263 Mich. 316, 248 N.W. 634 (1933).

280. Adadow v. Perry, 225 Mich. 286, 196 N.W. 190 (1923).

281. Kowalski v. Rusin, 242 Mich. 1, 217 N.W. 768 (1928).

Albright v. Stockhill, 208 Mich. 468, 175 N.W. 252 (1919) (honest difference of opinion).

Pound v. Clum, 204 Mich. 28, 170 N.W. 41 (1918) (equal means of knowledge).

George v. Spencer, 56 Mich. App. 249, 223 N.W.2d 736 (1974) (real estate salesman's representation to purchaser that he had parties interested at specified sum was mere "puffing").

Examination of property by purchaser

Purchasers, who examined house alone and stated to husband as they were leaving that they thought they would purchase the place and who later in the day examined premises again when real estate salesman was present, did not rely on alleged fraudulent representation by salesman that property had been appraised in husband's divorce case at $6,600 and purchasers were not entitled to relief when they learned about a year later that husband had placed a value of $4,500 on the property in his divorce suit.—Windham v. Morris, 370 Mich. 188, 121 N.W.2d 479 (1963).

Full opportunity to examine property

In an action to set aside for fraud purchase of land, where it appeared that plaintiff had full opportunity to examine land and its situation and partly did so, action will not lie for false representations about value of land.—Hammer v. Martin, 205 Mich. 359, 171 N.W. 419 (1919).

282. Burlingame v. B.E. Taylor Realty Co., 247 Mich. 109, 225 N.W. 562 (1929) (representation that lot would increase in value in certain amount and could be readily resold).

expected and intended, or if the representations prevent the vendee from making inquiries that he or she would otherwise make.[283]

Where statements as to the value of land are coupled with concealment or misrepresentation as to material facts, there may be ground for avoiding the contract.[284] A misrepresentation with respect to the market price or value of real estate may constitute a remediable misrepresentation of fact.[285]

§ 460.   —Vendee's Fraud and False Representations

A vendor acting to his or her damage in selling property in reliance on false or fraudulent representations of the vendee as to material matters may rescind the contract. But where the elements of actionable fraud are absent, the vendor may not secure relief on that ground.

A vendor induced to sell land to his or her damage in reliance on the fraud or false representations of the vendee concerning a material matter may avoid the contract.[286] The vendor may be entitled to rescission if he or she is induced to sell in exchange for personal property that the vendee has misrepresented with respect to matters of value,[287] or where the vendor is induced to sell by fraudulent promises of the vendee.[288] In such cases, the contract is not void, but merely voidable at the vendor's option, and the vendor may stand on the contract if he or she so desires.[289]

On the other hand, if the elements of remediable fraud are absent, the vendor may not avoid a contract for the sale of land on the ground of the alleged fraud or misrepresentation of the vendee.[290] Thus, the vendee's misrepresentation of value of personal property exchanged for real property is not always grounds for rescission

283. Hammer v. Martin, 205 Mich. 359, 171 N.W. 419 (1919).

284. Pound v. Clum, 204 Mich. 28, 170 N.W. 41 (1918).

Van Looyengoed v. Allencrest Gardens Corp., 265 Mich. 182, 251 N.W. 317 (1933) (concealment of fact that there was no local market for lots sold).

285. Reese v. Elliott, 216 Mich. 620, 185 N.W. 693 (1921).

Hammer v. Martin, 205 Mich. 359, 171 N.W. 419 (1919) (that vendor represents that land is worth certain sum is different from saying that its market value is certain amount, the first being merely an expression of opinion, while latter is statement of fact).

286. Kimmel v. Peach, 240 Mich. 697, 216 N.W. 374 (1927).

Grand Rapids, Grand Haven & Muskegon R. Co. v. Stevens, 143 Mich. 646, 107 N.W. 436 (1906).

Storrs v. Scougale, 48 Mich. 387, 12 N.W. 502 (1882) (long course of deceit).

White v. Mitchell, 38 Mich. 390 (1878) (vendors may rescind a sale procured by fraud).

287. Graham v. Moffett, 119 Mich. 303, 78 N.W. 132 (1899) (bank stock).

288. Dirr v. Adler, 262 Mich. 688, 247 N.W. 783 (1933) (vendees' fraudulent promise to assume mortgage and relieve vendor of liability thereon).

No intent to keep promise

One who fraudulently, and with no purpose of fulfillment, procures conveyance in consideration of agreement to obtain conveyance of other lands to grantor, and then retains title and possession, may be compelled in equity to pay the value of premises as if on a completed sale to him or her.—Merrill v. Allen, 38 Mich. 487 (1878).

289. Dunks v. Fuller, 32 Mich. 242 (1875).

290. Kent v. Matheson, 276 Mich. 316, 267 N.W. 847 (1936).

Jefferson Land Co. v. Kannowski, 233 Mich. 211, 206 N.W. 351 (1925).

Davis v. Phillips, 85 Mich. 198, 48 N.W. 513 (1891).

No fraud in law

A contract for the sale of land worth $9,000 for $1,000 cash, and the balance in payments of $500

of a contract for the sale of the real property.[291] The vendor's lack of reliance upon the vendee's statements also precludes rescission for the vendee's false representations.[292]

Concealment. The vendee's concealment of material facts, coupled with misrepresentations that prevent investigation, may constitute good grounds for refusal of the court to enforce a contract of sale against the vendor.[293]

Generally, a prospective purchaser is under no duty to disclose facts or possible opportunities within his or her knowledge that materially affect the value of the property.[294] Similarly, the vendee is not guilty of fraudulent concealment because of failure to disclose the purpose of his or her own purchase,[295] or to advise the vendor of probable future developments that might increase the value of the property.[296]

§ 461. Illegality

The object and provisions of a contract for the sale of land must not violate law or public policy.

The object and provisions of a contract for the sale of land must be such as do not violate law or public policy, and a contract violative of constitutional guaranties is invalid.[297] In order to bring this rule into operation, however, there must be something in the provisions of the contract that violates the law.[298]

Land Division Act. The Land Division Act deals with the making, approving,

yearly, including interest, was not a fraud in law.—Armstrong v. Martin, 171 Mich. 291, 137 N.W. 143 (1912).

291. Williams v. Spurr, 24 Mich. 335 (1872).

292. Reduction of income

Contract to buy real estate was not voided by purchaser's opinion that monthly installments under another contract taken over by vendor would be reduced, where it appeared that the vendor did not rely on such expression of opinion.—Glanbin v. Kousin, 249 Mich. 603, 229 N.W. 417 (1930).

293. Swimm v. Bush, 23 Mich. 99 (1871) (in that case, relief will not be refused merely because a sharp business man would not have been deceived in the same circumstances; the ground of redress is that the arts were designed to overreach the person dealt with, and that the latter, without fault or unreasonable neglect, was actually defrauded thereby).

294. Jones v. Keene, 2002 Mich. App. LEXIS 1031 (Mich. Ct. App. July 9, 2002).

Zaschak v. Traverse Corp., 123 Mich. App. 126, 333 N.W.2d 191 (1983).

295. Dorow v. Smith, 247 Mich. 320, 225 N.W. 533 (1929).

Stuart v. Dorow, 216 Mich. 591, 185 N.W. 662 (1921).

296. Furman v. Brown, 227 Mich. 629, 199 N.W. 703 (1924).

Burt v. Mason, 97 Mich. 127, 56 N.W. 365 (1893) (building of railroad).

297. Bloomfield Estates Improvement Ass'n v. City of Birmingham, 479 Mich. 206, 737 N.W.2d 670, 2007 Mich. LEXIS 1578 (2007).

Proctor & Assocs. v. Van Renken, 1997 Mich. App. LEXIS 1916 (Mich. Ct. App. Dec. 9, 1997)

Child-bartering agreement

Former wife's notarized statement wherein she gave to former husband any claim she had in marital home was result of "child-bartering agreement," as delivery of statement was conditioned on former husband's relinquishment of custody of parties' children to her, and was contrary to public policy and unenforceable.—Stinebaugh v. Bristol, 132 Mich. App. 311, 347 N.W.2d 219 (1984).

298. Bradway v. Miller, 200 Mich. 648, 167 N.W. 15 (1918) (agreement for title to be shown to be marketable by abstract of title is good).

Ratification

That salesman signed name of former prospective purchaser to land contract and assignment of it without authority, to give new purchaser benefit of down payment, did not warrant rescission by new purchaser as assignee, where owners ratified as-

filing, recording, altering, and vacating of plats; the recording of plats, on subdivided property; and the reservation of easements for utilities in vacated streets and alleys; and provides a penalty for violation of its provisions.[299] Under the Land Division Act, any sale of land subdivided in violation of its provisions is voidable at the option of the purchaser. That violation subjects the seller to the forfeiture of consideration received or pledged for the property, together with damages sustained by the purchaser recoverable in an action at law.[300]

If a violation of the act with respect to a property is cured, the right to void the contract of sale is extinguished, unless the purchaser has suffered harm.[301]

A purchaser of real property who participates in the illegal subdivision of the land that he or she then purchases is not eligible to subsequently void the contract of sale for the land.[302]

§ 462.　Waiver and Estoppel

The right to avoid a contract for the sale of land may be lost by waiver or estoppel. Violation of the Seller Disclosure Act or the Land Division Act is not subject to waiver or estoppel as against the purchaser.

signment.—Leslie v. Kennedy, 249 Mich. 553, 229 N.W. 469 (1930).

299. MCLS §§ 560.101 et seq.

300. MCLS § 560.267.

Quiet title action

The Land Division Act primarily governs the relationship between property holders and public regulatory bodies. Purchasers may void the sale of land that was "subdivided or otherwise partitioned or split in violation of" the Land Division Act, and they may further recover damages and return of any consideration. Defendants instead seek completion of the sale with a penalty levied against the seller. Even if there was an actual violation of the statute, it allows a buyer to back out if the land was improperly divided. It is not to be invoked to manipulate a one-sided deal that would result in conveyance of the entirety of the realty at a lower price than agreed to by the parties. In any event, there is no violation. Plaintiff intended to convey the whole property upon payment of the default judgment arising out of the promissory note, which was part of the original transaction conveying the property. Further, pursuant to the trial court's amended judgment, upon completion of the sale, plaintiff shall convey a deed that accurately describes the undivided property. Defendant's quiet title action was properly dismissed.—Rochau v. Horan, 2005 Mich. App. LEXIS 3091 (Mich. Ct. App. Dec. 13, 2005).

Violation as proof of negligence

Plaintiffs who purchased land from a subdivision developer had no grounds for a common-law negligence claim against the developer's vendor for a defect in the quality of the water under the subdivision; however, where the vendor was the platter of the subdivision and the plaintiffs alleged that he had violated the requirements of the Subdivision Control Act to ensure an adequate quantity and quality of water as some proof of their negligence claim, they should be allowed to amend their pleadings to address that claim and develop the legal and factual issues during a new trial.—Christy v. Glass, 415 Mich. 684, 329 N.W.2d 748 (1982).

301. Roose v. Parklane Homes Corp., 59 Mich. App. 542, 229 N.W.2d 838 (1975).

302. Bad deal

Land contract purchaser would not be entitled to rescission of sale as allegedly in violation of Land Division Act in light of contract manifesting cooperation between seller and purchaser in platting, recording, and selling subdivided parcels included in land, and their joint recording of subject plat some five months before purchaser sought rescission, thereby curing any noncompliance, at which time purchaser sought to extricate himself from contract in order to avoid "bad deal."—Roose v. Parklane Homes Corp., 59 Mich. App. 542, 229 N.W.2d 838 (1975).

The right to rescind a contract for the sale of land may be lost by estoppel[303] or by waiver.[304] A party to a contract failing to rescind within a reasonable time after discovery of fraud invalidating the contract will be precluded from rescission.[305]

A purchaser is not precluded from securing a decree rescinding a contract for false representations because of his or her failure to complain of the false representations when seeking a voluntary rescission before bringing suit.[306]

Violation of Seller Disclosure Act. The Seller Disclosure Act allows the vendee to terminate a contract for sale of land on grounds of the vendor's failure to properly disclose the requisite information concerning the condition of the property being sold until after the execution of a contract for sale, within the limited statutory deadlines after the execution of the contract.[307] If the vendee accepts performance of the contract, his or her right to rescind under the Seller Disclosure Act is extinguished.[308]

Violation of Land Division Act. A case decided under a provision of the former Plat Act,[309] similar to a provision of the Land Division Act,[310] ruled that the purchaser's right to assert the invalidity of a contract on the grounds of violation of a statutory provision voiding a contract for sale of land that has been subdivided in violation of subdivision rules is not affected by any action or inaction on the part of a purchaser otherwise constituting waiver or estoppel.[311]

---

303. Sulzberger v. Steinhauer, 235 Mich. 253, 209 N.W. 68 (1926) (tender).

304. Acceptance under conditions

Purchasers who, after claimed defects were known, agreed property was accepted on certain conditions, which vendors fully performed, waived right to rescind.—Pariseau v. Trinity Bldg. Co., 254 Mich. 213, 236 N.W. 239 (1931).

Fraud

The right to rescind for fraud may be waived.—Dertinger v. Lathrup, 251 Mich. 476, 232 N.W. 213 (1930).

Dinnan v. Bloomfield Hills Land Co., 214 Mich. 54, 181 N.W. 986 (1921).

Where purchaser of land under fraudulent representations as to trees and fertility made payments after learning of the fraud, he waived it.—Draft v. Hesselsweet, 194 Mich. 604, 161 N.W. 864 (1917).

Paying taxes

Where land contract required purchaser to pay taxes, purchaser failed to pay taxes, vendors obtained judgment for taxes against purchaser, purchaser acquired knowledge of vendors' misrepresentation of water and sewage facilities and two months thereafter, on advice of attorneys, paid judgment and 30 days thereafter rescinded the contract, such payment, without more, was not a waiver by purchaser of the alleged fraud and was not an affirmance of the contract.—Le Roy Constr. Co. v. McCann, 356 Mich. 305, 96 N.W.2d 757 (1959).

305. Hovey v. Plesum, 250 Mich. 650, 231 N.W. 106 (1930) (contract to purchase hotel).

Barker v. Finlay, 200 Mich. 166, 166 N.W. 996 (1918) (six years' delay after discovery of fraud).

306. McKenzie v. Bennett, 241 Mich. 570, 217 N.W. 773 (1928).

307. MCLS § 565.954.

308. MCLS § 565.954.

Annual Survey of Michigan Law; June 1, 2004 - May 31, 2005: Real Property, 52 Wayne L. Rev. 941 (2006).

309. Taunt v. Moegle, 344 Mich. 683, 75 N.W.2d 48 (1956) (since the prohibitory features of the plat act of 1929 are aimed at the subdivider and seller rather than the lot purchaser, contracts of sale made in violation thereof are at instance of the purchase void. He may with or without aid of § 78a the plat act of 1929 so treat the contract, and no action or inaction on his part otherwise constituting waiver or estoppel will prevent him from alleging its invalidity or seeking its rescission (MCLS § 560.78a (1948), repealed by 1967 Pub. Act 288)).

Compare Roose v. Parklane Homes Corp., 59 Mich. App. 542, 229 N.W.2d 838, 1975 Mich. App. LEXIS 1376 (1975).

310. MCLS § 560.267.

311. Taunt v. Moegle, 344 Mich. 683, 75 N.W.2d 48 (1956).

§ 463.   Ratification

A right to rescind a contract for the sale of land may be lost by ratification.

A party to a contract for the sale of land who has a right to rescind may lose that right by affirming and ratifying the contract.[312] Thus, if fraud in the sale of property is discovered while the contract is executory, the purchaser's subsequent payment of the purchase price affirms the contract and precludes rescission for fraud.[313]

Qualified acts or statements ordinarily cannot amount to a ratification.[314] After the withdrawal of an intending purchaser under an unauthorized contract of an agent, the vendor cannot bind the purchaser by a ratification of the contract.[315]

§ 464.   Evidence as to Contracts

In actions involving the existence and validity of contracts for the sale of land, the burden of proof rests on the party having the affirmative of the issue, and any competent and material evidence relevant to the issues is admissible.

In an action to cancel a contract for the sale of land, one claiming that the contract signed by the parties was never intended to be binding on either has the burden of sustaining that claim.[316]

Fraud is never presumed but must be proved.[317] A party seeking to invalidate a contract on the ground of fraud has the burden of proving fraud.[318] That party also

---

312. Roszczewski v. Jozwiak, 225 Mich. 670, 196 N.W. 359 (1923).

Refusal to vacate

Where a grantee refuses to make further payments under a land contract because of defects in title, and on notice of forfeiture and demand for possession refuses to vacate, claiming a right to withhold the balance of the price until title is perfected, he affirms the contract and limits his remedy for recovery for defects to an action at law for damages.—Corbett v. Schulte, 119 Mich. 249, 77 N.W. 947 (1899).

313. Achenbach v. Mears, 272 Mich. 74, 261 N.W. 251 (1935).

Continuing performance affirms contract

Purchasers, continuing to make payments on land contracts, entering into modified agreement, and making payments thereunder after discovering vendor's fraud, elected to affirm contract and lost right to rescind it.—Harry & Max Dunitz, Inc., v. Meinecke, 260 Mich. 586, 245 N.W. 524 (1932).

Tilling and paying for farm

Purchasers of farm tilling it for year, making payment, and paying taxes on the land, were not entitled to rescission for misrepresentation that farm produced $5,100 yearly income.—Lapicki v. Jones, 258 Mich. 126, 241 N.W. 801 (1932).

314. Connor v. Buhl, 115 Mich. 531, 73 N.W. 821 (1898).

315. Baldwin v. Schiappacasse, 109 Mich. 170, 66 N.W. 1091 (1896).

316. Roosevelt Park Protestant Reformed Church v. London, 293 Mich. 547, 292 N.W. 486 (1940).

317. McKay v. Smith, 234 Mich. 367, 208 N.W. 450 (1926).

Induced mistake

Where rescission of land contract is sought on ground of unilateral mistake induced by fraud, that fraud inducing mistake must be proved, for fraud cannot be presumed, but must be proved by party alleging it.—Kruger v. Agnor, 321 Mich. 131, 32 N.W.2d 365 (1948).

318. Steele v. Shaffer, 241 Mich. 632, 217 N.W. 777 (1928).

McKenzie v. Bennett, 241 Mich. 570, 217 N.W. 773 (1928).

has the burden of proving the falsity of the representation,[319] and his or her own reliance on it.[320] A party claiming a defense to an action to rescind for fraud on the basis of the complaining party's knowledge of the falsity of the representation has the burden of showing timely complete knowledge on the complainant's part.[321]

In an action involving the existence and validity of an alleged contract for the sale of land, any competent and material evidence relevant to the issues is admissible.[322] Parol evidence may be admitted with respect to certain issues.[323]

§ 465.   —Weight and Sufficiency

In an action involving the existence and validity of a contract to sell land, the party having the affirmative of the issue must prove his or her case by a preponderance of the evidence, and fraud invalidating the contract must be established by clear and convincing evidence.

In an action involving the existence and validity of a contract to sell land, the party having the affirmative of the issue must prove his or her case by a preponderance of the evidence.[324] A party contending that a contract signed was never intended to be binding on either of the parties must prove that contention by

Albright v. Stockhill, 208 Mich. 468, 175 N.W. 252 (1919).

Head v. Benjamin Rich Realty Co., 55 Mich. App. 348, 222 N.W.2d 237 (1974).

319. Lapicki v. Jones, 258 Mich. 126, 241 N.W. 801 (1932).

320. Burlingame v. B.E. Taylor Realty Co., 247 Mich. 109, 225 N.W. 562 (1929).

321. Sautter v. Ney, 365 Mich. 360, 112 N.W.2d 509 (1961).

322. Stacey v. Mikolowski, 367 Mich. 550, 116 N.W.2d 757 (1962).

Dated instrument

A dated instrument, signed by defendant, reciting receipt of certain money from plaintiff, to apply on purchase price of a certain amount, for certain land, balance to be paid at a certain time, was competent evidence, not only of the date and amount of payment, but also of a contract to sell and convey the land named.—Skiba v. Gustin, 161 Mich. 358, 126 N.W. 464 (1910).

Limiting effect

In an action to rescind a contract for the purchase of land for misrepresentations that it was suitable for diversified farming, in view of instruction limiting it, evidence that it was not worth the price paid was properly received.—Houder v. Reynolds, 195 Mich. 256, 161 N.W. 856 (1917).

Prior proposed contract

In vendor's suit to rescind contract on ground of fraud, copy of earlier contract never consummated was admissible as minimizing likelihood that defendant made fraudulent representations to induce more favorable contract.—Taylor v. Ward, 264 Mich. 118, 249 N.W. 473 (1933).

323. Delivery of papers to third person

In an action on a written contract to sell land, to be paid for in part by the conveyance of other land to plaintiffs, defendant may show by parol that the papers executed were placed in the hands of a third person, to be delivered when defendant's wife assented to the transaction and his attorney approved plaintiff's title.—Dikeman v. Arnold, 71 Mich. 656, 40 N.W. 42 (1888).

Mistake

Court must accept parol evidence to determine whether there was mutual mistake or unconscionable conduct that warrants rescission or reformation of a written contract.—Detroit Edison Co. v. Malburg, 148 F. Supp. 361 (D. Mich. 1957).

324. Allison v. Ward, 63 Mich. 128, 29 N.W. 528 (1886).

False representations

Purchaser, seeking rescission, must show by preponderance of evidence that vendor's agents made alleged false representations respecting improvements.—McKenzie v. Bennett, 241 Mich. 570, 217 N.W. 773 (1928).

convincing evidence.[325]

Evidence of mutual mistake or unconscionable conduct justifying rescission or reformation of a written contract giving an option to purchase land must be clear and convincing.[326]

In weighing the credibility of the evidence, it is proper to consider all pertinent factors.[327]

Under the circumstances disclosed in particular cases, a party may be entitled to a ruling that the evidence is sufficient to establish various issues,[328] such as that a contract for sale never existed,[329] that the opposing party understood that a disputed sales contract was in force,[330] or the amount agreed upon as the purchase price.[331] Under the evidence, a party may be entitled to a ruling finding fraud and misrepresentations,[332] including false representations concerning improvements,[333] the nature and quality of the soil,[334] and the salability and value of the land.[335]

325. Hornbeck v. Midwest Realty, Inc., 287 Mich. 230, 283 N.W. 39 (1938).

326. Detroit Edison Co. v. Malburg, 148 F. Supp. 361 (D. Mich. 1957).

327. Lapicki v. Jones, 258 Mich. 126, 241 N.W. 801 (1932) (delay in complaining).

Payment of taxes

On the question whether a father agreed to convey a piece of property to his daughter, the fact that it was assessed to him, in whose name the title continued to stand, was of no importance, while the payment of the taxes by the daughter's husband who was living on the property with her was significant.—Fairfield v. Barbour, 51 Mich. 57, 16 N.W. 230 (1883).

328. Grasman v. Jelsema, 70 Mich. App. 745, 246 N.W.2d 322 (1976).

Dassance v. Nienhuis, 57 Mich. App. 422, 225 N.W.2d 789 (1975).

Sufficient for jury

Evidence sufficient to raise question for jury as to whether money paid by plaintiff was under oral contract to purchase property, so that she was entitled to recover after ouster.—Croy v. Hawkins' Estate, 228 Mich. 107, 199 N.W. 679, 1924 Mich. LEXIS 752 (1924).

329. Stepanian v. Moskovitz, 232 Mich. 630, 206 N.W. 359 (1925).

330. George v. Smilanski, 238 Mich. 700, 214 N.W. 61, 1927 Mich. LEXIS 706 (1927).

331. Summer v. Shanahan, 267 Mich. 182, 255 N.W. 187 (1934).

Barker v. Finlay, 200 Mich. 166, 166 N.W. 996 (1918).

332. Ball v. Sweeney, 354 Mich. 616, 93 N.W.2d 298 (1958).

Hafner v. A.J. Stuart Land Co., 246 Mich. 465, 224 N.W. 630 (1929).

Head v. Benjamin Rich Realty Co., 55 Mich. App. 348, 222 N.W.2d 237 (1974).

Morykwas v. McKnight, 37 Mich. App. 304, 194 N.W.2d 522 (1971).

Vormelker v. Oleksinski, 32 Mich. App. 498, 189 N.W.2d 135 (1971).

Lightner v. Karnatz, 258 Mich. 74, 241 N.W. 841 (1932) (fraud in sale of lots).

City Inv. Co. v. Zimni, 255 Mich. 388, 238 N.W. 170 (1931) (fraud of vendor's agent).

McKay v. Smith, 234 Mich. 367, 208 N.W. 450 (1926) (evidence sufficient to show material misrepresentation by vendor relied on by purchaser).

333. McKenzie v. Bennett, 241 Mich. 570, 217 N.W. 773 (1928).

Sewer

In purchaser's action against vendors to rescind land contract for sale of lots upon which no water or sewage facilities existed, the evidence, including evidence that newspaper advertisement contained words "water and sewer" and that inspection by corporate purchaser's officers disclosed the presence of fire hydrants, was sufficient to show that purchaser relied on false statements, published by vendors, that such facilities were then available to each lot.—Le Roy Constr. Co. v. McCann, 356 Mich. 305, 96 N.W.2d 757 (1959).

334. Gyles v. Stadel, 252 Mich. 349, 233 N.W. 339 (1930).

Hall v. Proctor, 221 Mich. 400, 191 N.W. 205 (1922).

Character of soil and condition of orchard

Evidence showed that vendors induced purchasers to purchase farm and part with their business in part payment for the farm, by false representations

On the other hand, particular evidence may be sufficient to prove affirmatively the absence of fraud[336] or undue influence[337] invalidating a land contract. Similarly the evidence may be sufficient to establish mental competence,[338] or, on the other hand, mental incapacity.[339]

Under other circumstances the evidence may be insufficient to establish particular matters,[340] such as an agreement for the sale of land,[341] a promise arising

about value of the farm, character of its soil, and condition of orchards and vineyard.—Martin v. Critton, 211 Mich. 506, 179 N.W. 38 (1920).

335. Kefuss v. Whitley, 220 Mich. 67, 189 N.W. 76 (1922).

336. Knight v. Behringer, 329 Mich. 24, 44 N.W.2d 852 (1950).

Balen v. Burgeson, 187 Mich. 621, 154 N.W. 30 (1915).

337. In re Conant Estate, 130 Mich. App. 493, 343 N.W.2d 593 (1983).

338. Frischkorn v. Fitzgerald, 215 Mich. 106, 183 N.W. 756 (1921).

Mentally capable

In action by administrator for estate of 82-year-old decedent, challenging alleged mental capacity of decedent to execute a contract about four months prior to her death whereby she sold her home to defendants for $7,000 less than it was allegedly worth, evidence sustained finding that decedent was mentally capable of executing contract and that defendants had not obtained property fraudulently from decedent.—Klein v. Kent, 356 Mich. 122, 95 N.W.2d 864 (1959).

Nervous vendor

Conflicting evidence established that vendor, even though extremely nervous due to illness and use of intoxicating liquor, was mentally competent to contract when he executed offer to purchase realty.—Czeizler v. Radke, 309 Mich. 349, 15 N.W.2d 665 (1944).

Weak and bedridden vendor

In administrator's action to have contract for sale of realty executed by deceased as vendor declared void on ground deceased, who was in a weak condition, bedridden, and unable to read during last years of her life, was mentally incompetent to execute the contract, evidence of competency was sufficient to support denial of relief on that ground.—Straley v. Polifronio, 295 Mich. 251, 294 N.W. 401 (1940).

339. Star Realty, Inc. v. Bower, 17 Mich. App. 248, 169 N.W.2d 194 (1969).

Ill and aged woman

In proceeding to set aside contract executed by ill and aged woman, evidence sustained finding that mental condition of woman at time of execution of contract was such that she was not able to understandingly enter into contract.—Fitch v. Taklo, 339 Mich. 701, 64 N.W.2d 627 (1954).

340. Septic tank permits

In suit by purchaser of subdivision containing 91 lots against vendors for partial rescission of land contract on grounds of fraud, misrepresentation, failure of consideration and mistake after purchaser had constructed 49 residences and thereafter was refused septic tank permits, evidence that purchaser's agents sought information from brokers about the character of the soil in subdivision, that they appreciated the importance thereof, that they were familiar with building operations generally, that the provision of the sanitation code requiring septic tank permits had been adopted after brokers advertised property as "Ready to build now" and that percolation tests, of which purchaser had knowledge, indicated that soil throughout subdivision varied greatly, established that purchaser had not been induced to enter into contract by fraud and misrepresentation.—A & M Land Dev. Co. v. Miller, 354 Mich. 681, 94 N.W.2d 197 (1959).

341. Brill v. Brill, 75 Mich. App. 706, 255 N.W.2d 739 (1977).

Lack of full description

A sale of land was not made out by an entry on the books of the vendors and by their receipts for purchase money, where the land was not fully described and did not belong to them, and the actual owners only assented to the sale verbally.—Ayres v. Gallup, 44 Mich. 13, 5 N.W. 1072 (1880).

Reconveyance

Evidence was held insufficient to establish contract to reconvey interest in lots previously acquired through exchange of property.—Wojciechowski v. Mack, 239 Mich. 167, 214 N.W. 210 (1927).

from an agreement to sell land,[342] or duress invalidating the contract.[343] Under the circumstances of particular cases, the evidence may be insufficient to establish fraud or misrepresentation,[344] as with respect to the amount of rentals received from the property,[345] its value,[346] its boundaries,[347] its condition,[348] the cost of necessary repairs on it,[349] improvements on it,[350] the quantity of timber on it,[351] or the widening of a street or road.[352] Particular evidence may be insufficient to establish a fraudulent concealment invalidating the contract,[353] or the vendee's knowledge of

342. Use of condemnation award

In vendor's suit for rescission of land contract, evidence was insufficient to establish vendee's agreement to use condemnation award, payable to vendee, for erection of building.—Taylor v. Ward, 264 Mich. 118, 249 N.W. 473 (1933).

343. Knight v. Behringer, 329 Mich. 24, 44 N.W.2d 852 (1950).

Stated condition

Fact that purchasers, who had been tenants of prior purchaser and had remained in possession following default of prior purchaser, had been told that if they wished to acquire any interest in property they must accept contract offered to them, was not sufficient to indicate duress.—Broaden v. Doncea, 340 Mich. 564, 66 N.W.2d 216 (1954).

344. Detroit Edison Co. v. Malburg, 148 F. Supp. 361 (D. Mich. 1957).

Vargo v. Ihlenfeldt, 359 Mich. 265, 102 N.W.2d 550 (1960).

O'Conner v. Bamm, 335 Mich. 438, 56 N.W.2d 250, 1953 Mich. LEXIS 537 (1953) (no fraud or intentional wrongdoing on part of purchaser).

Kaulsky v. Selberg, 319 Mich. 208, 29 N.W.2d 154 (1947).

Vincent v. McIntyre, 244 Mich. 112, 221 N.W. 136 (1928).

Parsons v. Washburn, 245 Mich. 140, 222 N.W. 92 (1928) (evidence failed to establish fraud of cashier or assistant cashier of bank through whom plaintiff purchased vendors' rights in land contract).

Connivance of agent not proved

Evidence did not show plaintiff's agents sold lots at fraudulent undervaluation or that agent fraudulently connived with purchaser to purchase lots, and that they jointly reaped benefits.—Jefferson Park Land Co. v. Pascoe, 246 Mich. 96, 224 N.W. 420 (1929).

345. Haord v. Vandecar, 233 Mich. 47, 206 N.W. 329 (1925).

346. Similar sales

Representation that lot was worth contract price was not shown untrue under evidence of similar sales, and was not ground for cancellation.—Burlingame v. B.E. Taylor Realty Co., 247 Mich. 109, 225 N.W. 562 (1929).

347. Underwood v. Towne, 201 Mich. 55, 166 N.W. 1020 (1918).

348. A & M Land Dev. Co. v. Miller, 354 Mich. 681, 94 N.W.2d 197 (1959).

Haord v. Vandecar, 233 Mich. 47, 206 N.W. 329 (1925).

Lower v. Walters, 230 Mich. 395, 202 N.W. 937 (1925) (existence of Canada thistles on farm).

Building

In suit to rescind contract for purchase of farm, on ground that defendants had fraudulently represented that buildings were in good condition, whereas they were infested with termites, evidence that one of the defendants stated that house was a "nice house" and a "good house" was insufficient to show fraudulent misrepresentations warranting rescission.—Urban v. Doolan, 282 Mich. 271, 276 N.W. 445 (1937).

Summer resort

Purchaser of summer resort business seeking rescission failed to establish falsity of any material representations made to him by vendors regarding condition of property or earnings of business, and upon which he was entitled to rely.—Smith v. Taber, 362 Mich. 619, 107 N.W.2d 761 (1961).

349. Cost of repairs

Evidence produced by purchasers of home, who made extensive repairs to the home following purchase, was insufficient to establish falsity of representation by real estate salesman that cost of repairs would not exceed $2,000.—Windham v. Morris, 370 Mich. 188, 121 N.W.2d 479 (1963).

350. Garner v. Pierce, 277 Mich. 115, 268 N.W. 830 (1936).

351. Nebel v. Sullivan, 245 Mich. 642, 224 N.W. 409 (1929).

352. Berman v. Vigliotti, 337 Mich. 454, 60 N.W.2d 428 (1953).

Burlingame v. B.E. Taylor Realty Co., 247 Mich. 109, 225 N.W. 562 (1929) (evidence in suit to cancel deed did not show representation that contracts had been let for widening road was not true in fact).

353. Dorow v. Smith, 247 Mich. 320, 225 N.W. 533 (1929).

the falsity of representations that the vendee relied on.[354]

The evidence may be insufficient to show intoxication of one of the parties precluding that party's ability to make a binding contract,[355] or to establish a mutual mistake,[356] or undue influence exercised on one of the parties to the contract.[357]

A party may be entitled to a ruling that the evidence is insufficient to establish confidential or fiduciary relations between the parties to a land contract.[358]

Stuart v. Dorow, 216 Mich. 591, 185 N.W. 662 (1921).

354. Sautter v. Ney, 365 Mich. 360, 112 N.W.2d 509 (1961).

355. Himelson v. Galusz, 309 Mich. 512, 15 N.W.2d 727 (1944).

Ability to remember

In purchaser's action to set aside contract on the ground that he was intoxicated at the time it was entered into, evidence was insufficient to prove intoxication, in view of purchaser's testimony in which he detailed with minuteness the negotiations and conversations that took place at the execution of the contract.—Lapadat v. Copeland, 226 Mich. 329, 197 N.W. 547 (1924).

356. Construction of contract

Mutual mistake in contract for sale of property was not shown because vendee was first party in contract, and contract authorized "first party" to mortgage property when it was mutually understood that vendor was to have such right, where, up to that point in contract, neither party had been denominated as first or second party, and naming vendor as first party was universal custom.— Smith v. Rattray, 231 Mich. 218, 203 N.W. 844 (1925).

357. Knight v. Behringer, 329 Mich. 24, 44 N.W.2d 852 (1950).

Janiszewski v. Shank, 230 Mich. 189, 202 N.W. 949 (1925).

358. Parsons v. Washburn, 245 Mich. 140, 222 N.W. 92 (1928).

No inference supported

Fact that defendant's aged father reposed implicit confidence in defendant was not alone sufficient to create a fiduciary relationship between them and the mere fact that father and son lived together for many years did not give rise to the inference that confidential relations existed casting on the son the burden of negativing alleged fraud, duress, undue influence, or overreaching on his part in a real estate transaction between them.— Knight v. Behringer, 329 Mich. 24, 44 N.W.2d 852 (1950).

Chapter 16

CONSTRUCTION AND OPERATION OF CONTRACT FOR SALE OF LAND

§ 481. General Rules

A contract for the sale of land should be so construed as to effectuate the intent of the parties as expressed in their agreement when construed as a whole, and its operation and effect must be determined from the language employed considered in light of all the circumstances of the case.

Library References

Michigan Digest
John G. Cameron, Jr., Michigan Real Estate Forms
LexisNexis® Automated Michigan SCAO Forms
Thompson on Real Property, Thomas Edition (David A. Thomas, ed.)
Powell on Real Property® (Michael Allan Wolf, ed.)
Purchase and Sale of Real Property (Karl B. Holtzschue, ed.)

Law Reviews

Lawrence R. Shoffner, Real Property Law: Real Evidence: Special Rules for Real Estate Disputes, 80 Mich. B.J. 28 (2001).

The main rule of construction of contracts for the sale of lands is to ascertain and give effect to the intention of the parties as expressed in the agreement.[359] In determining the parties' intention, the court must construe the contract as a whole,[360] including any related documents.[361] But documents related to a separate transaction do not come into play.[362]

Ambiguities in a contract are be construed most strongly against the party preparing the contract, whether that party is the vendor[363] or the vendee.[364] This rule

---

359. Picard v. Shapero, 255 Mich. 699, 239 N.W. 264 (1931).

Crane v. O'Reiley, 8 Mich. 312 (1860).

360. Cousins v. Melvin F. Lanphar & Co., 312 Mich. 715, 20 N.W.2d 783 (1945).

361. Deane v. Rex Oil & Gas Co., 325 Mich. 625, 39 N.W.2d 204 (1949) (purchase agreement and escrow agreement must be read together to determine intent of parties).

362. Heinze v. Poulson, 250 Mich. 379, 230 N.W. 145 (1930) (voiding clause in gas and oil agreement did not avoid contract for sale of same land between parties, executed same day).

Breach of security agreement for personalty did not constitute default under land contract

Court would not imply an extension of strict terms of acceleration clause in land contract, in situation where parties also executed security agreement and assignment, where emphasis of different agreements as a whole was on remedies

of vendor in case of a default in obligation of land contract; under such circumstances court would not imply that a breach of some obligation under one of personal property security agreements, which provided merely additional security for same debt, constituted a default under land contract, so that debtors had no right to accelerate balance due for breach of covenant, contained in assignment, not to transfer liquor license.— Benincasa v. Mihailovich, 31 Mich. App. 473, 188 N.W.2d 136 (1971).

363. Keller v. Paulos Land Co., 381 Mich. 355, 161 N.W.2d 569 (1968).

Olsen v. Fry, 234 Mich. 233, 207 N.W. 803 (1926).

Keller v. Paulos Land Co., 5 Mich. App. 246, 146 N.W.2d 93 (1966), aff'd, 381 Mich. 355, 161 N.W.2d 569 (1968).

Prepared by agent

Contract for sale of realty as drawn by vendor's agent was required to be construed strictly against

applies even if the party supplied a preprinted form contract.[365]

Where a clause in a printed form of contract is left blank with respect to a matter that could be inserted, the clause forms no part of the contract for purposes of construction.[366]

The operation and effect of contracts for the sale of lands and the resulting rights and liabilities of the parties must be determined from the language of the contract as construed in light of the circumstances surrounding the case.[367] When it is doubtful whether a contract or conveyance covers land, the lack of an acknowledgment is entitled to weight in determining the probable intent of the grantor.[368] Under a memorandum agreement for sale of land providing that the buyer agreed to sign a contract within a specified time, it is not the duty of the buyer to prepare and tender the formal contract.[369]

What law governs. A contract for the sale of land signed in another state and to be performed in the other state is a contract of the foreign state and controlled by its laws.[370]

§ 482. Subject Matter

A description in a contract for the sale of real property is acceptable if it discloses with sufficient certainty what the intention of the grantor is with respect to the quantity and location of the land to which reference is made so that its identification is practicable.

It is required that an adequate description of the land be included in the

vendor if there was any ambiguity in it.—Randall v. Douglass, 321 Mich. 492, 32 N.W.2d 721 (1948).

364. Ambiguity

Any ambiguity in written contract for sale of land prepared by purchasers must be resolved against them, regardless of whether ambiguity resulted from language used or from striking a paragraph of offer, by which contract was initiated, with reference to consummation of sale.—Friedman v. Winshall, 343 Mich. 647, 73 N.W.2d 248 (1955).

365. Printed form

Where contract was prepared by vendor or furnished by it on a printed form, any uncertainty in the terms of contract was to be construed against vendor and its assignee and most favorably to the purchasers.—Cousins v. Melvin F. Lanphar & Co., 312 Mich. 715, 20 N.W.2d 783 (1945).

366. Holcomb v. Czenkusch, 222 Mich. 376, 192 N.W. 548 (1923).

367. Hager v. Rey, 209 Mich. 194, 176 N.W. 443 (1920).

Clee v. Seaman, 21 Mich. 287 (1870).

Olsen v. Fry, 234 Mich. 233, 207 N.W. 803 (1926) (contract to improve premises "before" and "in front of" all lots entitled purchaser of corner lot to improvements on both sides of lot).

Meaning of "as is"

Meaning of phrase "as is" as it appears in contracts dealing with sale of personalty has no similarly accepted meaning in contract dealing with realty.—Partrich v. Muscat, 84 Mich. App. 724, 270 N.W.2d 506 (1978).

Points

Seller has no legal obligation absent terms of binding contract to pay "points."—Wilson v. Romeos, 387 Mich. 664, 199 N.W.2d 208 (1972).

Where contract for sale of realty is silent on question of points, no agreement by seller to pay premium is inferred.—Wilson v. Romeos, 387 Mich. 664, 199 N.W.2d 208 (1972).

368. Price v. Haynes, 37 Mich. 487 (1877).

369. Hager v. Rey, 209 Mich. 194, 176 N.W. 443 (1920).

370. Frank's Nursery Sales, Inc. v. American Nat'l Ins. Co., 388 F. Supp. 76 (E.D. Mich. 1974).

Aropa Corp. v. King's Estate, 279 Mich. 418, 272 N.W. 728 (1937).

contract. A description is acceptable if it discloses with sufficient certainty what the intention of the grantor is with respect to the quantity and location of the land to which reference is made so that its identification is practicable.[371]

The description of property must identify the property when it is read in light of the circumstances of possession, ownership, situation of the parties, and their relation to each other and to the property, as they are when negotiations take place and the writing is made.[372]

The particular real estate forming the subject matter of a contract of sale depends on the intention of the parties as revealed by a proper construction of their agreement. If a contract specifically describes the land and provides for a conveyance by warranty deed, the land and not the title acquired by the vendor under a deed forms the subject matter of the contract.[373] A particular description in a land contract ordinarily prevails over a general description.[374] If necessary, the general description will be rejected as surplusage.[375]

A description of the property to be sold by street numbers indicates that the parties intended the land on which any building stands and contiguous property used in connection with a business conducted in that building and hence appurtenant to it.[376]

Selection of land. Where a contract to convey several lots gives the grantee an option to select others in lieu of those to be laid out, the grantor has no right to compel the acceptance of any undesignated lots.[377] The grantor may not prevent the grantee from making a selection by so platting new lots as not to conform in size with the lots designated.[378] If the contract provides that the vendor is to convey

---

371. Gerstenberger Farms v. Grimes, 2010 Mich. App. LEXIS 726 (Mich. Ct. App. Apr. 22, 2010).

Dmc v. Int'l Transmission Co., 2008 Mich. App. LEXIS 347 (Mich. Ct. App. Feb. 19, 2008).

Churchill v. Swarthout, 2006 Mich. App. LEXIS 1119 (Mich. Ct. App. Apr. 11, 2006).

Zaher v. Simon, 2004 Mich. App. LEXIS 1385 (Mich. Ct. App. June 3, 2004).

Zurcher v. Herveat, 238 Mich. App. 267, 605 N.W.2d 329 (1999).

372. Wozniak v. Kuszinski, 352 Mich. 431, 90 N.W.2d 456, 1958 Mich. LEXIS 459 (1958).

Churchill v. Swarthout, 2006 Mich. App. LEXIS 1119 (Mich. Ct. App. Apr. 11, 2006).

Zurcher v. Herveat, 238 Mich. App. 267, 605 N.W.2d 329 (1999).

Sunshine Homes, Inc. v. Nieman, 1997 Mich. App. LEXIS 2275 (Mich. Ct. App. Nov. 21, 1997).

373. Ickler v. Mullen, 196 Mich. 616, 162 N.W. 954 (1917).

Error as to ownership does not defeat obligation to convey

Where both parties in executing buy-sell agreement for property "owned by" vendor intended to contract for property with straight western boundary line but vendor was mistaken as to actual extent of property that it owned, binding contract existed for sale of property with straight western boundary line.—Goodwin, Inc. v. Coe, 392 Mich. 195, 220 N.W.2d 664 (1974) (abrogated on other grounds as stated in Converge, Inc. v. Topy Am., Inc., 316 Fed. Appx. 401, 2009 U.S. App. LEXIS 4917, 2009 FED App. 185N (6th Cir.) (6th Cir. Mich. 2009)).

374. Doelle v. Read, 329 Mich. 655, 46 N.W.2d 422 (1951).

375. Ickler v. Mullen, 196 Mich. 616, 162 N.W. 954 (1917).

376. Street numbers

Where contract for sale of property on which store building was located described property by street numbers only, contract would be construed as including sheds and ten-foot strip in back of store building that were used in connection with building.—Tandy v. Knox, 313 Mich. 147, 20 N.W.2d 844 (1945).

377. Robinson v. Cromelein, 15 Mich. 316 (1867).

378. Robinson v. Cromelein, 15 Mich. 316 (1867).

certain lots, and that the purchaser has the right to substitute others, on the failure of the purchaser to select others, the grantor may not do so, but must convey the lots originally specified in the contract.[379]

Quantity of land. Under Michigan law, the phrase "more or less" is ordinarily employed in land contracts to account for possible differences in measurement by different surveyors and not to indicate an assumption of the risk of overage or deficiency.[380] A sale of land containing a stated number of acres "more or less" constitutes a sale by the acre.[381] A statement of acreage does not prevail against a definite description, although it may be valuable to explain an otherwise ambiguous description of the property.[382]

Exceptions and reservations. A subsequent agreement of the parties may cure a want of certainty in contractual provisions as to exceptions and reservations.[383]

§ 483.   Purchase Price

It is essential that an enforceable real estate sales contract either set forth the price to be paid by the purchaser or furnish a basis from which the price may be ascertained.

It is essential that an enforceable real estate sales contract either set forth the price to be paid by the purchaser or furnish a basis from which the price may be ascertained.[384]

Contractual provisions with respect to the purchase price to be paid for land must be construed to effectuate the intention of the parties,[385] such as where there is a provision for sale by the acre.[386]

---

379. Robinson v. Cromelein, 15 Mich. 316 (1867).

380. Detroit Edison Co. v. Malburg, 148 F. Supp. 361 (D. Mich. 1957).

381. Detroit Lumber Co. v. Arbitter, 252 Mich. 99, 233 N.W. 179 (1930).

382. Doelle v. Read, 329 Mich. 655, 46 N.W.2d 422 (1951).

383. Roadway

Want of certainty in contract for conveyance of land, which provided that vendee would have roadway laid on premises, was cured by a subsequent mutual agreement locating roadway on boundary of land sold.—Levandowski v. Althouse, 136 Mich. 631, 99 N.W. 786 (1904).

384. In re Estate of Trainor, 2009 Mich. App. LEXIS 2591 (Mich. Ct. App. Dec. 17, 2009).

Zurcher v. Herveat, 238 Mich. App. 267, 605 N.W.2d 329 (1999).

Usage of "TBD"

Defendants also contend that the use of "TBD" made the terms indefinite such that the contract is unenforceable, with supporting language that discusses the general requirements of certainty as to

price. However, the same original source also provides that indefiniteness in terms can be made sufficiently definite and certain by reference to "evidence of established customs." In addition, when the intention of the parties can be determined, a contract with indefinite or ambiguous terms is enforceable. Here, two witnesses testified that in Muskegon County, the common usage of "TBD" meant that buyers would work out the details of a mortgage with a lender. Further, the evidence showed the intention of the parties was that the buyers would obtain a mortgage, but work out the details with a lender later. Therefore, even if "TBD" is an indefinite term, it is capable of being made definite such that the contract is enforceable.—Renouf v. Heller, 2005 Mich. App. LEXIS 1698 (Mich. Ct. App. July 14, 2005).

385. Montgomery v. Montgomery, 58 Mich. 441, 25 N.W. 390 (1885).

386. Burchard v. Frazer, 23 Mich. 224 (1871).

Payment to co-owner

Contract provision for payment to co-owner of tract, on release of lots on pro rata basis of $1,500 per acre, did not oblige her to accept one half of amount so computed.—Hutton v. Nardin, 238 Mich. 689, 214 N.W. 247 (1927).

A sale at a specified price less points is not a sale at the amount specified.[387]

A contract of sale that ultimately includes land of adjoining property owner adversely possessed by vendor for period necessary to perfect title generally does not require vendee to compensate the adjoining owner for the land adversely possessed.[388]

Indefiniteness respecting the method of payment of the purchase price of a contract, such as where a contract provides that the terms of payment are to be left for future negotiation, renders the contract unenforceable and precludes the recovery of damages in an action for breach of the alleged contract.[389]

Sale subject to mortgage. A conveyance of land subject to mortgage is a simple deed of whatever interest, estate, or equity the grantor has after satisfaction of the mortgage debt out of the property sold. The agreement to convey real estate for a specified sum subject to mortgage means that the price payable is that sum without deduction because of the mortgage.[390]

§ 484.   Time of Performance and Payment

The intention of the parties as revealed by the terms of their contract governs with respect to the time of performance and payment of a contract for the sale of land.

Where the parties to a contract for the sale of land make the time of performance definite, effect will be given to that provision.[391] If conveyance is to be made on payment, the vendee is entitled to a conveyance on payment or tender of

387. Wilson v. Romeos, 387 Mich. 664, 199 N.W.2d 208 (1972).

388. Adjoining owners

Where south property line of purchasers' property was properly 15 feet south of point where legal description in land contract placed south line because adjoining landowners had acquiesced in line so located, adjoining landowners were not entitled to compensation for 15 feet they were required to convey to make legal description in purchasers' land contract conform to occupational description.—Tarrants v. Goudie, 32 Mich. App. 432, 188 N.W.2d 900 (1971).

389. Zurcher v. Herveat, 238 Mich. App. 267, 605 N.W.2d 329 (1999).

Determining consideration

Where grandson testified that the consideration was $ 50,000, daughter testified that the consideration on the handwritten note she saw was either $ 50,000 or $ 60,000. The daughter's son could not recall a purchase price on the agreement he saw. The grandmother's nurse stated, "all I know is $ 50,000 for the house . . . that's all I know." The second quitclaim deed the grandmother executed listed the amount of consideration as one dollar. Based on this evidence, the probate court found that the plaintiffs and one defendant agreed that he

would purchase the Property for $ 50,000. The court stated that "[t]his finding is based upon the undisputed testimony of Bryan, and is buttressed at least in part by testimony from the daughter and grandson, relating to the content of the writing both saw and the fact that the purchase price was acceptable to the grandfather and, by implication or tacit agreement, [his wife]." Based on the record, and again deferring to the probate court on matters of credibility, we are not left with a definite and firm conviction that the probate court made a mistake in finding that the consideration was $ 50,000.—In re Estate of Trainor, 2009 Mich. App. LEXIS 2591 (Mich. Ct. App. Dec. 17, 2009).

390. Clark v. Thompson, 83 F. Supp. 133 (D. Mich. 1949).

391. Brotman v. Roelofs, 70 Mich. App. 719, 246 N.W.2d 368 (1976).

"Outlaw" of mortgage

Where a mortgage stated that it was to secure the purchase money of land, and was to be paid at a fixed time, if a mortgage then on the property had to be discharged from record, or would "outlaw," the term "outlaw," as used, referred to the time when by law the mortgage would be presumed to be paid.—Curtis v. Goodenow, 24 Mich. 18 (1871).

the purchase price,[392] or on payment or tender of the last installment where provision is made for payment in installments.[393] The vendor is not entitled to time to make title, but only to a reasonable time to execute a conveyance, after payment of the contract price has been made.[394]

When the vendee has performed under a contract those conditions for receiving conveyance of the property, the vendor must convey the property to the vendee by deed as specified in the contract or otherwise by an appropriate deed. The obligation to convey remains a continuing executory obligation on the part of the vendor until the vendor performs it.[395] The vendor may assign responsibility to convey to an assignee, in which case the vendor remains secondarily liable for the conveyance.[396] Upon the vendor's performance, the vendor may require the vendee to execute a discharge of the land contract in the same manner as a mortgage is discharged.[397]

Ordinarily, the purchaser is entitled to a reasonable time for investigation of the title before he or she becomes obligated to make payment of the purchase price.[398]

If a land contract fails to fix the time of possession, in absence of contrary evidence, it will be assumed that the parties intended transfer of possession within a reasonable time after the execution of the contract.[399]

The parties may waive provisions as to the time of performance of the contract.[400]

Concurrent acts. The intention of the parties as revealed by a construction of their agreement governs in determining whether the acts to be performed by them are concurrent.[401] Where the contract provides for delivery of possession by the vendor when the deal is closed, the purchaser may not be put in default for refusing to close the deal before a tenant in possession vacates or is removed.[402] If the parties intend that a covenant for the payment of the purchase price and a covenant for improvement are to run concurrently, the vendee's covenant to surrender the

---

392. Haight v. Salter, 260 Mich. 6, 244 N.W. 209 (1932).

393. Haight v. Salter, 260 Mich. 6, 244 N.W. 209 (1932).

394. Haight v. Salter, 260 Mich. 6, 244 N.W. 209 (1932).

395. MCLS § 565.360.

396. MCLS § 565.360.

397. MCLS § 565.360.

398. Allen v. Atkinson, 21 Mich. 351 (1870).

Encumbrance

Because vendee has right to good title, when there is appearance of encumbrance of record, vendee has right to demand reasonable time for investigation.—Frederick v. Hillebrand, 199 Mich. 333, 165 N.W. 810 (1917).

399. Tucson v. Farrington, 396 Mich. 169, 240 N.W.2d 464 (1976).

Hyne v. Pool, 2004 Mich. App. LEXIS 911 (Mich. Ct. App. Apr. 13, 2004).

Zurcher v. Herveat, 238 Mich. App. 267, 605 N.W.2d 329 (1999).

400. Sorge v. Dickie, 199 Mich. 251, 165 N.W. 781 (1917) (waiver may be shown by acts).

401. Covenants were concurrent

Where contract for conveyance of realty provided that, upon payment of purchase price and surrender of purchase contract by vendee, vendor, who had covenanted to make improvements, would deliver deed for property, contract contemplated that covenants for payment of price and improvements should run concurrently so as to require performance of covenant to improve as condition to recovery of price.—Palmer v. Fox, 274 Mich. 252, 264 N.W. 361 (1936).

402. Engel v. Tate, 203 Mich. 679, 170 N.W. 105 (1918).

contract on payment of the price is dependent on the vendor's covenant to make improvements and deliver a deed, so as to require performance of the covenant as a condition to the right of action by one party against the other.[403]

Provisions as to credit. Under a contract containing provisions concerning credit or installment payments, the time and conditions governing the making of deferred payments must be determined in compliance with the intention of the parties as revealed by the contract.[404] The same rule applies to provisions as to payment of interest.[405] Under an installment contract requiring the purchasers to pay the whole amount within five years, the vendors suing after the expiration of five years can recover the whole amount due.[406]

A contract for the sale of land may validly provide for acceleration of payments by the vendee in event of the vendee's default in the payment of any installment.[407] While those clauses are generally valid and enforceable,[408] the equities of a particular case may warrant that the acceleration clause not be enforced against the vendee.[409]

While an acceleration clause in a land contract is clearly valid, in view of the severity of the remedy, a court may refuse to imply that such a clause exists if the contract does not provide for it.[410]

On the other hand, a land contract may include a provision that expressly or implicitly prevents prepayment of the full balance owed on it, rather than payment

403. Palmer v. Fox, 274 Mich. 252, 264 N.W. 361 (1936).

404. Wiersma v. Nordella, 260 Mich. 574, 245 N.W. 520 (1932).

Proctor v. Plumer, 112 Mich. 393, 70 N.W. 1028 (1897).

405. Wiersma v. Nordella, 260 Mich. 574, 245 N.W. 520 (1932).

Welling v. Strickland, 161 Mich. 235, 126 N.W. 471 (1910) (interest payable monthly).

Payments and interest

Provision for payments each six months was construed as on account of both principal and interest, additional payment of interest not being required.—Hager v. Rey, 209 Mich. 194, 176 N.W. 443 (1920).

406. Scott v. Tierney, 263 Mich. 136, 248 N.W. 573 (1933).

407. Young v. Zavitz, 365 Mich. 354, 112 N.W.2d 493 (1961).

Brody v. Crozier, 242 Mich. 660, 219 N.W. 643 (1928).

Crosby v. Crosby, 2000 Mich. App. LEXIS 2737 (Mich. Ct. App. Feb. 11, 2000).

Windorf v. Ferris, 154 Mich. App. 201, 397 N.W.2d 268 (1986).

Larson v. Pittman, 3 Mich. App. 348, 142 N.W.2d 479 (1966) (entire unpaid balance).

408. Crosby v. Crosby, 2000 Mich. App. LEXIS 2737 (Mich. Ct. App. Feb. 11, 2000).

Bishop v. Brown, 118 Mich. App. 819, 325 N.W.2d 594 (1982).

409. Washburn v. Michailoff, 240 Mich. App. 669, 613 N.W.2d 405, 2000 Mich. App. LEXIS 94 (2000).

State-William Partnership v. Gale, 169 Mich. App. 170, 425 N.W.2d 756 (1988).

Breach of security agreement for personalty did not constitute default under land contract

Court would not imply an extension of strict terms of acceleration clause in land contract, in situation where parties also executed security agreement and assignment, where emphasis of different agreements as a whole was on remedies of vendor in case of a default in obligation of land contract; under such circumstances court would not imply that a breach of some obligation under one of personal property security agreements, which provided merely additional security for same debt, constituted a default under land contract, so that debtors had no right to accelerate balance due for breach of covenant, contained in assignment, not to transfer liquor license.—Benincasa v. Mihailovich, 31 Mich. App. 473, 188 N.W.2d 136 (1971).

410. Benincasa v. Mihailovich, 31 Mich. App. 473, 188 N.W.2d 136 (1971).

on an installment basis.[411]

§ 485.   —Time as of the Essence

A provision making time of performance of the essence of a contract of sale is valid and enforceable. In the absence of such a stipulation, time ordinarily is not of the essence.

A provision making time of performance of the essence of a contract of sale is valid and enforceable.[412] In determining whether or not the parties have made time of the essence, the court is guided by their intent as revealed by the provisions of their agreement.[413]

A party to a contract for sale of land may be entitled to a ruling that the parties to a particular contract made time of performance of its essence.[414]

In the absence of a provision making time of the essence, time is not of the essence of the contract for sale of land.[415] The mere statement of dates when payments are to be made does not alone render time of the essence.[416]

Where time of performance is not of the essence of the contract, performance

411. Limitation on principal paid each year

Where contract for sale of realty provided that purchasers should in no year after the first pay more than $3,000 on principal, vendors were not required to accept accelerated full payment of purchaser price and trial court properly refused to order transfer of property to the purchasers.—Spangler v. Carlisle, 70 Mich. App. 288, 245 N.W.2d 720 (1976).

412. Not against public policy

Provision in contract that time is of the essence and that purchaser's failure to perform covenants of contract gives vendor option to declare full balance of principal and accrued interest immediately due is harsh, but is not outlawed by public policy and is not invalid or unenforceable.—Bedford v. Tetzlaff, 338 Mich. 102, 61 N.W.2d 60 (1953).

413. Sobczak v. Kotwicki, 347 Mich. 242, 79 N.W.2d 471 (1956).

414. Jennison v. Leonard, 88 U.S. 302, 22 L. Ed. 539 (1875).

Plas v. Aldrich, 238 Mich. 343, 213 N.W. 80 (1927).

Nedelman v. Meininger, 24 Mich. App. 64, 180 N.W.2d 37 (1970).

Grade v. Loafman, 314 Mich. 364, 22 N.W.2d 746 (1946) (date of obtaining mortgage loan commitment).

Clear implication

Where written agreement for sale of city lots prepared by purchasers provided for execution of executory contract and for closing to take place

after sewer and water facilities had been brought to intersection of specified streets without expense to purchasers, provided that those facilities were available at specified intersection within 105 days and, if not thus available, agreement was void, that language clearly implied that the parties intended that time of closing had to be of the essence of agreement, particularly where purchasers subsequently consented to extension of time for making sewer and water facilities available.—Friedman v. Winshall, 343 Mich. 647, 73 N.W.2d 248 (1955).

415. Waller v. Lieberman, 214 Mich. 428, 183 N.W. 235 (1921).

Brotman v. Roelofs, 70 Mich. App. 719, 246 N.W.2d 368 (1976).

Time held not of essence of contract

Solomon v. Shewitz, 185 Mich. 620, 152 N.W. 196 (1915).

Munroe v. Edwards, 87 Mich. 112, 49 N.W. 465 (1891).

Munroe v. Edwards, 86 Mich. 91, 48 N.W. 689 (1891).

Gram v. Wasey, 45 Mich. 223, 7 N.W. 762 (1881).

416. Range v. Davison, 242 Mich. 73, 218 N.W. 789 (1928).

Strictness not favored

Although equity will hold defaulting party to contract specifically declaring time to be essence thereof, strict forfeitures without notice and last chance to perform are not favored, and time is not of essence in land contract merely stating time when payments shall be made.—Elbom v. Pavsner, 225 Mich. 213, 196 N.W. 442 (1923).

is required in a reasonable time.[417]

Waiver. Although time is of the essence of the contract, nevertheless, a strict performance may be waived by the party entitled to insist upon it.[418] Thus, the acceptance of past due payments waives the time provision.[419]

§ 486.   Dependent or Independent Stipulations

Stipulations in a contract for the sale of realty ordinarily are regarded as dependent, particularly where concurrent, but where it is clear that the parties intended them to be independent, the courts will give effect to such intention.

Covenants in a contract for the sale of realty are construed as dependent unless an intention to the contrary clearly appears.[420] If the acts or covenants of the parties are concurrent and to be performed at the same time, the covenants are dependent in character.[421]

However, the intention of the parties is the controlling consideration and prevails over all technical forms of expression.[422] When the parties intended stipulations to be independent, the courts will construe them to be independent.[423]

§ 487.   Conditions and Provisos

The parties to a contract for the sale of realty may make it subject to conditions and provisos.

The parties to a contract for the sale of realty may make it subject to such conditions and provisos as they see fit.[424] These conditions constitute a part of the contract.[425] They must be duly complied with by the respective party or parties.[426] Ordinarily, a substantial compliance suffices.[427]

Upon the fulfillment of the condition, the relief to which any party is entitled

---

417. Nedelman v. Meininger, 24 Mich. App. 64, 180 N.W.2d 37 (1970).

418. Ranck v. Springer, 333 Mich. 671, 53 N.W.2d 678 (1952) (waiver by conduct).

419. Whitley v. Tessman, 324 Mich. 215, 36 N.W.2d 724 (1949).

420. Palmer v. Fox, 274 Mich. 252, 264 N.W. 361 (1936).

Sutton v. Meyering Land Co., 248 Mich. 601, 227 N.W. 783 (1929).

Folkerts v. Marysville Land Co., 236 Mich. 294, 210 N.W. 231 (1926) (covenant to improve and covenant to purchase and pay price were dependent).

421. Palmer v. Fox, 274 Mich. 252, 264 N.W. 361 (1936).

Joseph v. Rottschafer, 248 Mich. 606, 227 N.W. 784 (1929).

422. Palmer v. Fox, 274 Mich. 252, 264 N.W. 361 (1936).

Benincasa v. Mihailovich, 31 Mich. App. 473, 188 N.W.2d 136 (1971).

423. Brow v. Gibraltar Land Co., 249 Mich. 662, 229 N.W. 604 (1930).

Bilansky v. Hogan, 190 Mich. 463, 157 N.W. 13 (1916) (provisions for securing purchase price and for improvements).

424. Modern Globe, Inc. v. 1425 Lake Drive Corp., 340 Mich. 663, 66 N.W.2d 92 (1954).

Hayman Management Co. v. Dura Corp., 45 Mich. App. 522, 206 N.W.2d 754 (1973).

425. Friedman v. Winshall, 343 Mich. 647, 73 N.W.2d 248 (1955).

426. Michigan State Bank v. Hammond, 1 Doug. 527 (Mich. 1845).

Greenspan v. Rehberg, 56 Mich. App. 310, 224 N.W.2d 67 (1974).

427. Abraham v. Stewart, 83 Mich. 7, 46 N.W. 1030 (1890).

ordinarily vests in that party.[428]

If a contract for the sale of land is on a condition precedent, it does not become effective or obligate the parties until the happening of the event or the performance of the condition on which the sale is conditioned.[429]

On the other hand, where a proper construction of the contract shows no intent to impose conditions or provisos, a contract is regarded as unconditional in character.[430]

A condition may be waived, and the waiver shown by the party's conduct.[431]

Forfeiture. Conditions working a forfeiture are not favored, are strictly limited by the terms of the contract, and may not be enlarged by construction.[432]

428. Liquidated damages

Vendor was entitled to retain $1,000 deposit under agreement providing that vendor may retain $1,000 as liquidated damages in event of default by purchaser by reason of purchaser's failure to obtain board of zoning appeals approval, where purchaser's application for nonconforming use was denied.—Jonna v. Diversey Corp., 368 Mich. 231, 118 N.W.2d 471 (1962).

429. Modern Globe, Inc. v. 1425 Lake Drive Corp., 340 Mich. 663, 66 N.W.2d 92 (1954) (approval of stockholder).

Tentative arrangement

Where arrangement whereby stepfather agreed to convey farm to stepson in consideration of services was at the outset merely tentative and parties were to "try it out" and if mutually satisfied arrangement should become operative, contractual status was dependent on condition precedent.—Daugherty v. Poppen, 316 Mich. 430, 25 N.W.2d 580 (1947).

430. Soloman v. Western Hills Dev. Co., 88 Mich. App. 254, 276 N.W.2d 577 (1979).

McCall v. Freedman, 35 Mich. App. 243, 192 N.W.2d 275 (1971).

Sieradzki Inv. Co. v. Texas Twp., 15 Mich. App. 430, 166 N.W.2d 669 (1968).

State of business

Where brother allegedly orally agreed to pay to construct new house for sister and to convey realty to sister, in consideration for sister's taking care of their mother, sister had deed put in name of brother, and his wife, sister and mother moved into house and brother thereafter stated that house belonged to sister, that he would give her a deed in a year or two and that he would increase her income when business permitted but brother never delivered deed, agreement to convey realty was not conditioned on business conditions and sister was entitled to specific performance of it.—Mc-

Farland v. Kinnee, 337 Mich. 484, 60 N.W.2d 324 (1953).

431. Time not made of the essence

Condition, in offer to purchase realty, that purchaser obtain property zoning for gas station and obtain necessary permits and approvals within 60 days, was waived where vendors did not notify purchasers after expiration of 60 days that contract was regarded as terminated, and relied on lapse of time only after purchaser obtained such zoning and permits, particularly where neither offer nor acceptance made time of essence.—Al-Oil, Inc. v. Pranger, 365 Mich. 46, 112 N.W.2d 99 (1961).

Zoning

Provision in offer to purchase agreement that purchase was subject to purchasers' obtaining rezoning for mobile home court for all or any part of property that they might petition for was permissive, not mandatory, and inured solely to benefit of purchasers who were entitled to waive it.—Bliss v. Carter, 26 Mich. App. 177, 182 N.W.2d 54 (1970).

432. Ortmann v. First Nat'l Bank, 49 Mich. 56, 12 N.W. 907 (1882).

Breach of security agreement for personalty did not constitute default under land contract

Court would not imply an extension of strict terms of acceleration clause in land contract, in situation where parties also executed security agreement and assignment, where emphasis of different agreements as a whole was on remedies of vendor in case of a default in obligation of land contract; under such circumstances court would not imply that a breach of some obligation under one of personal property security agreements, which provided merely additional security for same debt, constituted a default under land contract, so that debtors had no right to accelerate balance due for breach of covenant, contained in assignment, not to transfer liquor license.—Benincasa v. Mihailovich, 31 Mich. App. 473, 188 N.W.2d 136 (1971).

§ 488.   Effect of Executory Contract on Title

Under an executory contract, the vendee acquires equitable title to the realty, but the legal title remains in the vendor as security for the purchase price.

Under an executory contract for the sale of real property, the vendee acquires equitable title to the property,[433] is regarded as the beneficial owner of the property,[434] and has the right to possession.[435]

The vendor retains the legal title to the land as security for payment of the purchase price.[436] He or she holds it in trust for the vendee.[437] The vendee is entitled

---

433. Taylor Acquisitions, L.L.C. v. City of Taylor, 313 Fed. Appx. 826, 2009 U.S. App. LEXIS 3424, 2009 FED App. 148N (6th Cir.) (6th Cir. Mich. 2009).

In re Dukes, 24 B.R. 404, 1982 Bankr. LEXIS 2991 (Bankr. E.D. Mich. 1982).

Barker v. Klingler, 302 Mich. 282, 4 N.W.2d 596 (1942).

Bishop v. Hannan Real Estate Exchange, 267 Mich. 575, 255 N.W. 599 (1934).

In re Estate of Williams, 2009 Mich. App. LEXIS 1288 (Mich. Ct. App. June 9, 2009).

McMahon Helicopter Servs., And Brian McMahon, Plaintiffs/Counter-Defendants-Appellants v. Mid-West Dev., 2007 Mich. App. LEXIS 1685 (Mich. Ct. App. June 26, 2007).

Hall v. Independence Twp., 2001 Mich. App. LEXIS 1251 (Mich. Ct. App. Aug. 14, 2001).

Shaw v. Joquico, 2001 Mich. App. LEXIS 2647 (Mich. Ct. App. Aug. 28, 2001).

Zurcher v. Herveat, 238 Mich. App. 267, 605 N.W.2d 329 (1999).

Tidwell v. Dasher, 152 Mich. App. 379, 393 N.W.2d 644 (1986).

Ross Properties v. Sheng, 151 Mich. App. 729, 391 N.W.2d 464 (1986).

Pittsfield Charter Twp. v. City of Saline, 103 Mich. App. 99, 302 N.W.2d 608 (1981).

General Electric Co. v. Levine, 50 Mich. App. 733, 213 N.W.2d 811 (1973).

Administrator's contract

An administrator's contract, executed by him solely under powers of attorney granted him by decedent's heirs, to sell decedent's land, was efficacious to vest equitable title to it in purchaser, although heirs retained legal title as security for payment of purchase price.—Fowler v. Cornwell, 328 Mich. 89, 43 N.W.2d 73 (1950).

Equitable title not dependent on subsequent receipt of deed

An owner acquired a one-half interest in property at the time he and his partner entered into a land contract with the vendor and it was unnecessary for the owner to establish that he subsequently received a deed from the vendor, because his interest in the property was already proved by the land contract; a land contract vendee is vested with equitable title, and the vendee's interest is an interest in the real estate.—Ligon v. City of Detroit, 276 Mich. App. 120, 739 N.W.2d 900 (2007).

434. Marquette v. Michigan Iron & Land Co., 132 Mich. 130, 92 N.W. 934 (1903).

Upon payment in full

Although, pending making of contract for sale of realty, prospective purchaser cannot, either in law or in chancery, be considered owner of land, when making of contract is complete, land is thereafter regarded in equity as property of vendee, subject to rights of vendor under contract of purchase.—Rosenthal v. Shapiro, 333 Mich. 302, 52 N.W.2d 859 (1952).

435. Jennison v. Leonard, 88 U.S. 302, 22 L. Ed. 539 (1875).

In re Jeffers' Estate, 272 Mich. 127, 261 N.W. 271, 1935 Mich. LEXIS 451 (1935) (vendee, after execution of contract, became equitable owner entitled to possession except as otherwise stipulated in contract).

436. Vereyken v. Annie's Place, 1990 U.S. Dist. LEXIS 6431, 90-1 U.S. Tax Cas. (CCH) P50298 (E.D. Mich. 1990).

Gilford v. Watkins, 342 Mich. 632, 70 N.W.2d 695 (1955).

Barker v. Klingler, 302 Mich. 282, 4 N.W.2d 596 (1942).

In re Jeffers' Estate, 272 Mich. 127, 261 N.W. 271, 1935 Mich. LEXIS 451 (1935).

Tidwell v. Dasher, 152 Mich. App. 379, 393 N.W.2d 644 (1986).

Ross Properties v. Sheng, 151 Mich. App. 729, 391 N.W.2d 464 (1986).

437. Jennison v. Leonard, 88 U.S. 302, 22 L. Ed. 539 (1875).

Fowler v. Cornwell, 328 Mich. 89, 43 N.W.2d 73 (1950).

to a transfer of the legal title to the land on making payment of the purchase price.[438] However, the purchaser has merely a contingent equitable interest subject to cancellation for default in performance on the purchaser's part at any time before the purchaser has paid the contract price in full.[439]

Distinguished from mortgage. The rights of a mortgagor and mortgagee differ from those of a vendor and vendee in that the mortgagor holds the deed and the mortgagee has a lien, whereas the vendor holds the deed and the vendee has an equitable interest.[440]

§ 489.   Evidence and Questions of Law and Fact

There is a rebuttable presumption that a contract for the sale of land was entered into on the date of the instrument evidencing it. The construction of an unambiguous contract is a question of law for the court.

There is a presumption that a contract for the sale of land was entered into on the date of the instrument evidencing it, but this presumption is rebuttable.[441]

In accordance with the general rules governing the weight and sufficiency of evidence in civil actions, a party to a contract for the sale of land may be entitled to a ruling that particular evidence adduced with respect to construction and operation of a contract is sufficient[442] or insufficient[443] to show various facts or matters.

Questions of law and fact. The construction of a contract for the sale of land is a matter of law for the court when the contract is not ambiguous.[444]

Commer v. Potter, 232 Mich. 263, 205 N.W. 172 (1925).

Curry v. Curry, 213 Mich. 309, 182 N.W. 98 (1921) (trust relations are element of contract).

438. Hooper v. Van Husen, 105 Mich. 592, 63 N.W. 522, 1895 Mich. LEXIS 897 (1895).

439. Jackson v. West, 224 Mich. 578, 194 N.W. 1000 (1923).

440. Lutz v. Dutmer, 286 Mich. 467, 282 N.W. 431 (1938).

441. Goldberg v. Mitchell, 322 Mich. 662, 34 N.W.2d 515 (1948).

442. Lantis v. Cook, 342 Mich. 347, 69 N.W.2d 849 (1955) (construction of option clause).

Fowler v. Cornwell, 328 Mich. 89, 43 N.W.2d 73 (1950) (administrator acted within scope of authority in making contract).

Goldberg v. Mitchell, 322 Mich. 662, 34 N.W.2d 515 (1948) (contract was invalid).

Culver v. Castro, 126 Mich. App. 824, 338 N.W.2d 232 (1983) (adequate financing was condition precedent to performance).

443. Monroe v. Bixby, 330 Mich. 353, 47 N.W.2d 643 (1951) (payment for furniture).

444. Kotcher v. Temrowski, 282 Mich. 44, 275 N.W. 760 (1937).

Chapter 17

MODIFICATION OR RESCISSION

A. IN GENERAL

§ 501. Agreement to Modify or Merge

Until consummated by deed, a contract for the sale of land is open to modification or merger by or into a subsequent agreement of the parties.

Library References

> Michigan Digest
> John G. Cameron, Jr., Michigan Real Estate Forms
> LexisNexis® Automated Michigan SCAO Forms
> Thompson on Real Property, Thomas Edition (David A. Thomas, ed.)
> Powell on Real Property® (Michael Allan Wolf, ed.)
> Purchase and Sale of Real Property (Karl B. Holtzschue, ed.)

Law Reviews

> Evan F. Rosen, A New Approach to Section 363(F)(3), 109 Mich. L. Rev. 1529 (2011); Lawrence M. Dudek and Marilynn K. Smyth, Real Property Law: Construction Liens: How Lien Law in Michigan Affects Commercial And Residential Property, 82 MI Bar Jnl. 26 (2003).

Until consummated by deed, a contract for the sale of land may be modified or merged into a new contract by a subsequent agreement of the parties.[445] The modification governs the rights of the parties.[446] To the extent that the modification

---

445. Burstein v. Alldis, 234 Mich. 1, 208 N.W. 31 (1926).

Kelsey v. Pendill, 109 Mich. 334, 67 N.W. 327 (1896).

Ortmann v. First Nat'l Bank, 49 Mich. 56, 12 N.W. 907 (1882).

Stepanian v. Moskovitz, 232 Mich. 630, 206 N.W. 359 (1925) (previous oral negotiations or agreements merged into subsequent contract).

Evidence held insufficient to show agreement of modification

Johnson v. Douglas, 281 Mich. 247, 274 N.W. 780 (1937).

Pappas v. Harrah, 221 Mich. 460, 191 N.W. 221 (1922).

Operation and effect of agreement

Where vendor and purchaser, on discovering that record title to undivided one-half interest in realty sold was in estate of vendor's deceased sister, agreed that vendor take necessary steps to obtain full title whereupon sale would be consummated, vendor having obtained full title could not discharge obligations under written contract to sell by offering to return binder payment, although contract provided that if title was not good, binder payment would be refunded.—Todd v. Ratz, 313 Mich. 111, 20 N.W.2d 830 (1945).

Termination of right under original contract

Purchasers' contract to exchange land for vendors' equity in contract for sale of building on other land terminated parties' rights under sale contract.—Joseph v. Rottschafer, 248 Mich. 606, 227 N.W. 784 (1929).

446. De Land v. Jacobstein, 251 Mich. 191, 230 N.W. 943 (1930) (vendor required to foreclose under new contract).

Contract superseded

Although building contractor, as vendor, and purchasers entered into subsequent contract for sale of land covering same subject as first agreement, for sale of land and construction of building, terms of two agreements were inconsistent since second land contract involved sale of smaller parcel for lower price, and therefore second contract superseded first agreement.—Culver v. Castro, 126 Mich. App. 824, 338 N.W.2d 232 (1983).

Proof of title

Agreement to accept guaranty of title superseded provision in contract of sale requiring ven-

renews rights of parties, it waives objections of breaches of the prior contract.[447]

The courts have sustained parol agreements of this character.[448] On that basis, the time for conveyance or payment under a written contract may be extended by parol agreement.[449] An agreement in the nature of an option and agreements for the extension of time for payment should be construed together when they all relate to the same conditional purchase.[450]

But a subsequent agreement made dependent on the happening of an event does not affect the original contract if the event does not occur.[451]

An agreement setting aside or modifying specific provisions of a written contract must be an express agreement.[452] Therefore, it may be invalidated by uncertainty in its terms.[453] It is essential that the minds of the parties meet with respect to the claimed modification agreement.[454]

A subsequent agreement to change or modify the contract may be invalidated by fraud or by the incapacity of one of the parties to the agreement of modification.[455] But the right to rescind the modification for fraud may be waived.[456]

Consideration. A contract modifying a contract of sale generally must be supported by a consideration.[457] But no consideration is requisite if the case falls within the purview of a statute providing that an agreement to change or modify any

dor to furnish abstract.—McDonald v. Houseman-Spitzley Corp., 250 Mich. 509, 231 N.W. 74 (1930).

447. Default

Prior defaults are waived by entry into modified contract.—Gardner v. Thomas R. Sharp & Sons, 279 Mich. 467, 272 N.W. 871 (1937).

448. Buccilli v. Padgen, 231 Mich. 393, 204 N.W. 130 (1925).

449. Bugajski v. Siwka, 200 Mich. 415, 166 N.W. 863 (1918).

Frazer v. Hovey, 195 Mich. 160, 161 N.W. 887 (1917).

Loveridge v. Shurtz, 111 Mich. 618, 70 N.W. 132 (1897).

Kennedy v. Brady, 43 Mich. App. 760, 204 N.W.2d 779 (1972).

Gardner v. Batsakes, 13 Mich. App. 454, 164 N.W.2d 707 (1968).

450. Burstein v. Alldis, 234 Mich. 1, 208 N.W. 31 (1926).

451. De Vries v. Meyering Land Co., 248 Mich. 128, 226 N.W. 824 (1929) (letter signed only by one of purchasers of lots was not binding, where consent was conditional on securing consent of others).

452. Johnson v. Douglas, 281 Mich. 247, 274 N.W. 780 (1937) (contract setting aside or modifying specific provisions of written land contract concerning interest cannot be implied).

453. Schneider v. Levy, 256 Mich. 184, 239 N.W. 326 (1931) (agreement by vendor to extend time of payment, where time may or may not arrive in distant future, is void for uncertainty).

454. Low v. Low, 314 Mich. 370, 22 N.W.2d 748 (1946).

455. Incompetence

Where original contract for sale of farm from mother to son provided that mother was to have her support from son for life and at time of execution of rider relieving son of responsibility for supporting mother, mother's physical faculties were somewhat impaired, and she was apparently unable to protect herself, rider was canceled and original provision restored.—Low v. Low, 314 Mich. 370, 22 N.W.2d 748 (1946).

456. De Land v. Jacobstein, 251 Mich. 191, 230 N.W. 943 (1930).

457. Peters v. Dorr, 263 Mich. 318, 248 N.W. 635 (1933).

August v. Collins, 240 Mich. 23, 214 N.W. 951 (1927).

Straley v. Polifronio, 295 Mich. 251, 294 N.W. 401 (1940) (sufficient consideration shown).

Oral agreement

An oral agreement to modify a contract for the sale of land is invalid where not supported by a consideration.—Singer v. Hoffman Cake Co., 281 Mich. 371, 275 N.W. 177 (1937).

contract in respect of personal or real property is not invalid because of the absence of consideration if it is in writing and signed by the party against whom it is to be enforced.[458]

§ 502. Agreement to Rescind

The parties to a contract for the sale of land may effect its rescission by mutual agreement.

A contract for the sale of land may be rescinded by express or implied agreement of the parties to it.[459] To constitute a mutual rescission of a contract for the sale of land, there must of necessity be a mutual release of further obligations under the contract and a restoration of the status quo.[460]

One party may give the other an express option to rescind the contract of sale.[461]

An agreement to rescind is implied if the parties execute a lease to the property from the vendor to the vendee evidencing an understanding by both that the contract for sale is completely terminated.[462] An agreement to rescind is also implied when a vendee, having failed to pay installments and taxes as required by the contract, and having been served with notice to vacate, leaves the premises and surrenders his or her rights under the contract.[463]

To make a surrender of the contract by the purchaser that terminates the rights of the parties under the contract, the surrender must have been by operation of law or must have been voluntary and accepted by the vendor.[464]

On the other hand, no rescission is established where the minds of the parties have not met on a rescission agreement or where their conduct does not amount to a mutual rescission.[465]

§ 503. Abandonment

Either the vendor or the vendee may abandon his or her rights under a contract for the sale of land.

Mervez v. Petchesky, 259 Mich. 507, 244 N.W. 144 (1932).

Schneider v. Levy, 256 Mich. 184, 239 N.W. 326 (1931).

458. MCLS § 566.1.

459. Denler & Denler Land Co. v. Eby, 277 Mich. 360, 269 N.W. 203 (1936).

Krause v. McDermott, 274 Mich. 28, 263 N.W. 788 (1936).

Baker v. Lambers, 261 Mich. 86, 245 N.W. 578 (1933).

Harel Builders, Inc. v. Parklane Homes, Inc., 30 Mich. App. 83, 185 N.W.2d 898 (1971).

460. Gaval v. Wojtowycz, 13 Mich. App. 504, 164 N.W.2d 724 (1968).

461. Peters v. Fagan, 244 Mich. 46, 221 N.W. 274 (1928).

462. Judd v. Carnegie, 324 Mich. 583, 37 N.W.2d 558 (1949).

463. Miner v. Boynton, 129 Mich. 584, 89 N.W. 336 (1902).

Annett v. Stout, 322 Mich. 457, 34 N.W.2d 42 (1948) (acceptance of surrender).

Effect of surrender

A vendor who takes from his or her vendee a voluntary surrender of a contract takes it subject to all obligations assumed by the latter to third parties and is obligated to perform as to vendee's contract.—Stark v. Robar, 339 Mich. 145, 63 N.W.2d 606 (1954).

464. Merdzinski v. Modderman, 263 Mich. 173, 248 N.W. 586 (1933) (evidence held insufficient to show surrender by operation of law).

Hall v. Proctor, 221 Mich. 400, 191 N.W. 205 (1922).

Grunow v. Salter, 118 Mich. 148, 76 N.W. 325 (1898).

465. Obremski v. Dworzanin, 322 Mich. 285, 33 N.W.2d 796 (1948).

The rights of either vendor or vendee under a contract for the sale of land may be lost by abandonment.[466] Proof of abandonment must show an explicit waiver of contract rights.[467]

The abandonment need not be in writing, but may be inferred from the circumstances or a course of conduct inconsistent with continuance of the contract.[468]

Abandonment of a contract by the vendee is shown where the vendee positively and absolutely refuses to perform its conditions.[469] The vendee's abandonment is thus exhibited by his or her failure to make payments as they fall due accompanied by other circumstances inconsistent with continuance of the contract.[470] The vendee's abandonment is also shown by the vendee's conduct clearly showing an intention to abandon the contract.[471]

On the other hand, the conduct of the purchaser that is entirely consistent with the continuance of the contract in full force and effect does not evince an abandonment by the purchaser.[472]

Whether the purchaser's conduct amounts to an abandonment of the contract is a question for the jury under conflicting evidence.[473] But conduct that is so decisive and unambiguous as to leave no room for doubt may justify the court in

---

Gaval v. Wojtowycz, 13 Mich. App. 504, 164 N.W.2d 724 (1968).

466. Houghton v. Collins, 344 Mich. 175, 73 N.W.2d 208 (1955).

Annett v. Stout, 322 Mich. 457, 34 N.W.2d 42 (1948).

Welsh v. Richards, 41 Mich. 593, 2 N.W. 920 (1879) (eliminating rights of vendee's creditors).

467. Gault v. Van Zile, 37 Mich. 22 (1877).

Insufficient evidence

Evidence did not establish that written contract for the sale of improved realty was abandoned by the parties.—Tiley v. Chapman, 320 Mich. 173, 30 N.W.2d 824 (1948).

468. Annett v. Stout, 322 Mich. 457, 34 N.W.2d 42 (1948).

469. Collins v. Collins, 348 Mich. 320, 83 N.W.2d 213 (1957).

Tiley v. Chapman, 320 Mich. 173, 30 N.W.2d 824 (1948).

Dundas v. Foster, 281 Mich. 117, 274 N.W. 731 (1937).

Gaval v. Wojtowycz, 13 Mich. App. 504, 164 N.W.2d 724 (1968).

470. Houghton v. Collins, 344 Mich. 175, 73 N.W.2d 208 (1955).

Tiley v. Chapman, 320 Mich. 173, 30 N.W.2d 824 (1948).

Dundas v. Foster, 281 Mich. 117, 274 N.W. 731 (1937).

Lake Erie Land Co. v. Chilinski, 197 Mich. 214, 163 N.W. 929 (1917).

Narut v. Williams, 293 Mich. 376, 292 N.W. 336 (1940) (failure to make payments under contract accompanied by purchase of other property).

471. Tiley v. Chapman, 320 Mich. 173, 30 N.W.2d 824 (1948).

Gaval v. Wojtowycz, 13 Mich. App. 504, 164 N.W.2d 724 (1968).

Leasing of other premises

Vendees were deemed to have abandoned contract by virtue of leasing and occupying premises as tenants for several years after one of them had been served with a notice of forfeiture of the contract for failure to comply with contract's terms.—Dundas v. Foster, 281 Mich. 117, 274 N.W. 731 (1937).

472. Tiley v. Chapman, 320 Mich. 173, 30 N.W.2d 824 (1948).

Operation of farm

Where purchasers paid all taxes and assessments on land purchased on a contract, kept it adequately insured in their names, made valuable improvements on it, occupied a house on it, farmed the land, sold timber, and collected all rents, they would not be deemed to have abandoned the contract.—Collins v. Collins, 348 Mich. 320, 83 N.W.2d 213 (1957).

473. Collins v. Collins, 348 Mich. 320, 83 N.W.2d 213 (1957).

deciding the issue as a matter of law.[474]

B.   RESCISSION BY VENDOR

§ 511.   Vendor's Right to Rescind

A vendor may rescind a contract for the sale of land on proper grounds, including failure of consideration, the vendee's fraud, or mutual mistake. The vendor rescinds by any appropriate words or conduct.

Where proper grounds exist, a vendor may rescind a contract for the sale of land.[475] Proper grounds for rescission of a contract for the sale of real property by the vendor under the contract include the failure of the vendee's consideration,[476] and fraud and deceit on the part of the vendee,[477] or mutual mistake.[478]

Dundas v. Foster, 281 Mich. 117, 274 N.W. 731 (1937).

Gaval v. Wojtowycz, 13 Mich. App. 504, 164 N.W.2d 724 (1968).

Abandonment as bearing on rescission

Abandonment of possession by purchasers and resumption of possession by the seller, while not in itself amounting to a rescission of a contract for sale of land, is a circumstance to be considered by jury in determining whether rescission in fact was made.—Hall v. Proctor, 221 Mich. 400, 191 N.W. 205 (1922).

474. Collins v. Collins, 348 Mich. 320, 83 N.W.2d 213 (1957).

Tiley v. Chapman, 320 Mich. 173, 30 N.W.2d 824 (1948).

Dundas v. Foster, 281 Mich. 117, 274 N.W. 731 (1937).

Gaval v. Wojtowycz, 13 Mich. App. 504, 164 N.W.2d 724 (1968).

475. Ronczkowski v. Jozwiak, 230 Mich. 327, 203 N.W. 105 (1925).

Swain v. Baldwin, 54 Mich. 119, 19 N.W. 773 (1884).

Equitable Remedies and Principled Discretion: The Michigan Experience, 74 U. Det. Mercy L. Rev. 609 (1997).

476. Shepardson v. Stevens, 77 Mich. 256, 43 N.W. 918 (1889).

Swain v. Baldwin, 54 Mich. 119, 19 N.W. 773 (1884).

Assignment without consideration

Where defendants asserting validity of assignment of purchaser's interest in land contract contended that assignment was executed for valuable consideration, trial judge's finding, contrary to defendants' claim, that assignment was not in fact executed for valuable consideration supported

judge's conclusion that assignment should be cancelled.—Johnson v. Wynn, 38 Mich. App. 302, 196 N.W.2d 313 (1972).

Condition precedent not fulfilled because of complainant's action

Purchasers could not properly terminate purchase agreement on ground that one of conditions precedent to closing was not satisfied, where the condition was a matter over which purchasers had some control and they made little or no effort to fulfill the condition.—Ihlenfeldt v. Guastella, 42 Mich. App. 384, 202 N.W.2d 327 (1972).

477. Fraud in assent to contract, *supra*, Chapter 15.

Ronczkowski v. Jozwiak, 230 Mich. 327, 203 N.W. 105 (1925).

Roberts v. Saffell, 280 Mich. App. 397, 760 N.W.2d 715 (2008).

M & D, Inc. v. McConkey, 231 Mich. App. 22, 585 N.W.2d 33 (1998).

Silent Fraud: Is It Time to Speak to Speak Up?, 15 T.M. Cooley L. Rev. 455 (1998).

Burden of proof shifted

Where, in suit seeking rescission of contract to purchase motel business because of misrepresentation as to profits of business, plaintiff proved the misrepresentation and its materiality, burden of proof then shifted to defendant to prove that plaintiff's allegation of reliance on the misrepresentation was as false as the representation.— Papin v. Demski, 17 Mich. App. 151, 169 N.W.2d 351, aff'd, 383 Mich. 561, 177 N.W.2d 166 (1970).

Fraudulent practices

Court of Appeals decision upholding summary judgment grounded on failure to state claim upon which relief could be granted would be reversed and cause remanded for trial on complaint for rescission of real estate purchase agreement con-

An affirmative rescission by the vendor is a condition precedent to maintenance of the suit for rescission.[479] The vendor's permissible means of rescinding a contract for the sale of real estate include any appropriate words or conduct.[480]

While the vendor's conveyance of property subject to a contract for sale to

ditioned on securing mortgage from defendant corporate mortgagee that knew of plaintiff's circumstances and allegedly knew or should have known of alleged fraudulent practices by real estate company and thereby became integral part of fraudulent transaction that caused plaintiffs to abandon premises as uninhabitable.—Jeminson v. Montgomery Real Estate & Co., 396 Mich. 106, 240 N.W.2d 205 (1976).

Innocent misrepresentation

Where land contract vendors' innocently false representation that building could be used as seven-family apartment was actionable fraud, in view of plaintiffs-purchasers' reliance, and of cross-defendant city's authority to stop use as violation of state housing law, though it was valid nonconforming use under city zoning code, purchasers were properly granted rescission of contract.—Kroninger v. Anast, 367 Mich. 478, 116 N.W.2d 863 (1962).

Rescission of contract prevents application of laches

In action to recover moneys paid under land contract that was rescinded because of defendant sellers' fraud in guaranty against violations of city electrical code, defense of laches was not available to defendants in view of facts that action was one at law rather than in equity, that plaintiff purchasers asserted their rights promptly upon becoming aware of violations, and that defendants resold premises for same amount for which they purchased them, thereby obviating prejudice to defendants.—Head v. Benjamin Rich Realty Co., 55 Mich. App. 348, 222 N.W.2d 237 (1974).

Withholding after-acquired information

Purchasers of trailer park premises pursuant to two contracts intended by parties as single transaction were entitled to rescission of sale on record disclosing that, in interim between signing of first and second contracts, health department officials notified defendant sellers that because of inadequate septic tank system, resulting in standing water in drain field on premises, defendants could no longer operate same number of trailer park units, and that defendants fraudulently concealed such information from purchasers by advising them not to apply for health department license until following year and by stating that standing water could be covered with earth fill so as to comply with health department regulations, thereby breaching their duty to disclose after-acquired information rendering inaccurate prior representations which were true at time originally

made pursuant to agreement calling for transfer of current health department license without record of violations against it.—Morykwas v. McKnight, 37 Mich. App. 304, 194 N.W.2d 522 (1971).

478. Mutual mistake in assent to contract, *see, supra,* Chapter 15.

Dingeman v. Reffitt, 152 Mich. App. 350, 393 N.W.2d 632 (1986).

Expert assessment

Where defendant, experienced real estate agent and civil engineer, had volunteered statement that construction of dam had eliminated possibility of damage to warehouse by flooding, plaintiff purchaser, who desired warehouse to store furniture, had right to rely on representation in making deposit, recovery of which he sought after election not to complete transaction following discovery that possibility of flooding had not been eliminated.—People's Furniture & Appliance Co. v. Healy, 365 Mich. 522, 113 N.W.2d 802 (1962).

Not proper remedy

Where vendors intended to sell and vendees intended to purchase rental income property, rescission of contract on grounds of mutual mistake was not proper remedy even where property had no value either as income-producing property or as single-family residence, where there was persuasive indication that the parties considered that the risk as related to present condition should lie with the purchaser.—Lenawee County Bd. of Health v. Messerly, 417 Mich. 17, 331 N.W.2d 203 (1982).

Unilateral mistake gives no cause of action

Plaintiffs, who sought rescission of $6,500 land purchase contract on ground of mistake on discovery one year later that husband vendor had placed $4,500 valuation on property in divorce action wherein he was awarded property at that valuation were properly denied relief, since mistake was not mutual and fraud was not proved.—Windham v. Morris, 370 Mich. 188, 121 N.W.2d 479 (1963).

479. Lightner v. Karnatz, 258 Mich. 74, 241 N.W. 841 (1932).

480. Plas v. Aldrich, 238 Mich. 343, 213 N.W. 80 (1927).

Ives v. Bank of Lansingburg, 12 Mich. 361 (1864) (taking release).

Forcible dispossession of vendee by vendor

Unlawful ouster of vendee may act as rescission by vendor if accepted by vendee.—Schon v. Lawrence, 258 Mich. 543, 242 N.W. 745 (1932).

third parties may effect a rescission of the contract,[481] a conveyance under the contract for sale to one party to the contract and a third party does not rescind the contract with respect to a party to the contract not receiving a conveyed interest without a novation.[482]

§ 512. Actions

Equity has jurisdiction of a suit for rescission of a land contract. The vendee must refuse tender of the consideration from the vendor in order to contest the vendor's rescission of the contract.

Equity has jurisdiction of a suit for rescission of a land contract.[483] Rescission in equity is not a matter of right but rests in the sound discretion of the court.[484] Each case involving attempted rescission of a contract for the sale of real property must be decided on its own particular facts.[485]

A vendor will be refused the remedy of rescission if he or she fails to show adequate grounds for it[486] or if another remedy would be fairer to the parties.[487]

The law does not require action to rescind before the defrauded person is

481. Hornbeck v. Midwest Realty, Inc., 287 Mich. 230, 283 N.W. 39 (1938).

Himebaugh v. Chalker, 261 Mich. 80, 245 N.W. 576 (1932).

Atkinson v. Scott, 36 Mich. 18 (1877).

482. Partner and third party

Defendant partner, who had been divested of vendee's interest in partnership land contract by virtue of partnership dissolution agreement prior to conveyance of 2 of 18 subdivision lots by vendor to other partner as party to contract and to stranger, could not escape liability for damages after purchasers' default on ground that conveyance by vendor constituted rescission of land contract.—Greenbrier Homes v. Cook, 1 Mich. App. 326, 136 N.W.2d 27 (1965).

483. Ronczkowski v. Jozwiak, 230 Mich. 327, 203 N.W. 105 (1925).

Equity jurisdiction of court allows it to order other relief available to parties

De novo examination of briefs and record disclosed that trial judge, after denying rescission of contract for sale of land and certain equipment as requested by vendor, had awarded purchasers proper amount in accounting after a dispute arose concerning effective date of sale of land and equipment.—Robinett v. Roundhouse, 15 Mich. App. 27, 166 N.W.2d 6 (1968).

484. Kavanau v. Fry, 273 Mich. 166, 262 N.W. 763 (1935).

Lenawee County Bd. of Health v. Messerly, 417 Mich. 17, 331 N.W.2d 203 (1982).

Robinett v. Roundhouse, 15 Mich. App. 27, 166 N.W.2d 6 (1968).

Equities against rescission

Lapse of time and change of conditions, such as value of real estate, militate against remedy of rescission if another appears more just.—Browne v. Briggs Commercial & Development Co., 271 Mich. 191, 259 N.W. 886 (1935).

Evidence did not support rescission

In action to have set aside sale of plaintiff's home to defendants under contract requiring defendants to pay specified sum monthly for 60 months or until death of plaintiff before expiration of 60 months, and reciting that plaintiff was also being given an agreement of support in that home not to exceed five years, evidence did not establish either failure of defendants to support plaintiff adequately or nonpayment of balance due under contract.—O'Conner v. Bamm, 335 Mich. 438, 56 N.W.2d 250 (1953).

485. Schnitz v. Grand River Ave. Development Co., 271 Mich. 253, 259 N.W. 900 (1935).

486. Kent v. Matheson, 276 Mich. 316, 267 N.W. 847 (1936) (vendee's payment two days after vendor refused qualified tender).

Real Property Law: Real Evidence: Special Rules for Real Estate Disputes, 80 Mich. B.J. 28 (2001).

487. Ignorance of need for security

Where a contract between a son and his parents, whereby the latter were to convey the homestead to the former in consideration of his undertaking to support them for life, was not unconscionable, and was deliberately adopted, and a conveyance was made in pursuance of it, but conveyancer, through ignorance, did not provide any proper security for

reasonably certain that he or she has been defrauded, but requires that the person act with reasonable promptness after becoming reasonably certain.[488] But the doctrine of laches has no application in a suit to cancel a deed and a land contract that are void as against public policy.[489] The question of whether rescission is taken within a reasonable time after the cause of action is a fact question to be decided by the jury in view of all of the facts and circumstances of the case.[490]

The vendee must refuse tender of the consideration from the vendor in order to contest the vendor's rescission of the contract.[491]

§ 513.   Remedy

Upon rescission, the parties must be placed in the *statu quo ante*. Therefore, the vendor must tender the entire consideration received back to the vendee.

Upon rescission, the parties must be placed in the *statu quo ante*.[492]

Ordinarily, the vendor, in order to rescind, must restore or tender to the vendee the consideration received by the vendor[493] unless return of the consideration would be valueless to either party.[494]

In the absence of voluntary return of consideration by the vendor, the vendee may obtain recovery of what the vendee has paid the vendor.[495] The vendee may also obtain judgment for an allowance for the value of improvements he or she has placed on the land,[496] less the value of the use of the premises during his or her occupancy.[497]

A vendor of a contract for the sale of real property who rescinds cuts off the right of any remedy under the contract.[498]

parents, the contract would not be rescinded, but relief would be given as for a mistake, and execution of proper security decreed.—Van Donge v. Van Donge, 23 Mich. 321 (1871).

488. Cole Lakes, Inc. v. Linder, 99 Mich. App. 496, 297 N.W.2d 918 (1980).

489. Geel v. Valiquett, 292 Mich. 1, 289 N.W. 306 (1940).

490. Cole Lakes, Inc. v. Linder, 99 Mich. App. 496, 297 N.W.2d 918 (1980).

491. Insufficient tender

Purchaser's agent having expressly refused tendered refund of binder payment, delivery of payment to agent concealed in an envelope did not relieve vendor of obligation under written contract to sell realty, even though purchaser did not return the money contained in envelope.—Todd v. Ratz, 313 Mich. 111, 20 N.W.2d 830 (1945).

492. Bacon v. Fox, 267 Mich. 589, 255 N.W. 340 (1934).

493. Scadin v. Sherwood, 67 Mich. 230, 34 N.W. 553 (1887).

Krell v. Cohen, 214 Mich. 590, 183 N.W. 53 (1921) (note).

Aylesworth v. Camp, 171 Mich. 164, 137 N.W. 83 (1912) (cash payment).

494. Plas v. Aldrich, 238 Mich. 343, 213 N.W. 80 (1927).

495. Hornbeck v. Midwest Realty, Inc., 287 Mich. 230, 283 N.W. 39 (1938).

In re Reason's Estate, 276 Mich. 376, 267 N.W. 863 (1936).

Himebaugh v. Chalker, 261 Mich. 80, 245 N.W. 576 (1932).

496. Kimmel v. Peach, 240 Mich. 697, 216 N.W. 374 (1927).

497. Himebaugh v. Chalker, 261 Mich. 80, 245 N.W. 576 (1932).

498. Ives v. Bank of Lansingburg, 12 Mich. 361 (1864) (rescission prevents claim for purchase price).

Dispossession of vendee

Vendors' dispossession of defaulting vendee without forfeiture was repudiation and rescission

An "as is" clause in a contract for the sale of land is an indication that the parties intended the purchasers to bear both the risks and the benefits of sale and precludes the vendor from seeking rescission on the ground of mutual mistake.[499]

Similarly, if a vendor takes a course of action that affirms the contract, including giving the vendee a notice of forfeiture, he or she generally may not then rescind it.[500] The vendor must pursue other remedies in that case.[501]

C. RESCISSION BY VENDEE

§ 521. Vendee's Right to Rescind

The vendee may rescind a contract for the sale of land or sue for its rescission where adequate grounds exist, and the grant or denial of a rescission is addressed to the sound discretion of the court.

The vendee may rescind the contract or sue for its rescission if adequate grounds exist.[502] That the vendor is guilty of a breach of a covenant or condition of the contract is grounds for the vendee's rescission.[503] The vendee also has grounds to rescind a contract for sale of real property if the vendor has sold the property to a third party,[504] if the vendor has failed to comply with the Land Division Act,[505] if the vendor is guilty of fraud,[506] if the vendor failed to make required mortgage

---

of contract, entitling vendee to restoration of statu quo.—Schon v. Lawrence, 258 Mich. 543, 242 N.W. 745 (1932).

499. Dingeman v. Reffitt, 152 Mich. App. 350, 393 N.W.2d 632 (1986).

500. Plas v. Aldrich, 238 Mich. 343, 213 N.W. 80 (1927).

Proceeding under contract

By proceeding under contract after discovery of actual situation and falsity of representations made by vendors of stock in restaurant business, purchasers waived right to rescind.—D'Alessandro v. Hooning, 365 Mich. 66, 112 N.W.2d 114 (1961).

Repudiation not shown

Vendor's procurance of insurance on building on premises sold was not repudiation of land contract or eviction of purchasers' tenant, such as would authorize purchasers' recovery of payments made on contract.—Sriro v. Dunn, 265 Mich. 112, 251 N.W. 370 (1933).

501. Vendor's remedies, *see, infra,* Chapter 20.

502. Himebaugh v. Chalker, 261 Mich. 80, 245 N.W. 576 (1932).

Potter v. Ranlett, 116 Mich. 454, 74 N.W. 661 (1898).

Davis v. Strobridge, 44 Mich. 157, 6 N.W. 205 (1880) (acquiescence of purchaser in vendor's ouster of purchaser).

Equitable Remedies and Principled Discretion: The Michigan Experience, 74 U. Det. Mercy L. Rev. 609 (1997).

503. Covenant to improve

Purchaser was entitled to cancellation of contract, where vendor failed to make improvements provided for thereby within time required.—Martin v. Mortenson, 263 Mich. 381, 248 N.W. 844 (1933); Brow v. Gibraltar Land Co., 249 Mich. 662, 229 N.W. 604 (1930).

Covenant to improve and covenant to purchase and pay price being dependent in contract of sale, failure to comply with former was ground for rescission.—Folkerts v. Marysville Land Co., 236 Mich. 294, 210 N.W. 231 (1926).

Possession

Where purchaser's attorney informed vendor that he came to settle up contract, demanded return of money for failure to give possession and threatened suit, contract being in his hand while talking, there was a sufficient rescission.—Lackovic v. Campbell, 225 Mich. 1, 195 N.W. 798 (1923).

504. Sale to another

A purchaser of land who has made a part payment of the price and afterward finds that subsequent to his purchase the owner sold the lands to another person can treat the contract as rescinded.—Atkinson v. Scott, 36 Mich. 18 (1877).

payments,[507] if the parties made a mutual mistake,[508] or if there has been a failure of consideration.[509]

When the vendee sues in equity for a rescission, the grant or denial of relief is addressed to the sound discretion of the court,[510] which will decide each case on its own facts.[511]

The vendee may not rescind or be granted a rescission of a land purchase contract if the result would be inequitable.[512] The vendee's rescission would be inequitable where the vendee waited for several years before seeking a rescission and then did so only after property values began to decline.[513] Similarly, the fact that

Waiver of rescission after sale to another must be affirmative

Where vendor under contract had once disabled itself from performance by conveying property without mention of contract vendee's interest to a purchaser other than one named in contract, contract purchaser could treat contract as rescinded and vendor could not again re-establish liability on part of contract purchaser without some affirmative act on contract purchaser's part.—In re Reason's Estate, 276 Mich. 376, 267 N.W. 863 (1936).

505. MCLS § 560.267.

506. Barnhardt v. Hamel, 207 Mich. 232, 174 N.W. 182 (1919).

Lightner v. Karnatz, 258 Mich. 74, 241 N.W. 841 (1932) (vendee's default in payment of purchase price did not prevent rescission for vendor's fraud).

Fraudulent representation

Where purchaser was induced to buy land on representation that tracts on both sides of land purchased would remain as high-grade subdivisions but after sale vendor without purchaser's knowledge vacated plats of adjoining tracts.—Labadie v. Boehle, 288 Mich. 223, 284 N.W. 707 (1939).

507. Stellberger v. Scaduto, 264 Mich. 199, 249 N.W. 825 (1933).

Wilson v. Lingon, 260 Mich. 134, 244 N.W. 426 (1932).

508. Mutual mistake

Purchasers who charged that they were induced to buy home for $6,500 on representation of real estate salesman that it had been appraised in husband's divorce case at a value of $6,600 were not entitled to rescission of contract on ground of mutual mistake when purchasers subsequently learned that it had been valued at $4,500 by husband in the divorce case.—Windham v. Morris, 370 Mich. 188, 121 N.W.2d 479 (1963).

509. Younger v. Caroselli, 251 Mich. 533, 232 N.W. 378 (1930) (contract could be rescinded for failure of consideration through vendor's fault in

constructing driveway too narrow and building inaccessible garage).

510. Harris v. Axline, 323 Mich. 585, 36 N.W.2d 154 (1949).

Bechard v. Bolton, 316 Mich. 1, 24 N.W.2d 422 (1946).

Schnitz v. Grand River Ave. Development Co., 271 Mich. 253, 259 N.W. 900 (1935).

511. Dolecki v. Perry, 277 Mich. 679, 270 N.W. 184 (1936).

Schnitz v. Grand River Ave. Development Co., 271 Mich. 253, 259 N.W. 900 (1935).

512. Bechard v. Bolton, 316 Mich. 1, 24 N.W.2d 422 (1946).

Weider v. Rogman, 285 Mich. 539, 281 N.W. 318 (1938).

Kavanau v. Fry, 273 Mich. 166, 262 N.W. 763 (1935).

Amster v. Stratton, 259 Mich. 683, 244 N.W. 201 (1932).

Delay in making improvements

Purchaser could not rescind for vendor's delay in making improvements, where time was not essence of contract and there was practical performance before attempted rescission and full performance before trial.—Shpargel v. Emerson Land Co., 258 Mich. 222, 241 N.W. 891 (1932).

Right to abstracts

Where vendors, required to furnish abstract showing merchantable title upon completion of contract, furnished title policies, and purchasers retained policies for months, thereafter returning them without complaint or demand for abstracts, and offered vendors no fair opportunity precisely to perform their obligation, purchasers were not entitled to rescission until vendors had fair opportunity to furnish abstracts.—Probst v. Kennedy, 270 Mich. 583, 259 N.W. 333 (1935).

513. Schnitz v. Grand River Ave. Development Co., 271 Mich. 253, 259 N.W. 900 (1935).

the purchase proved a bad bargain does not entitle the vendee to a rescission of the contract.[514] The failure of the vendor to give information that the vendor is not obligated to furnish is also not grounds for the vendee's rescission.[515]

The vendee is not entitled to rescission for a claimed breach of covenant or condition by the vendor when the facts do not substantiate the claim.[516] Similarly, a vendee may not secure a rescission on an unsubstantiated contention that there was a failure of consideration.[517]

Ordinarily, a vendee in default is not entitled to rescind the contract.[518] If a vendee is in default in making late payments that are accepted by the vendor, the vendee is not entitled to rescind on the ground of the vendor's delay in conveying the property after demand and offer of payment.[519] But a vendee in default in payment of the purchase price may still rescind the contract for sale of real estate on the basis of the vendor's fraud.[520]

Deficiency in quantity. While the vendee may rescind the contract for a material deficiency in the quantity of land contracted for, this rule is inapplicable when the deficiency is not so material as to affect the enjoyment of the land and may be compensated by an abatement in the price.[521] The vendor's good faith offer to make good the deficiency bars rescission by the vendee, and in that case, the vendor must be given a reasonable opportunity to do so.[522]

Title defect. A material defect in the title to the property may support a rescission by the vendee.[523] But a defect that is of a minor character and subject to be cured is ordinarily no ground for rescission.[524] In any event, the vendor may not

514. Lapadat v. Copeland, 226 Mich. 329, 197 N.W. 547 (1924).

515. Gardner v. Thomas R. Sharp & Sons, 279 Mich. 467, 272 N.W. 871 (1937) (status of mortgage indebtedness).

516. Installation of gasoline pump

A contract for sale of gasoline station was not breached by vendor's failure to install gasoline pump when requested, where written agreement for purchase, and unsigned land contract admittedly embodying the terms agreed on, did not so require.—Slaggert v. Case, 319 Mich. 200, 29 N.W.2d 280 (1947).

Substitution of building restriction

Substitution, for contract provision restricting lots sold and majority of lots of subdivision, of general restriction limiting entire subdivision to single residences was mere technical breach not warranting purchaser's rescission.—Rosenthal v. Triangle Development Co., 261 Mich. 462, 246 N.W. 182 (1933).

517. Schnitz v. Grand River Ave. Development Co., 271 Mich. 253, 259 N.W. 900 (1935).

Violation of master deed did not defeat consideration

Violation by vendor of restriction in master deed limiting use of lots abutting specified high-

way to business purposes by construction of three bungalows on restricted lots was not such a substantial failure of consideration as to purchasers of other business lots as to warrant rescission of purchase, but merely gave rise to action for damages.—Abbate v. Shelden Land Co., 303 Mich. 657, 7 N.W.2d 97 (1942).

518. Stryker v. Marschner, 274 Mich. 205, 264 N.W. 344 (1936).

519. Miller v. Smith, 276 Mich. 372, 267 N.W. 862 (1936).

520. Lightner v. Karnatz, 258 Mich. 74, 241 N.W. 841 (1932).

521. Harris v. Axline, 323 Mich. 585, 36 N.W.2d 154 (1949).

Steinbach v. Hill, 25 Mich. 78 (1872).

522. Hathaway v. Hudson, 256 Mich. 694, 239 N.W. 859 (1932).

523. Bechard v. Bolton, 316 Mich. 1, 24 N.W.2d 422 (1946).

Ihlenfeldt v. Guastella, 42 Mich. App. 384, 202 N.W.2d 327 (1972).

524. Bonninghausen v. Hall, 267 Mich. 347, 255 N.W. 205 (1934).

be placed in default for defect of title or inability to convey by tender of performance by the purchaser and demand on the vendor before expiration of the time fixed by the contract for the making of the conveyance.[525]

Election to rescind and notice. Ordinarily, a vendee electing to rescind the contract must notify the vendor to that effect.[526]

§ 522. Conditions Precedent

A vendee seeking rescission of the contract must offer to do equity and comply with all conditions precedent.

Generally, a vendee seeking rescission of the contract must offer to do equity.[527] In the absence of waiver by the vendor,[528] the vendee must comply with all conditions precedent, such as performing or tendering performance of his or her own part of the contract[529] and demanding performance by the vendor.[530]

In that regard, the vendee must also place the vendor *in statu quo*.[531] The vendee must tender the contract back to the vendor,[532] or provide a release to the vendor from the contract.[533] A vendee who has received title to an interest in the land must reconvey or tender a release from the conveyance.[534]

Where the vendor categorically refuses an attempted rescission by the vendee,

MacLeod v. Hamilton, 254 Mich. 653, 236 N.W. 912 (1931).

525. Walcrath Realty Co. v. Van Dyke, 263 Mich. 316, 248 N.W. 634 (1933).

526. Converse v. Blumrich, 14 Mich. 109 (1866).

Notice was sufficient

Purchasers' notice to vendor of rescission of contract to purchase realty because vendor did not have merchantable title, mailed to person who had been active on behalf of vendor in negotiations and disputes arising out of contract and also to real estate agent employed by vendor's father who had represented vendor in the sale was sufficient notice of rescission.—Porter v. Ridge, 310 Mich. 425, 17 N.W.2d 239 (1945).

The bringing of a suit within a few days after payment of money toward the purchase of land operated as notice to vendor of refusal of purchasers to go ahead with the deal under new terms imposed.—Duncombe v. Tromble, 219 Mich. 8, 188 N.W. 367 (1922).

527. Hathaway v. Hudson, 256 Mich. 694, 239 N.W. 859 (1932).

528. Lackovic v. Campbell, 225 Mich. 1, 195 N.W. 798 (1923) (by refusing to deal with purchaser's counsel, where he gave notice of rescission and demanded return of money, vendor waived tender of a written release before suit to rescind).

529. Stryker v. Marschner, 274 Mich. 205, 264 N.W. 344 (1936).

Failure of vendee's performance bars rescission

Purchasers could not properly terminate purchase agreement because one of the conditions precedent to closing was not satisfied, where such condition involved matter over which purchasers had some control and they made little or no effort to fulfill the condition.—Ihlenfeldt v. Guastella, 42 Mich. App. 384, 202 N.W.2d 327 (1972).

530. Rush v. Emmons, 285 Mich. 542, 281 N.W. 319 (1938).

531. National Bank of Sturgis v. Levanseler, 115 Mich. 372, 73 N.W. 399 (1897).

Impossibility of returning possession

Placing of vendor *in statu quo* was a requisite to rescission of contract to purchase realty, and could not be accomplished where, shortly before purchaser instituted action for rescission, building on realty was padlocked for a year because of illegal use.—Smith v. Highland Park State Bank, 309 Mich. 226, 15 N.W.2d 142 (1944).

532. Sloman v. Allen, 252 Mich. 578, 233 N.W. 421 (1930) (duty to tender back contract).

533. Tender of release

Purchaser sued for installments on contract and not tendering release to vendor of her contract interest before suit was not entitled to rescind.—Walcrath Realty Co. v. Van Dyke, 263 Mich. 316, 248 N.W. 634 (1933).

534. Interest transferred

Where vendee merely sought to surrender contract physically to vendors or successor, without

the vendor may not contend that the tender of rescission is insufficient.[535] After the vendor's default, the vendee may rescind without paying or tendering the balance of the purchase price.[536]

§ 523.   Time for Rescission; Laches and Waiver

A vendee may lose his or her right to rescind where the vendee delays an unreasonable time after discovery of the ground for rescission, and the right may be lost by reason of laches, waiver, or estoppel.

A vendee with knowledge of the grounds on which he or she is entitled to rescind may lose that right where he or she delays to exercise it for an unreasonable time.[537] That is even more likely if the delay is accompanied by a change of circumstances that makes it impracticable for the vendee to place the vendor in statu quo.[538] Thus, the vendee's delay may preclude rescission of the land contract for duress,[539] fraud,[540] or defects in the title.[541]

While lapse of time alone is not necessarily decisive on the issue of waiver,[542]

any attempt to transfer interest acquired, vendee did not rescind contract and could not recover purchase price paid.—Barker v. Fordville Land Co., 264 Mich. 95, 249 N.W. 491 (1933).

535. Cox v. Holkeboer, 200 Mich. 86, 166 N.W. 1004 (1918).

536. Brow v. Gibraltar Land Co., 249 Mich. 662, 229 N.W. 604 (1930).

537. Rush v. Emmons, 285 Mich. 542, 281 N.W. 319 (1938).

Bennett v. Hickey, 112 Mich. 379, 70 N.W. 900 (1897).

Continued performance

Where vendor's alleged failure to improve lots in subdivision was of long standing and fully known to purchaser, who continued in performance of contract, purchaser was not entitled to rescind contract on account of that failure.—Jacobs v. Dearborn Holding Co., 270 Mich. 55, 258 N.W. 208 (1935).

Duty to act promptly

Purchaser intending to rescind for defect of title must do so promptly after discovering defect.—Colby v. Plymouth Road Development Corp., 251 Mich. 663, 232 N.W. 237 (1930).

538. Changes in value

A vendee, claiming right to rescind contract, must act promptly after accrual of such right, and if he or she continues to treat property as his or her own with view of seeing whether its market value increases or declines before deciding whether to rescind, vendee will not be permitted to rescind.—Pesciarelli v. Trestain, 288 Mich. 89, 284 N.W. 656 (1939).

539. Haldane v. Sweet, 55 Mich. 196, 20 N.W. 902 (1884) (purchaser of land made payments from time to time, and allowed more than six years to elapse since last payment without seeking redress).

540. Warren v. Hugo Scherer Estate, 272 Mich. 254, 261 N.W. 319 (1935).

Achenbach v. Mears, 272 Mich. 74, 261 N.W. 251 (1935).

Roszczewski v. Jozwiak, 225 Mich. 670, 196 N.W. 359 (1923) (it is duty of purchaser after he learns that he has been defrauded, if he intends to rescind, to do so promptly, and not do anything inconsistent with ownership of vendor).

Wylie v. Gamble, 95 Mich. 564, 55 N.W. 377 (1893) (false representations as to quantity of timber).

Delay after discovery

Where a purchaser of a fruit farm discovered fraudulent representations of the vendor in September, 1904, but continued thereafter to make payments under his contract, insisting on the right to a reduction in the price, an abandonment and attempted rescission of the contract in April, 1905, were ineffective, and did not entitle him to recover the purchase money paid.—Mestler v. Jeffries, 145 Mich. 598, 108 N.W. 994 (1906).

541. Hart v. Copper Dist. Power Co., 289 Mich. 150, 286 N.W. 191 (1939).

Roose v. Parklane Homes Corp., 59 Mich. App. 542, 229 N.W.2d 838 (1975).

542. Colby v. Plymouth Road Development Corp., 251 Mich. 663, 232 N.W. 237 (1930).

a lapse of time combined with a change of condition may be sufficient to militate against the vendee's exercise of the remedy of rescission.[543]

Whether the vendee's right of rescission of an executory contract is defeated by laches, waiver, estoppel, or election of remedies must be decided by the particular facts of the case involved.[544]

The vendee will not lose the right of rescission if the delay is caused by the vendor,[545] or if the vendee acted promptly after discovery of the ground for rescission.[546]

Under the circumstances, a party may be entitled to a ruling that the vendee has or has not lost the right to rescind because of laches[547] or on the ground of waiver or estoppel.[548]

Premature rescission. Ordinarily, a vendee is not entitled to rescind for failure

Adams v. Grant, 247 Mich. 60, 225 N.W. 647 (1929).

543. Pesciarelli v. Trestain, 288 Mich. 89, 284 N.W. 656 (1939).

Browne v. Briggs Commercial & Development Co., 271 Mich. 191, 259 N.W. 886 (1935).

544. Dolecki v. Perry, 277 Mich. 679, 270 N.W. 184 (1936).

545. Taylor v. Fry, 255 Mich. 333, 238 N.W. 274 (1931).

Beloskursky v. Jozwiak, 221 Mich. 316, 191 N.W. 16 (1922).

Allen v. Talbot, 170 Mich. 664, 137 N.W. 97 (1912).

Vendor's promises and excuses

A purchaser's right to rescind his contract for fraud of vendors was not waived by his subsequent execution of notes for the portion of the purchase money that vendors represented would be covered by sale of lots, where, at the time of execution of notes, purchaser was still lulled into security by promises made and excuses offered by vendors.—Kefuss v. Whitley, 220 Mich. 67, 189 N.W. 76 (1922).

546. Lurie v. Schoenberg, 252 Mich. 90, 233 N.W. 192 (1930).

547. Warren v. Hugo Scherer Estate, 272 Mich. 254, 261 N.W. 319 (1935) (seven years' delay supported laches).

Berg v. Hessey, 268 Mich. 599, 256 N.W. 562 (1934) (laches for five years' delay).

Laches not shown

Labadie v. Boehle, 288 Mich. 223, 284 N.W. 707 (1939).

Purchasers going into possession of income property January 15, 1929, and filing suit for rescission, August 29, 1929, for false representations, were not barred by laches.—Chanler v.

Venetian Properties Corp., 254 Mich. 468, 236 N.W. 838 (1931).

Delay, in order to test productivity of soil by season's cropping, was not laches preventing rescission of sale of land on ground of fraud.—Gyles v. Stadel, 252 Mich. 349, 233 N.W. 339 (1930).

La Force v. Caspian Realty Co., 242 Mich. 646, 219 N.W. 668 (1928).

That purchasers of house and lot continued in possession for six months, repeatedly demanding remedying of defects and making of changes, and made payments under contract after many of defects were known to them, does not bar their right to cancellation of contract and relief against forfeiture provided therein, where extent of defendant's fraud as to condition of house was not discovered until long after they went into possession.—Culver v. Avery, 161 Mich. 322, 126 N.W. 439 (1910).

548. Dolecki v. Perry, 277 Mich. 679, 270 N.W. 184 (1936).

Danto v. Kunze, 255 Mich. 135, 237 N.W. 390 (1931).

Kreibich v. Martz, 119 Mich. 343, 78 N.W. 124 (1899).

Bennett v. Hickey, 112 Mich. 379, 70 N.W. 900 (1897).

Affirmative action ratified agreement after grounds for rescission

Vendees, who purchased lake property for resale for resort purposes, waived right to rescind for alleged misrepresentations as to value and estimate of probable gain because of their affirmative action of replatting and making readjustments with purchasers of lots from vendors.—Berg v. Hessey, 268 Mich. 599, 256 N.W. 562 (1934).

Later agreement waived right

Purchaser of land, who, after discovering fraud practiced upon him entered into arrangement for restitution, surrendered his contract, but later made

of title or defects in the title before the time when the vendor is obligated to convey the property.[549]

§ 524.   Operation and Effect of Rescission

A vendee's valid rescission of a contract for the sale of land abrogates the rights of the parties thereunder, but ordinarily each is entitled to be put *in statu quo*.

Given that the vendee's valid rescission abrogates the contract and terminates the rights of the parties under it, after rescission, the vendee may not recover items for loss of wages and the expense of moving to the premises.[550] Similarly, the vendee may not recover an item for rental that the vendor's agent had agreed inured to him or her after the purchase.[551]

In the event of a rescission for fraud, the vendee is not entitled to a recovery that puts the vendee in a better position than if the land had been as represented.[552] But the vendee is entitled to be placed *in statu quo*,[553] such as by reimbursement from the vendor of payments to the vendor and of taxes on the property, with interest.[554]

A vendee who rescinds after having been in possession of the property for a considerable period must account for the reasonable rental value of the property during the time of his or her possession.[555] The vendee's advance of sums for taxes and interest must be offset by the reasonable rental value due vendors for the use of the land prior to cancellation of a contract for purchase of real property.[556]

§ 525.   Actions for Rescission

A vendee's action for rescission of a contract for the sale of land is equitable in nature, and the relief granted will be

agreement with vendor for continued possession, waived any right to rescind on ground of such fraud.—Jensen v. Evans, 230 Mich. 199, 202 N.W. 969 (1925).

Waiver or estoppel not shown

Purchasers participating in attempts at settlement did not waive right to rescind real estate contract for fraud, where no one was injured, and there were not acts indicating waiver.—Holbrook v. Blick, 256 Mich. 396, 240 N.W. 26 (1932).

Rescission was not waived by purchaser's using property and taking rentals.—La Force v. Caspian Realty Co., 242 Mich. 646, 219 N.W. 668 (1928).

Folkerts v. Marysville Land Co., 236 Mich. 294, 210 N.W. 231 (1926).

Jandorf v. Patterson, 90 Mich. 40, 51 N.W. 352 (1892).

549. Walcrath Realty Co. v. Van Dyke, 263 Mich. 316, 248 N.W. 634 (1933).

Detroit Fidelity & Surety Co. v. Bushman, 260 Mich. 115, 244 N.W. 251 (1932).

550. Cox v. Holkeboer, 200 Mich. 86, 166 N.W. 1004 (1918).

551. Cox v. Holkeboer, 200 Mich. 86, 166 N.W. 1004 (1918).

552. Cox v. Holkeboer, 200 Mich. 86, 166 N.W. 1004 (1918).

553. Cutter v. Wait, 131 Mich. 508, 91 N.W. 753 (1902) (where vendees were induced to enter into contract of sale by false representations, they had, on rescission, right to place themselves in statu quo by removing improvements made, as far as it could be done without injury to the freehold remaining).

554. Cox v. Holkeboer, 200 Mich. 86, 166 N.W. 1004 (1918).

555. Bechard v. Bolton, 316 Mich. 1, 24 N.W.2d 422 (1946).

Allen v. Talbot, 170 Mich. 664, 137 N.W. 97 (1912).

556. McKnight v. Broedell, 212 F. Supp. 45 (E.D. Mich. 1962).

determined by equitable principles as applied to the facts of the particular case.

An action by the vendee for rescission of a contract for the sale of land is equitable in nature and governed by equitable considerations.[557] In a vendee's equitable suit to rescind a contract of sale of realty, the vendee's reconveyance or tender before suit is unnecessary.[558]

In this type of action, the courts apply the general rules with respect to parties,[559] pleadings,[560] evidence,[561] and trial.[562]

The purchaser has the burden of establishing facts appealing to the court's discretion and entitling the purchaser to equitable relief of rescission.[563] It is a question of fact for the jury to determine whether the vendee has acted with reasonable promptness after learning that he or she has been defrauded.[564]

The nature and extent of relief granted in a vendee's suit for rescission are for the court to determine under equitable principles as applied to the facts of the particular case.[565] The court has discretion to determine the terms and conditions under which rescission of contract to purchase house may be granted to the

---

557. Probst v. Kennedy, 270 Mich. 583, 259 N.W. 333 (1935).

McHugh v. Trinity Bldg. Co., 254 Mich. 202, 236 N.W. 232 (1931) (complaint to rescind contract for false representations gave court equitable jurisdiction).

Time cause of action accrues

Plaintiffs, who received, as part of consideration for sale of realty, a contract for purchase of land, were held not required to wait until default occurred on that contract before bringing suit for fraud, because their right of action arose when fraud was committed, restitution offered, and notice of rescission given.—Ronczkowski v. Jozwiak, 230 Mich. 327, 203 N.W. 105 (1925).

558. Lightner v. Karnatz, 258 Mich. 74, 241 N.W. 841 (1932).

Tender of amount due is not necessary

Purchaser could sue in equity to rescind contracts for sale of land without tendering amount due and demanding deed.—Himebaugh v. Chalker, 261 Mich. 80, 245 N.W. 576 (1932).

559. Lapadat v. Copeland, 226 Mich. 329, 197 N.W. 547 (1924) (one of two purchasers of certain land could not join other purchaser in suit to cancel contracts, without authority to so do from other purchaser).

560. Beacock v. People's Lumber Co., 253 Mich. 403, 235 N.W. 200 (1931) (pleading and stipulation by purchasers, showing house purchased was defective in construction, subject to mechanics' liens and mortgages, contrary to vendor's representations, stated case for rescission).

561. Rush v. Emmons, 285 Mich. 542, 281 N.W. 319 (1938) (evidence sustained decree denying to purchasers cancellation and rescission of contract).

Evidence does not support rescission

Evidence supported finding that assignee of land contract was first to default and that such default caused vendor to default in mortgage payments and payments for taxes on the property, so that vendor was entitled to foreclose land contract and assignee was not entitled to rescission.—Roberts v. Rubin, 13 Mich. App. 652, 164 N.W.2d 740 (1968).

Misrepresentation and reliance

In purchasers' action for rescission of contract for purpose of motel, evidence disclosed that there were false representation by vendors concerning expenses of business and that purchasers relied on statement of income and expenses which inaccurately reflected expenses connected with business during that year.—Papin v. Demski, 383 Mich. 561, 177 N.W.2d 166 (1970).

562. Probst v. Kennedy, 270 Mich. 583, 259 N.W. 333 (1935).

563. Kavanau v. Fry, 273 Mich. 166, 262 N.W. 763 (1935).

564. Zadel v. Simon, 221 Mich. 180, 190 N.W. 700 (1922).

565. Martin v. Mortenson, 263 Mich. 381, 248 N.W. 844 (1933) (on cancellation of contract subject to trust mortgage securing bondholders, vendee is not entitled to decree requiring repayment of purchase price installments from trust fund without establishing trustee's possession of money paid by vendee).

vendee.[566] Thus, a purchaser under a land contract, who seeks remedies for injuries caused by allegedly fraudulent misrepresentations of vendor under the theory of rescission may also recover damages for losses sustained as a direct result of the misrepresentation.[567]

566. Beacock v. People's Lumber Co., 253 Mich. 403, 235 N.W. 200 (1931).

567. Mock v. Duke, 20 Mich. App. 453, 174 N.W.2d 161 (1969).

Chapter 18

PERFORMANCE OF CONTRACT FOR SALE OF LAND

§ 531.   Title of Vendor

Generally, a vendor is obligated to furnish the vendee with a marketable title. A marketable title is one free from encumbrances and assuring the vendee quiet and peaceful enjoyment of the property.

Library References

Michigan Digest
LexisNexis® Automated Michigan SCAO Forms
John G. Cameron, Jr., Michigan Real Estate Forms
Powell on Real Property® (Michael Allan Wolf, ed.)
Thompson on Real Property, Thomas Edition (David A. Thomas, ed.)

Law Reviews

Department: Section Brief: Real Property Law Section, 90 MI Bar Jnl. 58 (2011); David E. Nykanen, Real Property, 55 Wayne L. Rev. 575 (2009); Stephen R. Estey and Danielle Graceffa, Real Property, 54 Wayne L. Rev. 387 (2008); Naseem Stecker and Mike Eidelbes, Up Front: Real Property and Consumer Law Sections Team up on "Ask The Lawyer" to Discuss Mortgage Foreclosures, 87 MI Bar Jnl. 8 (2008); Gregg A. Nathanson, Feature: Real Property Law: What's New in Residential Transactions?, 86 MI Bar Jnl. 16 (2007); Jerome P. Pesick and Ronald E. Reynolds, Feature: Real Property Law: Recent Changes in Eminent Domain Law, 86 MI Bar Jnl. 22 (2007); David E. Nykanen and Jason C. Long, Annual Survey of Michigan Law; June 1, 2004 - May 31, 2005: Real Property, 52 Wayne L. Rev. 941 (2006); Daniel J. Schairbaum, Annual Survey of Michigan Law: June 1, 2003 - May 31, 2004: Real Property, 51 Wayne L. Rev. 881 (2005); Jerome P. Pesick, Real Property Law: Eminent Domain: Calculating Just Compensation in Partial Taking Condemnation Cases, 82 MI Bar Jnl. 34 (2003); Lawrence R. Shoffner, Real Property Law: Real Evidence: Special Rules for Real Estate Disputes, 80 MI Bar Jnl. 28 (2001).

Generally, the vendor is under an obligation to convey a merchantable or marketable title.[568] A contract to convey may be valid although the vendor does not own the premises, in which case the vendee's remedy is an action for damages.[569]

A marketable title is one free from encumbrances and assuring the vendee

---

568. Marketable title, *see, supra,* Chapter 1.

Fix v. Amiot, 251 Mich. 124, 231 N.W. 114 (1930).

Cole v. Cardoza, 441 F.2d 1337 (6th Cir. Mich. 1971).

Weaver v. Richards, 144 Mich. 395, 108 N.W. 382 (1906) (obligated to convey title which is unassailable on the face of record as well as in fact).

Reliance upon language in conveyance describing grantor as a single man, *see* 41 Mich. S.B.J. 23 (Jan. 1962).

Dispute between third persons

Litigation pending between third persons, in which the lands in question are involved, but that does not attempt to attack title of vendor, affords no excuse to vendee for declining the deed.— Curran v. Rogers, 35 Mich. 221 (1876).

Misdescription

Title that rests on deed essentially misdescribing property conveyed is not marketable.— Bradway v. Miller, 200 Mich. 648, 167 N.W. 15 (1918).

Titles by descent, devise, or sale in course of administration were not marketable

Fix v. Amiot, 251 Mich. 124, 231 N.W. 114 (1930).

Litchfield v. Tunnicliff, 118 Mich. 383, 76 N.W. 760 (1898).

569. Brin v. Michalski, 188 Mich. 400, 154 N.W. 110 (1915).

quiet and peaceful enjoyment of the property.[570] A title need not be actually bad in order to render it unmarketable, because it will be so regarded if a reasonably prudent person, familiar with the facts, would refuse to accept the title in the ordinary course of business.[571] Thus, a title is unmarketable if there is sufficient doubt or uncertainty to render it reasonably possible that the title may be involved in litigation.[572] There must, however, be a reasonable doubt of the validity of the vendor's title in order to render it unmarketable.[573]

A vendee has the duty to investigate the title of the vendor and to take notice of defects in title that the vendee has the means to discover. The vendee must make every inquiry that due diligence compels.[574] If the vendee does not use due diligence to seek out defects in title, he or she is chargeable with the burden of any that he or she would have discovered exercising due diligence.[575]

Ordinarily, a purchaser knowing of defects in the vendor's title at the time that the purchaser enters into the contract cannot refuse to perform his or her part in the

---

570. Bartos v. Czerwinski, 323 Mich. 87, 34 N.W.2d 566 (1948).

Delnay v. Woodruff, 244 Mich. 456, 221 N.W. 614 (1928).

Barnard v. Brown, 112 Mich. 452, 70 N.W. 1038 (1897).

Madhavan v. Sucher, 105 Mich. App. 284, 306 N.W.2d 481 (1981).

Tax notes: United States Supreme Court rewrote joint property law and created title problems, *see* 62 Mich. S.B.J. 636 (1983).

Effect on marketability of title of discrepancy in name of grantor or mortgagor, *see* 41 Mich. S.B.J. 18 (Jan. 1962).

571. McKnight v. Broedell, 212 F. Supp. 45 (E.D. Mich. 1962).

Klais v. Danowski, 373 Mich. 281, 129 N.W.2d 423 (1964).

Escher v. Bender, 338 Mich. 1, 61 N.W.2d 143 (1953).

Deane v. Rex Oil & Gas Co., 325 Mich. 625, 39 N.W.2d 204 (1949).

Bartos v. Czerwinski, 323 Mich. 87, 34 N.W.2d 566 (1948).

Madhavan v. Sucher, 105 Mich. App. 284, 306 N.W.2d 481 (1981).

572. McKnight v. Broedell, 212 F. Supp. 45 (E.D. Mich. 1962).

Klais v. Danowski, 373 Mich. 281, 129 N.W.2d 423 (1964).

Escher v. Bender, 338 Mich. 1, 61 N.W.2d 143 (1953).

Bartos v. Czerwinski, 323 Mich. 87, 34 N.W.2d 566 (1948).

Effect on marketability of title of delay in recording conveyance, *see* 41 Mich. S.B.J. 21 (Jan. 1962).

Forcing doubtful title on vendee

Doubtful title may not be forced on defendant by decree for specific performance.—Frankiewicz v. Konwinski, 246 Mich. 473, 224 N.W. 368 (1929).

573. Filled land

In view of reasonable doubt as to validity of title of vendors, riparian owners, of land claimed by Michigan on basis that it was filled-in land and was lakeward of ordinary high-water mark, title was unmarketable.—McKnight v. Broedell, 212 F. Supp. 45 (E.D. Mich. 1962).

Rejection of financing by financial institution

Financial institution's refusal to make mortgage loan is worthy of consideration, but not conclusive on question whether title is unmarketable.—Delnay v. Woodruff, 244 Mich. 456, 221 N.W. 614 (1928).

Title was marketable

Where there was no agreement concerning sale of property, except receipt for deposit, deposit did not constitute cloud upon title and did not create unmarketable title.—Henry v. Rouse, 345 Mich. 86, 75 N.W.2d 836 (1956).

574. Schweiss v. Woodruff, 73 Mich. 473, 41 N.W. 511 (1889).

575. Schweiss v. Woodruff, 73 Mich. 473, 41 N.W. 511 (1889).

Inquiry notice

Title searcher may be chargeable with inquiry notice when ambiguity is encountered.—American Federal Sav. & Loan Ass'n v. Orenstein, 81 Mich. App. 249, 265 N.W.2d 111 (1978).

absence of an express stipulation or agreement to that effect.[576]

Where the contract contains particular requirements concerning the character of title to be conveyed, the vendor must comply with those requirements.[577]

Where a contract for the sale of land contains no agreement to cancel if the abstract fails to show a merchantable title, and the abstract does so fail, the vendee may elect to receive back the deposit and release the vendor or to accept an inferior title.[578] A contract that does contain stipulations about the rights of the parties in event of the vendor's being unable to furnish a marketable title does control their rights.[579]

Actions for specific performance. Specific performance of a contract for the sale of real property is an equitable remedy within the sound discretion of the circuit court.[580]

§ 532.   —Record Title

A marketable title must be one of record. Anyone having an unbroken chain of title of record for 40 years generally has a marketable title of record.

Generally, a person having legal capacity to own land in Michigan, who has an unbroken chain of title of record to any interest in land for 40 years, has a marketable record title to the land, subject only to those claims and defects that are

576. Daly v. Kramer, 235 Mich. 581, 209 N.W. 926 (1926).

Reliance on own title examination

Even though purchaser relied on its own title examination when it contracted, and there was no fraud or misleading by vendor, action for damages on account of vendor's inability to convey title as agreed cannot be defeated unless purchaser knew of defect when it first contracted.—Crocker v. Ingersoll Engineering & Constructing Co., 249 F. 31 (6th Cir. Mich. 1918).

577. Ford v. Wright, 114 Mich. 122, 72 N.W. 197 (1897).

Insurable title

Where purchasers on November 17 requested a policy of title insurance, procurement of title insurance commitment on December 19 was within a reasonable time and purchasers had no valid cause to rescind the contract.—Worley v. McCarty, 354 Mich. 599, 93 N.W.2d 269 (1958).

"Perfect" title

A land contract providing for a title that is perfect calls for more than a warranty deed, and the vendee is not bound to rest upon covenants.—Platt v. Newman, 71 Mich. 112, 38 N.W. 720 (1888).

578. Sorge v. Dickie, 199 Mich. 251, 165 N.W. 781 (1917).

579. De Propris v. Smith, 342 Mich. 457, 70 N.W.2d 712 (1955).

Shubow v. W.X.Y.Z., Inc., 23 Mich. App. 111, 178 N.W.2d 143 (1970).

Right to refuse under contract

Where agreement for purchase provided that if title to land was not merchantable and acceptable to purchaser, moneys paid in escrow were to be returned, and purchaser, during period for search, obtained certain outstanding interests, but necessity remained for bringing proceedings to quiet title, purchaser was justified in refusing to accept title and vendor was not entitled to specific performance of the agreement.—Deane v. Rex Oil & Gas Co., 325 Mich. 625, 39 N.W.2d 204 (1949).

Satisfaction of purchaser

Under a sale of land by an administrator with the will annexed, providing for refunding of the partial payment if the title was not "satisfactory," the purchaser may refuse to complete the purchase, because he or she was not satisfied that the administrator had authority to give title under the power given the executor in the will.—Green v. Russell, 103 Mich. 638, 61 N.W. 885 (1895).

580. Specific performance, M.L.P.2d Remedies.

Zurcher v. Herveat, 238 Mich. App. 267, 605 N.W.2d 329 (1999).

not extinguished or barred by law. However, no one has such a marketable record title by reason of the applicable statute if the land in which the interest exists is in the hostile possession of another.[581]

While a title acquired by adverse possession may be a good and marketable title,[582] it does not become a marketable title of record until there has been a judicial determination and a recording of the decree granting title by adverse possession.[583]

§ 533.   —Easements and Encumbrances

In the absence of specific provision to the contrary in the contract, a vendor must convey property without easements or encumbrances on it.

In the absence of a specific provision to the contrary, the vendor must convey a title that is free from easements[584] and encumbrances.[585] An encumbrance is anything that constitutes a burden on the title.[586]

On the other hand, alleged encumbrances do not render the title unmarketable if the encumbrances are invalid,[587] or if the vendee created them.[588] Also, encumbrances for which the contract itself specifically provides do not render the title unmarketable.[589]

---

581. Marketable title, *see, supra*, Chapter 1.

MCLS § 565.101.

Fowler v. Doan, 261 Mich. App. 595, 683 N.W.2d 682 (2004).

People ex rel. Gazlay v. Murray, 54 Mich. App. 685, 221 N.W.2d 604 (1974) (act does not apply against state).

Researching online real estate records in Michigan, *see* 80 Mich. B.J. 22 (2001).

The 40-year marketable title act: A reappraisal, *see* 37 U. Det. L.J. 422 (1960).

582. Escher v. Bender, 338 Mich. 1, 61 N.W.2d 143 (1953).

Barnard v. Brown, 112 Mich. 452, 70 N.W. 1038 (1897).

583. Escher v. Bender, 338 Mich. 1, 61 N.W.2d 143 (1953).

Deane v. Rex Oil & Gas Co., 325 Mich. 625, 39 N.W.2d 204 (1949).

584. Colby v. Plymouth Road Development Corp., 251 Mich. 663, 232 N.W. 237 (1930) (pipeline right of way).

Platt v. Newman, 71 Mich. 112, 38 N.W. 720 (1888).

Easement as encumbrance

An easement for oil pipe line and telegraph or telephone lines was an encumbrance that prevented purchaser of land from obtaining marketable title within land contract requiring conveyance of marketable title.—Porter v. Ridge, 310 Mich. 425, 17 N.W.2d 239 (1945).

585. Dikeman v. Arnold, 71 Mich. 656, 40 N.W. 42 (1888).

Building restrictions

Building restriction in deed is encumbrance and cloud on title.—Hyman v. Boyle, 239 Mich. 357, 214 N.W. 163 (1927).

Ogooshevitz v. Warijas, 203 Mich. 664, 169 N.W. 820 (1918).

Condition subsequent

A condition subsequent in a deed, prohibiting use of premises for certain occupations deemed nuisances in first-class residence districts, constituted an apparent or prima facie encumbrance, which rendered the title of the grantee nonmarketable.—Ingersoll Engineering & Constr. Co. v. Crocker, 228 F. 844 (6th Cir. Mich. 1915).

586. Porter v. Ridge, 310 Mich. 425, 17 N.W.2d 239 (1945).

Madhavan v. Sucher, 105 Mich. App. 284, 306 N.W.2d 481 (1981).

587. Walkley v. Bostwick, 49 Mich. 374, 13 N.W. 780 (1882).

Paid mortgage

Where mortgagees have no right of possession until foreclosure, a mortgage that has been paid, though not discharged of record, is not an encumbrance, and does not justify a purchaser in refusing to take a proper deed, on the ground that the title is not clear.—Curran v. Rogers, 35 Mich. 221 (1876).

Title by adverse possession. A contract to convey land "in fee and unencumbered" is satisfied by tender of a deed conveying a title that the vendor has acquired by adverse possession.[590]

§ 534.   —Objections to Title and Waiver

A vendee has the duty to investigate the title of the vendor and to take notice of defects in title that the vendee has the means to discover. A vendee is under no duty specifically to point out to the vendor objections to the title unless so required by the contract. Objections to the title are subject to waiver.

A vendee has the duty to investigate the title of the vendor and to take notice of defects in title that the vendee has the means to discover. The vendee must make every inquiry that due diligence compels.[591] If the vendee does not use due diligence to seek out defects in title, he or she is chargeable with the burden of any that he or she would have discovered exercising due diligence.[592]

In the absence of provisions therefor in the contract, a vendee is not bound to point out specific defects in the title before rescinding the contract where the contract does allow the vendee to rescind for lack of good title.[593]

The vendee may waive objections to the title.[594] The vendee waives the right to rescind for title defect by continuing to perform under the contract after discovering the defect.[595] The vendee waives the right to an unencumbered title by consenting to the execution of a mortgage.[596] The vendee also waives the right to object to a title defect by bringing a suit for specific performance of the contract to

---

588. Maser v. Gibbons, 280 Mich. 621, 274 N.W. 352 (1937) (encumbrances created, induced, or suffered by purchaser under contract of sale cannot be urged as objection to title, nor do they constitute breach of warranty in vendor's deed, and same rule applies to assignee or agent of vendee).

589. Sloan v. Holcomb, 29 Mich. 153 (1874).

Mortgage

Under contract for sale of land providing for mortgages, purchaser is not relieved from payment solely because property is mortgaged.—Langley v. Kirker, 247 Mich. 443, 225 N.W. 931 (1929).

590. Barnard v. Brown, 112 Mich. 452, 70 N.W. 1038 (1897).

591. Schweiss v. Woodruff, 73 Mich. 473, 41 N.W. 511 (1889).

592. Schweiss v. Woodruff, 73 Mich. 473, 41 N.W. 511 (1889).

Inquiry notice

Title searcher may be chargeable with inquiry notice when ambiguity is encountered.—Ameri-

can Federal Sav. & Loan Ass'n v. Orenstein, 81 Mich. App. 249, 265 N.W.2d 111 (1978).

593. No notice of defect to vendor

Where agreement for purchase provided that moneys paid in escrow were to be returned if title to land was not marketable and acceptable to purchaser, purchaser could reject contemplated purchase on discovery of substantial defect that reasonably required proceeding to quiet title, without making objection known to vendor within period of option.—Deane v. Rex Oil & Gas Co., 325 Mich. 625, 39 N.W.2d 204 (1949).

594. Frazer v. Hovey, 195 Mich. 160, 161 N.W. 887 (1917).

Schwartz v. Woodruff, 132 Mich. 513, 93 N.W. 1067 (1903).

595. Payment with knowledge of restrictions

Purchaser with knowledge of building restrictions waived right to rescind contract requiring conveyance free of encumbrances after making payments without protest.—Hyman v. Boyle, 239 Mich. 357, 214 N.W. 163 (1927).

596. Langley v. Kirker, 247 Mich. 443, 225 N.W. 931 (1929).

obtain marketable title.[597]

Facts that do not unequivocally show acceptance of the title by the vendee do not constitute a waiver.[598]

§ 535.   —Curing Defects

Generally, a vendor is not in default if any defects in the title are cured before the time set for conveyance.

It is not essential that the vendor have a perfect title at the time of the execution of the contract. Generally, the vendor is not in default if his or her title has been perfected by the time for conveyance to the vendee.[599] While a vendor must use reasonable diligence to cure defects in the title,[600] the vendee may not complain of the vendor's failure to begin necessary proceedings before the time specified in the contract.[601] After defects have been cured in compliance with contract requirements, the title becomes marketable.[602]

A vendor who agrees to convey marketable title must bear the expense of obtaining it.[603]

On the other hand, a vendor who fails to perfect his or her title in compliance with the contract for sale of real property is in default.[604] After payment of the contract price, the vendor is not entitled to time to make title, but only to a

597. Cameron v. Sowicka, 248 Mich. 616, 227 N.W. 717 (1929).

Levin v. Hamilton, 233 Mich. 203, 206 N.W. 526 (1925).

Possession pending suit

Purchasers were not estopped, merely because they were enjoying possession when their suit for specific performance was started, to insist on vendors' performance of their contract obligation to deliver marketable title.—Klais v. Danowski, 373 Mich. 281, 129 N.W.2d 423 (1964).

Subsequent waiver

Where the purchaser of realty under a contract providing for clear title refused to perform because a clear title was not shown and elected to have the initial payment returned, he was not, upon the seller's refusal to return the payment and insistence that he was bound, precluded from subsequently waiving the defect in the title and insisting on specific performance.—Ogooshevitz v. Warijas, 203 Mich. 664, 169 N.W. 820 (1918).

598. Deane v. Rex Oil & Gas Co., 325 Mich. 625, 39 N.W.2d 204 (1949).

Colby v. Plymouth Road Development Corp., 251 Mich. 663, 232 N.W. 237 (1930).

599. Chappus v. Lucke, 246 Mich. 272, 224 N.W. 432 (1929).

Silfver v. Daenzer, 167 Mich. 362, 133 N.W. 16 (1911).

Deed to another

Purchaser could not rescind contract because of vendor's deed to another, where vendor reacquired title and tendered title when suit was commenced.—Jaerling v. Longsdorf, 254 Mich. 558, 236 N.W. 862 (1931).

Encumbrance released before damage

A vendee may not complain of an encumbrance that was released to the vendor before damage resulted.—Raffel v. Epworth, 107 Mich. 143, 64 N.W. 1052 (1895).

600. La Force v. Caspian Realty Co., 242 Mich. 646, 219 N.W. 668 (1928).

601. Lutz v. Dutmer, 286 Mich. 467, 282 N.W. 431 (1938).

602. Lower v. Walters, 230 Mich. 395, 202 N.W. 937 (1925).

603. Cost of curing defect

Provision of land sale contract that purchasers were satisfied with marketability of title as shown by abstract did not cast upon purchasers cost of establishing title where vendors agreed in contract to furnish marketable title and claim which was asserted by state did not appear in abstract.—Klais v. Danowski, 373 Mich. 281, 129 N.W.2d 423 (1964).

604. Wexler v. Poe, 245 Mich. 442, 222 N.W. 715 (1929).

reasonable time in which to execute the conveyance.[605]

§ 536. —Furnishing Abstract

Where the contract so requires, a vendor must furnish an abstract showing marketable title.

A vendor must comply with the terms of a contract that requires the vendor to furnish an abstract of title to the vendee.[606] After receiving it, the vendee is entitled to a reasonable time to have counsel examine the abstract.[607] If, however, the vendee files an action for specific performance, it renders the vendor's failure to deliver an abstract as required by the contract immaterial.[608]

Where the contract requires the vendor to furnish an abstract showing a clear or marketable title and the vendor provides an abstract showing less than marketable title, the vendor has not performed his or her obligation.[609] The purchaser need not accept an abstract offered by a vendor that fails to show marketable title.[610] The merchantability of the title must appear on the face of the abstract.[611] The vendor fails to meet his or her obligation in this regard by offering proof of title in other forms.[612]

605. Lawfulness of contract

Lawfulness of contract to sell real estate not owned by vendor does not extend contract time for delivering deed, in that vendor must take steps to acquire title in anticipation of his duty to deliver deed.—Haight v. Salter, 260 Mich. 6, 244 N.W. 209 (1932).

606. Sobczak v. Kotwicki, 347 Mich. 242, 79 N.W.2d 471 (1956).

607. Approval by Veterans Administration

Where both parties agreed that money would be paid to vendors and conveyance made to purchasers upon approval of vendors' title after loan was approved by veterans administration, vendors could not complain that money was not tendered until after 90-day period contemplated by contract within which purchasers were to finance transaction, in view of their refusal to give veterans administration's attorney abstract for title examination, in light of contract provision that if marketable title can be conveyed, sale shall be consummated within 90 days after delivery of abstract.—Sobczak v. Kotwicki, 347 Mich. 242, 79 N.W.2d 471 (1956).

608. Levin v. Hamilton, 233 Mich. 203, 206 N.W. 526 (1925).

609. Bradway v. Miller, 200 Mich. 648, 167 N.W. 15 (1918).

Walker v. Gillman, 127 Mich. 269, 86 N.W. 830 (1901).

610. Barber v. Lang, 237 Mich. 98, 211 N.W. 70 (1926).

611. Wexler v. Poe, 245 Mich. 442, 222 N.W. 715 (1929).

Lake Erie Land Co. v. Chilinski, 197 Mich. 214, 163 N.W. 929 (1917).

Lack of showing of marketable title in abstract

Abstract of title, showing foreclosure of mortgage by advertisement, without showing that mortgage contained power of sale, does not show good title in vendor.—Bryan v. Straus Bros. & Co., 157 Mich. 49, 121 N.W. 301 (1909).

Parol proof

If an abstract does not on its face show a merchantable title, and it requires parol proof to establish the fact that the title is a merchantable one, a contract agreeing to furnish an abstract showing a merchantable title is not complied with.—Lake Erie Land Co. v. Chilinski, 197 Mich. 214, 163 N.W. 929 (1917).

612. Facts not in record

Where vendor agreed to furnish abstract showing marketable title, it was not compliance with this requirement that other facts showed vendor to have title good in law, though not in record.—Bradway v. Miller, 200 Mich. 648, 167 N.W. 15 (1918).

Prescriptive title

Contract by which one party agreed to furnish abstract showing clear title to land involved is not complied with by furnishing clear title by prescription, or title not established of record.—

§ 537.　Conveyance and Delivery of Possession

A vendor is under a duty to convey, or tender conveyance, in compliance with the terms of the contract, and to deliver possession of the property to the vendee. The vendor's obligation to convey remains a continuing executory obligation on the part of the vendor until the vendor performs it.

In the absence of waiver or excuse, the vendor must convey or tender conveyance of the property in compliance with the terms of the contract.[613] The vendor's obligation to convey remains a continuing executory obligation on the part of the vendor until the vendor performs it.[614] The vendor may assign responsibility to convey to an assignee, in which case the vendor remains secondarily liable for the conveyance.[615] Upon the vendor's performance, the vendor may require the vendee to execute a discharge of the land contract in the same manner as a mortgage is discharged.[616]

The vendor's tender or conveyance must be timely.[617]

The vendor may not withhold conveyance of the property because the vendee is violating use restrictions in the land contract.[618]

A vendee may not interpose objections to a conveyance or tender on grounds

Ogooshevitz v. Arnold, 197 Mich. 203, 163 N.W. 946 (1917).

613. MCLS § 565.361.

Deed executed to "estate" is defective tender

Vendor's tender to administrator of deceased purchaser's estate of deed executed to estate of decedent was insufficient as tender, because estate of decedent was not a person who could be a grantee under law of Florida, where the realty was located, or under the law of Michigan.—In re Reason's Estate, 276 Mich. 376, 267 N.W. 863 (1936).

Tender from third person is valid

Tender of title that satisfies requirements of a contract for conveyance of land free and unencumbered is not objectionable because it comes not directly from party to contract, but from a third person.—Kimball v. Goodburn, 32 Mich. 10 (1875).

Use of language appropriate to create easement

Where a contract for the conveyance of land provided that the vendee agreed to cause a roadway to be laid on the premises, it was obviously intended to create an easement on the vendee's property, and the vendor was entitled to have the easement evidenced by appropriate language in the deed.—Levandowski v. Althouse, 136 Mich. 631, 99 N.W. 786 (1904).

Usual covenants must be in deed

Under a contract to convey land, which is silent as to the deed to be given, purchaser is entitled to a deed with those covenants as are usual by the custom of the place where the land lies.—Gault v. Van Zile, 37 Mich. 22 (1877); Allen v. Hazen, 26 Mich. 142 (1872); Dwight v. Cutler, 3 Mich. 566 (1855).

614. MCLS § 565.361.

615. MCLS § 565.361.

616. MCLS § 565.361.

617. Conveyance on payment

Where contract required conveyance on payment, purchaser is entitled to conveyance on payment or tender of purchase price.—Haight v. Salter, 260 Mich. 6, 244 N.W. 209 (1932).

Too late

Where purchaser, after vendor failed to perfect its title, rescinded and sued at law for return of payments, vendor's tender of deed was too late.—Smith v. Hubert Land Co., 261 Mich. 464, 246 N.W. 183 (1933).

618. No longer had ownership interest

Where purchasers paid purchase price in full under land contract but vendors refused to convey on ground that purchasers were using property in violation of restriction in land contract but there

that the vendee has already waived.[619] A vendee who has been put in possession of the property cannot sustain a refusal to accept a deed by the fact that it is not tendered punctually.[620] A vendee may not object to a tendered deed because of its recital of party-wall rights that would be implied without the provision.[621]

Where the vendee has attempted to rescind the contract, the vendor is not required to tender performance except as a prerequisite to a suit for specific performance.[622] If a vendee's covenants to pay installments of interest and taxes are not dependent on conveyance or tender of conveyance by the vendor, the latter may maintain an action for the interest and taxes that he or she paid without any tender.[623]

The Estates and Protected Individuals Code sets forth powers and responsibilities of personal representatives of estates[624] and trustees of testamentary trusts[625] subject to an executory contract for the sale of land requiring a conveyance to the purchaser.

A party entitled to a conveyance of a property under a land contract or a discharge of the contract upon the conveyance may bring an action compelling the conveyance or discharge. That action is under the statute[626] providing for compelling discharge of a mortgage. A party with the duty to convey a property or discharge a land contract is subject to penalties for the failure to do so.[627]

Delivery of possession. Delivery of possession is generally essential to transfer of a good title. A vendor obligated to deliver possession on a certain day does not absolve him- or herself from the failure to do so by tendering, on delivery of the contract, an assignment of a lease on the property together with a check for rent collected after the date of the contract and a letter to the tenant directing him or her to attorn, where the tender is refused by the vendee.[628]

Quantity of land. The terms of the contract control as to the quantity and

---

was no showing that vendors owned any other adjacent parcels at time of entering into contract and record failed to disclose that vendors had any interest in other property in that vicinity, vendors' interest in contract having ceased upon payment of purchase price in full, vendors were unable to enforce restriction.—Kotesky v. Davis, 355 Mich. 536, 94 N.W.2d 796 (1959).

619. Weadock v. Champe, 193 Mich. 553, 160 N.W. 564 (1916) (one given option on building, having expressed himself satisfied with leases on it, cannot object to tendered deed because made subject to existing tenancies).

Partial legal title did not waive remainder

One who is entitled to a full conveyance waives nothing by taking a conveyance from the owner of a part interest in the legal title, and still retains his right to demand the remainder.—Lamore v. Frisbie, 42 Mich. 186, 3 N.W. 910 (1879).

Purported deed did not waive right to valid deed

Fact that defendants, who were entitled by the condition of a contract to a legal conveyance of

lands, accepted the paper purporting to be a deed, would not constitute performance of condition by the plaintiff; they would not be concluded from objecting to its sufficiency.—Thompson v. Richards, 14 Mich. 172 (1866).

620. Curran v. Rogers, 35 Mich. 221 (1876).

621. Weadock v. Champe, 193 Mich. 553, 160 N.W. 564 (1916).

622. McArthur v. City of Cheboygan, 156 Mich. 152, 120 N.W. 575 (1909).

623. Foley v. Dwyer, 122 Mich. 587, 81 N.W. 569 (1900).

624. MCLS § 700.3715.

625. MCLS § 700.7817.

626. MCLS § 565.44.

627. MCLS § 565.361.

628. Sanders v. Detlaff, 218 Mich. 471, 188 N.W. 446 (1922).

measurements of the land that the purchaser is entitled to receive and the vendor is obligated to convey. The rights of the parties must be adjusted in compliance with those terms.[629] If the vendor misrepresents the extent or area of the land and induces the vendee to incur a liability for land that the vendor is unable to convey, the effect of the transaction is a fraud in law on the vendee even though both parties acted in good faith.[630]

§ 538. Payment of Purchase Price

The vendee must pay the purchase price in compliance with contractual requirements.

A vendee of land is obligated under a contract for sale of real property to pay the purchase price, and on payment of the purchase money, the vendee acquires an interest in the land.[631]

To be sufficient the payment must be made in compliance with the terms of the contract.[632] If a vendee is not able to deliver property that is to be taken as a part of the purchase price, the value of that exchanged property must be added to the monetary amount payable.[633]

Ordinarily, the vendee's note does not amount to an absolute payment of the purchase price.[634] The parties may agree that the note of the vendee constitutes payment on the contract.[635] Whether the vendor has accepted a note as absolute payment depends on the understanding of the parties.[636]

§ 539. —Tender

Generally, the vendee is obligated to make a sufficient tender of the purchase price, but the vendee may be excused

629. Heyer v. Lee, 40 Mich. 353 (1879) (vendee entitled to part of farm containing barn).

Improvements

Where one, knowing that he has title to but part of lot, gives deed to whole, and takes mortgage for price, and grantee goes into possession, and makes improvements before learning of defect in his title, damage sustained by reason of such defect must be deducted from amount found due on foreclosure of mortgage.—Rockwell v. Wells, 104 Mich. 57, 62 N.W. 165 (1895).

630. Baughman v. Gould, 45 Mich. 481, 8 N.W. 73 (1881).

631. Gustin v. Union School Dist. of Bay City, 94 Mich. 502, 54 N.W. 156 (1893).

632. Full payment shown under evidence

In action to quiet title to lands purchased on contract by plaintiff's husband, since deceased, evidence showed that contract price was fully paid.—Fowler v. Cornwell, 328 Mich. 89, 43 N.W. 73 (1950).

Time of payment

Under provision of land sale contract that if marketable title can be conveyed, sale is to be consummated within 90 days after delivery of abstract, until abstract was properly tendered by vendors, and purchasers were allowed sufficient time within which to examine abstract, purchasers were not in default.—Sobczak v. Kotwicki, 347 Mich. 242, 79 N.W.2d 471 (1956).

633. Neuschafer v. Rockwell, 206 Mich. 571, 173 N.W. 373 (1919).

634. Baker v. Lambers, 261 Mich. 86, 245 N.W. 578 (1933).

Presumption

There is presumption that vendor did not accept purchaser's note as absolute payment.—Plas v. Aldrich, 238 Mich. 343, 213 N.W. 80 (1927).

635. Lent v. Dickinson, 331 Mich. 257, 49 N.W.2d 167 (1951) (where promissory note was accepted as part payment of initial payment under land contract, amount of note would be credited on land contract as payment).

Burchard v. Frazer, 23 Mich. 224 (1871).

636. Plas v. Aldrich, 238 Mich. 343, 213 N.W. 80 (1927).

from doing so where the vendor has clearly indicated that the vendor will not accept it.

The vendee must make a sufficient tender of the purchase money to preserve his or her rights under the contract and to avoid being in default.[637] The vendee must actually produce and offer the purchase price to the vendor.[638] The tender may be made to an authorized agent of the vendor or to a third person to whom the vendor has transferred his or her rights.[639]

A sufficient tender that the vendor rejects is equivalent to a full compliance with the contract and entitles the vendee to enforce his or her rights under the contract.[640]

The tender is insufficient if the vendee makes it on conditions not incorporated in the contract.[641] However, a vendor may not refuse to accept a tender of overdue payments merely because at the time of the tender the purchaser has quitclaimed part of the land involved to a third person.[642]

Keeping tender good. Generally, the vendee must keep the tender good, but there may be circumstances excusing the vendee from doing so. One such instance is when the vendor refuses to deliver a deed simultaneous to accepting tender.[643]

When tender not required. The vendee is excused from tendering the purchase money if it would be useless because the vendor has indicated that he or she will not accept it.[644] The vendee must only make reasonable efforts to secure the vendor's acceptance of tender.[645] The vendor's repudiation of the contract and refusal to

637. Tenney v. Springer, 121 Mich. App. 47, 328 N.W.2d 566 (1982) (valid tender).

638. Pappas v. Harrah, 221 Mich. 460, 191 N.W. 221 (1922).

Certified check accepted

Tender by purchaser of property of a certified check rather than cash to owners of property was adequate, legal, and stopped the further running of interest on principal, where no complaint was made by owners of the sufficiency of tender at time it was made.—Keller v. Paulos Land Co., 381 Mich. 355, 161 N.W.2d 569 (1968).

639. Zadigian v. Gard, 223 Mich. 147, 193 N.W. 783 (1923).

640. Ebert v. Parle, 216 Mich. 60, 184 N.W. 402 (1921).

Tender of interest extinguishes right to rescission

A vendor's right to declare a forfeiture, and recover possession, on a default in payment of interest on the contract, is lost by a tender of the interest, even though he or she refuses it.—Hill v. Carter, 101 Mich. 158, 59 N.W. 413 (1894).

641. Changed condition

Tender of purchase price of gasoline station, conditioned upon receipt of deed without restriction requiring petroleum products to be purchased exclusively from vendors for 15 years, was ineffectual where restriction had been agreed upon and was valid only as to petroleum products resold in intrastate commerce.—Slaggert v. Case, 319 Mich. 200, 29 N.W.2d 280 (1947).

642. Malys v. W.C. Hood Realty Corp., 229 Mich. 110, 200 N.W. 943 (1924).

643. Consideration

When vendee in contract tenders money in performance of the contract, vendor has no right to money, except on condition of simultaneous delivery of deed; and hence in action against vendor for breach of such contract it is not necessary to show that tender has been kept good by payment of money into court.—Allen v. Atkinson, 21 Mich. 351 (1870).

644. Miller v. Smith, 140 Mich. 524, 103 N.W. 872 (1905).

Weinburgh v. Saier, 303 Mich. 640, 6 N.W.2d 921 (1942) (tender excused and interest payments suspended).

645. Need for formal tender obviated

Where vendee under contract which specified no place for making payment had made reasonable efforts to locate vendor for purpose of making installment payment and cash had been offered to bank for payment to vendor, but check was substituted upon request of bank, when refusal of

accept payment comprise a waiver of tender.[646]

§ 540.   —Amount

The vendee must pay or tender the full amount of the purchase price plus interest and expenses due, less any authorized deductions.

The vendee must pay or tender the full amount of the purchase price plus interest due[647] and expenses,[648] less any authorized deductions.[649]

The court has the power to determine when the contract provides that interest begins to accrue.[650] The court may also excuse the payment of interest for reasons of equity.[651]

The vendor is entitled to interest as provided by the contract, even if he or she is responsible for a delay in final performance of the contract, unless the contract provides otherwise.[652] The willful default of the vendor may bar his or her right to interest.[653]

If due to a mistake as to the land, the parties have to adjust the contract price to reflect the land actually conveyed, the vendee is entitled to interest on any excess payment to the vendor.[654]

vendor to receive check was predicated upon delay in making payment, need for more formal and legal tender of cash was obviated.—Bilandzija v. Shilts, 334 Mich. 421, 54 N.W.2d 705 (1952).

646. Range v. Davison, 242 Mich. 73, 218 N.W. 789 (1928).

Refusal to perform option

Tavern owners' refusal to perform option which gave broker right to purchase tavern including liquor license excused further tenders or offer to perform by broker.—Caughey v. Ames, 315 Mich. 643, 24 N.W.2d 521 (1946).

647. Picard v. Shapero, 255 Mich. 699, 239 N.W. 264 (1931).

Jennison v. Stone, 33 Mich. 99 (1875).

648. Reimbursement of seller

Where the purchaser of a farm as part payment agreed to deliver a truck to a seller, it was no excuse for the purchaser's failure to deliver the truck that the manufacturing company, whose agent he was, refused to accept the seller's notes, and the seller had to be reimbursed for the agreed amount of money paid down on the truck by way of deduction from the consideration for the farm.—Neuschafer v. Rockwell, 206 Mich. 571, 173 N.W. 373 (1919).

649. *See, infra*, § 541.

650. Dennis v. Sharer, 56 Mich. 224, 22 N.W. 879 (1885).

Covell v. Cole, 16 Mich. 223 (1867).

651. Jones v. Berkey, 181 Mich. 472, 148 N.W. 375 (1914).

Hager v. Rey, 209 Mich. 194, 176 N.W. 443 (1920) (interest in advance not due).

Allen v. Atkinson, 21 Mich. 351 (1870) (additional interest not demandable on contract while purchaser is not in default).

Payment of interest excused on deferred payment

Under contract for sale of land, providing merely for payment of certain sum in 10 days, and balance at rate of $15 or more per month, vendor was not entitled to interest on deferred payment.— Murphy v. Frank P. Miller Corp., 229 Mich. 162, 200 N.W. 974 (1924).

652. Wilcox v. Commonwealth Realty & Trust Co., 248 Mich. 527, 227 N.W. 678 (1929).

653. Wilcox v. Commonwealth Realty & Trust Co., 248 Mich. 527, 227 N.W. 678 (1929).

654. Interest on excess

Where the vendors contracted to convey a 40-foot lot actually containing only 36 feet, and where both parties were mistaken as to the size of the lot described in the contract, while the contract would not be rescinded the purchasers were entitled to an abatement of price in the amount of the value of a four-foot deficiency and to a rebate for interest paid on the excess purchase price from the date of the contract, but were required to pay interest on the net price from the date of the contract notwithstanding the purchasers made a

§ 541.   —Abatement or Deductions

A vendee is entitled to an abatement or deduction from the purchase price where it would be inequitable for the vendor to receive the full amount agreed upon.

Generally, a vendee is entitled to an abatement or deduction from the purchase price when circumstances render it inequitable for the vendor to receive the full price agreed upon.[655] The inequity may be sufficient in the case of a defect in the title,[656] or a deficiency in the quantity[657] or quality[658] of the estate.

On the other hand, the vendee is not entitled to an abatement or deduction from the purchase price if it would be inequitable to grant the vendee one.[659] It would be inequitable if an alleged defect in the title is not established,[660] or if both parties knew of a deficiency of title and there was no fraud.[661] In addition, if the land conveyed fails to comply in all respects with its description in the land contract, the vendee is not entitled to a deduction from the purchase price where the description in the contract is of a purely incidental and immaterial character.[662]

tender of the balance due the vendors when they arranged for a mortgage loan in order to pay the balance due.—Harris v. Axline, 323 Mich. 585, 36 N.W.2d 154 (1949).

655. Ginsburg v. August, 257 Mich. 404, 241 N.W. 172 (1932) (contract to purchase house entitling purchaser to deduct for stone delivered either to vendor or another builder permitted deduction for stone furnished to latter, notwithstanding vendor did not approve order).

656. Borkowski v. Kolodziejski, 332 Mich. 589, 52 N.W.2d 348 (1952).

657. Borkowski v. Kolodziejski, 332 Mich. 589, 52 N.W.2d 348 (1952).

Harris v. Axline, 323 Mich. 585, 36 N.W.2d 154 (1949).

Baughan v. Mortgage & Contract Co., 263 Mich. 248, 248 N.W. 611 (1933).

Interest on excess

Where the vendors contracted to convey a 40-foot lot actually containing only 36 feet, and where both parties were mistaken as to the size of the lot described in the contract, while the contract would not be rescinded the purchasers were entitled to an abatement of price in the amount of the value of a four-foot deficiency and to a rebate for interest paid on the excess purchase price from the date of the contract, but were required to pay interest on the net price from the date of the contract notwithstanding the purchasers made a tender of the balance due the vendors when they arranged for a mortgage loan in order to pay the balance due.—Harris v. Axline, 323 Mich. 585, 36 N.W.2d 154 (1949).

Usual remedy is damages

Shortage in land area may be adequately compensated by abatement of part of purchase price, and an abatement of purchase price, and not rescission, was proper remedy for fraud in misrepresenting quantity, where shortage was not discovered for five years, and it did not appear that purchasers bought land for use that would be hindered by the shortage.—Browne v. Briggs Commercial & Development Co., 271 Mich. 191, 259 N.W. 886 (1935).

658. Borkowski v. Kolodziejski, 332 Mich. 589, 52 N.W.2d 348 (1952).

659. National Bank of Sturgis v. Levanseler, 115 Mich. 372, 73 N.W. 399 (1897).

Forbes v. Forbes, 112 Mich. 630, 71 N.W. 171 (1897).

Settling of dirt

Purchaser under contract for sale of land was held not entitled to allowance for cost of replacing dirt necessitated by settling of that used to level lot.—McDonald v. Houseman-Spitzley Corp., 250 Mich. 509, 231 N.W. 74 (1930).

660. Thompson v. Noble, 108 Mich. 26, 65 N.W. 746 (1895).

661. Newman v. Bump, 245 Mich. 665, 224 N.W. 321 (1929).

662. Brick veneer

In suit by purchaser for abatement pro tanto of contract price for lot with store building, which was described in contract as brick veneer building, but which was discovered, when adjoining build-

§ 542.　—Default or Delay

While mere failure of the vendee to make prompt payment will not of itself terminate the contract, nevertheless, in the absence of legal excuse or waiver, the vendor has a right to forfeit the contract for the vendee's failure to comply with its provisions respecting payment.

A default or delay in payment of the purchase price does not of itself terminate the contract.[663] In the absence of waiver or excuse for the default, the vendor may be justified in declaring the contract forfeited,[664] especially if time or payment is made of the essence of the contract.[665] Although a default in time of payment may justify an acceleration of the payments due under the terms of the contract for sale, vendors under a land contract could not exercise their option to accelerate the entire unpaid balance after the purchasers made a valid tender of delinquent installments.[666]

The vendee is excused from complying with the contract provisions respecting payment if performance, or part performance, is prevented by the conduct of the

ing was torn down, to be veneered with brick on only three sides, purchaser was not entitled to relief where description of building as brick veneer was merely incidental to description of property and parties did not rely particularly on expression.—Andros v. Sanford, 280 Mich. 73, 273 N.W. 397 (1937).

663. Range v. Davison, 242 Mich. 73, 218 N.W. 789 (1928).

Muirhead v. McCullough, 234 Mich. 52, 207 N.W. 886 (1926).

Sparling v. Bert, 1 Mich. App. 167, 134 N.W.2d 840 (1965).

Normal course of mails

Where payment of monthly installment on purchase of land was mailed but not delivered in normal course of mails, vendors were not entitled to foreclose on basis of late payment.—Hoch v. Hitchens, 122 Mich. App. 142, 332 N.W.2d 440 (1982).

664. Lippman v. Cort, 240 Mich. 366, 215 N.W. 528 (1927).

Verran v. Blacklock, 60 Mich. App. 763, 231 N.W.2d 544 (1975).

McWilliams v. Urban American Land Development Co., 37 Mich. App. 587, 194 N.W.2d 920 (1972).

Interest redeemed

Where defaulting vendee has offered to pay vendor through checks remitted by his purchaser, he has redeemed his interest as required by statute.—Tenney v. Springer, 121 Mich. App. 47, 328 N.W.2d 566 (1982).

Vendee becoming mere tenant

Right to declare a forfeiture, in case of default in making payments, is a part of contract, and on default and declaration of forfeiture, contract constitutes vendee a mere tenant holding over without permission and gives vendor immediate right of possession.—Nash v. State Land Office Board, 333 Mich. 149, 52 N.W.2d 639 (1952).

665. Chappus v. Lucke, 246 Mich. 272, 224 N.W. 432 (1929) (failure to pay at appointed time justifies immediate forfeiture).

Default after extension

Where vendee failed to make primary payment, but secured extension of one week and again failed to make payment, refusal of vendor to continue with land contract five days afterward was justified, where time was of essence.—Caplan v. Rausch, 235 Mich. 693, 209 N.W. 812 (1926).

666. Sindlinger v. Paul, 428 Mich. 161, 404 N.W.2d 212 (1987).

Boening v. Schaefer, 284 Mich. 621, 279 N.W. 917 (1938).

Dumas v. Helm, 15 Mich. App. 148, 166 N.W.2d 306 (1968).

Larson v. Pittman, 3 Mich. App. 348, 142 N.W.2d 479 (1966).

Right to accelerate not shown

Where contracts contained acceleration clauses providing that entire amount owing was due and payable in case of default if proceedings were taken to enforce the contracts in equity, and vendor after default brought summary proceedings before court for possession of property, entire amount was not due under contracts.—Lent v. Dickinson, 331 Mich. 257, 49 N.W.2d 167 (1951).

vendor or results from the latter's failure to comply with the vendor's own obligations under the contract.[667] These grounds include where the vendor has failed to offer a clear title[668] or has not furnished an agreed abstract.[669]

However, the vendee's claim that nonpayment or delay in payment is occasioned by the fault of the vendor must be sustained under the law and evidence.[670] It will not be sustained if the vendee knew of the want of title in the vendor and payment was not made dependent on title.[671]

Extra payments paid in advance do not necessarily relieve the vendee from continuing to pay subsequent installments when due per the terms of the contract.[672]

§ 543.   —Waiver or Estoppel

The right of the vendor to insist on prompt payment may be lost by waiver or estoppel.

The right of the vendor to insist on prompt payment may be lost by waiver or estoppel.[673] Waiver may be express or implied.[674]

667. Tarrants v. Goudie, 32 Mich. App. 432, 188 N.W.2d 900 (1971).

Mulvihill v. Westgate, 306 Mich. 202, 10 N.W.2d 827 (1943) (possibility of litigation between grantor and wife).

Equity to deny forfeiture

Court of equity has power to relieve defaulting land contract purchaser from forfeiture and to compel specific performance by vendor if in court's judgment to do otherwise would result in unreasonable forfeiture.—Rothenberg v. Follman, 19 Mich. App. 383, 172 N.W.2d 845 (1969).

Reasonable attempt to pay

Where contract neither specified place for making of payments nor address of vendor, vendee who made ten trips in attempt to locate vendor or bank at which contract was located and payment was to be made, and who attempted to make payment to vendor's attorney, had made reasonable effort to comply with requirements for payment of installment, and forfeiture would not be allowed by equity because of delay in making payment, when purchaser had paid amount thereof into court, because where vendees had attempted within reasonable time to perform on their part, and later check was refused by vendor, equity would not enforce a forfeiture against them.—Bilandzija v. Shilts, 334 Mich. 421, 54 N.W.2d 705 (1952).

668. Ogooshevitz v. Warijas, 203 Mich. 664, 169 N.W. 820 (1918).

Bartlett v. Smith, 146 Mich. 188, 109 N.W. 260 (1906) (existence of encumbrance).

669. Ludwig v. Hall, 234 Mich. 478, 208 N.W. 436 (1926).

Standard Oil Co. v. Murray, 214 Mich. 299, 183 N.W. 55 (1921).

670. Heath v. Gloster, 260 Mich. 85, 244 N.W. 237 (1932).

Neuschafer v. Rockwell, 206 Mich. 571, 173 N.W. 373 (1919).

Possible foreclosure did not justify default

Possible foreclosure of mortgage afforded no defense against mortgagors' claim for past-due payments under contract to purchase mortgaged premises, in view of remedy given vendee by contract in that event.—Urban, 265 Mich. 415, 251 N.W. 537 (1933).

Vendor's mortgage did not give right to stop payments

Conditions of consent by contract purchaser to vendor's giving mortgage lien superior to contract were held not violated by mortgage containing power of sale on foreclosure for default, so as to excuse purchaser from making further payments.—Shapero v. Picard, 235 Mich. 481, 209 N.W. 576 (1926).

671. Chappus v. Lucke, 246 Mich. 272, 224 N.W. 432 (1929).

672. Minchella v. Fredericks, 138 Mich. App. 462, 360 N.W.2d 896 (1984).

673. Kudner v. Miller, 244 Mich. 49, 221 N.W. 154 (1928).

Standard Oil Co. v. Murray, 214 Mich. 299, 183 N.W. 55 (1921).

Ingersoll v. Horton, 7 Mich. 405 (1859).

Implied waiver may be shown by the acts of the parties.[675] The vendor's acceptance of past due payments waives the time of payment.[676] That waiver may last only until a subsequent demand.[677]

A claim of waiver, however, must be substantiated by proof inconsistent with the assertion of the right claimed to be waived.[678] Mere forbearance by the vendor does not of itself constitute a waiver.[679]

Waiver of the time of payment may be shown by an agreed extension of time.[680] After the expiration of the extension, the vendor may designate a reasonable time for performance.[681] A vendor who waives strict compliance with respect to the time of payment by accepting late payments may reform the situation by giving the vendee notice of his or her intention to require prompt payment in the future.[682]

Vendee in hospital

Where, under contract for sale of land, buyer's assignee had to make payment on particular date, that agreement was waived by act of seller, who did not insist on payment, because buyer's assignee at time was in hospital for operation, but wrote that seller would wait until buyer was in position to attend to his affairs.—Waller v. Lieberman, 214 Mich. 428, 183 N.W. 235 (1921).

674. Express or implied waiver

Although the law gives a vendor the benefit of remedies for defaults of a purchaser, the vendor may waive such remedies, expressly or by implication, and, if a purchaser in default is recognized by the vendor as having existing rights under the contract, the default becomes quiescent, and a valid forfeiture will have to await a new default, or at least a quickening of the old one, by demand for performance of the contract and reasonable opportunity afforded such a purchaser to awaken from the repose of imagined security.—Collins v. Collins, 348 Mich. 320, 83 N.W.2d 213 (1957).

675. Ranck v. Springer, 333 Mich. 671, 53 N.W.2d 678 (1952).

676. Miller v. Smith, 276 Mich. 372, 267 N.W. 862 (1936).

Zadigian v. Gard, 223 Mich. 147, 193 N.W. 783 (1923).

Repeated acceptance

If vendor repeatedly accepts payments after they are due from purchaser and habitually indulges purchaser in delinquency, vendor thereby waives, as to future payments, strict compliance with the terms of the contract as regards time of payment, and vendor must give preliminary notice or demand before he can declare a forfeiture, and

if forfeiture is declared without the preliminary notice, and action is instituted, the waiver may be used in defense of the action.—Collins v. Collins, 348 Mich. 320, 83 N.W.2d 213 (1957).

677. No demand for years

Where uncle in 1931 paid niece $450 down on house and written receipt stated that $250 balance was due, and niece lived with uncle in house until 1947 when she moved out but made no demand for payment until 1948, niece waived performance of payment of balance until she made demand.—Ranck v. Springer, 333 Mich. 671, 53 N.W.2d 678 (1952).

678. Narut v. Williams, 293 Mich. 376, 292 N.W. 336 (1940).

Herpel v. Herpel, 162 Mich. 606, 127 N.W. 763 (1910) (failure to institute ejectment proceedings).

Deeds to others

Where vendee had not made a bona fide effort to comply with obligations under contract for sale of land, forfeiture was declared, and thereafter vendor deeded to others several lots covered by sales contract, this did not take away her right to a forfeiture for vendee's default in making payments.—Donnelly v. Lyons, 173 Mich. 515, 139 N.W. 246 (1913).

679. Singer v. Hoffman Cake Co., 281 Mich. 371, 275 N.W. 177 (1937).

680. Pangburn v. Sifford, 216 Mich. 153, 184 N.W. 512 (1921).

Waller v. Lieberman, 214 Mich. 428, 183 N.W. 235 (1921) (oral or written agreement).

681. Levin v. Hamilton, 233 Mich. 203, 206 N.W. 526 (1925) (two weeks not unreasonable).

682. Collins v. Collins, 348 Mich. 320, 83 N.W.2d 213 (1957).

Chapter 19

RIGHTS AND LIABILITIES OF PARTIES

A. AS BETWEEN THEMSELVES

§ 551. In General

The general rule is that a vendee in possession under an executory contract to purchase is estopped to deny the vendor's title and may not acquire a title adverse to that of the vendor. Also, a vendor ordinarily is estopped to claim a title inconsistent with that which he or she has agreed to convey to the vendee.

Library References

Michigan Digest
LexisNexis® Automated Michigan SCAO Forms
John G. Cameron, Jr., Michigan Real Estate Forms
Powell on Real Property® (Michael Allan Wolf, ed.)
Thompson on Real Property, Thomas Edition (David A. Thomas, ed.)

Law Reviews

Department: Section Brief: Real Property Law Section, 90 MI Bar Jnl. 58 (2011); David E. Nykanen, Real Property, 55 Wayne L. Rev. 575 (2009); Stephen R. Estey and Danielle Graceffa, Real Property, 54 Wayne L. Rev. 387 (2008); Naseem Stecker and Mike Eidelbes, Up Front: Real Property and Consumer Law Sections Team up on "Ask The Lawyer" to Discuss Mortgage Foreclosures, 87 MI Bar Jnl. 8 (2008); Gregg A. Nathanson, Feature: Real Property Law: What's New in Residential Transactions?, 86 MI Bar Jnl. 16 (2007); Jerome P. Pesick and Ronald E. Reynolds, Feature: Real Property Law: Recent Changes in Eminent Domain Law, 86 MI Bar Jnl. 22 (2007); Michigan - May 31, 2005: Real Property, 52 Wayne L. Rev. 941 (2006); Daniel J. Schairbaum, Annual Survey of Michigan Law: June 1, 2003 - May 31, 2004: Real Property, 51 Wayne L. Rev. 881 (2005); Jerome P. Pesick, Real Property Law: Eminent Domain: Calculating Just Compensation in Partial Taking Condemnation Cases, 82 MI Bar Jnl. 34 (2003); Lawrence R. Shoffner, Real Property Law: Real Evidence: Special Rules for Real Estate Disputes, 80 MI Bar Jnl. 28 (2001).

Generally, a vendee in possession under an executory contract is estopped to dispute the title of the vendor.[683] Thus, when a vendee of land purchases a paramount title to that of the vendor, the vendee is considered to be purchasing for the benefit of the vendor.[684] The vendee may not acquire title adverse to that of the vendor,[685] including by or in reliance on a claim based on a tax title.[686]

683. Pungs v. Hilgendorf, 289 Mich. 46, 286 N.W. 152 (1939).

Felt v. Methodist Educational Advance, 251 Mich. 512, 232 N.W. 178 (1930).

Wolf v. Holton, 92 Mich. 136, 52 N.W. 459 (1892).

684. Wilkinson v. Green, 34 Mich. 221 (1876).

Purchase for vendee's benefit

Vendees of half of tract from corporate purchaser, which had contracted to buy whole tract but had defaulted and had stipulated to dismissal of appeal from judgment of restitution for assignee of vendor and against corporate purchaser, were entitled to purchase whole tract for vendees' benefit and protection after expiration of 90 days following date of entry of judgment in circuit court.—Parrish v. Michigan Properties Corp., 2 Mich. App. 49, 138 N.W.2d 517 (1965).

685. Walker v. Woods, 308 Mich. 24, 13 N.W.2d 193 (1944).

Ford Heights Land Co. v. Schanert, 279 Mich. 693, 273 N.W. 318 (1937) (foreclosure of mortgage on purchaser's interest in purchased realty did not abrogate purchase contract or entitle purchaser to obtain title adverse to contract vendor).

686. Darby v. Freeman, 304 Mich. 459, 8 N.W.2d 137 (1943).

However, to make the rule applicable, it is always essential that the case presents the mutuality and certainty necessary to constitute an estoppel generally.[687] In addition, the general rule does not apply if the vendee is in possession under a parol contract invalid under the statute of frauds.[688] Moreover, a vendee in a contract for the purchase of land of which the vendee is already in possession under an adverse title is not estopped by the contract to deny the title of the vendor.[689]

While it has been held that the doctrine of caveat emptor has been replaced by the doctrine of implied warranty of fitness in cases involving the purchase of new residential dwelling houses,[690] land contracts in which the vendor surrenders control, title, and possession to the vendee are governed by the doctrine of caveat emptor.[691] However, the vendor has duty to disclose to the purchaser any concealed condition known to the vendor that involves an unreasonable danger.[692]

Estoppel of vendor. Generally, a vendor is estopped to acquire and assert as against the purchaser a title inconsistent with that which the vendor has contracted to convey.[693]

Expenses and losses. Although a vendee takes possession as the trustee for the vendor and cannot acquire for his or her own benefit a title hostile to that of the vendor, the vendee is entitled in equity to reimbursement for reasonable advances

---

Ball v. Harpham, 140 Mich. 661, 104 N.W. 353 (1905).

Simons v. Rood, 129 Mich. 345, 88 N.W. 879 (1902).

Curran v. Banks, 123 Mich. 594, 82 N.W. 247 (1900).

Straw purchase

Purchaser in possession under contract and liable for taxes cannot claim under tax titles taken in son's name who later deeded to purchaser.—Tyler v. Burgeson, 229 Mich. 268, 201 N.W. 185 (1924).

Title inuring to benefit of vendor

Purchaser of real estate on contract with agreement to pay back taxes, thereafter failing to pay such taxes and purchasing property from state at tax sale, thereby attempting to cut off former owner's rights, could not obtain any advantage in court of equity based on deed received from state, and any interest acquired inures to benefit of former owner.—Walker v. Woods, 308 Mich. 24, 13 N.W.2d 193 (1944).

687. No estoppel

In contract of quitclaim of vendor's interest in land, an agreement by him that vendee may enter on and cultivate land does not import transfer of possession; and in action for possession by vendor, vendee is not estopped to deny plaintiff's title because requisite mutuality and certainty to sustain estoppel are wanting.—Clee v. Seaman, 21 Mich. 287 (1870).

688. Ball v. Harpham, 140 Mich. 661, 104 N.W. 353 (1905).

689. Donahue v. Klassner, 22 Mich. 252 (1871).

690. Weeks v. Slavik Builders, Inc., 24 Mich. App. 621, 180 N.W.2d 503, aff'd, 384 Mich. 257, 181 N.W.2d 271 (1970).

Implied warranty of habitability

The implied warranty of habitability that accompanies the sale of new homes applies only to the sale of new homes by a builder-vendor as part of a real estate transaction; the implied warranty did not apply where the purchaser of a new home engaged the services of a general contractor to construct a new home on land already owned.—Smith v. Foerster-Bolser Constr., Inc., 269 Mich. App. 424, 711 N.W.2d 421 (2006).

691. Christy v. Glass, 415 Mich. 684, 329 N.W.2d 748 (1982).

Roberts v. Saffell, 280 Mich. App. 397, 760 N.W.2d 715 (2008).

692. Exceptions

Vendor is liable for injuries resulting from failure to make disclosure of unreasonably dangerous condition or for efforts to actively conceal that condition.—Stewart v. Isbell, 155 Mich. App. 65, 399 N.W.2d 440 (1986).

693. Jeffery v. Hursh, 45 Mich. 59, 7 N.W. 221 (1880) (vendor in possession of land, neglecting to pay taxes thereon, cannot rely on title derived from sale for such taxes to defeat his own conveyance, which he has not perfected by delivery of possession).

expended in fortifying the vendor's title.[694]

More than one vendee. A party who sues to recover a half interest in a land contract for the purchase of realty has the burden of proving the charge that his or her co-purchaser acted fraudulently in procuring the vendor to execute a new contract.[695]

Destruction of property or taking by eminent domain. In the absence of an express provision to the contrary in the contract, when neither the legal title nor possession of the property has been transferred, and all or a material part of the property has been destroyed without fault of the purchaser, or is taken by eminent domain, the vendor cannot enforce the contract. The purchaser is entitled to recover any part of the purchase price that he or she has paid.[696]

If, however, the legal title or the possession of the property has been transferred, and there is no express provision to the contrary in the contract, on destruction of all or any part of the property, without fault of the vendor, or the taking of the property by eminent domain, the purchaser is not relieved from a duty to pay the price, nor is the purchaser entitled to recover any portion of the price that he or she has paid.[697]

§ 552.   Possession and Control of Property

In the absence of a stipulation to that effect in the contract, the vendee is not entitled to possession of the property while the contract remains executory, and if the vendee goes into possession, the vendee does so as a mere tenant at will or licensee.

An executory contract that does not purport to convey title or possessory interest confers on the vendee no right to possession.[698] If the vendee goes into possession under those conditions, the vendee is merely a tenant at will[699] or a licensee.[700] In other words, in the absence of a different provision in the contract, the right to possession remains in the vendor and the vendee is not entitled to possession until payment of the purchase price[701] and receipt of the deed.[702] However, the contract may provide for possession by the vendee, in which case the vendee is

---

694. Petroski v. Minzgohr, 144 Mich. 356, 108 N.W. 77 (1906).

695. Annett v. Stout, 322 Mich. 457, 34 N.W.2d 42 (1948).

696. MCLS § 565.701.

697. MCLS § 565.701.

698. Sibley v. Ross, 88 Mich. 315, 50 N.W. 379 (1891).

699. Murphy v. McIntyre, 152 Mich. 591, 116 N.W. 197 (1908).

Crane v. O'Reiley, 8 Mich. 312 (1860).

700. Gault v. Stormont, 51 Mich. 636, 17 N.W. 214 (1883) (verbal permission as mere license).

701. Bowerman v. Newaygo Circuit Judge, 353 Mich. 535, 91 N.W.2d 879 (1958).

Spaulding v. Wyckoff, 320 Mich. 329, 31 N.W.2d 71 (1948).

Emmons v. State Land Office Board, 305 Mich. 406, 9 N.W.2d 657 (1943).

Polczynski v. Nowicki, 227 Mich. 415, 198 N.W. 976 (1924) (overruled in part on other grounds by Rosenthal v. Shapiro, 333 Mich. 302, 52 N.W.2d 859 (1952)).

Sanders v. Detlaff, 218 Mich. 471, 188 N.W. 446 (1922).

702. Way v. Root, 174 Mich. 418, 140 N.W. 577 (1913).

Druse v. Wheeler, 22 Mich. 439 (1871).

entitled to it on those terms.[703] In this connection, the right to possession may be implied in the contract.[704]

In the passing of title and possession, the vendor and the vendee never own the property simultaneously, so that the vendor may not enforce a restriction in the contract against the vendee.[705]

Crops and timber. Generally, ripe but unsevered crops pass by a conveyance of the land.[706] But the rights of the vendor and vendee with respect to crops and timber may be specified by the provisions of the contract.[707]

Rents. The right to rents already due does not pass with conveyance of the land unless the contract stipulates it.[708] But a vendor wrongfully withholding a contract for the sale of a city lot after completion of a house on the lot is liable for the reasonable rental value of the premises.[709] Where applicable, the provisions of the contract are controlling with respect to the rights of the parties to rents.[710]

---

703. Spaulding v. Wyckoff, 320 Mich. 329, 31 N.W.2d 71 (1948).

Bowerman v. Newaygo Circuit Judge, 353 Mich. 535, 91 N.W.2d 879 (1958) (enforcement).

704. Lackovic v. Campbell, 225 Mich. 1, 195 N.W. 798 (1923).

Vendee's agreement to improve land

Even though a contract for the purchase of land says nothing as to the purchaser's taking immediate possession, he is entitled to do so, where he agreed to improve the property to a certain extent during the first year, and to set out fruit trees.—Corning v. Loomis, 111 Mich. 23, 69 N.W. 85 (1896).

705. Restriction on use of property

Where vendors under land contract containing restrictions on use of property refused to perform on ground that purchasers were violating restriction, but it was not alleged that vendors or any other prior common owner of this and adjacent parcels had imposed restrictions during period of common ownership upon parcel in question or the other parcels, vendors could not claim right to enforce restriction on theory of reciprocal negative easements.—Kotesky v. Davis, 355 Mich. 536, 94 N.W.2d 796 (1959).

706. Tripp v. Hasceig, 20 Mich. 254 (1870).

707. Nelson v. Graff, 12 F. 389 (C.C.D. Mich. 1882) (cutting of timber as wrongful conversion).

Jennison v. Stone, 33 Mich. 99 (1875).

Johnson v. Moore, 28 Mich. 3 (1873).

Lange v. Muskegon Booming Co., 63 Mich. 589, 30 N.W. 593 (1886).

Yeisley v. Bennett, 121 Mich. 422, 80 N.W. 114 (1899) (vendor had title to hay grown on designated land during years stipulated).

Duty to account

Where corporation, after selling land to be paid for as disposed of or logged by purchaser, sold timber on part of such land to another, it was required to account for proceeds of such timber.—American Cedar & Lumber Co. v. Gustin, 236 Mich. 351, 210 N.W. 300 (1926).

Removal of nursery stock

Under agreement in deed to nursery land providing that sellers could operate nursery business until certain date, when buyers agreed to pay for removal of remaining live inventory, buyers were liable to sellers for cost of removal of all nursery stock that could not have been sold or otherwise disposed of in operation of business until stated date, where sellers moved all of their stock before that time.—Emerson v. Powers, 366 Mich. 616, 115 N.W.2d 320 (1962).

708. Konopka v. Cislo, 258 Mich. 615, 242 N.W. 786 (1932).

Pendill v. Eells, 67 Mich. 657, 35 N.W. 754 (1888).

Deceased owner

Tenant who occupied premises up to short time before landlord's death is not liable to subsequent purchaser for rent during that time; tenant's liability is to estate of deceased landlord.—Williams v. Williams, 118 Mich. 477, 76 N.W. 1039 (1898).

709. Glanbin v. Kousin, 249 Mich. 603, 229 N.W. 417 (1930).

710. Bouker v. Spicer, 6 N.W. 117 (Mich. 1880).

No liability under contract

Vendees of approximately half of tract that corporate purchaser had contracted to buy were not liable to pay corporate purchaser reasonable

§ 553.   Taxes, Assessments, and Insurance

Generally speaking, the provisions of the contract are controlling with respect to the liability of vendor and vendee between themselves for taxes and assessments, and the right to insurance proceeds will be determined in compliance with the equities of the case and the provisions of the insurance policy.

In any real estate transaction between private parties in the absence of any agreement to the contrary, the seller is responsible for that portion of the annual taxes levied during the 12 months immediately preceding, but not including, the day title passes, from the levy date or dates to, but not including, the day title passes. The buyer is responsible for the remainder.[711]

However, provisions of law relative to assessment and collection of taxes from the vendor as the legal owner or from a vendee in possession and adoption of cumulative remedies against both do not necessarily control with respect to the ultimate liability for taxes and assessments as between the parties.[712] To the extent that the contract for sale specifies the parties' respective liabilities, the terms of the contract govern.[713] A contract that calls for delivery of a warranty deed free of all liens and encumbrances requires the vendor to pay taxes and assessments on the property, even if they are not determined under judicial process until after the

rent for time for which vendees had use of land while they were making payments to purchaser, against which vendor's assignee obtained judgment of restitution because of default, although vendees thereafter purchased entire tract from assignee, including portion vendees had contracted to purchase from corporate purchaser.—Parrish v. Michigan Properties Corp., 2 Mich. App. 49, 138 N.W.2d 517 (1965).

711. MCLS § 211.2.

United States v. Michigan, 346 F. Supp. 1277 (E.D. Mich. 1972) (taxable status that Michigan realty acquires on December 31 was matter of public record constituting notice to all future vendees).

712. Harrington v. Hilliard, 27 Mich. 271 (1873).

713. Marks-Fiske-Zeiger Co. v. American Bushings Corp., 250 Mich. 583, 230 N.W. 919 (1930) (installments of paving assessment which became lien prior to contract date were held payable by vendor under contract requiring conveyance free of liens unless subsequently accruing).

Cornell v. Norton, 188 Mich. 187, 154 N.W. 77 (1915).

Jacobs v. Union Trust Co., 155 Mich. 233, 118 N.W. 921 (1908).

Richmond v. Robinson, 12 Mich. 193 (1864).

"Current taxes" includes unpaid special assessments already assessed

Under paragraph of contract which provided that all taxes and assessments that were lien upon land at date of closing had to be paid by seller, excepting current taxes, insurance premiums, interests, rents, and water bills, if any, which were prorated and adjusted as of date of closing, the words "current taxes" were intended to include unpaid portion of special assessments, which although a lien on the property, were not payable for several years to come.—First Baptist Church v. Solner, 341 Mich. 209, 67 N.W.2d 252 (1954).

Subsequent taxes

A contract to convey, subject to all taxes thereafter assessed against the contract or the interest in lands created by it, will not be so construed as to call on the purchaser to assume subsequent taxes on the lands conveyed.—Minthorn v. Haines, 169 Mich. 169, 134 N.W. 1113 (1912).

Taxes "due and/or payable"

Exceptions provision of real estate sales contract that specified that vendor was to pay all taxes "due and/or payable" at time of closing required vendor to pay all taxes for year in which sale occurred, notwithstanding that taxes were not due and payable until after closing on date of levy, since taxes for year became due on last day of preceding year.—Bomarko, Inc. v. Rapistan

conveyance to the vendee.[714]

If the contract is silent on the point, liability may be determined in compliance with the equities of the case.[715]

Where a vendor has paid taxes or assessments, he or she may be granted[716] or denied[717] a refund or a reimbursement therefor in accordance with the circumstances disclosed in the particular case.

Insurance. In the absence of an agreement as to application of fire insurance money, a vendee has no right to direct its application.[718] If there is a contract provision, then the proceeds of a fire insurance policy will be applied in accordance with the provisions of the contract, the insurance policy, and the equities of the case.[719]

§ 554. Repairs and Improvements

The provisions of the contract ordinarily control in respect of the rights and liabilities of the vendor and vendee with respect to repairs and improvements.

The provisions of a contract for sale of real property are controlling with

Corp., 207 Mich. App. 649, 525 N.W.2d 518 (1994).

714. Amount of assessment

Where assessment for public improvement, which constituted lien at time of execution of land contract, obligating vendor to pay all taxes and assessments, constituting lien at that time, and convey land by warranty deed free and clear of all liens and encumbrances accruing prior to date of contract, was thereafter validated by court decree, except as to its amount, which was set aside, vendor was liable for larger assessment for that improvement imposed after delivery of warranty deed.—Gawron v. Robert Development Corp., 362 Mich. 577, 107 N.W.2d 878 (1961).

715. Benefits and costs

Where purchasers of undivided half of wild timber lands, under contract silent as to possession and payment of taxes, lumber the lands, and receive half benefits of lumbering, they are liable for one-half taxes levied after purchase.—Thompson v. Noble, 108 Mich. 26, 65 N.W. 746 (1895).

Taxes assessed the day after conveyance

Where parties to contract had fully agreed on all terms, and had met to consummate agreement, taxes accruing next day, of which nothing had been said, were payable by purchaser.—Sayers v. McKeever, 211 Mich. 249, 178 N.W. 650 (1920).

716. Waller v. Lieberman, 214 Mich. 428, 183 N.W. 235 (1921).

Vendee becoming vendor

Right of vendee contracting for resale of premises to recover assessment money that city re-

funded to vendee's grantee was not altered by fact that purchase price on resale was used for paying off encumbrances and taxes and that resale purchaser obtained warranty deed direct from original vendor.—Weintraub v. H.B. Earhart, Inc., 273 Mich. 668, 263 N.W. 765 (1935).

717. No tender of deed

No recovery can be had in an action of debt to recover taxes paid by a vendor upon a land contract that provided that if purchasers failed to pay taxes, amount of taxes could be added to the amount due on contract, where no tender of a deed was made to defendants, there being no obligation to pay any particular sum of money independent of obligation of plaintiff to convey.—Carter v. Reaume, 159 Mich. 160, 123 N.W. 539 (1909).

718. Shaw v. Cramton, 256 Mich. 293, 239 N.W. 366 (1931).

Kudner v. Miller, 244 Mich. 49, 221 N.W. 154 (1928).

719. Assigned property

Under fire policy providing for payment of loss to vendor and vendee's assignee as their respective interests may be, decree directing that amount due vendor be paid him on his furnishing proper deed, and balance be paid assignee who had sold property after fire was proper.—Bennett v. Johnson, 256 Mich. 557, 239 N.W. 888 (1932).

Payment to vendor on vendee's policy

Decree directing fire insurance money credited on purchasers' contract policy providing for loss payable to vendors as interest might appear was equitable.—Shaw v. Cramton, 256 Mich. 293, 239 N.W. 366 (1931).

respect to the obligations and liabilities of vendor and vendee as to repairs[720] and improvements[721] on the premises.

If the vendor's contractual obligation is impossible to perform, it becomes inoperative.[722]

The absence of a provision in the contract for sale making the vendor responsible for improvements leaves it for the vendee to pay for them.[723]

Provisions of a contract for sale of real property concerning payment for improvements may be unconscionable if they allow one party to benefit unreasonably at the expense of the other.[724]

§ 555. Assignment of Contract

A vendor may not convey the land to a third person without consent of the vendee. The vendee's assignment of his or her interest under the contract does not release the vendee from his or her obligations to the vendor in the absence of the latter's express agreement to that effect.

After entering into a contract for the sale of land, a conveyance of the land by the vendor, to a third person, without consent of the original vendee, violates the contract.[725] But a vendee who entrusts an assignment signed in blank to an agent

720. Representation written into contract

Representation written into contract made vendor liable to purchaser for reasonable and necessary cost of putting plumbing, lighting, and heating system in a proper usable condition, provided purchaser notified him of defects with reasonable promptness after discovery.—Goodspeed v. Nichols, 231 Mich. 308, 204 N.W. 122 (1925).

721. Tyler v. Burgeson, 229 Mich. 268, 201 N.W. 185 (1924).

Robinson v. Batzer, 195 Mich. 235, 161 N.W. 879 (1917).

Sheard v. Welburn, 67 Mich. 387, 34 N.W. 716 (1887).

722. Breach of covenant not shown

A vendor did not breach covenant for improvements to be made by it, where some of improvements were already in at time of contract of purchase and covenant requiring vendor to establish a sanitary sewer to connect with village sewer system when established could not be fulfilled because of failure of village to construct sewage system.—Robinson v. Grosse Pointe Shores Realty Co., 281 Mich. 184, 274 N.W. 758 (1937).

723. Reservation of life estate

Where plaintiff sold land to defendant on monthly payments for the life of plaintiff, and reserved a life estate, permanent improvements made by defendant of his own accord will be presumed to have been made for his own benefit,

and so not to entitle him to credit therefor on such payments.—Herpel v. Herpel, 162 Mich. 606, 127 N.W. 763 (1910).

724. Clause not relied on

That contract between vendor and purchaser gave vendor option to declare unconscionable forfeitures of amounts paid for improvements by purchaser in case of latter's default would not vitiate contract, where in suit vendor did not stand upon such provisions, but sought only equitable judgment.—Brown v. Brown, 194 Mich. 578, 161 N.W. 823 (1917).

725. Hornbeck v. Midwest Realty, Inc., 287 Mich. 230, 283 N.W. 39 (1938).

In re Reason's Estate, 276 Mich. 376, 267 N.W. 863 (1936).

Breach of non-assignment clause, *see* 17 Wayne L. Rev. 651 (1971).

Land contracts as security devices, *see* 12 Wayne L. Rev. 391 (1966).

No lack of vendor's consent in reassignment to original vendee

Where purchaser assigned her purchaser's interest to assignee, with vendors' consent and assignee made a reassignment of it, as security for payment of purchase price of notes, to original purchaser whom vendors had accepted in the first instance as purchaser under the contract, original purchaser could not be heard to assert invalidity of transactions between herself and assignee on ground of

may not hold the vendor liable for delivering a deed to the vendee's assignee.[726]

The vendee's assignment of a contract does not release the vendee from his or her obligations to the vendor unless the latter expressly agrees that the vendee is released.[727] The vendor's consent to the assignment does not operate of itself to release the vendee from his or her obligations under the original contract.[728] The vendor's failure to notify the vendee of the assignee's default does not operate to release the vendee from his or her obligations.[729]

With respect to the vendor, the vendee's assignee of a land becomes the principal debtor, and the vendee-assignor becomes surety on the contractual obligations.[730]

A vendee may take a reassignment from his or her assignee in order to gain security for the purchase price on the assignment.[731]

B.   AS AGAINST THIRD PERSONS

§ 561.   General Principles

The title of a vendee under a contract to purchase land is superior to that of third persons taking with notice or not for value, and a subsequent purchaser from the vendor with actual or constructive notice of a prior contract for sale of the land takes it subject to the contract.

A subsequent purchaser from the vendor with notice, actual or constructive, of a prior contract covering the same land takes it subject to the contract irrespective of whether or not that purchaser has received a deed.[732] That purchaser is not entitled to recover amounts expended for mortgage payments and improvements on

vendors' nonconsent.—Vande Vorren v. McCall, 360 Mich. 199, 103 N.W.2d 350 (1960).

726. North Detroit Land Co. v. Rominiecki, 257 Mich. 239, 241 N.W. 221 (1932).

727. Barnard v. Huff, 252 Mich. 258, 233 N.W. 213 (1930) (overruled in part by People's Sav. Bank v. Geistert, 253 Mich. 694, 235 N.W. 888 (1931)).

Greenbrier Homes v. Cook, 1 Mich. App. 326, 136 N.W.2d 27 (1965) (without novation, assignment by defendant partner to codefendant partner of vendee's interest in partnership land contract did not release defendant partner from obligation under contract).

728. Foley v. Dwyer, 122 Mich. 587, 81 N.W. 569 (1900).

729. Taylor v. Groll, 288 Mich. 590, 286 N.W. 88 (1939).

730. Krueger v. Campbell, 264 Mich. 449, 250 N.W. 285 (1933).

731. Default by assignee

In suit for decree confirming in plaintiff sole purchaser's interest under land contracts, wherein cross bill prayed for decree confirming title thereto in defendant, wherein it was revealed that defendant had assigned her purchaser's interest to plaintiff with vendors' consent and that plaintiff had made reassignment thereof, as security for payment of purchase price notes to defendant, court should have found amount of plaintiff's indebtedness to defendant, required his payment thereof to her within a reasonable time, to be determined by court, and provided by decree that, upon his default, title to purchaser's interest should become absolute in defendant as against claims of plaintiff.—Vande Vorren v. McCall, 360 Mich. 199, 103 N.W.2d 350 (1960).

732. Cousins v. Melvin F. Lanphar & Co., 312 Mich. 715, 20 N.W.2d 783 (1945).

Purchase from heirs

Person purchasing land from heirs, with notice of equitable rights of deceased prior purchaser's

a property that the purchaser actually knows was the subject of the previous sale.[733]

Encumbrances and charges antedating land contract. The vendee ordinarily takes the land subject to encumbrances and charges on it antedating the contract the existence of which he or she had notice.[734] The purchaser of land on which there is an unrecorded mortgage, of which the purchaser has no notice at the time of the conveyance, but notice of which the purchaser is given after he or she has made part payment, can be protected, as a bona fide purchaser without notice only as to the amount paid before notice.[735]

§ 562.   Creditors of Vendor or Vendee

A levy by execution is valid against all prior grantees and mortgagees of whose claims the party interested in the lien has neither actual nor constructive notice. The interest of the vendee is, however, subject to the rights of the vendee's own creditors.

Under the Revised Judicature Act of 1961, a levy by execution is valid against all prior grantees and mortgagees of whose claims the party interested in the lien has neither actual nor constructive notice, until the lien is discharged or five years have passed, whichever comes first.[736] On the other hand, if the vendor attempted a conveyance but misdescribed the property, that property is subject to execution.[737]

The vendee's possession of land under a bond for title affords notice to the creditors of the vendor.[738]

Creditors of vendee. A vendee having a valuable interest in the premises holds them subject to the rights of his or her creditors.[739]

In the absence of a binding contract for the sale of land, as in the case of a contract defective for want of consideration, the vendee has no interest in the land

---

widow, acquired no better title than his grantors held.—Fowler v. Cornwell, 328 Mich. 89, 43 N.W.2d 73 (1950).

Quitclaim deed

Where grantee accepted quitclaim deed with knowledge that grantor had previously entered into a land contract, quitclaim deed, although valid, was subject to land contract.—Mulvihill v. Westgate, 306 Mich. 202, 10 N.W.2d 827 (1943).

733. Vermeylen v. Knight Inv. Corp., 73 Mich. App. 632, 252 N.W.2d 574 (1977).

734. Smith v. Graham, 34 Mich. 302 (1876).

Taylor v. Whitmore, 35 Mich. 97 (1876) (mortgage).

Perkins v. Perkins, 16 Mich. 162 (1867) (lien for alimony).

735. Warner v. Whittaker, 6 Mich. 133 (1858).

736. MCLS § 600.6051.

Good title

Under former statute, that notice of levy of execution was not recorded, that no return of levy was endorsed on writ and filed with county clerk, that no notice of levy was served on judgment debtor, and that two of three notices of sale were posted in township rather than in city where property was located, did not avoid title acquired without knowledge thereof by judgment creditor at sheriff's sale, in view of debtor's knowledge of levy, posting, and change in date of sale.—Cross v. Fruehauf Trailer Co., 354 Mich. 455, 93 N.W.2d 233 (1958).

737. Balch v. Jaycox, 122 Mich. 624, 81 N.W. 564 (1900) (conveyance from husband to wife).

738. Atkinson v. Akin, 197 Mich. 289, 163 N.W. 1024 (1917) (open and exclusive possession).

739. Welsh v. Richards, 41 Mich. 593, 2 N.W. 920 (1879).

that is subject to sale on execution.[740]

§ 563.   Purchasers From Vendee

A provision in a contract to purchase land that no transfer of the vendee's interest shall be binding as against the vendor unless a duplicate of the papers evidencing the transfer shall be delivered to the latter is valid and enforceable. Generally, a subpurchaser buying from the vendee takes only the interest of the vendee.

A provision in a contract to purchase land, that no assignment or conveyance by the vendee creates a liability against the vendor unless a duplicate copy is delivered to the latter, is valid and enforceable.[741] This type of provision is designed to give the vendor actual notice of any transaction whereby any person might acquire from the vendee any right or interest in the vendee's interest in and to the contract and the premises described in it.[742] The divesting of any or all of the vendee's interest or the creation by the vendee in another of any character of interest in the land purchased or the premises is within the clause's scope.[743]

When a vendor is notified of the vendee's sale of the vendee's interest, the vendor holds the legal title subject to the equitable estate acquired by the subpurchaser.[744] However, the subpurchaser takes only the rights of the vendee and is subject to all defenses good as against the latter.[745]

Generally, a vendor not in privity of contract with a subpurchaser is not liable to the latter for the fulfillment of the contract between the vendee and the subpurchaser.[746] A subcontract between an assignee of the vendee and a subpurchaser does not entitle the subpurchaser to make payment to the vendor and

740. Salisbury v. Butler Bros., 245 Mich. 6, 222 N.W. 109 (1928).

741. Stover v. Bryant & Detwiler Improvement Corp., 329 Mich. 482, 45 N.W.2d 364 (1951) (quitclaim deed as within provision).

Breach of non-assignment clause, *see* 17 Wayne L. Rev. 651 (1971).

742. Stover v. Bryant & Detwiler Improvement Corp., 329 Mich. 482, 45 N.W.2d 364 (1951) (such provision was not for purpose of satisfying vendor's idle curiosity but to enable vendor to act advisedly at all times and to take steps necessary to protect its own interests).

743. Stover v. Bryant & Detwiler Improvement Corp., 329 Mich. 482, 45 N.W.2d 364 (1951).

744. Rubenstine v. Powers, 215 Mich. 434, 184 N.W. 589 (1921).

745. Craig v. Black, 249 Mich. 485, 229 N.W. 411 (1930).

German Corp. v. Negaunee German Aid Soc'y, 172 Mich. 650, 138 N.W. 343 (1912).

McGough v. Hopkins, 172 Mich. 580, 138 N.W. 210 (1912).

Title under land contract

Vendees of holders of land contract were estopped to deny owners' legal title until payment of full purchase price of original contract, where vendees had knowledge that holders possessed only equitable title to property.—Pellerito v. Weber, 22 Mich. App. 242, 177 N.W.2d 236 (1970).

746. Kraushaar v. Bunny Run Realty Co., 298 Mich. 233, 298 N.W. 514 (1941) (rights with respect to bathing beach).

Oakman v. Marino, 241 Mich. 591, 217 N.W. 794 (1928) (subpurchaser not entitled to recover damages from vendor because of restrictions running with land).

Negligence

Vendor, in his capacity as vendor, had no duty to subvendees on basis of which liability could be imposed upon him on negligence theory because of problems subvendees had with water supply in their homes; where vendee knew of water problems, it was its duty to inform subvendees of problems and, even if vendor had failed to disclose or actively concealed water problems, which he did not, his only liability would be to vendee.—

demand performance by the vendor until the subcontract is declared an equitable assignment of the original contract.[747]

A vendor's assignee need not convey to a subpurchaser until the purchase price is paid on the original contract even though full payment by the subpurchaser has been made on the subcontract.[748]

§ 564. Assignment by Vendor

An assignee of the vendor succeeds to the vendor's rights but takes subject to the equities existing between the original parties.

An assignee of the vendor, who is the purchaser of an equitable interest in a nonnegotiable contract, takes subject to all the rights and equities existing between the original parties.[749] An assignment by the vendor of a contract for the sale of land results in the assignee's succeeding to all rights of the vendor, but does not confer any right in the land itself.[750]

Where the vendor on assigning a contract guarantees payment by the vendee, on default in payment the vendor's assignee may call on the vendor for payment or may proceed to enforce the contract.[751] In the absence of a novation or of statute, the vendor's assignee may not recover against a defaulting assignee of the vendee.[752] A provision in a contract requiring the vendor's written consent to the vendee's assignment of the vendee's interest is enforceable by an assignee of the vendor.[753]

A person for whose benefit a promise is made by way of contract has by statute the same right to enforce that promise that the person would have if it were made directly to the person as promisee.[754] Under this statute, the vendor may bring an action at law under a land contract against the vendee's assignee who assumes

Christy v. Glass, 415 Mich. 684, 329 N.W.2d 748 (1982).

747. Puziol v. Kastle, 231 Mich. 100, 203 N.W. 665 (1925).

748. Jefferson v. Wagman, 261 Mich. 678, 247 N.W. 92 (1933).

749. Stephens v. Coryell, 169 Mich. 48, 134 N.W. 1094 (1912).

750. Cousins v. Melvin F. Lanphar & Co., 312 Mich. 715, 20 N.W.2d 783 (1945) (effect of tender).

Windmill Point Land Co. v. Jackson, 269 Mich. 50, 256 N.W. 619 (1934).

James S. Holden Co. v. Applebaum, 263 Mich. 507, 248 N.W. 882 (1933).

751. Mortgage & Contract Co. v. Linenberg, 260 Mich. 142, 244 N.W. 428 (1932).

752. Smith v. Ebert, 274 Mich. 373, 264 N.W. 406 (1936).

Kirker v. Larson, 252 Mich. 136, 233 N.W. 177 (1930).

753. Windmill Point Land Co. v. Jackson, 269 Mich. 50, 256 N.W. 619 (1934).

754. MCLS § 600.1405.

Constitutional as applied

This statute was held, so far as applicable to suit for specific performance of land contract against purchaser's assignee, to be constitutional, being remedial in character.—Lutz v. Dutmer, 286 Mich. 467, 282 N.W. 431 (1938).

Rebuilding of premises

In nonjury action by alleged third-party beneficiary to recover sums owing on materials supplied to rebuild fire-damaged premises at request of land contract vendee, court's findings that vendor authorized vendee as its agent to incur rebuilding expenses and undertook to pay such expenses regardless of its recovery on prior insurance policy was not against clear preponderance of evidence.—Lidke v. Jackson Vibrators, Inc., 379 Mich. 294, 150 N.W.2d 737 (1967).

and agrees to pay the land contract.[755]

§ 565. Assignment by Vendee

In the absence of a restriction in the contract, the vendee may assign his or her interest in a contract for the sale of real property. A restriction in the contract on the vendee's right to assign is not an illegal restraint on alienation of real property.

In the absence of restrictions against assignment, the vendee may assign his or her interest. The vendor may not attack the validity of the assignment on the ground that there is no consideration for it, or for other reasons that may render it subject to attack by the assignor.[756]

Restrictions against assignment of the vendee's interest without the consent of the vendor are generally valid.[757] These provisions are of course subject to waiver.[758] However, the failure of the parties to an assignment of a land contract to secure the requisite consent of the vendor does not void assignment as between them or permit either party to repudiate the assignment.[759]

Restraint on alienation. A no-assignment clause in a land contract is not invalid as being in restraint of the power of alienation of real property. It does not bar assignment of the contract, but merely reflects an agreement between the contracting parties themselves as to the method by which an assignment or conveyance affects the rights of the vendor.[760] Therefore, the owners of an equitable interest in real estate under a contract have a right to contract with a third person that they will sell and convey the property to that third person, although the assignment of the contract to that third person is subject to all the defenses that the owner of the fee might make when the assignee demanded a conveyance.[761]

755. Lutz v. Dutmer, 286 Mich. 467, 282 N.W. 431 (1938).

756. Hickman v. Chaney, 155 Mich. 217, 118 N.W. 993 (1908).

757. Stover v. Bryant & Detwiler Improvement Corp., 329 Mich. 482, 45 N.W.2d 364 (1951).

Jankowski v. Jankowski, 311 Mich. 340, 18 N.W.2d 848 (1945) (executory land contract).

Sloman v. Cutler, 258 Mich. 372, 242 N.W. 735 (1932).

Conveyance includes mortgage

Term "conveyance" in no-assignment clause of land contract reflecting vendor's refusal to be bound by any assignment or conveyance except by one acceptable to him embraces a mortgage of the lands involved.—National Lumber Co. v. Goodman, 371 Mich. 54, 123 N.W.2d 147 (1963).

758. Zeidler v. Burlingame, 260 Mich. 596, 245 N.W. 527 (1932).

Distasio v. Gervazio, 234 Mich. 482, 208 N.W. 440 (1926) (acceptance of payments from assignee).

Maday v. Roth, 160 Mich. 289, 125 N.W. 13 (1910) (parol waiver).

Sloman v. Cutler, 258 Mich. 372, 242 N.W. 735 (1932).

Peters v. Canfield, 74 Mich. 498, 42 N.W. 125 (1889).

759. McCluskey v. Winisky, 373 Mich. 315, 129 N.W.2d 400 (1964).

760. National Lumber Co. v. Goodman, 371 Mich. 54, 123 N.W.2d 147 (1963).

761. Cutler v. Lovinger, 212 Mich. 272, 180 N.W. 462 (1920).

Restraint on alienation

Provision in contract for sale of land against assigning purchaser's interest under it did not

§ 566.   —Operation and Effect of Assignment

An assignment of the vendee's interest passes the vendee's equitable title to the assignee and creates a privity of estate, but not of contract, between the assignee and the vendor.

The vendee's assignment of his or her interest transfers to the assignee the vendee's equitable title to, or present interest in, the land, together with the right to obtain final title on full performance.[762] The effect of the assignment is to create a privity of estate between the assignee and the vendor.[763] But the assignment does not of itself create a privity of contract between the parties.[764]

Assignment for security. A vendee who assigns his or her interest for the purpose of security retains the equitable interest and, on satisfaction of the obligation secured, is entitled to a reassignment.[765]

§ 567.   —Rights of Assignee

The vendee's assignee acquires the rights of the assignor under the contract, and may recover for breach of contract or for fraud.

The vendee's assignee acquires all the rights of the assignor.[766] But those rights are subject to existing equities between the original parties.[767]

An assignee under an assignment to which the vendor has not assented under a requirement of consent in the land contract that is personal to the vendee is not

prevent purchaser from assigning his interest subject to defenses available against him, because, if it did, it would be an unlawful restriction on power to alienate realty.—Hull v. Hostettler, 224 Mich. 365, 194 N.W. 996 (1923).

762. Gorman v. Butzel, 272 Mich. 525, 262 N.W. 302 (1935).

General Electric Co. v. Levine, 50 Mich. App. 733, 213 N.W.2d 811 (1973).

763. Gorman v. Butzel, 272 Mich. 525, 262 N.W. 302 (1935).

764. Gorman v. Butzel, 272 Mich. 525, 262 N.W. 302 (1935).

765. Krueger v. Campbell, 264 Mich. 449, 250 N.W. 285 (1933) (rule applies even though assignment is on its face unconditional).

766. All rights and remedies

Assignee of purchaser under contract is entitled to same right as original purchaser, and all remedies that were open to assignor for enforcement of obligation are available to assignee.—Lutz v. Dutmer, 286 Mich. 467, 282 N.W. 431 (1938).

767. Boraks v. Siegel, 366 Mich. 308, 115 N.W.2d 126 (1962).

Crumrine v. Bernstein, 249 Mich. 420, 228 N.W. 685 (1930).

Heiden Realty Co. v. Brown, 243 Mich. 578, 220 N.W. 699 (1928).

Oakman v. Marino, 241 Mich. 591, 217 N.W. 794 (1928).

Clarke v. Bussard, 220 Mich. 304, 189 N.W. 873 (1922).

Failure to cure breach after service of forfeiture notice

An unrecorded assignment of a vendee's interest in a contract for deed was void against a bona fide purchaser, and because a bankruptcy trustee possessed the rights of a bona fide purchaser the trustee could avoid the transfer; when the land contract vendor served a forfeiture notice on the vendee for nonpayment of money due under the contract, and the vendee or the assignee failed to cure the breach within 15 days, the contract was forfeited and the only property right left to the vendee or its assignee was the statutory right of redemption, meaning that the vendee no longer had a right to purchase the property that it could assign.—In re Casa Colonial Ltd. Partnership (Visuron Partnership v. Corcoran), 375 B.R. 779 (E.D. Mich. 2007).

entitled to force a release and conveyance of the title from the vendor.[768]

The assignee of the vendee may be entitled to recover against the vendor for the latter's breach of contract,[769] or to recover for fraud of the vendor[770] or of the assignor.[771]

Between themselves, multiple assignees of an interest in a land contract hold the interest in the manner as agreements between them provide.[772]

§ 568.   —Liabilities of Assignee

The mere assignment of a contract to purchase land by the vendee does not impose a personal liability to the vendor on the assignee, but where the latter expressly assumes that liability, the vendor may be charged accordingly.

The mere assignment of a contract to purchase land does not of itself impose a personal liability to the vendor on the assignee.[773] That rule is especially applicable when the assignment is made merely as a security for debt.[774] It is predicated on the ground that there is a lack of privity of contract between the assignee and the vendor.[775]

Although personal liability may be enforced by means of a deficiency decree

---

768. Tender of balance was ineffectual

Mortgagees of vendee's interest in certain of lots covered by land contract could not force release and conveyance of title to such lots by tendering to vendor amount which vendee owed thereon where mortgagees had not obtained vendor's acceptance of mortgage as required by land contract's no-assignment clause and where land contract was one of personal nature between vendor and vendee.—National Lumber Co. v. Goodman, 371 Mich. 54, 123 N.W.2d 147 (1963).

769. Garwood v. Burton, 265 Mich. 408, 251 N.W. 564 (1933).

770. Sweet v. Shreve, 262 Mich. 432, 247 N.W. 711 (1933).

Cole Lakes, Inc. v. Linder, 99 Mich. App. 496, 297 N.W.2d 918 (1980).

Lack of benefit of fraud is no defense

Vendor executing sham contract containing false statements about value of property was liable to assignee of contract for damages, even though vendor received no benefit from fraud.—Hall-Doyle Equity Co. v. Crook, 245 Mich. 24, 222 N.W. 215 (1928).

771. Laches not shown

Assignee of land contract was held not barred by four months' delay to assert assignor's fraud, where delay resulted from attorney's advice and plaintiff's ignorance of true situation.—Hall-Doyle Equity Co. v. Crook, 245 Mich. 24, 222 N.W. 215 (1928).

772. Partnership

Where vendees assigned land contract to members of alleged partnership of which vendees were members, vendees and assignees held title as tenants in common, each being considered as wholly and severally seized of his share.—Lutz v. Dutmer, 286 Mich. 467, 282 N.W. 431 (1938).

773. In re Cole, 29 F. Supp. 382 (D. Mich. 1939).

Smith v. Ebert, 274 Mich. 373, 264 N.W. 406 (1936).

Allen v. King, 265 Mich. 306, 251 N.W. 329 (1933).

General Electric Co. v. Levine, 50 Mich. App. 733, 213 N.W.2d 811 (1973).

Making of payments

The assignee of land contract who did not, in assignment, assume and agree to make land contract payments was not liable for any deficiency on foreclosure of contract, in absence of showing of any oral agreement to make payments, notwithstanding assignee had made payments for several years.—Taylor v. Groll, 288 Mich. 590, 286 N.W. 88 (1939).

774. Biltmore Land Co. v. Lundblad, 271 Mich. 130, 260 N.W. 137 (1935).

Biltmore Land Co. v. Munro's Estate, 271 Mich. 125, 260 N.W. 135 (1935).

775. Allen v. King, 265 Mich. 306, 251 N.W. 329 (1933).

on foreclosure of the contract where the assignee has assumed the obligations of the vendee, no such decree may be rendered in the absence of an assumption of liability by the assignee.[776] The assignment does not relieve the assignor-vendee of liability on the contract.[777] The land itself remains liable for the purchase money so that the vendor may compel the assignee to pay the price or surrender the land, or have it sold to satisfy the debt.[778]

The assignee of a contract for the purchase of land is personally liable to the vendor if the assignee expressly assumes the obligations of the contract.[779] The assignee's assumption of that liability under a land contract constitutes adequate consideration to the vendor for the vendor's consent.[780] The terms of the assignment agreement limit the extent of the assignee's assumed liabilities.[781]

The vendee may enforce the assignee's agreement to assume and pay the amount unpaid on a land contract.[782] On the foreclosure of the contract, that liability may be enforced by a deficiency judgment against the assignee.[783]

Tapert v. Schultz, 252 Mich. 39, 232 N.W. 701 (1930).

People's Sav. Bank v. Geistert, 253 Mich. 694, 235 N.W. 888 (1931) (privity of obligation between vendors and vendee in land contract did not carry over to assignee of vendee by quitclaim deed).

776. People's Sav. Bank v. Geistert, 253 Mich. 694, 235 N.W. 888 (1931).

777. Midland County Sav. Bank v. T.C. Prouty Co., 158 Mich. 656, 123 N.W. 549 (1909).

778. Lutz v. Dutmer, 286 Mich. 467, 282 N.W. 431 (1938).

779. Copeman v. Takken, 262 Mich. 674, 247 N.W. 778 (1933).

Sharrer v. MacDonald, 261 Mich. 544, 246 N.W. 220 (1933).

Roberts v. Rubin, 13 Mich. App. 652, 164 N.W.2d 740 (1968).

780. Windmill Point Land Co. v. Jackson, 269 Mich. 50, 256 N.W. 619 (1934).

Sloman v. Cutler, 258 Mich. 372, 242 N.W. 735 (1932) (executory contract).

781. Amount specified

In action to foreclose land contracts, assumption by defendant's assignee of obligation to pay plaintiff specified amount does not include additional expenditures by plaintiff.—Lowrie & Robinson Lumber Co. v. Rubin, 245 Mich. 224, 222 N.W. 169 (1928).

Inconsistent terms

An agreement by the assignee of a contract for the sale of lands made with his assignor, to pay the vendor "the balance due" on the contract, "amounting as near as can be estimated," to an amount which, by a mistake on the part of the

vendor in rendering a statement to the vendee, is much greater than the amount actually due, does not bind the assignee to pay any more than is actually due, with interest computed in the manner recognized by the original parties.—Peters v. Canfield, 74 Mich. 498, 42 N.W. 125 (1889).

Limits of assignment

The liability of the assignee of a contract who has assumed and agreed to pay the balance of the purchase price cannot be extended beyond the limits of his contract of assumption.—Lutz v. Dutmer, 286 Mich. 467, 282 N.W. 431 (1938).

782. Krueger v. Campbell, 264 Mich. 449, 250 N.W. 285 (1933).

783. Frischkorn Land Co. v. Whitley, 273 Mich. 11, 262 N.W. 724 (1935).

Bouchard v. Edwards, 265 Mich. 266, 251 N.W. 322 (1933) (on vendees' and their assignees' default, vendors had right to cease soliciting further payments, foreclose contract, and seek deficiency decree).

Johnson v. Bangs-McCutcheon, 260 Mich. 120, 244 N.W. 253 (1932).

Hamburger v. Russell, 255 Mich. 696, 239 N.W. 267 (1931).

Despite absence of privity

Assumption by assignee of liability as between vendee and assignee rendered assignee subject to deficiency decree on vendor's foreclosure of land contract, notwithstanding absence of privity of contract between vendor and assignee.—Zeidler v. Burlingame, 260 Mich. 596, 245 N.W. 527 (1932).

Equitable remedy

Vendor under contract has equitable remedy against assignee of vendee on assignee's promise to pay purchase price, and equitable doctrine of avoidance of multiplicity of suits and affording

Under the Revised Judicature Act of 1961, a person for whose benefit a promise is made by way of contract has by statute the same right to enforce that promise that the person would have if it were made directly to the person as promisee.[784] Under this statute, the vendor may bring an action at law under a land contract against the vendee's assignee who assumes and agrees to pay the land contract.[785] It is, however, essential that the agreement be sufficient to show that the assignee did assume personal liability before he or she may be so charged.[786]

Furthermore, execution of a written agreement whereby the vendor consents to the purchaser's assignment of the contract and the assignee assumes the obligation of the purchaser gives the vendor the right to proceed either at law or in equity to enforce the contract against the assignee.[787]

As between the vendee and the vendee's assignee who has assumed the debt, the assignee becomes the principal debtor and the vendee becomes a surety of the vendor's interests under the land contract.[788] Any material change in the contract by the assignee and the vendor releases the vendee from the suretyship obligation.[789]

§ 569.   —Mode and Sufficiency of Assignment

Although ordinarily an assignment must be in writing, in the absence of contractual or statutory restrictions, an assignment need not be in any particular form, and it is unnecessary for it to be acknowledged.

full relief and protecting all rights supports deficiency decree against vendee's assignee.—Barnard v. Huff, 252 Mich. 258, 233 N.W. 213 (1930) (overruled in part by People's Sav. Bank v. Geistert, 253 Mich. 694, 235 N.W. 888 (1931)).

784. MCLS § 600.1405.

Constitutional as applied

This statute was held, so far as applicable to suit for specific performance of land contract against purchaser's assignee, to be constitutional, being remedial in character.—Lutz v. Dutmer, 286 Mich. 467, 282 N.W. 431 (1938).

Rebuilding of premises

In nonjury action by alleged third-party beneficiary to recover sums owing on materials supplied to rebuild fire-damaged premises at request of land contract vendee, court's findings that vendor authorized vendee as its agent to incur rebuilding expenses and undertook to pay such expenses regardless of its recovery on prior insurance policy was not against clear preponderance of evidence.—Lidke v. Jackson Vibrators, Inc., 379 Mich. 294, 150 N.W.2d 737 (1967).

785. Change from common law

Under prior similar statute, court ruled that former rule that an assumption promise made to the assignor was not enforceable by the vendor in an action at law was no longer in effect.—Lutz v. Dutmer, 286 Mich. 467, 282 N.W. 431 (1938).

786. Smith v. Ebert, 274 Mich. 373, 264 N.W. 406 (1936).

Assignee's signature

Manner in which assignee of purchaser under contract affixes signature to assignment containing assumption clause does not fix liability of assignee to vendor for deficiency, because assignee is bound by accepting assignment.—Frischkorn Land Co. v. Whitley, 273 Mich. 11, 262 N.W. 724 (1935).

In equity, assignee of land contract agreeing to fulfill all of its conditions and who by his acts accepts assignment becomes liable to vendor for deficiency on foreclosure even though assignee did not attach signature to assignment.—Van Dellen v. Castetter, 265 Mich. 700, 253 N.W. 191 (1934).

787. Chicago Boulevard Land Co. v. Nutten, 268 Mich. 541, 256 N.W. 541 (1934).

788. Barnard v. Huff, 252 Mich. 258, 233 N.W. 213 (1930) (overruled in part by People's Sav. Bank v. Geistert, 253 Mich. 694, 235 N.W. 888 (1931)).

789. McCurdy v. Van Os, 290 Mich. 492, 287 N.W. 890 (1939).

Gorman v. Butzel, 272 Mich. 525, 262 N.W. 302 (1935).

Generally, the assignment of a contract for the sale of real property must be in writing.[790] In the absence of controlling contractual or statutory provisions, an assignment of the contract need not be in any particular form.[791] As between the parties, an assignment does not have to be acknowledged.[792]

A provision in a land contract forbidding its assignment unless a duplicate is furnished to the vendor is generally valid.[793]

A court will overturn an assignment of a land contract that transfers equity to the assignee for consideration that is so grossly inadequate that it shocks the conscience of the court.[794] The assignee's assumption of the vendee's personal liability under a land contract constitutes adequate consideration to the vendor for the vendor's consent.[795]

§ 570.   —Rescission and Cancellation

An assignment of a contract to purchase land may be rescinded or canceled for fraud, but the right of rescission must be timely exercised.

An assignment of a contract to purchase land may be cancelled or rescinded for fraud.[796] The assignee's rescission of a lien on the property because the vendor is guilty of fraud enabling the purchaser to make an assignment gives the assignee the right to judgment impressed against the land for the amount of the assignee's payment to the purchaser.[797]

On the other hand, if the vendor is guilty of no fraud, the assignee in an action

790. Krueger v. Campbell, 264 Mich. 449, 250 N.W. 285 (1933).

791. Lent v. Dickinson, 331 Mich. 257, 49 N.W.2d 167 (1951).

Hickman v. Chaney, 155 Mich. 217, 118 N.W. 993 (1908).

792. North Detroit Land Co. v. Rominiecki, 257 Mich. 239, 241 N.W. 221 (1932).

793. William F. Nance Realty Co. v. Wood-Wardowski Co., 242 Mich. 110, 218 N.W. 680 (1928).

794. Consideration

Peace of mind that assignors, husband and wife, obtained from knowing that they did not have to worry about ramifications of defaulting on land contract, including loss of employment by financially pressed husband, did not, in addition to recited $1.05 consideration, constitute adequate consideration for transfer of an equity in property worth approximately $12,000.—Rose v. Lurvey, 40 Mich. App. 230, 198 N.W.2d 839 (1972).

No evidence of inadequacy of consideration for assignment

On appeal from circuit court's finding in proceedings to foreclose interest of assignors of vendee interest in land contract, assignors' claim of inadequacy of consideration in assignment which recited consideration and under which assignee assumed assignors' debt was unfounded where there was no proof of inadequacy and question was never presented to trial court.—McCluskey v. Winisky, 373 Mich. 315, 129 N.W.2d 400 (1964).

795. Windmill Point Land Co. v. Jackson, 269 Mich. 50, 256 N.W. 619 (1934).

Sloman v. Cutler, 258 Mich. 372, 242 N.W. 735 (1932) (executory contract).

796. Hearns v. Hearns, 333 Mich. 423, 53 N.W.2d 315 (1952).

Crumrine v. Bernstein, 249 Mich. 420, 228 N.W. 685 (1930).

Spencer v. Hill, 336 Mich. 22, 57 N.W.2d 314 (1953) (fraud proved in mother's suit to cancel assignment to daughter).

Zaleski v. Niemiec, 247 Mich. 312, 225 N.W. 600 (1929) (fraud not proved).

Failure to tender

Suit to set aside assignments of contract for fraud was held not barred for plaintiffs' failure to tender back what they received.—Crumrine v. Bernstein, 249 Mich. 420, 228 N.W. 685 (1930).

797. Holbrook v. Blick, 256 Mich. 396, 240 N.W. 26 (1932).

to rescind may have no relief as against the vendor.[798] Similarly, the assignee's ignorance of the law affords no ground for rescission.[799]

A vendee's assignee seeking to rescind the assignment must exercise his or her right of rescission in due time or it will be barred.[800]

§ 571. Injuries to Property by Third Persons

A vendee without possessory rights at the time of alleged injury to the property by a third person may not maintain an action on that basis, but a vendee in possession may sue for a trespass on the property.

A vendee under a contract to purchase land who has acquired no possessory rights at the time of injury to the property cannot maintain an action for damages.[801] However, a vendee in possession of the property may maintain an action against a third person for trespass on the land,[802] even though the vendee has not paid the vendor the entire purchase price.[803]

The vendor cannot give an adjoining landowner permission to trespass upon the property held by a land-contract vendee for any purpose.[804]

§ 572. Actions between Vendor or Vendee and Third Persons

Under the rules governing civil actions generally, which apply in actions between a vendor or vendee and third persons, the party having the affirmative of an issue has the burden of proof.

The general rules governing civil actions apply in actions between vendor or vendee and third persons.[805]

Accordingly, a vendor of land under land contract is entitled to sue for waste of the land by a purchaser from an assignee of the vendee's interest under the land

798. Hubar v. Hartman Finance Corp., 256 Mich. 602, 240 N.W. 77 (1932).

799. Basis for assignment

Where wife joined husband in mortgage on home and in assigning land contracts, to satisfy partly husband's embezzlement of money, her motive being to do right thing and only incidentally to save husband from prosecution, she could not thereafter have her acts set aside on ground that she did not know that law would not have compelled her to do as she did.—Skillman v. M.J. Clark Memorial Home, 229 Mich. 547, 201 N.W. 453 (1924).

800. Laches

A vendee's assignee, making payments under land contract, with knowledge of vendor's breaches of covenants, for 34 months after assignment, and waiting 8 years before asserting right to return property and receive back money paid, lost right to rescind contract.—Pesciarelli v. Trestain, 288 Mich. 89, 284 N.W. 656 (1939).

801. Des Jardins v. Thunder Bay River Boom Co., 95 Mich. 140, 54 N.W. 718 (1893).

Moyer v. Scott, 30 Mich. 345 (1874) (subsequent deed from vendor does not save suit).

802. Oyler v. Fenner, 264 Mich. 519, 250 N.W. 296 (1933).

803. Gates v. Comstock, 107 Mich. 546, 65 N.W. 544 (1895).

804. Repair of wall

Fact that a plaintiff suing for a trespass on the property is a land-contract vendee does not give the defendant, adjoining landowner, the right to go upon premises to repair the defendant's wall on securing permission from plaintiff's vendor.—Dickel v. State Land Office Board, 308 Mich. 614, 14 N.W.2d 515 (1944).

805. Gram v. Wasey, 45 Mich. 223, 7 N.W. 762 (1881).

contract.[806] An assignee of a written contract for the sale of land may bring an action to enforce it in his or her own name.[807]

The party having the affirmative of an issue concerning a vendee's interest in land under an executory contract has the burden of proving it.[808] A party to an action to enforce a contract for the sale of land involving third parties may seek a ruling whether the evidence is sufficient to show liability under the contract,[809] reassignment of the contract,[810] the bad faith of a reassignment,[811] that the assignee is entitled to title,[812] or that the assignee is an innocent purchaser.[813]

In an action by a vendor against a purchaser's assignee for waste, evidence bearing on the good faith of the assignee in selling timber from the land is admissible.[814]

C. GOOD-FAITH PURCHASERS

§ 581. In General

The doctrine affording protection to a bona fide purchaser against prior equities of which the purchaser lacks notice is based on the theory that, in reliance on the legal title, the purchaser has parted with something of value so that to deprive that purchaser of the legal title would work an injustice.

Every conveyance of real estate that is not recorded is void as against a subsequent purchaser in good faith and for a valuable consideration whose conveyance is first duly recorded.[815]

806. Cutting of timber

Vendors of land, from which timber was cut and removed by purchaser from assignee of vendee's interest in contract were entitled to recover damages for waste in amount by which fair market value of property was reduced.—Campeau v. Hobbs, 259 Mich. 93, 242 N.W. 850 (1932).

807. Cook v. Bell, 18 Mich. 387 (1869).

808. Frischkorn Land Co. v. Whitley, 273 Mich. 11, 262 N.W. 724 (1935).

Real Property Law: Real Evidence: Special Rules for Real Estate Disputes, 80 Mich. B.J. 28 (2001).

809. Burrell v. Scott, 300 Mich. 385, 1 N.W.2d 582 (1942) (insufficient).

810. Showing of reassignment

Evidence established that assignment of purchasers' interest in contract was made under agreement between assignors and vendor bank that assignors surrender their interest in contract that they obtained through an assignment in consideration of bank releasing assignors from further liability.—McCurdy v. Van Os, 290 Mich. 492, 287 N.W. 890 (1939).

811. Krysinski v. Whipple, 248 Mich. 195, 226 N.W. 828 (1929) (sufficient).

812. Burden not met

Assignee of purchaser's interest in land contract failed to sustain burden of proving that he was entitled to have deed from assignor's predecessors to assignor set aside or that assignor had to convey property to assignee.—Lewis v. Brown, 24 Mich. App. 252, 180 N.W.2d 93 (1970).

813. Clarke v. Bussard, 220 Mich. 304, 189 N.W. 873 (1922) (insufficient).

814. Campeau v. Hobbs, 259 Mich. 93, 242 N.W. 850 (1932).

815. MCLS § 565.29.

Hearn v. Bank of New York (In re Hearn), 337 B.R. 603 (E.D. Mich. 2006).

Michigan Fire & Marine Ins. Co. v. Hamilton, 284 Mich. 417, 279 N.W. 884 (1938) (mortgage is conveyance within meaning of this section).

Christensen v. Christensen, 126 Mich. App. 640, 337 N.W.2d 611 (1983).

Evans v. Holloway Sand & Gravel, Inc., 106 Mich. App. 70, 308 N.W.2d 440 (1981).

The doctrine of equity protects a bona fide purchaser against prior equities of which he or she lacks notice. It is based on the theory that in reliance on the legal title, the bona fide purchaser has parted with a consideration of value or divested him- or herself of some legal right or been induced to change his or her position so that a deprivation of the legal title would work the bona fide purchaser an injustice.[816]

A plea of bona fide purchase without notice must aver not only a want of notice at the time of the purchase, but also at the time of its completion, and the payment of the money.[817]

The defense of a bona fide purchase may be interposed only by the bona fide purchaser him- or herself or by someone claiming through the bona fide purchaser.[818] No question as to the person's integrity or the purely moral quality of his or her conduct in making the purchase is involved in determining whether or not one is a bona fide purchaser.[819]

A purchaser's failure to exercise the highest degree of diligence and care does not prevent the purchaser being regarded as a bona fide purchaser.[820]

§ 582. Mode and Form of Conveyance

To enable one to claim the rights of a bona fide purchaser, the purchaser must take by regular conveyance. However, a quitclaim deed is sufficient where the case falls within the statute protecting holders by quitclaim.

Generally, to entitle one to claim rights as a bona fide purchaser without notice, the person must receive title to the real property by a regular conveyance.[821]

Avoidance of mortgage interest

Assignee's mortgage interest was avoided when neither the mortgage nor the assignment was recorded with the county as required by MCLS § 565.29 and the assignee could not establish that res judicata, laches, or equitable estoppel applied as a defense to the avoidance.—Hearn v. Bank of New York (In re Hearn), 337 B.R. 603 (E.D. Mich. 2006).

Drain easement

A drain easement that is not recorded with register of deeds as required by this act is void as against subsequent purchasers in good faith, notwithstanding it is recorded with the drain commissioner pursuant to statute.—Allen v. Bay County Rd. Comm'n, 10 Mich. App. 731, 160 N.W.2d 346 (1968).

Release of right-of-way

Release of right-of-way for construction and maintenance of drain was conveyance of real estate, within this act, and where not recorded, was void as against subsequent, good-faith purchaser of property.—Peaslee v. Dietrich, 365 Mich. 338, 112 N.W.2d 562 (1961).

816. In re Mazzetti, 22 B.R. 538 (Bankr. E.D. Mich. 1982) (under Michigan law, equitable mortgages are enforceable against original parties but are not enforceable against subsequent bona fide purchasers such as trustee in bankruptcy).

817. Thomas v. Stone, Walk. Ch. 117 (Mich. 1843) (no bona fide purchase).

818. Blanchard v. Tyler, 12 Mich. 339 (1864).

819. Battershall v. Stephens, 34 Mich. 68 (1876).

820. Cherry River Nat'l Bank v. Wallace, 329 Mich. 384, 45 N.W.2d 332 (1951).

Holly Lumber & Supply Co. v. Friedel, 271 Mich. 425, 261 N.W. 70 (1935).

821. Hardy v. Heide, 291 Mich. 542, 289 N.W. 246 (1939).

Eaton v. Trowbridge, 38 Mich. 454 (1878) (good conveyance shown).

Option to lease not an interest in property

A party that obtained an option to lease property was not a bona fide purchaser for value without

Thus, in the absence of a writing as required by the statute of frauds,[822] a person may not successfully claim to be a bona fide purchaser.[823]

Quitclaim deed. The fact that a good-faith purchaser's first recorded conveyance is in the form or contains the terms of a deed of quitclaim and release does not affect the question of the good faith of that subsequent purchaser, or constitute in itself notice to the bona fide purchaser of any unrecorded conveyance of the same real estate or part of it.[824] Thus, a purchaser acquiring title by quitclaim deed may be regarded as a bona fide purchaser and entitled to protection as such.[825]

If a case does not fall within the protection of the statutory rule, a grantee in a quitclaim deed is not regarded as a bona fide purchaser and takes only the interest of the grantor.[826] Thus, an unrecorded deed is only invalid against purchaser who takes without notice of that deed.[827]

Forged deed. There can be no such thing as a bona fide holder under a forged deed whose good faith confers any rights against the party whose name has been forged, or those claiming under that purchaser.[828] If a deed is forged, those innocently acquiring interests under the forged deed are in no better position respecting the title than if they had purchased with notice.[829]

notice of unrecorded building and use restrictions of a deed because an option to lease land does not constitute an interest in property; an option to lease does not transfer an interest in land until it is exercised, and at the time the party exercised its option it had actual notice that the property was subject to restrictions.—Johnson Family Ltd. P'ship v. White Pine Wireless, LLC, 281 Mich. App. 364, 761 N.W.2d 353 (2008).

Taking by divorce decree

A wife took title to premises granted her by a decree of divorce, subject to the outstanding equities against it.—Holden v. Butler, 173 Mich. 116, 138 N.W. 1071 (1912).

822. M.L.P.2d Frauds, Statute of.

MCLS § 566.106.

Statute of frauds not implicated

When an oral agreement related to the money generated by real property rather than that creating or transferring an interest in the real estate itself, the statute of frauds was not implicated.— Comerica Bank v. Goldman (In re Handelsman), 266 Mich. App. 433, 702 N.W.2d 641 (2005).

823. Hardy v. Heide, 291 Mich. 542, 289 N.W. 246 (1939).

824. MCLS § 565.29.

825. Smelsy v. Safety Inv. Corp., 310 Mich. 686, 17 N.W.2d 868 (1945).

826. Runyon v. Smith, 18 F. 579 (C.C.D. Mich. 1883) (taking of quitclaim deed puts grantee on inquiry, and precludes his or her claiming rights of bona fide purchaser without notice).

Baker v. Humphrey, 101 U.S. 494, 25 L. Ed. 1065 (1880).

Grahl v. Malkemus, 240 Mich. 387, 215 N.W. 295 (1927).

Backus v. Cowley, 162 Mich. 585, 127 N.W. 775 (1910).

Messenger v. Peter, 129 Mich. 93, 88 N.W. 209 (1901).

Hoffman v. Simpson, 121 Mich. 501, 80 N.W. 1133 (1899).

827. Whetstone v. Michigan Consol. Gas Co., 219 F. Supp. 121 (E.D. Mich. 1963).

Donohue v. Vosper, 189 Mich. 78, 155 N.W. 407 (1915), aff'd, 243 U.S. 59, 37 S. Ct. 350, 61 L. Ed. 592 (1917) (one taking title to land by quitclaim takes with notice of defects in his or her grantor's title, and subject to previous unrecorded warranty deeds).

828. Leidel v. Ballbach, 345 Mich. 201, 75 N.W.2d 860 (1956).

Austin v. Dean, 40 Mich. 386 (1879).

Fraudulent manipulation

Procuring grantor's signature by fraudulent manipulation of papers constitutes forgery and precludes acquisition of interests under forged instrument.—Horvath v. National Mortg. Co., 238 Mich. 354, 213 N.W. 202 (1927).

829. Leidel v. Ballbach, 345 Mich. 201, 75 N.W.2d 860 (1956).

Skupinski v. Provident Mortg. Co., 244 Mich. 309, 221 N.W. 338 (1928).

§ 583.   Notice

To constitute one a bona fide purchaser of land, the person must be without notice of prior equities of others, and where the purchaser acquires notice before payment of the purchase price, the person loses his or her status as a bona fide purchaser with respect to future payments.

Absence of notice of a prior title or interest is essential to render one a good-faith purchaser[830] entitled to the voiding of a conveyance recorded after his or her deed of purchase.[831] A person who has actual notice of prior equities will not be so regarded.[832] Accordingly, a mortgagee who had notice of a prior, unrecorded mortgage on a property cannot be a good-faith purchaser.[833]

In the absence of actual or constructive notice of prior equities, a vendee is protected as a bona fide purchaser.[834] The burden of proving notice, either actual or constructive, as against subsequent purchaser who has his or her deed first recorded, is on the party alleging notice.[835] A claim that defendants are not purchasers in good faith fails in absence of proof that defendants had knowledge of, or took part in, allegedly fraudulent transactions preceding their purchase.[836]

Time of notice. To make one a bona fide purchaser of land, a person must actually have paid the purchase money before receiving notice of a claim against the land.[837] A purchaser without a deed is protected by his or her good faith only as far as the purchaser has made payments before receiving notice of prior equities.[838]

830. Hosley v. Holmes, 27 Mich. 416 (1873).

Fitzhugh v. Barnard, 12 Mich. 104 (1863).

831. MCLS § 565.29.

Johnson Family L.P. v. White Pine Wireless, LLC, 281 Mich. App. 364, 761 N.W.2d 353 (2008).

Christensen v. Christensen, 126 Mich. App. 640, 337 N.W.2d 611 (1983).

832. Lake Erie Land Co. v. Chilinski, 197 Mich. 214, 163 N.W. 929 (1917) (one who read vendor's contract to sell to another was not a bona fide purchaser).

Russell v. Glantz, 57 Mich. App. 44, 225 N.W.2d 191 (1974).

Dealing through interpreter

Person seeking to charge a vendee with notice of prior equities precluding him from being a bona fide purchaser must show that an interpreter through whom the deal was made actually told the vendee of prior equities known to the interpreter.—Highstone v. Burdette, 61 Mich. 54, 27 N.W. 852 (1886).

Parol notice

Parol notice to person that deed in chain of title was mortgage in effect charged him with knowledge.—Goodman v. Rott, 242 Mich. 198, 218 N.W. 761 (1928).

833. Michigan Nat'l Bank & Trust Co. v. Morren, 194 Mich. App. 407, 487 N.W.2d 784 (1992).

834. Howe Mach. Co. v. Claybourn, 6 F. 438 (C.C.D. Mich. 1881).

Hull v. Swarthout, 29 Mich. 249 (1874).

835. Ooley v. Collins, 344 Mich. 148, 73 N.W.2d 464 (1955).

836. Assignee of contract for sale

In action to impress lien upon real estate in hands of defendants claiming through mortgagors and against assignee of purchase contract, evidence was insufficient to support claim that defendants were not purchasers in good faith in absence of proof that defendants had knowledge of, or took part in, allegedly fraudulent transactions preceding their purchase.—Ooley v. Collins, 344 Mich. 148, 73 N.W.2d 464 (1955).

837. Fraser v. Fleming, 190 Mich. 238, 157 N.W. 269 (1916).

Palmer v. Williams, 24 Mich. 328 (1872).

Blanchard v. Tyler, 12 Mich. 339 (1864).

Warner v. Whittaker, 6 Mich. 133 (1858).

838. Wiles v. Shaffer, 175 Mich. 704, 141 N.W. 599 (1913).

Notice to third person. Notice to a third person employed by a vendee to interest another in assumption of the contract to purchase land is not notice to that other, because the third person employee is the agent of the original vendee and not of the person sought to be charged with notice.[839]

§ 584.   —Constructive Notice

Constructive notice will preclude one from taking free of prior equities as a bona fide purchaser. A purchaser must use ordinary caution when discerning whether facts of which he or she is given notice raise a concern about the quality of the title.

A person having constructive notice of outstanding title or rights of others in real property that the person is purchasing is not a good faith purchaser[840] entitled to the voiding of a conveyance recorded after his or her deed of purchase.[841] The knowledge of facts that should put a prudent person on inquiry will charge a subsequent purchaser with notice.[842] A purchaser must use ordinary caution when discerning whether facts of which he or she is given notice raise a concern about the quality of the title that the purchaser is seeking to acquire.[843] A purchaser will be charged with notice not only of facts actually known but also of other facts that a

Dickenson v. Wright, 56 Mich. 42, 22 N.W. 312 (1885).

Reimbursement for moneys paid

Bona fide purchaser from record owner was entitled to reimbursement from equitable owner for payments made on contract before notice of latter's rights.—Ballona v. Petex, 234 Mich. 273, 207 N.W. 836 (1926).

839. Hamburger v. Veness, 232 Mich. 341, 205 N.W. 84 (1925).

840. Associated Truck Lines, Inc. v. Baer, 346 Mich. 106, 77 N.W.2d 384 (1956).

841. MCLS § 565.29.

Christensen v. Christensen, 126 Mich. App. 640, 337 N.W.2d 611 (1983).

Bankruptcy trustee

Where debtors refinanced their real property prior to filing a bankruptcy petition, but the mortgage was not recorded until after the petition was filed, the bankruptcy trustee was a bona fide purchaser who took the property free of the unrecorded mortgage; the disclosure of the mortgagee's interest in the debtors' schedules filed with their petition did not provide the trustee with constructive notice that would defeat his bona fide purchaser status, because the trustee attained his status at the time the case was commenced, and the status could not be undone by information contained in the petition—Kohut v. Quicken Loans,

Inc. (In re Wohlfeil), 322 B.R. 302 (E.D. Mich. 2005).

842. Kastle v. Clemons, 330 Mich. 28, 46 N.W.2d 450 (1951).

Gardner v. Gardner, 123 Mich. 673, 82 N.W. 522 (1900).

Dassance v. Nienhuis, 57 Mich. App. 422, 225 N.W.2d 789 (1975).

843. Smelsey v. Guarantee Finance Corp., 310 Mich. 674, 17 N.W.2d 863 (1945).

Extent of easement

A purchaser of land subject to an easement who is in possession of such facts as would lead a reasonable person to make further inquiries into the extent of the easement should be taken to have had notice of those facts which he would have discovered had he used ordinary diligence and, therefore, does not qualify as a bona fide subsequent purchaser without notice of those facts.—Lakeside Associates v. Toski Sands, 131 Mich. App. 292, 346 N.W.2d 92 (1983).

Ordinary caution

Where a purchaser of realty has knowledge of such facts as would lead any honest man, using ordinary caution, to make further inquiries concerning possible rights of another in the realty, but he fails to make them, he is chargeable with notice of what such inquiries and exercise of ordinary caution would have disclosed.—Kastle v. Clemons, 330 Mich. 28, 46 N.W.2d 450 (1951).

reasonably diligent investigation would disclose.[844] However, it is sufficient if the vendee exercises good faith and reasonable diligence. If the vendee does so then he or she is a bona fide purchaser, notwithstanding that there may be outstanding equities not revealed by the diligent care on his or her part.[845]

But a purchaser always has the duty to investigate the title of the vendor and to take notice of defects in title that the vendee has the means to discover. The vendee must make every inquiry that due diligence compels. If the vendee does not use due diligence to seek out defects in title, he or she is chargeable with the burden of any that he or she would have discovered exercising due diligence.[846]

Matters putting vendee on notice. A vendee may be put on notice as to prior rights or equities by the filing of a notice of levy on the land,[847] or by the fact that a mortgage alleged to have been merged with a deed from mortgagor to mortgagee has not been discharged of record.[848] The vendee may also be put on notice requiring further inquiry by recitals in the contract,[849] by open possession of the property by an unexpected party,[850] or by provisions contained in the probate records.[851] A vendee is chargeable with notice of whatever appears in the chain of

844. Kastle v. Clemons, 330 Mich. 28, 46 N.W.2d 450 (1951).

Oliver v. Sanborn, 60 Mich. 346, 27 N.W. 527 (1886).

Norris v. Hill, 1 Mich. 202 (1849) (where purchaser cannot make out title but by deed that leads him or her to another fact, he or she is presumed to have knowledge of that fact).

845. Cherry River Nat'l Bank v. Wallace, 329 Mich. 384, 45 N.W.2d 332 (1951).

Federman v. Van Antwerp, 276 Mich. 344, 267 N.W. 856 (1936).

Holly Lumber & Supply Co. v. Friedel, 271 Mich. 425, 261 N.W. 70 (1935).

Description as "trustee"

Fact that grantor in deed conveying title described itself as trustee was held not such notice to grantee as required him to look up grantor's power to so act or to investigate implication of term so employed.—Calvert v. Bowman, 271 Mich. 229, 259 N.W. 896 (1935).

Execution blank

Knowledge by one of purchasers that vendors executed deeds in blank as to grantee's name did not necessarily prevent purchasers from being innocent purchasers.—Kurbel v. O'Hair, 256 Mich. 680, 240 N.W. 57 (1932).

846. Schweiss v. Woodruff, 73 Mich. 473, 41 N.W. 511 (1889).

Christensen v. Christensen, 126 Mich. App. 640, 337 N.W.2d 611 (1983).

Inquiry notice

Title searcher may be chargeable with inquiry notice when ambiguity is encountered.—American Federal Sav. & Loan Ass'n v. Orenstein, 81 Mich. App. 249, 265 N.W.2d 111 (1978).

847. L. Starks Co. v. Eppink, 185 Mich. 233, 151 N.W. 676 (1915).

Barnard v. Campau, 29 Mich. 162 (1874).

848. Cook v. Foster, 96 Mich. 610, 55 N.W. 1019 (1893).

849. Burton v. Freund, 243 Mich. 679, 220 N.W. 672 (1928) (contract reciting conveyance of vacated alley put purchaser on inquiry, as respected his status as innocent purchaser and laches of abutting owners).

850. In re Fletcher Oil Co., 124 B.R. 501 (E.D. Mich. 1990).

Smelsey v. Guarantee Finance Corp., 310 Mich. 674, 17 N.W.2d 863 (1945).

Occupancy

Mere occupancy of certain premises is not notice to the buyer of the premises of a claim of a competing interest in the property by the occupant where occupant does not make any claim of any interest in the face of property being sold to the buyer.—Christensen v. Christensen, 126 Mich. App. 640, 337 N.W.2d 611 (1983).

851. Appeal of Moores, 84 Mich. 474, 48 N.W. 39 (1891) (probate records were notice to purchaser that tract was sold without authority of court, and was still subject to legacy).

title through which he or she claims.[852] But matters appearing in the chain of title that would not put a prudent person on inquiry do not affect the status of a vendee as a bona fide purchaser.[853]

The record of deeds not in the chain of title of a bona fide purchaser does not constitute notice to the purchaser.[854]

§ 585.   —Records

The statutes provide for the recording of instruments conveying title or other interest in lands and contain provisions as to notice. Where there has been a substantial compliance with statutory requirements, the record affords notice of facts set forth in an instrument or as to which the record reasonably suggests inquiry, whether or not the purchaser has examined the record.

The statutes provide for the recording of instruments conveying title or other interests in land.[855]

A vendee is chargeable with notice of whatever appears in the chain of title through which he or she claims.[856] A purchaser always has the duty to investigate the title of the vendor and to take notice of defects in title that the vendee has the means to discover. The vendee must make every inquiry that due diligence compels. If the vendee does not use due diligence to seek out defects in title, he or she is chargeable with the burden of any that he or she would have discovered exercising due diligence.[857] But matters appearing in the chain of title that would not put a prudent person on inquiry do not affect the status of a vendee as a bona fide purchaser.[858]

A duly recorded instrument affords notice of all facts expressly set forth in it.[859] An instrument constitutes notice of other material facts that an inquiry that it reasonably suggests will reveal.[860]

A person is obligated to search the record and is not entitled to rely on a mere

852. Kerschensteiner v. Northern Michigan Land Co., 244 Mich. 403, 221 N.W. 322 (1928).

Houseman v. Gerken, 231 Mich. 253, 203 N.W. 841 (1925).

Fitzhugh v. Barnard, 12 Mich. 104 (1863).

853. Jennings v. Dockham, 99 Mich. 253, 58 N.W. 66 (1894).

854. Meacham v. Blaess, 141 Mich. 258, 104 N.W. 579 (1905).

855. M.L.P.2d Deeds.

MCLS §§ 565.201 et seq.

Researching Online Real Estate Records in Michigan, 80 Mich. B.J. 22 (2001).

856. Kerschensteiner v. Northern Michigan Land Co., 244 Mich. 403, 221 N.W. 322 (1928).

Houseman v. Gerken, 231 Mich. 253, 203 N.W. 841 (1925).

Fitzhugh v. Barnard, 12 Mich. 104 (1863).

857. Schweiss v. Woodruff, 73 Mich. 473, 41 N.W. 511 (1889).

Inquiry notice

Title searcher may be chargeable with inquiry notice when ambiguity is encountered.—American Federal Sav. & Loan Ass'n v. Orenstein, 81 Mich. App. 249, 265 N.W.2d 111 (1978).

858. Jennings v. Dockham, 99 Mich. 253, 58 N.W. 66 (1894).

859. Bartkowiak v. Bartkowiak, 286 Mich. 623, 283 N.W. 49 (1938).

860. Fischer v. Lauhoff, 222 Mich. 128, 192 N.W. 605 (1923).

Stetson v. Cook, 39 Mich. 750 (1878).

abstract.[861]

The record may afford notice of the character of the vendor's estate,[862] exceptions[863] and restrictions,[864] dedication of an alley,[865] and outstanding interests of other persons,[866] such as easements,[867] liens, encumbrances, and mortgages,[868] and a timber permit.[869]

On the other hand, the record affords constructive notice only of what appears on its face or is reasonably suggested as a proper matter for inquiry.[870]

Destruction of record. The notice implied from a statutory record is not defeated by the loss or accidental destruction of the record after the record has been

861. McGinn v. Tobey, 62 Mich. 252, 28 N.W. 818 (1886).

862. Life estate

Purchasers from a life tenant are charged with notice appearing of record in the chain of title that vendor had only a life estate.—Lowry v. Lyle, 226 Mich. 676, 198 N.W. 245 (1924).

863. Wait v. Baldwin, 60 Mich. 622, 27 N.W. 697 (1886).

Murray v. Buikema, 54 Mich. App. 382, 221 N.W.2d 193 (1974).

864. Arlt v. King, 328 Mich. 645, 44 N.W.2d 195 (1950) (restrictions as to use).

Subdivision

Those who acquired lots in subdivision after recordation of restrictions permitting commercial use of specified lot, and had no knowledge of unrecorded restrictions limiting all lots in subdivision to residential use, were put on notice that specified lot was not included in residential use restrictions and were not entitled to injunction against commercial use of such lot.—Dykstra v. Huizinga, 362 Mich. 420, 107 N.W.2d 767 (1961).

Where restrictions in deeds to subdivided land were of record question for determination would not be whether subdivider's general plan of restriction was binding on property, but would be whether restrictions as set forth in deeds were to be interpreted in light of general plan as restricting subdivision to residence purposes.—Smith v. First United Presbyterian Church, 333 Mich. 1, 52 N.W.2d 568 (1952).

865. Purchasers of adjoining property

Recorded plat showing an alley was notice to purchasers of adjoining property of the dedication of the alley, which notice was strengthened by express reference to alley in deeds, and purchasers took subject to rights of other adjoining owners therein.—Lirones v. Andrews, 312 Mich. 423, 20 N.W.2d 259 (1945).

866. In re Mazzetti, 22 B.R. 538 (Bankr. E.D. Mich. 1982).

Woolfitt v. Histed, 208 Mich. 308, 175 N.W. 286 (1919).

867. Sanborn v. McLean, 233 Mich. 227, 206 N.W. 496 (1925) (reciprocal negative easement).

McQuade v. Wilcox, 215 Mich. 302, 183 N.W. 771 (1921).

868. Stearns Lighting & Power Co. v. Central Trust Co., 223 F. 962 (6th Cir. Mich. 1915).

Piech v. Beaty, 298 Mich. 535, 299 N.W. 705 (1941) (second mortgage).

Michigan Fire & Marine Ins. Co. v. Hamilton, 284 Mich. 417, 279 N.W. 884 (1938) (recording statute applicable to mortgages).

Babcock v. Young, 117 Mich. 155, 75 N.W. 302 (1898) (record of mortgage as notice of lien).

Expansion of mortgage debt

Where an original recorded mortgage and note provided for the payment of a single $47,000 debt, a subsequent unrecorded expansion of the debt was not effective against a third party to deprive it of bona fide purchaser status; the third party had no legal duty to undertake an inquiry into the debt underlying the mortgage to determine whether the debt remained the same.—Church & Church, Inc. v. A-1 Carpentry, 281 Mich. App. 330, 766 N.W.2d 30 (2008), reversed on other grounds, 483 Mich. 885, 759 N.W.2d 877 (2009).

Personalty

Although recording of realty mortgage does not give notice of chattel provisions, filing or recording of later mortgage specifically referring to prior mortgage in office where prior mortgage should have been filed or recorded gives constructive notice of prior mortgage and of its contents.—Detroit Trust Co. v. Detroit City Service Co., 262 Mich. 14, 247 N.W. 76 (1933).

Fact that real estate mortgage was recorded was no notice to purchasers that it covered personal property.—Security Trust Co. v. Tuller, 243 Mich. 570, 220 N.W. 795 (1928).

869. Kerschensteiner v. Northern Michigan Land Co., 244 Mich. 403, 221 N.W. 322 (1928).

870. Calvert v. Bowman, 271 Mich. 229, 259 N.W. 896 (1935).

Lucas v. Parks, 84 Mich. 202, 47 N.W. 550 (1890).

duly filed.[871]

§ 586.   —Defective Instruments and Records

An instrument not entitled to record does not afford notice of facts recited in it. Where the record is defective, the vendee may nevertheless rely on it in the absence of notice of error.

The actual recording of a deed not entitled to record[872] is ineffectual as notice.[873] If a recorded instrument fails to describe the land sufficiently to identify it with reasonable certainty, the record is not notice to subsequent bona fide purchasers.[874] However, under a statute, no conveyance made in good faith and on a valuable consideration is wholly void by reason of any defect in statutory requisites as to sealing, signing, attestation, or acknowledgment.[875]

The recording laws cannot be made by equitable construction to embrace cases not within them, or to give constructive notice of things the records do not show. For that reason, if a mistake is made in recording, the subsequent purchaser has a right, in the absence of actual notice of the mistake, to rely on the record as showing the true facts.[876]

§ 587.   —Priorities and Time of Recording

The claimant with the earlier recorded instrument conveying an interest in land generally is accorded priority.

871. Heim v. Ellis, 49 Mich. 241, 13 N.W. 582 (1882).

872. MCLS §§ 565.201 et seq.

873. Loomis v. Brush, 36 Mich. 40 (1877).

Lack of proper acknowledgment is not fatal

Kerschensteiner v. Northern Michigan Land Co., 244 Mich. 403, 221 N.W. 322 (1928) (unacknowledged instruments attached to deed were entitled to record, and when recorded constituted notice under recording laws).

Lariverre v. Rains, 112 Mich. 276, 70 N.W. 583 (1897).

Brown v. McCormick, 28 Mich. 215 (1873).

874. Savidge v. Seager, 175 Mich. 47, 140 N.W. 951 (1913).

Description held sufficient to afford notice

The record of a conveyance of a block of a certain number, according to a recorded plat, which is referred to, is sufficient to put a subsequent purchaser of the tract including such block on inquiry, although on the plat as recorded the blocks are not numbered; and, failing to make any inquiry, he is chargeable with notice of the conveyance.—Schweiss v. Woodruff, 73 Mich. 473, 41 N.W. 511 (1889).

875. MCLS § 565.604.

Statutes read together

This statute was not repealed by MCLS § 565.47, forbidding the record of deeds without due acknowledgment; latter statute is simply intended to diminish the frequency of occasions for applying the former law.—Brown v. McCormick, 28 Mich. 215 (1873).

876. Lowry v. Bennett, 119 Mich. 301, 77 N.W. 935 (1899).

Barnard v. Campau, 29 Mich. 162 (1874).

Mortgage recorded as deed

Where a deed, absolute on its face, but intended as a mortgage, was recorded as a deed, recorded deed does not give constructive notice that it was intended as security.—Johnson v. Cook, 179 Mich. 117, 146 N.W. 343 (1914).

Policy of law

The policy of the recording laws requires that, where grantees seek to protect latent equities in property deeded to them, deed must contain an intelligible hint that there are equities that a conveyance of the legal title will not impugn.—Van Slyck v. Skinner, 41 Mich. 186, 1 N.W. 971 (1879).

Generally, the instrument first recorded is accorded priority over claims based on subsequently recorded instruments.[877]

To receive priority, a recorded instrument must perfect title in the interest purported to be conveyed or secured.[878] As of March 31, 1997,[879] a recorded instrument of encumbrance does not perfect most encumbrances unless at the time of its recording it is accompanied by documentation of the facts that support the encumbrance and proof of service of actual notice upon the recorded owner of the encumbered real property.[880]

A purchaser is affected with notice of a deed prior in date to the one under which his or her grantor claimed, even though recorded subsequent to it.[881]

§ 588.   —Possession

A third person's possession of property affords a subsequent purchaser constructive notice of the claims, rights, and interests of the possessor, provided the character and extent of the possession compel inquiry.

Possession of realty by one other than the vendor affords constructive notice to the purchaser of the right, title, interest, or claim of the person in possession.[882] That notice is equivalent to constructive notice by the record.[883] The notice afforded by possession of the land by a third person prevents a prospective purchaser from becoming a bona fide purchaser.[884]

The mere occupancy of certain premises is not notice to the buyer of the

877. Bonninghausen v. Hansen, 305 Mich. 595, 9 N.W.2d 856 (1943).

Ameriquest Mortg. Co. v. Alton, 273 Mich. App. 84, 731 N.W.2d 99 (2006).

Cheboygan County Constr. Code Dep't v. Burke, 148 Mich. App. 56, 384 N.W.2d 77 (1985).

Presumption

The presumption in favor of one who holds the earliest record title cannot be destroyed without proof of an earlier right based on superior equities.—First Nat'l Bank v. McAllister, 46 Mich. 397, 9 N.W. 446 (1881).

Recording in different counties

Where a deed, prior to one under which a party claims, is first recorded in the county where the lands in controversy are situated, it becomes immaterial, on the issue of notice of such prior deed, that the later deed was first recorded in another county.—Munroe v. Eastman, 31 Mich. 283 (1875).

878. MCLS § 565.25.

879. 1996 Pub. Act 526.

880. MCLS § 565.25.

881. Cook v. French, 96 Mich. 525, 56 N.W. 101 (1893).

882. Smelsey v. Guarantee Finance Corp., 310 Mich. 674, 17 N.W.2d 863 (1945).

American Cedar & Lumber Co. v. Gustin, 236 Mich. 351, 210 N.W. 300 (1926).

Kushler v. Weber, 182 Mich. 224, 148 N.W. 418 (1914) (where property conveyed was in possession of third person at time of execution of deed, possession was notice to grantee of the claim of third person).

Baldwin v. Baldwin, 166 Mich. 157, 131 N.W. 555 (1911).

Howatt v. Green, 139 Mich. 289, 102 N.W. 734 (1905).

Matteson v. Vaughn, 38 Mich. 373 (1878).

883. Kastle v. Clemons, 330 Mich. 28, 46 N.W.2d 450 (1951).

Wild v. Wild, 266 Mich. 570, 254 N.W. 208 (1934).

Smelsey v. Guarantee Finance Corp., 310 Mich. 674, 17 N.W.2d 863 (1945) (constructive notice of title by possession is a legal deduction from fact of possession and is equal to constructive notice by record).

884. Stamp v. Steele, 209 Mich. 205, 176 N.W. 464 (1920).

premises of a claim of a competing interest in the property by the occupant where such occupant does not make any claim of any interest in the face of the property being sold to the buyer.[885]

Character and extent of possession. To constitute notice of the possessor's rights, the possession, use, or occupancy of the land must indicate to a reasonably prudent person that the possessor claims rights to the property.[886] The nature of the land may affect how possession is shown.[887] Generally, possession and occupancy of land is not sufficient notice to subsequent purchasers if it is not open, manifest, and unequivocal.[888] Moreover, the purchaser is chargeable only with notice of the possessor's claim to as much of the land as he or she actually occupies.[889]

The possession of the land by a third person that puts a reasonably prudent purchaser on inquiry is sufficient notice to prevent the purchaser from being a bona fide purchaser.[890] Possession that is actual,[891] that is open, manifest, and unequivocal,[892] that is open, notorious, and exclusive,[893] or that is open and visible[894] suffices to put the purchaser on notice.

§ 589.   —By Particular Person

The possession of a person occupying land under a deed affords notice of that person's rights to subsequent purchasers. The force of the notice is broken, however, if on inquiry the occupant disclaims title.

885. Leidel v. Ballbach, 345 Mich. 201, 75 N.W.2d 860 (1956).

Christensen v. Christensen, 126 Mich. App. 640, 337 N.W.2d 611 (1983).

886. American Cedar & Lumber Co. v. Gustin, 236 Mich. 351, 210 N.W. 300 (1926).

Apparently abandoned farm

Where, at the time purchasers visited a farm, they found it unoccupied, no barn on the premises, windows on one building boarded up, and blinds closed on the other building, no tracks in the snow indicating there was any one in or about the farm, plaintiff's possession was not such as to constitute notice of their interest in the property.—Fischer v. Lauhoff, 222 Mich. 128, 192 N.W. 605 (1923).

887. American Cedar & Lumber Co. v. Gustin, 236 Mich. 351, 210 N.W. 300 (1926) (possession of wild, uncultivated land need not be evidenced in same way as that of improved land).

888. Atwood v. Bearss, 47 Mich. 72, 10 N.W. 112 (1881).

889. Robertson v. Smith, 191 Mich. 660, 158 N.W. 207 (1916) (barn of adjoining owner projecting slightly over boundary line).

890. Oconto Co. v. Lundquist, 119 Mich. 264, 77 N.W. 950 (1899) (timber operations apparent).

891. Holmes v. Deppert, 122 Mich. 275, 80 N.W. 1094 (1899).

Allen v. Cadwell, 55 Mich. 8, 20 N.W. 692 (1884).

Full knowledge

A purchaser of lands in the actual possession of third persons, having full knowledge of that possession and of rights claimed by them, cannot assert equities against them that could not have been asserted by his or her grantor.—Dunks v. Fuller, 32 Mich. 242 (1875).

Maintenance of lawn and driveway

Actual and unequivocal possession of part of a lot to a certain line, shown by possessor's location of clothesline post and maintenance of lawn and driveway, was sufficient notice, to one purchasing an adjoining part of lot, of the possessor's claim to line.—Vanden Berg v. Devries, 220 Mich. 484, 190 N.W. 226 (1922).

892. Kastle v. Clemons, 330 Mich. 28, 46 N.W.2d 450 (1951).

Miner v. Wilson, 107 Mich. 57, 64 N.W. 874 (1895) (fenced property).

893. Fischer v. Lauhoff, 222 Mich. 128, 192 N.W. 605 (1923).

Goodman v. Fangert, 204 Mich. 66, 170 N.W. 29 (1918).

Delosh v. Delosh, 171 Mich. 175, 137 N.W. 81 (1912).

894. Woodward v. Clark, 15 Mich. 104 (1866).

The possession of a person occupying land under a deed affords notice of that person's rights to subsequent purchasers.[895] So does the possession of a vendee holding under a land contract,[896] or that of a subvendee,[897] or of a person in possession of land with the right to cut and sell timber.[898]

Actual possession of land by a tenant in common is sufficient to put others on inquiry.[899] Possession by the grantee of a tenant in common conveying in fee parcels of the estate in common puts all parties in interest on inquiry.[900]

A purchaser of land is bound to take notice of the rights of a tenant in possession.[901] A purchaser is charged with notice of all facts pertinent to those rights that would be revealed on a prudent and reasonable inquiry into the matter.[902] The force of the notice is broken, however, if on inquiry the tenant disclaims title.[903] If, in the case of a tenant occupying premises, the record shows a lease under which the tenant is entitled to possession, his or her possession will be referred to the recorded lease, and a subsequent purchaser will not be charged with notice of any other undisclosed equity that the tenant may have.[904]

895. Wild v. Wild, 266 Mich. 570, 254 N.W. 208 (1934).

Unrecorded deed

The failure of a grantee who is in possession of the land to record his deed does not render it void as to subsequent purchasers, since possession is notice to all the world of the holder's rights.—Hommel v. Devinney, 39 Mich. 522 (1878).

A grantee in possession of land has a title to it against all the world, whether or not his deed is recorded.—Brady v. Sloman, 156 Mich. 423, 120 N.W. 795 (1909).

896. Wild v. Wild, 266 Mich. 570, 254 N.W. 208 (1934).

Bartlett v. Smith, 146 Mich. 188, 109 N.W. 260 (1906) (unrecorded contract).

Full notice

Immediate possession and constant occupancy by one who holds under a land contract operates as full notice of his or her rights under the contract to a subsequent purchaser, so far, at least, as concerns enclosed premises.—Seager v. Cooley, 44 Mich. 14, 5 N.W. 1058 (1880).

Vendee's possession against assignee of vendor

Fact that purchasers under land contract had been in possession of property since inception of contract constituted notice to vendor's assignee and holder of mortgage executed thereafter, of purchaser's rights under contract.—Cousins v. Melvin F. Lanphar & Co., 312 Mich. 715, 20 N.W.2d 783 (1945).

897. Jefferson v. Wagman, 261 Mich. 678, 247 N.W. 92 (1933).

898. American Cedar & Lumber Co. v. Gustin, 236 Mich. 351, 210 N.W. 300 (1926).

899. Schmidt v. Steinbach, 193 Mich. 640, 160 N.W. 448 (1916).

900. Pellow v. Arctic Mining Co., 164 Mich. 87, 128 N.W. 918 (1910).

901. Higginbotham v. Phillips, 192 Mich. 49, 158 N.W. 130 (1916) (subtenant).

Brady v. Sloman, 156 Mich. 423, 120 N.W. 795 (1909).

Starkey v. Horton, 65 Mich. 96, 31 N.W. 626 (1887).

902. Smelsy v. Safety Inv. Corp., 310 Mich. 686, 17 N.W.2d 868 (1945) (99-year lease).

Lambert v. Weber, 83 Mich. 395, 47 N.W. 251 (1890).

Burden of inquiry

Where lease granted lessee first right and option to purchase from the "undersigned" the premises at any time during the term of the lease but not until after a specified date, the lessees' possession of the premises at the time the optionors conveyed them to defendants within three weeks after execution of the lease and option was notice to defendants of the lessee's rights in the premises placing a burden of inquiry upon them.—Associated Truck Lines, Inc., v. Baer, 346 Mich. 106, 77 N.W.2d 384 (1956).

903. Trumpower v. Marcey, 92 Mich. 529, 52 N.W. 999 (1892) (title to tree).

904. Inconsistent unrecorded instrument

In purchaser's action for rent under recorded lease against tenant in possession at time of purchase, who relied on unrecorded memorandum inconsistent with lease, judgment for purchaser was affirmed by divided court.—Hull v. Gafill Oil Co., 263 Mich. 650, 249 N.W. 24 (1933).

That a person conveys land to his or her spouse, and the spouse continues to live there with the person, does not afford sufficient notice to subsequent purchasers to answer the purpose of recording the deed.[905] If a person has left his or her spouse and is living apart, the spouse's continued occupation of the premises as his or her homestead affords notice of the spouse's claim of ownership to a purchaser acquiring title from the person, although a deed from the spouse to the person is on record.[906]

In the case of joint possession of land by parent and child, the child's occupancy does not afford notice of any claim of title or right in the child under an alleged lease, the presumption being that the child's possession was subservient to that of the parent.[907] That a mother conveys her dower interest to a child in exchange for income from the land, and continues to reside on the premises, affords sufficient notice to prevent the child's spouse from successfully claiming the rights of a bona fide purchaser.[908] However, a parent conveying to a child may have to make a claim of title above and beyond his or her occupancy in order to put a prospective purchaser on notice.[909]

Mere retention of possession after conveyance of land does not necessarily afford notice that the grantors still claim rights in the premises inconsistent with those conveyed.[910]

§ 590.   —Effect of Notice

The effect of notice of outstanding rights is to prevent a purchaser from becoming a bona fide purchaser and to make that person take subject to existing rights or equities. Even an unrecorded deed is good as against subsequent purchasers with notice.

A purchaser of land with notice of outstanding rights in another is not a bona fide purchaser but takes subject to those existing rights or equities.[911] The purchaser

---

905. Atwood v. Bearss, 47 Mich. 72, 10 N.W. 112 (1881).

906. Stevens v. Castel, 63 Mich. 111, 29 N.W. 828 (1886).

907. Nagelspach v. Shaw, 146 Mich. 493, 109 N.W. 843 (1906).

908. Holden v. Butler, 173 Mich. 116, 138 N.W. 1071 (1912).

909. No claim of interest

Where a mother, who had deeded her home to her son so that he could get a mortgage and take care of her and the property, knew that her son was offering the property for sale and made no claim of interest therein, her occupancy did not preclude the purchasers' claim that they were innocent purchasers for value without notice of the rights of the mother.—Leidel v. Ballbach, 345 Mich. 201, 75 N.W.2d 860 (1956).

910. Abbott v. Gregory, 39 Mich. 68 (1878).

Bloomer v. Henderson, 8 Mich. 395 (1860).

911. Wiles v. Shaffer, 175 Mich. 704, 141 N.W. 599 (1913).

Austin v. Dean, 40 Mich. 386 (1879) (knowledge of dispute).

Notice of actual interests

A purchaser of land from one who himself holds under a contract of purchase, who knows that three other persons are interested with his vendor in the venture, is thereby charged with notice of their actual interests in the land.—Schwartz v. Woodruff, 132 Mich. 513, 93 N.W. 1067 (1903).

Notice that deed was actually a mortgage

Stockholder of grantee corporation accepting deed after record showing claim that deed was in reality mortgage was not bona fide purchaser.—McLaughlin v. Majestic Development Corp., 247 Mich. 498, 226 N.W. 256 (1929).

acquires no better title than that of his or her vendor.[912]

One buying land with notice of a prior sale is not entitled to protection as a bona fide purchaser.[913] The fact of a prior conveyance or encumbrance brought to the knowledge of a subsequent purchaser makes his or her interest subject to that conveyance or encumbrance.[914]

A purchaser of land with notice that his or her grantor is under contract to convey it to another obtains the rights as the grantor or vendor had, including the right to subsequent payments.[915]

A purchaser for value, with notice of a previous contract to convey that is void under the statute of frauds, acquires good title, because by the sale, the grantor elects to treat the former contract as void.[916]

Much as one who holds under an unrecorded deed, the holder of an unrecorded equitable interest in property has no claim against a good-faith purchaser of the property.[917] Such a right will not even overcome a prior unrecorded deed.[918]

Unrecorded deed. An unrecorded deed is good as against subsequent

---

912. Williams v. Flood, 63 Mich. 487, 30 N.W. 93 (1886).

Warner v. Sibley, 53 Mich. 371, 19 N.W. 40 (1884).

Purchaser from life tenant

A purchaser of land from the life tenant who, after a mortgage foreclosure for nonpayment of interest, obtained a deed thereto from the mortgagee who purchased at the foreclosure sale, is not an innocent purchaser where he knew the facts; and he acquires only the interest of the life tenant.—McCall v. McCall, 159 Mich. 144, 123 N.W. 550 (1909).

Right to rent

Where defendant deeded property to a grantee who was to construct a building and lease it to the defendant and the grantee deeded the land to plaintiffs, who had knowledge of the defendant's relationship with its grantee from the outset, and defendant had paid rent to its grantee for occupancy between certain dates, the plaintiff was not entitled to recover additional rental for the same dates on the ground that the defendant had paid the rental to the wrong person.—Adeline Realty Co. v. Michigan Bell Tel. Co., 355 Mich. 22, 93 N.W.2d 912 (1959).

913. Zadigian v. Gard, 223 Mich. 147, 193 N.W. 783 (1923).

Hains v. Hains, 69 Mich. 581, 37 N.W. 563 (1888) (one accepting deed, knowing of existence of prior unrecorded contract of his grantor for sale of land, and failing to inquire of other party to such contract with respect to it, is not bona fide purchaser, whatever may have been his grantor's representations in the matter).

Ryerson v. Eldred, 18 Mich. 12 (1869).

Actual knowledge of oral contract

Where plaintiff at time of purchasing lot and building from defendant had actual knowledge of prior oral contract under which defendant sold that lot, and building to be erected on it, to third person, prior contract was valid as against plaintiff; but, where plaintiff was defrauded by defendant's misrepresentations that third person had defaulted, plaintiff in suit for specific performance or, in the alternative, for rescission was properly given a personal decree against defendant and a lien on premises.—Buccilli v. Padgen, 231 Mich. 393, 204 N.W. 130 (1925).

914. E.B. Millar & Co. v. Olney, 69 Mich. 560, 37 N.W. 558 (1888).

Oliver v. Olmstead, 112 Mich. 483, 70 N.W. 1036 (1897) (lease).

Deed as security

Where an agent of a lumber company, in consideration of lumber supplied for a building by him, takes a deed of the lot and building from the owner, and thereafter conveys to a trustee for the company, the latter and its grantees take the property subject to all equities existing in favor of the first owner against the agent.—Rundle v. Spencer, 67 Mich. 189, 34 N.W. 548 (1887).

915. American Cedar & Lumber Co. v. Gustin, 236 Mich. 351, 210 N.W. 300 (1926).

916. Messmore v. Cunningham, 78 Mich. 623, 44 N.W. 145 (1889).

917. Advance to vendee

One who advances money without security, to enable another to purchase land which he had reason to believe was sold in fraud of the rights of a former contract purchaser, is without any equi-

purchasers with notice.[919] A purchaser with notice of a prior unrecorded deed is not at liberty to rely, without further inquiry, upon a search of the records, and the fact that no such deed is found recorded.[920] Furthermore, a purchaser with knowledge of a prior unrecorded deed who thereafter records his or her own deed before the unrecorded deed is placed on record acquires no title.[921]

However, where a purchaser, after learning that a prior purchaser may have some interest in the property under an unrecorded contract to purchase land, makes a reasonable but unsuccessful attempt to locate the prior purchaser, and duly searches the records without avail, he or she may be regarded as a purchaser in good faith.[922] In the absence of notice or adverse use, a vendee is not obligated to inquire concerning the precise terms of outstanding but unrecorded deeds that may affect the title.[923]

Purchaser with notice from bona fide purchaser. Generally, a person having notice of existing equities who purchases from a good-faith purchaser is protected by the want of notice on the part of his or her vendor.[924]

Privies of vendee. The estate of a vendee who dies after purchasing property with notice of an interest is also precluded from having good-faith status with respect to that interest.[925]

§ 591. Consideration

In order to constitute a vendee a bona fide purchaser, the vendee must have paid a sufficient consideration.

ties as a bona fide encumbrancer on the land to secure his loan.—Simon v. Brown, 38 Mich. 552 (1878).

918. Bona fide status not shown

A transfer of lands worth $1,000 for a present payment of $25, which was not designed as a sale of the lands, but as a trade for an indefinite amount to be ascertained afterwards, and to depend on the success of the adventure, is not such a dealing as will invest the grantee with a right which by force of the registry law is sufficient to overcome a prior unrecorded deed.—Battershall v. Stephens, 34 Mich. 68 (1876).

919. Oliver v. Sanborn, 60 Mich. 346, 27 N.W. 527 (1886).

Munroe v. Eastman, 31 Mich. 283 (1875).

Farmers & Mechanics' Bank v. Bronson, 14 Mich. 361 (1866).

Fraudulent character of deed

Where a grantee knew, before he acquired the property, of a prior unrecorded deed that grantor claimed was secured through fraud, he could not, in suit by prior grantee, avail himself of the defense of fraud, which is purely equitable and available only to grantor.—Cochran Timber Co. v. Fisher, 190 Mich. 478, 157 N.W. 282 (1916).

Notice was insufficient

Large sign on premises, reading: "Modern Homes Building Company owners of this property will build 200 houses here," followed by name of agent, who subsequently arranged for assumption of his purchase agreement with true owner by one to whom he afterward executed quitclaim deed, was held not sufficient notice to put latter on inquiry as to prior interest of one claiming under purchase agreement given him by such agent.—Hamburger v. Veness, 232 Mich. 341, 205 N.W. 84 (1925).

920. Shotwell v. Harrison, 30 Mich. 179 (1874).

921. Dennis v. Dennis, 119 Mich. 380, 78 N.W. 333 (1899).

Munroe v. Eastman, 31 Mich. 283 (1875).

922. Federman v. Van Antwerp, 276 Mich. 344, 267 N.W. 856 (1936).

923. Harr v. Coolbaugh, 337 Mich. 158, 59 N.W.2d 132 (1953).

924. Haab v. Moorman, 332 Mich. 126, 50 N.W.2d 856 (1952).

925. Michigan Nat'l Bank & Trust Co. v. Morren, 194 Mich. App. 407, 487 N.W.2d 784 (1992).

In order to constitute a vendee a good-faith purchaser as against existing equities or prior conveyances of which the vendee had no notice, the vendee's deed must be supported by a valuable consideration.[926] To entitle a vendee of lands to the status of a good-faith purchaser without notice of a prior unrecorded encumbrance, the vendee must have paid the purchase money[927] or have become bound for it in such a way that a court cannot relieve the vendee of the payment.[928]

Thus, a vendee who provides only a note in consideration is not in a position to be a good-faith purchaser[929] until he or she begins making payments on the note.[930]

A person who takes by inheritance or without having given any consideration is not a good-faith purchaser.[931]

§ 592. Failure to Record Deed or Other Instrument

The recording statute is designed to protect innocent purchasers, who take free of existing equities unknown to them and not disclosed by the record.

By statute, every conveyance of realty not recorded is void as against any subsequent purchaser in good faith for a valuable consideration whose conveyance is the first duly recorded.[932] The purpose of the recording law is to represent the true state of title in the public records and thus to protect innocent purchasers.[933] The design of the recording laws is to prevent fraud in real estate transactions by

926. Bigelow v. Sheehan, 150 Mich. 507, 114 N.W. 389 (1907).

Grand Rapids Nat'l Bank v. Ford, 143 Mich. 402, 107 N.W. 76 (1906).

Williams v. Williams, 118 Mich. 477, 76 N.W. 1039 (1898).

Stone v. Welling, 14 Mich. 514 (1866).

Hanold v. Owen, 64 Mich. 439, 31 N.W. 420 (1887) (sufficient consideration).

927. White v. McGarry, 47 F. 420 (C.C.D. Mich. 1880).

Stone v. Welling, 14 Mich. 514 (1866).

Unrecorded deed valid pending payment

An unrecorded conveyance is valid as against a subsequent purchaser until the latter shows that he has paid purchase price; mere institution of suit by him to quiet title does not make him a bona fide purchaser.—Smith v. Williams, 44 Mich. 240, 6 N.W. 662 (1880).

928. Thomas v. Stone, Walk. Ch. 117 (Mich. 1843).

929. No payment

The making and depositing in escrow of the note of the vendee to be delivered to the vendor when the vendee was given a good title to, and possession of, the land contracted for is not such a payment of money as entitles the vendee to the

rights of a bona fide purchaser for value.—Lambert v. Weber, 83 Mich. 395, 47 N.W. 251 (1890).

930. Payment on note prior to notice of defect

One who claims as a bona fide purchaser, but who has only given his notes, must also show that he had made payment thereon before notice of the defect in his grantor's title.—Watson v. Melchor, 42 Mich. 477, 4 N.W. 200 (1880).

931. Whetstone v. Michigan Consol. Gas Co., 219 F. Supp. 121 (E.D. Mich. 1963).

932. MCLS § 565.29.

Christensen v. Christensen, 126 Mich. App. 640, 337 N.W.2d 611 (1983).

Lakeside Associates v. Toski Sands, 131 Mich. App. 292, 346 N.W.2d 92 (1983) (owners of interests in land cannot protect those interests unless they properly record them).

Researching online real estate records in Michigan, see 80 Mich. B.J. 22 (2001).

Failure of adverse possessor to record his interest as not affecting his title, even as to bona fide purchaser, 8 Wayne L. Rev. 219, 225 (1961).

933. Harr v. Coolbaugh, 337 Mich. 158, 59 N.W.2d 132 (1953).

Michigan Fire & Marine Ins. Co. v. Hamilton, 284 Mich. 417, 279 N.W. 884 (1938) (effect of recording acts not extended by construction).

securing certainty and publicity in such dealings, and purchasers should have their conveyance seasonably recorded.[934]

Therefore, a purchaser may rely on the record.[935] In the absence of other notice, the purchaser in good faith takes free of all equities not disclosed by the record.[936] Thus, an unrecorded deed is invalid against a subsequent purchaser having no notice of its existence.[937]

§ 593.   Title and Rights of Bona Fide Purchaser

An innocent purchaser for value acquires an indefeasible title and takes free of all existing rights and equities as to which he or she is not chargeable with notice.

The title of a bona fide purchaser is indefeasible in equity and in law.[938] Such a purchaser is protected with respect to all prior rights and equities concerning which he or she is not chargeable with notice.[939] Those rights and equities may include liens and encumbrances[940] or rights with respect to removal of fixtures.[941]

The grantee under a deed of gift cannot assert title to property as against the rights of bona fide purchasers intervening before the deed to the grantee became effective.[942]

§ 594.   Evidence

A subsequent purchaser who has recorded a deed is presumed to be a bona fide purchaser as against the unrecorded claims of others, and the burden of proving the contrary rests on the party asserting it.

934. Atwood v. Bearss, 47 Mich. 72, 10 N.W. 112 (1881).

935. Haab v. Moorman, 332 Mich. 126, 50 N.W.2d 856 (1952).

936. Smelsy v. Safety Inv. Corp., 310 Mich. 686, 17 N.W.2d 868 (1945).

Russell v. Myers, 32 Mich. 522 (1875) (prior unrecorded sale of timber).

Priority of lease

Valid oil and gas lease took precedence over prior unrecorded contract for sale under which purchaser had not been in actual possession.—Doctor v. Muskegon Oil Corp., 246 Mich. 62, 224 N.W. 398 (1929).

937. Whetstone v. Michigan Consol. Gas Co., 219 F. Supp. 121 (E.D. Mich. 1963).

Smith v. Williams, 44 Mich. 240, 6 N.W. 662 (1880).

Burns v. Berry, 42 Mich. 176, 3 N.W. 924 (1879).

Lakeside Associates v. Toski Sands, 131 Mich. App. 292, 346 N.W.2d 92 (1983).

938. Skupinski v. Provident Mortg. Co., 244 Mich. 309, 221 N.W. 338 (1928).

Beidler v. City Bank of Battle Creek, 172 Mich. 381, 137 N.W. 717 (1912).

939. Roth v. Smilay, 251 Mich. 381, 232 N.W. 220 (1930).

Sauer v. Fischer, 247 Mich. 283, 225 N.W. 518 (1929).

Soloman v. Western Hills Dev. Co., 110 Mich. App. 257, 312 N.W.2d 428 (1981).

940. Messmore v. Maerz, 149 Mich. 331, 112 N.W. 980 (1907).

941. Removal of cabins

Right to remove cabins erected by assignee of lessee's interest under unrecorded lease from purchaser under land contract, existing by reason of lease provision and fact that cabins constituted trade fixtures, was not enforceable against bona fide purchasers of the land for value after termination of lease interest by forfeiture of purchaser's rights under land contract for default in payments thereunder.—Tilchin v. Boucher, 328 Mich. 355, 43 N.W.2d 885 (1950).

942. Meade v. Robinson, 234 Mich. 322, 208 N.W. 41 (1926).

There is a presumption that a subsequent purchaser who is first to have his or her deed recorded is a bona fide purchaser without notice.[943] The burden of proving notice is on the party alleging it.[944]

Generally, a person acquiring title from a fraudulent grantor has the burden of proving that he or she paid value and took without notice of the fraud.[945]

Admissibility. Competent, relevant, and material evidence tending to prove or disprove actual knowledge of another's prior interest is admissible.[946]

Weight and sufficiency. In reviewing a trial court's determination on the evidence whether a vendee is a good-faith purchaser, an appellate court does not overturn the findings of the factfinder unless they are clearly erroneous under the facts on the record.[947]

A party to a case involving a claim that a vendee is a bona fide purchaser may seek a ruling whether the evidence is sufficient to show that the vendee party is[948] or is not[949] a bona fide purchaser, that the vendee had actual[950] or constructive[951]

943. Harr v. Coolbaugh, 337 Mich. 158, 59 N.W.2d 132 (1953).

Federman v. Van Antwerp, 276 Mich. 344, 267 N.W. 856 (1936).

944. Ooley v. Collins, 344 Mich. 148, 73 N.W.2d 464 (1955).

945. Osten-Sacken v. Steiner, 356 Mich. 468, 97 N.W.2d 37 (1959).

Hardy v. Heide, 291 Mich. 542, 289 N.W. 246 (1939).

Letson v. Reed, 45 Mich. 27, 7 N.W. 231 (1880).

946. Evidence of actual knowledge

Where one of four tenants in common assumed to and did convey the entire land, and the grantee of two of the other tenants brought an action for title and possession and sought to show that defendant was informed of the outstanding title of plaintiff's grantors at the time of his purchase by the interpreter through whom the sale was made, evidence was competent.—Highstone v. Burdette, 61 Mich. 54, 27 N.W. 852 (1886).

947. Port Inv. Co. v. Anderson, 23 Mich. App. 103, 178 N.W.2d 157 (1970).

Real property law: Real evidence: Special rules for real estate disputes, *see* 80 Mich. B.J. 28 (2001).

948. Leidel v. Ballbach, 345 Mich. 201, 75 N.W.2d 860 (1956).

Cherry River Nat'l Bank v. Wallace, 329 Mich. 384, 45 N.W.2d 332 (1951).

Kurbel v. O'Hair, 256 Mich. 680, 240 N.W. 57 (1932).

Port Inv. Co. v. Anderson, 23 Mich. App. 103, 178 N.W.2d 157 (1970).

Dalton v. Miller, 248 Mich. 253, 226 N.W. 826 (1929) (deed in form was mortgage in fact).

Range v. Davison, 242 Mich. 73, 218 N.W. 789 (1928) (assignee).

Ignorance of prior agreement

Evidence supported finding that plaintiffs, in accepting conveyance of farm property pursuant to their agreement to care for grantor during his lifetime, were purchasers in good faith, without knowledge of unrecorded pool agreement in oil and gas royalties which grantor had previously entered into, so that pool agreement was not binding as against plaintiffs' rights in the property.—Mark v. Bradford, 315 Mich. 50, 23 N.W.2d 201 (1946).

Vendor's spouse

In action to recover one-half interest as purchaser in land contract, evidence was sufficient to show that purchaser and co-purchaser surrendered their purchasers' interest in contract, and that such surrender was accepted by vendor, and that under new contract executed by vendor to co-purchaser's wife, wife was bona fide purchaser, who was entitled to her rights as such.—Annett v. Stout, 322 Mich. 457, 34 N.W.2d 42 (1948).

949. Osten-Sacken v. Steiner, 356 Mich. 468, 97 N.W.2d 37 (1959).

Dyksterhouse v. Ohl, 330 Mich. 599, 48 N.W.2d 122 (1951).

Smelsey v. Guarantee Finance Corp., 310 Mich. 674, 17 N.W.2d 863 (1945).

Hardy v. Heide, 291 Mich. 542, 289 N.W. 246 (1939).

American Cedar & Lumber Co. v. Gustin, 236 Mich. 351, 210 N.W. 300 (1926) (evidence showed knowledge or notice of prior purchase).

notice, that possession by third parties did[952] or did not[953] constitute notice to the purchaser, or that the purchaser's transaction was undertaken with an absence of good faith.[954]

Jury questions. Conflicting evidence concerning notice of a prior interest presents a question of fact for the factfinder to determine.[955]

On the other hand, if the evidence as to the bona fide status of a purchaser is undisputed, the application of the law to the facts is decided by the court as a matter of law.[956]

Vendee's vendor

Evidence justified finding that neither defendants' predecessor in title who purchased land from plaintiff's grantor after conveyance to plaintiff, nor defendants, were purchasers in good faith so as to entitle defendants to priority over plaintiff because deeds under which defendants claimed were recorded before plaintiff's deed was recorded.—Taskey v. Paquette, 324 Mich. 143, 36 N.W.2d 876 (1949).

950. Dassance v. Nienhuis, 57 Mich. App. 422, 225 N.W.2d 789 (1975) (overruled on other grounds by G & D Co. v. Durand Milling Co., 67 Mich. App. 253, 240 N.W.2d 765 (1976)).

Finner v. Weilnau, 243 Mich. 624, 220 N.W. 669 (1928) (lease).

Goodman v. Rott, 242 Mich. 198, 218 N.W. 761 (1928) (ostensible deed was mortgage).

Misner v. Stange, 203 Mich. 411, 169 N.W. 938 (1918) (liens).

951. Solomon v. Shewitz, 185 Mich. 620, 152 N.W. 196 (1915) (put on inquiry).

Absence of good faith

The testimony of a notary, who took the acknowledgment of an assignment of a land certifi-cate, that it was executed after the filing of a lis pendens, and evidence of an absurdly small consideration, and of subsequent attempts to get advantage of the claimant of the land, warrant a finding that the assignment was not made in good faith before the filing of the lis pendens.—Warner v. Sibley, 53 Mich. 371, 19 N.W. 40 (1884).

952. Chandler v. Clark, 151 Mich. 159, 115 N.W. 65 (1908) (unrecorded deed).

953. Ballona v. Petex, 234 Mich. 273, 207 N.W. 836 (1926) (vacant lot).

954. Absence of good faith

The testimony of a notary, who took the acknowledgment of an assignment of a land certificate, that it was executed after the filing of a lis pendens, and evidence of an absurdly small consideration, and of subsequent attempts to get advantage by claimant of the land, warrant a finding that the assignment was not made in good faith before the filing of the lis pendens.—Warner v. Sibley, 53 Mich. 371, 19 N.W. 40 (1884).

955. Goodman v. Fangert, 204 Mich. 66, 170 N.W. 29 (1918).

956. Oliver v. Sanborn, 60 Mich. 346, 27 N.W. 527 (1886).

Chapter 20

REMEDIES OF VENDOR

§ 601.   Available Remedies

A vendor who does not repudiate and rescind a contract from the beginning has remedies in affirmance of the contract for sale consisting of summary process upon forfeiture of the land contract, foreclosure of the land contract or equitable lien, an action for the purchase money, a suit for damages arising from breach of contract, or an action for specific performance.

Library References

> Michigan Digest
> John G. Cameron, Jr., Michigan Real Estate Forms
> Midwest Transaction Guide
> Thompson on Real Property, Thomas Edition (David A. Thomas, ed.)
> Powell on Real Property® (Michael Allan Wolf, ed.)

Law Reviews

> Kimberly A. Breitmeyer, Residential Builder Corporation Owners: Now Liable Under The Michigan Consumer Protection Act, 85 MI Bar Jnl. 28 (2006); Carl W. Herstein, Annual Survey Of Michigan Law, June 1, 1999 - May 31, 2000: Real Property, 47 Wayne L. Rev. 669 (2001); Lawrence R. Shoffner, Real Property Law: Real Evidence: Special Rules For Real Estate Disputes, 80 Mich. B.J. 28 (2001).

If the contract provides for it, and all the contractual conditions are met, a vendor may repudiate and rescind a contract for the sale of real property and require that the parties be put back into the statu quo that existed prior to the contract.[957]

Otherwise, in affirmance of the contract, under the present legal framework, summary proceedings are the customary form of action against a defaulting purchaser under a land contract. Their aim is to obtain a resumption of the installment payments.[958] Of course, if the purchaser is not in physical possession of the land or possession can be recovered peaceably, the purchaser's rights may be declared forfeited by the seller without proceedings in court if notice of forfeiture is duly given.[959]

---

957. Rescission by vendor, *see, supra*, Chapter 17.

958. Gruskin v. Fisher, 405 Mich. 51, 273 N.W.2d 893 (1979).

959. Rescission of land contract, *see, supra*, Chapter 17.

Sachs v. City of Detroit, 257 F. Supp. 2d 903, 2003 U.S. Dist. LEXIS 6637 (E.D. Mich. 2003).

Nash v. State Land Office Board, 333 Mich. 149, 52 N.W.2d 639 (1952).

Shamie v. Flynn, 2001 Mich. App. LEXIS 2082 (Mich. Ct. App. July 17, 2001).

Linden Inv. Co. v. Frank Minca, Ernestine Minca, Joseph A. Kephart, Richard F. Kinkle, Estate of Louise Nettlow, 1999 Mich. App. LEXIS 2865 (Mich. Ct. App. Oct. 5, 1999).

Day v. Lacchia, 175 Mich. App. 363, 437 N.W.2d 400 (1989).

Rothenberg v. Follman, 19 Mich. App. 383, 172 N.W.2d 845 (1969).

Necessity of forfeiture

Where no forfeiture of the rights of the vendee has occurred, a valid reentry by the vendor may not be had even if peaceable possession is obtained.—Maday v. Roth, 160 Mich. 289, 125 N.W. 13 (1910).

In addition to summary process for possession on the basis of the forfeiture or termination of an executory land contract, the vendor may also seek foreclosure of the land contract, payment of the balance of the purchase price under a contract allowing that remedy, or bring a simple action for damages consisting of the unpaid installments on the land contract.[960]

The common-law action of ejectment no longer exists as a remedy following a land contract forfeiture. Summary proceedings are the exclusive remedy based upon forfeiture[961] where the vendee does not voluntarily surrender possession after the vendor's notice of forfeiture.[962]

Sellers are no longer at liberty immediately after forfeiture of a land contract to seize possession of the premises and put buyers out on the street.[963]

In the absence of a breach of the contract by the vendee, the vendor has no right to take or recover possession from the vendee who is in possession under the terms of the contract.[964]

Actions for specific performance. Specific performance of a contract for the sale of real property is an equitable remedy within the sound discretion of the circuit court.[965]

Action for title, interest, or possession. No action for title to, interest in, or possession of real property under the Revised Judicature Act of 1961 may be maintained by a person for the recovery of premises sold under a land contract the possession of which may be obtained by summary proceedings upon the forfeiture of the land contract.[966]

§ 602.   Election of Remedies

In comparison with an action for foreclosure or for money damages, summary proceedings upon forfeiture of the land contract move expeditiously and generally accomplish their purpose of persuading the purchaser to cure the arrears in payment on a land contract.

A judgment for possession for the vendor in summary process upon a forfeiture of the land contract merges and bars any claim for money due under the contract at the time of trial. It does not merge or bar any other claim for relief.[967]

960. Gruskin v. Fisher, 405 Mich. 51, 273 N.W.2d 893 (1979).

961. Minchella v. Fredericks, 138 Mich. App. 462, 360 N.W.2d 896 (1984).

962. Gruskin v. Fisher, 405 Mich. 51, 273 N.W.2d 893 (1979).

963. Gruskin v. Fisher, 405 Mich. 51, 273 N.W.2d 893 (1979).

964. Cook v. Hopkins, 68 Mich. 514, 36 N.W. 790 (1888).

965. Specific performance, M.L.P.2d Remedies.

Van Dyke v. City of Warren & Downtown Dev. Auth., 2010 Mich. App. LEXIS 2517 (Mich. Ct. App. Dec. 28, 2010).

Malburg v. Wayne J. Lennard & Sons, 2003 Mich. App. LEXIS 2090 (Mich. Ct. App. Aug. 28, 2003).

Zurcher v. Herveat, 238 Mich. App. 267, 605 N.W.2d 329 (1999).

966. MCLS § 600.2932.

967. MCLS § 600.5750.

Gruskin v. Fisher, 405 Mich. 51, 273 N.W.2d 893 (1979).

Thus, although a judgment for possession has been entered, the vendor may seek to recover damages other than arrears owed by the vendee until the vendor obtains a writ of restitution.[968] The writ of restitution bars claims for damages due under the contract subsequent to the time of the issuance of the writ.[969]

Summary proceedings for possession of property are outside the realm of normal rules concerning merger and bar so as to enable the proceedings to be handled expeditiously. Therefore, the dismissal with prejudice of a vendor's suit for summary possession of real estate does not preclude the vendor's subsequent suit for reformation of contract, mistake, breach of lease agreement, breach of contract, guaranty, and unjust enrichment.[970]

In comparison with an action for foreclosure or for money damages, summary proceedings move expeditiously and generally accomplish their purpose of persuading the purchaser to cure the arrears in payment. But if the purchaser is not going to catch up on payment, then the vendor has to make an election of remedies. The vendor may accept possession or, if he or she wants a deficiency judgment, abandon the summary proceedings prior to taking possession in favor of a foreclosure.[971]

A vendor who forecloses after obtaining a judgment of forfeiture in summary proceedings that the vendee refuses to redeem will be seen differently when he or she asks the circuit court in the foreclosure action for a prompt adjudication of the foreclosure. In that light, the vendor does not appear to be taking advantage of the vendee who failed to redeem.[972]

The election of remedies means that the vendor cannot obtain possession

Unpaid taxes

The plain language of Mich. Comp. Laws § 600.5750 leads to the conclusion that a claim for unpaid taxes is barred. Such taxes are "money payments." Where, at the time of the judgment, they are "in arrears under the contract," a judgment for money damages to recover those amounts is barred by a forfeiture. The fact that they are payable to the taxing authorities rather than to a land contract vendor is of no consequence.—Michigan Nat'l Bank v. Cote, 451 Mich. 180, 546 N.W.2d 247, 1996 Mich. LEXIS 758 (1996).

968. Michigan Nat'l Bank v. Cote, 451 Mich. 180, 546 N.W.2d 247, 1996 Mich. LEXIS 758 (1996).

Gruskin v. Fisher, 405 Mich. 51, 273 N.W.2d 893 (1979).

969. MCLS § 600.5750.

Gruskin v. Fisher, 405 Mich. 51, 273 N.W.2d 893 (1979).

Ames v. Maxson, 157 Mich. App. 75, 403 N.W.2d 501, 1987 Mich. App. LEXIS 2283 (1987).

No award for money due after issuance of writ

Judgment for possession after forfeiture of executory contract and the issuance of a writ of restitution bars any claim for money payments that would have become due under the contract subsequent to the issuance of the writ.—Van Elsacker v. Erzberger, 137 Mich. App. 552, 357 N.W.2d 891 (1984).

970. J.A.M. Corp. v. AARO Disposal, Inc., 461 Mich. 161, 600 N.W.2d 617 (1999).

Simpson v. JP Morgan Chase Bank, N.A., 2010 Mich. App. LEXIS 1851 (Mich. Ct. App. Sept. 30, 2010).

In re Barbara Hroba Trust, 2008 Mich. App. LEXIS 2061 (Mich. Ct. App. Oct. 16, 2008).

971. Gruskin v. Fisher, 405 Mich. 51, 273 N.W.2d 893 (1979).

Durda v. Chembar Development Corp., 95 Mich. App. 706, 291 N.W.2d 179, 1980 Mich. App. LEXIS 2510 (1980).

Past due payments

If the past-due payments and other material breaches are not timely cured, the contract is forfeited.—In re Delex Management, 155 B.R. 161, 1993 Bankr. LEXIS 816, 24 Bankr. Ct. Dec. (LRP) 552, 29 Collier Bankr. Cas. 2d (MB) 125 (Bankr. W.D. Mich. 1993).

972. Gruskin v. Fisher, 405 Mich. 51, 273 N.W.2d 893 (1979).

under summary process and, after being unable to sell the property, commence foreclosure proceedings and seek a deficiency judgment. Thus, the market value of the property and the duration of the land contract are factors weighed by the vendor in selecting between forfeiture and foreclosure.[973]

§ 603.   Summary Proceedings Upon Forfeiture

A vendor may maintain summary proceedings to recover possession of land from a vendee in default under an executory contract for any reason for which the land contract permits forfeiture of the land contract.

A person entitled to premises may recover possession of the premises by summary proceedings after the occupant's forfeiture of the premises under the express conditions or covenants of any executory contract for the purchase of lands or tenements.[974] The district court, municipal courts, and common pleas court of Detroit have jurisdiction over summary process proceedings.[975]

The vendor may bring a summary process action for possession under an executory land contract if the property is vacant or is occupied by the vendee, another party to the contract, an assignee of the contract, or a third party.[976] The vendor is entitled to possession even as against a vendee who has gone into possession by the vendor's permission if the vendee is not entitled to retain possession under the terms of the contract.[977]

However, the vendor may not bring summary process to gain possession after forfeiture on the basis of an acceleration clause in the land contract.[978]

In a case falling within the scope of this subject-matter jurisdiction, the vendor may recover possession of the land by summary proceedings.[979] If the vendor proceeds in accordance with the terms of the contract and has not parted with title to the property, the court may not consider equitable defenses interposed by the

---

973. Gruskin v. Fisher, 405 Mich. 51, 273 N.W.2d 893 (1979).

974. MCLS § 600.5726.

975. MCLS § 600.5704.

M.L.P.2d Landlord and Tenant, Chapter 13, Summary Eviction Proceedings.

Redemption is absolute

Notice of forfeiture required to be sent by land contract vendor as condition precedent to commencement of proceedings under summary proceedings statute is insufficient to support eviction and does not preclude purchaser from statutory right to cure default at any time during proceedings and as late as six months thereafter under certain circumstances.—Gruskin v. Fisher, 405 Mich. 51, 273 N.W.2d 893 (1979).

976. MCR 4.202.

Surrender after filing does not moot summary process

A summary proceeding under prior similar stat-

ute instituted by vendors after default by the vendees was not fatally defective because the vendees voluntarily surrendered possession without issuance of a writ of restitution.—Kraushaar v. Bunny Run Realty Co., 298 Mich. 233, 298 N.W. 514 (1941).

977. Gault v. Stormont, 51 Mich. 636, 17 N.W. 214 (1883).

978. MCLS § 600.5726.

Day v. Lacchia, 175 Mich. App. 363, 437 N.W.2d 400 (1989).

Minchella v. Fredericks, 138 Mich. App. 462, 360 N.W.2d 896, 1984 Mich. App. LEXIS 2970 (1984).

979. *See* Tilchin v. Boucher, 328 Mich. 355, 43 N.W.2d 885 (1950), Megantz v. Cooke, 282 Mich. 213, 275 N.W. 823 (1937); and Stevens v. Most, 251 Mich. 23, 231 N.W. 47 (1930) (all decided under prior similar statute).

vendee in a summary process action.[980] The vendor is entitled to a writ of restitution against a vendee who does not redeem or interpose a valid defense.[981] Thus, the vendor's breach of the executory contract, not resulting in liquidated damages, cannot be pleaded by the purchaser as a defense in summary proceedings to recover possession after forfeiture.[982]

With respect to the vendor's right to institute summary proceedings, the right to forfeit the contract on default is not lost on appointment of a receiver for the vendee.[983] Similarly, the vendor's default on a mortgage does not preclude him or her from declaring a forfeiture of a land contract where the vendee has defaulted first.[984] A vendee in possession may not defeat the vendor's right to recover possession for nonpayment of the purchase price on the ground that the title is unmarketable.[985]

Nonexclusive character of remedy. The remedy of summary proceedings to recover possession of the land subject to an executory land contract is not exclusive in character, and is in addition to other legal, equitable, or statutory remedies.[986]

Action for title, interest, or possession. No action for title to, interest in, or possession of real property under the Revised Judicature Act of 1961 may be maintained by a person for the recovery of premises sold under land contract the possession of which may be obtained by summary proceedings upon the forfeiture of the land contract.[987]

§ 604.   —Waiver of Right to Forfeiture

The vendor may by waiver or estoppel lose the right to summary proceedings upon the forfeiture of the land contract.

The vendor may lose his or her right to a forfeiture of a contract for the sale

---

980. Grylls v. Hergiton, 268 Mich. 35, 255 N.W. 334 (1934) (decided under prior similar statute).

Rescission by purchaser

Purchasers' rescission of land contract could not be had in vendor's summary proceeding under prior similar statute to oust purchasers.—Pine Shores Realty Co. v. Parker, 253 Mich. 300, 235 N.W. 163 (1931).

981. Walker v. Lind, 280 Mich. 61, 273 N.W. 392 (1937) (decided under prior similar statute).

Gould v. Young, 143 Mich. 572, 107 N.W. 281, 1906 Mich. LEXIS 693 (1906) (decided under prior similar statute).

Default in paying mortgage interest

Vendor's default in paying mortgage interest becoming due after notice of forfeiture was no defense in summary proceeding under prior similar statute.—Picard v. Shapero, 255 Mich. 699, 239 N.W. 264 (1931).

982. Rosenthal v. American Constr. & Realty Co., 262 Mich. 91, 247 N.W. 117 (1933) (decided under prior similar statute).

983. Rowe v. William Ford & Co., 257 Mich. 646, 241 N.W. 889 (1932) (decided under prior similar statute).

984. Singer v. Hoffman Cake Co., 281 Mich. 371, 275 N.W. 177 (1937).

Vendee's fault

Vendor in default in making payments on mortgage, was held not precluded from forfeiting land contract, where purchaser was largely responsible for vendor's default, and could have protected herself under contract.—Heath v. Gloster, 260 Mich. 85, 244 N.W. 237 (1932).

985. Jordan v. Morony, 250 Mich. 593, 231 N.W. 80 (1930) (with respect to defense of suit for possession, if title is defective, purchaser must surrender possession of premises and sue for damages).

986. MCLS § 600.5750.

987. MCLS § 600.2932.

of land by waiver or estoppel.[988]

Proposing the payment of interest on late payments, prior to giving notice of rescission, does not comprise a waiver of the right to rescind.[989] Giving notice of forfeiture on one ground does not waive the right to rescind on another valid ground for doing so.[990]

A prior rescission of the land contract by the purchaser does not constitute a waiver of forfeiture subsequently declared by the vendor.[991]

Waiver after declaration of forfeiture. A vendor who has duly declared the intent to obtain a forfeiture and has notified the vendee of that intent may nonetheless thereafter waive the right of forfeiture by subsequent acts clearly inconsistent with it.[992]

The receipt of partial payment that is made prior to the deadline to cure in the notice of judgment of forfeiture does not waive the right to a writ of restitution.[993]

However, the vendor cannot, without the consent of the vendee, waive a forfeiture that the vendor has declared.[994]

§ 605.   —Conditions Precedent

Notice of forfeiture is a condition precedent to maintenance of summary proceedings, but the notice does not preclude the vendor's subsequent selection of another affirmative cause of action in response to the vendee's breach of the contract.

The forfeiture of the contract by notice from the vendor[995] is a prerequisite to commencement of a summary process action for possession of the property subject to a land contract.[996] When a contract for the sale of land is sufficient to give the

---

988. Balesh v. Alcott, 257 Mich. 352, 241 N.W. 216 (1932).

Kimball v. Goodburn, 32 Mich. 10 (1875).

Waiver or estoppel not shown

Vendors were not precluded from declaring forfeiture because of negligible default for which purchasers were responsible.—Langley v. Kirker, 247 Mich. 443, 225 N.W. 931 (1929).

989. No tender made

Where parties entered into a preliminary agreement providing that plaintiffs would purchase a motel and restaurant and paid $2,000 down as a binder, alleged insistence by the defendants upon 6% interest that came up only after the plaintiffs had informed the defendants of their inability to carry out the agreement was not a waiver of any tender by the plaintiffs where there was no valid tender of the amount due or express waiver.—Duiven v. Brakesman, 356 Mich. 1, 95 N.W.2d 868 (1959).

990. Welling v. Strickland, 161 Mich. 235, 126 N.W. 471 (1910).

991. Windmill Point Land Co. v. Strickland, 264 Mich. 79, 249 N.W. 464 (1933).

992. Krell v. Cohen, 214 Mich. 590, 183 N.W. 53 (1921).

993. Reinecke v. Sheehy, 47 Mich. App. 250, 209 N.W.2d 460 (1973).

994. Chicago Boulevard Land Co. v. Apartment Garages, Inc., 245 Mich. 448, 222 N.W. 697 (1929).

995. Wilson v. Taylor, 457 Mich. 232, 577 N.W.2d 100, 1998 Mich. LEXIS 1295 (1998).

Gruskin v. Fisher, 405 Mich. 51, 273 N.W.2d 893 (1979).

Mervez v. Petchesky, 259 Mich. 507, 244 N.W. 144 (1932).

Malys v. W.C. Hood Realty Corp., 229 Mich. 110, 200 N.W. 943 (1924).

Miner v. Dickey, 140 Mich. 518, 103 N.W. 855 (1905).

996. Wilson v. Taylor, 457 Mich. 232, 577 N.W.2d 100, 1998 Mich. LEXIS 1295 (1998).

vendee the right of possession, the vendee's failure to make the stipulated payments does not of itself entitle the vendor to immediate possession without notice of forfeiture.[997]

Under the Revised Judicature Act of 1961, the vendee has 15 days, or a longer time under the contract, to cure a default or breach of an executory contract for sale of real property after being served with written notice of forfeiture from the vendor.[998] The notice of forfeiture must contain the statutorily required information.[999]

While a land contract vendor has the right to possession of the premises 15 days after service of the notice of forfeiture on the vendee, or later if the contract so states, that right may only be enforced after the writ of restitution is issued and cannot be enforced even then if the vendee prevents the writ from issuing by timely paying the redemption price.[1000] The function of the notice is to inform the vendee that he or she faces court action if the default is not cured.[1001]

One result of that fact is that the vendor does not have to accept a surrender of the premises by the vendee in response to the notice. The vendor may choose to obtain relief under the summary proceedings despite the offer of surrender.[1002] A vendee under a contract giving the vendor the election to forfeit for the vendee's default, where vendee acquiesces in the forfeiture and surrenders possession to the vendor, thereby loses all rights in the premises.[1003]

The notice of forfeiture may be served personally, or to certain persons at the premises, or to the last known address of the vendee, or by first-class mail.[1004] As a last resort, service may be made under the relevant statute[1005] by publication.[1006]

It is essential that the vendor first give notice of the intention to terminate prior to an equitable action for rescission, and the failure to notify all parties is grounds for voiding the resulting judgment.[1007] The vendee can probably waive notice of forfeiture, however.[1008]

Gruskin v. Fisher, 405 Mich. 51, 273 N.W.2d 893 (1979).

997. Corning v. Loomis, 111 Mich. 23, 69 N.W. 85 (1896).

998. MCLS § 600.5728.

999. MCLS § 600.5728.

1000. De Spelder v. De Spelder, 1997 Mich. App. LEXIS 3843 (Mich. Ct. App. Mar. 7, 1997).

Durda v. Chembar Development Corp., 95 Mich. App. 706, 291 N.W.2d 179 (1980).

1001. Gruskin v. Fisher, 405 Mich. 51, 273 N.W.2d 893 (1979).

1002. Gruskin v. Fisher, 405 Mich. 51, 273 N.W.2d 893 (1979).

1003. Kennedy v. Ford, 183 Mich. 481, 149 N.W. 1013 (1914).

1004. MCLS § 600.5730.

1005. MCLS §§ 554.301, 554.302.

1006. MCLS § 600.5730.

1007. Zadigian v. Gard, 223 Mich. 147, 193 N.W. 783 (1923).

John v. McNeal, 167 Mich. 148, 132 N.W. 508 (1911).

Peters v. Canfield, 74 Mich. 498, 42 N.W. 125 (1889).

Reinecke v. Sheehy, 47 Mich. App. 250, 209 N.W.2d 460 (1973).

Sparling v. Bert, 1 Mich. App. 167, 134 N.W.2d 840 (1965).

1008. Crane v. O'Reiley, 8 Mich. 312 (1860).

Notice mailed to last known address

Provision in a contract that notice of forfeiture is sufficient if mailed to the last-known post office address of the vendee is for the mutual benefit of both parties; in absence of vendee's advising

A vendor's notice of forfeiture may be sufficient even though it is not given before repossession.[1009]

A vendor must have title at the time of giving notice of the forfeiture of the contract for sale of the property.[1010]

§ 606.   —Parties, Pleadings, and Process

The vendor's assignee may maintain summary proceedings to recover the land upon the vendee's forfeiture of the land contract. The pleadings and service of summons are specified by statute.

The vendor's assignee may bring summary proceedings for the recovery of possession of the land.[1011]

Necessary parties to a summary process action on forfeiture of an executory contract for the sale of real property include the vendee under the contract, any person claiming an interest in the real property, and any person in possession of the premises who is not released from liability.[1012] The vendee's assignee is a proper party to such an action.[1013]

Pleadings. The complaint in a summary process action on forfeiture of an executory contract for the sale of real property must state the original selling price, the principal balance due, the amount in arrears on the contract, and the particulars of any other alleged material breach. It must have a copy of the notice of forfeiture and proof of service of the notice attached to it.[1014]

Within the jurisdiction set out in court rules, a party to a summary proceeding on the forfeiture of an executory contract for the sale of real property may join

---

vendor of a change of address, a notice sent to the last-known post office address suffices; purchaser's application for title abstract to abstract division of vendor's agent was not notice of change of address requiring vendors to send forfeiture declaration to new address.—Alper v. Oakman, 260 Mich. 499, 245 N.W. 504 (1932).

Notice waived

Where notice to quit and notice of forfeiture were waived, it was unnecessary to serve written declaration of forfeiture, and unequivocal act of vendor indicating that vendor treated contract as ended would constitute binding election to rescind.—Balesh v. Alcott, 257 Mich. 352, 241 N.W. 216 (1932).

1009. Emmons v. Easter, 62 Mich. App. 226, 233 N.W.2d 239 (1975).

Marketable title

Marketable title is one of such character as should assure to the vendee the quiet and peaceful enjoyment of the property, which must be free from incumbrance. An incumbrance is anything which constitutes a burden upon the title, such as a right-of-way, a condition which may work a

forfeiture of the estate, a right to take off timber, or a right of dower. A title may be regarded as "unmarketable" where a reasonably prudent man, familiar with the facts, would refuse to accept title in the ordinary course of business, and it is not necessary that the title actually be bad in order to render it unmarketable.—Madhavan v. Sucher, 105 Mich. App. 284, 306 N.W.2d 481 (1981).

1010. Premature notice

Where a contract provided that if the vendee, who was to take immediate possession and pay the balance of the purchase price in three years, made default in payment, he should forfeit both lands and the sums paid, and the vendor had no title to part of the lands sold, a notice of forfeiture given before the vendor had acquired title was a nullity, and could not operate as a notice upon his subsequently acquiring title.—Getty v. Peters, 82 Mich. 661, 46 N.W. 1036 (1890).

1011. Vos v. Dykema, 26 Mich. 399 (1873).

1012. MCR 4.202.

1013. Porter v. Barrett, 233 Mich. 373, 206 N.W. 532 (1925).

1014. MCR 4.202.

claims and counterclaims for damages for various causes of action. But the court may order separate disposition of the claim for possession and claims for damages.[1015] Claims for damages other than those that become due under the contract may be joined with a land contract forfeiture action in district court so long as the damages sought do not exceed the monetary jurisdictional limit of the district court. If the damages sought are in excess of the district court's monetary jurisdictional limit, the damages claims must be brought in circuit court even though the forfeiture action remains in the district court.[1016]

Process. Service of the complaint and requisite summons[1017] must be in accordance with the general provisions of the Michigan Court Rules of 1985.[1018]

Proper service of summons is essential to institution of a summary proceeding for recovery of possession of land.[1019]

§ 607.   —Trial and Evidence

The court hearing a summary process action on the forfeiture of an executory land contract may hold hearings on all issues, order joinder of parties, allow additional pleadings, and make and enforce writs and orders.

The court hearing a summary process action on the forfeiture of an executory land contract may hold hearings on all issues, order joinder of parties, allow additional pleadings, and make and enforce writs and orders.[1020] Any party may request a jury trial.[1021]

On the trial of a summary proceeding to recover possession of land sold under an executory contract, it is not erroneous to fail to present questions of law to the

---

1015. MCLS § 600.5739.

MCR 4.202.

1016. Michigan Nat'l Bank v. Cote, 451 Mich. 180, 546 N.W.2d 247, 1996 Mich. LEXIS 758 (1996).

Ames v. Maxson, 157 Mich. App. 75, 403 N.W.2d 501 (1987).

Equitable defenses

Plaintiff's mere invocation of equitable defenses and counter-claims in the circuit court were also insufficient to divest the district court of jurisdiction.—Thomas v. Gutowski, 2002 Mich. App. LEXIS 2206 (Mich. Ct. App. Dec. 20, 2002).

Incidental damages

Reason for enacting prior statute, providing in part that money judgment may be rendered in action for breach of land contract against any defendant over whom court has personal jurisdiction and that if claim for money exceeds jurisdiction of court, the court must hear claim for possession but dismiss claim for money, was to allow award of incidental damages when they fell within jurisdictional amount of district court, and

the statute was not intended to allow recovery of portion of contract price after notice of forfeiture has been given.—Hayes v. Kent Real Estate Co., 44 Mich. App. 196, 205 N.W.2d 52 (1972).

1017. *See* MCLS § 600.5735 and MCR 2.102, 4.202.

1018. MCR 2.105, 4.202.

1019. Barnes v. Curry, 232 Mich. 532, 205 N.W. 484 (1925) (substituted service unwarranted under facts).

Proceeding a nullity

Summary proceeding to obtain possession of land after forfeiture was a nullity for want of proper service of summons.—Crenshaw v. Granet, 237 Mich. 367, 211 N.W. 636 (1927).

1020. MCR 4.202.

Real Property Law: Real Evidence: Special Rules for Real Estate Disputes, 80 Mich. B.J. 28 (2001).

1021. MCLS § 600.5738.

jury.[1022]

In summary proceedings for possession of real estate, the burden is on the plaintiff vendor to prove the essential elements of his or her cause of action.[1023] The defendant vendee is not required to proceed with any defense until there has been some proof showing that the vendor is entitled to possession.[1024] Then, where the vendee asserts payment, the vendee has the burden of proving it.[1025]

The party having the affirmative of an issue has to establish it by a preponderance of the proof.[1026]

Whether evidence manifests an intent to not accept a tender offer to cure a forfeiture for default under an executory contract for the sale of real property is a question for the jury.[1027]

Default. If a defendant in a vendor's summary process action for possession

1022. No question of fact

Refusal to submit to jury items of setoff relating to fire insurance moneys was not error where testimony conclusively showed that amount credited in each instance from insurance money was correct.—Yaroch v. La Body, 288 Mich. 354, 284 N.W. 906 (1939).

1023. Frye v. Mielke, 266 Mich. 501, 254 N.W. 182 (1934).

1024. Frye v. Mielke, 266 Mich. 501, 254 N.W. 182 (1934).

1025. Frye v. Mielke, 266 Mich. 501, 254 N.W. 182 (1934).

Burden sustained

Signed entry on land contract as to principal and interest paid deceased vendor, and balance of principal due, afforded prima facie evidence of payment and was sufficient to sustain purchaser's burden of proof thereof in administrator's action to recover possession, where jury, on disputed evidence, found vendor's signature was genuine and all evidence of circumstances of payment was excluded.—Frye v. Mielke, 271 Mich. 182, 259 N.W. 883 (1935).

1026. Nelson v. Smith, 161 Mich. 363, 126 N.W. 447 (1910) (evidence insufficient to show vendor's waiver of forfeiture clause).

Payment by note shown

In vendor's proceeding to recover possession of land for purchaser's default, vendor's admission that promissory note of purchaser was accepted as part payment of initial payment on one contract was sufficient to sustain holding that note was accepted as a payment, and evidence supported finding as to amount of credit to be allowed purchaser.—Lent v. Dickinson, 331 Mich. 257, 49 N.W.2d 167 (1951).

Right to restitution shown

Evidence was sufficient to entitle vendor's assignee to judgment of restitution against defaulting purchaser.—Heath v. Gloster, 260 Mich. 85, 244 N.W. 237 (1932).

Time not of essence of contract

Evidence of vendor's failure to take steps to declare forfeiture for a three-year period during which monthly payments under the contract were not made as stipulated justifies an assumption that time was not of the essence of the contract.—Malys v. W.C. Hood Realty Corp., 229 Mich. 110, 200 N.W. 943 (1924).

1027. "Is paid" language

Where plaintiff manifested an intent not to accept tender of payment, refused to provide defendants with actual figures necessary to allow defendants to proceed with the sale of the property, and defendants' attorney attempted to effect a meeting with plaintiff through plaintiff's attorney for purposes of paying the amount of the judgment, but plaintiff refused, such a scenario, where a defendant evinces readiness, willingness, and ability to tender payment for purposes of redemption, but plaintiff, by acts or words, indicates that tender would not be accepted, satisfies "is paid" language of the statute.—Tenney v. Springer, 121 Mich. App. 47, 328 N.W.2d 566, 1982 Mich. App. LEXIS 3616, 37 A.L.R.4th 279 (1982).

Vendor wanted to keep property

In an action seeking to enforce redemption under land contract, entry of summary judgment for defendants for lack of genuine issue of material fact was reversible error in light of plaintiff's affidavits alleging that defendant's attorney was making himself unavailable for receipt of plaintiff's tender of payment, and that defendant's attorney stated that defendant wanted to keep property and that he could not accept payment, thereby raising genuine issue of material fact as to whether defendant had manifested intent not to accept tender of payment.—Karakas v. Dost, 67 Mich. App. 161, 240 N.W.2d 743 (1976).

upon forfeiture under an executory contract for the sale of real property fails to appear at trial, the court may adjourn the hearing for up to seven days or enter a default and hear the plaintiff's evidence. Upon sufficient proof, the court may enter a default judgment, which must be sent to the defendant and inform the defendant of his or her pending eviction and possible liability for damages.[1028]

If a plaintiff fails to appear, the court may adjourn the hearing for up to seven days or enter a default judgment and order costs to the defendant.[1029]

§ 608.   —Judgment and Writ

The judgment in a summary process action on the forfeiture of an executory land contract must, among other things, provide for the terms and conditions for the issuance of the writ of restitution. The writ of restitution, when issued, bars further right of redemption on the contract.

In accordance with the Michigan Court Rules of 1985, the judgment in a summary process action on the forfeiture of an executory land contract must, among other things, provide for the terms and conditions for the issuance of the writ of restitution, describe the right to appeal, determine other rights as necessary, and be mailed or delivered to the parties to the action.[1030]

A judgment for the vendor must specify the amount due or in arrears at the time of trial. This amount constitutes the amount that the vendee or other defendant must pay with costs to redeem and preclude the issuance of a writ of possession to enforce the judgment. Costs are to be determined in accordance with the rules generally applicable to civil actions.[1031] However, the amount required to be paid to redeem property from forfeiture after the breach of a land contract cannot include any accelerated indebtedness by reason of the contract breach.[1032]

In case the plaintiff in summary proceedings is entitled to possession of the premises in a proceeding upon any executory contract for the purchase of real estate, no writ of restitution may issue for 90 days after judgment. If the purchaser has paid

---

1028. MCR 4.202.

1029. MCR 4.202.

1030. MCR 4.202.

1031. MCLS § 600.5741.

MCR 4.202.

1032. MCLS § 600.5726.

Day v. Lacchia, 175 Mich. App. 363, 437 N.W.2d 400 (1989).

Judgment of possession after forfeiture

Where land contract was recorded and contract payments were made but eventually fell into default, respondent sought a judgment of possession after forfeiture in the district court, naming co-purchaser, only, as the defendant. When co-purchaser failed to redeem the property, respondent obtained an October 18, 2005, consent judgment of possession after land contract forfeiture. Eventually, petitioner discovered the forfeiture and sued for specific performance, asserting that the estate was prepared to pay the accelerated contract price but that respondent refused to accept the tender and therefore would not provide to plaintiff the warranty deed to the entire 80 acres. In her trial brief, petitioner argued that respondent's failure to provide notice, as required by the summary proceedings court rules, rendered the district court proceedings null and void. Petitioner noted that a land contract vendor has only four possible options when a vendee defaults: do nothing; get the vendees to release their interest ("deed back"); accelerate the balance and pursue foreclosure in the circuit court (where a judicial sale, subject to redemption, will take place); or proceed to forfeiture, which essentially sets aside the contract.— Loree v. Mich. Reserves, Inc. (In re Estate of West), 2009 Mich. App. LEXIS 1289 (Mich. Ct. App. June 11, 2009).

more than 50% of the purchase price provided for in the contract, no writ of restitution may issue for 6 months.[1033] The vendee's payment of the amount due within the period prescribed by statute warrants denial to the vendor of a writ of restitution.[1034]

Upon the expiration of the redemption period, the vendor may apply for the writ of restitution. The verified, written application must describe any payments made by the defendant and whether the vendor has complied with any conditions of the judgment. If any amount of the judgment has been paid, the court must hold a hearing prior to issuing a writ of restitution.[1035]

Within the jurisdiction set out in court rules, a party to a summary proceeding on the forfeiture of an executory contract for the sale of real property may join claims and counterclaims for damages for various causes of action.[1036] In summary proceedings based on forfeiture of a land contract, the vendor may at the court's discretion recover damages incidental to forfeiture proceedings from a vendee who has defaulted. A defaulting land contract vendee who remains in possession of property and does not redeem is liable for the reasonable rental value from that date that the period for cure expires until he or she vacates the property. Allowing the vendor to recover from a defaulting vendee both the property and the reasonable rental value for the time that the vendee remains in possession and does not redeem is neither inconsistent nor double recovery for the vendor.[1037]

Provision is made by statute for either party to appeal to the circuit court from the judgment of the district court, and for the filing of an appeal bond under court rules.[1038] The filing of an appeal and bond stays the tolling of the respective redemption period following the judgment.[1039] The appealing party must file bond to stay proceedings within a reasonable time after the judgment of possession is entered.[1040]

Effect of judgment for vendor and writ of restitution. A judgment for

---

1033. MCLS § 600.5744.

Bankruptcy estate

Because a vendee under a land contract had paid less than 50% of the purchase price, the vendee had 90 days after entry of a judgment of foreclosure to redeem the contract; where the vendee failed to redeem within the statutory 90-day period, and filed for bankruptcy two days after the expiration of the redemption period, the vendee did not have any rights to the property at the time of the bankruptcy filing and the property was not part of the bankruptcy estate (MCLS § 600.5744).—In re Horton, 302 B.R. 198, 2003 Bankr. LEXIS 1651 (Bankr. E.D. Mich. 2003).

1034. Lambton Loan & Inv. Co. v. Adams, 132 Mich. 350, 93 N.W. 877 (1903).

1035. MCR 4.202.

1036. MCLS § 600.5739.

MCR 4.202.

1037. Durda v. Chembar Development Corp., 95 Mich. App. 706, 291 N.W.2d 179 (1980).

Holdover rent

Holdover rent is essentially an action against a vendee (defendant) for the reasonable rental value after default on a land contract. Recovery is allowed on the theory of an implied promise to pay. Thus, it is not an action based on tort or an action for "property damage" to which the allocation of fault provisions would apply.—Wilson v. Henry, 2006 Mich. App. LEXIS 341 (Mich. Ct. App. Feb. 9, 2006).

1038. MCLS § 600.5753.

1039. MCLS § 600.5744.

In re Horton, 302 B.R. 198, 2003 Bankr. LEXIS 1651 (Bankr. E.D. Mich. 2003).

Sun Valley Foods Co. v. Ward, 460 Mich. 230, 596 N.W.2d 119 (1999).

Sun Valley Foods Co., 2003 Mich. App. LEXIS 2879 (Mich. Ct. App. Nov. 13, 2003).

1040. Sun Valley Foods Co. v. Ward, 460 Mich. 230, 596 N.W.2d 119 (1999) (there is no requirement that the bond to stay proceedings be

possession for the vendor in summary process merges and bars any claim for money due under the contract at the time of trial. It does not merge or bar any other claim for relief.[1041] Thus, although a judgment for possession has been entered, the vendor may seek to recover damages other than arrears owed by the vendee until the vendor obtains a writ of restitution.[1042] Unpaid real estate taxes that a vendee is required to pay under a land contract are money payments due or in arrears, and judgment for possession bars a claim for their recovery.[1043]

The issuance of the writ of restitution, including after vendee's failure to pay in full or cure completely within the statutory redemption period, bars all equitable right of redemption on an executory contract for the sale of real property.[1044] The writ of restitution also bars claims for damages due under the contract subsequent to the time of the issuance of the writ.[1045]

Neither the judgment for possession nor the writ of restitution bars any other

---

filed within 10 days after the judgment of possession is entered).

Motion for new trial

If an appeal is taken or a motion for new trial is filed before the expiration of the period during which the writ of restitution shall not be issued and if a bond to stay proceedings is filed, the period during which the writ shall not be issued shall be tolled until the disposition of the appeal or motion for new trial is final.—Sun Valley Foods Co., 2003 Mich. App. LEXIS 2879 (Mich. Ct. App. Nov. 13, 2003).

1041. MCLS § 600.5750.

Mazur v. Young, 507 F.3d 1013, 2007 U.S. App. LEXIS 26631, 2007 FED App. 455P (6th Cir.) (6th Cir. Mich. 2007).

Gruskin v. Fisher, 405 Mich. 51, 273 N.W.2d 893 (1979).

Gayles v. Deutsche Bank Nat'l Trust Co., 2010 Mich. App. LEXIS 2040 (Mich. Ct. App. Oct. 21, 2010).

1300 LaFayette East Coop., Inc. v. Savoy, 284 Mich. App. 522, 773 N.W.2d 57, 2009 Mich. App. LEXIS 1377 (2009).

Patulski v. Thompson, 2008 Mich. App. LEXIS 1913 (Mich. Ct. App. Sept. 30, 2008).

Subsequent suit

Summary proceedings for possession of property are outside the realm of normal rules concerning merger and bar so as to enable the proceedings to be handled expeditiously; therefore, the dismissal with prejudice of plaintiff's suit for summary possession of real estate did not preclude plaintiff's subsequent suit for reformation of contract, mistake, breach of lease agreement, breach of contract, guaranty, and unjust enrichment.—J.A.M. Corp. v. AARO Disposal, Inc., 461 Mich. 161, 600 N.W.2d 617 (1999).

1042. Gruskin v. Fisher, 405 Mich. 51, 273 N.W.2d 893 (1979).

1043. Michigan Nat'l Bank v. Cote, 451 Mich. 180, 546 N.W.2d 247 (1996).

Claim for money payments due

Defendant contends that plaintiffs' claim under the guaranty constitutes a "claim for money payments due or in arrears under the contract at the time of trial" within the meaning of § 5750 and that, since plaintiffs elected to institute forfeiture proceedings and to obtain a writ of restitution, the claim against defendant is barred. The claim against defendant as guarantor is simply not a post-forfeiture claim for "money payments due or in arrears under *the [land] contract*." Instead, the claim is one for liability under the wholly separate and discrete *guaranty contract*. Although that liability is certainly related to the land contract and the original transaction between buyer and plaintiffs, defendant is not being sued for amounts he owes under that contract; rather, his liability arises solely from the guaranty, as he was not even a party to the land contract. Moreover, § 5750 expressly provides that the remedy provided by summary proceedings is "in addition to, and not exclusive of, other remedies, either legal, equitable or statutory."—Richard v. 380 Fair Assocs., 2006 Mich. App. LEXIS 2518 (Mich. Ct. App. Aug. 15, 2006).

.1044. MCLS § 600.5744.

Accord Tilchin v. Boucher, 328 Mich. 355, 43 N.W.2d 885 (1950) and Titus v. Cavalier, 276 Mich. 117, 267 N.W. 799 (1936) (both decided under prior statute).

1045. MCLS § 600.5750.

Gruskin v. Fisher, 405 Mich. 51, 273 N.W.2d 893 (1979).

Gayles v. Deutsche Bank Nat'l Trust Co., 2010 Mich. App. LEXIS 2040 (Mich. Ct. App. Oct. 21, 2010).

Richard v. 380 Fair Assocs., 2006 Mich. App. LEXIS 2518 (Mich. Ct. App. Aug. 15, 2006).

forms of legal, equitable, or statutory relief available to either party.[1046]

Judgment for vendee. If the judgment is in favor of the vendee or other defendant, that party is entitled to costs taxed and assessed as for other civil judgments.[1047]

Costs. The Revised Judicature Act of 1961 provides for allowing and, within the statutory limits, taxing of costs on the respective parties.[1048]

§ 609.   —Redemption

A writ of restitution is only issued in a summary process action upon the forfeiture of a land contract after the expiration of the redemption period in which no redemption is completed and upon the plaintiff's motion.

Under the Revised Judicature Act of 1961, in case the plaintiff in summary proceedings is entitled to possession of the premises in a proceeding upon any executory contract for the purchase of real estate, no writ of restitution may issue for 90 days after judgment.[1049] If the purchaser has paid more than 50% of the purchase price provided for in the contract, no writ of restitution may issue for 6 months.[1050] For these purposes, the purchase price means the original selling price for the property as set forth on the face of the land contract. It does not include unpaid taxes or insurance premiums allocated to the purchaser.[1051]

The vendee of the land contract may pay the amount awarded plus costs and cure all material breaches of the executory contract before the time for issuance of the writ of restitution and thereby stop the issuance of the writ altogether.[1052] That tender may be made to the vendor, the vendor's attorney, or the court.[1053] The

No award for money due after issuance of writ

Judgment for possession after forfeiture of executory contract and the issuance of a writ of restitution bars any claim for money payments that would have become due under the contract subsequent to the issuance of the writ.—Van Elsacker v. Erzberger, 137 Mich. App. 552, 357 N.W.2d 891 (1984).

1046. MCLS § 600.5750.

1047. MCLS § 600.5747.

1048. MCLS § 600.5759.

1049. MCLS § 600.5744.

Geno Enterprises v. Newstar Energy USA, Inc., 2003 Mich. App. LEXIS 1341 (Mich. Ct. App. June 5, 2003).

Day v. Lacchia, 175 Mich. App. 363, 437 N.W.2d 400 (1989).

Summary eviction

A summary eviction judgment *must* state the amount of past-due rent that, if timely paid, will allow a defendant to remain in possession of the premises. But unlike an ordinary damages award,

and unlike the award of costs, the amount of past-due rent is not a judgment for damages enforceable by a writ of execution.—1300 LaFayette East Coop., Inc. v. Savoy, 284 Mich. App. 522, 773 N.W.2d 57, 2009 Mich. App. LEXIS 1377 (2009).

1050. MCLS § 600.5744.

Entingh v. Grooters, 236 Mich. App. 458, 600 N.W.2d 415 (1999).

1051. Entingh v. Grooters, 236 Mich. App. 458, 600 N.W.2d 415 (1999).

1052. MCLS § 600.5744.

Redemption is absolute

Notice of forfeiture required to be sent by land contract vendor as condition precedent to commencement of proceedings under summary proceedings statute is insufficient to support eviction and does not preclude purchaser from statutory right to cure default at any time during proceedings and as late as six months thereafter under certain circumstances.—Gruskin v. Fisher, 405 Mich. 51, 273 N.W.2d 893 (1979).

1053. Pankey v. New Century Mortg. Corp., 392 B.R. 710, 2008 U.S. Dist. LEXIS 64678 (E.D. Mich. 2008).

vendee needs to pay only the amount of the judgment to preclude the issuance of the writ of restitution. While some other non-monetary material breach, as specified in the judgment for possession, might need to be cured to preclude the issuance of a writ of restitution, the amount specified in the judgment is the only monetary payment that needs to be made to preclude the issuance of a writ of restitution in a land contract forfeiture proceeding. The failure to make monthly payments during the redemption period is not a material breach sufficient to justify issuance of the writ of restitution.[1054]

The mailing of a personal check in the amount due on the last day provided for payment constitutes payment of judgment within the time prescribed within the meaning of the statute providing that a writ of restitution in summary proceedings to recover real property may not issue on a judgment of possession for nonpayment of money owed by a defaulting land contract vendee if, "within time provided," amount of judgment is "paid" to the vendor.[1055] On the other hand, the land contract vendee's placement of the default amount in escrow with a title insurer is only an offer of tender, not an unconditional tender of funds to the vendor, and thus does not constitute a redemption.[1056]

This right to redeem is entirely statutory in nature and cannot be diminished by either express or implied terms of the contract purporting to determine what constitutes "paid" or "within time provided."[1057]

The vendor is not required to give the vendee any notice of the expiration of the statutory period for redemption.[1058] On the other hand, the vendor may not wrongfully prevent or reject tender. The vendor's action in that regard supports a cause of action to enforce the vendee's right of redemption under the executory land contract.[1059]

Flynn v. Korneffel, 451 Mich. 186, 547 N.W.2d 249 (1996) (deposit with title insurer is not tender).

Lamberton Group v. J.S. Realty, Inc., 2000 Mich. App. LEXIS 2242 (Mich. Ct. App. May 30, 2000).

Karakas v. Dost, 67 Mich. App. 161, 240 N.W.2d 743 (1976).

Checks payable to vendor and mortgagee

A defaulting vendee on a land contract has redeemed his interest as required by the summary proceedings statute for the recovery of possession of premises where the defaulting vendee has offered to pay the vendor through checks remitted by a purchaser from the defaulting vendee and payable to the mortgagee of the property as well as to the vendor, thereby permitting the defaulting vendee to make the vendor whole while protecting the defaulting vendee's equity in the subject property.—Tenney v. Springer, 121 Mich. App. 47, 328 N.W.2d 566 (1982).

1054. Wilson v. Taylor, 457 Mich. 232, 577 N.W.2d 100 (1998).

Richard v. 380 Fair Assocs., 2006 Mich. App. LEXIS 2518 (Mich. Ct. App. Aug. 15, 2006).

1055. Birznieks v. Cooper, 405 Mich. 319, 275 N.W.2d 221 (1979).

1056. Flynn v. Korneffel, 451 Mich. 186, 547 N.W.2d 249 (1996).

Alternative Solutions Of Kalamazoo v. Cooper, 2003 Mich. App. LEXIS 2627 (Mich. Ct. App. Oct. 21, 2003).

1057. Birznieks v. Cooper, 405 Mich. 319, 275 N.W.2d 221 (1979).

1058. Pappas v. Harrah, 221 Mich. 460, 191 N.W. 221 (1922) (decided under prior statute).

1059. Manuel v. Atlas Mortg. Corp., 1996 Mich. App. LEXIS 815 (Mich. Ct. App. Nov. 1, 1996).

Karakas v. Dost, 67 Mich. App. 161, 240 N.W.2d 743 (1976).

No prevention of redemption shown

Land contract vendors did not fraudulently prevent redemption where vendee disclosed details of redemption on last day of redemption period and where vendors were unintentionally unavailable, but prepared to accept redemption money if ten-

The issuance of the writ of restitution, including after vendee's failure to pay in full or cure completely within the statutory redemption period, bars all equitable right of redemption on an executory contract for the sale of real property.[1060] In summary proceedings to recover real property, a writ of restitution may not issue pursuant to a judgment for possession because of the land contract vendee's nonpayment of money if, within the time prescribed by the statute, the amount of the judgment is paid to the vendor.[1061]

§ 610.   Lien

A vendor may have either an express or an implied lien on the land for the purchase money even if he or she has taken no security. It is not even an equitable lien until declared and established by judicial decree.

A vendor may have an express lien on the land for the purchase money, which is a lien by contract and not by implication; or, independently of contract, the vendor may have a lien implied in equity if he or she has taken no security.[1062] Thus, as a rule, a court hearing a case in equity will raise an implied vendor's lien in favor of a vendor who has conveyed legal title without taking security for the unpaid purchase price.[1063] The vendor's right to a lien is not confined to cases in which

dered.—Flynn v. Korneffel, 451 Mich. 186, 547 N.W.2d 249 (1996).

Performance not excused

Performance could not be excused on the ground that appellants tried to tender payment but were prevented from doing so by appellees' refusal to attend the scheduled closing in October 1998 for the property. As the party having the burden of proof on this issue, it was incumbent on appellants to at least set forth specific facts showing a genuine issue of material fact for trial on this issue in the trial court. The appellants failed to meet their burden to show a genuine issue of material fact.—A & E Holdings v. Consumers Petroleum Profit Sharing Trust, a/k/a C & F Admin. Trust, Consumers Petroleum Emples. Retirement Trust, C & F Holding Corp., C & F Liquidating Trust, William Feldman, & Doreen Carroll, Personal Representative of the Estate of Frank Carroll, 2003 Mich. App. LEXIS 519 (Mich. Ct. App. Feb. 25, 2003).

1060. MCLS § 600.5744.

1061. Birznieks v. Cooper, 405 Mich. 319, 275 N.W.2d 221 (1979).

1062. Lyon v. Clark, 132 Mich. 521, 94 N.W. 4 (1903).

Curtis v. Clarke, 113 Mich. 458, 71 N.W. 845 (1897).

Reliance on lien

A vendor's lien on the sale of land is based on an implied agreement, and the circumstances of the sale must show that it was the intention of the

parties that the sale was made and credit given for the purchase price in reliance on the lien.— Richards v. Lewis L. Arms Shingle & Lumber Co., 74 Mich. 57, 41 N.W. 860 (1889).

1063. Vereyken v. Annie's Place, Inc., 1990 U.S. Dist. LEXIS 6431 (E.D. Mich. May 16, 1990), aff'd, 964 F.2d 593 (6th Cir. Mich. 1992) (Sixth Circuit Court of Appeals explained on appeal that the vendor's interest is much greater than a lien; in Michigan, the vendor under a land contract for the sale of real property retains legal title to the real property subject to an equitable obligation to convey legal title to the vendee upon full payment of the purchase money).

Paternoster v. Van Meaghen, 298 Mich. 274, 299 N.W. 80 (1941) (part of purchase price).

Berberian v. Guaranty Trust Co., 257 Mich. 159, 241 N.W. 149 (1932).

Donovan v. Donovan, 85 Mich. 63, 48 N.W. 163 (1891).

Dunton v. Outhouse, 64 Mich. 419, 31 N.W. 411 (1887).

Sokolowski v. Peoples Sav. & Loan Ass'n, 23 Mich. App. 609, 179 N.W.2d 197 (1970).

Balance of purchase price

Under agreement to sell certain lot and erect dwelling house on it, vendor is entitled to lien for balance of purchase price, even though he gave deed to premises before erection of dwelling house was complete.—Shaw v. Tabor, 146 Mich. 544, 109 N.W. 1046 (1906).

there is a sale of the legal title, but extends also to sales of an equitable right or interest.[1064]

The lien of the grantor after conveyance is a mere equitable charge on the land. Strictly speaking, it is not even an equitable lien until declared and established by judicial decree.[1065] The vendor's lien is in the nature of a mortgage and must be for a certain amount known to exist at the time of its creation.[1066] It can exist only as collateral to a debt created simultaneously with the sale.[1067] No lien will be implied when it is impossible to state the amount of the purchase price of the land,[1068] or when there are no equities in favor of the vendors justifying implication of a lien.[1069]

One furnishing purchase money. A person who has furnished another with the money with which to buy land may, where such other fails to comply with the agreement to give a mortgage, be entitled to a vendor's lien on the land.[1070]

Amount and extent of lien. Generally, a vendor's lien will not be extended to cover estimated damages resulting from fraudulent misrepresentations by the purchaser.[1071] In the absence of an agreement to that effect, the vendor will acquire no lien on personal property that the purchaser, on taking possession, moves onto the

Well-settled doctrine

The doctrine is well settled that a vendor of land, if he has taken no security, although he has made an absolute conveyance by deed, acknowledging full payment of the consideration, yet retains an equitable lien for the purchase money, unless there be an express or implied waiver and discharge of it.—Brown v. Porter, 2 Mich. N.P. 12 (1870).

1064. Lavin v. Lynch, 203 Mich. 143, 168 N.W. 1024 (1918).

Ortman v. Plummer, 52 Mich. 76, 17 N.W. 703, 1883 Mich. LEXIS 460 (1883).

1065. Lutz v. Dutmer, 286 Mich. 467, 282 N.W. 431 (1938).

1066. Equitable mortgages, *see, infra,* Chapter 24.

Balow v. Teutonia Farmers' Mut. Fire Ins. Co., 77 Mich. 540, 43 N.W. 924 (1889).

1067. Palmer v. Sterling, 41 Mich. 218, 2 N.W. 24 (1879).

1068. Warner v. Bliven, 127 Mich. 665, 87 N.W. 49 (1901).

Hiscock v. Norton, 42 Mich. 320, 3 N.W. 868 (1879).

1069. Dunton v. Outhouse, 64 Mich. 419, 31 N.W. 411 (1887) (lien denied where transaction tainted with fraud).

Hiscock v. Norton, 42 Mich. 320, 3 N.W. 868 (1879).

Palmer v. Sterling, 41 Mich. 218, 2 N.W. 24 (1879) (no lien in case of gift of land).

"Purchaser" ignorant of transactionA person cannot become a purchaser by a transaction of which he is wholly ignorant, nor can there be, as against him, a vendor's lien for a purchase price that he never agreed to pay.—Weare v. Linnell, 29 Mich. 224 (1874).

Payne v. Avery, 21 Mich. 524 (1870).

1070. Williams v. Rice, 60 Mich. 102, 26 N.W. 846 (1886).

Promise of mortgage

Where one party advances money to another on faith of verbal agreement by the latter to secure its payment by a mortgage upon certain lands, which is not executed, or which, if executed, is so defective or informal as to fall short of being a duly executed mortgage, lien impressed by equity on such land in favor of the creditor who advances the money attaches on the advancement thereof, and for the same length of time as the debt, and waiver may not be implied from the act of the creditor in receiving a mortgage which is ineffective as a specific lien, nor is the equitable mortgage merged in such instrument subsequently executed.—Schram v. Burt, 111 F.2d 557 (6th Cir. Mich. 1940).

1071. Value of personality given as payment

Where vendor agrees to accept chattels in payment of price, he cannot affirm contract, and maintain lien for deficiency arising from failure of property given him to equal its represented value, on theory that to that extent consideration was not paid.—Graham v. Moffett, 119 Mich. 303, 78 N.W. 132 (1899).

premises.[1072]

Priority. A vendor's lien has priority over assignees in bankruptcy or a general assignee for the benefit of creditors.[1073]

§ 611.   —Assignment

A vendor's lien is assignable. The assignee of a vendor's interest in an executory contract may sue at law or may foreclose the vendor's lien.

A vendor's lien is assignable.[1074] But if a vendor under an executory contract for the sale of land trades his or her rights to another, that party may become the owner of the contract with the power to enforce it only on a conveyance to that party of the property and assignment of the contract.[1075] The assignee of a vendor's interest in an executory contract may sue at law or may foreclose the vendor's lien.[1076]

The vendor's assignee takes subject to all defenses existing between the original parties.[1077] The rights and liabilities of the assignee are adjusted in accordance with the equities of the case.[1078]

§ 612.   —Termination

A vendor's lien may be terminated by express release or by waiver. The vendee's final payment of the debt upon which a vendor's lien is based extinguishes the vendor's lien.

The vendee's final payment of the debt upon which a vendor's lien is based extinguishes the vendor's lien.[1079]

1072. Midland County Sav. Bank v. T.C. Prouty Co., 158 Mich. 656, 123 N.W. 549 (1909).

1073. Lyon v. Clark, 132 Mich. 521, 94 N.W. 4 (1903).

1074. Lavin v. Lynch, 203 Mich. 143, 168 N.W. 1024 (1918).

1075. Jackson v. West, 224 Mich. 578, 194 N.W. 1000 (1923).

1076. Mortgage & Contract Co. v. Linenberg, 260 Mich. 142, 244 N.W. 428 (1932) (option to proceed in equity).

Assignee had no lien under vendor's contract

Where an executory contract for the sale of land did not provide for forfeiture, and created no lien for the unpaid purchase money, and no security therefor except insurance on the buildings, the demand of the vendor's assignee holding the legal title is based on an ordinary money debt secured by the contract.—Midland County Sav. Bank v. T.C. Prouty Co., 158 Mich. 656, 123 N.W. 549 (1909).

1077. Peterson v. Poloms, 250 Mich. 311, 230 N.W. 184 (1930) (fraud).

Quail v. Wayne Circuit Judge, 249 Mich. 425, 228 N.W. 775 (1930).

1078. Worsham v. McCall, 262 Mich. 154, 247 N.W. 181 (1933).

Rosenthal v. Wilson, 244 Mich. 220, 221 N.W. 177 (1928) (liability for deductions).

Nowatarski v. Dusza, 218 Mich. 443, 188 N.W. 369 (1922).

Warden v. Sawyer, 215 Mich. 250, 183 N.W. 911 (1921).

1079. In re Dukes, 24 B.R. 404, 1982 Bankr. LEXIS 2991 (Bankr. E.D. Mich. 1982).

Thomas v. Dutkavich, 2010 Mich. App. LEXIS 2049 (Mich. Ct. App. Oct. 28, 2010).

See Vereyken v. Annie's Place, Inc., 964 F.2d 593 (6th Cir. Mich. 1992) (stating that the term "vendor's lien" is far from accurate since the legal title held by the vendor under the doctrine of

A vendor's lien may be lost by an express release of it.[1080] The vendor may also waive it,[1081] or abandon it by conduct inconsistent with retention of the lien,[1082] such as by taking an independent security for payment of the purchase price.[1083]

On the other hand, if the circumstances are consistent with retention of the lien, no waiver occurs.[1084] Thus, the vendor does not lose the lien by taking an unsecured note[1085] or bond[1086] of the vendee for the purchase price, or by exhausting his or her remedies at law.[1087] Moreover, waiver of the lien cannot be inferred from the fact that the parties may not have contemplated an assertion of the lien in the first instance.[1088]

§ 613.   —Enforcement of Lien

A vendor's lien may be enforced in the same manner that an equitable mortgage may be enforced. Thus, the usual mode of enforcing a vendor's lien in equity is by a sale of the property to which it is attached.

Generally, a vendor's lien may be enforced in the same manner that an equitable mortgage[1089] may be enforced.[1090] The long-standing rule allows fore-closure of equitable mortgages by complaint for judicial sale.[1091] Thus, the usual

---

equitable conversion is "clearly a much greater estate than a lien").

1080. Sloan v. Holcomb, 29 Mich. 153 (1874) (one holding vendor's lien may release lien, and hold only personal securities to which it is collateral).

Termination by release not shown

McClure v. Edward J. Meyer Southfield Woods Corp., 254 Mich. 686, 236 N.W. 907 (1931).

MacLeod v. Hamilton, 254 Mich. 653, 236 N.W. 912 (1931).

Pine Shores Realty Co. v. Parker, 253 Mich. 300, 235 N.W. 163 (1931).

1081. Baker v. Lambers, 261 Mich. 86, 245 N.W. 578 (1933).

Donovan v. Donovan, 85 Mich. 63, 48 N.W. 163 (1891).

1082. Baker v. Lambers, 261 Mich. 86, 245 N.W. 578 (1933) (accepting surrender of vendees' rights).

Alienation not bar after reconveyance

The alienation by a vendor, subject to a contract to convey, is no bar to vendor's suit to foreclose lien after a reconveyance to him or her.—Jones v. Bowling, 117 Mich. 288, 75 N.W. 611 (1898).

1083. Ortman v. Plummer, 52 Mich. 76, 17 N.W. 703, 1883 Mich. LEXIS 460 (1883) (mortgage).

In re Palmer, 1 Doug. 422 (Mich. 1844).

Sears v. Smith, 2 Mich. 243 (1851) (taking obligation of third person).

1084. Lyon v. Clark, 132 Mich. 521, 94 N.W. 4 (1903).

Curtis v. Clarke, 113 Mich. 458, 71 N.W. 845 (1897).

Berberian v. Guaranty Trust Co., 257 Mich. 159, 241 N.W. 149 (1932) (vendor's intention not to assert lien did not afford evidence of waiver).

Schmidt v. Gaukler, 156 Mich. 243, 120 N.W. 746 (1909) (supplemental agreement did not show waiver where expressly providing to contrary).

1085. Berberian v. Guaranty Trust Co., 257 Mich. 159, 241 N.W. 149 (1932).

Lyon v. Clark, 132 Mich. 521, 94 N.W. 4 (1903).

Allowance of note against decedent's estate

Vendor's lien was not waived by securing allowance of note for balance of purchase price against deceased purchaser's estate.—Berberian v. Guaranty Trust Co., 257 Mich. 159, 241 N.W. 149 (1932).

1086. Brown v. Porter, 2 Mich. N.P. 12 (1870).

1087. Pariseau v. Trinity Bldg. Co., 254 Mich. 213, 236 N.W. 239 (1931).

Zeigler v. Valley Coal Co., 150 Mich. 82, 113 N.W. 775 (1907) (vendor, by exhausting his remedy at law, in suit to recover debt, does not waive lien, but may thereafter enforce lien in equity).

1088. Berberian v. Guaranty Trust Co., 257 Mich. 159, 241 N.W. 149 (1932).

1089. Equitable mortgages, *see, infra,* Chapter 23.

mode of enforcing a vendor's lien in equity is by a sale of the property to which it is attached.[1092]

The enforcement of a vendor's lien is peculiarly within the equitable jurisdiction of a court.[1093] A vendor's lien may be enforced by the vendor although the vendor still retains the legal title to the property.[1094]

Sale under a decree foreclosing a vendor's lien passes the title to the purchaser at the sale together with all incidental rights.[1095]

The amount of the judgment or decree granted in an action to enforce a vendor's lien must be determined by the facts and circumstances involved, regard being had to equitable principles, and the rights of the parties in the particular case.[1096]

There can be no such thing as a strict foreclosure of a vendor's lien, which would cut off the right of redemption.[1097]

A vendee may be entitled to an injunction restraining enforcement of the vendor's lien on proper grounds, such as fraud or failure of consideration.[1098]

Limitations and laches. A vendor's suit to enforce the vendor's lien may be barred by limitations or laches.[1099]

Pleading. A complaint to establish and enforce a vendor's lien must set forth the essential elements of the plaintiff's cause of action, by setting forth the contract

1090. Fitzhugh v. Maxwell, 34 Mich. 138 (1876).

1091. Foreclosure by judicial sale, *see, infra,* Chapter 32.

Martin v. McReynolds, 6 Mich. 70 (1858).

1092. Mere money debt

The claim of a vendor in a land contract is but an ordinary money debt secured by the contract; and his proceedings to enforce the lien upon the land should be governed by the analogies of proceedings to enforce other equitable liens, and be executed by a sale to satisfy the amount due.—Fitzhugh v. Maxwell, 34 Mich. 138 (1876).

1093. Genyk v. Nagrich, 255 Mich. 189, 237 N.W. 525 (1931).

Craig v. Black, 249 Mich. 485, 229 N.W. 411 (1930).

Wood v. Schoolcraft, 145 Mich. 653, 108 N.W. 1075 (1906).

1094. Walker v. Casgrain, 101 Mich. 604, 60 N.W. 291 (1894).

1095. Rule applied when conveyance to third person

Where vendor of real estate sold on contract thereafter established his lien for unpaid balance of purchase price and for back taxes paid by him

and purchased premises at sale pursuant to decree establishing lien, and thereafter conveyed premises to another, that purchaser had the same right as against original purchaser as might be asserted by vendor.—Walker v. Woods, 308 Mich. 24, 13 N.W.2d 193 (1944).

1096. Wood v. Schoolcraft, 145 Mich. 653, 108 N.W. 1075 (1906) (measure of damages in case of co-tenancy).

Kulling v. Kulling, 124 Mich. 56, 82 N.W. 847 (1900) (allowance of interest).

1097. Fitzhugh v. Maxwell, 34 Mich. 138 (1876).

1098. Sufficiency of evidence

Evidence, in action by purchaser to enjoin foreclosure of land contract, was insufficient to show purchaser had been fraudulently induced to consent to vendor's giving mortgage lien superior to contract.—Shapero v. Picard, 235 Mich. 481, 209 N.W. 576 (1926).

1099. Laches not shown

Fact that suit to enforce vendor's lien was brought three years after vendor secured allowance of note for balance of purchase price against deceased purchaser's estate afforded no defense to suit, where estate was not adversely affected thereby.—Berberian v. Guaranty Trust Co., 257 Mich. 159, 241 N.W. 149 (1932).

of sale with reasonable certainty and the consideration and terms of payment.[1100] Waiver of a vendor's lien cannot be relied on unless pleaded.[1101]

Evidence. Generally, there is a presumption that the vendor has a lien on the land for unpaid and unsecured purchase money.[1102] The burden of refuting that presumption rests upon the vendee.[1103] The burden of establishing the waiver of the vendor's lien rests upon the party alleging the waiver.[1104]

One suing to enforce a vendor's lien must by clear evidence prove the contract of purchase,[1105] and the consideration and terms of payment.[1106] On the other hand, one seeking to show waiver of a vendor's lien is required to adduce clear and convincing proof of waiver.[1107]

Disposition of proceeds. The Michigan Court Rules of 1985 provide generally for the distribution of proceeds from the foreclosure of real property by judicial sale.[1108] A decree for the sale of land to satisfy a vendor's lien must allow the lienor to purchase and direct that the proceeds be applied first to payment of the debt, the costs, and the residue, if any, to be paid to the debtor. It is erroneous to order payment of the money into court to be divided between the parties as their interests may appear.[1109]

§ 614. Foreclosure of Land Contracts

The foreclosure of a land contract is conducted in the same manner as the foreclosure of a mortgage, and the general rules of procedure apply except as may otherwise be prescribed by law.

By the express terms of the Revised Judicature Act of 1961[1110] and the Michigan Court Rules of 1985,[1111] the foreclosure of a land contract is conducted in the same manner as the foreclosure of a mortgage, and the general rules of procedure apply except as may otherwise be prescribed by law.[1112] Under this law, a proceeding to foreclose a land contract is purely statutory in origin.[1113]

1100. Dunton v. Outhouse, 64 Mich. 419, 31 N.W. 411 (1887).

Mowrey v. Vandling, 9 Mich. 39 (1860).

Fraud

A bill to enforce an equitable lien for the purchase money of land, and alleging fraud, need only set forth the substance and result of the alleged fraudulent transaction.—Merrill v. Allen, 38 Mich. 487 (1878).

1101. Zeigler v. Valley Coal Co., 150 Mich. 82, 113 N.W. 775 (1907).

1102. Dunton v. Outhouse, 64 Mich. 419, 31 N.W. 411 (1887).

1103. Dunton v. Outhouse, 64 Mich. 419, 31 N.W. 411 (1887).

Sears v. Smith, 2 Mich. 243 (1851).

1104. Zeigler v. Valley Coal Co., 150 Mich. 82, 113 N.W. 775 (1907).

1105. Mowrey v. Vandling, 9 Mich. 39 (1860).

1106. Waterfield v. Wilber, 64 Mich. 642, 31 N.W. 553 (1887).

Mowrey v. Vandling, 9 Mich. 39 (1860).

1107. Zeigler v. Valley Coal Co., 150 Mich. 82, 113 N.W. 775 (1907).

1108. MCR 3.410.

1109. Johnson v. Fowler, 68 Mich. 1, 35 N.W. 764 (1888).

1110. MCLS §§ 600.3101 et seq.

1111. MCR 3.410.

1112. Foreclosure of mortgages and land contracts by judicial sale, *see, infra,* Chapter 32.

1113. Stewart v. Isbell, 155 Mich. App. 65, 399 N.W.2d 440 (1986).

The circuit courts have jurisdiction to foreclose land contracts.[1114]

Under the Revised Judicature Act of 1961, actions for foreclosure of a land contract are equitable in nature.[1115]

When a complaint is filed for the foreclosure of a land contract, the court has the power to order a sale of the premises that are the subject of the land contract or that part of the premises that is sufficient to discharge the amount due on the land contract plus costs.[1116]

No action for title to, interest in, or possession of land may be maintained for the recovery of premises sold under a land contract by a person who is entitled to foreclose the land contract.[1117]

§ 615.   Actions for Purchase Money

A vendor may sue for the remainder of a purchase price under an acceleration clause in a land contract upon fulfillment of the contractual conditions for exercising that right.

A vendor may sue for the remainder of a purchase price under an acceleration clause in a land contract upon fulfillment of the contractual conditions for exercising that right.[1118] The vendor on default by the vendee under a contract to purchase land may treat the contract as continuing in force and sue for the payments due.[1119]

Default of vendor. Where the vendor has defaulted in his or her obligations under the contract, the vendor may be denied the right to recover unpaid installments of the purchase price.[1120]

Parties. Both the purchaser under a contract for the sale of land and the

1114. Windorf v. Ferris, 154 Mich. App. 201, 397 N.W.2d 268, 1986 Mich. App. LEXIS 2819 (1986).

Minchella v. Fredericks, 138 Mich. App. 462, 360 N.W.2d 896, 1984 Mich. App. LEXIS 2970 (1984).

Bishop v. Brown, 118 Mich. App. 819, 325 N.W.2d 594 (1982).

1115. MCLS § 600.3180.

1116. Stewart v. Isbell, 155 Mich. App. 65, 399 N.W.2d 440 (1986).

1117. MCLS § 600.2932.

See, infra, Chapter 32, regarding foreclosure of mortgages and land contracts by judicial sale.

1118. Gruskin v. Fisher, 405 Mich. 51, 273 N.W.2d 893 (1979).

Crosby v. Crosby, 2000 Mich. App. LEXIS 2737 (Mich. Ct. App. Feb. 11, 2000).

Windorf v. Ferris, 154 Mich. App. 201, 397 N.W.2d 268, 1986 Mich. App. LEXIS 2819 (1986).

Bishop v. Brown, 118 Mich. App. 819, 325 N.W.2d 594 (1982).

1119. Gruskin v. Fisher, 405 Mich. 51, 273 N.W.2d 893 (1979).

Ashbaugh v. Sauer, 268 Mich. 467, 256 N.W. 486 (1934).

Chicago Boulevard Land Co. v. Apartment Garages, Inc., 245 Mich. 448, 222 N.W. 697 (1929).

Amount

Where a purchaser repudiates a land contract and the purchaser's checks aggregating $500 were given as the first payment and returned by the bank unpaid, and where the vendor resold the land for $500 less than the contract price, the vendor may not maintain an action based on the failure to pay the checks.—Epstein v. Rosenfield, 222 Mich. 358, 192 N.W. 717 (1923).

1120. Failure to pay taxes and mortgage interest

Vendor defaulting in making agreed payments of taxes and mortgage interest and principal could not recover unpaid installments on land contract.—Pack v. Mackay, 261 Mich. 348, 246 N.W. 144 (1933).

purchaser's assignee are proper parties defendant in an action to enforce payment of the purchase money.[1121]

§ 616. —Conditions Precedent

Performance of conditions precedent is essential to maintenance of an action for the purchase price.

There must be due compliance with all conditions precedent before a vendor becomes entitled to sue the vendee for the purchase money.[1122] Under a contract that fixes no time for performance of the vendor's obligations, the vendor's performance is not a condition precedent to the right to secure payments from the vendee on the date that the land contract does fix.[1123]

If the covenants in a contract for the sale of land as to payment of the purchase price and as to conveyance of title are mutual and dependent, the vendor may not maintain an action for the purchase price without first conveying or tendering a deed.[1124] If the vendee arbitrarily refuses tender of a deed and other instruments required by a contract for the sale of land, without asking for time in which to examine the documents, the tender is sufficient.[1125]

The rule requiring conveyance or tender of a deed before maintaining an action for the purchase price is a rule of procedure and not of substantive law, so that the rule applies in Michigan irrespective of the rule that may prevail in a foreign jurisdiction where the land is located.[1126]

Under a contract clearly indicating that payment of the price precedes the conveyance, the vendor may maintain an action for the price without a conveyance

---

1121. Lutz v. Dutmer, 286 Mich. 467, 282 N.W. 431 (1938).

1122. Cinderizing street

Where covenants, in contract for conveyance of realty, that vendee would pay installments of purchase price in five years and that vendor would "cinderize or gravel the streets," were dependent, vendor's failure to cinderize street in front of vendee's lot was a material breach of covenant to improve, precluding vendor's assignee from recovering balance of price of lot.—Palmer v. Fox, 274 Mich. 252, 264 N.W. 361 (1936).

Waiver of time limit

When purchaser of realty secured permits, the obtaining of which within 60 days had been condition of offer to purchase, vendors could have recovered purchase price of property if purchaser had failed to carry out contract, even though permits were secured after more than 60 days had elapsed.—Al-Oil, Inc. v. Pranger, 365 Mich. 46, 112 N.W.2d 99 (1961).

1123. Lamar v. Detroit Apartments Corp., 237 Mich. 206, 211 N.W. 643 (1927).

1124. Geel v. Valiquett, 292 Mich. 1, 289 N.W. 306 (1940).

McColl v. Wardowski, 280 Mich. 374, 273 N.W. 736 (1937).

St. John v. Richard, 272 Mich. 670, 262 N.W. 437 (1935).

Tender by vendor's assignee

A proper tender of deed by assignee of vendor's interest was necessary before an action for the balance due on a land contract could be maintained.—Bradway v. Netzorg, 298 Mich. 198, 298 N.W. 501 (1941).

1125. Bradway v. Netzorg, 298 Mich. 198, 298 N.W. 501 (1941) (deed and abstract).

1126. Geel v. Valiquett, 292 Mich. 1, 289 N.W. 306 (1940).

Canadian law inapplicable

A vendor who did not tender deed could not recover from purchasers entire balance due under executory contract for sale of land in Canada on ground that contract was governed by Canadian law and that it was unnecessary to tender deed as condition precedent to suing for balance of purchase price, since question was one of procedure or remedy and not one of substantive law, and hence law of forum prevailed.—McColl v. Wardowski, 280 Mich. 374, 273 N.W. 736 (1937).

or tender.[1127] If the vendees suing to recover payments made an attempt to rescind on the ground of failure of consideration, the vendor is not required to tender a deed as a condition precedent to suing for recovery of the balance due on the purchase price.[1128]

§ 617.   —Defenses

Rescission or repossession upon forfeiture of the contract affords a good defense to an action for the purchase money, and fraud, illegality, or a defect in title may also constitute a valid defense to such an action.

It is a good defense to the vendor's action for the purchase price that the contract has been rescinded.[1129] The vendee may also raise the defense that the vendor has regained possession under a writ of possession following a forfeiture of the contract to the vendor.[1130]

Vendors are not entitled to money deposited under a contract for the sale of land after the deal has fallen through and they have sold the property putting it out of their power to convey.[1131] However, the fact that the vendors are in default in mortgage payments does not defeat recovery of installments due under a contract from a vendee who is responsible for the default.[1132] Similarly, the breach of a broker's promise to resell a lot within a specified time affords no defense to the vendee when sued by the vendor for overdue installments on the contract.[1133]

That the vendor knows that the vendee's use of the property is illegal is not a defense to the vendor's action.[1134]

Defect in title. A defect in, or failure of, title ordinarily affords a defense to an action for the purchase money.[1135] However, if the vendor has a good title at the time fixed for performance, it is no defense that he or she lacked good title at the time of execution of the contract.[1136] Moreover, the vendee may not properly complain of a defect in title due to the vendee's fault.[1137]

Estoppel or laches. A vendee may lose the right to interpose a defense because

---

1127. Loud v. Pomona Land & Water Co., 153 U.S. 564, 14 S. Ct. 928, 38 L. Ed. 822 (1894).

1128. Robinson v. Grosse Pointe Shores Realty Co., 281 Mich. 184, 274 N.W. 758 (1937).

1129. Ives v. Bank of Lansingburg, 12 Mich. 361 (1864) (rescission by taking release from vendee).

1130. Gruskin v. Fisher, 405 Mich. 51, 273 N.W.2d 893 (1979).

1131. Bushaw v. Darling, 227 Mich. 383, 198 N.W. 883 (1924).

1132. Dibble v. Harrow, 262 Mich. 509, 247 N.W. 732 (1933).

1133. Cavanaugh v. Van Dam, 264 Mich. 383, 249 N.W. 880 (1933).

1134. Mere knowledge of illegal intent

Mere knowledge on the part of the vendor that his vendee at the time of the purchase of property intends to use it for an illegal purpose will not prevent his recovering from the vendee the value of the property.—Webber v. Donnelly, 33 Mich. 469 (1876).

1135. Redding v. Lamb, 81 Mich. 318, 45 N.W. 997 (1890) (where there is failure of title to lands, a breach of covenant of seizin may be set up as defense to action for purchase money).

1136. Rogers v. Eaton, 181 Mich. 620, 148 N.W. 348 (1914).

1137. Dibble v. Harrow, 262 Mich. 509, 247 N.W. 732 (1933).

Sale for taxes

The purchaser cannot interpose as a defense that taxes levied subsequent to the making of the

of estoppel[1138] or laches.[1139]

Setoff or recoupment; fraud. In a proper case, a vendee sued for the purchase money may set off or recoup damages that the vendee has sustained.[1140] It is not essential to the vendee's right of setoff or recoupment for fraud of the vendor that the vendee offers or has the right to rescind.[1141] However, the right of the vendee to recoup an excess in price due to the vendor's misrepresentation concerning the property is defeated if the misrepresentation is not willful.[1142]

Misrepresentations by a co-vendee do not entitle the vendee to interpose fraud as a defense to the vendor's action for the purchase money.[1143]

§ 618.   —Trial and Evidence

On the trial of an action for purchase money, the instructions must state the law correctly and conform to the issues and proof, and any competent evidence is admissible where relevant and material to the issues involved.

On the trial of an action for the purchase money, the instructions must state the law correctly and conform to the issues and proof.[1144] On conflicting evidence, the questions of fact are for the determination of the jury.[1145]

Evidence. In an action for the purchase price of land, competent evidence that is relevant and material to the issues involved is admissible.[1146] The deed must be introduced in evidence when the vendor seeks recovery for an alleged excess in the quantity of land conveyed by a contract for sale of real property.[1147]

The weight and sufficiency of the evidence adduced in actions for the purchase

---

contract that he had duty to pay, had not been paid, and that land had been sold and a tax deed given for it.—Pringle v. Wagnoer, 110 Mich. 612, 68 N.W. 423 (1896).

1138. Manley v. Saunders, 27 Mich. 347 (1873).

Morman v. Harrington, 118 Mich. 623, 77 N.W. 242 (1898) (estoppel not shown).

1139. Cavanaugh v. Van Dam, 264 Mich. 383, 249 N.W. 880 (1933) (five years' delay in asserting fraud).

1140. Dickenson v. Wright, 56 Mich. 42, 22 N.W. 312 (1885) (in action for unpaid balance on land contract, it is proper to show, by way of recoupment, that, in consequence of institution of suit involving validity of plaintiff's title, payments were deferred by mutual agreement, and that meanwhile timber on land was so far destroyed by fire as to lessen value of land).

1141. Sloman v. Allen, 252 Mich. 578, 233 N.W. 421 (1930).

Morman v. Harrington, 118 Mich. 623, 77 N.W. 242 (1898).

1142. Baughman v. Gould, 45 Mich. 481, 8 N.W. 73 (1881).

1143. Stevens v. Stott, 270 Mich. 637, 259 N.W. 157 (1935).

1144. Dikeman v. Arnold, 71 Mich. 656, 40 N.W. 42 (1888) (erroneous to omit defendant's theory).

1145. Morman v. Harrington, 118 Mich. 623, 77 N.W. 242 (1898).

1146. Real Property Law: Real Evidence: Special Rules for Real Estate Disputes, 80 Mich. B.J. 28 (2001).

Fraudulent representations

Defendant could show fraudulent representations by persons other than vendor, where jury were instructed that, unless defendant relied solely on false representations by vendor, vendor could recover.—Morman v. Harrington, 118 Mich. 623, 77 N.W. 242 (1898).

Record of suit for possession

The record in suit for possession of real property under forfeiture of executory land contract is admissible as evidence in action on note for price of land.—Reeves v. Kelly, 30 Mich. 132 (1874).

1147. Lewis v. Pond, 45 Mich. 46, 7 N.W. 236 (1880).

price to establish various issues involved in the case are determined in compliance with the general rules.[1148]

§ 619.   —Amount of Recovery

Generally, a vendor suing for the purchase price of property may recover the amount due under the contract less any deductions to which the vendee may be entitled.

Generally, the amount recoverable in an action for the purchase money depends on the terms of the contract or other instrument on which the action is brought. A vendor affirming the contract and suing for the purchase money is entitled to recover whatever amount is due under it.[1149]

In determining the amount due, the court will deduct credits to which the purchaser is entitled, such as payments or amounts assumed on account of the purchase price.[1150]

§ 620.   Actions for Damages

A vendor may choose to maintain an action for damages against a vendee failing or refusing to perform the vendee's obligations under the contract.

A vendor may choose to maintain an action for damages against a vendee failing or refusing to perform the vendee's part of the contract for sale of real property.[1151] Accordingly, the vendor may claim breach of contract where nonpayment constitutes breach under the terms of a contract for sale of real property.[1152] In

---

1148. Newman v. Banker, 131 Mich. 89, 90 N.W. 1027 (1902) (evidence was sufficient to show that bank to which defendants made payment for land purchased from plaintiff was acting as latter's agent).

1149. Scott v. Tierney, 263 Mich. 136, 248 N.W. 573 (1933) (whole amount due following default as to installments).

Rogers v. Eaton, 181 Mich. 620, 148 N.W. 348 (1914) (recovery of interest).

Computation in case of fraud

Where a vendor of land agrees to accept in payment stock owned by the vendee, at the price paid for it by him, and the vendee misrepresents the price paid, the vendor may treat the difference between the price actually paid by the vendee for the stock and that at which he accepted it from him as the balance due on the purchase, and maintain assumpsit for its recovery.—Hidey v. Swan, 111 Mich. 161, 69 N.W. 225 (1896).

Judgment as not excessive

In action by buyer against seller for damages for the sale to buyer of a herd of cattle infected with Bangs disease, wherein defendants brought a cross-action for the balance due on the purchase

price of dairy farm, cattle, and equipment, in the sum of $10,093.59, net judgment of $5,550 for defendants after reduction by a remittitur was not excessive.—Hoekzema v. Van Haften, 320 Mich. 683, 31 N.W.2d 841 (1948).

1150. Nugent v. Teachout, 67 Mich. 571, 35 N.W. 254 (1887).

1151. Gruskin v. Fisher, 405 Mich. 51, 273 N.W.2d 893 (1979).

Spangler v. Carlisle, 70 Mich. App. 288, 245 N.W.2d 720 (1976).

After retaking possession

Under a contract for the sale of realty, providing that on failure of the vendee to perform the contract the vendor shall have the right to declare the same void, retain whatever has been paid thereon, and retake possession, where the vendee has abandoned the contract, and the vendor has retaken possession, the latter may maintain an action for damages for the breach of contract.— Allen v. Mohn, 86 Mich. 328, 49 N.W. 52 (1891).

1152. Pleadings adequate

Vendors adequately pled breach of contract by purchasers regarding land sale contract, where

addition, the vendor may recover damages for the vendee's continued occupancy between the notice of forfeiture and the issuance of writ of restitution in summary proceedings for possession following the forfeiture of an executory land contract.[1153] Furthermore, the vendor may sue for damages resulting from the purchaser's breach of the agreement to turn over, as part of the purchase price, notes of the vendor that are held by the vendee.[1154]

A vendor may sue for damages under an acceleration clause of a land contract so long as the conditions precedent stated in the contract are fulfilled.[1155]

On the other hand, the ending of the vendor's rights to acquire title by virtue of a time limitation in a contract with the owner of the property, and the subsequent acquisition of title by the vendee directly from the owner, do not confer on the vendor a right to maintain an action for breach of contract on the ground that the vendor was wrongfully deprived of profits that would have resulted from consummation of the real estate transaction.[1156]

§ 621.   —Trial and Evidence

The instructions in a vendor's action for damages must conform to the issues and proof, and the vendor may have to prove the ability to perform his or her part of the contract and prove the damages that the vendor seeks to recover.

If a vendor sues for damages on the vendee's default and no evidence of the value of the land is offered, the court may properly direct a verdict in favor of the defendant vendee.[1157]

While there is some authority that the vendor must tender a deed before

---

contract, incorporated by reference in complaint, indicated that failure of purchasers to make monthly payments constituted nonperformance of obligation due, even though personal liability of purchasers was nonexistent.—Woody v. Tamer, 158 Mich. App. 764, 405 N.W.2d 213 (1987).

1153. Visuron Ltd. P'ship v. Corcoran (In re Casa Colonial Ltd P'ship), 375 B.R. 779, 2007 U.S. Dist. LEXIS 56956 (E.D. Mich. 2007)

Ames v. Maxson, 157 Mich. App. 75, 403 N.W.2d 501, 1987 Mich. App. LEXIS 2283 (1987).

Durda v. Chembar Development Corp., 95 Mich. App. 706, 291 N.W.2d 179 (1980).

1154. Transfer to stranger

Where a grantor conveys land in consideration of a certain sum in cash and all of the notes that he has made to the grantee, and the grantee without the knowledge of the grantor, omits from the list of notes one which he had transferred to a stranger, the grantor may sue to recover the value of the outstanding note.—Reed v. Reed, 108 Mich. 498, 66 N.W. 381 (1896).

1155. Forfeiture

Under a land contract providing that once default occurred vendor has the right to immediate possession and that the vendor may, "without notice to purchaser," declare all unpaid money remaining under contract forthwith due and payable, acceleration of payment due from purchasers is proper upon vendor's notice of intention demanding payment in full of all past-due payments and declaring that if payments were not made forfeiture would be declared.—Reinecke v. Sheehy, 47 Mich. App. 250, 209 N.W.2d 460 (1973).

1156. Home Farm Corp. v. Simi, 293 Mich. 683, 292 N.W. 529 (1940).

1157. McColl v. Wardowski, 280 Mich. 374, 273 N.W. 736 (1937).

McNeal v. Tuori, 107 Mich. App. 141, 309 N.W.2d 588 (1981).

bringing a suit for damages,[1158] and that the failure to tender is grounds for directed verdict,[1159] there is other authority to the effect that no tender of a deed is necessary,[1160] and no showing of ability to perform is required.[1161] Other authority provides for different measures of damages depending on whether the vendee has title or not.[1162]

The vendor must prove the damages that he or she seeks to recover.[1163] If the vendor establishes the breach of contract and damages, the factfinder has a duty to weigh the evidence and, if possible, make a reasonable determination of damages.[1164] Immaterial matters need not be proved.[1165]

In a situation where the damages are measured by the difference between the contract price and the market value of the property, the vendor has the burden of proving the market value of the property at the time of breach.[1166] Determination of the market value of the real property must include consideration of possible market changes due to economic conditions between the breach and subsequent resale unless the sale occurred proximately to the breach. A plaintiff in an action for damages for breach of a contract to purchase real property need not pinpoint the market value of the property at the exact moment of breach. Evidence of the proximity of the contract offer, listing price, or opinion of market value to the time of the breach, the source of that evidence, and the resale price may be considered by the trier of fact in determining the market value.[1167]

If evidence of the resale price is the only evidence of market value, the plaintiff has the burden of establishing that the resale occurred within a reasonable time, at the highest price obtainable, under terms as favorable as the original contract, and that there has not been a decline in market value.[1168]

The instructions in a vendor's suit for damages must conform to the issues and evidence in the case and submit to the jury all issues of fact proper for their

1158. Roycraft v. Northville Six Mile Co., 358 Mich. 466, 100 N.W.2d 223 (1960).

Home Farm Corp. v. Simi, 293 Mich. 683, 292 N.W. 529 (1940) (by conveying title).

1159. McColl v. Wardowski, 280 Mich. 374, 273 N.W. 736 (1937).

1160. McColl v. Wardowski, 280 Mich. 374, 273 N.W. 736 (1937).

Stewart v. McLaughlin's Estate, 126 Mich. 1, 85 N.W. 266 (1901).

Greenbrier Homes v. Cook, 1 Mich. App. 326, 136 N.W.2d 27 (1965).

1161. McColl v. Wardowski, 280 Mich. 374, 273 N.W. 736 (1937).

Stewart v. McLaughlin's Estate, 126 Mich. 1, 85 N.W. 266 (1901).

Greenbrier Homes v. Cook, 1 Mich. App. 326, 136 N.W.2d 27 (1965).

1162. *See, infra,* § 622.

1163. McLeod v. Hunt, 128 Mich. 124, 87 N.W. 101 (1901).

1164. Oakwood of Cambridge v. Kapsa, 2010 Mich. App. LEXIS 932 (Mich. Ct. App. May 20, 2010).

McNeal v. Tuori, 107 Mich. App. 141, 309 N.W.2d 588 (1981).

1165. Clemens v. Conrad, 19 Mich. 170 (1869).

1166. Oakwood of Cambridge v. Kapsa, 2010 Mich. App. LEXIS 932 (Mich. Ct. App. May 20, 2010).

McNeal v. Tuori, 107 Mich. App. 141, 309 N.W.2d 588 (1981).

1167. McNeal v. Tuori, 107 Mich. App. 141, 309 N.W.2d 588 (1981).

1168. McNeal v. Tuori, 107 Mich. App. 141, 309 N.W.2d 588 (1981).

consideration and supported by the evidence.[1169]

§ 622. —Amount of Recovery

If the vendor has not tendered a deed, the measure of the vendor's damages for the vendee's breach is the difference between the amount agreed to be paid and the market value of the land at the time of breach. If the vendee has been put into possession and the vendor has tendered a deed, the measure of damages is the full purchase price less whatever has been paid on account.

The question of tender in a suit for damages on a defaulted land contract directly affects the amount of recovery.[1170] If the vendor has not tendered a deed before bringing suit for the vendee's failure to perform a land contract, the measure of damages is the difference between the amount due on the contract and the value of the land at the time that the vendee breaches the contract.[1171] Where, however, the vendee has been put into possession and the vendor has tendered a proper deed, the measure of damages is the purchase price that the vendee is to pay under the contract.[1172]

Where the vendee abandons the contract, the measure of damages is the difference between the contract price and the value of the land at the time of abandonment and re-entry, less whatever has been paid.[1173]

Consequential damages for breach of a contract to purchase real property may be recovered in addition to general damages where the damage was foreseeable and was a natural consequence of the breach.[1174]

But if the contract is terminated by forfeiture, the vendor may not recover as damages the compensation that the vendor paid his or her agents for negotiating the contract.[1175]

1169. When request properly refused

In an action for the value of land that plaintiffs allege defendant agreed to exchange for land conveyed by them, where issue of delivery and acceptance of plaintiffs' deed at the time alleged is fairly submitted to the jury, it is proper to refuse to charge that the action is for the price of defendant's land, and not for damages for his not conveying, and that the fact that he contracted to convey and then refused would not sustain the action; if plaintiffs' deed was accepted, the contract, which specifies the purchase price, is material.—Dikeman v. Arnold, 78 Mich. 455, 44 N.W. 407 (1889).

1170. McColl v. Wardowski, 280 Mich. 374, 273 N.W. 736 (1937).

1171. Roycraft v. Northville Six Mile Co., 358 Mich. 466, 100 N.W.2d 223 (1960).

McColl v. Wardowski, 280 Mich. 374, 273 N.W. 736 (1937).

St. John v. Richard, 272 Mich. 670, 262 N.W. 437 (1935).

McNeal v. Tuori, 107 Mich. App. 141, 309 N.W.2d 588 (1981).

MacRitchie v. Plumb, 70 Mich. App. 242, 245 N.W.2d 582 (1976).

Carter v. Reaume, 159 Mich. 160, 123 N.W. 539 (1909) (rule applied in action by assignee).

1172. Curran v. Rogers, 35 Mich. 221 (1876).

1173. Allen v. Mohn, 86 Mich. 328, 49 N.W. 52 (1891).

1174. McNeal v. Tuori, 107 Mich. App. 141, 309 N.W.2d 588 (1981).

Cost of survey, abstract, and attorney fees, but not interest on purchase price

Where vendee breached his contract to purchase land, vendor was entitled to money paid for a survey, abstract, and attorney's fees, but not to interest on the purchase price where the land had greatly increased in value and had been in the possession of the vendor.—Biddle v. Biddle, 202 Mich. 160, 168 N.W. 92 (1918).

Chapter 21

REMEDIES OF VENDEE

§ 641.   Recovery of Purchase Money Paid

A vendee may recover purchase money paid where the consideration fails for want of a valid contract of sale, or where the vendor fails or refuses to convey the property called for under the contract.

Library References

> Michigan Digest
> John G. Cameron, Jr., Michigan Real Estate Forms
> Midwest Transaction Guide
> Thompson on Real Property, Thomas Edition (David A. Thomas, ed.)
> Powell on Real Property® (Michael Allan Wolf, ed.)

Law Reviews

> Jeffery A. Cojocar, "As Is" Clauses: The Law Behind "As Is" Clauses in Residential Real Estate Transactions, 84 MI Bar Jnl. 35 (2005); Lawrence R. Shoffner, Real Property Law: Real Evidence: Special Rules for Real Estate Disputes, 80 Mich. B.J. 28 (2001).

A vendee may recover purchase money paid if the consideration fails for want of a valid contract of sale,[1176] or if the vendor fails or refuses to convey the property called for under the contract.[1177]

If the vendor repudiates or rescinds the contract, the vendee may likewise treat the contract as at an end and recover the purchase money paid.[1178] Thus, the vendee may recover when the vendor transfers the property to a third person.[1179]

1175. Hubbard v. Epworth, 69 Mich. 92, 36 N.W. 801 (1888).

1176. Taylor v. Fry, 255 Mich. 333, 238 N.W. 274 (1931).

Oral contract

Money paid on oral agreement for the purchase of land may be recovered as paid without consideration, if there is no possession given so as to take the case out of the statute of frauds.—Scott v. Bush, 26 Mich. 418 (1873).

1177. Koploy v. Dilworth, 238 Mich. 157, 213 N.W. 108 (1927) (person contracting for corner lots is not bound to take inside lots, but may recover purchase money paid).

Williams v. Polgar, 43 Mich. App. 95, 204 N.W.2d 57 (1972), aff'd, 391 Mich. 6, 215 N.W.2d 149 (1974).

1178. Woodliff v. Al Parker Sec. Co., 233 Mich. 154, 206 N.W. 499 (1925).

Robinson v. Batzer, 195 Mich. 235, 161 N.W. 879 (1917).

Weaver v. Aitcheson, 65 Mich. 285, 32 N.W. 436 (1887).

Davis v. Strobridge, 44 Mich. 157, 6 N.W. 205 (1880).

Dispossession of vendee

Vendors' dispossession of defaulting vendee without forfeiture was repudiation and rescission of contract, entitling vendee to restoration of statu quo.—Schon v. Lawrence, 258 Mich. 543, 242 N.W. 745 (1932).

Repudiation not shown

Vendor's procurance of insurance on building on premises sold was not repudiation of land contract or eviction of purchasers' tenant, such as would authorize purchasers' recovery of payments made on contract.—Sriro v. Dunn, 265 Mich. 112, 251 N.W. 370 (1933).

1179. Hornbeck v. Midwest Realty, Inc., 287 Mich. 230, 283 N.W. 39 (1938).

In re Reason's Estate, 276 Mich. 376, 267 N.W. 863 (1936).

Atkinson v. Scott, 36 Mich. 18 (1877).

Transfer subject to vendee's rights

A conveyance to one having actual knowledge of a contract of sale previously made does not

Furthermore, the vendee may be entitled to the value of improvements that he or she has made on the property.[1180]

However, a vendee who has voluntarily forfeited his or her rights under a land contract by default in payments may not recover amounts already paid on the contract.[1181] The vendee is not entitled to amounts paid where the contract has been abrogated,[1182] or where it validly provides for a forfeiture in the event of default in payment.[1183]

A vendee otherwise entitled to recover back purchase money paid may lose the right of recovery through waiver or estoppel.[1184]

Defects in title. Where, in violation of the contract, the vendor fails to convey or tender a merchantable title, the vendee may rescind the contract and recover the purchase price paid.[1185]

entitle the vendee under the contract to rescind and recover back partial payments.—Kreibich v. Martz, 119 Mich. 343, 78 N.W. 124 (1899).

1180. Davis v. Strobridge, 44 Mich. 157, 6 N.W. 205 (1880).

1181. Buyers made no valid tender

Buyers under a purchase agreement of a motel and restaurant were not entitled to recover the $2,002 down payment made under the agreement on the theory that the vendors had refused to perform by insisting upon a condition unstated in the agreement of payments of 6% interest on the unpaid balance of the purchase price where the buyers never made a valid tender of the amount due.—Duiven v. Brakesman, 356 Mich. 1, 95 N.W.2d 868 (1959).

Per contract

Where preliminary purchase agreement provided purchasers were to give written notice of any objection to title and that following that notice vendors were entitled to 30 days to remedy objection or to obtain title insurance, vendors, in absence of notice, had right to assume that title tendered by them was sufficient, and where vendors kept their property off market for about two months in anticipation of fulfillment of contract, they were justified upon purchasers' default to retain deposit as liquidated damages, as provided in agreement.—Ihlenfeldt v. Guastella, 42 Mich. App. 384, 202 N.W.2d 327 (1972).

1182. After judgment for restitution

After judgment for restitution was entered in summary proceedings brought by vendor, after forfeiture, purchaser's assignee could not rescind for vendor's breach of contract and bring suit to recover money paid on it, because contract was then entirely abrogated.—Rosenthal v. American Constr. & Realty Co., 262 Mich. 91, 247 N.W. 117 (1933).

1183. Nelson v. Hacker, 278 Mich. 383, 270 N.W. 720 (1936).

Crenshaw v. Granet, 237 Mich. 367, 211 N.W. 636 (1927) (that possession was taken without valid summary proceeding did not relieve purchaser from force and effect of valid forfeiture previously declared).

Time of essence

Where installment land contract provided that time was of its essence, and that on purchaser's failure to perform the vendor should have right to declare contract void and to retain money paid thereon, the purchaser on forfeiture of contract for nonpayment of amount due thereon was not entitled to an accounting for money paid before forfeiture.—Security Inv. Co. v. Meister, 214 Mich. 337, 183 N.W. 183 (1921).

1184. Geel v. Goulden, 168 Mich. 413, 134 N.W. 484 (1912).

Negotiations as to payment

A vendee under a contract of sale waives right to rescind by reason of a conveyance of land by vendor to another, who took subject to that contract, where, with knowledge of the facts, he negotiates with him as to payments under the contract.—Kreibich v. Martz, 119 Mich. 343, 78 N.W. 124 (1899).

Waiver not shown

Vendors having been unable to procure mortgage agreed upon, purchasers' unaccepted proposal of a modification whereby they would procure a mortgage and give vendors a second mortgage for vendors' equity in property did not constitute a waiver of purchasers' right to recover deposit.—Maxey v. Proctor, 343 Mich. 453, 72 N.W.2d 198 (1955).

1185. Porter v. Ridge, 310 Mich. 425, 17 N.W.2d 239 (1945) (property subject to perpetual easement).

Failure to acquire and convey within reasonable time

Where vendors did not have title nor acquire title and make conveyance within reasonable time

On the other hand, where the vendee enters and occupies the land for a prolonged period, the vendee may not recover the entire amount of the purchase price paid on the vendor's failure to convey a marketable title in pursuance of the contract.[1186] In addition, purchasers who notify the vendors of the termination of the agreement within a period of less than 30 days after making a deposit and thereby do not give the vendor a reasonable time to provide title as allowed under the contract may be estopped to claim recovery of their deposit.[1187]

Quitclaim deed. In the absence of fraud, the consideration that the vendee has paid for a quitclaim deed cannot be recovered because the grantor lacks good title to the land.[1188]

Fraud of vendor. Where the vendor has been guilty of fraud in connection with the sale of land, the vendee may rescind the contract and recover the purchase money paid.[1189]

Overpayment. Where the vendee has overpaid the vendor with respect to the purchase price, the vendee is entitled to recover the amount of the overpayment.[1190]

Compelling conveyance. A party entitled to a conveyance of a property under a land contract may bring an action compelling the conveyance. That action is under the statute[1191] providing for compelling discharge of a mortgage. A party with the duty to convey a property is subject to penalties for the failure to do so.[1192]

§ 642.   —Vendee's Lien and Its Enforcement

Where a contract for the sale of land has been rescinded and the vendee is entitled to recover purchase money paid, the vendee has a lien on the land as against the vendor for

given by purchaser after payment of last installment, purchaser was held entitled to rescind and recover purchaser price.—Haight v. Salter, 260 Mich. 6, 244 N.W. 209 (1932).

1186. Todd v. McLaughlin, 125 Mich. 268, 84 N.W. 146 (1900).

1187. Henry v. Rouse, 345 Mich. 86, 75 N.W.2d 836 (1956).

1188. Cartier v. Douville, 98 Mich. 22, 56 N.W. 1045 (1893).

Tax title

Where the holder of a tax title conveys by quitclaim deed, both parties acting in good faith, believing that the deed conveyed a valid title, grantee is not entitled to recover back the consideration on a failure of the title.—Thorkildsen v. Carpenter, 120 Mich. 419, 79 N.W. 636 (1899).

1189. Barker v. Fordville Land Co., 264 Mich. 95, 249 N.W. 491 (1933).

Barnhardt v. Hamel, 207 Mich. 232, 174 N.W. 182 (1919).

Head v. Benjamin Rich Realty Co., 55 Mich. App. 348, 222 N.W.2d 237 (1974).

Smith v. Michigan Realty & Constr. Co., 175 Mich. 600, 141 N.W. 635, 1913 Mich. LEXIS 829 (1913) (person led to make contract of purchase through false representations may disaffirm sale, tender reconveyance, with demand for purchase money, and on refusal bring suit to recover it).

Laubengayer v. Rohde, 167 Mich. 605, 133 N.W. 535 (1911) (may recover purchase price with interest).

Right to rely on representations

Fact that buyer of warehouse might have ascertained from others that possibility of flooding of warehouse had not been eliminated was no defense to buyer's action to recover down payment, where buyer had a right to rely on agent's representations regarding allegedly slight possibility of flooding.—People's Furniture & Appliance Co. v. Healy, 365 Mich. 522, 113 N.W.2d 802 (1962).

1190. Dinnan v. Bloomfield Hills Land Co., 214 Mich. 54, 181 N.W. 986 (1921).

Byrnes v. Martin, 67 Mich. 399, 34 N.W. 688 (1887).

1191. MCLS § 565.44.

1192. MCLS § 565.361.

such money, and the lien may be enforced against an
assignee of the vendor who is not a bona fide purchaser.

Where a contract for the sale of land has been rescinded and the vendee is
entitled to recovery of the purchase money paid, the vendee has a lien on the land
for the money as against the vendor.[1193] This lien may be enforced against assignees
of the vendor who are not bona fide purchasers.[1194]

However, a purchaser who knew that the purported vendor was in fact acting
for others and who made improvements to the property prior to closing without
inquiring as to the nature of the purported vendor's authority is not entitled to an
equitable lien against the property for the improvements made.[1195]

An opportunity to pay must be afforded before foreclosure of a vendee's
lien.[1196]

A vendee's suit to enforce his or her lien for the amount paid on a contract
because of alleged fraud of the vendors was maintainable in chancery.[1197]

§ 643.   —Proceedings

A vendee may sue for recovery of purchase money paid at
law, or, where the legal remedy is inadequate, may proceed
in equity. Generally, only the vendor who received the
money is subject to suit for its recovery.

A vendee seeking to recover purchase money paid may sue at law for
rescission and recovery of the purchase money,[1198] or, where the legal remedy is
inadequate, may proceed in equity,[1199] provided the contract has not been rescinded.[1200] Money paid as the purchase price of land can be recovered in an action
for money had and received, whether the consideration fails for want of title or of

---

1193. Beacock v. People's Lumber Co., 253
Mich. 403, 235 N.W. 200 (1931).

Younger v. Caroselli, 251 Mich. 533, 232 N.W.
378 (1930).

Lockwood v. Bassett, 49 Mich. 546, 14 N.W.
492 (1883).

Analogy to vendor's lien

A vendee who has paid the purchase money
punctually has a lien, as against the vendor,
analogous to that of a vendor against a vendee who
has not paid the purchase money.—Payne v.
Atterbury, Harrington Ch. 414 (Mich. 1842).

Vendor's default

Where a contract for the sale of land fails
through the vendor's default, the purchaser is
entitled to a lien upon the land for repayment of
what he has paid under the contract.—Robinson v.
Campbell, 222 Mich. 111, 192 N.W. 644 (1923).

1194. Hafner v. A.J. Stuart Land Co., 246
Mich. 465, 224 N.W. 630 (1929).

1195. Snider v. Dunn, 11 Mich. App. 39, 160
N.W.2d 619 (1968).

1196. Hafner v. A.J. Stuart Land Co., 246
Mich. 465, 224 N.W. 630 (1929).

1197. German Bundesheim Soc'y v. Schmidt,
242 Mich. 139, 218 N.W. 664 (1928).

1198. Von Hoene v. Barber, 215 Mich. 538,
184 N.W. 526 (1921) (overruled on other grounds
by Witte v. Hobolth, 224 Mich. 286, 195 N.W. 82
(1923)).

Loudon v. Carroll, 130 Mich. 79, 89 N.W. 578
(1902) (action by grantee for rescission of executed contract of sale of land and recovery of
purchase money may be maintained at law, when
reconveyance is tendered).

1199. Younger v. Caroselli, 251 Mich. 533,
232 N.W. 378 (1930).

1200. Head v. Benjamin Rich Realty Co., 55
Mich. App. 348, 222 N.W.2d 237 (1974).

a valid contract to convey.[1201]

Generally speaking, a vendee's suit to recover purchase money paid, brought after rescission of a contract for the sale of land, lies only against the vendors who received the money.[1202] However, where there are several vendors, a recovery of the purchase money may be had against all of them.[1203]

The liability of a vendor's assignee is no greater than the total of payments that he or she received from the purchaser.[1204]

Time to sue. A suit to recover money paid under a land contract for the sale of land is not premature because the invalidity of the contract is adjudicated in an action subsequently brought to recover the balance due on the contract.[1205] An equitable action for the recovery of purchase money paid may be barred by laches.[1206]

§ 644.   —Conditions Precedent

For an action at law, it is a condition precedent to recovery back of purchase money paid that the vendee rescind the contract, demand the money, and tender back anything that he or she may have received.

A vendee seeking to recover purchase money paid under a contract of sale must rescind the contract as a condition precedent to maintenance of such an action at law.[1207] Rescission as a prerequisite to a suit at law for return of the consideration paid requires that demand be made for the return of the money and that the party seeking rescission tender back any interest acquired under the contract.[1208]

1201. Wright v. Dickinson, 67 Mich. 580, 35 N.W. 164 (1887).

1202. Barker v. Fordville Land Co., 264 Mich. 95, 249 N.W. 491 (1933).

Corporate officers of vendor not liable

In chancery suit for rescission of land contracts, purchaser, although entitled to rescission and restitution of purchase money from vendor corporation, could not recover anything from corporation's president and sales manager not party to contracts, even if he participated in fraud and received commission from corporation.—Van Looyengoed v. Allencrest Gardens Corp., 265 Mich. 182, 251 N.W. 317 (1933).

1203. Zadel v. Simon, 221 Mich. 180, 190 N.W. 700 (1922).

1204. Hafner v. A.J. Stuart Land Co., 246 Mich. 465, 224 N.W. 630 (1929) (personal money decree against assignees of vendor, in suit by purchasers for rescission for fraud, will be limited to payments received by assignees from purchasers).

1205. Wright v. Dickinson, 67 Mich. 580, 35 N.W. 164 (1887).

1206. Smith v. Highland Park State Bank, 309 Mich. 226, 15 N.W.2d 142 (1944).

Rescission of contract prevents application of laches

In action to recover moneys paid under land contract that was rescinded because of defendant sellers' fraud in guaranty against violations of city electrical code, defense of laches was not available to defendants in view of facts that action was one at law rather than in equity, that plaintiff purchasers asserted their rights promptly upon becoming aware of violations, and that defendants resold premises for same amount for which they purchased them, thereby obviating prejudice to defendants.—Head v. Benjamin Rich Realty Co., 55 Mich. App. 348, 222 N.W.2d 237 (1974).

1207. Thomas v. Reece, 333 Mich. 598, 53 N.W.2d 505 (1952).

Lightner v. Karnatz, 258 Mich. 74, 241 N.W. 841 (1932).

1208. Peters v. Fagan, 244 Mich. 46, 221 N.W. 274 (1928).

Lack of rescission

Where plaintiff contracted to purchase vacant lots from defendants, in absence of evidence that

However, demand and tender may be excused where they would be futile.[1209] Thus, a vendee rescinding the contract and seeking a return of purchase money paid is not required to tender the remainder due on the purchase and demand a deed if doing so would be useless because the vendor is unable to convey good title.[1210] When the vendor insists on inserting conditions in the conveyance not called for by the agreement, the vendor may not complain, in the vendee's suit at law for recovery of purchase money paid, that the vendee has to first give notice of rescission and demand performance by the vendor.[1211]

Generally, a vendee seeking to recover the money paid on a land contract must place the vendor in statu quo so far as feasible.[1212] But a vendee rescinding for failure of consideration is not required to put the parties *in statu quo* before the vendee may recover his or her investment if this cannot be done.[1213] When the vendee is not in a position to tender back or return what he or she has received, the vendee's failure to do so may be excused and a deduction made to adjust the equities of the parties.[1214]

§ 645.　—Pleading, Evidence, and Trial

The plaintiff's initial pleading in an action to recover purchase money paid must state a cause of action. The burden rests on the purchaser to prove a defect in the vendor's title, and on the trial of actions to recover purchase money paid, the court must instruct the jury correctly as to the law.

In accordance with the general rules, the plaintiff's initial pleading must state a cause of action and is sufficient if it does so.[1215] Under the usual rules, there generally must be no variance between the pleadings and the proof.[1216]

plaintiff had at any time demanded return of money or notified defendants of her intention to rescind, plaintiff had no cause of action for return of consideration based upon theory of rescission.—Thomas v. Reece, 333 Mich. 598, 53 N.W.2d 505 (1952).

1209. Thomas v. Reece, 333 Mich. 598, 53 N.W.2d 505 (1952).

Stockham v. Cheeney, 62 Mich. 10, 28 N.W. 692 (1886).

1210. Smith v. Hubert Land Co., 261 Mich. 464, 246 N.W. 183 (1933).

Wright v. Dickinson, 67 Mich. 580, 35 N.W. 164 (1887).

1211. Duncombe v. Tromble, 219 Mich. 8, 188 N.W. 367 (1922).

1212. Wright v. Dickinson, 67 Mich. 590, 42 N.W. 849 (1889).

Wright v. Dickinson, 67 Mich. 580, 35 N.W. 164 (1887).

1213. Younger v. Caroselli, 251 Mich. 533, 232 N.W. 378 (1930).

1214. Consumption of certain articles

In a suit to rescind a contract for the purchase of farm on the ground of fraudulent representation by the vendor, that plaintiff was unable to return certain feed, potatoes, and apples delivered with the farm, because they had been consumed, did not defeat the right to recover the amount paid on contract, because jury could deduct value of that property.—Zadel v. Simon, 221 Mich. 180, 190 N.W. 700 (1922).

1215. Quail v. Wayne Circuit Judge, 249 Mich. 425, 228 N.W. 775 (1930).

Recovery on common counts

Recovery of money paid on contract rescinded for fraud may be had under the common counts.—Lackovic v. Campbell, 225 Mich. 1, 195 N.W. 798 (1923).

1216. Silfver v. Daenzer, 167 Mich. 362, 133 N.W. 16 (1911).

Mestler v. Jeffries, 145 Mich. 598, 108 N.W. 994 (1906).

Evidence. Generally, there is a presumption that the vendor has title, and to avoid the effects of a tender of a deed, the burden rests upon the vendee to show defects in the vendor's title.[1217] Competent evidence relevant and material to the issues of the case is admissible.[1218] Evidence failing to meet that requirement is inadmissible.[1219] The party having the affirmative of the issue must prove it by a preponderance of the evidence, and under the circumstances disclosed in particular cases the evidence was sufficient to establish various issues.[1220]

Trial. The instructions of the court should conform to the issues of the case and inform the jury correctly concerning the law.[1221]

§ 646. —Amount of Recovery

> **A successful vendee may recover the purchase money paid, with interest, less the value of whatever use of the premises that the vendee may have enjoyed.**

A successful vendee may recover the purchase price that the vendee paid to the vendor,[1222] with interest,[1223] and the reasonable value of any improvements that the vendee may have made in good faith,[1224] less the value of whatever use of the premises that the vendee may have enjoyed.[1225]

The vendee may also recover damages suffered by reason of losses and expenses incurred naturally and reasonably as a result of the vendor's fraud.[1226]

§ 647. Damages for Breach of Contract

> **Among other remedies, a vendee may bring an action to recover damages sustained as a result of the vendor's breach of a contract for the sale of real property.**

1217. Baxter v. Aubrey, 41 Mich. 13, 1 N.W. 897 (1879).

1218. Dikeman v. Arnold, 78 Mich. 455, 44 N.W. 407 (1889).

1219. Wright v. Dickinson, 67 Mich. 590, 42 N.W. 849 (1889).

Immaterial evidence

In action to recover difference between what plaintiff paid defendant for land and what it cost defendant, defendant having agreed to sell it at cost and misrepresented price, evidence of what it was worth is immaterial.—Straus Land Corp. v. Dupuis, 207 Mich. 399, 174 N.W. 129 (1919).

1220. Holmes v. Robert Oakman Land Co., 260 Mich. 378, 244 N.W. 509 (1932) (evidence sustained finding that rescission of real estate contract was not waived by laches and payments).

Sutton v. Meyering Land Co., 248 Mich. 601, 227 N.W. 783 (1929) (vendor's inability to complete improvements within time stipulated).

Hall v. Proctor, 221 Mich. 400, 191 N.W. 205 (1922) (rescission of contract).

Kefuss v. Whitley, 220 Mich. 67, 189 N.W. 76 (1922) (knowledge of co-vendor's misrepresentations).

Head v. Benjamin Rich Realty Co., 55 Mich. App. 348, 222 N.W.2d 237 (1974) (repair expenses).

1221. Cossett v. O'Riley, 160 Mich. 101, 125 N.W. 39 (1910).

Wright v. Dickinson, 67 Mich. 590, 42 N.W. 849 (1889).

1222. Hornbeck v. Midwest Realty, Inc., 287 Mich. 230, 283 N.W. 39 (1938).

1223. Davis v. Strobridge, 44 Mich. 157, 6 N.W. 205 (1880).

1224. Himebaugh v. Chalker, 261 Mich. 80, 245 N.W. 576 (1932).

Head v. Benjamin Rich Realty Co., 55 Mich. App. 348, 222 N.W.2d 237 (1974).

1225. Himebaugh v. Chalker, 261 Mich. 80, 245 N.W. 576 (1932).

Amster v. Stratton, 259 Mich. 683, 244 N.W. 201 (1932).

1226. Head v. Benjamin Rich Realty Co., 55 Mich. App. 348, 222 N.W.2d 237 (1974).

Among other remedies, a vendee may sue for damages resulting from the vendor's breach of contract.[1227] This type of action is an action at law.[1228] While the vendee may sue for specific performance of a land contract,[1229] the vendee may nevertheless be entitled to damages for breach of contract even though the facts are such that under the circumstances specific performance cannot be awarded.[1230]

An action for damages for the vendor's breach of a land contract may lie even though the conditions are such that the vendor cannot perform.[1231]

The vendee may recover against the vendor for damages sustained as a result of the vendor's false representations concerning the land.[1232]

Where, at the request of the vendee, the deed is made to the vendee's spouse, the deed does not pass to the spouse any right of action that the vendee would have had for the vendor's failure to pay off encumbrances in compliance with the provisions of a contract for the sale of land.[1233]

A vendee defaulting in the payment of installments on designated dates, who thereby forfeits the contract, may not maintain an action for breach of the contract by the vendor.[1234]

§ 648. —Conditions Precedent

A vendee suing for damages for the vendor's breach of the contract thereby elects to stand on the contract and so need

1227. McCall v. Freedman, 35 Mich. App. 243, 192 N.W.2d 275 (1971).

Additional remedy

Purchaser is not limited to remedy by rescission and action at law for return of consideration but he may affirm contract and sue at law by action for damages because of its breach.—Thomas v. Reece, 333 Mich. 598, 53 N.W.2d 505 (1952).

1228. Rosenthal v. American Constr. & Realty Co., 262 Mich. 91, 247 N.W. 117 (1933).

1229. M.L.P.2d Remedies.

McCall v. Freedman, 35 Mich. App. 243, 192 N.W.2d 275 (1971).

1230. Miller v. Smith, 140 Mich. 524, 103 N.W. 872 (1905).

Allen v. Atkinson, 21 Mich. 351 (1870) (action for damages lies although vendee has waived right to specific performance).

Tenancy by the entirety

Husband's contract to sell realty held by himself and wife under tenancy by entirety, though not susceptible of specific performance nor valid to affect in any way either her or his title, has validity between him and purchaser as foundation of an action for damages for breach of it.—Way v. Root, 174 Mich. 418, 140 N.W. 577 (1913).

1231. Dikeman v. Arnold, 78 Mich. 455, 44 N.W. 407 (1889).

Homestead

Action will lie for damages for breach of contract to convey land not signed by wife, although contracting party is married and the property concerned is homestead.—Droppers v. Marshall, 203 Mich. 173, 168 N.W. 1001 (1918).

Titleless vendor

That purchaser who had been admitted into possession made terms with owner of paramount title, vendor having by decree in chancery been declared to have no title to land, does not deprive purchaser of right to recover against his vendor on account of breach of agreement to convey title.—Bugajski v. Siwka, 200 Mich. 415, 166 N.W. 863 (1918).

1232. Fuller v. Bilz, 161 Mich. 589, 126 N.W. 712 (1910).

Absence of intent to deceive is no defense

One who misrepresents the quality and value of his land, intending to influence, and actually influencing, another to buy it, is liable in case for resulting damages even though he was innocent of any intention to deceive.—Holcomb v. Noble, 69 Mich. 396, 37 N.W. 497 (1888).

1233. Norton v. Colgrove, 41 Mich. 544, 3 N.W. 159 (1879).

1234. Jones v. Berkey, 181 Mich. 472, 148 N.W. 375 (1914).

not rescind as a condition precedent to maintenance of the action.

Given that an action for damages is based on affirmation of the contract, it is unnecessary for the vendee to rescind the contract, or to restore possession of the premises in order to maintain the action.[1235]

If the vendor has by decree in equity been declared to have no title to the land that the vendor contracted to sell and in possession of which the vendor placed the vendee, in order to recover for the breach of the contract, the vendee need not tender the vendor the sum remaining due under the contract and demand a deed.[1236]

When a vendee tenders the price, the vendor generally has no right to the money except on condition of simultaneous delivery of the deed, and in an action against the vendor for breach of the contract it is not necessary to show that the tender has been kept good.[1237]

Whether a contract interposes a condition precedent on the vendor's performance of the contract depends on the intention of the parties to the land contract.[1238]

§ 649.   —Pleading, Evidence, and Trial

The vendee's complaint in an action for damages is sufficient where it states a cause of action based on an affirmance of the contract. The party having the affirmative of the issue has the burden of proof in such actions, and on the trial questions of fact are for the jury.

The vendee's complaint for damages for breach of a contract for the sale of land is sufficient if it states a cause of action based on the theory of an affirmance of the contract and a suit for breach of it.[1239] Evidence within the issues made by the complaint is admissible.[1240]

Evidence. As in other civil actions, in a purchaser's action to recover damages for the vendor's breach of contract the burden of proof rests on the party having the affirmative of the issue.[1241] Competent evidence relevant and material to the issues

---

1235. Way v. Root, 174 Mich. 418, 140 N.W. 577 (1913).

1236. Bugajski v. Siwka, 200 Mich. 415, 166 N.W. 863 (1918).

1237. Allen v. Atkinson, 21 Mich. 351 (1870).

1238. Mortgage application

In nonjury action for specific performance of home purchaser contract providing, inter alia, that plaintiff buyers were to apply for FHA mortgage in specific amount, pursuant to which buyers prepared application papers and were otherwise ready to perform, trial court's finding that buyers performed contract, even though defendant sellers actually submitted application papers to lending institution which refused mortgage, was not clearly erroneous on record disclosing that sub-

mission of application papers was not condition precedent to performance of contract, but that seller had agreed to submit papers to lender and that, upon refusal of loan, sellers notified buyers by mail without explaining reasons for rejection and sold property to others at higher price.— McCall v. Freedman, 35 Mich. App. 243, 192 N.W.2d 275 (1971).

1239. Thomas v. Reece, 333 Mich. 598, 53 N.W.2d 505 (1952).

1240. Holcomb v. Noble, 69 Mich. 396, 37 N.W. 497 (1888) (under declaration that land was represented to be of certain value, representations that it was of that value for farming may be shown).

1241. Gitson v. Yale Land Co., 212 Mich. 292, 180 N.W. 593 (1920).

involved is admissible,[1242] but evidence failing to meet those standards is inadmissible.[1243] The party having the affirmative of the issue must prove it by a preponderance of the proof. A party to the action is entitled to a ruling whether the evidence on a particular issue is sufficient[1244] or insufficient.[1245]

Trial. On the trial of a vendee's action for damages against the vendor, questions of fact are for the jury.[1246]

§ 650.   —Amount of Recovery

The vendee suing for damages for the vendor's breach of a contract for the sale of land is entitled to recover such damages as arise as the fair and natural result of the vendor's breach.

The damages to which a vendee is entitled on a breach of a contract for the sale of land are those that arise as the fair, legal, and natural result, under all the circumstances, of the vendor's breach.[1247] Thus, under the circumstances disclosed

1242. Bartlett v. Smith, 146 Mich. 188, 109 N.W. 260 (1906).

1243. De Vries v. Meyering Land Co., 248 Mich. 128, 226 N.W. 824 (1929).

1244. Thomas v. Reece, 333 Mich. 598, 53 N.W.2d 505 (1952) (damages on theory of affirmance of contract and vendor's breach).

De Vries v. Meyering Land Co., 248 Mich. 128, 226 N.W. 824 (1929) (verdict for $3,000 for loss of bargain to purchasers of lots on account of breach of contract to create adjoining lake).

Gitson v. Yale Land Co., 212 Mich. 292, 180 N.W. 593 (1920) (data for ascertainment of damages as against contention that verdict was speculative).

Findings of trial judge

In actions for damages in amounts of costs of repairing dwelling houses constructed by defendant and sold and conveyed to plaintiffs, fact finding of trial judge, hearing case without jury, that houses were not constructed with good workmanship and in compliance with federal requirements was not against clear preponderance of evidence, as required to warrant reversal of judgment for plaintiffs.—Allen v. Currier Lumber Co., 337 Mich. 696, 61 N.W.2d 138 (1953).

No condition precedent

In nonjury action for specific performance of home purchaser contract providing, inter alia, that plaintiff buyers were to apply for FHA mortgage in specific amount, pursuant to which buyers prepared application papers and were otherwise ready to perform, trial court's finding that buyers performed contract, even though defendant sellers actually submitted application papers to lending institution which refused mortgage, was not clearly erroneous on record disclosing that sub-

mission of application papers was not condition precedent to performance of contract, but that seller had agreed to submit papers to lender and that, upon refusal of loan, sellers notified buyers by mail without explaining reasons for rejection and sold property to others at higher price.—McCall v. Freedman, 35 Mich. App. 243, 192 N.W.2d 275 (1971).

1245. Fleischer v. Buccilli, 13 Mich. App. 135, 163 N.W.2d 637 (1968) (damages to purchasers as result of failure of vendors to deliver policy of title insurance or abstract of title as required by contract).

Value of lot

Evidence, including testimony of defendant that, so far as he remembered, similar lots had sold for between $10,000 and $12,000, though he did not remember when those similar lots were sold for such prices, was insufficient to justify finding that land was worth $12,000 at time defendant breached contract to sell real property.—Soloman v. Western Hills Dev. Co., 110 Mich. App. 257, 312 N.W.2d 428 (1981).

1246. Phillips v. Gamble, 227 Mich. 689, 199 N.W. 712 (1924) (whether tender was sufficient to stop running of interest).

Offer to pay

In action for breach of written option giving plaintiff right to purchase property, including transfer of liquor license, whether plaintiff offered to pay cost of new license was for jury.—Caughey v. Ames, 315 Mich. 643, 24 N.W.2d 521 (1946).

1247. Award for deficiency in quantity of land was adequate

Baughan v. Mortgage & Contract Co., 263 Mich. 248, 248 N.W. 611 (1933).

in particular cases, the measure of damages for the vendor's breach of a contract for the sale of land may be the market value of the land less the contract price,[1248] or the difference between the agreed price and the value of the land at the time of the breach.[1249] A vendee who fails to obtain a good title may be awarded the difference between the value of the premises with a good title and their value with the defective title conveyed.[1250]

In the absence of a showing of bad faith or wrongful conduct, the benefit of the bargain damage due to the vendor's failure to convey marketable title will not be awarded.[1251] Thus, if the vendor of land is unable to perform the contract of sale made in good faith, the measure of damages is the consideration money plus interest and expenses.[1252]

The cost of restoring the property to suitable use in the manner the vendee intended to use it are appropriate damages for the vendor's breach of contract rendering the property unusable for that purpose.[1253]

Where the vendor fails to give the vendee possession on the agreed date and later does give the vendee possession, the vendee may recover the fair rental value

Particular amounts

In action for breach of written option giving plaintiff right to purchase property, $729 as damages awarded plaintiff were not speculative where verdict was supported by the testimony and was less than the $1,000 profit which plaintiff lost because of such breach.—Caughey v. Ames, 315 Mich. 643, 24 N.W.2d 521 (1946).

In lot purchasers' action for vendor's breach of agreement to make street improvements, where the lot at time of trial had the same physical characteristics as farm land as when purchased, and where purchasers had paid $1,200 therefor, evidence sustained verdict of $425 for purchasers.—Gitson v. Yale Land Co., 212 Mich. 292, 180 N.W. 593 (1920).

Value of bonus

The vendee is not entitled to recover for the value of a bonus that he might have received for a lease of the land by him if the vendor had duly performed.—Bucuss v. Schuler, 254 Mich. 690, 236 N.W. 908 (1931).

1248. Bucuss v. Schuler, 254 Mich. 690, 236 N.W. 908 (1931).

Allen v. Atkinson, 21 Mich. 351 (1870).

Jaye v. Tobin, 42 Mich. App. 756, 202 N.W.2d 712 (1972) (action against subdivision owner for breach of purchase contracts for lots in subdivision).

1249. Craine v. Miller, 240 Mich. 357, 215 N.W. 355 (1927).

Zimmerman v. Miller, 206 Mich. 599, 173 N.W. 364 (1919).

Bugajski v. Siwka, 200 Mich. 415, 166 N.W. 863 (1918).

Stewart v. McLaughlin's Estate, 126 Mich. 6, 87 N.W. 218 (1901).

Michigan Alternativ e Hous. v. Delta Commerce Props., 1998 Mich. App. LEXIS 1420 (Mich. Ct. App. May 5, 1998).

Soloman v. Western Hills Dev. Co., 110 Mich. App. 257, 312 N.W.2d 428 (1981) (if vendor commits fraud in land contract).

No damages

Where contract price for sale of property to plaintiff was $7,000, and value of property at time of breach occurring when property was sold to another was $7,000, as determined by sale price, plaintiff was not entitled to damages for breach.—Port Inv. Co. v. Anderson, 23 Mich. App. 103, 178 N.W.2d 157 (1970).

1250. Stockham v. Cheeney, 62 Mich. 10, 28 N.W. 692 (1886).

1251. Walch v. Crandall, 164 Mich. App. 181, 416 N.W.2d 375 (1987).

1252. Hammond v. Hannin, 21 Mich. 374 (1870).

Soloman v. Western Hills Dev. Co., 110 Mich. App. 257, 312 N.W.2d 428 (1981).

1253. Bliss v. Carter, 26 Mich. App. 177, 182 N.W.2d 54 (1970) (sand and topsoil removed from property subject to contract to purchase were necessary for purposes for which purchasers purchased property, so that cost of replacing removed sand and topsoil was an authorized measure of damages).

for the period during which the vendee was kept out of possession.[1254] If the vendee accepts an existing tenancy and receives the rent from the tenant, the amount of rent received is properly deducted from the damage found in the vendee's favor in an action for breach of a covenant against encumbrances.[1255]

A seller of real property who notwithstanding a contract to sell, refuses to convey or conveys to a third party, acts in bad faith, and the damages to the buyer may be measured by the benefit of the bargain.[1256] Where a vendor in an unrecorded land contract sells the land to a third person, in an action by the vendee for breach of the contract, the measure of damages is the payments made and the reasonable value of the improvements made in good faith, less the value of the use of the premises.[1257]

Interest. The purchaser, if admitted into possession, is not allowed to recover interest on purchase money payments without being charged with the rental value of the premises during the time that he or she is in possession.[1258]

Nominal damages. In a vendee's action for breach of a contract for the sale of land, in the event of proof of a material breach, the vendee is entitled to a directed verdict for at least nominal damages.[1259]

1254. Sanders v. Detlaff, 218 Mich. 471, 188 N.W. 446 (1922).

1255. Edwards v. Clark, 83 Mich. 246, 47 N.W. 112 (1890).

1256. Mickam v. Joseph Louis Palace Trust, 849 F. Supp. 516, 1993 U.S. Dist. LEXIS 20101, 73 A.F.T.R.2d (RIA) 698, 94 TNT 12-10 (E.D. Mich. 1993).

Walch v. Crandall, 164 Mich. App. 181, 416 N.W.2d 375, 1987 Mich. App. LEXIS 2821 (1987).

Soloman v. Western Hills Dev. Co., 110 Mich. App. 257, 312 N.W.2d 428 (1981).

1257. Bartlett v. Smith, 146 Mich. 188, 109 N.W. 260 (1906).

Improvements

Corporate purchaser that breached its contract to sell approximately half of tract it purchased in that assignee of vendor obtained judgment of restitution against corporate purchaser because of default on land contract was liable to vendees not only for amount vendees paid corporate purchaser but also for cost of improvements vendees had placed upon property, in view of inurement of those improvements to benefit of assignee when judgment was secured.—Parrish v. Michigan Properties Corp., 2 Mich. App. 49, 138 N.W.2d 517 (1965).

1258. Crocker v. Ingersoll Engineering & Constructing Co., 249 F. 31 (6th Cir. Mich. 1918).

1259. Gitson v. Yale Land Co., 212 Mich. 292, 180 N.W. 593 (1920).

Purchaser unable to perform

Where purchaser was unable to perform on final date set for closing of real estate purchase contract, he was precluded from being awarded benefit of his bargain, and where he failed to offer evidence of any incidental damages, he was properly awarded nominal damages along with costs.—Derosia v. Austin, 115 Mich. App. 647, 321 N.W.2d 760 (1982).

Chapter 22

EXCHANGE OF PROPERTY

§ 671. Contracts for Exchange

The legal effect of a contract of exchange for property is, in general, the same as that of a contract of sale.

Library References

> Michigan Digest
> John G. Cameron, Jr., Michigan Real Estate Forms
> Midwest Transaction Guide
> Thompson on Real Property, Thomas Edition (David A. Thomas, ed.)
> Powell on Real Property® (Michael Allan Wolf, ed.)
> Purchase and Sale of Real Property (Karl B. Holtzschue, ed.)

Law Reviews

> Stephen R. Estey and Danielle Graceffa, Real Property, 54 Wayne L. Rev. 387 (2008); Nadia E. Nedzel, Reviving Protection for Private Property: A Practical Approach To Blight Takings, 2008 Mich. St. L. Rev. 995 (2008); Lenin E. Lopez, A Matter of Semantics: Should Tenancies-In-Common be Treated as Securities or Real Estate Interests?, 8 J. Bus. & Sec. L. 1 (2007); Gregg A. Nathanson, Real Property Law: What's New In Residential Transactions?, 86 MI Bar Jnl. 16 (2007).

The legal effect of a contract for exchange of property is generally the same as that of a contract of sale. In both cases the title is absolutely transferred. Both types of transactions are governed by the same rules of law for practical purposes.[1260]

A claimed sale may actually be an exchange notwithstanding the placing of values upon the properties exchanged.[1261] An apparent exchange may be a sale.[1262]

Making of the contract. With respect to the making of a contract for exchange involving real property, the statute of frauds comes into play.[1263]

Lands owned by an infant or incompetent may be given in exchange upon court order pursuant to statute.[1264]

Insofar as the wife's dower interest is concerned, it is provided by statute, in effect, that, where a husband exchanges lands, his widow may not have dower in both but must make her election. If she evinces no election by proceeding within one

---

1260. Hunt v. Fenlon, 313 Mich. 644, 21 N.W.2d 906 (1946).

1261. Exchange

A contract whereby plaintiff was to convey an equity in property in consideration of defendant's conveyance of an equity in other property, each to assume a mortgage, to furnish an abstract of title, and to deliver possession, was a contract for an exchange of properties.—Hamburger v. Berman, 203 Mich. 78, 168 N.W. 925 (1918).

1262. Payment in goods

A contract for a present sale of a growing crop is as valid, if made for a price to be paid in

merchandise, as if made for money.—Crapo v. Seybold, 36 Mich. 444 (1877).

Where property is taken at a fixed money price, the transfer amounts to a sale, whether the price is paid in cash or in goods.—Picard v. McCormick, 11 Mich. 68 (1862).

1263. M.L.P.2d Frauds, Statute of.

MCLS § 566.108.

1264. Graham v. Nippress, 222 Mich. 386, 192 N.W. 683, 1923 Mich. LEXIS 699 (1923).

Hunt v. Stevens, 174 Mich. 501, 140 N.W. 992, 1913 Mich. LEXIS 491 (1913).

Young v. Blanchard, 165 Mich. 340, 130 N.W. 694, 1911 Mich. LEXIS 807 (1911).

year after the husband's death to recover her dower in the lands given in exchange, she is deemed to have elected to take dower in the lands received.[1265]

Assuming that a contract is not meant to be conditioned on procurement of the spouse's signature, the fact that a party to a contract for exchange of real property cannot perform it without his or her spouse's signature does not render the contract void as between the parties to it.[1266]

A factual issue may be raised, however, as to when a contract for exchange becomes effective.[1267] An issue may be raised, particularly in cases involving realty, whether the wife of a party to the contract has knowingly become a party to it.[1268] Where property to be exchanged under the terms of a contract was a homestead owned by a husband and wife as tenants by the entireties, such fact was stated, in effect, to be significant in determining whether the contract was to be effective without the wife's signature.[1269]

A want of meeting of the minds in the making of a contract for exchange may be cured by the subsequent conduct of a party if the conduct amounts to ratification or estoppel to deny ratification.[1270]

Passing of title. Whether a transaction is a sale or an exchange, the passing of title to the respective items or parcels of property depends upon the intention of the parties, and may be, but is not necessarily, mutual or simultaneous.[1271]

§ 672.   Warranties

A warranty of title is implied in law in an exchange of property. The Seller Disclosure Act requires parties to a contract to exchange certain real property to disclose specified material defects within the knowledge of the party giving the property in the exchange.

1265. MCLS § 558.2.

1266. Dikeman v. Arnold, 78 Mich. 455, 44 N.W. 407 (1889).

1267. Wife's signature

Where husband signed contract for purchase of real estate by husband and wife providing for the conveyance by the husband and wife of land, held by them as tenants by entirety, as part of purchase price, with the intention that the wife should subsequently sign the contract, and the wife thereafter refused to sign, and vendors knew that the land to be conveyed to them was owned by them as tenants by entirety, the husband could recover from the vendors a portion of the purchase price paid by him at the time when he signed the contract, since it was not intended by the parties that the contract should become a valid contract until signed by the wife.—Rothstein v. Weeks, 224 Mich. 548, 195 N.W. 49 (1923).

1268. Zeigen v. Roiser, 200 Mich. 328, 166 N.W. 886 (1918).

1269. Rothstein v. Weeks, 224 Mich. 548, 195 N.W. 49 (1923).

1270. Ratification of terms

Defendant who, after discovering that plaintiff was expecting him, under terms of the contract, to assume responsibilities under a lease held by plaintiff, corrected a mistake in his own deed to plaintiff upon the exchange, and within five days thereafter sold and delivered the stock of goods received from plaintiff and put it out of his power to place plaintiff in statu quo, if plaintiff wished to rescind, was estopped to deny ratification of contract terms as testified to by plaintiff.—Harlow v. Jaseph, 183 Mich. 500, 149 N.W. 1047 (1914).

1271. Exchange

Title to the property of one of the parties to a contract of exchange may pass before he has acquired title to that for which it is exchanged.—Pratt v. Wickham, 133 Mich. 356, 94 N.W. 1059 (1903).

Sale

An agreement to sell a growing crop of wheat for 100 bushels of oats did not transfer title to the wheat, so long as the oats remained undelivered and mingled with other oats of the purchaser of the wheat.—Crapo v. Seybold, 35 Mich. 169 (1876).

In an exchange of properties, a warranty of title is implied in law, just as in a contract of sale.[1272]

Seller Disclosure Act. The disclosure requirements of the Seller Disclosure Act apply to the transfer of any interest in real estate consisting of not less than one or more than four residential units whether by sale, exchange, installment land contract, lease with an option to purchase, any other option to purchase, or ground lease coupled with proposed improvements by the purchaser or tenant, or a transfer of stock or an interest in a residential cooperative.[1273]

§ 673. Performance

Generally, a contract for exchange of property must be performed according to its terms.

Generally, a valid contract for exchange of property must be performed according to its terms, and a party cannot be compelled to accept performance not in conformity with the contract.[1274]

Objections to title, however, must advance a true cloud on the title.[1275] Even title defects that are remedied prior to court action will not allow cancellation of the contract.[1276]

Sometimes, equities arising out of a contract for exchange of properties warrant the requiring of complete performance, despite a petition for cancellation on the ground of title irregularities.[1277]

In an exchange of property based on appraisals, misrepresentations made to the appraisers render the affected appraisal nonbinding upon the other party in a suit for specific performance.[1278]

A party who has not performed or tendered performance under a contract for exchange of property cannot ordinarily complain of the default of the other

1272. Hunt v. Sackett, 31 Mich. 18 (1875) (personal property).

1273. Seller Disclosure Act, *see, supra,* Chapter 15.

MCLS § 565.952.

Brown v. Ind. Bldg. Sys. LLC, 2010 Mich. App. LEXIS 1199 (Mich. Ct. App. June 29, 2010).

Roberts v. Saffell, 280 Mich. App. 397, 760 N.W.2d 715, 2008 Mich. App. LEXIS 1756 (2008).

Stigmatized Property Law: To Disclose or Not to Disclose, that is the Question for Michigan Residential Sellers, 85 MI Bar Jnl. 34 (2006).

1274. Lack of title
Where the parties to an exchange agree to furnish abstracts showing marketable record title, a party cannot be compelled to accept an abstract showing title in a stranger, the party furnishing such abstract claiming title under a land contract not shown by the abstract.—Efrusy v. Mack, 219 Mich. 85, 188 N.W. 374 (1922).

1275. Bolstered tax title
Where plaintiff claimed that land conveyed to him under an agreement to exchange was encumbered with a tax title, and the court found that defendant's grantor had obtained a quitclaim deed from the holder of the tax title, and had conveyed to defendant by deed of warranty, plaintiff was not entitled to a decree rescinding the agreement.—Pirgandi v. Fay, 128 Mich. 630, 87 N.W. 888 (1901).

1276. Defects in deed
Where, at the time of an exchange of land, the deed to plaintiff was not signed by the grantor's wife, and had only one witness, but such defects were subsequently remedied, and the deed redelivered, plaintiff had no ground for complaint.—Pirgandi v. Fay, 128 Mich. 630, 87 N.W. 888 (1901).

1277. Bojarski v. Milus, 226 Mich. 475, 198 N.W. 182 (1924).

1278. Sutliff v. Dayton, 106 Mich. 179, 65 N.W. 522 (1895) (goods).

party.[1279]

Performance excused or avoided. The destruction of a farm dwelling by fire after execution of a contract for exchange that gave no immediate right to possession, and while a condition precedent was still unfulfilled, released the purchasers.[1280]

On the other hand, parties to a contract for exchange cannot avoid performance by having the contract recorded, notwithstanding a provision that the contract, if recorded, becomes void.[1281]

§ 674. Fraud

An inspection of the property to be received in an exchange, or an opportunity to inspect, may preclude the party receiving the property from complaining of misrepresentation.

Fraud in execution of instrument. A land exchange contract will not be set aside at the instance of a party who signs the contract after having heard it read, on the ground that he or she was misled as to its contents, unless very good reason exists for so doing, even though the person cannot read or write English.[1282]

Good faith. Where a party has made false representations to induce an exchange, and those representations have been relied upon, it is immaterial that they were made in good faith, and not fraudulently and only in reckless disregard of the truth.[1283] Similarly, fraudulent representations of material facts, if made and relied upon, are actionable even though made in good faith.[1284]

Person making representation. A principal is, of course, chargeable with fraud on the part of his or her agent, because the principal cannot be permitted to profit by the agent's fraud.[1285] A principal cannot defend a fraudulent exchange on the ground of irregularities by other parties induced by the principal's agent.[1286] Where parties exchanged their farm for that of others, they could not rescind without showing fraudulent participation by the other parties, although they had made a bad bargain in reliance on their own agent's assurances.[1287]

Knowledge or opportunity to inspect. Knowledge of the matters respecting which misrepresentations are made,[1288] or even an opportunity to inspect the

1279. Frankiewicz v. Konwinski, 246 Mich. 473, 224 N.W. 368 (1929).

Efrusy v. Mack, 219 Mich. 85, 188 N.W. 374 (1922).

1280. Frankiewicz v. Konwinski, 246 Mich. 473, 224 N.W. 368 (1929).

1281. Cohen v. Bredfeld, 241 Mich. 173, 216 N.W. 376 (1927).

1282. Dennis v. Slyman, 216 Mich. 202, 184 N.W. 584 (1921).

1283. Hillier v. Carpenter, 206 Mich. 594, 173 N.W. 386 (1919).

1284. Weinberg v. Ladd, 199 Mich. 164, 165 N.W. 711 (1917).

1285. Upell v. Bergman, 246 Mich. 82, 224 N.W. 404 (1929).

Chaffee v. Raymond, 241 Mich. 392, 217 N.W. 22 (1928).

1286. Reich v. Schmidt, 242 Mich. 130, 218 N.W. 671 (1928).

1287. Roe v. Albain, 255 Mich. 491, 238 N.W. 205 (1931).

1288. Federal seizure

Where parties had knowledge, at the time of entering into an exchange agreement, that the

property to be received in exchange,[1289] may preclude relief on the ground of fraud.

On the other hand, one who inspects property to be received in an exchange does not thereby preclude him- or herself from relief from subsequent fraudulent statements.[1290] The fact that one has seen realty to be received in an exchange does not in all cases bar the individual from relief, even with respect to fraudulent representations made at the time of the inspection.[1291]

Waiver or estoppel to claim fraud. A person does not waive fraud by signing a contract containing a "self-reliance clause." This type of clause is ineffective as a defense against a charge of fraud.[1292]

On the other hand, misrepresentations as to the amount of goods on hand in a business are waived by the plaintiff's operation of the business for five or six weeks after taking possession of it and discovering the amount of goods actually on hand.[1293]

§ 675.   —Nature of Misrepresentation

Misrepresentations as to the value of property offered in an exchange may, but do not usually, constitute actionable fraud.

Value. Generally, an exaggeration of the value of property to be exchanged, without more, and under ordinary circumstances, does not vitiate the transaction.[1294] A party who exaggerates the value of his or her own property can hardly complain

property had been padlocked by federal authorities, they were not entitled to rescission on the ground of fraud.—Barkovits v. Veres, 254 Mich. 543, 236 N.W. 857 (1931).

1289. Open to observation

Where representations as to the building that plaintiffs received on a trade concerned matters open to plaintiffs' observation, the rule of caveat emptor was applicable.—Kowalski v. Rusin, 242 Mich. 1, 217 N.W. 768 (1928).

Value of building

Where the complaining parties had ample opportunity to examine a building and to procure an estimate of its cost, but failed to do so, they could not rescind on the ground that the value of the building had been misrepresented.—Achenbach v. Mears, 272 Mich. 74, 261 N.W. 251 (1935).

Value of store merchandise

Where parties who exchanged a farm for a store had ample opportunity to examine the merchandise and to procure an inventory, examination and appraisal thereof, but did not do so, they could not complain that the representations as to the value of the merchandise were false.—Achenbach v. Mears, 272 Mich. 74, 261 N.W. 251 (1935).

1290. Hubert v. Joslin, 285 Mich. 337, 280 N.W. 780 (1938).

1291. Ignorance of defrauded parties

Where plaintiffs were Polish immigrants without knowledge of the value of land in the county and without experience in farming, and with little knowledge of the American language, and false representations as to value were made with knowledge of plaintiffs' ignorance and with expectation and purpose that such representations would be relied upon, plaintiffs were not precluded from relief by fact that they saw the farm before trading city property for it.—Szarkowski v. Pfister, 262 Mich. 226, 247 N.W. 163 (1933).

1292. Hubert v. Joslin, 285 Mich. 337, 280 N.W. 780 (1938).

1293. Saba v. Miller, 327 Mich. 363, 41 N.W.2d 894 (1950).

1294. Bowen v. Stocklin, 215 Mich. 341, 183 N.W. 946 (1921).

Matter of opinion

False statements about value will rarely void an exchange of properties, since value is usually a matter of opinion, and statements concerning value can rarely be supposed to have induced an exchange without negligence on part of complaining party.—Achenbach v. Mears, 272 Mich. 74, 261 N.W. 251 (1935).

about the other party's exaggeration.[1295]

Furthermore, a party who has a store or other business to dispose of usually has a right to claim whatever value he or she desires for it, without invalidating a bargain, particularly where it is being traded for something else.[1296]

There are exceptions to the general rule, however, depending upon such relevant factors as any calculated purpose to deceive, and the respective knowledge and experience of the parties.[1297]

> The contention made is that the statement of value was a mere matter of opinion, and cannot be made the basis of an action for fraud. This is a statement of the general rule, but the rule established by the weight of authority is that false statements of value intentionally made to one who is in ignorance of the quality and value, under circumstances indicating a purpose that such statements are to be relied upon, and where the party to whom they are made has no opportunity to examine the property, may be treated as an affirmation of fact and fraudulent.[1298]

But in any case, a claimed exaggeration of value must be sustained under the

Potential resale

Representation of vendors exchanging property, based on expectations of sale, that they had purchaser at stated price, was not actionable fraud.—Feldpausch v. Hendershot, 245 Mich. 694, 224 N.W. 407 (1929).

Valuation of equity

Defendants' statement, given to induce land exchange, that equity was nearly $6,000 was not fraudulent, though $6,000 was not the amount actually paid.—Mielke v. Tucker, 241 Mich. 449, 216 N.W. 919 (1928).

1295. Mutual overvaluation

Evidence of overvaluation by defendant was insufficient to show fraud warranting cancellation of land exchange contract, in view of plaintiff's overvaluation of his own property.—Kaiser v. Wojewoda, 237 Mich. 620, 213 N.W. 83 (1927).

1296. Achenbach v. Mears, 272 Mich. 74, 261 N.W. 251 (1935).

1297. Szarkowski v. Pfister, 262 Mich. 226, 247 N.W. 163 (1933).

Asserted expert knowledge

False representations that property could be sold for certain price, and was worth certain amount largely exceeding actual value, of which defendants professed expert knowledge, sustained decree rescinding exchange contract for fraud.—O'Neill v. Kunkle, 244 Mich. 653, 222 N.W. 110 (1928).

Silent misrepresentation

Where defendants, who dealt in realty, procured owner of farm to give her son land contract reciting consideration of $7,000 and other consideration, and had contract assigned to themselves without consideration, plaintiffs, in exchanging lands with defendants, were entitled to believe, and act on belief, that value of farm as fixed by owner was in excess of the $7,000 contract price.—Schliska v. Ross, 230 Mich. 225, 203 N.W. 81 (1925).

1298. Pinch v. Hotaling, 142 Mich. 521, 106 N.W. 69 (1905).

Knowledge of ignorance

Plaintiffs, who were Polish immigrants, without knowledge of value of land in county, with no experience in farming, prone to rely upon statements made to them, stand on a different footing than they would if, from knowledge of farming in county and experience therewith, they had traded for land therein; then their knowledge of the value of the land visited might estop them from claiming fraud; but plaintiffs were city dwellers, with no knowledge of value of farms in county, no experience in farming there or elsewhere, with little knowledge of the American language, and the statements made to them by defendants were made with knowledge of plaintiffs' ignorance, for the purpose of being relied upon and with such expectation and such statements of value, though in the form of opinion, relied upon by plaintiffs to whom they were made, constitute actionable fraud.—Szarkowski v. Pfister, 262 Mich. 226, 247 N.W. 163 (1933).

Gothe v. Kakis, 257 Mich. 364, 241 N.W. 136 (1932).

evidence.[1299]

Income from a business or rental property. Under the circumstances of particular cases, it is actionable fraud to misrepresent the profits of a business,[1300] or to represent falsely that a building from which the complaining party expected income was occupied and that the mortgage on it would be extended,[1301] or to misrepresent the amount of income from rental property.[1302]

A decline in profits in a business after it is acquired in an exchange does not support a claim of fraud, especially when the new owner's actions may have caused the decline.[1303]

Location of property. False representations as to the location of property to be exchanged may be actionable.[1304]

Encumbrances. False representations about encumbrances upon the property to be exchanged may be actionable, at least if the person making the representations professes to have knowledge that there are no encumbrances except those that he or she discloses.[1305] On the other hand, the defendant's statement, in reference to a prior mortgage, "that there was none so far as he knew" is such a representation as

1299. Mortgage

Representation of vendors exchanging property that mortgage was "good as gold" was not fraudulent, in view of experience of purchasers and testimony indicating that the mortgage was a sound investment.—Feldpausch v. Hendershot, 245 Mich. 694, 224 N.W. 407 (1929).

1300. Profits from mill

Parties misrepresenting profits from and condition of mill, for which owner executed lease, instead of agreed land contract, in exchange for equity in realty, conveyed to his wife by lessees known to have no other source of income than mill to make required payments, which were prohibitively large, were guilty of fraud, warranting rescission of trade.—Bacon v. Fox, 267 Mich. 589, 255 N.W. 340 (1934).

1301. Rental property

Where defendant agreed to exchange her entire property for a building of plaintiff's, misrepresentations by plaintiff that the building was occupied, and that the mortgage on it would be extended, were material, since defendant would have no means, except the receipts from the property, with which to satisfy the mortgage.—Kanar v. Schuster, 222 Mich. 282, 192 N.W. 562 (1923).

1302. Hillier v. Carpenter, 206 Mich. 594, 173 N.W. 386 (1919).

1303. Change of sales staff

The fact that, after an exchange of a farm for a store in a small town, and after a change of the sales force in the store, sales in it diminished, does not establish fraud, however.—Achenbach v. Mears, 272 Mich. 74, 261 N.W. 251 (1935).

1304. Lake frontage

Builder taking, for subdivision, property erroneously believed to have considerable lake frontage, and so represented, was properly allowed to rescind.—Mann v. Pearson, 249 Mich. 211, 228 N.W. 678 (1930).

Town lots

False representations concerning location of town lots, affecting their value, warranted rescission.—Salata v. Dylewski, 234 Mich. 331, 207 N.W. 895 (1926).

1305. Upell v. Bergman, 246 Mich. 82, 224 N.W. 404 (1929).

Claimed discount on vendor's lien

One exchanging lot for equity in farm property on false representation of defendants' broker that defendants' vendor, who had $2,450 due him on a land contract by which he had sold to defendants, had consented to accept $1,500 in full payment, was entitled to rescission.—Chaffee v. Raymond, 241 Mich. 392, 217 N.W. 22 (1928).

Profession of knowledge

Where defendant, for the purpose of obtaining plaintiff's property in exchange for a mortgage, asserted to him, as a fact of which he professed to have knowledge, that there was no prior mortgage on the land, when he knew or had good reason to believe the contrary, or no good reason to believe his assertion to be true, it seems he would be liable as for a fraudulent representation, and the plaintiff might have rescinded the contract and claimed his property.—Bristol v. Braidwood, 28 Mich. 191 (1873).

comes within the maxim of caveat emptor.[1306]

Promissory misrepresentation. If a person in the course of negotiating an exchange of property promises to do something in the future, the mere failure to fulfill that promise does not constitute actionable fraud,[1307] so long as the parties deal on an equal basis.[1308]

If, however, the person making such a promise has the intention, at the time of the making of the promise, not to fulfill it, the promissory representation may constitute actionable fraud.[1309] As a corollary, where fraud is committed partly by false promises and partly by false representations of fact, the promissory representations, made as part of a scheme to defraud, are actionable.[1310]

Character of the property. A misrepresentation, if material, as to the character of land offered in exchange is actionable.[1311]

Misrepresentation as to title or right of possession. Where defendant represents that he or she has a good title to property, and makes an exchange with the plaintiffs, but, on attempting to take possession, the plaintiffs find another party occupying the premises with the consent of defendant, under an agreement to work around the premises, which work has been done, and where that occupant declines to vacate, a legal fraud has been perpetrated on the plaintiffs.[1312]

Pendency of padlocking proceeding. Although the defendants, at the time of entering into an exchange contract, conceal the fact that the government has commenced proceedings to padlock the property offered by defendants, that concealment is not grounds for rescission where a bond is given to the government

1306. Bristol v. Braidwood, 28 Mich. 191 (1873).

1307. Promise to protect from foreclosure

Chattel mortgagee's breach of agreement to protect one receiving in exchange a farm and personal property on it, from foreclosure within a year following the purchase of the land, resulting in loss of the personal property, did not constitute the basis for an action to rescind for fraud; the agreement being simply a promise to do something in the future.—Dennis v. Slyman, 216 Mich. 202, 184 N.W. 584 (1921).

1308. Promise to erect dwelling houses

Failure of vendors exchanging property to fulfill promises to erect dwelling houses would not render contract void, where parties dealt on equal basis.—Feldpausch v. Hendershot, 245 Mich. 694, 224 N.W. 407 (1929).

1309. Promises to lend and to employ

Where complainants, who were the owners of a growing business with assets amounting to over $4,000, were induced by defendants to incorporate and transfer the stock to defendant machinery company in exchange for certain of its stock that was of little value, and to induce complainants to make the transfer, defendants represented that defendant company would advance capital so that complainants' business would improve, that the stock of defendant company would net a return of 6%, and that complainants would be given positions as department managers in defendant's business; all of which were untrue, complainants were entitled to rescission of the exchange on grounds of deceit.—Allen v. Pulfer, 159 Mich. 616, 124 N.W. 525 (1910).

1310. Szarkowski v. Pfister, 262 Mich. 226, 247 N.W. 163 (1933).

1311. Przytulski v. Jozwiak, 230 Mich. 521, 202 N.W. 924 (1925).

Hubert v. Joslin, 285 Mich. 337, 280 N.W. 780 (1938) (nature and productivity of soil).

Not misrepresented

Defendant was not fraudulently misrepresenting in describing his lands, offered in exchange, as bordered on two sides by a river, where lands previously deeded to city were excepted and conveyance to the city was construed as conveyance only of a right of flowage and not an unconditional grant of a fee title.—Chanter v. Roberts, 322 Mich. 545, 33 N.W.2d 923 (1948).

1312. Austin v. Ash, 232 Mich. 251, 205 N.W. 155 (1925).

and the premises are never in fact padlocked.[1313]

§ 676.   Rescission

Generally, one who has been defrauded in an exchange of properties may elect to rescind the exchange.

Grounds. A party seeking to rescind an exchange on the ground of fraud must "establish such a case of fraud as to prevent the passing of the title."[1314]

The representation that property is not subject to a mortgage, when it is in fact subject to a mortgage, is grounds for rescission of a contract for the exchange of property.[1315]

In a suit to cancel an exchange of property induced by false representations, the appropriate relief is rescission of the contract and restoration of the parties to their former status. A judgment allowing the culpable party to retain the property received in the exchange and granting other relief is therefore improper, particularly where both parties make propositions for settlement based on rescission.[1316]

A breach of warranty as to title or as to an encumbrance upon the property received in exchange justifies rescission.[1317]

A default in performance of the terms of the exchange contract may justify rescission, as where one defaulted in paying taxes and failing to settle a second mortgage.[1318] If one party departs from a special contract for the delivery of specific articles from each to the other, the other party might treat it as rescinded. If, by the terms of the contract, concurrent acts are to be performed, with respect to the delivery of property by one party and the payment of the price by the other, if either party refuses performance, the other may treat the contract as abandoned, and justify rescission.[1319]

On the other hand, mere inadequacy of consideration, where both parties to an exchange of lands have opportunity and ability to exercise independent judgment about the value, and where no fraud or misrepresentation is shown, will not justify rescission.[1320]

1313. Mielke v. Tucker, 241 Mich. 449, 216 N.W. 919 (1928).

1314. Achenbach v. Mears, 272 Mich. 74, 261 N.W. 251 (1935).

1315. Chattel mortgage

Defendant's misrepresentation, in connection with an agreement to exchange his grocery and meat business for the plaintiff's residence, that defendant owned the fixtures free and clear of any lien or encumbrance, whereas in fact his vendor had retained title to the fixtures as though part of the realty in a land contract of sale to defendant, entitled plaintiff to rescind the agreement, even though the plaintiff, as purchaser in good faith from one in possession, might have been able to establish title to the fixtures as against the defendant's vendor.—Saba v. Miller, 327 Mich. 363, 41 N.W.2d 894 (1950).

1316. Hillier v. Carpenter, 206 Mich. 594, 173 N.W. 386 (1919).

1317. Deprivation under mortgage

The taking from one's possession, by virtue of a valid chattel mortgage, of property received in exchange on a horse trade, would, though the exchange had been executed, authorize a rescission of the contract.—Hunt v. Sackett, 31 Mich. 18 (1875).

1318. Dysarz v. Mack, 245 Mich. 9, 222 N.W. 94 (1928).

1319. Stahelin v. Sowle, 87 Mich. 124, 49 N.W. 529 (1891).

1320. Vernon v. Antona, 222 Mich. 83, 192 N.W. 681 (1923).

Election of remedies. Generally, one who has a ground for rescission of a property exchange must elect whether to repudiate or affirm the contract, i.e., whether he or she will rescind or pursue other remedies. If the exchange is affirmed, he or she will be precluded from rescinding, the theory being that he or she cannot pursue an inconsistent course by treating the agreement as void while retaining or seeking to obtain that which he or she was to receive under it.[1321]

Where a party claiming to have been defrauded signs a receipt in the nature of a compromise after knowledge of any false representations, he or she is precluded from rescinding.[1322]

On the other hand, the fact that a plaintiff, when he or she tenders back to defendant a deed, demands payment for the personal property that the plaintiff has given in exchange, does not preclude rescission.[1323]

Restoration of statu quo. Rescission proceeds upon the principle of restoring, so far as practicable, the parties to their original positions. A party is ordinarily not entitled to rescind unless that party is able to restore what he or she has received.[1324] Thus, where a person has lost, by foreclosure or forfeiture, the property received, that person is not in a position to rescind,[1325] unless the other party has an opportunity to redeem after rescission.[1326] Deterioration of the property before rescission may also be an element to be considered in this connection.[1327]

The rule requiring that the rescinding party be in a position to restore what he or she has received is not absolute. If the rescinding party has in good faith changed the property or lost it but the value of it is capable of ascertainment, rescission may

---

1321. Austin v. Ash, 232 Mich. 251, 205 N.W. 155 (1925).

Warnes v. Brubaker, 107 Mich. 440, 65 N.W. 276 (1895).

Disposition of property received

Where plaintiff exchanged his apartment house for an orange grove in November, 1919, and in January, 1920, examined the grove, but was dissatisfied, his failure to promptly tender a reconveyance and insist on a rescission, and his later disposal of the water rights connected with the grove, were an affirmance of the exchange, and barred his right to rescind.—Vernon v. Antona, 222 Mich. 83, 192 N.W. 681 (1923).

Use of property received

One who has been defrauded in the exchange of realty for a patent right and other property, and who, after ascertaining the fraud, makes use of the right conveyed to him, or retains and uses the other property constituting a part of the consideration of his conveyance, thereby ratifies and affirms the entire transaction, and cannot treat the agreement as void while retaining what he received under it.—Dunks v. Fuller, 32 Mich. 242 (1875).

1322. Parkyn v. Ford, 194 Mich. 184, 160 N.W. 531 (1916).

1323. Stevens v. Thompson, 98 Mich. 9, 56 N.W. 1041 (1893).

1324. Rule stated

Substantial return to the statu quo ante is of the essence of the action.—Papciak v. Morawski, 243 Mich. 157, 219 N.W. 601 (1928).

1325. Augustyn v. Zawacki, 250 Mich. 218, 229 N.W. 453 (1930).

Lemmon v. Kenas, 247 Mich. 378, 225 N.W. 558 (1929).

Vernon v. Antona, 222 Mich. 83, 192 N.W. 681 (1923).

Papciak v. Morawski, 243 Mich. 157, 219 N.W. 601 (1928).

1326. Place v. Brown, 37 Mich. 575 (1877).

1327. Deterioration

Conceding that one exchanging city property for a farm was defrauded, he was not entitled to rescind where he learned of the fraud on April 1, 1918, and took no steps to rescind until May, 1920, after suit had been brought to foreclose a mortgage for the difference in the prices of the two places, and in the meantime had permitted the farm to run down and deteriorate in value while the other parties had made considerable improvements on the property received by them, and made no offer to place the other parties *in statu quo* beyond an offer to reconvey.—Bowen v. Stocklin, 215 Mich. 341, 183 N.W. 946 (1921).

still be had.[1328]

In any case, however, the ability to make a substantial restoration is sufficient.[1329] Nothing less, however, will suffice.[1330]

Although the party seeking to rescind must ordinarily be able to restore substantially what he or she has received, the converse is not necessarily true. In a case where the defendant assignees of a land contract parted with plaintiffs' property received in an exchange, before plaintiffs sought to rescind for fraud, the decree properly required defendants to repay the value of the plaintiffs' equity in it.[1331]

It follows from the nature of rescission and the principle of restoration of the statu quo ante that a decree rescinding an exchange must provide for reconveyance by the defendants rather than their payment of the trade price or value. This is true though the defendants have made only a belated offer to reconvey.[1332]

In order to more completely restore the parties to their original positions, or to approximate those positions, some adjustments of minor equities, such as by way of accounting, may be warranted in connection with a decree of rescission.[1333]

Tender. In considering whether a tender of property received in an exchange is necessary in connection with rescission, a distinction must be made between

1328. Szarkowski v. Pfister, 262 Mich. 226, 247 N.W. 163 (1933).

1329. Inconsequential value of property used

Directed verdict in suit to rescind realty trade for fraud was properly denied, where value of personalty used by grantee was not consequential.—Lindow v. Mudge, 247 Mich. 624, 226 N.W. 656 (1929).

Stock of goods

Contention that defendants could not be put in statu quo because condition and amount of stock of goods was different from what it was at time of exchange did not preclude rescission of agreement for exchange of plaintiff's residence for grocery and meat business on ground of fraud and misrepresentations, where stock of goods as of date of repossession by defendants was substantially the same as at time of exchange.—Saba v. Miller, 327 Mich. 363, 41 N.W.2d 894 (1950).

Woodcutting

Cutting of 48 cords of wood on farm did not preclude rescission of contract whereby farm was exchanged for city property.—Szarkowski v. Pfister, 262 Mich. 226, 247 N.W. 163 (1933).

1330. Restoration of boot money only

Plaintiff and defendant exchanged stoves, plaintiff receiving $2 on the exchange. Several weeks afterwards plaintiff, claiming to have been defrauded, tendered the $2 but not the stove to the defendant, and demanded her stove. Defendant refused to accept the money or return the stove. This was not a sufficient compliance with the rule

requiring one who seeks to rescind a contract on the ground of fraud to place the other party in statu quo.—Johnson v. Flynn, 97 Mich. 581, 56 N.W. 939 (1893).

1331. Schliska v. Ross, 230 Mich. 225, 203 N.W. 81 (1925).

1332. Bacon v. Fox, 267 Mich. 589, 255 N.W. 340 (1934).

1333. Bacon v. Fox, 267 Mich. 589, 255 N.W. 340 (1934).

Gothe v. Kakis, 257 Mich. 364, 241 N.W. 136 (1932).

Accounting for loss

Where plaintiff was entitled to rescind agreement for exchange of her residence for defendants' grocery and meat business on ground of fraud and misrepresentation, plaintiff was also entitled to an accounting for loss attributable to fraud and not to plaintiff's mismanagement, default or neglect.—Saba v. Miller, 327 Mich. 363, 41 N.W.2d 894 (1950).

Disbursements and benefits

Court in decreeing rescission of exchange contract and restoration of statu quo properly considered disbursements, benefits, and like as between parties.—Mezak v. Fox, 253 Mich. 326, 235 N.W. 172 (1931).

Payments and rent

Defrauded transferee of land contract must account for payments received on it and have credit for rent on property exchanged.—Gadzinski v. Rola, 246 Mich. 10, 224 N.W. 334 (1929).

rescission effected or attempted by the defrauded party him- or herself, and a suit for a decree of rescission. In an action at law, based on rescission, a tender is a prerequisite. In an equitable action, however, the rule is not so rigid. There, the complaint must proffer return of what has been received. The decree will place the parties in their original positions as far as possible.[1334]

Accordingly, on the one hand, one cannot reclaim personal property the person has traded without returning or tendering property received,[1335] and, on the other hand, a tender is not necessary where one seeks a decree of rescission,[1336] at least if the bill for rescission expresses an offer or willingness to place defendant in *statu quo* or to return what has been received.[1337]

If an exchange agreement remains wholly executory on the defendant's part, there is no occasion for restoration or tender.[1338]

In any case, tender is not necessary where the defendant's conduct shows that tender would be unavailing,[1339] or where the property received is absolutely worthless.[1340]

Whether there was a proper offer to return property received as part of a demand for rescission is determined under the facts of the case.[1341]

Equities of third parties. A purchaser under a subcontract, purchasing an equity in the original contract from one fraudulently securing it will, on cancellation, be required to proceed under the subcontract.[1342]

§ 677.   —Laches

One who claims to have been defrauded in an exchange of property generally must act promptly if he or she wishes to rescind the exchange.

1334. Chaffee v. Raymond, 241 Mich. 392, 217 N.W. 22 (1928).

1335. Johnson v. Flynn, 97 Mich. 581, 56 N.W. 939 (1893).

Offer to "trade back"

Where land has been conveyed in exchange for personal property, and the grantee seeks to repudiate the bargain for fraud, he cannot reclaim his goods without tendering a reconveyance; and a mere offer to "trade back," without such conveyance or tender, is no rescission.—Wilbur v. Flood, 16 Mich. 40 (1867).

1336. Augustyn v. Zawacki, 250 Mich. 218, 229 N.W. 453 (1930).

1337. Saba v. Miller, 327 Mich. 363, 41 N.W.2d 894 (1950).

Burns v. Misura, 228 Mich. 152, 199 N.W. 606 (1924).

1338. Heth v. Oxendale, 238 Mich. 236, 213 N.W. 133 (1927).

1339. Salata v. Dylewski, 234 Mich. 331, 207 N.W. 895 (1926).

1340. Sheldon Axle Co. v. Scofield, 85 Mich. 177, 48 N.W. 511 (1891).

Worthlessness

Evidence that a short time after an exchange of stoves between plaintiff and defendant, plaintiff was informed that the stove received of defendant was worthless, "worth not to exceed $3," does not establish a case of worthless property so as to absolve plaintiff from tendering a return of the property on rescinding the exchange.—Johnson v. Flynn, 97 Mich. 581, 56 N.W. 939 (1893).

1341. Offer to return

Grantor's telling the grantee corporation's president before bringing suit to set aside a deed conveying realty in exchange for hotel property, to "take your stuff and give me my stuff and we'll call it off," constituted a sufficient tender of restoration, if tender was a prerequisite to institution of the proceedings.—Touma v. Holly Lumber & Supply Co., 294 Mich. 96, 292 N.W. 576 (1940).

1342. Reich v. Schmidt, 242 Mich. 130, 218 N.W. 671 (1928).

A party who desires to rescind an exchange of real property for fraud must act promptly.[1343]

Generally, however, whether relief in the nature of rescission is to be withheld on the ground of laches depends in large measure on the facts and circumstances of the particular case, especially the extent to which the defendant has been prejudiced by the delay.[1344]

A delay of five months might be a bar to rescission under the circumstances,[1345] while a delay of three years may be excused under other circumstances.[1346] By way of analogy, a delay of three years before seeking relief by way of injunction against forfeiture may, under the circumstances of the case, likewise be excused.[1347]

§ 678. Remedies Other Than Rescission

An action for damages may be maintained for breach of a contract to exchange properties, or for fraud in connection therewith, providing the complaining party has not elected to rescind.

Claim and delivery action. Where title to personal property to be received in an exchange has passed, a claim and delivery action may lie to gain possession of it.[1348]

Assumpsit. The ground on which an action on the common counts in assumpsit is sustained on the rescission of a contract of exchange, where it is permitted at all, is that because the contract of exchange is rescinded, there is no longer any express contract existing. The law will thereupon do that which the equities of the case demand under the conditions in which the rescission has left the parties.[1349] Therefore, if one party executes and delivers the requisite deed, and the other party refuses to perform under an agreement for the exchange of land, the latter's refusal has the effect of rescinding the contract and raises an implied promise to pay for

1343. Theory

Person discovering that he has been defrauded in exchange of property must act promptly in order to be entitled to rescission, which proceeds upon theory that by reason of fraud title to property never passed.—Achenbach v. Mears, 272 Mich. 74, 261 N.W. 251 (1935).

1344. Heth v. Oxendale, 238 Mich. 236, 213 N.W. 133 (1927).

Relief not barred

Saba v. Miller, 327 Mich. 363, 41 N.W.2d 894 (1950).

Gothe v. Kakis, 257 Mich. 364, 241 N.W. 136 (1932).

Upell v. Bergman, 246 Mich. 82, 224 N.W. 404 (1929).

Schliska v. Ross, 230 Mich. 225, 203 N.W. 81 (1925).

1345. Store and stock of goods

Parties who exchanged farm for store and continued to conduct store some five months after discovery of alleged fraud held to have waived fraud complained of so as to bar suit for rescission.—Achenbach v. Mears, 272 Mich. 74, 261 N.W. 251 (1935).

1346. Heth v. Oxendale, 238 Mich. 236, 213 N.W. 133 (1927).

1347. Hubert v. Joslin, 285 Mich. 337, 280 N.W. 780 (1938).

1348. MCLS § 600.2920; MCR 3.105.

See M.L.P.2d Personal Property.

The former action was replevin. *See, e.g.,* Pratt v. Wickham, 133 Mich. 356, 94 N.W. 1059 (1903); Whitcraft v. Wolfe, 148 Mich. App. 40, 384 N.W.2d 400, 1985 Mich. App. LEXIS 3149 (1985).

1349. Hunt v. Sackett, 31 Mich. 18 (1875).

what that party has received upon it.[1350]

If a plaintiff contracts to exchange goods for certain lots, including one pointed out by the defendant, and subsequently discovers that the lot described in the contract is in another and different locality and of less value than the one pointed out, plaintiff cannot waive the tort and maintain assumpsit for the value of the lot.[1351]

Damages for breach. An action upon a contract of exchange of personal property, as for breach of warranty of title, is an affirmance of the contract. No act in disaffirmance of the trade, such as tendering back the deposit money, or demanding the property given in exchange, is necessary as a condition precedent to bringing the action.[1352]

By conduct amounting to an affirmance of the contract, however, a party may be precluded from interposing the defense of fraud in an action for the breach.[1353]

Specific performance. Where a contract for exchange provides fully for the manner and time in which title defects may be presented and passed upon, those provisions are binding in a suit for specific performance.[1354]

It follows from the principle, that a plaintiff who has not performed or tendered performance cannot ordinarily complain of the default of the other party, that a party cannot compel specific performance of a contract for exchange if that party is unable to establish his or her title to the property to be given in exchange.[1355]

Damages for fraud. Parties who have been defrauded in an exchange of property have a right to affirm the contract and, by complaint for equitable relief, require defendants to account for the fraud and to have a mortgage given by them cancelled if the damages recoverable equal the amount of the mortgage.[1356]

Injunction. If the defrauded parties desire to retain the property acquired in an exchange, they could, sue to recover damages in an equitable suit to enjoin forfeiture of the contract and to obtain a credit on it.[1357]

In such an action, under the circumstances of the case, a delay of three years before commencement of the suit may not bar the granting of the relief sought.[1358]

Appropriate relief. The court exercising its equity jurisdiction must give relief

---

1350. Dikeman v. Arnold, 78 Mich. 455, 44 N.W. 407 (1889).

1351. Reed v. Ismond, 110 Mich. 16, 67 N.W. 912 (1896).

1352. Hunt v. Sackett, 31 Mich. 18 (1875).

1353. Hamburger v. Berman, 170 N.W. 555 (Mich. 1919).

1354. Cohen v. Bredfeld, 241 Mich. 173, 216 N.W. 376 (1927).

1355. Real Property Law: Real Evidence: Special Rules For Real Estate Disputes, 80 Mich. B.J. 28 (2001).

Plaintiff's loss of evidence

Plaintiff was not entitled to specific performance of contract for exchange of properties, where plaintiff's paper evidence of title was lost through disappearance of depositary under escrow agreement.—Frankiewicz v. Konwinski, 246 Mich. 473, 224 N.W. 368 (1929).

1356. Vanek v. Soumar, 218 Mich. 282, 187 N.W. 396 (1922).

1357. Hubert v. Joslin, 285 Mich. 337, 280 N.W. 780 (1938).

1358. Delay in commencement of suit

Plaintiffs were not barred by laches from maintaining suit to enjoin forfeiture of land contract for

in accordance with the plaintiff's election upon proof of equities warranting it.[1359]

§ 679.   Procedure

Damages recoverable in an action for breach of a contract for exchange are those that are the natural, direct, and proximate result of the breach.

Pleading. An allegation of fraud is sufficient if the facts that are alleged show that defendant was active in the execution of the fraudulent transaction, whereby the plaintiff was induced to trade real estate, and that the defendant received a share of the proceeds.[1360]

Trial. In an action for breach of a contract to exchange properties, whether the title tendered is a marketable title is a legal question upon which the jury must be instructed.[1361]

In an action for the breach of a contract to exchange lands, an owner may testify to the actual value of the land that he or she has agreed to convey.[1362]

Damages. It follows from the nature of rescission and from the rule that a complaining party must elect whether to rescind or sue for damages for breach or for fraud that the relief to which a complaining party is entitled in a suit for rescission is, generally, a restoration of the property with which the party was induced to part. For that reason, a party obtaining a decree rescinding the trade of realty for fraud is entitled only to be put in statu quo ante. Money damages may be decreed only when reconveyance of the realty is impossible.[1363]

Similarly, it is error, in a suit to rescind, to allow damages to the plaintiff for expenses in going to and from the property, because those expenses do not enhance the value of the property.[1364]

An adjustment of minor equities in a suit for rescission may nevertheless be justified when, if adjustment for items such as repairs, improvements, taxes, and rentals is necessary to restore the parties to their respective prior positions.[1365]

the exchange of their Chicago property for defendants' farm and to obtain a credit on contract on ground of defendants' fraud, even though they waited 3 years and until after defendants had prosecuted lawsuit resulting in cancellation of $2,000 mortgage on farm, where plaintiffs were not experienced in business, had no money to bring suit, needed a place to stay, and had no opportunity to put in a crop to see what the result of their efforts would be.—Hubert v. Joslin, 285 Mich. 337, 280 N.W. 780 (1938).

1359. Cancellation of mortgage

Where the parties defrauded in connection with an exchange of property elect to affirm the contract and sue for cancellation of a mortgage given by them, and where the defendants asked no affirmative relief and the property previously owned by the plaintiffs had passed through several hands, had been neglected, and could not be returned in the same condition as at the time of the exchange,

plaintiffs were entitled to relief in accordance with their election, and chancery court erred in decreeing a rescission and requiring the plaintiffs to amend to conform to that theory.—Vanek v. Soumar, 218 Mich. 282, 187 N.W. 396 (1922).

1360. Watson v. Wagner, 202 Mich. 397, 168 N.W. 428 (1918).

1361. Frederick v. Hillebrand, 199 Mich. 333, 165 N.W. 810 (1917).

1362. Frederick v. Hillebrand, 199 Mich. 333, 165 N.W. 810 (1917).

1363. Bacon v. Fox, 267 Mich. 589, 255 N.W. 340 (1934).

1364. Austin v. Ash, 232 Mich. 251, 205 N.W. 155 (1925).

1365. Saba v. Miller, 327 Mich. 363, 41 N.W.2d 894 (1950).

Similarly, a lien may be impressed in connection with the adjustment.[1366]

In an action for breach in the nature of a refusal to convey, the proper measure of damages is the amount lost through the defendant's breach, to be ascertained as of the date of the breach.[1367] More specifically, damages are the fair market value, at the time of the breach, of the property that defendant promised to convey.[1368] In such a case, however, the damages do not include such incidental items as loss of wood and hay caused by the complaining party's belief that the contract would be fulfilled, and the consequent failure to provide a barn for the hay, or to cut the wood.[1369]

As for damages for fraud or misrepresentation, on affirmance of the contract, the measure of damages is the difference between the actual value of the property received in exchange and the value of it if it had been as it was represented to be.[1370]

Consistently, where a party is told that a deed in the chain of title to property that the party was receiving was security for a certain amount, the party is entitled to recover that amount with interest, less the amount actually secured by the deed.[1371]

On failure of title, the consideration for a conveyance given in exchange is not necessarily the measure of damages if the party receiving it has made sustained use of the property.[1372]

Where the breach occurs by reason of an encumbrance upon the property received and upon other property as well, the measure is not the value of the property given in exchange.[1373]

§ 680.   —Evidence

One seeking to rescind a contract for the exchange of property, on the ground of fraud, must establish the fraud by convincing evidence.

Incompetency to contract. The evidence may be insufficient to establish the mental incompetency of a party entering into a contract for the exchange of property.[1374]

Bacon v. Fox, 267 Mich. 589, 255 N.W. 340 (1934).

Mezak v. Fox, 253 Mich. 326, 235 N.W. 172 (1931).

Gadzinski v. Rola, 246 Mich. 10, 224 N.W. 334 (1929).

1366. Lien impressed

In accounting incident to rescission of exchange of property, defendants were entitled to mortgage on property reconveyed to plaintiffs for difference in amount defendants had paid on it and expenditures plaintiff made on property plaintiff reconveyed.—Gothe v. Kakis, 257 Mich. 364, 241 N.W. 136 (1932).

1367. Hamburger v. Berman, 203 Mich. 78, 168 N.W. 925 (1918).

1368. Dikeman v. Arnold, 71 Mich. 656, 40 N.W. 42 (1888).

1369. Frederick v. Hillebrand, 199 Mich. 333, 165 N.W. 810 (1917).

1370. Hubert v. Joslin, 285 Mich. 337, 280 N.W. 780 (1938).

1371. Goodman v. Rott, 242 Mich. 198, 218 N.W. 761 (1928).

1372. Hunt v. Middlesworth, 44 Mich. 448, 7 N.W. 57 (1880).

1373. Hunt v. Sackett, 31 Mich. 18 (1875).

1374. Hake v. Youngs, 254 Mich. 545, 236 N.W. 858 (1931).

Richardson v. Brown, 247 Mich. 298, 225 N.W. 488 (1929).

Execution of instrument. Evidence on the question whether a person executed an assignment of a land contract for the purpose of making an exchange of property and not, as defendant claims, for the purpose of securing a loan, may sustain a judgment for defendant in a suit for equitable relief.[1375]

Delivery of instrument. Evidence may be sufficient to support a finding that delivery of an assignment in connection with an exchange of property was not contrary to instructions of the assignor and was therefore authorized.[1376]

Fraud. Fraud is never presumed or lightly inferred.[1377] At least convincing evidence is necessary.[1378]

The evidence may show that acts of a party to an exchange constitute a badge of fraud set up in anticipation of a claim of fraud.[1379]

The courts have ruled on the sufficiency of the evidence in cases involving fraud with respect to the valuation of property offered in the exchange,[1380] income

---

1375. Zeigen v. Roiser, 200 Mich. 328, 166 N.W. 886 (1918).

1376. Krysinski v. Whipple, 248 Mich. 195, 226 N.W. 828 (1929).

1377. Vernon v. Antona, 222 Mich. 83, 192 N.W. 681 (1923) (no fraud in exchange of orange grove for apartment).

1378. Rule stated

A party seeking rescission of a contract for exchange of real property on the ground of fraud must establish the fraud by convincing evidence.—Zimmerman v. Feldman, 217 Mich. 390, 186 N.W. 495 (1922).

Standard of proof

Generally, fraud must be proved by "clear and convincing" evidence rather than by the preponderance of the evidence. Traxler v. Ford Motor Co., 227 Mich. App. 276, 576 N.W.2d 398 (1998); Allstate Ins. Co. v. Maroki, 2002 Mich. App. LEXIS 1343 (Mich. Ct. App. Sept. 24, 2002). But, as explained by the Court of Appeals in Mina v. General Star Indem. Co., 218 Mich. App. 678, 555 N.W.2d 1 (1996), rev'd in part on other grounds, 455 Mich. 866, 568 N.W.2d 80, 1997 Mich. LEXIS 1627 (1997), there are decisions both ways on this issue. The most recent decisions require "clear and convincing" proof. *See, e.g.,* Harmonie Club Enterprises v. TCF Natl Bank, 2007 Mich. App. LEXIS 1431 (Mich. Ct. App. May 24, 2007); Colby v. Zimmerman, 2001 Mich. App. LEXIS 1974 (Mich. Ct. App. Oct. 12, 2001); Flynn v. Korneffel, 451 Mich. 186, 547 N.W.2d 249 (1996). There are earlier Michigan decisions stating that the preponderance of evidence standard is applicable. *See, e.g.,* Achenbach v. Mears, 272 Mich. 74, 261 N.W. 251 (1935); Kukielka v. Ranyak, 229 Mich. 13, 200 N.W. 964 (1924); Leser v. Smith, 212 Mich. 558, 180 N.W. 464 (1920).

Insufficient proof

Whether or not defendant, who on exchanging property with plaintiff for a mortgage, represented in reference to a prior mortgage that there was none so far as he knew, could be liable under clear and distinct proof that he in fact did know there was a prior mortgage, he cannot be held liable on proof simply that someone had told him he had heard that there was a prior mortgage.—Bristol v. Braidwood, 28 Mich. 191 (1873).

1379. Affidavit by other party to exchange

In trade of realty for a gristmill, an affidavit signed by a complaining party at the time of the transaction, to the effect that she had investigated the mill, that her husband was an experienced miller, and that no representations as to profits from the mill were made by the defendants, must be considered a badge of fraud exacted by the defendants' attorney to build up a defense against an anticipated charge of fraud.—Bacon v. Fox, 267 Mich. 589, 255 N.W. 340 (1934).

1380. Gothe v. Kakis, 257 Mich. 364, 241 N.W. 136 (1932).

Shultz v. McCarty, 253 Mich. 445, 235 N.W. 215 (1931).

Noble v. Shears, 230 Mich. 376, 202 N.W. 921 (1925).

Leser v. Smith, 212 Mich. 558, 180 N.W. 464 (1920) (value of farms).

McKenzie v. Call, 176 Mich. 198, 142 N.W. 370 (1913).

Mutual overvaluation

Evidence of overvaluation by defendant was insufficient to show fraud warranting cancellation of land exchange contract, in view of plaintiff's overvaluation.—Kaiser v. Wojewoda, 237 Mich. 620, 213 N.W. 83 (1927).

or receipts from a business or rental property offered in exchange,[1381] encumbrances or amounts due on the purchase price of property offered in exchange,[1382] the character of land offered in exchange,[1383] the identity of property shown with that ultimately exchanged,[1384] the right to make a transfer required by the contract for exchange,[1385] the potential for resale of the property exchanged,[1386] and workmanship and materials on a dwelling offered in exchange.[1387]

Realty and stock of goods

Trial court's findings, based on conflicting evidence that plaintiffs, who exchanged farm for city realty and hardware business, did not establish fraud as to value of realty, but established a deceptive overvaluation of hardware stock, were warranted.—Kukielka v. Ranyak, 229 Mich. 13, 200 N.W. 964 (1924).

Value and income

Where complainant exchanged his farm for apartment building owned by defendant, evidence showed that defendant made false representations concerning value of and income derived from apartment building, and that complainant in making the exchange relied on those representations, which were either fraudulently made or made in reckless disregard of the truth.—Hillier v. Carpenter, 206 Mich. 594, 173 N.W. 386 (1919).

1381. Hillier v. Carpenter, 206 Mich. 594, 173 N.W. 386 (1919).

Saba v. Miller, 327 Mich. 363, 41 N.W.2d 894 (1950) (grocery and meat business).

Bacon v. Fox, 267 Mich. 589, 255 N.W. 340 (1934) (mill).

Shultz v. McCarty, 253 Mich. 445, 235 N.W. 215 (1931) (theater property).

1382. Dennis v. Slyman, 216 Mich. 202, 184 N.W. 584 (1921).

McKenzie v. Call, 176 Mich. 198, 142 N.W. 370 (1913).

Bristol v. Braidwood, 28 Mich. 191 (1873).

Claimed discount on amount due

Evidence required finding of fraudulent representation by agent of defendant exchanging equity that defendant's vendor, who had money coming on contract for sale to defendant, had consented to take discount.—Chaffee v. Raymond, 241 Mich. 392, 217 N.W. 22 (1928).

1383. Przytulski v. Jozwiak, 230 Mich. 521, 202 N.W. 924 (1925) (farm lands).

Clark v. Purchase, 226 Mich. 374, 197 N.W. 518 (1924) (farm lands).

1384. Identity of lot

Evidence that purchaser transferred $4,900 property for interest in $1,200 lot, and was shown different lot of greater value, showed fraud sufficient to cancel transaction.—Gadzinski v. Rola, 246 Mich. 10, 224 N.W. 334 (1929).

1385. Right to transfer

In suit to rescind an exchange of property, evidence showed that defendant had been guilty of fraud and misrepresentation, having known he was prohibited from transferring by contract under which he held.—Rodenhouse v. De Golia, 198 Mich. 402, 164 N.W. 488 (1917).

1386. Larzelere v. Conlin, 234 Mich. 337, 207 N.W. 802 (1926).

1387. Ponke v. Rusinowski, 241 Mich. 629, 217 N.W. 765 (1928).

Chapter 23

NATURE AND VALIDITY OF MORTGAGES

A. THE NATURE OF MORTGAGES

§ 701. General Considerations

A "mortgage" is a lien on real estate securing payment or performance of an obligation, but a mortgage does not give the mortgagee title to the property. Any agreement sufficient to constitute a valid regular real estate mortgage suffices to effect a mortgage on an interest in a land contract.

Library References

Michigan Digest
John G. Cameron, Jr., Michigan Real Estate Forms
Midwest Transaction Guide
Thompson on Real Property, Thomas Edition (David A. Thomas, ed.)
Powell on Real Property® (Michael Allan Wolf, ed.)
Real Estate Financing

Law Reviews

Ryan E. Scharar, The Limits Of Securitization: Why Bankruptcy Courts Should Substantively Consolidate Predatory Sub-Prime Mortgage Originators and Their Special Purpose Entities, 2008 Mich. St. L. Rev. 913 (2008); Naseem Stecker and Mike Eidelbes, Up Front: Real Property and Consumer Law Sections Team up on "Ask The Lawyer" to Discuss Mortgage Foreclosures, 87 MI Bar Jnl. 8 (2008); Howard A. Lax, Recognizing Mortgage Fraud, 86 MI Bar Jnl. 34 (2007); Eric C. Bartley, . . . And Federal Regulation for All: Federally Regulating the Mortgage Banking Industry, 2006 Mich. St. L. Rev. 477 (2006); Frederick L. Miller, Bait and Switch in the Mortgage Market: Coping with High-Rate Sleight of Hand, 85 MI Bar Jnl. 21 (2006); Kevin W. Kevelighan, Consumer Law: Consumer Mortgage Defense, 85 MI Bar Jnl. 32 (2006); Kevin W. Kevelighan, Consumer Mortgage Defense: Challenging Non-Judicial Foreclosures in District Court Summary Proceedings, 85 MI Bar Jnl. 32 (2006); Nicole Stelle Garnett, The Neglected Political Economy of Eminent Domain, 105 Mich. L. Rev. 101 (2006).

A "mortgage" is a lien on real estate securing payment or performance of an obligation, but a mortgage does not give the mortgagee title to the property.[1388]

1388. Livonia Prop. Holdings, L.L.C. v. 12840-12976 Farmington Rd. Holdings, L.L.C., 717 F. Supp. 2d 724, 2010 U.S. Dist. LEXIS 47595 (E.D. Mich. 2010).

Z & Z Leasing v. Graying Reel, 873 F. Supp. 51, 1995 U.S. Dist. LEXIS 466, 40 Env't Rep. Cas. (BNA) 1220, 25 Envtl. L. Rep. 20802 (E.D. Mich. 1995).

McKeighan v. Citizens Commercial & Sav. Bank, 302 Mich. 666, 5 N.W.2d 524 (1942).

Dan Allor Plumbing & Heating v. Abbey Homes, 2011 Mich. App. LEXIS 932 (Mich. Ct. App. May 19, 2011).

Prime Fin. Servs. LLC v. Vinton, 279 Mich. App. 245, 761 N.W.2d 694, 2008 Mich. App. LEXIS 1192, 65 U.C.C. Rep. Serv. 2d (CBC) 867 (2008).

PTPS, Inc. v. B & B Inv. Group, 1997 Mich. App. LEXIS 3795 (Mich. Ct. App. Mar. 7, 1997).

Foote v. Pontiac, 161 Mich. App. 60, 409 N.W.2d 756 (1987) (real estate mortgage).

Purchase money mortgage

A purchase money mortgage is a mortgage or security device taken back to secure the performance of an obligation incurred in the purchase of the property; two mortgages at issue were purchase money mortgages, where in both cases the mortgagor gave the mortgage to secure repayment of the funds used to purchase the real property.— Qassis v. Republic Bank (In re Luna Pier Land Dev., LLC), 325 B.R. 735, 2005 Bankr. LEXIS 949, 44 Bankr. Ct. Dec. (LRP) 218 (Bankr. E.D. Mich. 2005).

Nonetheless, a mortgage is an interest in land,[1389] yet only a chose in action.[1390]

A mortgage of land is regarded as a conveyance within the meaning of the recording laws.[1391] However, "a mortgage, being a mere security for the debt or liability secured by it, the debt or liability secured is the principal and the mortgage is but an incident or accessory."[1392]

The validity of a mortgage of real estate is generally governed by the law of the state where the mortgaged property is situated.[1393] Even if a mortgage is valid by the laws of the state where it is executed, if it does not comply with the laws of the state where the mortgaged land is situated, it cannot be enforced there. A provision in a mortgage, valid in the state where made, cannot be enforced in the state in which proceedings are commenced when it is in violation of the public policy of the latter state.[1394]

Such matters as mortgages of personal property,[1395] mortgages fraudulent as to creditors or subsequent purchasers,[1396] rights of mortgagors and mortgagees as to fixtures,[1397] mortgage insurance,[1398] and subrogation to the rights of mortgagees,[1399] are discussed elsewhere.

Land contract mortgages. The statutes providing for the mortgaging of all or a part of either a vendor's or vendee's interests in a land contract provide that any agreement sufficient to constitute a valid regular real estate mortgage suffices to effect a mortgage on an interest in the land contract.[1400]

§ 702. Mortgages Distinguished From Other Transactions

A mortgage is to be distinguished from a conditional sale, a lease, and a trust.

1389. Aetna Mortg. Co. v. Dembs, 13 Mich. App. 686, 164 N.W.2d 771 (1968).

1390. Plasger v. Leonard, 312 Mich. 561, 20 N.W.2d 296 (1945).

1391. MCLS § 565.35.

Stover v. Bryant & Detwiler Improvement Co., 329 Mich. 482, 45 N.W.2d 364 (1951).

Bankruptcy

Because the real property was sold at a pre-petition foreclosure sale, only the right of redemption, not the property itself, became part of the bankruptcy estate.—In re Jones, 233 B.R. 799, 1999 Bankr. LEXIS 544, 41 Collier Bankr. Cas. 2d (MB) 1392 (Bankr. E.D. Mich. 1999).

1392. In re Estate of Goodwin, 362 Mich. 456, 107 N.W.2d 881 (1961).

Ginsberg v. Capitol City Wrecking Co., 300 Mich. 712, 2 N.W.2d 892, 1942 Mich. LEXIS 669 (1942).

1393. Fitch v. Remer, 9 F. Cas. 181, 1860 U.S. App. LEXIS 453 (C.C.D. Mich. 1860) (No. 4,836).

Barras v. Youngs, 185 Mich. 496, 152 N.W. 219 (1915).

Bankruptcy

Because debtor's confirmed plan did not include any provision to redeem real property sold at a pre-petition foreclosure sale, creditor was entitled to relief from the automatic stay so that it could pursue eviction proceedings even though the plan did provide for cure of the default and creditor had not objected to the plan confirmation (MCLS § 600.3240).—In re Jones, 233 B.R. 799, 1999 Bankr. LEXIS 544, 41 Collier Bankr. Cas. 2d (MB) 1392 (Bankr. E.D. Mich. 1999).

1394. Curtis v. Mueller, 184 Mich. 148, 150 N.W. 847 (1915).

1395. *See* M.L.P.2d Personal Property, M.L.P.2d Secured Transactions.

1396. *See* M.L.P.2d Fraudulent Conveyances.

1397. *See, supra*, Chapter 3.

1398. *See* M.L.P.2d Insurance.

1399. *See* M.L.P.2d Subrogation.

1400. MCLS § 565.358.

A mortgage is to be distinguished from other transactions of a similar nature but having different elements or characteristics.[1401]

A mortgage of real property is to be distinguished from a conditional sale by the fact that the former is merely security for the payment of a debt, or for the performance of some other condition, while the latter is a sale for a price paid or to be paid, to become absolute on the occurrence of a particular event, or is a purchase accompanied by an agreement to resell on certain conditions.[1402] A conveyance that extinguishes the debt and gives the grantor an option to rescue the property by payment or relinquish the property by nonpayment is a sale with the privilege of repurchase, and is not a mortgage.[1403]

However, in the absence of facts showing the intention of the parties, courts exercising equity jurisdiction incline to construe a deed with a condition to be a mortgage.[1404] A former court of chancery would not permit a transaction that was in substance a mortgage to have the effect of a sale.[1405]

On the question whether a certain instrument is a mortgage or a lease, an agreement in which one party, in consideration of a promise to pay a certain amount, let to another a parcel of land for a year, agreeing to prepare the land and plant it, and authorizing the latter to enter the premises and harvest the same, is a lease and not a mortgage.[1406]

A mortgage is also to be distinguished from a trust.[1407] Whether an instrument is to be treated as a mortgage or a trust instrument within the statutory definition[1408] generally depends on the intention of the parties as gathered from the whole instrument.[1409]

1401. Curtis v. Sheldon, 47 Mich. 262, 11 N.W. 151, 1882 Mich. LEXIS 626 (1882).

Ellis v. Brown, 29 Mich. 259 (1874).

Campau v. Chene, 1 Mich. 400 (1850).

"Shifting Risk To The Dumbest Guy In The Room" – Derivatives Regulation after the Wall Street Reform and Consumer Protection Act, 11 J. Bus. & Sec. L. 1 (2010).

Re-Examining The Role Of Private Property In Market Democracies: Problematic Ideological Issues Raised By Land Registration, 25 Mich. J. Int'l L. 467 (2004).

1402. Blumberg v. Beekman, 121 Mich. 647, 80 N.W. 710 (1899).

Campau v. Chene, 1 Mich. 400 (1850).

1403. Sauer v. Fischer, 247 Mich. 283, 225 N.W. 518 (1929).

1404. Swetland v. Swetland, 3 Mich. 482 (1855).

1405. Cornell v. Hall, 22 Mich. 377 (1871).

Understanding at the time

Where land was mortgaged to a surety on an appeal bond, and was afterwards conveyed to the surety by an absolute conveyance, and the surety paid the judgment debt, but it was understood at the time of the conveyance that the mortgagor could pay the debt himself, or defeat the judgment by legal proceedings, which he attempted to do, the deed operated as a mortgage, and not a conditional sale.—Sowles v. Wilcox, 127 Mich. 166, 86 N.W. 689 (1901).

1406. Stadden v. Hazzard, 34 Mich. 76 (1876).

1407. Comstock v. Howard, Walk. Ch. 110 (Mich. 1843).

Trust mortgage

Where purchaser of equity of redemption in property conveyed to a party who signed bonds and executed trust indenture to his grantor as trustee by way of security in which rents were assigned as additional security, instrument was a trust mortgage, notwithstanding that for time being bonds were held by trustee, where parties intended trust mortgage.—Giblin v. Detroit Trust Co., 270 Mich. 293, 258 N.W. 635 (1935).

1408. MCLS § 554.213.

1409. Union Guardian Trust Co. v. Nichols, 311 Mich. 107, 18 N.W.2d 383 (1945).

Reichert v. Guaranty Trust Co., 261 Mich. 315, 246 N.W. 132 (1933) (trustee named in corporate capacity).

§ 703. Subject Matter

Any property that may be sold may be mortgaged to secure a debt.

Generally, any kind of property that may be sold or conveyed may be mortgaged to secure a debt.[1410] This general rule is applicable to a situation in which a contract for the sale of land remains executory. Under those circumstances, where no deed has been executed, the vendor may mortgage his or her rights in the contract.[1411]

A person cannot lawfully mortgage property, however, unless the person has a present valid title or interest in the property that is sought to be encumbered.[1412] Where a mortgagor has no title to the property, such as where the title that the mortgagor asserts is not merely defeasible but is absolutely void, the mortgage creates no interest in the premises.[1413] Where a deed to the premises in question is forged, a mortgage given by the grantee in the forged deed will also fail to create any lien on the land in favor of the mortgagee.[1414]

Condominiums. Each condominium unit of an established condominium project is a sole property subject to being mortgaged independently of other units in the project.[1415]

Land contract mortgage. A land contract mortgage does not have to specifically identify the interest encumbered as a vendor's or a vendee's interest.[1416]

§ 704. Debt or Obligation

Any obligation capable of reduction to money or its equivalent may be secured by a mortgage. The rate of interest that may be charged in a mortgage may be subject to Michigan's strict usury laws.

There can be no mortgage unless there is a debt to be secured thereby, or some

1410. Brown v. Phillips, 40 Mich. 264 (1879).

Glaser's Elevator & Lumber Co. v. Lee Homes, Inc., 65 Mich. App. 328, 237 N.W.2d 312 (1975) (vested remainder interest in testamentary trust).

A Simple Explanation Of Some Legal And Economic Aspects Of The Financial Meltdowns Of Banks, 89 MI Bar Jnl. 38 (2010).

Coping with the Specter of Urban Malaise in a Postmodern Landscape: The Need for a Detroit Land Bank Authority, 84 U. Det. Mercy L. Rev. 521 (2007).

Alternative mortgage instruments: Authorizing and implementing price level adjusted mortgages, 16 U. Mich. J.L. Ref. 115 (1982).

Changing status of land contract in Michigan and advantages of two-party mortgage as alternative, 28 Wayne L. Rev. 239 (1981).

Standing timber

A mortgage on standing timber is a mortgage on

an interest in land.—Williams v. Hyde, 98 Mich. 152, 57 N.W. 98 (1893).

1411. MCLS §§ 565.356 et seq.

Union Guardian Trust Co. v. Rood, 261 Mich. 188, 246 N.W. 74 (1933).

1412. Mead v. Pinyard, 154 U.S. 620 (1876).

Doyle v. Mizner, 40 Mich. 160 (1879).

1413. Felcher v. Dutton, 265 Mich. 231, 251 N.W. 332 (1933).

1414. Horvath v. National Mortg. Co., 238 Mich. 354, 213 N.W. 202 (1927).

1415. MCLS § 559.161.

Contracts and Commercial Law, 56 Wayne L. Rev. 171 (2010).

1416. MCLS § 565.358.

obligation to pay money.[1417] A mortgage given to secure all existing debts of a mortgagor to the mortgagee is valid.[1418] A mortgage may cover future advances of debt as well as present liabilities.[1419]

On the other hand, a former chancery court had no power to enforce an agreement in a mortgage for the payment, in case of foreclosure, of a specified sum of money as attorney's fees,[1420] because the exaction of attorney's fees is inconsistent with public policy,[1421] and therefore invalid.[1422]

Under The Secondary Mortgage Loan Act, the principal of a mortgage loan on a residential secondary mortgage subject to the act[1423] may include only the allowed capitalized charges and fees.[1424]

Restrictions on interest rates. The rate of interest that may be charged in a mortgage may be subject to Michigan's strict usury laws.[1425] A usurious rate of interest is without effect.[1426]

1417. Ginsberg v. Capitol City Wrecking Co., 300 Mich. 712, 2 N.W.2d 892 (1942).

1418. Macomb County Sav. Bank v. Kohlhoff, 5 Mich. App. 531, 147 N.W.2d 418 (1967).

1419. MCLS § 565.902.

Citizens' Sav. Bank v. Kock, 117 Mich. 225, 75 N.W. 458 (1898).

Hyde v. Shank, 77 Mich. 517, 43 N.W. 890 (1889).

Newkirk v. Newkirk, 56 Mich. 525, 23 N.W. 206 (1885).

Payment of taxes

A provision of a mortgage that, on a failure of the mortgagor to pay the taxes on the mortgaged property, they may be paid by the mortgagee and added to the amount of the mortgage lien is valid.—Farwell v. Bigelow, 112 Mich. 285, 70 N.W. 579 (1897).

1420. Kittermaster v. Brossard, 105 Mich. 219, 63 N.W. 75 (1895).

1421. Damon v. Deeves, 62 Mich. 465, 29 N.W. 42 (1886).

1422. Bendey v. Townsend, 109 U.S. 665, 3 S. Ct. 482, 27 L. Ed. 1065 (1884).

Kittermaster v. Brossard, 105 Mich. 219, 63 N.W. 75 (1895).

Vosburgh v. Lay, 45 Mich. 455, 8 N.W. 91 (1881).

1423. MCLS § 493.51.

1424. MCLS § 493.72.

1425. M.L.P.2d Interest.

MCLS §§ 438.31 et seq., 438.41 et seq., 438.61 et seq., 438.101 et seq.

Barbour v. Handlos Real Estate & Bldg. Corp., 152 Mich. App. 174, 393 N.W.2d 581 (1986)

(nonqualified lender may only charge 11% interest on a mortgage, including finance charges; interest on a late payment may not exceed 10%).

Federal preemption on certain first mortgages

State usury laws applicable to wraparound mortgage notes are preempted by the Depository Institutions Deregulation and Monetary Control Act of 1980 where the otherwise acceptable wraparound mortgage note is secured by a first lien, is made after March 31, 1980, and is made by a qualified creditor.—Mitchell v. Trustees of United States Mut. Real Estate Inv. Trust, 144 Mich. App. 302, 375 N.W.2d 424 (1985).

Prepayment penalty

The free market interest rate for residential mortgages allowed by the Michigan usury statute applies as long as the particular subsections of the statute are satisfied; if the subsections are satisfied, then the restrictions on prepayment penalties apply, provided that the security for the mortgage is a single-family dwelling and the loan is not federally insured or guaranteed. Specifically, the statute prohibits the lender from charging a prepayment fee or penalty in excess of 1% of the amount of any prepayment made within 3 years of the date of the loan, or any prepayment fee or penalty at all thereafter, or from prohibiting any prepayment of the loan at any time; the Michigan usury statute is not preempted by section 501 of the federal Depository Institutions Deregulation and Monetary Control Act, and, as a result, lenders who make loans secured by first mortgages on residential property, except for certain alternative mortgage transactions, are prohibited from charging Michigan consumers prepayment fees or penalties outside of those allowed by the Michigan usury statute.—Nelson v. Assocs. Fin. Servs. Co. of Ind., Inc., 253 Mich. App. 580, 659 N.W.2d 635 (2002).

1426. M.L.P.2d Interest.

In addition, under The Secondary Mortgage Loan Act, the interest rate that may be levied on a residential secondary mortgage subject to the act[1427] must not exceed the rate that the Credit Reform Act[1428] allows.[1429]

§ 705.   Consideration

Valid consideration is necessary to the existence of a valid mortgage. Valid consideration for a mortgage may consist of detriment to one party or benefit to the other.

Although a mortgage may be sustained even though voluntarily given, except as to those who are defrauded by it,[1430] the general rule is that a valid consideration is essential to the validity of a mortgage.[1431] A mortgage jointly undertaken by married persons does not require separate consideration to the estate of each.[1432]

Valid consideration for a mortgage may consist of detriment to one party or benefit to the other.[1433] The act of a mortgagee in parting with the full amount of consideration named in the mortgage will constitute sufficient consideration for the mortgage, even though the mortgagor receives no part of the consideration.[1434]

A mortgage given to provide money to pay outstanding notes is for a valid consideration,[1435] as is a mortgage given in return for a relinquishment of dower rights.[1436]

A preexisting debt or liability is a valuable and sufficient consideration, and no new consideration need be given at the time of the execution of the mortgage.[1437] The release of an existing mortgage is sufficient consideration for the making of a

MCLS § 438.32.

1427. MCLS § 493.51.

1428. MCLS §§ 445.1851 et seq.

1429. MCLS § 493.71.

No federal preemption

Congress, in enacting the Depository Institutions Deregulation and Monetary Control Act of 1980, did not intend to include junior mortgages executed for refinancing purposes among the loan transactions exempted from state usury laws.—Mitchell v. Trustees of United States Mut. Real Estate Inv. Trust, 144 Mich. App. 302, 375 N.W.2d 424 (1985).

1430. Brigham v. Brown, 44 Mich. 59, 6 N.W. 97 (1880).

1431. Parks v. Sherman, 208 Mich. 697, 176 N.W. 583 (1920).

Part payment of purchase price

A mortgage given a contractor in part payment of purchase price was valid, having been assigned where owner recovered identical amount on contractor's bond for performance.—Stevens v. Garland, 198 Mich. 24, 164 N.W. 516 (1917).

1432. In re Rochkind, 128 B.R. 520 (Bankr. E.D. Mich. 1991).

1433. McPherson v. DeConick, 272 Mich. 578, 262 N.W. 415 (1935).

Litchfield v. Tunnicliff, 118 Mich. 383, 76 N.W. 760 (1898).

Laylin v. Knox, 41 Mich. 40, 1 N.W. 913 (1879).

1434. McPherson v. DeConick, 272 Mich. 578, 262 N.W. 415 (1935).

1435. Manning v. Rosenfield, 239 Mich. 459, 214 N.W. 424 (1927).

1436. Moss v. Van Wagnen, 249 Mich. 218, 228 N.W. 696 (1930).

1437. Lee State Bank v. McElheny, 227 Mich. 322, 198 N.W. 928 (1924).

Restitution

Mortgage securing note given for restitution of moneys obtained by mortgagor's husband under false pretenses, was supported by consideration where mortgagor wife was endorser on original obligations.—Wilhelm v. King Auto Finance Co., 259 Mich. 463, 244 N.W. 130 (1932).

refinanced mortgage substituting for the released mortgage.[1438]

A mortgage ceases to be an enforceable security when the consideration fails.[1439] A mortgagor who does not receive the amount of the debt secured by a mortgage may be entitled to rescind the mortgage.[1440] It is not a defense to an action for rescission of a mortgage securing negotiable instruments that the purchaser of the negotiable instruments might have found a defect in the mortgage. So long as the negotiable instrument is valid on its face, the purchaser is under no duty to inquire into the validity of a securing mortgage.[1441]

Similarly, a mortgage is unenforceable if it is for advances to be made to the mortgagor that have not been furnished.[1442] Where a note secured by a mortgage is given by an owner to a building contractor in payment for construction of a house, and part of the consideration is the contractor's promise to remedy defects, and the defects are not remedied, there is a failure of consideration.[1443]

Evidence. The burden of establishing the want or failure of consideration for a mortgage is on the party asserting it.[1444] The presumption that the representation of the debt in a mortgage is true can be overcome only by a preponderance of clear and convincing evidence.[1445] However, the consideration for a note secured by a mortgage may always be inquired into.[1446] Evidence is generally admissible to show want,[1447] or insufficiency,[1448] of consideration.

1438. Release of original mortgage only

Second mortgage exacted by a mortgagee, in addition to payment by a loan corporation in a refinancing transaction, was not invalid for want of consideration because the original obligation was released by the mortgagee in refinancing, since the agreement to release the original obligation and take bonds from the loan corporation was a sufficient consideration for the agreement to give a second mortgage, and the release was intended to affect only the original obligation and not the new second mortgage agreement.—Meek v. Wilson, 283 Mich. 679, 278 N.W. 731 (1938).

1439. Ginsberg v. Capitol City Wrecking Co., 300 Mich. 712, 2 N.W.2d 892, 1942 Mich. LEXIS 669 (1942).

1440. Franck v. Bedenfield, 197 Mich. App. 316, 494 N.W.2d 840 (1992).

1441. Mox v. Jordan, 186 Mich. App. 42, 463 N.W.2d 114 (1990).

M.L.P.2d Negotiable Instruments.

1442. Gray v. Lincoln Housing Trust, 229 Mich. 441, 201 N.W. 489 (1924).

Future credit not given

A mortgage given by a mortgagor on the understanding that he should have a future credit, and which the agent of the mortgagee, who took it, knew would not have been given except upon that understanding, cannot be enforced for a different purpose, and, where no future credit is given and no advances made, must be held to have been given without consideration.—Mizner v. Kussell, 29 Mich. 229 (1874).

1443. Gottesman v. Rheinfrank, 303 Mich. 153, 5 N.W.2d 701 (1942).

1444. McPherson v. DeConick, 272 Mich. 578, 262 N.W. 415 (1935).

Wiswall v. Ayres, 51 Mich. 324, 16 N.W. 667 (1883).

Sufficient evidence

Evidence, in action on note and for foreclosure of collateral mortgage, sustained finding that there was failure of consideration moving from promisee to the promisors.—Cummings v. Continental Machine Tool Corp., 371 Mich. 177, 123 N.W.2d 165 (1963).

1445. Miller v. Ashton, 241 Mich. 46, 216 N.W. 448 (1927).

Cady v. Burgess, 144 Mich. 523, 108 N.W. 414 (1906).

1446. Miller v. Ashton, 241 Mich. 46, 216 N.W. 448 (1927).

Cady v. Burgess, 144 Mich. 523, 108 N.W. 414 (1906).

Carpenter v. Buttrick, 41 Mich. 706, 3 N.W. 196 (1879) (property of church society).

1447. Smith v. Heinze, 305 Mich. 290, 9 N.W.2d 545 (1943) (well drilling).

Stevens v. Stevens, 181 Mich. 438, 148 N.W. 225 (1914).

§ 706.   Equitable Mortgages

Security transactions that fail to satisfy the requirements of a legal mortgage may be treated as mortgages in equity. An equitable mortgage may be constituted by any writing from which the intention to create a mortgage may be gathered.

The "rule is clearly established that where one party advances money to another upon the faith of a verbal agreement by the latter to secure its payment by a mortgage upon certain lands and improvements, which is not executed, or which, if executed, is so defective or informal as to fall short of being a duly executed mortgage, equity will impress upon such land and improvements a lien in favor of the creditor who advances the money for the security in satisfaction of his debt."[1449] As otherwise stated, a court has power to decree an equitable mortgage under proper circumstances and to construe an instrument in the form of an absolute conveyance as a security for the payment of a debt or performance of some other obligation.[1450] This doctrine of equitable mortgages is founded upon the maxim that regards that as done which was agreed to be done and should have been done, and in applying the rule the court will treat the subject matter respecting collateral consequences and incidences as if the act contemplated by the parties was done at the beginning of the transaction, always regarding the substance rather than the form of the agreement.[1451]

An equitable mortgage may be constituted by any writing from which the intention to create a mortgage may be gathered.[1452] Generally, an agreement in writing, intended to give a lien on real estate for the payment of a debt may be good

Evidence insufficient

On a bill to foreclose a mortgage, evidence under the cross-bill was insufficient to establish want of consideration by reason of his failure to convey the land to defendant.—Turney v. Combination Brick Co., 184 Mich. 439, 151 N.W. 590 (1915).

Mortgage reciting payment of loan was actually for future advance

Where note and mortgage executed to and approved by a Federal Housing Administration mortgagee recited that a loan of $5,500 had been made by the mortgagee, if the loan was actually made it would constitute a debt but it was permissible to show in mortgagors' suit for accounting that actually no consideration passed and that mortgage was to cover future advances.—Ginsberg v. Capitol City Wrecking Co., 300 Mich. 712, 2 N.W.2d 892 (1942).

1448. Higgins v. McGill, 207 Mich. 570, 175 N.W. 410 (1919).

1449. Schram v. Burt, 111 F.2d 557 (6th Cir. Mich. 1940).

Boyd v. Perry (In re Boyd), 185 B.R. 529 (Bankr. E.D. Mich. 1995).

Right to foreclose under equitable mortgage

An "equitable mortgage" is transaction that vests grantee-mortgagee with right to bring action for foreclosure in event that obligation of grantor as mortgagor is not performed.—In re Van Duzer, 390 Mich. 571, 213 N.W.2d 167 (1973).

1450. Judd v. Carnegie, 324 Mich. 583, 37 N.W.2d 558 (1949).

1451. Schram v. Burt, 111 F.2d 557 (6th Cir. Mich. 1940).

1452. Siegel v. Sharrard, 276 Mich. 668, 268 N.W. 775 (1936).

Cullins v. Magic Mortg., Inc., 23 Mich. App. 251, 178 N.W.2d 532 (1970).

Additions to installment contract

Where vendor, at purchaser's request, paid contractor part of cost of additional structures and added payment to installment contract, parties' intention expressed by agreement and reasonable inferences controls on question whether contract was mortgage.—Rowe v. William Ford & Co., 257 Mich. 646, 241 N.W. 889 (1932).

Equitable mortgage supported by ample evidence

Although, after plumbing contractor refused to complete work until $17,000 owing him was paid,

as an equitable mortgage.[1453] In this fashion, a contract in form may, through the parties' acts, be construed as a mortgage.[1454]

The assignment of the interest of a vendor or vendee in a contract for the sale of land as security for a debt creates an equitable mortgage.[1455] However, as against the vendor under a land contract, an assignment by the vendee does not give the assignee a mortgage lien on the property.[1456] Similarly, the contents of an assignment may evidence an intention not to create an equitable mortgage.[1457]

The doctrine of equitable mortgages is not, however, limited to written instruments intended as mortgages that, by reason of some formal defect, are inoperative without the court's aid, but also extends to a variety of parol transactions of that nature.[1458] Where a person advances money to another upon the faith of a verbal agreement by the latter to secure its payment by a mortgage that is not executed, or which, if executed, falls short of being a duly executed mortgage, equity will impress upon the mortgaged lands and improvements a lien in favor of the creditor who advances the money.[1459] The equitable lien thus created is controlled by the same equitable principles as that of the vendor of real estate for unpaid purchase money.[1460] It attaches on the advancement of the money and for the

financially troubled home builder, in return for loan of $35,000, signed assignment of his interest in certain realty as well as quitclaim deed of it, transaction amounted to an equitable mortgage, where builder had an equity of at least $76,000 and there was abundant evidence that parties intended transaction as a security interest.—Taines v. Munson, 19 Mich. App. 29, 172 N.W.2d 217 (1969).

1453. Sibley v. Ross, 88 Mich. 315, 50 N.W. 379 (1891).

Abbott v. Godfroy's Heirs, 1 Mich. 178 (1849).

Bank purchase

A bank purchased a building under a contract securing an unpaid balance of the price; cashier thereafter procured a loan from vendor for the bank, which it was agreed would be secured by the real estate, and by a sealed agreement, made and recorded, stating, as the amount due, the balance of the price and the loan, the land payments were extended; transaction was known and approved by the officers of the bank, and the cashier was authorized to procure loans; on that basis, vendor was entitled to a lien for the whole amount due him after the bank's insolvency.—Whitney v. Foster, 117 Mich. 643, 76 N.W. 114 (1898).

1454. Rowe v. William Ford & Co., 257 Mich. 646, 241 N.W. 889 (1932).

1455. Gunderman v. Gunnison, 39 Mich. 313 (1878).

Burden of proof

Contract vendees having asserted inadequacy of consideration in connection with their claim in foreclosure action that their assignment was equi-

table mortgage, had burden of proving contention, and failed to do so.—McCluskey v. Winisky, 373 Mich. 315, 129 N.W.2d 400 (1964).

Optional repayment

An assignment of a contract for the purchase of realty, conditioned that if the assignee paid certain liabilities, and the assignor failed to repay by a specified time, the assignee would own the contract absolutely, but if repaid, he should surrender all claim, is a mortgage.—Meigs v. McFarlan, 72 Mich. 194, 40 N.W. 246 (1888).

1456. Cheff v. Haan, 269 Mich. 593, 257 N.W. 894 (1934).

1457. Intention to defease

In a case wherein the vendees' interest under a contract to purchase realty had been assigned and the assignment contract was accompanied by a written agreement granting to the assignors an option to purchase the realty from the assignees, the Supreme Court held that the giving of such an option indicated that the assignors had parted with their interest in the realty contract and that no equitable mortgage resulted.—Porritt v. Stone, 340 Mich. 645, 66 N.W.2d 244 (1954).

1458. Schram v. Burt, 111 F.2d 557 (6th Cir. Mich. 1940).

Anderson v. Smith, 103 Mich. 446, 61 N.W. 778 (1895) (purchase and reconveyance).

Schultz v. Schultz, 117 Mich. App. 454, 324 N.W.2d 48 (1982) (fiduciary relationship).

1459. Schram v. Burt, 111 F.2d 557 (6th Cir. Mich. 1940).

1460. Schram v. Burt, 111 F.2d 557 (6th Cir. Mich. 1940).

same length of time as the debt. A waiver will not be implied from the act of the creditor in receiving the mortgage if it is ineffective, nor is the equitable mortgage thus created merged in the instrument subsequently executed.[1461] The equitable mortgagee's advances to the benefit of the property also do not engender a waiver or estoppel against the rights of the equitable mortgagor.[1462]

However, an equitable mortgage is not created in a transaction in which the prospective mortgagee fails to facially do everything necessary to secure a mortgage. In equity the court cannot overlook the requirements of the statute and the mortgagee's lack of thoroughness and diligence in protecting his or her own position.[1463]

§ 707.   Form and Contents of Mortgages

No particular form is necessary to constitute a mortgage, although a statutory form is provided, and the content required to constitute a valid mortgage is less than that necessary to constitute a recordable mortgage.

Under the statutes governing conveyances of real property,[1464] a mortgage must contain:[1465]

(1) a legal description of the property;

(2) the amount of the debt secured;

(3) the date of the note;

(4) the signature of the mortgagor; and

(5) the terms of repayment of the debt.

A mortgage note recorded as a mortgage must contain all of these elements to secure the note to the property.[1466] However, generally, the mortgage must only follow the substance of the words of conveyance specified in the statute.[1467]

However, a document satisfies the statutory requirements for an unrecorded mortgage if it recites that payment of loan is secured with a deed to property, the amount of the mortgage, the repayment date and interest rate, and the signature of the grantor.[1468] In particular, the statutory requirement for a statement of the marital

---

1461. Schram v. Burt, 111 F.2d 557 (6th Cir. Mich. 1940).

1462. Sham sale

Notwithstanding fact that equitable mortgagee after sham sale paid off land contract, paid taxes, and secured a buyer for property, equitable mortgagor did not lose right to claim interest in land because of laches, waiver, estoppel, and abandonment.—Taines v. Munson, 19 Mich. App. 29, 172 N.W.2d 217 (1969).

1463. Boyd v. Perry (In re Boyd), 185 B.R. 529 (Bankr. E.D. Mich. 1995).

1464. MCLS § 565.154.

1465. Boyd v. Perry (In re Boyd), 185 B.R. 529 (Bankr. E.D. Mich. 1995).

1466. Boyd v. Perry (In re Boyd), 185 B.R. 529 (Bankr. E.D. Mich. 1995) (parties' subsequent conduct cannot fill in for missing payment terms).

1467. United States v. Certain Real Property Located at 750 East Shore Drive, 800 F. Supp. 547 (E.D. Mich. 1992).

1468. United States v. Certain Real Property Located at 750 East Shore Drive, 800 F. Supp. 547 (E.D. Mich. 1992).

status of the parties,[1469] the identification of the mortgages drafter,[1470] and the notary[1471] that apply to the recording of a mortgage instrument, are not necessary in a document whose terms satisfy the statutory requirements for an unrecorded mortgage.[1472]

The parties to the mortgage must be described sufficiently so that their identity may be ascertained.[1473] The property must also be described with sufficient certainty to identify it or furnish a means by which it may be identified.[1474] A recorded cross-collateralization agreement that is not identified to the specific property does not provide notice to subsequent takers and therefore does not have priority over a subsequently recorded mortgage on the real property.[1475]

However, a mortgage does not fail merely because the property can be identified only with the aid of extrinsic proofs. It is always competent to connect the written description with the material subject matter by proof of the surrounding circumstances.[1476]

A mortgage to secure all existing debts, without specifying them, is not invalid for lack of certainty in the amounts secured.[1477]

The parties to a mortgage may insert conditions or stipulations in a mortgage

---

1469. MCLS § 565.221.

M.L.P.2d Deeds.

1470. MCLS § 565.201a.

M.L.P.2d Deeds.

Corporate entity as drafter

The statute requiring that each instrument presented for recording contain the name of the person who drafted the instrument is satisfied if a corporation is named as the drafter, because the term "person" includes a corporate entity; a mortgage presented for recording and listing a corporation as the person who drafted it was in recordable form.—Lim v. New Century Mortg. Corp. (In re Ammar), 368 B.R. 629 (Bankr. E.D. Mich. 2007).

1471. MCLS § 565.201.

M.L.P.2 Deeds.

1472. United States v. Certain Real Property Located at 750 East Shore Drive, 800 F. Supp. 547 (E.D. Mich. 1992).

1473. Brayton v. Merithew, 56 Mich. 166, 22 N.W. 259 (1885).

Corporate mortgagee

Earlier mortgages were not defective on basis that they were in mortgagee's name individually, although mortgagor contended that mortgagee stipulated at trial that his intention was that corporation be mortgagee.—Barbour v. Handlos Real Estate & Bldg. Corp., 152 Mich. App. 174, 393 N.W.2d 581 (1986).

1474. Slater v. Breese, 36 Mich. 77 (1877).

Wrong section did not create ambiguity

Where the description in a mortgage is "lot No. one (1) in section 20-eight (28), in the Forsyth or Porter farm in a city, being on the southwest corner of Fort and Sixth streets," and the lot was actually in section 18, there could be no ambiguity because there was no section 28 on the farm.—Cooper v. Bigly, 13 Mich. 463 (1865).

1475. Union Bank & Trust Co., N.A. v. Farmwald Dev. Corp., 181 Mich. App. 538, 450 N.W.2d 274 (1989).

1476. Slater v. Breese, 36 Mich. 77 (1877).

Mortgage of platted property must refer to plat

The Land Division Act (LDA) requires that mortgages of platted property refer to the plat and provides that mortgages that do not refer to the plat are not entitled to be recorded; the mortgage act and the recording act do not set forth the sole and exclusive requirements for valid mortgages and for properly recorded mortgages and the requirement of the LDA that conveyances of platted property refer to the plat is not inconsistent with, or precluded by, the requirements in the mortgage statute and the recording act.—Wells Fargo Home Mortg., Inc. v. Richardson (In re Brandt), 434 B.R. 493 (W.D. Mich. 2010).

1477. Michigan Ins. Co. v. Brown, 11 Mich. 265 (1863).

that do not deprive it of its essential attributes.[1478] It is competent for the parties to insert in the mortgage a covenant binding the mortgagor to pay the debt secured,[1479] such a promise eliminating the need for an accompanying note.[1480]

Under The Secondary Mortgage Loan Act, the instrument of a mortgage loan on a residential secondary mortgage subject to the act[1481] may not contain:[1482]

(1) a power of attorney to confess judgment;

(2) a waiver of the debtor's rights under a state or federal law;

(3) an assignment or order for payment of the debtor's income;

(4) any provision encouraging the debtor to incorporate; or

(5) an agreement by the debtor to payment of damages without a judgment.

Power of sale. A power of sale is not a necessary part of a mortgage.[1483] The validity of a mortgage is not affected by a defect in the power of sale.[1484]

Land contract mortgage. A land contract mortgage must be in the form provided for regular real estate mortgages.[1485]

§ 708. Execution and Delivery

A mortgage must be properly executed and acknowledged by the grantor to be valid. A mortgage delivered by the mortgagor must be accepted by the mortgagee in order to become effective.

A mortgage, in order to be valid and operative, must be duly executed.[1486] A mortgage is invalid if executed in blank, where the blanks are filled without the mortgagor's authority or consent.[1487] Each signatory's name must be legibly printed, typewritten, or stamped beneath his or her respective signature.[1488]

1478. Poole v. Horton, 45 Mich. 404, 8 N.W. 59 (1881).

1479. Cooklin v. Cooklin, 260 Mich. 69, 244 N.W. 232 (1932).

1480. Cooklin v. Cooklin, 260 Mich. 69, 244 N.W. 232 (1932).

1481. MCLS § 493.51.

1482. MCLS § 493.73.

1483. Cowles v. Marble, 37 Mich. 158 (1877).

Butler v. Ladue, 12 Mich. 173 (1863).

1484. State Bank of Bay City v. Chapelle, 40 Mich. 447 (1879).

1485. MCLS § 565.358.

1486. Van Mourik v. First Nat'l Bank in Mt. Clemens, 277 Mich. 46, 268 N.W. 806 (1936).

McPherson v. DeConick, 272 Mich. 578, 262 N.W. 415 (1935).

Wood v. Genett, 120 Mich. 222, 79 N.W. 199 (1899).

Ann Arbor Sav. Bank v. Ellison, 113 Mich. 557, 71 N.W. 873 (1897).

Visioneering, Inc. Profit Sharing Trust v. Belle River Joint Venture, 149 Mich. App. 327, 386 N.W.2d 185 (1986) (oral contract).

Execution to third person

It is not necessary that a mortgage be made directly to the beneficiary, but it may be made to a third person as well as to the creditor.—Adams v. Niemann, 46 Mich. 135, 8 N.W. 719 (1881).

1487. Stebbins v. Watson, 71 Mich. 467, 39 N.W. 721 (1888).

1488. MCLS § 565.201.

Michigan register of deeds practice, *see* 16 Mich. Real Prop. Rev. 91 (1989).

A mortgage of lands must be signed by the grantor.[1489] A mortgage must be acknowledged in order to be accepted for recording by the register of deeds of a county.[1490] But a mortgage does not have to be formally acknowledged to be valid between the parties to it.[1491]

Up until March 4, 2002,[1492] a mortgage that was required to be acknowledged would not be recorded by the register of deeds of a county unless the mortgage was duly witnessed.[1493] However, a mortgage did not have to be witnessed to be valid between the parties to it.[1494]

A mortgage delivered by the mortgagor must be accepted by the mortgagee in order to become effective.[1495] In this regard, the recording of the mortgage by the mortgagor may constitute sufficient delivery to the mortgagee.[1496] But where the mortgagee acquires possession of a mortgage which is placed in the hands of a third person to be delivered to the mortgagee on the happening of a certain contingency or the performance by the mortgagee of certain conditions, before the happening of the contingency, or without complying with the conditions, there is no completion of delivery to the mortgagee that makes the mortgage operative.[1497]

Land contract mortgages. A land contract mortgage must be executed and acknowledged in the same manner as a real estate mortgage.[1498]

B.   THE VALIDITY OF MORTGAGES

§ 711.   Validity of Mortgages In General

The proper mental capacity and the assent of the parties are necessary to the establishment of a valid mortgage.

The voluntary assent of the parties and the necessary mental capacity are essential to the validity of a mortgage.[1499] Thus, where it is shown that the mortgagor does not have sufficient mental capacity to comprehend the nature of his or her act, a mortgage that the mortgagor executes may be set aside.[1500] But if the mortgagor understood the transaction in question at the time of its making, the

---

1489. MCLS § 565.154.

1490. MCLS § 565.47.

1491. Turner v. Peoples State Bank, 299 Mich. 438, 300 N.W. 353 (1941).

1492. 2002 Pub. Act 23.

1493. MCLS § 565.47, prior to amendment by 2002 Pub. Act 23.

1494. Baker v. Clark, 52 Mich. 22, 17 N.W. 225 (1883).

1495. Shelden v. Erskine, 78 Mich. 627, 44 N.W. 146 (1889).

1496. Sessions v. Sherwood, 78 Mich. 234, 44 N.W. 263 (1889).

1497. Cressinger v. Dessenburg, 42 Mich. 580, 4 N.W. 269 (1880).

No request for delivery

A mortgage to a creditor was enclosed in an envelope, and left with a person, with directions to deliver it to the mortgagee when requested by the joint action of two persons, one of whom was the mortgagor; mortgagor refused to join in the request to deliver the mortgage; under these circumstances, there was no delivery.—Belding Sav. Bank v. Moore, 118 Mich. 150, 76 N.W. 368 (1898).

1498. MCLS § 565.358.

1499. Walter v. Walter, 297 Mich. 26, 297 N.W. 58 (1941).

Johnson v. Van Velsor, 43 Mich. 208, 5 N.W. 265 (1880).

1500. Holmes v. Martin, 123 Mich. 155, 81 N.W. 1072 (1900).

mortgagor cannot insist that it be set aside on the basis of his or her mental incapacity.[1501]

As to mortgages that are partially valid and partially invalid, it is generally true that if the parts are separable, the mortgage need not necessarily be void in its entirety, but may be enforced under its valid part.[1502]

§ 712. Mistake

A fundamental mistake of fact will invalidate a mortgage.

In the absence of fraud or other misconduct, the tendency of the courts is to uphold mortgages as against the contention of a mistake.[1503] Thus, a mortgagor generally will not be allowed relief where the mortgagor acts with full knowledge of all material facts and the mistake is due to the mortgagor's own inattention or carelessness.[1504]

The law requires very strong proof to support a charge of mistake. A mortgage generally will be enforced against lands that the mortgagor claims ought not to have been included on the mere ground that a mistake was made in the description.[1505] Likewise, a mortgage voluntarily executed will not be set aside on the ground of a mistake of law.[1506]

§ 713. Fraud

A mortgage procured by fraud may be invalidated. A mortgagor who does not receive the amount of the debt secured by a mortgage due to fraud may be entitled to rescind the mortgage.

A mortgage that the mortgagee has procured by fraud or misrepresentation may be invalidated by a court in equity.[1507] False representations by the vendor concerning the value of the property that induce the mortgagee to give a mortgage for more than it is really worth are grounds for invalidating the mortgage.[1508]

Flanigan v. Byers, 225 Mich. 66, 195 N.W. 820 (1923) (illiteracy).

1501. Lee v. Fiero, 120 Mich. 430, 79 N.W. 1125 (1899).

1502. Rood v. Winslow, 2 Doug. 68 (Mich. 1845).

1503. Roosenraad v. Sluiter, 276 Mich. 674, 268 N.W. 777 (1936).

1504. Boyd v. Perry (In re Boyd), 185 B.R. 529 (Bankr. E.D. Mich. 1995).

Roosenraad v. Sluiter, 276 Mich. 674, 268 N.W. 777 (1936).

Fraud by spouse

Wife was bound by a mortgage that included part of her lands, where her negligence enabled her husband to perpetrate a fraud.—Sponseller v. Kimball, 246 Mich. 255, 224 N.W. 359 (1929).

1505. Shepard v. Shepard, 36 Mich. 173 (1877).

1506. Skillman v. M.J. Clark Memorial Home, 229 Mich. 547, 201 N.W. 453 (1924).

1507. Hedler v. Manning, 252 Mich. 195, 233 N.W. 223 (1930).

Sackner v. Sackner, 39 Mich. 39 (1878) (family relationship).Terry v. Tuttle, 24 Mich. 206 (1872).

All parties bound

All of the beneficiaries in a trust mortgage are bound by the fraudulent representations made by a part of them to induce the giving of the security.—Crowley v. Langdon, 127 Mich. 51, 86 N.W. 391 (1901).

1508. John Schweyer & Co. v. Mellon, 196 Mich. 590, 162 N.W. 1006 (1917).

A mortgagor who does not receive the amount of the debt secured by a mortgage due to fraud may be entitled to rescind the mortgage.[1509]

A party attacking a mortgage on the ground that it is secured by fraud must establish the existence of all of the essential elements of fraud.[1510] But a court will closely scrutinize mortgages between persons in a close fiduciary or confidential relationship for fraud.[1511]

§ 714. Duress

Duress that coerces the mortgagor so as to deprive him or her of all free choice may invalidate a mortgage. Economic duress can exist in the absence of an illegal threat, so long as the threat is wrongful.

Generally, a mortgagor may invalidate a mortgage procured by duress.[1512] The duress must be of such a character that coerces the mind of the mortgagor and entirely deprives the mortgagor's act of all freedom and choice.[1513]

A mortgage is voidable if a party's consent is induced by an improper threat that leaves the victim no reasonable alternative. Economic duress can exist in the absence of an illegal threat, so long as the threat is wrongful. Even acts that are lawful and not in the nature of a tort can be wrongful under the right circumstances.[1514]

A mortgage executed by one spouse under a threat of a criminal prosecution against the other spouse may be invalidated on the ground of duress.[1515] This general rule may apply only to cases in which the arrest is unlawful or the threatened

---

1509. Franck v. Bedenfield, 197 Mich. App. 316, 494 N.W.2d 840 (1992).

1510. Seymour v. Powers, 255 Mich. 624, 238 N.W. 630 (1931).

Mizner v. Kussell, 29 Mich. 229 (1874).

Converse v. Blumrich, 14 Mich. 109 (1866).

Second mortgage

A second mortgage exacted by mortgagee in addition to payment by federal agency in refinancing transaction was not void for fraud where mortgagor understood that second mortgage was condition precedent to mortgagee's acceptance of payment from federal agency, and no fraudulent representations to mortgagor were shown.—Meek v. Wilson, 283 Mich. 679, 278 N.W. 731 (1938).

1511. Manning v. Rosenfield, 239 Mich. 459, 214 N.W. 424 (1927).

Fraud by son

Chancery will not aid an avaricious, 66-year-old, active and aggressive man to deprive his 85-year-old father of his home by refusing to cancel father's note and mortgage, obtained by son through fraudulent representation that he had interest in mortgaged land by inheritance from his deceased mother, who held title to it with father by

entireties.—Walter v. Walter, 297 Mich. 26, 297 N.W. 58 (1941).

1512. Benedict v. Roome, 106 Mich. 378, 64 N.W. 193 (1895).

1513. In re Rochkind, 128 B.R. 520 (Bankr. E.D. Mich. 1991) (creditor threatened to use power of his public office as judge to ruin debtor's husband for personal gain).

Detroit Nat'l Bank v. Blodgett, 115 Mich. 160, 73 N.W. 120 (1897).

1514. In re Rochkind, 128 B.R. 520 (Bankr. E.D. Mich. 1991).

1515. Bentley v. Robson, 117 Mich. 691, 76 N.W. 146 (1898) (charge of forgery).

Briggs v. Withey, 24 Mich. 136 (1871).

Embezzlement

A mortgage by the wife to secure the repayment of money embezzled by her husband, executed at the time she was first informed of her husband's crime, and after she had been told by the one whose money had been appropriated that he must have the money or the security, or that he would go on with the proceedings, may be set aside as

prosecution groundless or illegal.[1516]

The fact that a mortgagor executes a mortgage to induce another to endorse a note to secure the release from civil restraint of a third party who had misappropriated funds does not show duress invalidating the mortgage.[1517]

§ 715. Undue Influence

Undue influence is a ground for invalidating a mortgage.

Undue influence exerted on a mortgagor by a mortgagee, even though it does not constitute actual duress, may be sufficient to invalidate the instrument.[1518]

A son whose parents have executed a mortgage on their property to him in consideration that the son will support them, is bound to take no advantage of them. If the son obtained a mortgage on the parents' lands by reason of influence asserted due to his advantageous position, a former court of chancery would set aside the mortgage on the ground of that undue influence.[1519]

§ 716. Illegality

An illegal mortgage is invalid.

An illegal mortgage is generally invalid and unenforceable.[1520] This principle has often been applied to mortgages founded upon an illegal consideration,[1521] such as a mortgage executed for the purpose of preventing a criminal prosecution.[1522] A contractual obligation, or a conveyance, based on a promise, expressed or implied, to refrain from instituting or pressing a criminal charge or to obtain the suppression thereof, is opposed to public policy and is invalid on the ground of illegality of consideration.[1523]

A mortgage is similarly invalid when its consideration is an agreement to

having been obtained by duress.—Benedict v. Roome, 106 Mich. 378, 64 N.W. 193 (1895).

1516. Wilhelm v. King Auto Finance Co., 259 Mich. 463, 244 N.W. 130 (1932).

1517. Seymour v. Powers, 255 Mich. 624, 238 N.W. 630 (1931).

1518. Meech v. Lee, 82 Mich. 274, 46 N.W. 383 (1890).

Bowe v. Bowe, 42 Mich. 195, 3 N.W. 843 (1879).

Wartemberg v. Spiegel, 31 Mich. 400 (1875).

1519. Bowe v. Bowe, 42 Mich. 195, 3 N.W. 843 (1879).

1520. Koons v. Vauconsant, 129 Mich. 260, 88 N.W. 630 (1902).

Waterbury v. Andrews, 67 Mich. 281, 34 N.W. 575 (1887).

1521. Dierkes v. Wideman, 143 Mich. 181, 106 N.W. 735 (1906).

House of ill fame

A mortgage purporting on its face to be given to secure the repayment of money on certain conditions expressed in it is void where the money is in reality paid to the mortgagor to enable the mortgagee to conduct a house of ill fame.—McDonald v. Born, 135 Mich. 177, 97 N.W. 693 (1903).

1522. Hanson v. Loescher, 221 Mich. 387, 191 N.W. 30 (1922) (implied promise to drop prosecution).

Koons v. Vauconsant, 129 Mich. 260, 88 N.W. 630 (1902).

Restitution agreement

Conveyance of realty as security for performance of restitution agreement, executed in reliance upon implied promise that grantor would not be prosecuted for wrongfully appropriating funds of grantee, was repugnant to public policy and therefore void.—Groening v. Nowlen, 369 Mich. 28, 118 N.W.2d 998 (1963).

1523. Groening v. Nowlen, 369 Mich. 28, 118 N.W.2d 998 (1963).

interfere with the administration of the criminal law. The highest considerations of public policy require that such a bargain must not be allowed to stand.[1524]

§ 717.   Right To Contest Validity

The validity of a mortgage may be attacked by the mortgagor, the mortgagor's privies, and third persons whose interests are injuriously affected by the mortgage.

While the right to contest the validity of a mortgage is available to the mortgagor and those claiming under the mortgagor, as well as to third persons whose rights or interests are injuriously affected by the mortgage, persons whose rights the mortgage does not injuriously affect may not maintain an action challenging a mortgage.[1525]

However, the right to attack the validity of a mortgage may be lost by way of estoppel,[1526] or by waiver of the alleged ground of invalidity.[1527]

A mortgagor may also expressly or impliedly ratify a voidable mortgage.[1528] But where the coercive influence still exists, a ratification is ineffective.[1529]

§ 718.   Evidence as to Validity

The burden of proof is on one seeking to attack the validity of a mortgage to prove its invalidity. A preponderance of the evidence is necessary to establish the invalidity of a mortgage.

The burden of proof rests on the party attacking the validity of a duly executed mortgage to prove its invalidity.[1530] For that purpose, only relevant and material evidence is admissible on the issue of the mortgages validity.[1531]

A preponderance of the evidence is necessary to establish the invalidity of a

---

1524. Groening v. Nowlen, 369 Mich. 28, 118 N.W.2d 998 (1963).

Meech v. Lee, 82 Mich. 274, 46 N.W. 383 (1890).

1525. Wyoming Park Lumber & Fuel Co. v. Vander Ark, 291 Mich. 496, 289 N.W. 228 (1939).

1526. Sloan v. Holcomb, 29 Mich. 153 (1874).

1527. Orban v. Union Guardian Trust Co., 281 Mich. 644, 275 N.W. 662 (1937).

Waiver by subsequent lease

Mortgagors waived rights to cancel mortgage for fraud, where, after knowledge of circumstances, they leased mortgaged farm from purchaser at foreclosure sale.—Tacey v. State Bank of Linwood, 242 Mich. 258, 218 N.W. 676 (1928).

1528. Parks v. Sherman, 208 Mich. 697, 176 N.W. 583 (1920).

1529. Bentley v. Robson, 117 Mich. 691, 76 N.W. 146 (1898).

1530. Perrett v. Yarsdorfer, 37 Mich. 596 (1877).

Sloan v. Holcomb, 29 Mich. 153 (1874).

Smithson v. Michigan Bank, 32 Mich. App. 160, 188 N.W.2d 168 (1971) (fraud).

Real property law: Real evidence: Special rules for real estate disputes, 80 Mich. B.J. 28 (2001).

Duress

Where it is contended that a mortgage that was executed by the wife on her property under duress, to save her husband from imprisonment for obtaining money on a forgery, was on property paid for wholly or in part with the husband's money, so as to give the injured party a lien on it, that fact must be affirmatively proven.—Bentley v. Robson, 117 Mich. 691, 76 N.W. 146 (1898).

1531. Curtis v. Mueller, 184 Mich. 148, 150 N.W. 847 (1915).

mortgage.[1532] In various specific cases, a party has obtained of a ruling that the evidence was sufficient to establish the invalidity of a mortgage on the ground of fraud,[1533] failure of consideration,[1534] or illegality.[1535]

But in other cases the evidence was insufficient to establish invalidity on the ground of fraud,[1536] duress,[1537] or undue influence.[1538]

§ 719. Recording

A mortgage must be recorded to be effective as against third persons without notice of it, but is binding as between the

1532. Frickee v. Donner, 35 Mich. 151 (1876).

Hosley v. Holmes, 27 Mich. 416 (1873).

1533. Wartemberg v. Spiegel, 31 Mich. 400 (1875).

Matthews v. Aluminum Acceptance Corp., 1 Mich. App. 570, 137 N.W.2d 280 (1965) (constructive forgery or fraud).

Father v. son

In father's suit against his son for cancellation of note and second mortgage on plaintiff's land, evidence was sufficient to show that defendant obtained note and mortgage through fraudulent representation that he had interest in land by inheritance from his deceased mother, who held title to it with father by entireties.—Walter v. Walter, 297 Mich. 26, 297 N.W. 58 (1941).

1534. Cummings v. Continental Machine Tool Corp., 371 Mich. 177, 123 N.W.2d 165 (1963).

1535. Illegality of consideration

Evidence in suit to set aside deed to realty given as security for performance of agreement by grantor to repay funds of grantee wrongfully appropriated by grantor supported conclusion that grantor had executed restitution agreement and deed in reliance upon implied promise that he would not be prosecuted for misappropriation of funds.—Groening v. Nowlen, 369 Mich. 28, 118 N.W.2d 998 (1963).

1536. Folkringa v. State Mfg. & Lumber Corp., 258 Mich. 660, 242 N.W. 801 (1932).

Sponseller v. Kimball, 246 Mich. 255, 224 N.W. 359 (1929).

Dean v. Agaard, 243 Mich. 141, 219 N.W. 608 (1928).

Bennett v. Lashley, 237 Mich. 198, 211 N.W. 642 (1927).

Sellers v. Perry, 191 Mich. 619, 158 N.W. 144 (1916).

Home construction

In mortgagors' suit to set aside mortgage to finance construction of home whereby, through fraud of builder, they failed to receive check for mortgage proceeds, evidence did not show mort-

gagees participated in fraud.—Szatyn v. Wilde, 255 Mich. 461, 238 N.W. 238 (1931).

Mortgage for lease and disbursements

Finding that plaintiffs failed to carry burden of proving fraud on part of defendants in connection with transaction in which plaintiffs mortgaged premises owned by them and executed long term lease of premises to defendants and also assigned mortgage proceeds to defendants to be disbursed by them according to prearranged schedule was not against clear preponderance of evidence in action to set aside mortgage.—Smithson v. Michigan Bank, 32 Mich. App. 160, 188 N.W.2d 168 (1971).

Signature and delivery

In suit for cancellation of mortgage, where mortgagee filed a counterclaim for foreclosure, evidence did not justify finding of fraud, coercion, undue influence, or bad faith on part of mortgagee in securing signatures of mortgagors to mortgage and the delivery of the mortgage to the mortgagee.—Turner v. Peoples State Bank, 299 Mich. 438, 300 N.W. 353 (1941).

1537. Turner v. Peoples State Bank, 299 Mich. 438, 300 N.W. 353 (1941).

Remington v. Staring, 261 Mich. 136, 246 N.W. 63 (1933).

Coveney v. Pattullo, 130 Mich. 275, 89 N.W. 968 (1902).

Brooks v. Sullivan, 127 Mich. 8, 86 N.W. 1102 (1901).

Experienced mortgagor

In action to foreclose mortgages executed by experienced business woman who had considerable time for investigation, consultation, reflection and consideration of the matter, evidence with respect to alleged statement of president of mortgagee bank that woman's son, formerly bank president, was guilty of conduct for which he probably could be put in prison but that all would be forgiven if woman executed notes and mortgages, did not establish duress voiding the notes and mortgages.—Payne v. Cavanaugh, 292 Mich. 305, 290 N.W. 807 (1940).

1538. Roosenraad v. Sluiter, 276 Mich. 674, 268 N.W. 777 (1936).

parties without recording. A land contract mortgage must be recorded in the same manner as a real estate mortgage.

A mortgage of lands is a "conveyance" within the meaning of the recording laws.[1539] However, the object of laws requiring the recording of a mortgage[1540] is to give notice to third persons.[1541] Thus, between the parties to it, a mortgage is just as effective for all purposes without recording as it is with it.[1542]

Unless a mortgage is renewed within 30 years after its due date or the date of its recording by the recording of an affidavit of the amount unpaid or of an extension agreement, it will be considered as discharged of record.[1543] But this rule does not cause the lien of the mortgage to be discharged because of a failure to re-record.[1544]

Land contract mortgage. A land contract mortgage must be recorded in the same manner as a real estate mortgage. A land contract mortgage does not have to be filed under the Uniform Commercial Code.[1545]

1539. MCLS § 565.35.

Stover v. Bryant & Detwiler Improvement Corp., 329 Mich. 482, 45 N.W.2d 364 (1951).

Balen v. Mercier, 75 Mich. 42, 42 N.W. 666 (1889).

Researching online real estate records in Michigan, *see* 80 Mich. B.J. 22 (2001).

1540. MCLS § 565.29.

1541. Michigan Fire & Marine Ins. Co. v. Hamilton, 284 Mich. 417, 279 N.W. 884 (1938).

Mortgage on platted property must include legal description

A mortgage involving platted real estate that did not contain a legal description of the property, but included the street address and taxpayer identification number of the property, was "fatally defective" because it violated the requirements of two Michigan statutes that require all mortgages of platted property to include the caption of the plat and the lot number; the mortgage was a "mere nullity" and it provided no notice, constructive or otherwise.—Richardson v. Well Fargo Home Mortg., Inc. (In re Brandt), 421 B.R. 426 (W.D. Mich. 2009).

1542. Bacon v. Northwestern Mut. Life Ins. Co., 131 U.S. 258, 9 S. Ct. 787, 33 L. Ed. 128 (1889).

1543. MCLS § 565.382.

Michigan Fire & Marine Ins. Co. v. Hamilton, 284 Mich. 417, 279 N.W. 884 (1938).

Austin v. Anderson, 279 Mich. 424, 272 N.W. 730 (1937) (statute retroactive).

1544. Michigan Fire & Marine Ins. Co. v. Hamilton, 284 Mich. 417, 279 N.W. 884 (1938).

1545. MCLS § 565.358.

Chapter 24

ABSOLUTE DEED AS MORTGAGE

§ 731.   Necessary Conditions

An absolute deed may be shown to be a mortgage.

Library References

Michigan Digest
LexisNexis™ Automated Michigan SCAO Forms
John G. Cameron, Jr., Michigan Real Estate Forms
Powell on Real Property® (Michael Allan Wolf, ed.)
Thompson on Real Property, Thomas Edition (David A. Thomas, ed.)

Law Reviews

David E. Nykanen, Real Property, 55 Wayne L. Rev. 575 (2009); Stephen R. Estey and Danielle Graceffa, Real Property, 54 Wayne L. Rev. 387 (2008); Naseem Stecker and Mike Eidelbes, Up Front: Real Property and Consumer Law Sections Team up on "Ask The Lawyer" to Discuss Mortgage Foreclosures, 87 MI Bar Jnl. 8 (2008); Gregg A. Nathanson, Feature: Real Property Law: What's New in Residential Transactions?, 86 MI Bar Jnl. 16 (2007); David E. Nykanen and Jason C. Long, Annual Survey of Michigan Law; June 1, 2004 - May 31, 2005: Real Property, 52 Wayne L. Rev. 941 (2006); Daniel J. Schairbaum, Annual Survey of Michigan Law: June 1, 2003 - May 31, 2004: Real Property, 51 Wayne L. Rev. 881 (2005); Lawrence R. Shoffner, Real Property Law: Real Evidence: Special Rules for Real Estate Disputes, 80 MI Bar Jnl. 28 (2001).

A deed absolute on its face may be shown to be a mortgage.[1546] It was a well settled rule that a court of chancery had the power to decree that an instrument in the form of an absolute conveyance was in reality security for the payment of a debt,[1547] and where such a construction was given by the court, the instrument

---

1546. Alber v. Bradley, 321 Mich. 255, 32 N.W.2d 454 (1948).

Rossman v. Hutchinson, 289 Mich. 577, 286 N.W. 835 (1939).

Ruch v. Ruch, 159 Mich. 231, 124 N.W. 52 (1909).

Kunz v. Torcellini, 51 Mich. App. 742, 216 N.W.2d 479 (1974).

Exchange of improvements for money

Where building contractor agreed to pay off lot purchaser's land contract and back taxes and provide labor and materials toward constructing home on lot in exchange for disputed amount of money, conveyance of lot from lot purchaser to building contractor, while absolute on its face, constituted mortgage.—Kirkendall v. Heckinger, 403 Mich. 371, 269 N.W.2d 184 (1978).

1547. Porritt v. Stone, 340 Mich. 645, 66 N.W.2d 244 (1954).

Judd v. Carnegie, 324 Mich. 583, 37 N.W.2d 558 (1949).

Sauer v. Fischer, 247 Mich. 283, 225 N.W. 518 (1929).

Maginn v. Cashin, 196 Mich. 221, 162 N.W. 1009 (1917).

Schultz v. Schultz, 117 Mich. App. 454, 324 N.W.2d 48 (1982).

Grant v. Van Reken, 71 Mich. App. 121, 246 N.W.2d 348 (1976).

Taines v. Munson, 19 Mich. App. 29, 172 N.W.2d 217 (1969).

Advances to corporation

A deed from a corporation, absolute on its face, but given to secure advances made by a director, is a mortgage, and the corporation may convey the property in payment of its debts, subject to that mortgage, if valid.—Moore v. Universal Elevator Co., 122 Mich. 48, 80 N.W. 1015 (1899).

Husband and wife for husband's loan

Where a deed executed by husband and wife was in fact a mortgage to secure a loan to the husband, the instrument must be regarded as a mortgage as to both husband and wife.—Ehle v. Looker, 182 Mich. 248, 148 N.W. 378 (1914).

Payment by heirs

Where a deed on its face purporting to convey an absolute title to the grantee was merely to secure existing and prospective claims of a third person against the grantor, the grantor on paying the debt was entitled to a reconveyance, and,

would be regarded in chancery as a mortgage.[1548]

A transaction involving the lending of money and the giving of security in real property for it creates the relation of mortgagor and mortgagee, notwithstanding the fact that the instrument given is in the form of an absolute deed.[1549] More specifically, a conveyance of land in consideration of the assumption by the grantee of a certain indebtedness of the grantor, and a contemporaneous agreement that the latter may purchase the property for the amount of that indebtedness within a specified time, constitutes a mortgage, and the fact that possession is given to the grantee prior to payment of the amount does not affect the character of the transaction.[1550] The claim may be made not only against the vendor, but a co-vendee who secures an interest in the property in an apparently absolute transaction.[1551]

To render a conveyance that is absolute in its terms a mortgage, it must be a mortgage at its inception and can never become a mortgage by any subsequent act.[1552] On the other hand, an absolute deed given as security for a debt and treated by the court as a mortgage may subsequently be converted into an unconditional conveyance of the title to the property.[1553]

The defense of laches may bar a claim that a warranty deed constituted a mortgage.[1554]

---

where his heirs after his death paid the debt, they stood in his place, and could compel a conveyance.—Olney v. Brown, 163 Mich. 125, 128 N.W. 241 (1910).

1548. In re Van Duzer, 390 Mich. 571, 213 N.W.2d 167 (1973).

Simington v. Goldstein, 330 Mich. 536, 48 N.W.2d 116 (1951).

Alber v. Bradley, 321 Mich. 255, 32 N.W.2d 454 (1948).

Miskinis v. Bement, 301 Mich. 365, 3 N.W.2d 307 (1942).

Rossman v. Hutchinson, 289 Mich. 577, 286 N.W. 835 (1939).

1549. Reid v. Dowd, 257 Mich. 492, 241 N.W. 174 (1932).

Borrowing from bank

Where plaintiff borrowed money from defendant bank and to secure the debt executed deed to bank, and all interested parties treated plaintiff as owner of property subject to indebtedness owing bank, deed was a mortgage.—McKeighan v. Citizens Commercial & Sav. Bank, 302 Mich. 666, 5 N.W.2d 524 (1942).

Quitclaim deed

A quitclaim deed given by purchaser of realty to his son as security for money loaned to assist purchaser in carrying out the purchase contract, which son caused to be recorded as a mortgage, was a mere mortgage of the land.—Stover v. Bryant & Detwiler Improvement Corp., 329 Mich. 482, 45 N.W.2d 364 (1951).

1550. Clark v. Woodruff, 90 Mich. 83, 51 N.W. 357 (1892).

An attempt to have a deed, coupled with a land contract, declared to be a mortgage-loan transaction, *see* 7 Wayne L. Rev. 173 (1960).

1551. Co-vendee

One of two vendees named in a contract for deed, who claimed that the name of the other vendee was inserted to secure repayment to her of a sum loaned to him and paid to the vendors, had the burden of proving his claim.—Burns v. Stevens, 236 Mich. 447, 210 N.W. 483 (1926).

1552. Selik v. Goldman Realty Co., 240 Mich. 612, 216 N.W. 422 (1927).

Maginn v. Cashin, 196 Mich. 221, 162 N.W. 1009 (1917).

Swetland v. Swetland, 3 Mich. 482 (1855).

1553. Sauer v. Fischer, 247 Mich. 283, 225 N.W. 518 (1929).

Corrigan v. Aetna Life & Casualty, 140 Mich. App. 467, 364 N.W.2d 728 (1985).

1554. Laches

Where all facts relied on by grantors who sought to have warranty deed declared mortgage had been known to grantors seven years prior to institution of action to have warranty deed declared mortgage and grantees had made extensive repairs and improvements to property during that period, grantors were guilty of laches.—Staebler v. Buchanan, 45 Mich. App. 55, 205 N.W.2d 843 (1973).

A person who has no interest in the property conveyed cannot enforce an equitable mortgage under a deed conveying it.[1555]

§ 732. Circumstances Determining Character of Transaction

A court may consider the surrounding circumstances in determining whether an absolute deed is, in reality, a mortgage.

In determining whether a deed absolute in form is a mortgage, the court is not limited to the instrument itself, but may consider all the surrounding circumstances.[1556] The court will protect the necessities of a situation by looking through the form to the substance of a transaction in determining whether a deed absolute on its face is an equitable mortgage.[1557] An adverse financial condition of a grantor coupled with an inadequate purchase price for the property is sufficient to establish a deed absolute on its face to be an equitable mortgage.[1558]

The pecuniary embarrassment of the grantor, the grantor's indebtedness to the grantee, and the inadequacy of the consideration are circumstances the court looks to in determining the true character of the instrument.[1559]

Thus, the court in considering the surrounding circumstances determines whether the consideration involved is adequate,[1560] because inadequacy of consid-

---

1555. Interest foreclosed

Where a former owner of property loses all interest therein on the foreclosure of a mortgage by a receiver of a bank without any redemption, and the receiver conveys the premises to a third person pursuant to an oral agreement between the third person and the former owner that the former owner will receive the conveyance on repayment of the money to the third person, the instrument conveying the property to the third person will not be declared a mortgage, since the former owner has no interest subject to being mortgaged.—Bernstein v. Riseman, 282 Mich. 292, 276 N.W. 453 (1937).

1556. Darling v. Darling, 123 Mich. 307, 82 N.W. 48 (1900) (payment by wife).

Sanborn v. Sanborn, 104 Mich. 180, 62 N.W. 371 (1895).

Reilly v. Brown, 87 Mich. 163, 49 N.W. 557 (1891) (guardianship).

Stahl v. Dehn, 72 Mich. 645, 40 N.W. 922 (1888) (contracts for repurchase).

Cornell v. Hall, 22 Mich. 377 (1871).

Koenig v. Van Reken, 89 Mich. App. 102, 279 N.W.2d 590 (1979).

Understanding

In suit to declare deed an equitable mortgage and for accounting, evidence indicating that parties expressed an understanding that deed signed by illiterate plaintiff in defendant's attorney's office, transferring $11,000 property for $3,200 consideration, was merely security for plaintiff's

indebtedness to defendant in that amount warranted requested relief.—Lopez v. Lazaros, 369 Mich. 477, 120 N.W.2d 209 (1963).

1557. Koenig v. Van Reken, 89 Mich. App. 102, 279 N.W.2d 590 (1979).

1558. Schultz v. Schultz, 117 Mich. App. 454, 324 N.W.2d 48 (1982).

Koenig v. Van Reken, 89 Mich. App. 102, 279 N.W.2d 590 (1979).

1559. Taines v. Munson, 19 Mich. App. 29, 172 N.W.2d 217 (1969).

1560. Ellis v. Wayne Real Estate Co., 357 Mich. 115, 97 N.W.2d 758 (1959).

Jankowski v. Szpieg, 282 Mich. 397, 276 N.W. 493 (1937).

Mintz v. Soule, 182 Mich. 564, 148 N.W. 769 (1914).

Schmidt v. Barclay, 161 Mich. 1, 125 N.W. 729 (1910).

Malone v. Danforth, 137 Mich. 227, 100 N.W. 445 (1904) (no new consideration for warranty deed).

McMillan v. Bissell, 63 Mich. 66, 29 N.W. 737 (1886) (advancements to son-in-law).

No proof of inadequacy of consideration

On appeal from circuit court's finding in proceedings to foreclose interest of assignors of vendee interest in land contract, assignors' claim of inadequacy of consideration in assignment

eration is a strong indication that the parties did not consider the conveyance to be absolute.[1561] The inadequacy of consideration is generally the most important factor.[1562]

Another relevant factor may be whether the debt is extinguished by the delivery of the instrument.[1563]

That the original application preceding the deed was for a loan may be of weight and importance in determining whether a deed is in fact a mortgage.[1564]

The fact of a relationship between the parties to a complaint filed to have a deed construed as a mortgage has no force except as it is pertinent to the case.[1565]

Fraud and mistake are not essential to a cause seeking to establish that a conveyance absolute in form is in fact a mortgage.[1566]

§ 733.   —Intention of Parties

The intention of the parties at the time of the execution of the instrument is one of the most important factors in determining whether an absolute deed is a mortgage.

A circumstance to be considered by a court in determining whether a deed absolute in form was to be taken as a mortgage was the matter of the intention of the parties at the time of the execution of the instrument.[1567] The controlling criterion is the intention of the parties.[1568] This question of the intention of the parties must be considered in light of such other matters as how the parties

which recited consideration and under which assignee assumed assignors' debt was unfounded where there was no proof of inadequacy and question was never presented to trial court.—McCluskey v. Winisky, 373 Mich. 315, 129 N.W.2d 400 (1964).

1561. Sheets v. Huben, 354 Mich. 536, 93 N.W.2d 168 (1958).

Simington v. Goldstein, 330 Mich. 536, 48 N.W.2d 116 (1951).

Jankowski v. Szpieg, 282 Mich. 397, 276 N.W. 493 (1937).

Schultz v. Schultz, 117 Mich. App. 454, 324 N.W.2d 48 (1982).

Gross inadequacy

Gross inadequacy of price paid for property, or absence of price, is a strong circumstance indicating that security, and not actual sale, was what parties intended by a deed.—Maginn v. Cashin, 196 Mich. 221, 162 N.W. 1009 (1917).

Unequal bargaining positions

In determining whether deed absolute on its face may be declared equitable mortgage, adequacy of consideration may be considered as indication that parties did not consider conveyance to be absolute, especially where bargaining positions of parties were markedly unequal.—Grant v.

Van Reken, 71 Mich. App. 121, 246 N.W.2d 348 (1976).

1562. Taines v. Munson, 19 Mich. App. 29, 172 N.W.2d 217 (1969).

1563. Jankowski v. Szpieg, 282 Mich. 397, 276 N.W. 493 (1937).

1564. Ellis v. Wayne Real Estate Co., 357 Mich. 115, 97 N.W.2d 758 (1959).

1565. Tilden v. Streeter, 45 Mich. 533, 8 N.W. 502 (1881).

1566. Ferd L. Alpert Industries, Inc. v. Oakland Metal Stamping Co., 379 Mich. 272, 150 N.W.2d 765 (1967).

1567. Sheets v. Huben, 354 Mich. 536, 93 N.W.2d 168 (1958).

Simington v. Goldstein, 330 Mich. 536, 48 N.W.2d 116 (1951).

Alber v. Bradley, 321 Mich. 255, 32 N.W.2d 454 (1948).

Sauer v. Fischer, 247 Mich. 283, 225 N.W. 518 (1929).

1568. Sheets v. Huben, 354 Mich. 536, 93 N.W.2d 168 (1958).

themselves treated the instrument,[1569] including their acts in compliance with the recording laws.[1570]

In determining whether a deed absolute on its face is an equitable mortgage, the financial embarrassment of the grantor along with inadequate consideration, although not an infallible test, are indicative of the parties' intent not to consider conveyance to be absolute.[1571]

The intention of the parties respecting whether an absolute deed is a mortgage is solely a question of fact.[1572] A deed absolute in form will be construed as a mortgage if the proof is clear that it is the intention of the parties that the transfer be for purposes of security.[1573] Where it clearly appears that the parties intended the instrument as an absolute conveyance, the court will not obviate the legal effect of the instrument involved by declaring it to be a mortgage.[1574]

§ 734.   Defeasance

A deed absolute on its face will be held to be a mortgage where it conveys an estate subject to a defeasance.

Given that courts in equity have always favored the right of redemption, defeasible purchases are narrowly watched,[1575] and the question whether a conveyance amounts to a mortgage does not turn upon the question of whether or not there is an express agreement for a defeasance, but rather on the actual intention and understanding of the parties.[1576]

A deed that purports to be an absolute conveyance, but is intended to be made

---

Miskinis v. Bement, 301 Mich. 365, 3 N.W.2d 307 (1942).

Jankowski v. Szpieg, 282 Mich. 397, 276 N.W. 493 (1937).

Koenig v. Van Reken, 89 Mich. App. 102, 279 N.W.2d 590 (1979).

1569. Blumberg v. Beekman, 121 Mich. 647, 80 N.W. 710 (1899).

1570. Stover v. Bryant & Detwiler Improvement Corp., 329 Mich. 482, 45 N.W.2d 364 (1951).

1571. Koenig v. Van Reken, 89 Mich. App. 102, 279 N.W.2d 590 (1979).

1572. Miskinis v. Bement, 301 Mich. 365, 3 N.W.2d 307 (1942).

1573. Bernstein v. Riseman, 282 Mich. 292, 276 N.W. 453 (1937).

Ferd L. Alpert Industries, Inc. v. Oakland Metal Stamping Co., 3 Mich. App. 101, 141 N.W.2d 671 (1966), rev'd on other grounds, 379 Mich. 272, 150 N.W.2d 765 (1967).

1574. Cadman v. Peter, 12 F. 363 (C.C.D. Mich. 1882), aff'd, 118 U.S. 73, 6 S. Ct. 957, 30 L. Ed. 78 (1886).

City Lumber Co. v. Hollands, 181 Mich. 531, 148 N.W. 361 (1914).

Restrick Lumber Co. v. Wyrembolski, 164 Mich. 71, 128 N.W. 1083 (1910).

Stahl v. Dehn, 72 Mich. 645, 40 N.W. 922 (1888) (sale of lots).

Court gives effect to parties' intended relations

If a transaction involves something more than the mere loan of money, and the incidental deed with a land contract back is in accord with the intent and agreement of the parties, courts are bound to give effect to the contract as consummated, rather than to create and substitute a different contractual relation between the parties.—Reid v. Dowd, 257 Mich. 492, 241 N.W. 174 (1932).

1575. Stahl v. Dehn, 72 Mich. 645, 40 N.W. 922 (1888).

1576. Rossman v. Hutchinson, 289 Mich. 577, 286 N.W. 835 (1939).

Reid v. Dowd, 257 Mich. 492, 241 N.W. 174 (1932).

Jones v. Ireland, 225 Mich. 467, 196 N.W. 369 (1923).

Clark v. Woodruff, 90 Mich. 83, 51 N.W. 357 (1892).

defeasible by force of a deed of defeasance or other instrument for that purpose, does not defeat or affect the original conveyance as against any person other than the maker of the defeasance, or persons having actual notice of it, unless the instrument of defeasance is recorded in the county where the lands lie.[1577]

Generally, a deed made for the purpose of securing a debt, and accompanied by a contemporaneous agreement for a reconveyance of the property on payment of the debt and interest, is in legal effect a mortgage.[1578] If the owners of land convey it to secure a loan, and the grantee gives back a land contract, the transaction is a mortgage, so that the owners are not divested of the legal title to the land.[1579] Thus, although the existence of an option to repurchase is but a circumstance to be considered in favor of the existence of a mortgage, where the execution of a deed together with an agreement giving the grantor the right to repurchase the property on payment of a specified sum is intended by the parties merely as a security transaction to secure the repayment of the debt, the court will treat the deed as a mortgage.[1580]

However, the mere fact of an agreement to reconvey will not, in itself, turn an absolute conveyance into a mortgage.[1581] Accordingly, a deed made for a consideration paid at the time, whether the payment is made in cash or by the surrender and satisfaction of a precedent debt, under an agreement on the part of the grantee to allow the vendor to repurchase the property at a future day, for the same or an

1577. MCLS § 565.32.

Skupinski v. Provident Mortg. Co., 244 Mich. 309, 221 N.W. 338 (1928).

Good-faith purchaser

An unrecorded defeasance is void only against purchasers for a valuable consideration without actual notice of its existence.—Columbia Bank v. Jacobs, 10 Mich. 349 (1862).

Set aside warranty deed

In a suit to declare a deed to be a mortgage and to set aside a warranty deed from the grantor to third parties a decree dismissing the bill as to the third parties when plaintiff failed to establish his claim that they were not purchasers in good faith and for value was justified under this section.—Dalton v. Miller, 248 Mich. 253, 226 N.W. 826 (1929).

1578. Dow v. Chamberlin, 7 F. Cas. 983, 7 F. Cas. 983 (C.C.D. Mich. 1851) (No.4,037).

Denby v. Ozeran, 255 Mich. 477, 238 N.W. 218 (1931).

Levenson v. Cohen, 250 Mich. 31, 229 N.W. 433 (1930).

Skupinski v. Provident Mortg. Co., 244 Mich. 309, 221 N.W. 338 (1928).

Ferry v. Miller, 164 Mich. 429, 129 N.W. 721 (1911).

Enos v. Sutherland, 11 Mich. 538 (1863).

Deed to contractor

Deed to person contracting to erect dwelling and building and land contracts back to grantor, having been executed for purpose of security, constituted a "mortgage."—Titus v. Cavalier, 276 Mich. 117, 267 N.W. 799 (1936).

1579. Restrick Lumber Co. v. Wyrembolski, 164 Mich. 71, 128 N.W. 1083 (1910).

Clark v. Woodruff, 90 Mich. 83, 51 N.W. 357 (1892).

Jeffery v. Hursh, 58 Mich. 246, 25 N.W. 176, 27 N.W. 7 (1885).

Pierce v. Grimley, 77 Mich. 273, 43 N.W. 932 (1889) (conveyance to trustee).

Return of surplus land

A debtor conveyed certain lands to a trustee, to be sold for the payment of debts, and the deed provided that the surplus and all unsold lands be returned to him after deducting costs and expenses. It was properly treated as a mortgage.—State Bank of Bay City v. Chapelle, 40 Mich. 447 (1879).

1580. Spitzley v. Holmes, 256 Mich. 559, 240 N.W. 81 (1932).

McLaughlin v. Majestic Development Corp., 247 Mich. 498, 226 N.W. 256 (1929).

Grant v. Van Reken, 71 Mich. App. 121, 246 N.W.2d 348 (1976).

1581. Stahl v. Dehn, 72 Mich. 645, 40 N.W. 922 (1888).

advance price, does not convert the transaction into a mortgage.[1582] Similarly, although a conveyance of land contains a clause providing that the grantee is to reconvey upon receiving a certain sum within a specified time, that fact does not affect the construction of the instrument as a deed with an option to repurchase, if it appears that the repurchase is optional with the grantor and that the conveyance is made and accepted in payment of an existing debt.[1583]

§ 735. Presumptions and Burden of Proof

A deed absolute on its face creates a presumption that it is an absolute conveyance and not a mortgage.

A deed absolute on its face creates a presumption that the instrument is an absolute conveyance and not a mortgage.[1584] However, the continued possession of the land by the grantor long after the recording of the deed raises a presumption that the deed was intended as a mortgage,[1585] or at least that the grantor has retained some right in the land.[1586]

The party alleging that a deed absolute on its face was intended as a mortgage has the burden of proving that allegation.[1587] That burden is a heavy one.[1588]

However, where it is conceded that a deed absolute in form was intended as security, the burden is on the grantee to prove a contention that by a subsequent oral agreement it was changed to an absolute deed.[1589]

1582. Beecher v. Morse, 286 Mich. 513 (1938).

1583. Reed v. Bond, 96 Mich. 134, 55 N.W. 619 (1893).

Daniels v. Johnson, 24 Mich. 430 (1872).

Repayment within three years

The execution of a deed, in consideration of a certain sum and an agreement that the vendee must reconvey within three years upon a repayment of the money, did not constitute a mortgage, but an absolute conveyance with an option to repurchase.—Gogarn v. Connors, 188 Mich. 161, 153 N.W. 1068 (1915).

1584. Ellis v. Wayne Real Estate Co., 357 Mich. 115, 97 N.W.2d 758 (1959).

1585. Hulin v. Stevens, 53 Mich. 93, 18 N.W. 569 (1884).

1586. McKeighan v. Citizens Commercial & Sav. Bank, 302 Mich. 666, 5 N.W.2d 524 (1942).

Jankowski v. Szpieg, 282 Mich. 397, 276 N.W. 493 (1937).

Selik v. Goldman Realty Co., 240 Mich. 612, 216 N.W. 422 (1927).

1587. Schmidt v. Barclay, 161 Mich. 1, 125 N.W. 729 (1910).

Miller v. Peter, 158 Mich. 336, 122 N.W. 780 (1909).

Kellogg v. Northrup, 115 Mich. 327, 73 N.W. 230 (1897).

Tilden v. Streeter, 45 Mich. 533, 8 N.W. 502 (1881).

Grant v. Van Reken, 71 Mich. App. 121, 246 N.W.2d 348 (1976).

Additional structures

Where vendor, at purchaser's request, paid part of cost of additional structures and added payment to installment contract, those claiming that contract became mortgage had burden of proof.—Rowe v. William Ford & Co., 257 Mich. 646, 241 N.W. 889 (1932).

Co-vendee

One of two vendees named in a contract for deed, who claimed that the name of the other vendee was inserted to secure repayment to her of a sum loaned to him and paid to the vendors, had the burden of proving his claim.—Burns v. Stevens, 236 Mich. 447, 210 N.W. 483 (1926).

1588. Ferd L. Alpert Industries, Inc. v. Oakland Metal Stamping Co., 379 Mich. 272, 150 N.W.2d 765 (1967).

Schultz v. Schultz, 117 Mich. App. 454, 324 N.W.2d 48 (1982).

1589. Brennan v. Finn, 217 Mich. 584, 187 N.W. 353 (1922).

§ 736.   Admissibility of Evidence

Evidence of the circumstances surrounding the transaction is admissible in determining whether a deed absolute on its face was intended as a mortgage.

The court, in determining whether a deed absolute on its face was intended as a mortgage, will allow the admission of evidence of the circumstances surrounding the transaction and the conversation at the time of its consummation.[1590] The court must not exclude any evidence that tends to show what effect the parties meant the instrument to have.[1591] Evidence concerning the mental capacity of the grantor is relevant to show the relations of the parties and the nature of the transaction.[1592] It also is material where the value of the property greatly exceeded the consideration for the deed,[1593] or where the grantee paid no taxes on the land to which the grantee was given a deed.[1594]

The declarations and statements of the parties are admissible only in so far as they tend to prove the original intention of the parties, as formed and entertained at the time the deed was made.[1595]

Parol evidence. Although not admissible for the purpose of contradicting or varying the terms of the instrument itself,[1596] it is the general rule that parol evidence is admissible to prove that a deed absolute on its face was, in fact, intended as a mortgage.[1597] Parol evidence may prevail over other evidence in determining the parties' intent.[1598]

Conversely, it may also be shown by parol evidence that a deed was intended for the purpose of passing title and was not intended to have the effect of a mortgage.[1599]

Kunz v. Torcellini, 51 Mich. App. 742, 216 N.W.2d 479 (1974).

1590. Carveth v. Winegar, 133 Mich. 34, 94 N.W. 381 (1903).

Real Property Law: Real Evidence: Special Rules for Real Estate Disputes, 80 Mich. B.J. 28 (2001).

1591. Jeffrey v. Hursh, 49 Mich. 31, 12 N.W. 898 (1882).

1592. Reilly v. Brown, 87 Mich. 163, 49 N.W. 557 (1891).

1593. Selik v. Goldman Realty Co., 240 Mich. 612, 216 N.W. 422 (1927).

1594. Hulin v. Stevens, 53 Mich. 93, 18 N.W. 569 (1884).

1595. McMillan v. Bissell, 63 Mich. 66, 29 N.W. 737 (1886).

1596. Dow v. Chamberlin, 7 F. Cas. 983, 7 F. Cas. 983 (C.C.D. Mich. 1851) (No. 4,037).

1597. Ferd L. Alpert Industries, Inc. v. Oakland Metal Stamping Co., 379 Mich. 272, 150 N.W.2d 765 (1967).

Ellis v. Wayne Real Estate Co., 357 Mich. 115, 97 N.W.2d 758 (1959).

Rossman v. Hutchinson, 289 Mich. 577, 286 N.W. 835 (1939).

Jankowski v. Szpieg, 282 Mich. 397, 276 N.W. 493 (1937).

Petition of Selik, 246 Mich. 330, 224 N.W. 350 (1929).

1598. Collateral security for loan

Where a standard fire policy contained notice of a mortgage and land contract and the customary condition that, unless otherwise provided, it was void unless the insured's interest was other than unconditional and sole ownership in fee simple, parol evidence was admissible to show that absolute deed given by insured was for collateral security in nature of mortgage for money lent to him.—Gervickes v. Royal Exch. Assurance Co., 222 Mich. 103, 192 N.W. 654 (1923).

1599. Vollmer v. Coenis, 309 Mich. 319, 15 N.W.2d 654 (1944).

§ 737. Weight and Sufficiency of Evidence

In order to show that a deed absolute on its face was in reality intended as a mortgage, the evidence must be clear and convincing.

Although some decisions have ruled that a preponderance of the evidence is sufficient to show that a deed absolute on its face was intended as a mortgage,[1600] the appellate courts have more often resorted to other expressions, such as "clear,"[1601] "very clear,"[1602] "clear and convincing,"[1603] "clear and satisfactory,"[1604] "clear, irrefragable, and most convincing,"[1605] "convincing beyond reasonable controversy,"[1606] "sufficient to overcome the presumption that the instrument in question truly represents the transaction in its entirety,"[1607] or "a force of evidence sufficient to command the unhesitating assent of every reasonable mind."[1608]

In specific cases, the evidence was sufficient to establish that the instrument was intended primarily as security,[1609] and was therefore, in fact, a mortgage.[1610] In

1600. Samuels v. Detroit Trust Co., 223 Mich. 661, 194 N.W. 517 (1923).

Schmidt v. Barclay, 161 Mich. 1, 125 N.W. 729 (1910).

1601. Rathbone v. Maltz, 155 Mich. 306, 118 N.W. 991 (1909).

1602. Schultz v. Schultz, 117 Mich. App. 454, 324 N.W.2d 48 (1982).

1603. Ellis v. Wayne Real Estate Co., 357 Mich. 115, 97 N.W.2d 758 (1959).

Sheets v. Huben, 354 Mich. 536, 93 N.W.2d 168 (1958) (clear and satisfactory).

Staebler v. Buchanan, 45 Mich. App. 55, 205 N.W.2d 843 (1973).

Taines v. Munson, 19 Mich. App. 29, 172 N.W.2d 217 (1969).

1604. Porritt v. Stone, 340 Mich. 645, 66 N.W.2d 244 (1954).

Wilson v. Potter, 339 Mich. 247, 63 N.W.2d 413 (1954).

Judd v. Carnegie, 324 Mich. 583, 37 N.W.2d 558 (1949).

Rubenstine v. Powers, 215 Mich. 434, 184 N.W. 589 (1921).

Smith v. Smith, 177 Mich. 268, 143 N.W. 86 (1913).

Dalton v. Mertz, 173 Mich. 153, 138 N.W. 1055 (1912).

1605. Lucas v. Johnson, 339 Mich. 540, 64 N.W.2d 651 (1954).

Rehn v. Booth, 299 Mich. 311, 300 N.W. 100 (1941).

Polokoff v. Vebb, 226 Mich. 541, 198 N.W. 194 (1924).

Brennan v. Finn, 217 Mich. 584, 187 N.W. 353 (1922).

Kunz v. Torcellini, 51 Mich. App. 742, 216 N.W.2d 479 (1974).

Degree of proof not sufficient

In an action to have a deed absolute on its face declared a mortgage, evidence was not of that clear, irrefragable, and convincing character required to show that parties, when executing it, intended it to be other than the deed it purported to be.—Frolich v. Aikman, 194 Mich. 569, 161 N.W. 867 (1917).

1606. Tilden v. Streeter, 45 Mich. 533, 8 N.W. 502 (1881).

1607. Crane v. Read, 172 Mich. 642, 138 N.W. 223 (1912).

McArthur v. Robinson, 104 Mich. 540, 62 N.W. 713 (1895).

1608. Jankowski v. Szpieg, 282 Mich. 397, 276 N.W. 493 (1937).

1609. Muskegon Bank & Trust Co. v. Acterhoff, 366 Mich. 548, 115 N.W.2d 323 (1962).

Pettiford v. Weisenthal, 346 Mich. 339, 78 N.W.2d 177 (1956).

Miskinis v. Bement, 301 Mich. 365, 3 N.W.2d 307 (1942).

Carrier v. Caplan, 247 Mich. 38, 225 N.W. 581 (1929).

Petition of Selik, 246 Mich. 330, 224 N.W. 350 (1929).

Cady v. Burgess, 144 Mich. 523, 108 N.W. 414 (1906).

other cases, the evidence was insufficient to establish that the instrument was intended as a security instrument,[1611] and was therefore, in fact, an absolute conveyance.[1612]

If the evidence is sufficient to show that a conveyance in the form of an absolute deed secured advances, the vendee must show with sufficient evidence that an alleged subsequent oral agreement transformed the security into an absolute conveyance.[1613]

Kunz v. Torcellini, 51 Mich. App. 742, 216 N.W.2d 479 (1974).

Advance for labor and materials

Decree that deed given defendants who advanced money for labor and materials and supervised repair of building was mortgage was justified.—Crombez v. Liogre, 249 Mich. 506, 229 N.W. 419 (1930).

Assignment

Evidence, on a bill to declare an assignment of a land contract by complainant's wife to be a mortgage and for an accounting and discharge, established that the assignment was made as security for a loan.—Jackiewicz v. Siwka, 187 Mich. 165, 153 N.W. 688 (1915).

Money advancement

Evidence established that deed to defendants and plaintiff was intended to give latter interest as security for money advanced.—Domboorajian v. Domboorajian, 235 Mich. 668, 209 N.W. 846 (1926).

Signing of bail bond

Evidence established that warranty deed to realty executed by husband and wife as owners by the entireties was in fact merely a mortgage to secure grantee against loss by reason of signing bail bond for grantor husband and hence subsequent quitclaim deed by grantee to grantor wife merely operated to release the mortgage or lien against the realty.—Frankowich v. Frankowich, 323 Mich. 516, 35 N.W.2d 478 (1949).

1610. Lopez v. Lazaros, 369 Mich. 477, 120 N.W.2d 209 (1963).

Ellis v. Wayne Real Estate Co., 357 Mich. 115, 97 N.W.2d 758 (1959).

Sheets v. Huben, 354 Mich. 536, 93 N.W.2d 168 (1958).

Coyle v. Sheehan, 251 Mich. 586, 232 N.W. 222 (1930).

Selik v. Goldman Realty Co., 240 Mich. 612, 216 N.W. 422 (1927).

Rosen v. Booth, 224 Mich. 299, 194 N.W. 976 (1923).

1611. Wilson v. Potter, 339 Mich. 247, 63 N.W.2d 413 (1954).

Rehn v. Booth, 299 Mich. 311, 300 N.W. 100 (1941).

McFadden v. Huron Valley Bldg. & Sav. Ass'n, 255 Mich. 659, 239 N.W. 322 (1931).

Samuels v. Detroit Trust Co., 223 Mich. 661, 194 N.W. 517 (1923).

Swan v. Stevens' Estate, 206 Mich. 594, 173 N.W. 493 (1919).

Smith v. Smith, 177 Mich. 268, 143 N.W. 86 (1913).

1612. Cadman v. Peter, 118 U.S. 73, 6 S. Ct. 957, 30 L. Ed. 78 (1886).

Lucas v. Johnson, 339 Mich. 540, 64 N.W.2d 651 (1954).

Rowe v. William Ford & Co., 257 Mich. 646, 241 N.W. 889 (1932).

Reid v. Dowd, 257 Mich. 492, 241 N.W. 174 (1932).

Rubenstine v. Powers, 215 Mich. 434, 184 N.W. 589 (1921).

Staebler v. Buchanan, 45 Mich. App. 55, 205 N.W.2d 843 (1973).

Dismissal proper

Evidence established the dismissal on the merits of a bill to have a land contract declared a mortgage was proper.—Doudt v. Loveridge, 138 Mich. 295, 101 N.W. 1132 (1904).

1613. Brennan v. Finn, 217 Mich. 584, 187 N.W. 353 (1922) (insufficient evidence).

Chapter 25

CONSTRUCTION AND OPERATION OF MORTGAGES

§ 751. Intention of the Parties

Generally, the law of the state where the property is situated governs the construction and effect of a mortgage. The courts look to the intention of the parties and carry their intention into effect wherever possible.

Library References

Michigan Digest
LexisNexis™ Automated Michigan SCAO Forms
John G. Cameron, Jr., Michigan Real Estate Forms
Powell on Real Property® (Michael Allan Wolf, ed.)
Thompson on Real Property, Thomas Edition (David A. Thomas, ed.)

Law Reviews

David E. Nykanen, Real Property, 55 Wayne L. Rev. 575 (2009); Stephen R. Estey and Danielle Graceffa, Real Property, 54 Wayne L. Rev. 387 (2008); Naseem Stecker and Mike Eidelbes, Up Front: Real Property and Consumer Law Sections Team up on "Ask The Lawyer" to Discuss Mortgage Foreclosures, 87 MI Bar Jnl. 8 (2008); Gregg A. Nathanson, Feature: Real Property Law: What's New in Residential Transactions?, 86 MI Bar Jnl. 16 (2007); David E. Nykanen and Jason C. Long, Annual Survey of Michigan Law; June 1, 2004 - May 31, 2005: Real Property, 52 Wayne L. Rev. 941 (2006); Daniel J. Schairbaum, Annual Survey of Michigan Law: June 1, 2003 - May 31, 2004: Real Property, 51 Wayne L. Rev. 881 (2005); Lawrence R. Shoffner, Real Property Law: Real Evidence: Special Rules for Real Estate Disputes, 80 MI Bar Jnl. 28 (2001).

Generally, the law of the state where the property is situated governs the construction and effect of a mortgage.[1614] The character and legal effect of a mortgage in this state, and the rights, duties, and liabilities of the parties under it, are fixed by the law in force at the time of its execution; therefore, the statutes governing foreclosure are read into every mortgage and become a part of the contract.[1615]

The primary rule in construing a mortgage is to give effect to the intention of the parties, despite literal terms in derogation of the interior sense of the transaction.[1616]

Where a mortgage contains apparently contradictory or repugnant clauses, meaning will be given to all the words and clauses used, if possible.[1617] Similarly, where another written instrument, such as a note[1618] or a bond,[1619] is incorporated by reference into a mortgage, or is given as part of the same transaction, the two

1614. Union Guardian Trust Co. v. Building Sec. Corp., 280 Mich. 144, 273 N.W. 424 (1937).

1615. Bass v. Federal Land Bank, 300 Mich. 418, 2 N.W.2d 447 (1942).

Oades v. Standard Sav. & Loan Ass'n, 257 Mich. 469, 241 N.W. 262 (1932).

1616. Union Guardian Trust Co. v. Building Sec. Corp., 280 Mich. 144, 273 N.W. 424 (1937).

1617. Detroit Trust Co. v. Rivard, 315 Mich. 62, 23 N.W.2d 206 (1946).

1618. Guardian Depositors Corp. v. Wagner, 287 Mich. 202, 283 N.W. 29 (1938).

Grover v. Gratiot Macomb Development Co., 257 Mich. 26, 240 N.W. 66 (1932).

1619. Michigan Trust Co. v. Grand Rapids Hotel Co., 265 Mich. 328, 251 N.W. 414 (1933).

instruments must be read and construed together.[1620] The mortgage may be modified by the contents of the other writing.[1621]

Recitals are to be construed according to their natural and reasonable import.[1622] A mortgagor is not precluded from disputing the truth of a recital, such as that providing for consideration.[1623]

As a general rule, in construing an ambiguous mortgage, the intention of the parties may be determined from the consideration of extrinsic circumstances,[1624] including the construction placed on the mortgage by the parties.[1625] However, the contractual rights and liabilities of the parties to a mortgage cannot be implied, but must be found in the instrument.[1626] In that vein, the language of the instrument is to be construed most favorably to the mortgagee.[1627]

Land contract mortgages. The statute authorizing the securing of any debt or obligation that may be secured by a regular real estate mortgage to be secured by a mortgage on the interest of a vendor or vendee in a land contract specifically does not alter the effect of an otherwise enforceable provision of the land contract prohibiting or resulting in a default on the mortgage, sale, assignment, or

1620. Keagle v. Pessell, 91 Mich. 618, 52 N.W. 58 (1892) (will).

Abele v. McGuigan, 78 Mich. 415, 44 N.W. 393 (1889) (lease).

Stuart v. Worden, 42 Mich. 154, 3 N.W. 876 (1879) (deed).

1621. Irreconcilable contradiction

A mortgage is merely collateral to the debt represented by notes that constitute the primary contract, and that must govern where there is an irreconcilable contradiction between them and the mortgage concerning date on which the debt falls due.—Ferris v. Johnson, 136 Mich. 227, 98 N.W. 1014 (1904).

1622. Jerome v. Hopkins, 2 Mich. 96 (1851).

Damon v. Deeves, 62 Mich. 465, 29 N.W. 42 (1886) (error as to amount).

1623. Computation by court required

Where a mortgage executed by complainant in 1891 was attacked by him on the ground of want of consideration, and it appeared that the only consideration for it was the sum remaining due under a mortgage given in 1877, the recitals in the later mortgage were not conclusive on the question of consideration, but court had to determine by computation the actual amount so due.—Ruloff v. Hazen, 124 Mich. 570, 83 N.W. 370 (1900).

1624. Citizens' Bank of Saline v. Luenser, 264 Mich. 392, 249 N.W. 871 (1933).

Waters v. Gillies, 128 Mich. 608, 87 N.W. 881 (1901).

Agreement for subsequent conveyance

Evidence in suit to foreclose a mortgage was sufficient to authorize a finding that occupancy of land was based on an agreement for a subsequent conveyance; so that improvements thereon made by the person so in possession became part of the real estate, and were covered by a subsequent mortgage of the land.—Morley v. Quimby, 132 Mich. 140, 92 N.W. 943 (1903).

Tax payments

Payment of tax raises strong presumption that mortgage was not operative as security for greater amount than that on which tax was paid.—Carroll v. Chauret, 241 Mich. 338, 216 N.W. 913 (1928).

1625. French v. Case, 77 Mich. 64, 43 N.W. 1056 (1889).

Chase v. Brown, 32 Mich. 225 (1875).

Payment

Where, at the time of the making of a loan secured by a mortgage, there was no arrangement that the mortgage could not be paid according to its terms, evidence of subsequent statements by the mortgagee that he did not expect the mortgagor to pay the principal, and that he would have the money after the mortgagee's death, did not establish a binding promise on the mortgagee's part to forbear collection of the debt, there being no consideration to support it.—Trombly v. Klersy, 139 Mich. 209, 102 N.W. 638 (1905).

1626. Union Guardian Trust Co. v. Building Sec. Corp., 280 Mich. 144, 273 N.W. 424 (1937).

1627. Union Guardian Trust Co. v. Building Sec. Corp., 280 Mich. 144, 273 N.W. 424 (1937).

Stuart v. Worden, 42 Mich. 154, 3 N.W. 876 (1879).

encumbrance of the interest.[1628]

§ 752. Parties

A mortgage may be made jointly to two or more parties and to secure separate debts due to the mortgagees severally.

A "mortgagor" is a person who mortgages his or her property to another person.[1629] A mere owner of the equity of redemption is not a mortgagor, and the mortgagee cannot avail him- or herself of an agreement made by a mere owner of that equity to pay the mortgage if the owner is not a party to the mortgage or in any way liable for the debt secured by it.[1630]

A "mortgagee" is a person to whom a mortgage is made. It is not necessary that a mortgagee be only one person.[1631] A mortgage may be made jointly to two or more,[1632] and to secure separate debts due to the mortgagees severally.[1633]

Where the true owner of property makes the principal of a mortgage note payable to others, those other persons are parties to the contract and entitled to enforce it.[1634]

§ 753. Debts or Liabilities Secured

The character, terms, or amount of the debt or obligation secured by a mortgage are to be ascertained from the instrument.

In determining the character, terms, or amount of a debt secured by a mortgage, the elementary rule is to ascertain from the instrument in its entirety, and the surrounding circumstances, the intention of the parties.[1635]

1628. MCLS § 565.357.

Graves v. Am. Acceptance Mortg. Corp., 469 Mich. 608, 677 N.W.2d 829 (2004).

1629. Ballentine's Law Dictionary at 817 (3d ed. 1969).

1630. Stuart v. Worden, 42 Mich. 154, 3 N.W. 876 (1879).

1631. Death of joint mortgagee

A mortgage due to two or more persons jointly, on the death of any of them, passes to the survivor or survivors, and not to the personal representatives of the deceased.—Cote v. Dequindre, Walk. Ch. 64 (Mich. 1842).

1632. Cooley v. Kinney, 109 Mich. 34, 66 N.W. 674 (1896).

Mortgage by only one joint tenant

Where parties own property as joint tenants with full rights of survivorship, and only one tenant executes a mortgage on property, and the mortgaging tenant dies, the surviving joint tenant is not liable on the mortgage because that joint tenant was not a party to the mortgage, and the mortgage effectively terminates on the mortgaging joint tenant's death; the debt becomes an obligation of the decedent tenant's estate, but the property does not become an asset of the estate subject to foreclosure. In such a circumstance, no equitable mortgage is created because the only equity that the mortgagee seeks to have done is to save it from the mistake of not having insisted that the other joint tenant also pledge his or her interest in the property to secure the loan.—Townsend v. Chase Manhattan Mortg. Corp., 254 Mich. App. 133, 657 N.W.2d 741 (2002).

1633. Donovan v. Dwyer, 57 Mich. 561, 24 N.W. 857 (1885).

1634. Children of mortgagor

Where the principal of a mortgage note was made payable to the mortgagor's children, instead of to the person who furnished the consideration, the children were parties to the contract, and entitled to enforce it.—Palmer v. Bray, 136 Mich. 85, 98 N.W. 849 (1904).

1635. Engler v. Engler, 192 Mich. 361, 158 N.W. 836 (1916).

As a distinct security in itself,[1636] the mortgage secures the debt, and its terms limit the amount secured,[1637] while the note represents and evidences the debt.[1638]

A mortgage to secure all of the mortgagor's existing debt is valid.[1639]

Conversely, a mortgage that does not provide for the payment of interest on the amount secured will not be construed so as to require it.[1640]

It is not necessary that the debt secured by a mortgage exist at the time the mortgage is executed.[1641] The consideration named in the instrument does not limit the security for which a mortgage may stand if the intent to secure a future indebtedness is apparent from the whole instrument.[1642]

The use of testimonial evidence to determine the intent of the parties concerning the debts secured is permissible.[1643]

Support and maintenance. A mortgage may be given to secure the performance of a contract or undertaking by the mortgagor to furnish support and

Rundle v. Scully, 144 Mich. 62, 107 N.W. 694 (1906).

Resizing provision

Under Michigan law, the court construed the resizing mechanism of a commercial loan agreement as discretionary, not mandatory, where the agreement incorporated a note, which granted defendant mortgagee the "sole and absolute discretion" to resize, and the court rejected plaintiff mortgagor's contention that the provision of the loan agreement conflicted with the provision of the note; extrinsic evidence was inadmissible because the contract contained an integration clause and the contract language was unambiguous.—Wonderland Shopping Ctr. Venture L.P. v. CDC Mortg. Capital, Inc., 274 F.3d 1085 (6th Cir. Mich. 2001).

Term of mortgage

Where a mortgage stated that it was to secure the purchase money of land, and was to be paid at a fixed time, if a mortgage then on the property should be discharged from record, or should "outlaw," the term "outlaw," as used, referred to the time when by law the mortgage would be presumed to be paid.—Curtis v. Goodenow, 24 Mich. 18 (1871).

1636. Eaton v. Truesdail, 40 Mich. 1 (1879).

1637. Incorporation by reference

Mortgage securing "repayment of $1,050 according to terms of note" was security for repayment of $1,050 only, notwithstanding note promised payment of open account also.—Carroll v. Chauret, 241 Mich. 338, 216 N.W. 913 (1928).

Partnership indebtedness

Mortgage for $1,500, providing that when indebtedness of mortgagor and firm of which he was a member should be reduced to $3,500, the mortgage should be deemed satisfied, secured $1,500 of indebtedness until indebtedness was so reduced, and not merely the excess over $3,500.—Commercial State Sav. Bank v. Stevens, 180 Mich. 35, 146 N.W. 226 (1914).

Recitals in mortgage as controlling

Recital in deed given as security for loan determined amount of lien, regardless of recitals in note.—Continental Bank v. Kowalsky, 247 Mich. 348, 225 N.W. 496 (1929).

1638. Replacement note

Note executed to payee in place of other discounted by it was properly included with mortgage theretofore executed securing all liability.—Peninsular State Bank v. Miller, 254 Mich. 475, 236 N.W. 815 (1931).

1639. Michigan Ins. Co. v. Brown, 11 Mich. 265 (1863).

Macomb County Sav. Bank v. Kohlhoff, 5 Mich. App. 531, 147 N.W.2d 418 (1967).

1640. Visioneering, Inc. Profit Sharing Trust v. Belle River Joint Venture, 149 Mich. App. 327, 386 N.W.2d 185 (1986).

1641. Ginsberg v. Capitol City Wrecking Co., 300 Mich. 712, 2 N.W.2d 892, 1942 Mich. LEXIS 669 (1942).

1642. Citizens' Sav. Bank v. Kock, 117 Mich. 225, 75 N.W. 458 (1898).

Brackett v. Sears, 15 Mich. 244 (1867).

1643. No change to terms of mortgage

In equitable action to foreclose open-end mortgage that allegedly secured certain notes, court's proper admission of testimony to construe intent of parties did not constitute allowance of testimony to change terms of mortgage instrument.—Macomb County Sav. Bank v. Kohlhoff, 5 Mich. App. 531, 147 N.W.2d 418 (1967).

maintenance to the mortgagee or to another person.[1644]

§ 754.   —Indemnity Mortgages

Any mortgage given by way of indemnity is valid and enforceable, but only with respect to a liability or responsibility that has been assumed according to the terms of the mortgage.

A mortgage given by way of indemnity is not founded on a present debt, but meant to secure the mortgagee against loss or damage in consequence of a contingent liability or responsibility that the mortgagee has assumed or agreed to assume for and on behalf of the mortgagor, or the mortgagor's surety, endorser or otherwise. An indemnity mortgage is valid and enforceable, but only concerning a liability or responsibility that has been assumed according to the terms of the mortgage.[1645] The security of the mortgage will be strictly confined to the particular debt or liability, or class of debts or liabilities, specified in the condition. It cannot be diverted to other purposes or held as security for other debts, at least without the consent of the mortgagor. Likewise, an indemnity mortgage may by appropriate words be restricted to the securing of endorsements made, or other liabilities contracted, for the mortgagor within a certain limited time after its execution. In that case, it will be a continuing security during the specified time, but will not cover any obligations incurred after the end of the designated period.[1646]

An indemnity mortgage may be given to secure the mortgagee not only as against debts or liabilities for which he or she has already assumed responsibility or liability, but also to protect the mortgagee against loss or damage on endorsements or other liabilities that the mortgagee may in the future enter into for the benefit of the mortgagor.[1647]

In construing indemnity mortgages, the cardinal rule is to ascertain the intention of the parties from the language of the instrument, aided by extrinsic evidence in case of ambiguity, such as statements of the parties contemporaneous with the execution of the instrument.[1648]

§ 755.   —Extension of Security to Other Debts or Liabilities

Generally, where a mortgage is given to secure a specific debt, the security will not be extended to antecedent or subsequent debts unless the instrument so provides.

1644. French v. Case, 77 Mich. 64, 43 N.W. 1056 (1889).

1645. Albion State Bank v. Knickerbocker, 125 Mich. 311, 84 N.W. 311 (1900).

Expenditure not secured

A mortgage securing all obligations that the mortgagee may assume or become liable for by reason of paper endorsements or obligations he or she may make for the mortgagor does not secure a liability of the mortgagee arising from payment of outstanding note of mortgagor not endorsed by him or her.—Burt v. Gamble, 98 Mich. 402, 57 N.W. 261 (1894).

1646. Burt v. Gamble, 98 Mich. 402, 57 N.W. 261 (1894).

1647. Limit as to amount

A note previously endorsed by H. for W. is within a mortgage to secure "any and all accommodation indorsements made" by H. for W. up to the sum of $3,000, to which extent H. "agrees to indorse for W. . . . as from time to time required," the total of said endorsements in no event to exceed said sum of $3,000.—Holliday v. Snow, 129 Mich. 494, 89 N.W. 443 (1902).

1648. Albion State Bank v. Knickerbocker, 125 Mich. 311, 84 N.W. 311 (1900).

In the absence of a valid agreement of the parties, a mortgagee or deed of trust given to secure a particular debt, whether present or prospective, cannot be enforced as security for another and different debt.[1649] Thus, where a mortgage is given to secure a specific debt, the security will not be extended to antecedent[1650] or subsequent[1651] debts unless the instrument so provides and identifies in clear terms those intended to be secured.[1652]

A mortgage purporting to bind a mortgagor to pay all further or other sums of money and other indebtedness that might be due or owing from the mortgagor when the mortgage becomes due or is foreclosed covers only those demands directly arising out of dealings between the mortgagee and the mortgagor. This type of provision in a mortgage is sometimes referred to as a "dragnet clause."[1653]

The English doctrine of "tacking," in so far as it would permit the holder of a mortgage given for the express purpose of securing a particular debt to add to his or her claim any other debt or demand against the mortgagor and stretch the security of the mortgage to cover it also, is not recognized in this country, and this type of tacking is not permitted.[1654]

Agreement of parties. It is competent for the parties to a mortgage to agree that it shall stand as security for a debt or claim different from that described in the mortgage, or for a debt subsequently contracted. When the good faith of the arrangement is not impeached, the mortgage will be a valid security for the new debt as between the parties to it. Accordingly, the parties to a mortgage given to secure an existing debt for a sum certain may agree to make the mortgage a security for other debts or liabilities to be incurred in the future.[1655]

1649. Woodin v. Sparta Furniture Co., 59 Mich. 58, 26 N.W. 504 (1886).

1650. Gifford v. Hartson, 247 Mich. 217, 225 N.W. 578 (1929).

1651. Parkes v. Parker, 57 Mich. 57, 23 N.W. 458 (1885).

Holiday Inns, Inc. v. Susher-Schaefer Inv. Co., 77 Mich. App. 658, 259 N.W.2d 179 (1977).

Lands acquired by mortgagor's spouse

Where a husband mortgaged an undivided two thirds of certain land without inserting covenants of title, and his wife afterwards acquired the other undivided third to which he had no title when he gave the mortgage, the mortgagee's original rights were not affected, even if the husband furnished the money to pay for the third acquired by his wife.—McClure v. Holbrook, 39 Mich. 42 (1878).

1652. Macomb County Sav. Bank v. Kohlhoff, 5 Mich. App. 531, 147 N.W.2d 418 (1967).

Intended coverage

Mortgage executed for specific debt and land contracts given as additional security covered additional loan to mortgagor not specifically mentioned in it, but intended to be covered by mortgage.—Riess v. Old Kent Bank, 253 Mich. 557, 235 N.W. 252 (1931).

Printed clause

A printed omnibus clause in a mortgage extending it to debts not covered by the amount specifically stated seems to be to some extent counterbalanced by the presumption arising from the fact that the stamp on the mortgage corresponds to the specified sum.—Lashbrooks v. Hatheway, 52 Mich. 124, 17 N.W. 723 (1883).

1653. Co-mortgagors not covered individually

Mortgage agreement containing so-called "dragnet clause" covering only demands directly arising out of dealings between "mortgagor" and "mortgagee" and those debts entered into by "mortgagor" would be held not to include subsequent mortgage debt agreement entered into by only one of co-mortgagors regarding separate project, there being nothing in plain language of clause to indicate that it included subsequent debts of fewer than all persons designated as "mortgagor" thereunder.—Holiday Inns, Inc. v. Susher-Schaefer Inv. Co., 77 Mich. App. 658, 259 N.W.2d 179 (1977).

1654. Wing v. McDowell, Walk. Ch. 175 (Mich. 1843).

1655. Riess v. Old Kent Bank, 253 Mich. 557, 235 N.W. 252 (1931).

Claims purchased by mortgagee. A mortgagee, buying up claims held by third persons against his or her mortgagor, cannot include them in a mortgage from the mortgagor and compel their settlement as a condition to redemption, or have them included in a foreclosure decree, except in cases where no subsequent purchaser or lien creditor will be prejudiced. The mortgagor may consent to their inclusion, however.[1656] Even where the mortgage is so drawn as to cover any demands that the mortgagee may hold against the mortgagor, the mortgagee cannot, by virtue of the instrument, buy up outstanding claims against the mortgagor and include them in the security, unless a provision that the mortgagee may do so is clearly and unequivocally expressed. Generally, a stipulation of this character ordinarily can cover only those demands that arise directly out of dealings between the parties to the instrument.[1657]

Taxes and assessments. Where the mortgagor of realty neglects to pay taxes or assessments levied on the property during the continuance of the mortgage lien, the mortgagee has the right to pay them for his or her own protection. On making that payment, the mortgagee is entitled to add the amount to the principal of the mortgage debt and bring it within the security of the mortgage although the mortgage does not expressly authorize payment,[1658] or is silent as to the payment of taxes.[1659]

A mortgagee who pays the taxes is presumed to do so for the benefit or protection of the security, and not on the personal liability of the owner of the premises.[1660] The mortgagee has no right to intervene and pay the tax until it has been returned as delinquent, and it is evident that the mortgagor will not pay it.[1661]

Insurance. Generally, if the mortgagor violates a mortgage covenant to insure the property, the mortgagee may take out the insurance and add the cost to the principal sum secured by the mortgage.[1662]

Costs. The costs of an incomplete and ineffectual sale under a mortgage foreclosure may not be added to the amount due on the mortgage.[1663]

§ 756. Property Mortgaged and Estates of Parties

The property covered by a mortgage must be determined by the description contained in the mortgage itself.

A mortgage encumbers specific property. The nature, location, and extent of

Macomb County Sav. Bank v. Kohlhoff, 5 Mich. App. 531, 147 N.W.2d 418 (1967).

"Wraparound mortgage"

"Wraparound mortgage" is junior mortgage that secures promissory note with face amount equal to sum of principal balance of existing mortgage note plus any additional funds advanced by wraparound lender.—Mitchell v. Trustees of United States Mut. Real Estate Inv. Trust, 144 Mich. App. 302, 375 N.W.2d 424 (1985).

1656. Perrin v. Kellogg, 38 Mich. 720 (1878).

1657. Lashbrooks v. Hatheway, 52 Mich. 124, 17 N.W. 723 (1883).

1658. People's Wayne County Bank v. Wesolowska, 256 Mich. 45, 239 N.W. 367 (1931).

1659. G.F. Sanborn Co. v. Alston, 153 Mich. 463, 117 N.W. 625 (1908).

1660. New York Life Ins. Co. v. Erb, 276 Mich. 610, 268 N.W. 754 (1936).

1661. Pond v. Drake, 50 Mich. 302, 15 N.W. 466 (1883).

1662. Leland v. Collver, 34 Mich. 418 (1876).

1663. Birenberg v. Razgunas, 273 Mich. 292, 262 N.W. 914 (1935).

the property covered by a mortgage must be determined by the description of it contained in the mortgage itself, interpreted according to the established rules of construction, and aided by extrinsic evidence for purposes of identification and limitation, where that is necessary by reason of the uncertainty or ambiguity of the description.[1664] A mortgage will give the mortgagee no greater rights or interests than the mortgagor.[1665] Whatever defeats a mortgagor's title also defeats the lien of the mortgagee.[1666]

Generally, because a mortgage will give the mortgagee no greater rights or interests than the mortgagor possessed, a mortgage for the purchase money of land attaches to no property that the purchaser does not own at the time the mortgage is given, nor will covenants be implied that extend the mortgage to an after-acquired interest.[1667] Thus, a mortgage creates no right in an allegedly servient tenement if the mortgagor has no interest in the servient tenement at the time the mortgage is executed.[1668] However, the parties to an agreement that certain personalty is to be considered part of the realty as between the parties and is to be covered by the real estate mortgage, may stipulate that personalty subsequently placed upon the mortgaged premises is also to be considered part of the realty and subject to the mortgage.[1669]

The statutory foreclosure provision that unless the premises described in a mortgage deed are redeemed within the time limited for redemption, the deed becomes operative and vests in the grantee all the mortgagor's right, title, and interest in the property,[1670] does not enlarge any estate definitely limited in the mortgage, but, as between the original parties, may bind a subsequently acquired interest.[1671]

The description in bonds, such as that they are secured by a trust mortgage on a leasehold estate as set forth in an indenture of mortgage, must be construed in connection with the description in the mortgage in determining what property is mortgaged.[1672]

Fixtures. A mortgage of land covers all fixtures belonging to the realty, without special mention being made of them.[1673] But to maintain priority over other interests, the mortgage may have to be perfected as a fixture filing under the

---

1664. Anderson v. Baughman, 7 Mich. 69 (1859).

1665. Corporate mortgagor

In receiving a mortgage of corporate property, mortgagees must take it subject to duties or encumbrances that law attaches to enjoyment of property mortgaged, but not to such as may exist against the corporation without reference to that property.—Joy v. Jackson & Michigan Plank Road Co., 11 Mich. 155 (1863).

1666. Sloan v. Holcomb, 29 Mich. 153 (1874).

1667. Brown v. Phillips, 40 Mich. 264 (1879).

1668. Von Meding v. Strahl, 319 Mich. 598, 30 N.W.2d 363 (1948) (overruled as stated in

Schmidt v. Eger, 94 Mich. App. 728, 289 N.W.2d 851 (1980)).

1669. Guardian Depositors' Corp. v. Keller, 286 Mich. 403, 282 N.W. 194 (1938).

1670. MCLS § 600.3236 (foreclosure by advertisement).

MCLS § 600.3130 (foreclosure by judicial sale).

1671. Brayton v. Merithew, 56 Mich. 166, 22 N.W. 259 (1885) (decided under prior identical statute).

1672. Michigan Trust Co. v. Grand Rapids Hotel Co., 265 Mich. 328, 251 N.W. 414 (1933).

1673. Fixtures, *see, supra,* Chapter 3.

Tyler v. Hayward, 235 Mich. 674, 209 N.W. 801 (1926).

Uniform Commercial Code—Secured Transactions.[1674]

Appurtenances. A mortgage of land with the "appurtenances" covers such physical property and rights as are used with, and for the benefit of, the land and are reasonably necessary for its proper enjoyment.[1675]

Interest under contract of purchase. The mortgage given by one holding land under an executory contract for its purchase covers that equitable interest, whatever it may be, at the date of the mortgage, giving the mortgagee the right to complete the purchase if the mortgagor refuses to do so.[1676]

Rights of cestui que trust under a trust deed. If a deed of trust given as security for a debt imposes a duty on the trustee to sell the land and hold the proceeds in trust or distribute the proceeds, the interest of the beneficiary under the trust deed is personal property.[1677]

Exceptions and reservations. In determining the extent and location of the property covered by a reservation or exception in a mortgage, the court will attempt to ascertain and effectuate the intentions expressed in the instruments before it.[1678]

Adverse possession. The mortgagee cannot bar the mortgagor's equity of redemption by the mortgagee's mere assumption, evidenced by his or her giving a deed, that he or she has title in fee, nor can an occasional occupation under that deed, or any occupation short of a continuous and notorious one, be adverse to the right to redeem, and have the effect of barring the equity of redemption.[1679]

On the other hand, a stranger who occupies mortgaged land under an open claim of absolute ownership holds adversely to the mortgagee and the mortgagor from the beginning. The mortgagee cannot assert against the adverse possessor a right that could not be asserted by the mortgagor if the mortgage had not been made.[1680]

§ 757.   —Interests of Parties

A real estate mortgage is a mere security in the nature of a specific lien for debts and does not convey any title to the mortgagee.

1674. Priority of mortgages, *see, infra*, Chapter 26.

MCLS § 440.9334.

1675. Building

A real-estate mortgage on a lot, and the "tenements, hereditaments, and appurtenances," covers a wooden opera house that rests on sills on the ground, the roof being supported by the sides, and by iron columns on stone and wood foundations, the base of the stage and furnace of which are in excavations made for the purpose.—Miles v. McNaughton, 111 Mich. 350, 69 N.W. 481 (1896).

1676. Balen v. Mercier, 75 Mich. 42, 42 N.W. 666 (1889).

1677. After foreclosure

That rule is applicable to mortgage bonds and participation certificates even after foreclosure of mortgage if trustee, as purchaser at foreclosure sale, has right to sell property thus acquired and distribute proceeds.—Union Guardian Trust Co. v. Nichols, 311 Mich. 107, 18 N.W.2d 383 (1945).

1678. Exception

A mortgage of land, "except the life estate of the widow," covers the part of the land in which the widow has a life estate, subject only to that estate.—Caple v. Switzer, 122 Mich. 636, 81 N.W. 560 (1900).

1679. Humphrey v. Hurd, 29 Mich. 44 (1874).

1680. Schafer v. Hauser, 111 Mich. 622, 70 N.W. 136 (1897).

Contrary to the so-called "title theory" of mortgages under which a person who mortgages land that he or she holds conveys the legal title to the mortgagee,[1681] the "lien theory" obtains in this state.[1682] Under the lien theory, although a mortgage on real estate creates a contingent interest in the land that by foreclosure may become an absolute one,[1683] a mortgagee has no estate in the mortgaged land, but has only a chose in action.[1684] The title to the premises and the right of possession remain in the mortgagor until foreclosure.[1685]

The rights of the mortgagor and mortgagee differ from those of vendor and vendee, therefore, in that the mortgagor holds the fee and the mortgagee has a lien,[1686] while a vendor holds the fee and a vendee has an equitable interest.[1687]

When a mortgage has been paid, the mortgagee will not be allowed to dispute the title of the mortgagor or the mortgagor's grantee as a reason for refusing to discharge it.[1688]

Mortgage in form of deed. Although a mortgagee under a mortgage in the form of a deed holds legal title merely as security,[1689] a deed absolute given as a mortgage conveys legal title.[1690] While that deed is in chancery only a mortgage, another deed back is required to revest the title in the mortgagor.[1691]

A deed absolute on its face, given to secure money lent and redeemable by its payment, being a mortgage in chancery as between the parties, is also a mortgage as to those who purchase from them with notice.[1692]

Land contract mortgage. A vendor or vendee may subject any or all of his or

1681. Wing v. McDowell, Walk. Ch. 175 (Mich. 1843).

Stevens v. Brown, Walk. Ch. 41 (Mich. 1842).

1682. Z & Z Leasing v. Graying Reel, 873 F. Supp. 51 (E.D. Mich. 1995).

McKeighan v. Citizens Commercial & Sav. Bank, 302 Mich. 666, 5 N.W.2d 524 (1942).

Equitable Trust Co. v. Milton Realty Co., 263 Mich. 673, 249 N.W. 30 (1933).

Brink v. Freoff, 40 Mich. 610 (1879).

Wagar v. Stone, 36 Mich. 364 (1877).

Crippen v. Morrison, 13 Mich. 23 (1864).

Caruthers v. Humphrey, 12 Mich. 270 (1864).

1683. Union Guardian Trust Co. v. Nichols, 311 Mich. 107, 18 N.W.2d 383 (1945).

1684. Plasger v. Leonard, 312 Mich. 561, 20 N.W.2d 296 (1945).

Definition

Real estate mortgages are personal property, collateral to indebtedness for which they are given as security.—Kerschensteiner v. Northern Michigan Land Co., 244 Mich. 403, 221 N.W. 322 (1928).

1685. Z & Z Leasing v. Graying Reel, 873 F. Supp. 51 (E.D. Mich. 1995).

Dawson v. Peter, 119 Mich. 274, 77 N.W. 997 (1899).

1686. Z & Z Leasing v. Graying Reel, 873 F. Supp. 51 (E.D. Mich. 1995).

1687. Lutz v. Dutmer, 286 Mich. 467, 282 N.W. 431 (1938).

1688. Ormsby v. Barr, 22 Mich. 80 (1870).

1689. Fletcher v. Morlock, 251 Mich. 96, 231 N.W. 59 (1930).

1690. Skupinski v. Provident Mortg. Co., 244 Mich. 309, 221 N.W. 338 (1928).

Jordan v. Diltz, 240 Mich. 512, 215 N.W. 313 (1927).

People v. Andre, 153 Mich. 531, 117 N.W. 55 (1908).

1691. Farr v. Childs, 204 Mich. 19, 169 N.W. 868 (1918).

McArthur v. Robinson, 104 Mich. 540, 62 N.W. 713 (1895).

1692. Hurst v. Beaver, 50 Mich. 612, 16 N.W. 165 (1883).

her interests in a land contract to the lien of a land contract mortgage.[1693] Unless the parties agree otherwise, a land contract mortgage encumbers all of the respective vendor's or vendee's interests that are mortgaged in the same manner as a regular real estate mortgage.[1694]

§ 758.   —Acquisition of Outstanding Title

Whether the lien of a mortgage merges into the fee and extinguishes a mortgage debt when the mortgagee acquires fee title to the mortgaged property depends on the mortgagee's intention.

Whether the lien of a mortgage merges into the fee and extinguishes a mortgage debt when the mortgagee acquires fee title to the mortgaged property depends on the mortgagee's intention. If it is in the mortgagee's interest to preserve the lien separately from the fee, it will ordinarily be concluded that the mortgagee did not intend to merge the lien into the fee.[1695]

Under statutes applicable to general property taxes due prior to January 1, 1999, the purchaser of a tax title obtained an absolute title in fee simple.[1696] Nonetheless, under this statute, neither party to a mortgage could cut off the other's interest by bidding in the premises at a tax sale.[1697] However, the rule did not apply where the purchase of the tax title was made after the relation of mortgagor and mortgagee had been terminated.[1698]

Under this former rule, if a mortgagor suffered mortgaged land to be sold for delinquent taxes and acquired a tax title, either by direct purchase at the tax sale or by accepting a transfer from another person purchasing at the sale, the mortgagor did not thereby defeat the lien of the mortgage, and could not be permitted to set up the tax title in opposition to the rights of the mortgagee.[1699] In other words, a mortgagor of real estate, while in possession of the real estate, was obligated to pay the taxes assessed against him or her and could not, by purchasing the tax title on the sale of

---

1693. MCLS § 565.357.

1694. MCLS § 565.357.

Graves v. Am. Acceptance Mortg. Corp., 469 Mich. 608, 677 N.W.2d 829 (2004).

1695. No merger intended

Where mortgaged property was encumbered by a second mortgage when mortgagee holding first mortgage acquired fee by purchase at mechanics' lien foreclosure sale, it was contrary to mortgagee's interest to eliminate priority of its first mortgage by merger; hence, it was concluded that mortgagee did not intend to merge its fee and security interests.—Sylvania Sav. Bank Co. v. Turner, 27 Mich. App. 640, 183 N.W.2d 894 (1970).

1696. *Former* MCLS § 211.72, repealed by 1999 Pub. Act 123, effective December 31, 2003.

1697. Maxfield v. Willey, 46 Mich. 252, 9 N.W. 271 (1881).

1698. Foreclosure

Where mortgagee who had taken usurious interest foreclosed, and refused to redeem from third party's tax title, he was in no position to invoke the aid of equity to reinstate his interest in the premises, after mortgagor repurchased from holder of the tax title.—Napper v. Fitzpatrick, 194 Mich. 175, 160 N.W. 400 (1916).

Where a mortgagee purchased the premises at foreclosure sale, he may, after the period for redemption, be a purchaser at a tax sale, where they are sold for taxes that accrued when he was mortgagee.—Ensley v. Coolbaugh, 160 Mich. 299, 125 N.W. 279 (1910).

1699. Jacobsen v. Nieboer, 299 Mich. 116, 299 N.W. 830 (1941).

the property for taxes the mortgagor should have paid, defeat the mortgage.[1700]

Under this rule, the mortgagor's purchase was regarded as merely operating as a payment of the taxes, and as a redemption inuring to the mortgagee's benefit.[1701] In whose name the mortgagor repurchased the property was irrelevant.[1702]

The mortgagee's purchase of the land to which he or she held a mortgage at a tax sale gave the mortgagee no title that could be asserted against the mortgagor, because the purchase only amounted to a redemption from the sale and could not be considered an independent title.[1703] The mortgagor was entitled to an assignment of the tax certificate, upon payment of the amount paid for it, with interest.[1704] Similarly, a mortgagee who, acting in behalf of the mortgagor, takes a quitclaim deed from a judgment creditor after the mortgagor's time for redemption from the execution sale has expired, cannot by that act cut off the mortgagor's right to redeem on payment of the amount due.[1705]

Other statutes apply to property taxes levied after December 31, 1998, and do not provide for tax sales of tax-delinquent property.[1706] Those statutes provide that, whether the tax-foreclosed property is retained by a governmental unit or subsequently auctioned[1707] to a third party after the governmental unit takes title, the absolute title conveyed to the governmental unit extinguishes all outstanding recorded or unrecorded liens against the property except certain specified liens not including mortgages.[1708] Only a party who can prove that he or she did not receive notice of the tax foreclosure is entitled to sue the state, and a party can not sue the subsequent owner for damages for the value of his or her former interest in the tax-foreclosed property.[1709]

1700. Fells v. Barbour, 58 Mich. 49, 24 N.W. 672 (1885).

Connecticut Mut. Life Ins. Co. v. Bulte, 45 Mich. 113, 7 N.W. 707 (1881).

1701. Napper v. Fitzpatrick, 194 Mich. 175, 160 N.W. 400 (1916).

Estoppel

Where mortgagors expressly mortgaged and warranted to mortgagees title to land described in mortgage containing usual covenant by mortgagors to pay all taxes and at time mortgage was executed mortgagors were in default in payment of taxes and land was sold to state without knowledge of mortgages who failed to redeem; after title was absolute in state, land was sold to a third party and pursuant to so-called scavenger act mortgagors contracted for repurchase of land from state, mortgagors did not acquire title free and clear of mortgage encumbrance; equity considers that mortgagors redeemed land when they exercised their right as former owners to match highest bid at scavenger sale and mortgagors were "estopped" from claiming that mortgage lien was cut off.—Jacobsen v. Nieboer, 299 Mich. 116, 299 N.W. 830 (1941).

1702. Chamberlain v. Forbes, 126 Mich. 86, 85 N.W. 253 (1901).

1703. Porter v. Corbin, 124 Mich. 201, 82 N.W. 818 (1900).

1704. Baker v. Clark, 52 Mich. 22, 17 N.W. 225 (1883).

1705. Williams v. Bolt, 170 Mich. 517, 136 N.W. 472 (1912).

1706. MCLS §§ 211.78 et seq., enacted by 1999 Pub. Act 123, effective October 1, 1999.

1707. MCLS § 211.781, enacted by 1999 Pub. Act 123, effective October 1, 1999.

1708. MCLS § 211.78k, enacted by 1999 Pub. Act 123, effective October 1, 1999.

1709. MCLS § 211.781, enacted by 1999 Pub. Act 123, effective October 1, 1999.

Chapter 26

LIEN AND PRIORITY

§ 771. Mortgage Liens

A mortgage on realty vests a lien on the mortgaged premises in the secured parties.

Library References

Michigan Digest
LexisNexis® Automated Michigan SCAO Forms
John G. Cameron, Jr., Michigan Real Estate Forms
Powell on Real Property® (Michael Allan Wolf, ed.)
Thompson on Real Property, Thomas Edition (David A. Thomas, ed.)

Law Reviews

David E. Nykanen, Real Property, 55 Wayne L. Rev. 575 (2009); Stephen R. Estey and Danielle Graceffa, Real Property, 54 Wayne L. Rev. 387 (2008); Naseem Stecker and Mike Eidelbes, Up Front: Real Property and Consumer Law Sections Team up on "Ask The Lawyer" to Discuss Mortgage Foreclosures, 87 MI Bar Jnl. 8 (2008); Gregg A. Nathanson, Feature: Real Property Law: What's New in Residential Transactions?, 86 MI Bar Jnl. 16 (2007); David E. Nykanen and Jason C. Long, Annual Survey of Michigan Law; June 1, 2004 - May 31, 2005: Real Property, 52 Wayne L. Rev. 941 (2006); Daniel J. Schairbaum, Annual Survey of Michigan Law: June 1, 2003 - May 31, 2004: Real Property, 51 Wayne L. Rev. 881 (2005); Lawrence R. Shoffner, Real Property Law: Real Evidence: Special Rules for Real Estate Disputes, 80 MI Bar Jnl. 28 (2001).

A mortgage, or a deed of trust in the nature of a mortgage, on real estate vests a lien on the mortgaged premises in the secured parties.[1710]

The extent of a mortgage lien is determined by the provisions of the mortgage, rather than by the terms of the note secured,[1711] but the destruction of the paper evidence does not destroy the lien. A mortgage lien, such as a purchase money mortgage, that is purposely destroyed before it is recorded remains a valid and existing lien upon the lands as between the parties and all others claiming under it with notice.[1712]

Under equitable principles, a mortgagee is entitled to the whole mortgaged property as security for the secured debt. The mortgagee has a corresponding right to have the whole avails of the property applied in payment of the debt.[1713]

Land contract mortgages. A mortgage on an interest in a land contract that is recorded as a regular real estate mortgage takes priority over all mortgages, liens, security, and other interests in the specified interest in the land contract except those to which a real estate mortgage would be subordinate. The land contract mortgage does not have to be perfected under the Uniform Commercial Code.[1714]

§ 772. Duration of Lien

No suit or proceedings may be maintained to foreclose a mortgage on real estate unless they are commenced within

1710. McKeighan v. Citizens Commercial & Sav. Bank, 302 Mich. 666, 5 N.W.2d 524 (1942).

Dougherty v. Randall, 3 Mich. 581 (1855) (a mortgagee's lien before entry is not real estate).

1711. Carroll v. Chauret, 241 Mich. 338, 216 N.W. 913 (1928).

1712. Sloan v. Holcomb, 29 Mich. 153 (1874).

1713. In re Scofield Buggy Co., 89 Mich. 15, 50 N.W. 753 (1891).

1714. MCLS § 565.358.

15 years from the time the mortgage becomes due and payable, or within 15 years after the last payment was made on the mortgage.

No suit or proceedings may be maintained to foreclose a mortgage on real estate unless they are commenced within 15 years from the time the mortgage becomes due and payable, or within 15 years after the last payment was made on the mortgage.[1715]

In addition, a real estate mortgage that is not renewed by affidavit or extension agreement of record either within 30 years after the due date of the mortgage or, when the mortgage sets forth no due date, within 30 years after the recording of the mortgage, is discharged as a matter of law.[1716] Prior to the amendment of the statute setting forth this rule, the statute contained the now deleted provision that such a mortgage was to "be considered as discharged of record."[1717] Under that former language, a foreclosure in chancery was not precluded where no rights of third persons were involved.[1718] Contemporaneously with the amendment, the State Bar Committee on Title Standards was of the opinion that the deletion of the words "of record" abrogated the rule permitting foreclosure in chancery, and that the lien of such a mortgage is now discharged.[1719]

§ 773.   Waiver or Loss of Lien

A mortgagee may waive or defeat the lien created by a mortgage on realty by his or her acts or omissions. Generally, a mortgage lien is extinguished by a mortgage foreclosure sale.

A mortgagee may waive his or her mortgage lien.[1720] A mortgagee or his or her successor in interest may waive the priority of the mortgage in favor of another lien or mortgage by executing a written waiver on the mortgage or by a separate acknowledged instrument. This type of waiver, when recorded, is constructive notice of the waiver to all persons. A waiver of this sort is recorded in the same manner as mortgage discharges.[1721]

A mortgagee may lose the lien by his or her actions, such as by evading tender of payment.[1722]

A lien created by mortgage on a building or structure attached to the land in such a way as to make it a fixture is not defeated by a removal of the fixture to other premises.[1723] Thus, where after the execution of a mortgage on a lot and the buildings thereon, the buildings are removed to another lot without the mortgagee's

---

1715. Mortgage foreclosures, *see, infra*, Chapters 31, 32.

MCLS § 600.5803.

1716. MCLS § 565.382.

1717. *Former* MCLS § 565.382 (1948), prior to amendment by 1951 Pub. Act 8.

1718. Michigan Fire & Marine Ins. Co. v. Hamilton, 284 Mich. 417, 279 N.W. 884 (1938).

1719. 35 Mich. S.B.J. 119 (August 1956).

1720. Sibley v. Ross, 102 Mich. 158, 60 N.W. 460 (1894) (waiver not shown).

1721. MCLS § 565.391.

1722. Ferguson v. Popp, 42 Mich. 115, 3 N.W. 287 (1879).

1723. Johnson v. Bratton, 112 Mich. 319, 70 N.W. 1021 (1897).

consent, the mortgagee, or a bona fide assignee of the mortgagee, does not lose his lien thereon, as against one claiming under a sale and conveyance from the mortgagor, even though such purchaser may have had no knowledge that the buildings were so removed.[1724] However, the Uniform Commercial Code—Secured Transactions provides that a mortgage on fixtures may lose priority to a subsequent security interest in the fixture that is perfected under the code unless the real estate mortgage is earlier perfected with a fixture filing under the code.[1725]

Tax foreclosure. For property taxes levied after December 31, 1998, tax sales are eliminated, in favor of giving the foreclosing governmental unit an absolute title in the tax-foreclosed property that extinguishes all outstanding recorded or unrecorded liens against the property except certain specified liens not including mortgages.[1726] Only a party who can prove that he or she did not receive notice of the tax foreclosure is entitled to sue the state, and a party can not sue the subsequent owner for damages for the value of his or her former interest in the tax-foreclosed property.[1727]

Judicial sale of property. Generally, a mortgage lien is extinguished by a mortgage foreclosure sale.[1728] However, the parties may agree to an extension of the mortgage lien.[1729]

§ 774. Priority of Debt Secured by Same Mortgage

In general, notes secured by a single mortgage are entitled to equal treatment in the absence of an agreement to the contrary. However, if they are negotiable instruments, they take in order of perfection.

Under the common law, there is, in general, no priority as between several debts secured by one and the same mortgage. Presumptively, notes secured by a single mortgage are entitled to equal treatment.[1730] Thus, where there are several notes secured by a mortgage, no one of them has any priority or preference over the others by reason of its maturing at an earlier date, but all have an equal claim that must be paid ratably out of the land.[1731] One of the debts may have priority, however, if the creditor can show equities entitling the debt to a preference over the others.[1732] A debt secured by a mortgage along with other debt may also have

1724. Partridge v. Hemenway, 89 Mich. 454, 50 N.W. 1084 (1891).

1725. Fixture filings, *see, supra*, Chapter 3.

MCLS § 440.9334.

1726. MCLS § 211.78k, enacted by 1999 Pub. Act 123, effective October 1, 1999.

1727. MCLS § 211.78l, enacted by 1999 Pub. Act 123, effective October 1, 1999.

1728. Schram v. Pillon, 45 F. Supp. 942 (D. Mich. 1942).

1729. After execution sale

Where mortgage is given after execution sale of the premises, the lien of mortgage is not destroyed where a decree is entered by stipulation giving purchaser at execution sale a lien for his or her improvements and disbursements, and ordering a sale in default of payment of the lien, and where such sale is made and the property is bought for benefit of the mortgagor.—Seeley v. Sharrer, 112 Mich. 267, 70 N.W. 551 (1897).

1730. Sisson v. Hirons, 278 Mich. 553, 270 N.W. 784 (1936).

1731. Jennings v. Moore, 83 Mich. 231, 47 N.W. 127 (1890).

Wilcox v. Allen, 36 Mich. 160 (1877).

McCurdy v. Clark, 27 Mich. 445 (1873).

1732. Delay of foreclosure

Where the holder of notes secured by mortgage is induced by the representations of the holder of

priority if there is an agreement between the mortgagees, or holders of the mortgage interests, as to their respective priorities, or the mortgage creates senior and junior classes of claims.[1733]

The general rule also applies as between the holders of a number or series of bonds all secured by a mortgage or deed of trust, unless the holders have contracted otherwise.[1734]

However, if a security interest is assigned in debt secured by a mortgage, perfected security interests secured on the same mortgage generally receive priority according to time of perfection under the Uniform Commercial Code—Secured Transactions.[1735] Perfected security interests have priority over unperfected security interests in the same mortgage.[1736]

§ 775.   Priorities Between Mortgages in General

Successive mortgages on the same property are entitled to priority in the order in which they have attached as liens on the property.

In general, and aside from the question of priority of record, successive mortgages on the same property are entitled to priority in the order in which they have attached as liens on it.[1737] However, exceptional circumstances may render it equitably fair that a junior lien has priority.[1738]

The parties affected by a conflict may agree regarding the order of priority

other notes, maturing earlier, and secured by the same mortgage, to delay foreclosure proceedings, he does not acquire any preference, unless he has been damaged by relying on such representations.—Burhaus v. Mitchell, 42 Mich. 417, 4 N.W. 178 (1880).

1733. Dunham v. W. Steele Packing & Provision Co., 100 Mich. 75, 58 N.W. 627 (1894) (preferred creditors created).

Cross-collateralization agreement

Although mortgagee could properly cross-collateralize its loans, in absence of notice of cross-collateralization, junior mortgagee could not be bound by cross-collateralization agreement.—Union Bank & Trust Co., N.A. v. Farmwald Dev. Corp., 181 Mich. App. 538, 450 N.W.2d 274 (1989).

1734. C.P.A. Co. v. First Mortg. Bond Co., 287 Mich. 255, 283 N.W. 574 (1939).

1735. M.L.P.2d Personal Property.

MCLS § 440.9322.

1736. M.L.P.2d Personal Property.

MCLS § 440.9317.

1737. Beals v. Hale, 45 U.S. 37, 11 L. Ed. 865, 4 How. 37 (1846).

Rule stated

As between two mortgagees, where the equities of parties are equal, and neither has the legal title, the prior equity will prevail.—Wing v. McDowell, Walk. Ch. 175 (Mich. 1843).

1738. Foreclosure without recording lis pendens

Where junior mortgagee received and recorded junior mortgage four months after senior mortgagee of property began foreclosure proceedings without filing lis pendens notice and about two years prior to foreclosure sale, junior mortgagee, who was not a party to foreclosure proceedings, had all rights under second mortgage that it would have had if there had never been a foreclosure of senior mortgage.—National Acceptance Co. v. Mardigian, 259 F. Supp. 612 (E.D. Mich. 1966).

Mortgage given before delivery of deed

A grantee gave back a purchase-money mortgage before delivery of the deed. Afterwards, at the time the deed was actually delivered, this grantee mortgaged the premises to a third party, in whose presence the delivery was made, and who had no notice of the former mortgage. The second mortgage should be given precedence to the first.—Heffron v. Flanigan, 37 Mich. 274 (1877).

between two or more mortgages.[1739] Whether a party will be held to a subordination clause that is ambiguous depends on whether the party would have discovered the subordination by the exercise of due diligence in the inquiry that the ambiguity gives the party the duty to make.[1740] Where a first mortgagee agrees to subordinate his or her mortgage to a third mortgage, the first mortgage is also subordinate to the second mortgage as a result.[1741]

Under the statute making subsequent mortgagees subject to prior unrecorded mortgages of which the mortgagee has knowledge,[1742] the mortgagor's estate is imputed with the mortgagor's knowledge of the unrecorded mortgage.[1743]

A mortgage that is so defective that it cannot be sustained as a valid encumbrance on the property will be postponed to the lien of a junior mortgage free from objections and taken in good faith and without notice.[1744]

As between mortgages, neither of which is recorded, priority is ordinarily determined by priority of execution.[1745]

§ 776. Priorities Between Mortgages and Other Liens or Claims

As between a mortgage of real property and other liens on the premises, that which is first in time generally is first in right, unless that order of priority is modified by statute or by an agreement of the parties. A construction lien has priority when the mortgage is recorded subsequent to the first actual physical improvement.

In general, as between a mortgage, or a trust deed in the nature of a mortgage,

Notice of mortgage

Where a home buyer executed two mortgages to the property on the same day (for $216,000 to a bank to finance the purchase and for $17,100 to the builder to finance additional construction costs), the bank's mortgage had priority, even though the builder's mortgage was recorded first, because (1) the bank held a purchase money mortgage, and (2) the builder had notice of the banks' mortgage by virtue of its presence at the closing and signing of the HUD settlement listing the bank's mortgage.—In re Wade (LaSalle Bank v. Lim), 414 B.R. 161 (E.D. Mich. 2009).

1739. Gillam v. Barnes, 123 Mich. 119, 82 N.W. 38 (1900) (delay not affecting priority).

1740. Obvious ambiguity

Ambiguity in subordination clause in defendant's mortgage was so obvious as to put prudent person on inquiry notice, in view of fact that clause was ambiguous as to whether defendant's mortgage was subordinate to plaintiff's subsequently obtained mortgage.—American Federal Sav. & Loan Ass'n v. Orenstein, 81 Mich. App. 249, 265 N.W.2d 111 (1978).

1741. Union Bank & Trust Co., N.A. v. Farmwald Dev. Corp., 181 Mich. App. 538, 450 N.W.2d 274 (1989).

1742. MCLS § 565.29.

1743. Not a good-faith taker

Decedent who was aware of defendants' prior unrecorded mortgage at time he took second mortgage from them was not good faith purchaser under statute governing unrecorded conveyances, and accordingly, decedent's notice of cloud on title was properly imputed to personal representatives of decedent's estate on their purchase of mortgaged premises from defendants since it would be inequitable to confer on personal representatives the status of good-faith purchasers in performance of duties for which they were responsible as managers and distributors of decedent's estate assets.—Michigan Nat'l Bank & Trust Co. v. Morren, 194 Mich. App. 407, 487 N.W.2d 784 (1992).

1744. Stead v. Grosfield, 67 Mich. 289, 34 N.W. 871 (1887).

1745. Nibbelink v. Coopersville State Bank, 286 Mich. 1, 281 N.W. 415 (1938).

of real property and other liens or claims that may attach as liens on the premises, that which is first in time is first in right.[1746] The rule gives mortgages priority over subsequently recorded claims that have been reduced to judgment against the mortgagor.[1747] The fixed legal right of a mortgagee generally cannot be impaired by any equities subsequently arising against the objection of the mortgagee.[1748] Rights acquired prior to the mortgage cannot be asserted if the conduct of the holder of those rights renders their assertion unjust.[1749]

Nevertheless, a statute in force when the mortgage is made may operate to create a lien paramount to the lien of the mortgage,[1750] or to make a subsequently executed mortgage prior to other liens or claims.[1751] The order of priority between a mortgage and other liens or claims may be modified by agreement of the parties,[1752] or by express provision in the mortgage.[1753] In the absence of fraud or

1746. Williams & Works, Inc. v. Springfield Corp., 408 Mich. 732, 293 N.W.2d 304 (1980).

Stegeman v. Stegeman, 241 Mich. 508, 217 N.W. 885 (1928).

Columbia Bank v. Jacobs, 10 Mich. 349 (1862).

Cheboygan County Constr. Code Dep't v. Burke, 148 Mich. App. 56, 384 N.W.2d 77 (1985).

Equitable subrogation exception

A purchaser's interest in property it purchased after a federal tax lien was imposed on the property was subject to the tax lien, despite the fact that Michigan equitable subrogation principles provide an exception to the general rule that a federal tax lien has priority over subsequent interests acquired in the property. Under the exception, a person is subrogated to the rights of a mortgage holder if the person paid off the mortgage; while the purchaser paid off its seller's mortgage, it did so "voluntarily" so as to qualify for its own financing, and the equitable subrogation exception to the first-in-time rule applies only if the party was somehow "compelled" to make the payment.—Bednarowski & Michaels Dev., L.L.C. v. Wallace, 293 F. Supp. 2d 728 (E.D. Mich. 2003).

1747. Cheboygan County Constr. Code Dep't v. Burke, 148 Mich. App. 56, 384 N.W.2d 77 (1985).

1748. Adams v. Central City Granite Brick & Block Co., 154 Mich. 448, 117 N.W. 932 (1908).

Attachment lien

Lands were conveyed by A. to B. absolutely, and the conveyance registered; B. gave back a defeasance, which was not registered; defeasance was not void with respect to an attaching creditor of B., although without actual notice of its existence.—Columbia Bank v. Jacobs, 10 Mich. 349 (1862).

1749. Laches

Laches of purchaser defaulting under unrecorded land contract divested his claim to property

of any equitable standing against one foreclosing mortgage.—Smith v. O'Dell, 240 Mich. 185, 215 N.W. 408 (1927).

1750. Greenvault v. Farmers' & Mechanics' Bank, 2 Doug. 498 (Mich. 1847).

Mechanics' lien

Parties furnishing materials and labor, used in constructing building on land sold to builder by corporation taking purchase-money mortgage, were entitled, under statute and equities, to prior liens on building, but not land, as against both vendor and corporation loaning vendee money secured by another mortgage with knowledge that building was being constructed.—Winkworth Fuel & Supply Co. v. Bloomsbury Corp., 266 Mich. 298, 253 N.W. 304 (1934).

1751. Prior record of subsequent mortgage

Material supplier's lien was inferior to mortgage executed subsequent to furnishing of materials, where recorded mortgage stated that subsequent mortgage was to be executed.—Redford Lumber Co. v. Knight, 242 Mich. 695, 219 N.W. 686 (1928).

1752. Levitz v. Capitol Sav. & Loan Co., 267 Mich. 92, 255 N.W. 166 (1934).

Gillam v. Barnes, 123 Mich. 119, 82 N.W. 38 (1900).

Between contractor and builder

Where contractors agreed with builder that mortgage be procured and that contractors would accept note for any balance that mortgage proceeds left unsatisfied, and aided in procuring mortgage, mortgagee was entitled to priority over contractors to extent of sums employed in construction or actually paid contractors.—Heide v. Societatea Romana De Ajutor Si Cultura Banatiana, 262 Mich. 394, 247 N.W. 702 (1933).

1753. Mickle v. Gould, 42 Mich. 304, 3 N.W. 961 (1879).

misrepresentation,[1754] a mortgage subordination agreement is valid when based on a valuable consideration.[1755]

A construction lien has priority when the other interest is recorded subsequent to the first actual physical improvement.[1756] A mortgage recorded before the first actual physical improvement to the real property has priority over a construction lien to the extent that advances are made prior to the first improvement. Advances made after the first actual physical improvement also have priority over the lien claim of any lien claimant who waives his or her lien claim under the construction lien in accordance with the Construction Lien Act.[1757] A mechanic's lien takes precedence over a mortgage executed after the actual commencement of construction.[1758]

A recorded cross-collateralization agreement that is not identified to the

Recording

Where a subsequent mortgage contains a clause showing that it is made subject to a prior one, filing of prior mortgage is unnecessary to maintain priority.—Flory v. Comstock, 61 Mich. 522, 28 N.W. 701 (1886).

1754. Fraud not shown

In procuring of mortgage subordination agreement, true statement to mortgagee that parties wanted mortgagor's name off books and promise that mortgagor's grantee would assume and pay indebtedness did not show fraud, particularly where part of promise to pay indebtedness was carried out.—Levitz v. Capitol Sav. & Loan Co., 267 Mich. 92, 255 N.W. 166 (1934).

Lack of knowledge of fraud

Mortgagee taking mortgage, relying on public record of title and contract purchaser's written consent to vendor's giving mortgage lien superior to contract, without notice or knowledge of claim that consent was fraudulently obtained, was entitled to priority.—Shapero v. Picard, 235 Mich. 481, 209 N.W. 576 (1926).

1755. Lyle v. Vogt, 249 Mich. 465, 229 N.W. 448 (1930) (where land contract authorized mortgage, mortgage was good to extent of consideration advanced, though mortgagee had notice of contract's purpose).

From third party

That consideration for mortgage subordination agreement moved from mortgagor's grantee, a third party, rather than from party given priority, is immaterial.—Levitz v. Capitol Sav. & Loan Co., 267 Mich. 92, 255 N.W. 166 (1934).

1756. MCLS § 570.1119.

J.W. McCausey & Co. v. Gittleman, 201 Mich. 8, 166 N.W. 896 (1918).

Stevens v. Garland, 198 Mich. 24, 164 N.W. 516 (1917).

Kerr-Murray Mfg. Co. v. Kalamazoo Heat, Light & Power Co., 124 Mich. 111, 82 N.W. 801 (1900) (contract for materials subsequent to mortgage).

Stocker v. Tri-Mount/Bay Harbor Bldg. Co., 268 Mich. App. 194, 706 N.W.2d 878 (2005).

Portage Realty Corp. v. Baas, 100 Mich. App. 260, 298 N.W.2d 892 (1980) (percolation tests do not constitute commencement of construction).

A construction claimant's road map to recovery through payment bonds and liens, 76 Mich. B.J. 560 (1997).

Commencement of work without filing lis pendens

Delivery of materials or other commencement of work prior to recording of mortgage on property gave mechanics' liens priority even without filing of notice of lis pendens.—Williams & Works, Inc. v. Springfield Corp., 76 Mich. App. 541, 257 N.W.2d 160 (1977).

1757. MCLS § 570.1119.

A construction claimant's road map to recovery through payment bonds and liens, *see* 76 Mich. B.J. 560 (1997).

1758. Wallich Lumber Co. v. Golds, 375 Mich. 323, 134 N.W.2d 722 (1965).

River Rouge Sav. Bank v. S & M Bldg. Co., 359 Mich. 189, 101 N.W.2d 260 (1960).

Winkworth Fuel & Supply Co. v. Bloomsbury Corp., 266 Mich. 298, 253 N.W. 304 (1934).

Stephens Lumber Co. v. Townsend-Stark Corp., 228 Mich. 182, 199 N.W. 706 (1924).

Durant Constr., Inc. v. Gourley, 125 Mich. App. 695, 336 N.W.2d 856 (1983).

G.O. Lewis Co. v. Erving, 4 Mich. App. 589, 145 N.W.2d 368 (1966).

The validity of mechanics' liens claimed to be prior to real estate mortgages, *see* 7 Wayne L. Rev. 175 (1960).

Construction lien given priority

It is a basic proposition of mortgage law that a junior mortgagee's interest in property, if properly recorded before the commencement of proceedings to foreclose a senior encumbrance, is not cut off by the foreclosure unless the junior mortgagee is made a party to the proceedings; however, the

specific property does not provide notice to subsequent takers and therefore does not have priority over a subsequently recorded mortgage on the real property.[1759]

Executions and mortgages. In general, the holder of a recorded mortgage has priority over a subsequent execution.[1760] Thus, where one in good faith conveys lands, taking back a mortgage on them for future support, an execution subsequently levied on the land under a judgment on the grantor gives the judgment creditor no interest in the property.[1761]

Execution creditors of a mortgagor are generally entitled to priority over the mortgagee as to moneys advanced by the latter subsequently to their levies, unless the subsequent payments are made by a junior mortgagee in order to prevent the foreclosure of a lien superior to that of the creditors.[1762]

Although a judgment creditor who levies on land upon which there is a prior unrecorded mortgage fraudulent as to the creditor may be entitled to precedence over the mortgagee, the creditor cannot bid in the land and afterwards defeat the priority of the mortgage if the creditor has allowed other bidders and junior lienors to remain ignorant of the fact that the creditor intended to dispute priority, because that would permit the creditor to gain an unfair advantage in the bidding.[1763]

Where execution was levied on property subsequently mortgaged but no sale was made under such levy, the issuance of execution in a chancery suit in aid of execution on the judgment on which the prior levy was had was an abandonment of the prior execution. If the chancery decree made the judgment creditor's claim subject to the outstanding mortgage, the judgment creditor, on obtaining title under the chancery execution sale, was not entitled to have the title quieted as against the mortgagee.[1764]

Land contract mortgages. The mortgagee on a recorded land contract

---

law is not as precise when the junior mortgagee's interest is not recorded until after commencement of proceedings to foreclose the senior encumbrance. A party who takes an interest in property that is the subject of a foreclosure proceeding, and does so after a lis pendens has been properly filed, cannot move to prevent the confirmation of the foreclosure sale; where a contractor filed a mechanics' lien claim against property and several months later the owner of the property executed a mortgage on the property with a lender, and this mortgage was not recorded until 10 years later, and before the lender recorded its mortgage the contractor initiated foreclosure proceedings, the foreclosure of the contractor's lien extinguished the lien of the mortgagee where mortgagee did not redeem at the foreclosure sale. The contractor's purchase of the property at the foreclosure sale was not subject to the mortgagee's junior mortgagee, which was extinguished after the four-month redemption period expired; the junior mortgagee had constructive notice of the contractor's lien because the construction lien was recorded before the mortgage was executed and notice of lis pendens was filed before the mortgage was recorded.—Advanta Nat'l Bank v. McClarty, 257

Mich. App. 113, 667 N.W.2d 880 (2003).

1759. Union Bank & Trust Co., N.A. v. Farmwald Dev. Corp., 181 Mich. App. 538, 450 N.W.2d 274 (1989).

1760. Recording before sale

Where mortgage had been recorded before and its validity as encumbrance was not assailed at time of, execution sale under judgment against one of title holders, such sale and title acquired thereby by execution creditor were subject to the mortgage.—Pratt v. Mapes, 270 Mich. 501, 259 N.W. 142 (1935).

1761. Chandler v. Whitely, 100 Mich. 313, 58 N.W. 1011 (1894).

1762. Dummer v. Smedley, 110 Mich. 466, 68 N.W. 260 (1896).

1763. Belcher v. Curtis, 119 Mich. 1, 77 N.W. 310 (1898).

1764. Pratt v. Mapes, 270 Mich. 501, 259 N.W. 142 (1935).

mortgage is entitled to the same notices from a claimant on a prior lien or interest to which the land contract vendor or vendee would be entitled as the owner of the fee if the land contract were a mortgage on the fee. The mortgagee must be named in any action to enforce a prior lien or interest on the interest subject to the land contract mortgage. The mortgagee under a land contract mortgage has a right to redeem the land contract interest subject to the prior lien or interest.[1765]

§ 777. Priority of Mortgage for Purchase Money

Whether purchase money mortgages are exempt from the first-in-time rule of the race-notice statutes is a question currently before the Michigan Supreme Court.

The "race-notice" statutes[1766] provide that the first instrument concerning real estate to be recorded takes priority over later-recorded instruments. In a 2002 decision, the Michigan Supreme Court held that these statutes do not exempt purchase money mortgages from the "first-in-time" recording priority and that a purchase money mortgage therefore did not have precedence over a prior recorded lien on the same property. However, the Supreme Court subsequently granted rehearing in the case and vacated its decision. The Court of Appeals had held that a purchase money mortgage had priority over all other liens or interests, even those that were recorded previously.[1767] On reconsideration, the Supreme Court held that a mortgage does not qualify as a purchase money mortgage where the loan proceeds are used by the mortgagor to pay off a land contract debt and thereby acquire legal title to that property; because the mortgagor already had equitable title to the property already purchased pursuant to a land contract, the obligations incurred under the mortgage were not for the purpose of purchasing the property, but were used to discharge a debt.[1768] Therefore, it was not necessary for the Court to address the question of the possible priority of a purchase money mortgage.[1769]

Because the purchase money mortgage is, in effect, a limitation on the title that the mortgagor takes, rather than an encumbrance on the title conveyed, it outranks a mortgage previously given by the same mortgagor before the mortgagor took title to the property in an earlier part of the same transaction by which the mortgagor acquires title to the property.[1770]

Recorded purchase-money mortgages are not affected by subsequent recorded interests or claims to the land.[1771] Similarly, the mortgagee's interests in the mortgage are not affected by any previous conveyances or liens that, without the

---

1765. MCLS § 565.360.

1766. MCLS §§ 565.25, 565.29.

Tibble v. Consumers Credit Union (In re Koshar), 334 B.R. 889 (Bankr. W.D. Mich. 2005).

1767. Graves v. American Acceptance Mortg. Corp., 246 Mich. App. 1, 630 N.W.2d 383 (2001), rev'd, 467 Mich. 308, 652 N.W.2d 221 (2002), vacated, on reh'g, mot. granted, 2003 Mich. LEXIS 56 (Mich. Jan. 28, 2003).

1768. Graves v. Am. Acceptance Mortg. Corp., 469 Mich. 608, 677 N.W.2d 829 (2004) (on rehearing).

1769. Graves v. Am. Acceptance Mortg. Corp., 469 Mich. 608, 677 N.W.2d 829 (2004) (on rehearing).

1770. Fecteau v. Fries, 253 Mich. 51, 234 N.W. 113 (1931).

1771. Recording secures full rights under mortgage

Grantor of lands who, on taking back a purchase money mortgage, has both conveyances promptly and simultaneously recorded has done all the law requires of that grantor to protect his or her rights.—Heffron v. Flanigan, 37 Mich. 274 (1877).

knowledge of the mortgagee, the grantee may place on the record before obtaining title.[1772]

§ 778.   Priority of Record

As between two mortgages or a mortgage and another instrument affecting the same premises, the first one recorded is given priority in the absence of countervailing equities.

A recorded claim or lien against a property is notice to a person recording a subsequent mortgage on the property of the existence of that claim or lien.[1773] That recorded claim or lien has priority over a subsequently recorded mortgage on the property.[1774]

In the absence of other notice,[1775] the order of priority as between persons claiming liens on the same premises by mortgage or otherwise depends on the respective dates when they were recorded, or filed for record, rather than on the time of their execution.[1776] Thus, where the holder of land under an agreement for purchase executes a mortgage for a precedent debt on the holder's equitable interest, and after the holder's acquisition of the legal title, executes another, also for a precedent debt, and both are recorded, the mortgage of the equitable interest is entitled to priority.[1777]

§ 779.   Mortgagees as Bona Fide Purchasers

If a mortgage is supported by an actual present consideration and is given and taken in good faith, the mortgagee is regarded as a bona fide purchaser for value,

1772. Fecteau v. Fries, 253 Mich. 51, 234 N.W. 113 (1931).

1773. MCLS § 565.25.

Researching online real estate records in Michigan, see 80 Mich. B.J. 22 (2001).

1774. MCLS § 565.29.

1775. Mortgage first recorded was junior

Evidence sustained decree quieting title in first mortgagee under foreclosure, sale, purchase, and expiration of period of redemption, on ground that principal owner and active manager of private bank, which held a second mortgage in point of time of execution but first in time of recording, had actual knowledge of execution of first mortgage at time of execution of second mortgage.—Hope College Bd. of Trustees v. Read, 280 Mich. 335, 273 N.W. 589 (1937).

1776. Skupinski v. Provident Mortg. Co., 244 Mich. 309, 221 N.W. 338 (1928).

Hannah v. Carnahan, 65 Mich. 601, 32 N.W. 835 (1887).

Mitchell v. Trustees of United States Mut. Real Estate Inv. Trust, 144 Mich. App. 302, 375 N.W.2d 424 (1985) (wraparound mortgage on mortgagors' home, which was executed and recorded after bank recorded another mortgage on home, was subject to lien and thus did not have priority of first lien under Michigan recording law).

Determination of when mortgage recorded

In determining whether a mortgage was recorded within the applicable "relation-back" period under the preferential transfer provisions of the Bankruptcy Code (to determine if the creditor perfected its mortgage lien in the debtor's home within the required time after its creation), the relevant question under the Michigan "race-no-tice" recording statute is the date the register of deeds accepted the mortgage for recording; the date of acceptance is used, and not the later date when the register of deeds actually files the mortgage in its record book, regardless of whether register of deeds complies with its statutory obligation to maintain entry books.—Tibble v. Consumers Credit Union (In re Koshar), 334 B.R. 889 (Bankr. W.D. Mich. 2005).

1777. Edwards v. McKernan, 55 Mich. 520, 22 N.W. 20 (1885).

and as such is protected against adverse claims of which the mortgagee has no notice, actual or constructive.

If a mortgage, or a trust deed in the nature of a mortgage, is supported by an actual present consideration and is given and taken in good faith and without fraud, the mortgagee is to be treated as a bona fide purchaser for value,[1778] and as such is protected against unrecorded adverse claims of which he or she had no notice, actual or constructive.[1779] A mortgagee of a purchaser who holds under a deed absolutely void, although the mortgagee is innocent, is not protected.[1780]

A recorded cross-collateralization agreement that is not identified to the specific property does not provide notice to subsequent takers and therefore does not have priority over a subsequently recorded mortgage on the real property.[1781]

As against claim of fraud or mental incompetency. Although a conveyance of land may be voidable for fraud in the hands of the original grantee, if the grantee has given a mortgage on the premises to one advancing his or her money in good faith and without notice of the fraud, the claim of fraud cannot be set up against the mortgagee.[1782] The rule is otherwise, however, if knowledge of the fraud can be brought home to the mortgagee,[1783] such as where the mortgage is obtained by fraud or forgery.[1784]

Bona fide mortgagees of a grantee whose conveyance is absolutely void by reason of the grantor's insanity do not stand in the relation of bona fide purchasers and are not protected.[1785]

Preexisting debt. A creditor who takes a mortgage on realty merely as security for the payment of a debt or demand already due to the creditor, and without giving

---

1778. MCLS § 565.29.

1779. Shepard v. Shepard, 36 Mich. 173 (1877) (on a bill to foreclose a mortgage, evidence was insufficient to charge the mortgagee with notice of a prior unrecorded deed).

Foreclosure without recording lis pendens

Where junior mortgagee received and recorded junior mortgage four months after senior mortgagee of property began foreclosure proceedings without filing lis pendens notice and about two years prior to foreclosure sale, junior mortgagee, who was not a party to foreclosure proceedings, had all rights under second mortgage that it would have had if there had never been a foreclosure of senior mortgage.—National Acceptance Co. v. Mardigian, 259 F. Supp. 612 (E.D. Mich. 1966).

Incorrect legal description of property

A bankruptcy trustee had the right to avoid a mortgage against the debtor's property as a bona fide purchaser without notice where the mortgage contained an incorrect legal description of the property; the recorded mortgage on the wrong property did not provide a bona fide purchaser with constructive notice of the mortgagee's interest in the property, and no amount of inquiry into the property's chain of title would have revealed

the mortgage.—In re Vandenbosch (Moyer v. Edlund), 405 B.R. 253 (W.D. Mich. 2009).

1780. Forgery

There can be no bona fide holder under forgery with right against person whose name was forged.—Horvath v. National Mortg. Co., 238 Mich. 354, 213 N.W. 202 (1927).

1781. Union Bank & Trust Co., N.A. v. Farmwald Dev. Corp., 181 Mich. App. 538, 450 N.W.2d 274 (1989).

1782. Defendant charged with notice

Where complainants deeded to B. premises to enable him to raise money, not exceeding $8,500, to erect a building on the premises, and he borrowed thereon $1,150 from defendant, and did not do the work, the loss of the loan cannot be put on defendant having no knowledge of the fraud, even if charged with notice of complainants' rights.—McEwen v. Keary, 178 Mich. 6, 144 N.W. 524 (1913).

1783. Jackson, Lansing & Saginaw R. Co. v. Davison, 65 Mich. 437, 37 N.W. 537 (1888).

1784. Laprad v. Sherwood, 79 Mich. 520, 44 N.W. 943 (1890) (by agent of mortgagee).

1785. Sponable v. Hanson, 87 Mich. 204, 49 N.W. 644 (1891).

any new consideration or being induced to change his or her position in any manner, is not entitled to the protection accorded to a bona fide purchaser for value, as against prior liens or equities.[1786]

Although a mortgage is given to secure an antecedent debt, if, at the time and in consideration of the giving of a mortgage, the creditor grants a definite extension of the time for payment, this is such a new consideration as will give the creditor the character of a purchaser for value.[1787]

§ 780.   —Notice

A mortgage taken with notice, actual or constructive, of prior liens or encumbrances of the same realty, is subject to such prior liens or encumbrances. A recorded transaction regarding real estate is sufficient notice to subsequent takers in regard to that real estate.

Under common law, the general rule is that where a mortgagee at the time of taking the mortgage has knowledge or legal notice of a prior conveyance, mortgage, or other lien on the property, the mortgagee takes subject to it, and is not entitled to the protection of a bona fide purchaser.[1788]

Accordingly, a mortgagee of land is charged with notice of, and must take in subordination to, any conveyance or encumbrance of the premises that has been placed on the records before the execution of the mortgagee's mortgage.[1789] The mortgagee also takes subject to an agreement or judicial proceeding affecting the title to the land or creating a charge on it,[1790] providing the recording of it is regular, correct, and sufficient.[1791] Likewise, a mortgagee or purchaser from a life tenant is charged with notice of record in the chain of title that the mortgagor or vendor has only a life estate.[1792] But the mortgagee is not chargeable with notice of any conveyance or lien recorded after the mortgagee's mortgage.[1793]

On the other hand, without knowledge giving the mortgagee a reason for inquiry into some other possible ownership arrangement between titleholders of

1786. People's Sav. Bank v. Bates, 120 U.S. 556, 7 S. Ct. 679, 30 L. Ed. 754 (1887).

McGraw v. Henry, 83 Mich. 442, 47 N.W. 345 (1890).

Saenger v. Von Der Heide, 80 Mich. 152, 44 N.W. 1116 (1890).

Boxheimer v. Gunn, 24 Mich. 372 (1872).

On church property

Members taking mortgage on church property for antecedent debts were not innocent purchasers.—Horbal v. St. John's Greek Catholic Church, 260 Mich. 331, 244 N.W. 493 (1932).

1787. De May v. Defer, 103 Mich. 239, 61 N.W. 524, 1894 Mich. LEXIS 1134 (1894).

1788. Venske v. Smith, 265 Mich. 44, 251 N.W. 325 (1933) (recorded deed).

Lacny v. Alexander, 238 Mich. 312, 213 N.W. 88 (1927).

Michigan Lumber Yard v. Slater, 204 Mich. 670, 171 N.W. 513 (1919).

E.B. Millar & Co. v. Olney, 69 Mich. 560, 37 N.W. 558 (1888).

1789. Lines v. Weaver, 220 Mich. 244, 189 N.W. 847 (1922).

1790. Skupinski v. Provident Mortg. Co., 244 Mich. 309, 221 N.W. 338 (1928).

1791. Woods v. Love, 27 Mich. 308 (1873).

1792. Lowry v. Lyle, 226 Mich. 676, 198 N.W. 245 (1924).

1793. Stead v. Grosfield, 67 Mich. 289, 34 N.W. 871 (1887).

Shelden v. Warner, 45 Mich. 638, 8 N.W. 529 (1881).

Cooper v. Bigly, 13 Mich. 463 (1865).

record, a mortgagee has a right to rely on the notice of ownership that the recorded record gives the mortgagee.[1794]

Before releasing portions of the mortgaged premises, mortgagees need not examine the records, because the record of a later conveyance would not be notice to them; however, if they have notice of facts enough to put a prudent person upon inquiry, they are, of course, bound to examine the records and act accordingly.[1795]

A recorded cross-collateralization agreement that is not identified to the specific property does not provide notice to subsequent takers and therefore does not have priority over a subsequently recorded mortgage on the real property.[1796]

A mortgage taken with knowledge of a lessee's rights is subject to the lease, although the lease is unacknowledged and unrecorded.[1797]

Constructive notice. Constructive as well as actual notice to a mortgagee of prior conveyances or encumbrances will postpone the lien of the mortgage to the rights of their holders.[1798] The mortgagee is chargeable with notice if he or she is shown to have had knowledge of facts that would put a reasonably careful person on inquiry, and where that inquiry, carefully prosecuted in the right quarter, would have led to a discovery of the facts concerning the prior conveyance or encumbrance.[1799] The fact that the value of the land encumbered is not enough to secure two loans is significant, but not conclusive, of the fact that the second mortgagee has

1794. Mortgagor's mistake as to unrecorded ownership

A mortgagee who has received in good faith a mortgage executed by his debtor and wife, of property the title to which of record is in the husband, is not liable to have his mortgage invalidated as to a portion of the premises, on a claim by the wife that she holds such portion by an unrecorded deed from her husband, and that the portion was included in the mortgage by a mistake of her husband.—Shepard v. Shepard, 36 Mich. 173 (1877).

Notice of record not overcome by owners' handling of property between themselves

Where a mortgage is taken on property shown of record to be owned by the mortgagors as tenants in common, knowledge that the mortgagors were partners in actual possession of the land mortgaged down to the time the mortgage was executed will not be considered actual notice to the mortgagee of the fact that the land was the property of the partnership.—Hammond v. Paxton, 58 Mich. 393, 25 N.W. 321 (1885).

1795. Dewey v. Ingersoll, 42 Mich. 17, 3 N.W. 235 (1879).

1796. Union Bank & Trust Co., N.A. v. Farmwald Dev. Corp., 181 Mich. App. 538, 450 N.W.2d 274 (1989).

1797. Arnold v. Whitcomb, 83 Mich. 19, 46 N.W. 1029 (1890).

1798. Terry v. Tuttle, 24 Mich. 206 (1872).

Seiberling Tire & Rubber Co. v. State Bank of Fraser, 78 Mich. App. 587, 261 N.W.2d 13 (1977).

Inquiry required

Mortgagee is "put on inquiry" as to mortgagor's title if circumstances raise doubt in his mind, or would raise doubt in mind of man of ordinary prudence.—Lacny v. Alexander, 238 Mich. 312, 213 N.W. 88 (1927).

1799. Redman v. Murray W. Sales Co., 266 F. 272 (6th Cir. Mich. 1920) (one receiving a mortgage while building was being repaired is charged with notice of material supplier's right to lien).

Apparent forgery

One leaving fully executed note and mortgage with broker to procure loan was entitled to cancellation after broker's forgery, against innocent holder from whom broker obtained money, forgery being apparent.—Graham v. Sinderman, 238 Mich. 210, 213 N.W. 200 (1927).

Notice of lease

A prospective mortgagee examined the property, a large flouring mill, and was told that the water to run it was furnished by another company under a lease, and was told something of the terms of payment, but he did not know its terms, or that it was in writing; he was put upon inquiry as to its contents, including a mortgage clause in it for security of lessor.—Gordon v. Constantine Hydraulic Co., 117 Mich. 620, 76 N.W. 142 (1898).

no notice of a prior lien.[1800]

In order to protect him- or herself, a mortgagee must make an investigation where the existence of an earlier deed or lien in the chain of title is indicated by recitals in the mortgage that he or she is offered.[1801]

Possession as notice. Where at the time of the execution of a mortgage, a person other than the mortgagor is in actual possession of the mortgaged premises, that possession ordinarily is sufficient to put the mortgagee on inquiry as to the rights of the possessor.[1802] The mortgagee therefore takes the mortgage subject to those rights.[1803] Thus, the actual possession of land by a purchaser holding a deed, even though not recorded, or a contract for the purchase, ordinarily is notice of his or her rights to a party taking a mortgage on the land from the vendor, so that the lien of the mortgage can cover nothing more than the vendor's remaining rights or interests.[1804]

On the other hand, the continued possession by a grantor after the recording of his or her deed is presumed to be by sufferance of the grantee, and does not affect the status as an innocent purchaser of a mortgagee of the grantee.[1805] Similarly, that the nature of the possessory rights exhibited by common owners of a property is at variance with their title does not necessarily create a duty in the mortgagee to make inquiry.[1806]

§ 781.   Notice of Mortgage Affecting Priority

Any person acquiring rights in realty with notice of the existence of a prior mortgage ordinarily takes subject to the rights of the mortgagee.

A subsequent purchaser of land takes the property subject to the lien of a prior mortgage, if the purchaser takes it with actual or constructive notice of the existence of the mortgage and its terms, or with knowledge or facts that puts the purchaser on

---

1800. Matteson v. Blackmer, 46 Mich. 393, 9 N.W. 445 (1881).

1801. Case v. Erwin, 18 Mich. 434 (1869).

1802. Allen v. Cadwell, 55 Mich. 8, 20 N.W. 692 (1884).

1803. Householder

Company making construction loan, receiving mortgage on lot, must be charged with constructive notice of right of person occupying house on lot described.—Capitol Sav. & Loan Co. v. Standard Sav. & Loan Ass'n, 264 Mich. 550, 250 N.W. 309 (1933).

1804. Cousins v. Melvin F. Lanphar & Co., 312 Mich. 715, 20 N.W.2d 783 (1945).

Van Baalen v. Cotney, 113 Mich. 202, 71 N.W. 491 (1897).

Weisgerber v. Wisner, 55 Mich. 246, 21 N.W. 331 (1884).

Hubbard v. Smith, 2 Mich. 207 (1851).

Possession for one day

Possession of premises improved by house taken by purchaser in good faith and by virtue of his contract was such a constructive possession as to be notice of his rights to defendant loaning money on mortgage to the vendor on the following day, so that the mortgage was void as to the purchaser and his assignee.—Fraser v. Fleming, 190 Mich. 238, 157 N.W. 269 (1916).

1805. McEwen v. Keary, 178 Mich. 6, 144 N.W. 524 (1913).

1806. Notice of record not overcome by owners' handling of property between themselves

Where a mortgage is taken on property shown of record to be owned by the mortgagors as tenants in common, knowledge that the mortgagors were partners in actual possession of the land mortgaged down to the time the mortgage was executed will not be considered actual notice to the mortgagee of the fact that the land was the property of the partnership.—Hammond v. Paxton, 58 Mich. 393, 25 N.W. 321 (1885).

inquiry.[1807] Purchasers, however, take free from the lien of mortgages of which they lack notice.[1808]

Constructive notice of a prior mortgage has the same effect as actual notice in postponing to it the rights of a subsequent purchaser or encumbrancer taking with notice.[1809] Whatever is notice enough to excite attention, and puts a party on guard and calls for inquiry, is notice of everything to which inquiry might have led, and every unusual circumstance is a ground of suspicion and prescribes inquiry.[1810] As a rule, a grantee always takes with constructive notice of whatever appears in the conveyances constituting the chain of title, and this rule applies whether the grantee takes a mortgage that refers to another mortgage,[1811] or a prior unrecorded mortgage is expressly referred to in the deed to the junior mortgagee's mortgagor, and excepted from it.[1812]

Although a mortgage contains an imperfect or erroneous description of the premises intended to be conveyed, or omits portions of it, nevertheless, it is a valid lien as against a subsequent purchaser or encumbrancer having notice of the mortgage and of the mistake in it. Against that person, it may be reformed in equity or corrected by a new mortgage, without losing its priority of lien.[1813]

§ 782.   —Record of Mortgage as Notice

A subsequent purchaser or encumbrancer is charged with notice of the existence and terms of a duly recorded mortgage and will take subject to the lien of the mortgage.

The object served by the recording statutes is to give notice to third persons. Thus, as between the parties to it, a mortgage is just as effectual for all purposes without recording as it is with it.[1814] Furthermore, the constructive notice furnished by the record of a mortgage does not deprive a purchaser of the right to rely on the

---

1807. Fitzhugh v. Barnard, 12 Mich. 104 (1863).

Willcox v. Hill, 11 Mich. 256 (1863).

Mitchell v. Trustees of United States Mut. Real Estate Inv. Trust, 144 Mich. App. 302, 375 N.W.2d 424 (1985) (wraparound mortgage on mortgagors' home, which was executed and re-corded after bank recorded another mortgage on home, was subject to lien and thus did not have priority of first lien under Michigan recording law).

1808. Payne v. Avery, 21 Mich. 524 (1870).

Priorities: Bona fide purchasers, *see* 57 Mich. L. Rev. 685 (1959).

1809. Boxheimer v. Gunn, 24 Mich. 372 (1872).

1810. Michigan Mut. Life Ins. Co. v. Conant, 40 Mich. 530 (1879) (discrepancy as to descrip-tion).

1811. Kitchell v. Mudgett, 37 Mich. 81 (1877).

Baker v. Mather, 25 Mich. 51 (1872).

1812. Houseman v. Gerken, 231 Mich. 253, 203 N.W. 841 (1925).

1813. Kimble v. Harrington, 91 Mich. 281, 51 N.W. 936 (1892).

Omission from description

A mortgage was taken that by mistake omitted certain property it was intended to cover; third person, authorized to procure its correction, se-cured for himself a mortgage upon the whole, and offered the original mortgagee an interest in this mortgage to the amount of the former one, but the offer was declined; original mortgage remained in force and was rectified and foreclosed.—Hunt v. Hunt, 38 Mich. 161 (1878).

1814. Michigan Fire & Marine Ins. Co. v. Hamilton, 284 Mich. 417, 279 N.W. 884 (1938).

Trust mortgage

Where trust mortgage articles and notice of election of successor trustee were recorded, and trustee's signature followed by words "as trustee" were on agreement of sale of trust land before

vendor's positive statements, fraudulently made, that the property is unencumbered, nor will it prevent the purchaser from suing for the false representations.[1815]

Only a complete[1816] and valid recording of a mortgage on particular land by an officer having authority to do so,[1817] in the proper place and book,[1818] in full compliance with the registry statutes, constitutes constructive notice by record to a subsequent mortgagee or grantee of the same land.[1819]

Where there were several validly recorded mortgages on a particular piece of land, the mortgage last recorded was the one that was last in a former court of chancery.[1820] It is the date of recording that is important, and not the date of execution, and when two mortgages bear the same date of execution, it cannot be claimed that the earlier acknowledgment of the one recorded later shows that it is intended or given as a first security.[1821]

Although a subsequent purchaser or mortgagee of land has no actual notice of a prior mortgage or a deed of trust in the nature of a mortgage on it, nevertheless, if such mortgage or deed of trust is duly recorded before the subsequent transaction is put on the record, the subsequent purchaser or mortgagee will be charged with notice of the existence and terms of the mortgage, and of the lien that it creates, and will take subject to it.[1822] Where a purchaser under a second mortgage seeks relief against a party who holds under a first mortgage, on the theory that the first mortgage was not filed and recorded until after the second, the party cannot have relief where the first mortgage was filed prior to the party's mortgage, even though

purchaser signed agreement, purchaser was charged with notice of existence of trust and was bound to ascertain at his peril terms of trust and to make careful inquiry into authority of trustee to enter into a binding agreement of sale.—Sadow v. Losh, 38 Mich. App. 404, 196 N.W.2d 350 (1972).

1815. Weber v. Weber, 47 Mich. 569, 11 N.W. 389 (1882).

1816. Sinclair v. Slawson, 44 Mich. 123, 6 N.W. 207 (1880) (name of mortgagee omitted).

1817. Town clerk

A mortgage on standing timber is a mortgage on an interest in land, and the filing of it as a chattel mortgage in the town clerk's office, is not notice to a subsequent purchaser from the mortgagor.—Williams v. Hyde, 98 Mich. 152, 57 N.W. 98 (1893).

1818. Grand Rapids Nat'l Bank v. Ford, 143 Mich. 402, 107 N.W. 76 (1906).

Gordon v. Constantine Hydraulic Co., 117 Mich. 620, 76 N.W. 142 (1898).

Sufficiency of record

The entry of a mortgage filed for record in the entry book required by law to be kept until the mortgage was copied in full into the record constituted constructive notice to purchasers, and referred them to the mortgage on file for particu-

lars.—Sinclair v. Slawson, 44 Mich. 123, 6 N.W. 207 (1880).

1819. Beals v. Hale, 45 U.S. 37, 11 L. Ed. 865 (1846).

Security interest in mobile home

The Legislature's 2003 amendment of the Mobile Home Commission Act (MHCA) to add a section providing that a security interest in a mobile home affixed to real property may be perfected in the same manner as a lien on real property is not a "new law" that cannot be applied retroactively, but is rather a "clarification" of the Legislature's original intent; the amendment was the Legislature's response to the holding in *In re Kroskie*, 315 F.3d 644 (6th Cir. 2003), that the MHCA provided the exclusive method for perfecting a security interest in a mobile home.—Citicorp Trust Bank v. Meoli (In re Oswalt), 318 B.R. 817 (W.D. Mich. 2004), aff'd, 444 F.3d 524 (6th Cir. Mich. 2006).

1820. Titus v. Cavalier, 276 Mich. 117, 267 N.W. 799 (1936).

1821. Van Aken v. Gleason, 34 Mich. 477 (1876).

1822. Webber v. Ramsey, 100 Mich. 58, 58 N.W. 625 (1894).

Campbell v. Keys, 130 Mich. 127, 89 N.W. 720 (1902) (execution levied after recordation).

that filing occurred only two hours before the filing of the second mortgage.[1823]

Priority of record is not given superiority of lien if the instrument recorded transfers no present mortgageable interest entitled to recording,[1824] or if the prior recorded instrument is an agreement to mortgage to secure an indebtedness not then existing.[1825]

However, notice of a prior mortgage does not give notice of a pending action in foreclosure of that mortgage. If the foreclosing mortgagee fails to record a lis pendens, the subsequent mortgagee who records his or her mortgage subsequent to the filing of the action in foreclosure is entitled to exercise his or her rights as if the foreclosure never occurred.[1826]

Agreement as to priority. The order of priority between two mortgages that would ordinarily result from their relative positions on the record may be reversed by an agreement of the parties to that effect.[1827] The belated recording of a mortgage, the priority of which is expressly recognized in a previously recorded second mortgage, does not affect the rights of the respective parties.[1828]

Whether a party will be held to a subordination clause that is ambiguous depends on whether the party would have discovered the subordination by the exercise of due diligence in the inquiry that the ambiguity gives the party the duty to make.[1829]

Priority affected by fraud. Priority of record will not give superiority of lien to a mortgage that is marked by fraud or bad faith, as against a later recorded mortgage that is free from comparable objections. It is an indication of bad faith that no money has been advanced or paid under the mortgage claiming superiority.[1830]

Erroneous description of property. The record is not constructive notice concerning land not described in the property description, and, if the description of

1823. Hoffman v. McMorran, 52 Mich. 318, 17 N.W. 928 (1883).

1824. Equitable interest mortgaged

Where a person mortgages lands that he or she holds under a bond for a deed, the person conveys no legal interest in the bond, but only an equitable interest; and the registry of mortgage is not notice.—Wing v. McDowell, Walk. Ch. 175 (Mich. 1843).

1825. Agreement to mortgage

An agreement to mortgage premises to secure an indebtedness not then existing was acknowledged by the party to whom the mortgage was to be given, and was recorded; record could not operate as constructive notice to any one claiming as subsequent purchaser or encumbrancer from party who was to give the mortgage.—Farmers & Mechanics' Bank v. Bronson, 14 Mich. 361 (1866).

Mortgage for future credit prior only to extent of consideration paid.

Second mortgage given to raise funds for completing apartment recorded prior to first mortgage was taken in good faith, but valid as prior lien only for actual consideration paid.—Manning v. Rosenfield, 239 Mich. 459, 214 N.W. 424 (1927).

1826. National Acceptance Co. v. Mardigian, 259 F. Supp. 612 (E.D. Mich. 1966).

1827. Patterson v. Miller, 249 Mich. 89, 227 N.W. 674 (1929).

1828. Winkworth Fuel & Supply Co. v. Bloomsbury Corp., 266 Mich. 298, 253 N.W. 304 (1934).

1829. Obvious ambiguity

Ambiguity in subordination clause in defendant's mortgage was so obvious as to put prudent person on inquiry notice, in view of fact that clause was ambiguous as to whether defendant's mortgage was subordinate to plaintiff's subsequently obtained mortgage.—American Federal Sav. & Loan Ass'n v. Orenstein, 81 Mich. App. 249, 265 N.W.2d 111 (1978).

1830. Brigham v. Brown, 44 Mich. 59, 6 N.W. 97 (1880).

the property in a mortgage wholly fails to identify that intended to be encumbered, or by mistake is so expressed as to be applicable only to a different tract or lot, so that it could not be enforced without invoking the aid of a court in equity to reform it, the record of it is not notice to subsequent purchasers or lienors.[1831] If, however, the description is merely ambiguous or incomplete, it is sufficient to put such persons on inquiry; and, if it is apparent from the face of the record that there is a minor mistake or misdescription, which is capable of being corrected from other parts of the same instrument, or other details of the same description, it operates as a constructive notice.[1832]

§ 783.   Failure to Record Mortgage

An unrecorded mortgage is void as against any subsequent purchaser in good faith and for a valuable consideration of the same real estate or any portion of it whose conveyance is first duly recorded.

A mortgage is a conveyance[1833] subject to the requirement that if it is not recorded as provided by law, it is void as against any subsequent purchaser in good faith and for a valuable consideration, of the same real estate or any portion of it, whose conveyance is recorded before the mortgage.[1834] Generally, then, unless equitable considerations dictate otherwise,[1835] and in the absence of notice[1836]

1831. Barrows v. Baughman, 9 Mich. 213 (1861).

1832. Construction showing error

The error in the description in a mortgage appearing by construction, its record is notice to subsequent purchasers that the mortgage is upon the lot intended to be designated, and they take subject to it.—Anderson v. Baughman, 7 Mich. 69 (1859).

1833. MCLS § 565.35.

Jackson City Bank v. Campbell, 172 Mich. 541, 138 N.W. 254 (1912).

1834. MCLS § 565.29.

Michigan Fire & Marine Ins. Co. v. Hamilton, 284 Mich. 417, 279 N.W. 884 (1938).

Piech v. Beaty, 298 Mich. 535, 299 N.W. 705 (1941) (second mortgage).

Bankruptcy trustee

Where debtors refinanced their real property prior to filing a bankruptcy petition, but the mortgage was not recorded until after the petition was filed, the bankruptcy trustee was a bona fide purchaser who took the property free of the unrecorded mortgage; the disclosure of the mortgagee's interest in the debtors' schedules filed with their petition did not provide the trustee with constructive notice that would defeat his bona fide purchaser status, because the trustee attained his status at the time the case was commenced, and the status could not be undone by information con-

tained in the petition.—Kohut v. Quicken Loans, Inc. (In re Wohlfeil), 322 B.R. 302 (Bankr. E.D. Mich. 2005).

Federal government in forfeiture is not good-faith purchaser

Applicability of federal civil forfeiture statute to residence used by occupant to grow marijuana did not deprive innocent unrecorded mortgagees of their interest in residence as against that of federal government, where government was not "purchaser" within definition of Michigan statute voiding unrecorded mortgage conveyances as against subsequent purchasers in good faith for valuable consideration.—United States v. Certain Real Property Located at 750 East Shore Drive, 800 F. Supp. 547 (E.D. Mich. 1992).

Recipient of deed intended as mortgage is not good-faith purchaser

Finding of trial court in nonjury action that deed to plaintiffs was equitable mortgage was not clearly erroneous and thereby precluded plaintiffs from being deemed "purchasers in good faith" of legal title within meaning of such phrase as used in this section.—Bryce v. Jones, 394 Mich. 425, 230 N.W.2d 272 (1975).

1835. Concealment of intent to dispute priority

A judgment creditor who levied on land on which was a prior unrecorded mortgage, fraudulent as to him, cannot bid in the land, and afterwards defeat the priority of mortgage, where

either at the time of purchase or at the time of the payment of the consideration,[1837] a subsequent mortgagee or the mortgagee's assignee,[1838] or grantee for a valuable consideration,[1839] who first records his or her interest,[1840] takes land free from the liens of prior unrecorded mortgages.

However, no statute makes a failure to record a mortgage of land operate to void the instrument, as against an assignee or creditor of the mortgagor, who does not have the status of a bona fide purchaser.[1841]

Constructive notice. The doctrine is well settled that if a person taking a conveyance or encumbrance has notice of the time of the taking of it of an unrecorded mortgage or facts that put the person on inquiry that would lead to knowledge of its existence, then the person is bound by the notice and the person's lien is subject to that previous mortgage lien.[1842] The knowledge of a person who dies is imputed to his or her estate.[1843] A mortgage that is held from the record is

---

he allowed other bidders and junior lienors to remain ignorant of the fact that he intended to dispute priority, because that would permit him to gain an unfair advantage in bidding.—Belcher v. Curtis, 119 Mich. 1, 77 N.W. 310 (1898).

1836. Klanowski v. Nelson, 252 Mich. 530, 233 N.W. 404 (1930).

Effect of actual knowledge

Mortgage is junior to prior unrecorded mortgage where junior mortgagee took mortgage with actual knowledge of such prior unrecorded mortgage.—Matosh v. Metropolitan Trust Co., 262 Mich. 201, 247 N.W. 156 (1933).

1837. Warner v. Whittaker, 6 Mich. 133 (1858).

1838. Burns v. Berry, 42 Mich. 176, 3 N.W. 924 (1879).

Notice is question of fact

Where plaintiffs' claim that their unrecorded mortgage was entitled to priority over defendant's mortgage would be proved by a finding that defendant had actual knowledge of plaintiffs' mortgage before defendant took its mortgage, and issue of defendant's actual knowledge was disputed on record, summary judgment for defendant was unauthorized.—Cheff v. Bank of the Commonwealth, 40 Mich. App. 474, 198 N.W.2d 914 (1972).

1839. Belding Sav. Bank v. Moore, 118 Mich. 150, 76 N.W. 368 (1898).

1840. Klanowski v. Nelson, 252 Mich. 530, 233 N.W. 404 (1930) (recorded mortgage properly adjudged entitled to precedence over previously executed unrecorded mortgage).

Cancellation and re-mortgage

Mortgagee's acceptance of new mortgage and cancellation of old one does not in all cases deprive him of the right to have the lien of the

discharged mortgage continued against intervening liens of which he does not have knowledge, notwithstanding such intervening liens are recorded.—Schanhite v. Plymouth United Sav. Bank, 277 Mich. 33, 268 N.W. 801 (1936).

Creditor's lien

Under Michigan law, liens upon realty may be perfected by depositing notice of levy thereon with the Register of Deeds in the county where the land is located, and in view of fact that under Michigan law an unrecorded equitable mortgage does not bar perfection of a lien, bankrupt's unrecorded assignment of its interest in certain realty in consideration for an extension of credit, on the date of bankruptcy, was not a bar to perfection of a lien by another creditor, and therefore trustee took bankrupt's interest in the realty free of such equitable mortgage under ideal hypothetical creditor provisions of Bankruptcy Act.—In re Plymouth Glass Co., 171 F. Supp. 650 (D. Mich. 1957).

1841. Haug v. Third Nat'l Bank, 95 Mich. 249, 54 N.W. 888 (1893).

1842. Fifth Nat'l Bank v. Pierce, 117 Mich. 376, 75 N.W. 1058 (1898).

Mortgagor's possession of notes

One who purchases premises covered by an undischarged mortgage, the mortgagee being well known and easily accessible to him, and he having knowledge of facts sufficient to put a prudent person on inquiry, cannot claim to be a purchaser without notice of the equities of the mortgage simply because the mortgagor has possession of, and exhibits to him, the notes described in the mortgage; he stands in no better position than the mortgagor himself.—Boxheimer v. Gunn, 24 Mich. 372 (1872).

1843. Purchase of mortgaged premises

Decedent who was aware of defendants' prior unrecorded mortgage at time he took second mortgage from them was not good faith purchaser

good against creditors extending credit to a mortgagor with notice of the mortgage.[1844]

Judgment creditors. A creditor's lien recorded after the making of an unrecorded mortgage of which the holder of the lien has no notice at the time of the recording has priority over the unrecorded mortgage.[1845] This rule applies even to a portion of a property that is erroneously excluded from the description of property in a mortgage properly recorded on the remainder of the parcel.[1846]

A mortgage that is not recorded because it would impair the mortgagor's credit is a fraudulent conveyance as against a subsequent judgment creditor, who extended credit on the faith of the mortgagor's apparently unencumbered title to the land.[1847]

Absolute deed intended as a mortgage. An unrecorded deed of defeasance is void as against any person other than its maker, the maker's heirs or devisees, or persons having actual notice of it.[1848] If a deed is intended as a mortgage, it is void as against a prior mortgage where the instrument of defeasance is not recorded.[1849] A subsequent purchaser without notice of land conveyed absolutely but with an unrecorded defeasance,[1850] or an attaching creditor of the grantee,[1851] is not charged with notice of, and has priority over, the rights of the holder of the deed or instrument of defeasance.

§ 784.   Transactions Subsequent to Mortgage Affecting Priority; Estoppel

A superior equity may arise in favor of a junior mortgagee where a senior mortgagee acts to the prejudice of the junior mortgagee or to the impairment of his or her security, with actual knowledge of the existence of the junior mortgage.

In order to give a junior mortgage precedence over any senior one, there must

under statute governing unrecorded conveyances, and accordingly, decedent's notice of cloud on title was properly imputed to personal representatives of decedent's estate on their purchase of mortgaged premises from defendants because it would be inequitable to confer on personal representatives the status of good-faith purchasers in performance of duties for which they were responsible as managers and distributors of decedent's estate assets.—Michigan Nat'l Bank & Trust Co. v. Morren, 194 Mich. App. 407, 487 N.W.2d 784 (1992).

1844. Wattles v. Slater, 154 Mich. 666, 118 N.W. 486 (1908).

1845. MCLS § 600.6051.

Coleman v. Hoge, 313 Mich. 181, 20 N.W.2d 857 (1945).

1846. Half of parcel not included in description of recorded mortgage

Where certain parcel of bankrupt's land was mortgaged, but through mutual mistake description only included half of said parcel, as trustee in bankruptcy was vested with rights of creditor holding execution lien and had to be deemed to have complied with all requirements of former statute necessary to acquisition of such lien, trustee was entitled to priority over mortgage as to portion of parcel not included in mortgage, unless he had such actual or constructive notice.—In re Cobb, 14 F. Supp. 465 (D. Mich. 1936).

1847. Belcher v. Curtis, 119 Mich. 1, 77 N.W. 310 (1898).

1848. MCLS § 565.32.

Columbia Bank v. Jacobs, 10 Mich. 349 (1862).

1849. Carrier v. Caplan, 247 Mich. 38, 225 N.W. 581 (1929).

1850. Reid v. Dowd, 257 Mich. 492, 241 N.W. 174 (1932).

1851. Columbia Bank v. Jacobs, 10 Mich. 349 (1862).

be either an agreement to that effect or a superior equity in the junior mortgagee.[1852] Such an equity, however, arises from anything done by the senior mortgagee to the prejudice of the junior mortgagee, or to the impairment of the latter's security, with actual knowledge of the existence of the junior mortgage.[1853]

Substitution or renewal of mortgages. As a general rule, entering satisfaction of a mortgage and taking a new one, when designed by the parties to be merely a continuation of the first mortgage, and when the two acts are practically simultaneous or parts of the same transaction,[1854] is not an extinguishment of the mortgage, but a renewal of it, and does not give priority to an intervening judgment or mortgage creditor of the mortgagor.[1855] That is especially true if it is done in good faith, in ignorance of the existence of the intervening lien, and without any intention to release the lien of the mortgage.[1856]

Release or satisfaction. Generally, a release or satisfaction of a mortgage or deed of trust on the record inures to the benefit of a junior lienor or holder of an interest acquired subsequent to the execution of the mortgage or deed of trust, unless the release or satisfaction was made for a particular purpose only, not contemplating the displacement of the lien of a mortgage, of which fact the junior encumbrancer was cognizant.[1857] Purchasers or encumbrancers after a discharge is placed on the record are entitled to the protection afforded subsequent purchasers and encumbrancers in good faith as against unrecorded conveyances, and can be affected only by actual notice, or notice of facts that put them on inquiry.[1858]

As between a mortgagee whose mortgage is discharged of record solely through the act of a third person, which act is unauthorized by the mortgagee and for which the mortgagee is in no way responsible, and a person who is induced by that cancellation to believe that the mortgage has been cancelled in good faith, and who purchases title or accepts a mortgage on the property as security for a loan, the equities are balanced, and the lien of the mortgage first in order of time is

---

1852. Obtaining legal title of another

As between two mortgagees, where the equities of the parties are equal, the subsequent obtaining of the legal title in right of another and with notice of the prior equity will not aid the holder of the postponed equity.—Wing v. McDowell, Walk. Ch. 175 (Mich. 1843).

1853. James v. Brown, 11 Mich. 25 (1862) (release of part of lands).

Postponement to extent of injury

Anything done by the first mortgagee to the prejudice of the second mortgagee, with a knowledge of the second mortgage, must, to the extent of injury, postpone the first to the second mortgage.—Bailey v. Gould, Walk. Ch. 478 (Mich. 1844).

1854. Brown v. Dunckel, 46 Mich. 29, 8 N.W. 537 (1881).

1855. Eggeman v. Eggeman, 37 Mich. 435 (1877).

1856. Pritchard v. Kalamazoo College, 82 Mich. 587, 47 N.W. 31 (1890).

Cancellation and re-mortgage

Mortgagee's acceptance of new mortgage and cancellation of old one does not in all cases deprive him of the right to have the lien of the discharged mortgage continued against intervening liens of which he does not have knowledge, notwithstanding such intervening liens are recorded.—Schanhite v. Plymouth United Sav. Bank, 277 Mich. 33, 268 N.W. 801 (1936).

1857. Fee acquired by senior mortgagee

Where fee was acquired by first mortgagee who intended to keep mortgage alive, notwithstanding release given by first mortgagee, junior mortgagee who had notice of first mortgage did not thereby acquire a senior mortgage.—Titus v. Cavalier, 276 Mich. 117, 267 N.W. 799 (1936).

1858. Ferguson v. Glassford, 68 Mich. 36, 35 N.W. 820 (1888).

superior.[1859]

If a mortgage is released or satisfied through accident or mistake, it may be restored under equitable principles and given its original priority as a lien where the rights of innocent third parties will not be affected.[1860] Similarly, where the discharge, release, or satisfaction of a mortgage is the result of fraud, accident, or mistake, it does not inure to the benefit of a person acquiring an interest in the property who does not rely or advance anything on the faith of the discharge.[1861] A purchaser of the premises who has been informed by the mortgagor that the mortgage is still outstanding and held by a named person is charged with notice that the discharge was recorded by mistake, and is not protected by the record showing of the discharge.[1862]

Failure of consideration. On a failure of the consideration for which the release or satisfaction of a mortgage is executed, it may generally be set aside, at least as against a mere volunteer or a purchaser who pays only a nominal consideration and is chargeable with knowledge of the rights and equities of the parties.[1863]

Estoppel. A mortgagee of land may be estopped to assert the priority of his or her lien as against subsequent purchasers or encumbrancers by conduct or an omission on the mortgagee's part that operates as a forfeiture of the mortgagee's rights or that renders it unconscionable to enforce the fixed security to their prejudice.[1864] Whether the holder of a prior mortgage or lien is estopped to deny the validity of a later mortgage or lien depends on the question whether, within the principles of law applicable to the situation, the later mortgagee or lienholder has been misled by the prior mortgagee and is thereby prejudiced.[1865]

1859. Forged satisfaction

The record entry of a forged satisfaction of a mortgage, through no fault of the mortgagee, gives no priority to a subsequent mortgagee, who is deceived by it.—Keller v. Hannah, 52 Mich. 535, 18 N.W. 346 (1884).

1860. Schanhite v. Plymouth United Sav. Bank, 277 Mich. 33, 268 N.W. 801 (1936).

Sheldon v. Holmes, 58 Mich. 138, 24 N.W. 795 (1885).

1861. Beal v. Alschuler, 277 Mich. 66, 268 N.W. 813 (1936).

1862. Ferguson v. Glassford, 68 Mich. 36, 35 N.W. 820 (1888).

1863. Plasger v. Leonard, 316 Mich. 174, 25 N.W.2d 156 (1946).

1864. Laches

Without determining whether the doctrine of laches can be used as an affirmative defense when the recording statute otherwise controls, a court held that a mortgagee's two-year delay in recording its mortgage could not be used as a defense by another mortgagee on the issue of priority, because even though a two-year delay is "significant," the mortgagee recorded the mortgage as soon as it discovered its prior attorney had failed to do so, and took legal steps to protect its interest in property even before the mortgage was recorded.—Qassis v. Republic Bank (In re Luna Pier Land Dev., LLC), 325 B.R. 735 (Bankr. E.D. Mich. 2005).

Lack of fraudulent intent

The failure of the officers of a bank, in answering a general inquiry from another bank as to the character and standing of a customer, to disclose that the customer was indebted to their bank, and that it held liens on certain of his property, will not estop it to assert such liens as against a mortgage subsequently taken by the inquiring bank, in the absence of any fraudulent intent.—First Nat'l Bank v. Marshall & I. Bank, 83 F. 725 (6th Cir. Mich. 1897).

1865. No misleading acts shown

Where, after foreclosure of first mortgage, mortgagors waited until two months before right to redeem would have expired and then sold a portion of premises which were encumbered by recorded second mortgage, redeemed land from foreclosure, and secured release of land retained by them from second mortgage, failure of a second mortgagee, who did nothing to mislead purchasers to redeem from foreclosure, did not affect his lien nor extin-

The priority of a lien may be lost by laches, in that the principle that laches that causes a court in equity to look with favor on that defense is not mere delay, but delay that works disadvantage and prejudice to another, has been applied in determining the priority of liens on land.[1866]

Generally a second mortgagee, whose mortgage expressly recites the first mortgage or declares that it is taken subject to it, is estopped to deny the prior lien.[1867]

A mortgagee may be estopped by his or her fraud from asserting the priority of his or her lien.[1868] Thus, a mortgage fraudulently obtained and recorded by a third party through collusion with the mortgagor, during the interval of substituting a new mortgage for an old one, will be postponed to the substituted mortgage.[1869]

Future advance mortgages. A mortgage securing an indebtedness or other obligation that arises or is incurred after the mortgage has been recorded has priority with respect to the future advance as of the date of recording of the mortgage.[1870] A mortgage amended to secure an indebtedness or other obligation that arises or is incurred after the mortgage has been recorded has priority with respect to the future advance as of the date of recording of the amendment to the mortgage.[1871]

However, the statutes regulating future advance mortgages do not apply to a residential future advance mortgage,[1872] except to the extent the mortgage secures a protective advance[1873] unless the requisite statements are set forth in a conspicuous manner on the first page of the mortgage.[1874]

For those mortgages not covered by these statutory provisions, the debts

guish his mortgage and did not "estop" him from enforcing his mortgage against land sold to purchasers who had no actual notice of second mortgage.—Piech v. Beaty, 298 Mich. 535, 299 N.W. 705 (1941).

1866. Johnson v. Cook, 179 Mich. 117, 146 N.W. 343 (1914).

1867. Inconsistent positions

A party cannot affirm a mortgage in part by seeking foreclosure, and disaffirm it in part by asking that liens established by prior mortgages, and recognized in the mortgage sought to be foreclosed, be set aside.—Gow v. Collins & Parker Lumber Co., 109 Mich. 45, 66 N.W. 676 (1896).

1868. Corey v. Alderman, 46 Mich. 540, 9 N.W. 844 (1881).

1869. Waldo v. Richmond, 40 Mich. 380 (1879).

1870. MCLS § 565.902.

Future advance mortgage defined

A "future advance mortgage" is a mortgage that secures a future advance and is recorded; a future advance is an indebtedness or other obligation that arises after the mortgage has been recorded, whether or not the future advance was obligatory

or optional on the part of the mortgagee.—Citizens State Bank v. Nakash, 287 Mich. App. 289, 788 N.W.2d 839 (2010).

Not created by reference to unrecorded instrument

A future advance mortgage cannot be created by reference, but must be expressly created in a recorded instrument; a recorded mortgage's incorporation by reference of an unrecorded promissory note with a future advance clause did not create a future advance mortgage.—Citizens State Bank v. Nakash, 287 Mich. App. 289, 788 N.W.2d 839 (2010).

Priority of advances

The priority of all advances made in connection with a future advance mortgage relates back to the date when the mortgage was recorded; even future advances made after the execution and recording of a subsequent mortgage are superior to the interest of the subsequent mortgage.—Deutsche Bank Trust Co. Ams. v. Spot Realty, Inc., 269 Mich. App. 607, 714 N.W.2d 409 (2005).

1871. MCLS § 565.903.

1872. MCLS § 565.901.

1873. MCLS § 565.901.

1874. MCLS § 565.903a.

executed under a recorded mortgage agreement containing a future advances clause covering subsequent notes executed by a mortgagor have a right of priority dating to the time of their individual advancement to the mortgagor.[1875]

1875. Ladue v. Detroit & M.R. Co., 13 Mich. 380 (1865).

Seiberling Tire & Rubber Co. v. State Bank of Fraser, 78 Mich. App. 587, 261 N.W.2d 13 (1977).

Holiday Inns, Inc. v. Susher-Schaefer Inv. Co., 77 Mich. App. 658, 259 N.W.2d 179 (1977) (advances before subsequent recording have priority).

Chapter 27

RIGHTS AND LIABILITIES OF PARTIES

§ 791. Possession or Control of Property

A mortgagor is entitled to possession of the mortgaged property until foreclosure and expiration of the redemption period.

Library References

> Michigan Digest
> John G. Cameron, Jr., Michigan Real Estate Forms
> Midwest Transaction Guide
> Thompson on Real Property, Thomas Edition (David A. Thomas, ed.)
> Powell on Real Property® (Michael Allan Wolf, ed.)
> Real Estate Financing

Law Reviews

> Rita Subhedar, A Proposed State Response to the Michigan Housing Crisis, 11 J.L. Soc'y 173 (2010); Carl W. Hernstein, Annual Survey of Michigan Law, June 1, 1999–May 31, 2000: Real Property, 47 Wayne L. Rev. 669 (2001).

Under the Revised Judicature Act of 1961, summary process eviction proceedings against a person in possession of mortgaged premises may only be initiated after the expiration of the deadline for redemption following the foreclosure sale of the property.[1876] While the validity of a trust mortgage sale might be tested in summary proceedings in so far as invalidity appeared in the procedure, the underlying equities bearing on the instruments, legal capacity of the mortgagee, or trustee, and other matters wholly *de hors* the record, inclusive of an accounting, cannot be tried in those proceedings.[1877]

Another provision of the Revised Judicature Act of 1961 bars an action by a mortgagee or a mortgagee's assigns or representatives for the recovery of the mortgaged premises, until the title to the premises becomes absolute upon a foreclosure of the mortgage.[1878] Under a statute to that effect, a mortgagor is entitled to possession of the mortgaged premises,[1879] and is entitled to recover possession

---

1876. MCLS § 600.5714.

Agreement to extend redemption period

An agreement by the purchaser under foreclosure to extend the time of redemption and to permit the mortgagors to continue in occupancy which expressly preserved all rights, duties and liabilities of the parties, would not prevent summary proceedings to recover possession.—Audretsch v. Hurst, 126 Mich. 301, 85 N.W. 746 (1901).

1877. Reid v. Rylander, 270 Mich. 263, 258 N.W. 630 (1935).

1878. MCLS § 600.2932.

1879. Straus v. Barbee, 262 Mich. 113, 247 N.W. 125 (1933).

Hazeltine v. Granger, 44 Mich. 503, 7 N.W. 74 (1880).

Wagar v. Stone, 36 Mich. 364 (1877).

Deed intended as security

A deed absolute given by way of security conveys no right of possession, if the papers show that the relation between the parties to it is that of mortgagor and mortgagee, and that the mortgagor is left in possession under an arrangement that amounts to a defeasance of the deed.—Ferris v. Wilcox, 51 Mich. 105, 16 N.W. 252 (1883).

Policy of state

Policy of state, except as modified by statute relating to trust mortgages, is to save to mortgagors possession and benefits of mortgaged prem-

from the mortgagee at any time before those rights have been foreclosed in some manner.[1880] An exception to that rule is created by statutes relating to trust mortgages.[1881] Otherwise, a mortgagee or a mortgagee's representatives or assigns may not take possession of mortgaged premises until the title to the premises becomes absolute on foreclosure of the mortgage.[1882]

Accordingly, an unforeclosed mortgage gives no possessory right.[1883] A mortgagor of land is entitled to possession until foreclosure and does not forfeit that right by the failure to make payments as stipulated.[1884] A mortgagee cannot, before foreclosure, take and hold possession without the consent of the mortgagor.[1885] Likewise, the constructive possession of vacant lands, as between the mortgagor and the mortgagee, must be deemed to be in the mortgagor.[1886] An apparent abandonment by the mortgagor of land not under foreclosure gives no right to the mortgagee to enter upon the land in an attempt to reduce the indebtedness upon the mortgage.[1887]

§ 792.   —Agreement as to Possession

The mortgagor may, by a definite and clear agreement apart from the mortgage, grant to the mortgagee the right to possession.

The statutory provision[1888] that the mortgagee of land is not entitled to possession until after foreclosure is for the mortgagor's benefit, so that the mortgagor can waive it by permitting the mortgagee to take possession, which consent is good until revoked. But this type of agreement is not valid if it is contained in the mortgage. It must be separate and subsequent, and for a new consideration.[1889]

Thus, a mortgagee's possession not obtained by license of the mortgagor is tortious, and the mortgagor may be ejected.[1890] A mortgagor cannot be deprived of

---

ises, as against mortgagees, until expiration of redemption period.—Massachusetts Mut. Life Ins. Co. v. Sutton, 278 Mich. 457, 270 N.W. 748 (1936).

1880. Humphrey v. Hurd, 29 Mich. 44 (1874).

1881. MCLS § 554.212.

Assignment of rent clause

Where agent of trustee under trust mortgage had possession of property from inception of mortgage and default occurred in mortgage, trustee was entitled to continue in possession under assignment of rent clause without filing notice of default and serving copy on occupiers of premises, since such notice is to protect occupiers and there was no question of prejudice to them.—Giblin v. Detroit Trust Co., 270 Mich. 293, 258 N.W. 635 (1935).

1882. Detroit Fidelity & Surety Co. v. King, 264 Mich. 91, 249 N.W. 477 (1933).

Pines v. Equitable Trust Co., 263 Mich. 458, 249 N.W. 32 (1933).

Nusbaum v. Shapero, 249 Mich. 252, 228 N.W. 785 (1930).

1883. Lee v. Clary, 38 Mich. 223 (1878).

1884. Ferris v. Wilcox, 51 Mich. 105, 16 N.W. 252 (1883).

1885. Reading v. Waterman, 46 Mich. 107, 8 N.W. 691 (1881).

1886. Albright v. Cobb, 34 Mich. 316 (1876).

1887. Tudryck v. Mutch, 320 Mich. 86, 30 N.W.2d 512 (1948).

1888. MCLS § 600.2932.

1889. Byers v. Byers, 65 Mich. 598, 32 N.W. 831 (1887).

Morse v. Byam, 55 Mich. 594, 22 N.W. 54 (1885).

1890. Pierce v. Grimley, 77 Mich. 273, 43 N.W. 932 (1889).

Newton v. McKay, 30 Mich. 380 (1874).

his or her right to possession unless that power is clearly given to the mortgagee by the agreement of the parties.[1891] A contract giving the mortgagee possession of premises must be read in light of the policy of the state, and the contract must be so definite with respect to time that a lay mortgagor will know the rights surrendered without the necessity of obtaining a judicial construction of an uncertain contract.[1892]

Permission to the mortgagee to take possession of the mortgaged premises, given by the mortgagor's administrator after the administrator has parted with the title, is of no more force than if given by a stranger.[1893] Similarly, no agreement to which a surviving spouse is not a party can give a right of possession before foreclosure under a purchase money mortgage executed by a decedent, as against the survivor's possessory claims.[1894] Finally, a provision in a real estate mortgage that permits possession in the mortgagee on a mere default in payment will not be enforced.[1895]

But a mortgagor's subsequent specific contract giving a mortgagee possession of the premises will be enforced according to its terms.[1896]

If the mortgagor gives the mortgagee possession simultaneously with or after the execution of the mortgage, but without any definite agreement as to the time of possession, the mortgagee's tenure is temporary.[1897]

§ 793. Use and Management of Property in General

In general, the mortgagor may control and manage the mortgaged premises as the mortgagor sees fit.

The mortgagor, until actual foreclosure, is in possession by right, and not by sufferance, and may make such arrangements for the use of the property as any other person may.[1898]

Conditions precedent to ejectment by mortgagor

A mortgagee who is deliberately and intentionally put in possession by the mortgagor has rightful possession, and an action for possession cannot be brought against him by the mortgagor without some previous action, terminating his right and rendering his continuance in possession wrongful.—Reading v. Waterman, 46 Mich. 107, 8 N.W. 691 (1881).

1891. Bennos v. Waderlow, 291 Mich. 595, 289 N.W. 267 (1939).

Agreement with mortgagor's grantee

Contract whereby mortgagor's grantee voluntarily placed mortgagee in possession was valid.—Pines v. Equitable Trust Co., 263 Mich. 458, 249 N.W. 32 (1933).

1892. Massachusetts Mut. Life Ins. Co. v. Sutton, 278 Mich. 457, 270 N.W. 748 (1936).

1893. Newton v. McKay, 30 Mich. 380 (1874).

1894. Newton v. Sly, 15 Mich. 391 (1867).

1895. Hazeltine v. Granger, 44 Mich. 503, 7 N.W. 74 (1880).

1896. Massachusetts Mut. Life Ins. Co. v. Sutton, 278 Mich. 457, 270 N.W. 748 (1936).

Michigan Trust Co. v. Lansing Lumber Co., 103 Mich. 392, 61 N.W. 668 (1894) (enforcement in chancery).

1897. Massachusetts Mut. Life Ins. Co. v. Sutton, 278 Mich. 457, 270 N.W. 748 (1936).

1898. Ladue v. Detroit & M.R. Co., 13 Mich. 380 (1865).

Crippen v. Morrison, 13 Mich. 23 (1864).

Unjust enrichment

Where plaintiff contended that one defendant was unjustly enriched because plaintiff paid off the sellers' mortgage that defendant was allegedly required to pay, thereby extinguishing the sellers' mortgage, and that the other defendant was enriched because it would not have to defend against a title claim arising from the sellers' mortgage, the court disagreed.—Capital Title Ins. Agency v.

The mortgagor's grantee may contract to voluntarily turn over the operation and management of the mortgaged premises to the mortgagee.[1899] A mortgagee who takes possession by agreement may have general discretion over the operation of the property.[1900] However, until foreclosure, a mortgagee, though in possession for foreclosing, is not the owner, but, beyond securing payment due the mortgagee, is the owner's trustee.[1901]

A mortgagee in possession collecting the proceeds of the premises in payment of the mortgage debt is not entitled to compensation in the absence of an express agreement or of evidence from which one may be implied.[1902]

A mortgagee has the right to the whole security to meet the amount of the mortgage lien. The mortgagee cannot be compelled to take a part of the property that lessens the value of the mortgage security.[1903]

On the other hand, the mortgagee cannot elect a remedy for default in payment that consists of removal of severable resources from the property without the agreement of the mortgagor.[1904]

§ 794.   Rents and Profits

The mortgagor is entitled to the rents and profits of mortgaged property until foreclosure and expiration of the equity of redemption; however, a mortgagor's subsequent specific contract, based on a valuable consideration, giving the mortgagee the rents, is valid.

The general rule is that the mortgagor is entitled to the rents and profits from the mortgaged property until foreclosure and expiration of the equity of redemption.[1905]

Towne Mortg. Co., 2009 Mich. App. LEXIS 566 (Mich. Ct. App. Mar. 10, 2009).

Mortgagors who remained in possession of the property after the foreclosure sale did not have a claim in unjust enrichment for maintaining the property; the mortgagors had the use and enjoyment of the property during the time they maintained it and were in default on their mortgage.—Sweet Air Inv., Inc. v. Kenney, 275 Mich. App. 492, 739 N.W.2d 656 (2007).

1899. Pines v. Equitable Trust Co., 263 Mich. 458, 249 N.W. 32 (1933).

1900. Liquor in bar

Mortgagee of a hotel, who took possession of the mortgaged premises and leased them to a third person, was not obliged to allow the keeping of a bar for the sale of liquors there.—Curtiss v. Sheldon, 91 Mich. 390, 51 N.W. 1057 (1892).

1901. Fidelity Trust Co. v. Saginaw Hotels Co., 259 Mich. 254, 242 N.W. 906 (1932).

1902. Pomeroy v. Noud, 145 Mich. 37, 108 N.W. 498 (1906).

Gilluly v. Shumway, 144 Mich. 661, 108 N.W. 88 (1906).

Barnard v. Paterson, 137 Mich. 633, 100 N.W. 893 (1904).

1903. Webber v. Ramsey, 100 Mich. 58, 58 N.W. 625 (1894) (cutting of timber).

1904. Injunction from cutting timber

Chancery had jurisdiction of a suit to restrain the grantee in a deed intended as a mortgage from cutting timber on the lands and to ascertain whether the mortgage had been paid, and, if not, to determine the amount due and decree its payment.—Bigelow v. Thompson, 133 Mich. 334, 94 N.W. 1077 (1903).

1905. Smith v. Mutual Ben. Life Ins. Co., 362 Mich. 114, 106 N.W.2d 515 (1960).

Bennos v. Waderlow, 291 Mich. 595, 289 N.W. 267 (1939).

Pines v. Equitable Trust Co., 263 Mich. 458, 249 N.W. 32 (1933).

Straus v. Barbee, 262 Mich. 113, 247 N.W. 125 (1933).

However, a mortgagee or assignee of a mortgagee may obtain from the circuit court the appointment of a receiver to collect rents or profit from certain mortgaged properties whose mortgagor fails to pay taxes or insurance premiums on the property.[1906] This remedy applies equally to a land contract mortgage.[1907]

Agreements or stipulations. A mortgagor cannot be deprived of the right to the benefits of the mortgaged premises unless that power is clearly given to the mortgagee by the agreement of the parties.[1908] A mortgagor's subsequent specific contract giving the mortgagee the rents of the premises will be enforced according to its terms.[1909] A mortgagor may, in case of default, by an express agreement, place the mortgagee in possession with the duty to preserve the property and collect the rents and income.[1910] However, a contract giving the mortgagee the rents of the premises must be read in light of the policy of the state, and mortgagors must not be deprived of the rents unless the right is clearly given. The contract must be so definite as to time that a lay mortgagor will know the rights surrendered without the necessity of obtaining a judicial construction of an uncertain contract.[1911]

Accordingly, although the general rule that an assignment of rents and profits as additional security under a mortgage is invalid has been recognized, exceptions to the rule allow an independent assignment of rents to a mortgagee, subsequent to a mortgage, and based on a valuable consideration,[1912] and the granting to the

Deed intended as mortgage

A deed intended as a mortgage will not sustain a claim by the grantee for the rent of the premises if the grantor remains in possession.—Hulin v. Stevens, 53 Mich. 93, 18 N.W. 569 (1884).

1906. MCLS § 600.2927.

1907. MCLS § 565.359.

1908. Bennos v. Waderlow, 291 Mich. 595, 289 N.W. 267 (1939).

1909. Massachusetts Mut. Life Ins. Co. v. Sutton, 278 Mich. 457, 270 N.W. 748 (1936).

Additional security

Michigan law permits a mortgagor to grant to a mortgagee an assignment of rents as additional security and that the assignee/mortgagee's rights are perfected and binding against the assignor/mortgagor when such assignment is recorded and a default occurs in the terms and conditions of the mortgage.—In re Coventry Commons Assoc., 143 B.R. 837, 1992 U.S. Dist. LEXIS 12454 (E.D. Mich. 1992).

Termination of right to rents upon notice of default

Mortgagor's interest in rents made subject to assignment of rents to mortgagee was automatically terminated when mortgagees served notice of default upon mortgagor; debtor, which subsequently purchased mortgaged apartment complex from mortgagor, did not acquire any interest in rents.—In re P.M.G. Properties, 55 B.R. 864 (Bankr. E.D. Mich. 1985).

1910. Reichert v. Guaranty Trust Co., 261 Mich. 315, 246 N.W. 132 (1933).

1911. Massachusetts Mut. Life Ins. Co. v. Sutton, 278 Mich. 457, 270 N.W. 748 (1936).

1912. Kelly v. Bowerman, 113 Mich. 446, 71 N.W. 836 (1897) (assignment of rents of mortgaged property, to be recovered by mortgagee and applied upon the mortgage, is valid).

Extension of time as consideration

Extension of time for payment of mortgage indebtedness was sufficient valuable consideration for assignment of rents from mortgaged premises as additional security for payment of taxes, assessments, and insurance premiums, and assignment was valid.—Massachusetts Mut. Life Ins. Co. v. Ruetter, 268 Mich. 175, 255 N.W. 754 (1934).

Forbearance as consideration

Where mortgagor, in consideration of mortgagee's promise to forbear institution of foreclosure proceedings, assigned rentals from mortgaged premises to mortgagee "so long as bond and mortgages aforesaid are in default" and mortgagor "shall continue to manage and conduct" the mortgaged premises, continuance of the assignment was dependent upon the existence of but one condition, that being default in bonds and mortgage, as against contention that bonds and mortgage must continue to be in default and also that mortgagor must continue to manage and conduct the apartments.—Fox v. Detroit Trust Co., 285 Mich. 669, 281 N.W. 399 (1938).

mortgagee of the right to collect rents accruing during the redemption period following a sale under a decree of foreclosure.[1913] Such an assignment may be enforced by the mortgagee according to its terms,[1914] for the period of time specified.[1915]

Mortgagee in possession. If the mortgagee has lawfully obtained possession before foreclosure, it is his or her duty to receive the rents, but beyond securing payment of the debt due the mortgagee, he or she is in the position of a trustee for the mortgagor.[1916] Thus, a mortgagee in possession, in the absence of an express agreement on the condition of the tenancy, is liable for the annual rental of the land.[1917] The mortgagee also has the duty to account for the rents and profits of the property and to apply the net amount on the mortgage debt.[1918]

The duty to account for rents and profits is the same for a grantee under a deed that is in fact a mortgage as that for other mortgagees in possession.[1919]

As between different mortgagees. Rents belonging to a second mortgagee under an assignment in the mortgage need not be diverted for taxes, pending foreclosure, for the first mortgagee's benefit.[1920]

§ 795.   —Assignments of Rents

A statute authorizes an assignment to the mortgagee of rents in connection with a trust mortgage or with industrial or commercial property.

1913. Mutual Benefit Life Ins. Co. v. Wetsman, 277 Mich. 322, 269 N.W. 189 (1936).

1914. Discharge as manager

Where mortgagor, in consideration of mortgagee's agreement to forbear instituting foreclosure proceedings on mortgage, assigned income from mortgaged property to mortgagee "so long as bond and mortgage" are in default and mortgagor "shall continue to manage and conduct" the mortgaged premises, purchaser at bankruptcy sale could not by discharging mortgagor as manager disturb the assignment and acquire claim on the income from the property.—Fox v. Detroit Trust Co., 285 Mich. 669, 281 N.W. 399 (1938).

1915. Forbearance for reasonable time

There was no lack of consideration for mortgagor's assignment of rents, for which assignment plaintiff agreed to withhold foreclosure, but for no definite time, since, where no time is fixed, forbearance is for reasonable time.—Massachusetts Mut. Life Ins. Co. v. Sutton, 278 Mich. 457, 270 N.W. 748 (1936).

1916. Fidelity Trust Co. v. Saginaw Hotels Co., 259 Mich. 254, 242 N.W. 906 (1932).

1917. Byers v. Byers, 65 Mich. 598, 32 N.W. 831 (1887).

Liability under general rules

A mortgagee in possession pending or prior to foreclosure is accountable for the rental value of the property, subject to general rules respecting negligence and fault.—Brill v. Cherwin, 346 Mich. 507, 78 N.W.2d 122 (1956).

1918. Low v. Kalamazoo Circuit Judge, 61 Mich. 35, 27 N.W. 877 (1886).

1919. Miller v. Peter, 184 Mich. 142, 150 N.W. 554 (1915).

Weise v. Anderson, 134 Mich. 502, 96 N.W. 575 (1903).

Requirement of agreement

On bill by plaintiffs for specific performance of defendants' oral contract to enter into land contract, where defendants filed cross-bill averring that deed by which they had obtained title to property was taken as security for moneys loaned plaintiffs and asked that deed be decreed mortgage and prayed foreclosure thereof, and later petitioned for appointment of temporary receiver to collect monthly rentals and control property pending determination of suit on merits, trial court's order appointing receiver, which deprived plaintiffs of possession, income and control of property was error, in absence of agreement in mortgage allowing defendants in case of default, to income or possession pending foreclosure and averment of emergency to justify trial court's appointment of receiver.—Lendzion v. Senstock, 300 Mich. 346, 1 N.W.2d 567 (1942).

1920. Equitable Trust Co. v. Bankers' Trust Co., 268 Mich. 394, 256 N.W. 460 (1934).

Rents and profits of property mortgaged to the trustees under a trust mortgage or deed of trust may be assigned to the benefit of bondholders or holders of other obligations issued or to be issued by the trustees.[1921] This remedy applies equally to land contract mortgages.[1922]

The assignment of rents in a trust mortgage may be enforced by the trustee of the trust.[1923] The rule is designed for the benefit of bondholders and must be given effect to that end. The purpose of the rule is to put the trustee in the mortgagor's shoes until the debt is paid.[1924] The provision is permissive, not exclusive, and is not incident merely to foreclosure.[1925] The remedy is statutory and not allowed at common law, and must be construed in light of the rule that the mortgagee may not divest the mortgagor of possession until title becomes absolute on foreclosure.[1926]

Under the statute, an assignment of rents and profits of mortgaged property as further security may be in writing executed at or after execution of the mortgage.[1927] An assignment may take effect *in futuri*, as on default.[1928] The courts will determine whether a mortgage contains a sufficient assignment of rents and profits within the provisions of the statute.[1929]

Whether an instrument is a trust mortgage within the statutory definition[1930] depends largely on the intention of the parties when the instrument is executed.[1931] In that determination, all provisions of the instrument must be considered.[1932]

The trustee of the mortgage, as assignee, is entitled to all rents and profits resulting from the operation of the building, including rents collected from subtenants, and is not limited to the rent due the mortgagor landlord under the primary lease.[1933] The term "profits" as used in the statute does not include all business profits realized by a receiver through operation of the mortgaged plant,

1921. MCLS § 554.211.

1922. MCLS § 565.359.

1923. Equitable Trust Co. v. Simpson, 286 Mich. 460, 282 N.W. 215 (1938).

Union Guardian Trust Co. v. Lipsitz, 268 Mich. 209, 255 N.W. 766 (1934).

Equitable Trust Co. v. Milton Realty Co., 263 Mich. 673, 249 N.W. 30 (1933).

1924. Security Trust Co. v. Sloman, 252 Mich. 266, 233 N.W. 216 (1930).

1925. Reichert v. Guaranty Trust Co., 261 Mich. 315, 246 N.W. 132 (1933).

1926. Detroit Trust Co. v. Detroit City Service Co., 262 Mich. 14, 247 N.W. 76 (1933).

1927. Central Trust Co. v. Wolf, 262 Mich. 209, 247 N.W. 159 (1933).

Security Trust Co. v. Sloman, 252 Mich. 266, 233 N.W. 216 (1930).

1928. Union Guardian Trust Co. v. Lipsitz, 268 Mich. 209, 255 N.W. 766 (1934).

1929. Union Guardian Trust Co. v. Lipsitz, 268 Mich. 209, 255 N.W. 766 (1934).

Detroit Trust Co. v. Detroit City Service Co., 262 Mich. 14, 247 N.W. 76 (1933).

Bankers' Trust Co. v. Russell, 261 Mich. 579, 246 N.W. 504 (1933) (clause was insufficient).

1930. MCLS § 554.213.

1931. Union Guardian Trust Co. v. Zack, 274 Mich. 108, 264 N.W. 309 (1936) (use of word "trustee").

Reichert v. Guaranty Trust Co., 261 Mich. 315, 246 N.W. 132 (1933) (trustee named in corporate capacity).

1932. Equitable Trust Co. v. Milton Realty Co., 263 Mich. 673, 249 N.W. 30 (1933).

Secret agreement

As respects question whether mortgage is a trust mortgage, purchasers of bonds secured by mortgage are not required to go behind instrument to which bonds refer them, to discover secret agreement of parties.—Union Guardian Trust Co. v. Lipsitz, 268 Mich. 209, 255 N.W. 766 (1934).

1933. Abrin v. Equitable Trust Co., 271 Mich. 535, 261 N.W. 85 (1935).

including the use of inventory, receivables, and other unmortgaged assets.[1934] Neither the taking of possession nor the appointment of a receiver is a condition precedent to the trustee's collection of the assigned rents, and such right of collection may become effective on default and in advance of foreclosure proceedings.[1935] However, the trustee under the mortgage, in order to take advantage of the provision for assignment of rents and profits, must file a notice of default.[1936] The failure to file a notice will be deemed to be a waiver of the right to rents and profits prior to securing the appointment of a receiver on foreclosure.[1937]

Where a creditor and a debtor enter into a land contract and the senior trust mortgage is foreclosed, the rights under an assignment of rents by the trust mortgage are terminated and are not revived by the creditor's redemption from the foreclosure of the trust mortgage.[1938]

Mortgages on commercial or industrial property. The rents from any commercial or industrial property other than family residences or buildings containing five or fewer apartments may be assigned as security in addition to the property described in a mortgage.[1939] The court may appoint a receiver to enforce a provision of a mortgage to that effect upon the default of the mortgagor.[1940] This remedy applies equally to a land contract mortgage.[1941]

§ 796.   Taxes

> **A mortgagor in possession is obligated to pay the taxes on the property, but on the failure of the mortgagor to do so, it becomes the right of any mortgagee to pay the taxes. The parties to the mortgage may agree, as between themselves, as to which is responsible for the payment of taxes.**

Generally, a mortgagor in possession has the duty to pay the taxes on the property, but on the failure of the mortgagor to do so, it becomes the right of any mortgagee to pay the taxes. A payment by a mortgagee allows the mortgagee to increase the amount of his or her encumbrance in order to secure its repayment by the mortgagor.[1942] Thus, the mortgagee's lien for taxes exists only in connection with the mortgage. The discharge of the mortgage discharges the lien, which cannot thereafter be revived.[1943]

1934. Detroit Trust Co. v. Detroit City Service Co., 262 Mich. 14, 247 N.W. 76 (1933).

1935. Security Trust Co. v. Sloman, 252 Mich. 266, 233 N.W. 216 (1930).

1936. Detroit Properties Corp. v. Detroit Hotel Co., 258 Mich. 156, 242 N.W. 213 (1932).

Union Guardian Trust Co. v. Lipsitz, 268 Mich. 209, 255 N.W. 766 (1934) (notice to tenant).

1937. Detroit Properties Corp. v. Detroit Hotel Co., 258 Mich. 156, 242 N.W. 213 (1932).

1938. Bennos v. Waderlow, 291 Mich. 595, 289 N.W. 267 (1939).

1939. MCLS § 554.231.

1940. Smith v. Mutual Ben. Life Ins. Co., 362 Mich. 114, 106 N.W.2d 515 (1960) (receiver to collect rents and apply them to accrued interests, maintenance costs, insurance, taxes, and a deficiency until expiration of redemption period).

1941. MCLS § 565.359.

1942. Connecticut Mut. Life Ins. Co. v. Bulte, 45 Mich. 113, 7 N.W. 707 (1881).

Waste

Failure to pay taxes on mortgaged property, where income exceeded requirements for it, constituted "waste."—Nusbaum v. Shapero, 249 Mich. 252, 228 N.W. 785 (1930).

1943. Mortgage & Contract Co. v. First Mortg. Bond Co., 256 Mich. 451, 240 N.W. 39 (1932).

Although an early decision is to the contrary,[1944] the more recent decision of the Michigan Supreme Court indicates that a mortgagee generally is entitled to be reimbursed for money that he or she expends in paying delinquent taxes on the mortgaged premises, which it is the mortgagor's duty to pay.[1945]

In any event, the Revised Judicature Act of 1961 provides that a mortgagee or assignee of a mortgagee may obtain from the circuit court the appointment of a receiver to collect rents or profit from certain mortgaged properties whose mortgagor fails to pay taxes on the property.[1946] This remedy applies equally to a land contract mortgage.[1947]

A second mortgagee is under no obligation to protect the lien of the first mortgage by the payment of taxes.[1948] However, under statutes applicable to property taxes levied after December 31, 1998, which abolish tax sales of tax-delinquent property,[1949] whether the tax-foreclosed property is retained by a governmental unit or subsequently auctioned[1950] to a third party after the governmental unit takes title, the absolute title conveyed to the governmental unit extinguishes all outstanding recorded or unrecorded liens against the property except certain specified liens not including mortgages.[1951] Only a party who can prove that he or she did not receive notice of the tax foreclosure is entitled to sue the state, and, the party can not sue the subsequent owner for damages for the value of his or her former interest in the tax-foreclosed property.[1952]

The procedures for the revised tax foreclosure system allow the mortgagee of a property to be notified of any return of unpaid property taxes on the mortgaged property.[1953]

A mortgagee could not enforce in chancery a lien for money expended in redeeming the land from a tax foreclosure, where the mortgagee forecloses the mortgage and permits the mortgagor to redeem from the foreclosure sale, without making any claim for the lien.[1954]

When the terms of a mortgage on real property require the mortgagor to make periodic payments of sums allocated to an escrow account for the purpose of paying taxes on the property, the mortgagee must furnish the mortgagor with a statement within 60 days of the close of the calendar year. The statement must show the beginning balance of the escrow fund, total receipts received by the fund during the calendar year, an itemized statement of all expenditures from the fund during the calendar year, and the balance in the fund at the end of the calendar year.[1955] This annual statement is not required, however, if the mortgagee gives the mortgagor a

Hopkins v. Sanders, 172 Mich. 227, 137 N.W. 709 (1912).

1944. Raynsford v. Phelps, 43 Mich. 342, 5 N.W. 403 (1880).

1945. Buchta v. Lehmann, 263 Mich. 41, 248 N.W. 542 (1933).

1946. MCLS § 600.2927.

1947. MCLS § 565.359.

1948. Connecticut Mut. Life Ins. Co. v. Bulte, 45 Mich. 113, 7 N.W. 707 (1881).

1949. MCLS §§ 211.78 et seq.

1950. See MCLS § 211.78l.

1951. MCLS § 211.78k.

1952. MCLS § 211.78l.

1953. MCLS § 211.78a.

1954. Vincent v. Moore, 51 Mich. 618, 17 N.W. 81 (1883) (decided under prior redemption statutes).

1955. MCLS § 565.161.

monthly statement containing the same information.[1956]

Agreement as to tax liability. A mortgagor may agree to pay the tax against the mortgagee's interest.[1957] A tax assessment against a mortgagee, based on the mortgage, is within the mortgagor's covenant to pay all assessments "on or on account of the mortgage or the debt secured thereby."[1958] However, a stipulation in a mortgage requiring the mortgagor to pay all taxes that are levied by any lawful authority upon the mortgaged premises does not require the mortgagor to pay the taxes directed by a subsequent statute to be levied against the mortgagee's interest in the land.[1959]

§ 797.   Insurance

Under a covenant so providing, the mortgagor is required to keep the buildings on mortgaged real estate insured for the benefit of the mortgagee.

A covenant to the effect that the mortgagor will keep the building on the mortgaged premises insured for the benefit of the mortgagee is valid and binding.[1960] The breach of that covenant entitles the mortgagee to protect his or her security by taking out insurance.[1961]

The mortgagee may recover the expense of insurance coverage thus procured by the mortgagee.[1962] As an alternative, the Revised Judicature Act of 1961 provides that a mortgagee or assignee of a mortgagee may obtain from the circuit court the appointment of a receiver to collect rents or profit from certain mortgaged properties whose mortgagor fails to pay insurance premiums on the property.[1963] This remedy applies equally to a land contract mortgage.[1964]

On the other hand, if a mortgagee obtains insurance on his or her own account, and the premium is not paid by or charged to the mortgagor, the mortgagor cannot

---

1956. MCLS § 565.162.

1957. Common Council of Detroit v. Board of Assessors, 91 Mich. 78, 51 N.W. 787 (1892).

1958. Green v. Grant, 134 Mich. 462, 96 N.W. 583 (1903).

1959. Fuller v. Kane, 110 Mich. 549, 68 N.W. 267 (1896).

1960. Miller v. Aldrich, 31 Mich. 408 (1875).

Interest in insurance proceeds

Security interest in real property continues in insurance proceeds which result from destruction of real property, especially where vendee was contractually bound to obtain insurance for benefit of vendor, but failed to do so.—Warner v. Tarver, 158 Mich. App. 593, 405 N.W.2d 109 (1986).

Waste

Failure to pay insurance premium on mortgaged property, where income exceeded requirements

therefor, constituted "waste."—Nusbaum v. Shapero, 249 Mich. 252, 228 N.W. 785 (1930).

1961. Leland v. Collver, 34 Mich. 418 (1876).

Lender's right to purchase insurance

A mortgage lender did not breach its contractual obligations under a mortgage agreement by placing homeowners insurance on the borrower's property, where the terms of the mortgage obligated the borrowers to insure the property and provide the lender with evidence of insurance and permitted the lender to purchase insurance for the property and to charge the cost to the borrowers if the borrowers failed to maintain sufficient insurance on the property; borrowers failed to bring forth evidence to support their claim that they had maintained insurance on the property.—Mills v. Equicredit Corp., 344 F. Supp. 2d 1071, 2004 U.S. Dist. LEXIS 23904 (E.D. Mich. 2004).

1962. Walton v. Bagley, 47 Mich. 385, 11 N.W. 209 (1882).

1963. MCLS § 600.2927.

1964. MCLS § 565.359.

claim the benefit of a payment of the insurance.[1965]

A mortgage may irrevocably constitute the mortgagee as the agent to procure and renew all insurance on the buildings covered by the mortgage.[1966]

When the terms of a mortgage on real property require the mortgagor to make periodic payments of sums allocated to an escrow account for the purpose of paying insurance on the property, the mortgagee must furnish the mortgagor with a statement within 60 days of the close of the calendar year. The statement must show the beginning balance of the escrow fund, total receipts received by the fund during the calendar year, an itemized statement of all expenditures from the fund during the calendar year, and the balance in the fund at the end of the calendar year.[1967] This annual statement is not required, however, if the mortgagee gives the mortgagor a monthly statement containing the same information.[1968]

§ 798. Repairs, Improvements, and Condo Fees

A mortgagee in possession must make reasonable and necessary repairs; however, the mortgagee has no authority to improve the estate at the mortgagor's expense.

A mortgagee in possession must make reasonable and necessary repairs, and is liable for a willful default or gross neglect in this respect. The extent of the mortgagee in possession's duty to repair is dependent on the circumstances of the particular case. He or she must use reasonable means to preserve the estate and the property within the means furnished by the rents.[1969] A mortgagee in possession is not entitled to charge for repairs that are not necessary to save the estate from loss and injury.[1970]

Improvements. In general, a mortgagee in possession has no authority to improve the estate at the mortgagor's expense.[1971]

An equitable mortgagee who has caused improvements to be made on the property with the consent of the mortgagor is entitled to recover the cost of the improvements including the fair value of the mortgagee's labor expenses.[1972] The mortgagee is even entitled to payment when the labor that he or she furnished is in violation of the residential builders licensing act.[1973]

Where a person holds title to land to secure him- or herself for a payment that

---

1965. Pendleton v. Elliott, 67 Mich. 496, 35 N.W. 97 (1887).

1966. 1928–1930 Op. Atty. Gen. 183.

Carpenter v. Continental Ins. Co., 61 Mich. 635, 28 N.W. 749, 1886 Mich. LEXIS 952 (1886).

1967. MCLS § 565.161.

1968. MCLS § 565.162.

1969. Fidelity Trust Co. v. Saginaw Hotels Co., 259 Mich. 254, 242 N.W. 906 (1932).

1970. Barnard v. Paterson, 137 Mich. 633, 100 N.W. 893 (1904).

1971. Fidelity Trust Co. v. Saginaw Hotels Co., 259 Mich. 254, 242 N.W. 906 (1932).

1972. Discretion of court as to improvements

Where court was ordered by Supreme Court to make equitable determination, apart from any purported contract, of amount that property owners were required to pay for improvements made upon their lot, that determination rests within sound discretion of trial judge without regard to prior agreement.—Kirkendall v. Heckinger, 105 Mich. App. 621, 307 N.W.2d 699 (1981).

1973. Kirkendall v. Heckinger, 105 Mich. App. 621, 307 N.W.2d 699 (1981).

the person makes of his or her spouse's mortgage on the land, money spent by the person in improvements does not constitute a lien on the land.[1974]

When the terms of a mortgage on real property require the mortgagor to make periodic payments of sums allocated to an escrow account for the purpose of paying for improvements to the property, the mortgagee must furnish the mortgagor with a statement within 60 days of the close of the calendar year. The statement must show the beginning balance of the escrow fund, total receipts received by the fund during the calendar year, an itemized statement of all expenditures from the fund during the calendar year, and the balance in the fund at the end of the calendar year.[1975] This annual statement is not required, however, if the mortgagee gives the mortgagor a monthly statement containing the same information.[1976]

Condominium Fees. The mortgagee of a first mortgage of record or other purchaser of a condominium unit who obtains title to the condominium unit as a result of foreclosure of the first mortgage is not liable for the condominium assessments by the condominium association chargeable to the unit that become due prior to the person's acquisition of the title to the unit.[1977]

§ 799.   Waste

A mortgagee may secure an injunction to restrain the mortgagor from committing waste.

A mortgagee is entitled to have his or her mortgage security unimpaired by acts of the mortgagor. Therefore, the mortgagee may secure an injunction to restrain a mortgagor from committing waste.[1978]

Insofar as the mortgagee is concerned, waste has been held to be anything that tends to destroy the mortgage security.[1979] Thus, a mortgagee may maintain an equitable suit to enjoin the removal of timber that impairs the mortgage security.[1980] The nonpayment of taxes[1981] or insurance[1982] constitutes waste of the mortgage security.

In addition, in order to prevent waste of the property, the Revised Judicature Act of 1961 provides that a mortgagee or assignee of a mortgagee may obtain from the circuit court the appointment of a receiver to collect rents or profit from certain mortgaged properties whose mortgagor fails to pay taxes or insurance on the property.[1983] This remedy applies equally to a land contract mortgage.[1984]

1974. Darling v. Darling, 123 Mich. 307, 82 N.W. 48 (1900).

1975. MCLS § 565.161.

1976. MCLS § 565.162.

1977. MCLS § 559.158.

1978. Wilkinson v. Dunkley-Williams Co., 139 Mich. 621, 103 N.W. 170 (1905).

1979. Nusbaum v. Shapero, 249 Mich. 252, 228 N.W. 785 (1930).

1980. Collins v. Rea, 127 Mich. 273, 86 N.W. 811 (1901).

1981. Waste
Failure to pay taxes on mortgaged property, where income exceeded requirements for it, constituted "waste."—Nusbaum v. Shapero, 249 Mich. 252, 228 N.W. 785 (1930).

1982. Nusbaum v. Shapero, 249 Mich. 252, 228 N.W. 785 (1930).

1983. MCLS § 600.2927.

1984. MCLS § 565.359.

§ 800.   Powers and Duties of Trustee

The rights, powers, duties, and liabilities of a trustee are derived from, and measured by, the terms of the trust instrument.

The powers of a trustee in a deed of trust exist only in the terms creating the trust. Powers granted to the trustee in a deed of trust are not liberally construed. Their exercise must be consonant with the terms of the deed.[1985] Thus, the instrument must grant to the trustee authority to represent the bondholders.[1986] When in doubt as to the proper performance of his or her duties under the deed, or as to the manner of exercising the powers thereby conferred on him or her, it is the trustee's right and duty to apply to a court for its aid and direction.[1987] A court, however, will not interfere with a reasonable exercise of a discretionary power vested in a trustee by the terms of a trust mortgage.[1988]

As in the case of a trustee's rights and powers, the trustee in a trust deed must look to the terms of the instrument itself to determine his or her duties and liabilities.[1989] The trustee cannot use the subject of the trust, or the fiduciary relation to it, for the trustee's own personal benefit, advantage, or gain.[1990] However, the trustee cannot be held liable in damages if the trustee has not violated some duty or obligation, either express or implied, that he or she assumed in accepting the trust.[1991]

The statute[1992] relating to a trustee's acquisition, management, and disposition of property mortgaged to such trustee to secure bonds plainly contemplates that the subsequent acts of the trustee in maintaining, operating, and disposing of the property are for all the bondholders.[1993] In the absence of statutory authority, or some provision in the instrument which establishes the trust, nothing can be done by a majority of the bondholders, however large, that binds a minority without their

1985. Union Guardian Trust Co. v. Building Sec. Corp., 280 Mich. 144, 273 N.W. 424 (1937).

Sadow v. Losh, 38 Mich. App. 404, 196 N.W.2d 350 (1972).

1986. Sawyer Grant Land Co. v. McPherson, 19 F. Supp. 709 (D. Mich. 1935).

Implied powers

Where trust mortgage provided that trustee would do any and all things required of him by majority vote of noteholders but trustee had no duties which required him to sell land prior to natural expiration of equity of redemption, trustee had no implied power to sell land prior to expiration of equity of redemption.—Sadow v. Losh, 38 Mich. App. 404, 196 N.W.2d 350 (1972).

1987. Rudell v. Union Guardian Trust Co., 295 Mich. 157, 294 N.W. 132 (1940) (decree as res judicata).

1988. Union Guardian Trust Co. v. Stillman, 300 Mich. 27, 1 N.W.2d 439 (1942) (delay in commencing foreclosure suit).

1989. Union Guardian Trust Co. v. Stillman, 300 Mich. 27, 1 N.W.2d 439 (1942).

1990. Commissions on sale to trust

Corporate trustee, under trust deed providing for investment of funds derived from sale of bonds secured thereby in securities agreed on by trustees, was liable to mortgagor for secret profits from commissions received by it on its sale of municipal bonds to trust fund.—Calaveras Timber Co. v. Michigan Trust Co., 278 Mich. 445, 270 N.W. 743 (1936).

1991. Calaveras Timber Co. v. Michigan Trust Co., 278 Mich. 445, 270 N.W. 743 (1936).

1992. MCLS § 451.404.

1993. Straus v. Central Detroit Realty Co., 307 Mich. 669, 12 N.W.2d 402 (1943).

Settlement of foreclosure proceedings

Trustee under leasehold trust mortgage, after commencement of foreclosure proceedings on behalf of bondholders, would have had right to make settlement of it if it was for the best interest of the bondholders.—In re Detroit Metropolitan Corp., 289 Mich. 358, 286 N.W. 646 (1939).

consent.[1994]

A party dealing with a trustee under a recorded mortgage is charged with notice of the existence of the trust.[1995] If the trustee of a recorded trust mortgage exceeds the authority conferred by the mortgage in contracting with a party, the contract is invalid.[1996] It cannot be enforced in law or equity.[1997]

As a general rule, a trustee under a deed of trust is entitled to be reimbursed for all expenditures authorized or contemplated by the deed of trust. In a proper case, the trustee is entitled to compensation for his or her services in administering the trust.[1998]

§ 801.   Action on Debt

Generally, the creditor may sue on the debt or evidence of the debt without regard to the mortgage.

A mortgage creditor may sue on the debt or evidence of it as a substantive cause of action without regard to the mortgage.[1999] However, a suit independent of foreclosure proceedings was not authorized in chancery.[2000] By statute, a mortgage that does not contain an express covenant for payment, and no bond or other separate instrument to secure payment, gives the mortgagee only the remedy of taking the lands mentioned in the mortgage.[2001]

Similarly, the grantee of a deed absolute in form but intended as a mortgage cannot ordinarily maintain an action at law while retaining the title. The grantee's remedy is in equity to have the deed declared a mortgage, especially in a case where

---

1994. Bradley v. Tyson, 33 Mich. 337 (1876) (purchasing at foreclosure sale).

Waiver of payment

Under provisions of trust mortgage, holders of majority of outstanding bonds issued under the mortgage did not have right to direct trustee to waive payment of principal or interest on bonds for more than six months after they became due and payable.—Detroit Trust Co. v. Rivard, 315 Mich. 62, 23 N.W.2d 206 (1946).

1995. Sadow v. Losh, 38 Mich. App. 404, 196 N.W.2d 350 (1972).

1996. Sadow v. Losh, 38 Mich. App. 404, 196 N.W.2d 350 (1972).

1997. Sadow v. Losh, 38 Mich. App. 404, 196 N.W.2d 350 (1972).

1998. MCLS § 451.404.

Union Trust Co. v. Tonquish Temple Ass'n, 247 Mich. 36, 225 N.W. 572 (1929).

Retention of income property

A provision in a trust deed did not warrant trustee's retention of part of income of property as compensation for services.—Barras v. Youngs, 185 Mich. 496, 152 N.W. 219 (1915).

Summary testimony

In suit to foreclose trust mortgage on realty, summary testimony as to accounting of trustee, when not challenged by competent testimony, was sufficient to warrant approval of account.—Union Guardian Trust Co. v. Stillman, 300 Mich. 27, 1 N.W.2d 439 (1942).

1999. Action on bond

Holder of bond secured by mortgage was entitled to sue on bond at law notwithstanding provision therein vesting right of action on or under "this indenture" exclusively in trustee.—Mendelson v. Realty Mortg. Corp., 257 Mich. 442, 241 N.W. 154 (1932).

2000. Kollen v. Sooy, 172 Mich. 214, 137 N.W. 808 (1912).

Remedies available to holder of mortgage

Creditor holding real estate mortgage as security in event of nonpayment of debt had right to action at law on note, action at law on covenant in mortgage, foreclosure in equity with right to deficiency judgment in amount fixed by court's decree, and foreclosure by advertisement.—Guardian Depositors Corp. v. Powers, 296 Mich. 553, 296 N.W. 675 (1941).

2001. MCLS § 565.6.

there must be an accounting for rents and profits.[2002]

The pendency of foreclosure proceedings is no defense on the merits to an action at law for the debt.[2003] Thus, the statute[2004] providing in part that, while a bill to foreclose is pending and after decree, no proceedings may be had at law for the recovery of any part of the debt secured by the mortgage, unless the court hearing the foreclosure authorizes it, is intended merely to avoid unnecessary litigation and not to limit the remedy of the creditor. Accordingly, an action at law brought without the permission of the court hearing the foreclosure, being a mere irregularity, will not be restrained unless substantial rights are affected.[2005]

On the other hand, if the action for the debt results in a judgment for the money demanded in a foreclosure action, the foreclosure action may not be maintained unless the execution of the judgment is conclusively returned less than completely satisfied.[2006] Once the action for debt fails, the mortgagee may then foreclose the mortgage.[2007]

Furthermore, the court hearing a foreclosure of a trust mortgage or deed of trust may consolidate any actions for debt initiated by individual bondholders or

2002. Weise v. Anderson, 134 Mich. 502, 96 N.W. 575 (1903).

2003. Goodrich v. White, 39 Mich. 489 (1878).

2004. MCLS § 600.3105.

Action on deficiency decree does not require permission of court

Although leave of court was required by former statute before proceedings could be had for recovery of debts secured by mortgage or any part thereof, action upon a deficiency decree itself was a new and independent action and leave to begin such action was not required.—Union Guardian Trust Co. v. Rood, 308 Mich. 168, 13 N.W.2d 248 (1944).

2005. Steele v. Grove, 109 Mich. 647, 67 N.W. 963 (1896).

2006. MCLS § 600.3105.

Actions in separate states

Under Michigan statute precluding mortgage foreclosure proceedings on money judgment until execution on judgment has been returned unsatisfied, plaintiff mortgagee that obtained judgment in another state on note secured by properties in Michigan and other state, without stating amount of relief, could not obtain foreclosure in Michigan until court in other state determined amount of liability so as to permit defendant to satisfy debt and enable defendant to satisfy requirement for return of unsatisfied charges.—Southern Floridabanc, S.A. v. Feldman, 703 F. Supp. 627, 1989 U.S. Dist. LEXIS 652 (E.D. Mich. 1989).

Foreclosure

By its terms, MCLS § 600.3105 only prohibits a separate proceeding for recovery of a debt secured by a mortgage if a proceeding has already been initiated to recover the same debt secured by the same mortgage. Again, use of the word "the" before "debt" and "mortgage" limits a party holding a single debt secured by a single mortgage to the election of either judicial or statutory foreclosure by advertisement to prevent double recovery on the same debt.—Church & Church Inc. v. A-1 Carpentry, 281 Mich. App. 330, 766 N.W.2d 30, 2008 Mich. App. LEXIS 2033 (2008), affirmed in part and vacated in part on other grounds, affirmed on other grounds by, in part, 281 Mich. App. 330, 766 N.W.2d 30, 2008 Mich. App. LEXIS 2033 (2008).

Mortgagor protected from double recovery

Once a judicial foreclosure proceeding on the mortgage has begun, a subsequent action on the note is prohibited, absent court authorization, thereby protecting the mortgagor from double recovery.—Residential Funding Co., LLC v. Saurman, 2011 Mich. App. LEXIS 719 (Mich. Ct. App. Apr. 21, 2011).

2007. Note for improvements

Fact that plaintiff, who held assignment of land contract vendees' interest as security for promissory note given for improvements, had first attempted to collect note by proceeding against principal debtors, defendants' predecessors in interest, did not estop him from attempting to foreclose mortgage, his efforts to collect from principal debtors having failed.—Boraks v. Siegel, 366 Mich. 308, 115 N.W.2d 126 (1962).

holders of other securities secured by the mortgage with the foreclosure action.[2008]

2008. MCLS § 600.3105.

Chapter 28

ASSIGNMENT OF MORTGAGE OR DEBT

§ 811. In General

A mortgage is assignable. The necessary intention to assign may be implied in chancery

Library References

> Michigan Digest
> John G. Cameron, Jr., Michigan Real Estate Forms
> Midwest Transaction Guide
> Thompson on Real Property, Thomas Edition (David A. Thomas, ed.)
> Powell on Real Property® (Michael Allan Wolf, ed.)
> Real Estate Financing

Law Reviews

> Ryan E. Scharar, The Limits of Securitization: Why Bankruptcy Courts Should Substantively Consolidate Predatory Sub-Prime Mortgage Originators and their Special Purpose Entities, 2008 Mich. St. L. Rev. 913 (2008); Stephen R. Estey and Danielle Graceffa, Real Property, 54 Wayne L. Rev. 387 (2008); Michael A. Luberto, Real Property Law: Title Insurance for the General Practitioner: Some Insider Tips, 86 MI Bar Jnl. 28 (2007); Daniel J. Schairbaum, Annual Survey of Michigan Law, June 1, 2002 - May 31, 2003: Real Property, 50 Wayne L. Rev. 711 (2004); Byron D. Cooper, Researching Online Real Estate Records in Michigan, 80 Mich. B.J. 22 (2001).

In accordance with the modern rule respecting assignments of choses in action, a mortgage is assignable.[2009] Thus, a deed to land as security for a claim, and a land contract back to the debtor by the grantee, constitutes a mortgage that can be transferred as personal property by assignment.[2010]

A creditor who obtains no interest under the security instrument has nothing to assign to another creditor.[2011]

A nominal mortgagee who records the mortgage for the convenience of the real owner may refuse to assign it to the real owner until the expense of the recording is paid.[2012]

Validity. In general, an assignment procured by fraud or improper influence or which was the effect of mental incapacity may be set aside.[2013] However, the validity of an assignment of a mortgage is not impaired by a showing that the

---

2009. Holmes v. Holmes, 129 Mich. 412, 89 N.W. 47 (1902).

Legal or equitable assignment

The right of a mortgagee may be transferred either by a legal or an equitable assignment.— Densmore v. Savage, 110 Mich. 27, 67 N.W. 1103 (1896).

2010. Keller v. McConville, 175 Mich. 479, 141 N.W. 652 (1913).

2011. Gillam v. Barnes, 123 Mich. 119, 82 N.W. 38 (1900).

2012. Murphy v. Fleming, 69 Mich. 185, 36 N.W. 787 (1888).

2013. Terry v. Terry, 170 Mich. 330, 136 N.W. 448 (1912).

Frank v. Brown, 255 Mich. 415, 238 N.W. 237 (1931) (facts did not show fraud).

Cornell v. Crane, 113 Mich. 460, 71 N.W. 878 (1897) (representation as first mortgage).

Webster v. Bailey, 31 Mich. 36 (1875) (false representations honestly made).

Character of security

One may rescind a contract for the sale of mortgages on the ground of false representations regarding character of the security, though the purchaser acts only on suspicion regarding falsity of the representations, provided the purchaser can

assignor had a life interest only, so long as it does not diminish the bulk of the estate at the death of the life tenant.[2014]

A consumer who has the right to rescind a mortgage note under the federal Truth in Lending Act[2015] may rescind the note as against an assignee of the note.[2016]

Equitable assignments in general. In a proper case, the necessary intention to assign may be implied in chancery if there is a bequest of a mortgage.[2017] It may also be implied when there is a transaction amounting prima facie to a discharge of a mortgage, but that must be held an assignment in order to carry out the meaning of the parties and effect justice to all.[2018]

§ 812.   Requisites and Sufficiency of Assignment

Generally, an assignment of a mortgage should be in writing; however, a written assignment is not necessary in chancery.

The assignee of a mortgage is entitled to foreclose in chancery on proof of his or her purchase, without any written assignment.[2019] The assignment must be supported by a sufficient consideration to be valid between the parties.[2020]

A conveyance of all of one's right, title, and interest in land will pass the grantor's interest in a mortgage on the same land.[2021] A deed of property by an equitable mortgagee operates as an assignment of that mortgagee's security.[2022]

An assignment of a mortgage, without delivering the securities, does not transfer the securities, unless that is the intent of the parties.[2023]

---

subsequently prove that suspicions were well founded.—Simonds v. Cash, 136 Mich. 558, 99 N.W. 754 (1904).

Necessary showing of good faith

Law would not permit the assignment to stand where the assignee failed to explain the circumstances of the transaction and show its bona fides.—Snyder v. Snyder, 131 Mich. 658, 92 N.W. 353 (1902).

2014. Sutphen v. Ellis, 35 Mich. 446 (1877).

2015. 15 USCS § 1635.

2016. 15 USCS § 1641.

In re Estate of Burgin, 1998 Mich. App. LEXIS 2753 (Mich. Ct. App. Jan. 23, 1998) (defendant's right to rescission).

Franck v. Bedenfield, 197 Mich. App. 316, 494 N.W.2d 840 (1992) (that assignee is holder in due course is not defense).

2017. Densmore v. Savage, 110 Mich. 27, 67 N.W. 1103 (1896).

2018. New note and mortgage in absence of authority

That a new note and mortgage to take the place of an antecedent secured indebtedness of another

that was thereupon released are void for want of authority in the mortgagors, will not release mortgagors from payment of the debt, as chancery will treat the transaction as an assignment of the original debt and security.—Miller v. Childs, 120 Mich. 639, 79 N.W. 924 (1899).

2019. Pease v. Warren, 29 Mich. 9 (1874).

2020. Parks v. Sherman, 208 Mich. 697, 176 N.W. 583 (1920).

Weekly payments for life

The assignment of a mortgage in consideration of a specified weekly payment during the life of the mortgagee and his wife is based on a sufficient consideration where, if the mortgagee and his wife live to the age of expectancy as shown by the life tables, the assignee would pay all the mortgage is worth.—Parker v. Thomas, 126 Mich. 691, 86 N.W. 129 (1901).

2021. Niles v. Ransford, 1 Mich. 338 (1849).

2022. Maginn v. Cashin, 196 Mich. 221, 162 N.W. 1009 (1917).

2023. Fletcher v. Carpenter, 37 Mich. 412 (1877).

§ 813. —Notice or Record

An assignment of a mortgage may be recorded, but the record is not notice to the mortgagor so as to invalidate payment to the mortgagee.

A statute authorizes the recording of assignments of mortgages.[2024] Another statute makes the recording of all assignments of a mortgage a prerequisite to its foreclosure by advertisement.[2025] Under this latter statute, the assignments of mortgages that must be recorded before the mortgage can be foreclosed are those only that are voluntary. Transfers that result from the operation of law are not included.[2026]

An unrecorded assignment is ineffective against subsequent purchasers or assignees for value without notice.[2027]

On the other hand, although the recording of assignments of mortgages is authorized, the recording will not, in itself, "be deemed notice of such assignment to the mortgagor, his heirs or personal representatives, so as to invalidate any payments made by them, or either of them to the mortgagee."[2028]

If a mortgage secures a negotiable instrument, third persons may not be protected in their transactions with the record owner of the mortgage.[2029] The mortgagor may also have a defense against a transferee that he or she made payment to the original payee on the mortgage.[2030]

An assignee of a renewal mortgage securing nonnegotiable paper acquires no valid claim against the mortgagor of the original mortgage, where, without the latter's knowledge, the original mortgage is previously transferred to a third person in whose hands it is still outstanding.[2031]

Assignments of mortgages executed in other states are entitled to record only where the statutes relating to acknowledgment and so on are complied with.[2032]

§ 814. Transfer of Debt as Assignment of Mortgage

In general, anything that transfers the debt transfers the mortgage with it.

A mortgage being a mere security for the debt or liability secured by it, the debt or liability secured is the principal and the mortgage but an incident or

---

2024. MCLS § 565.25.

2025. MCLS § 600.3204.

2026. Miller v. Clark, 56 Mich. 337, 23 N.W. 35 (1885).

2027. Priority, *see, supra*, Chapter 26. MCLS §§ 565.29, 565.34, 565.35.

2028. MCLS § 565.33.

Goodale v. Patterson, 51 Mich. 532, 16 N.W. 890 (1883).

2029. Babcock v. Young, 117 Mich. 155, 75 N.W. 302 (1898).

Wilson v. Campbell, 110 Mich. 580, 68 N.W. 278 (1896).

2030. MCLS § 440.3305.

2031. Brooke v. Struthers, 110 Mich. 562, 68 N.W. 272 (1896).

2032. Gray v. Waldron, 101 Mich. 612, 60 N.W. 288 (1894).

Dohm v. Haskin, 88 Mich. 144, 50 N.W. 108 (1891).

accessory. Anything that transfers the debt transfers the mortgage with it.[2033] The transfer occurs even without the assignee's foreknowledge of the existence of the mortgage.[2034] The transfer of a note operates as an equitable assignment of the mortgage or deed of trust given to secure it.[2035]

Accordingly, the assignment of the mortgage by the mortgagee to one person after the mortgagee endorses the mortgage note to another is a nullity.[2036] A person who purchases a note secured by a mortgage and takes no legal transfer by endorsement of a note or assignment of the mortgage acquires only an equitable interest.[2037] But an equitable assignee of a debt secured by a mortgage is entitled to have the mortgage follow the debt.[2038] The assignee of a debt, secured by a mortgage, can enforce the payment of the debt out of the mortgaged estate even though the assignee has no assignment of the mortgage.[2039]

While a mortgage instrument is not a negotiable instrument,[2040] a note secured by a mortgage that qualifies as a negotiable instrument[2041] is transferable in accordance with the Uniform Commercial Code—Negotiable Instruments.[2042] When the note is transferred, the mortgage goes with it.[2043]

The assignee of a mortgage note subject to the Uniform Commercial Code—Negotiable Instruments who is a holder in due course[2044] has no duty to inquire into the validity of the underlying mortgage so long as the note is valid on

2033. Ginsberg v. Capitol City Wrecking Co., 300 Mich. 712, 2 N.W.2d 892, 1942 Mich. LEXIS 669 (1942).

Aiton v. Slater, 298 Mich. 469, 299 N.W. 149 (1941).

Atwood v. Schlee, 269 Mich. 322, 257 N.W. 712 (1934).

Loveridge v. Shurtz, 111 Mich. 618, 70 N.W. 132 (1897).

2034. Atwood v. Schlee, 269 Mich. 322, 257 N.W. 712 (1934).

2035. Jones v. Titus, 208 Mich. 392, 175 N.W. 257 (1919).

Martin v. McReynolds, 6 Mich. 70 (1858).

2036. McKeighan v. Citizens Commercial & Sav. Bank, 302 Mich. 666, 5 N.W.2d 524 (1942).

Atwood v. Schlee, 269 Mich. 322, 257 N.W. 712 (1934).

2037. Nelson v. Ferris, 30 Mich. 497 (1874).

2038. Briggs v. Hannowald, 35 Mich. 474 (1877).

2039. Cooper v. Ulmann, Walk. Ch. 251 (Mich. 1843).

2040. Fair v. Moody, 2008 Mich. App. LEXIS 2542 (Mich. Ct. App. Dec. 23, 2008).

Bibler v. Arcata Invs. 2, 2005 Mich. App. LEXIS 3025, 58 U.C.C. Rep. Serv. 2d (CBC) 244 (Mich. Ct. App. 2005).

Mox v. Jordan, 186 Mich. App. 42, 463 N.W.2d 114 (1990).

2041. M.L.P.2d Negotiable Instruments. MCLS § 440.3104.

2042. M.L.P.2d Negotiable Instruments. MCLS § 440.3203.

2043. Mox v. Jordan, 186 Mich. App. 42, 463 N.W.2d 114 (1990).

2044. M.L.P.2d Negotiable Instruments. MCLS § 440.3302.

Grand Pac. Fin. Corp. v. Capital, 2011 Mich. App. LEXIS 1226 (Mich. Ct. App. June 30, 2011).

Fair v. Moody, 2008 Mich. App. LEXIS 2542 (Mich. Ct. App. Dec. 23, 2008).

Metro Car Co. v. Hemker, 2005 Mich. App. LEXIS 3299 (Mich. Ct. App. Dec. 29, 2005).

Mox v. Jordan, 186 Mich. App. 42, 463 N.W.2d 114 (1990).

. . . And Federal Regulation For All: Federally Regulating the Mortgage Banking Industry, 2006 Mich. St. L. Rev. 477 (2006).

Holder in due course

Assignees who took assignment of three mortgages were holders in due course, because transaction was not bulk transfer that would take it out of ordinary course of business, and compensation of release of personal loans was adequate under MCLS § 440.3304.—Barbour v. Handlos Real Estate & Bldg. Corp., 152 Mich. App. 174, 393 N.W.2d 581 (1986).

its face.[2045] The existence of other mortgages on the mortgaged premises under the assignment does not affect the status of the assignee as holder in due course of the assigned mortgage.[2046]

A note may put its holder on notice of the existence of a collateral agreement, but that fact does not ordinarily put the holder on inquiry or constructive notice of the contents of or defenses to the collateral agreement. Even the receipt of a mortgage does not constitute actual notice of its payment terms in a case in which they are different from those on the note secured by the mortgage.[2047]

Transfer of part of debt or instrument secured. The assignment of a part of a debt secured by a mortgage, or of one of several notes secured by a mortgage, carries with it a proportional interest in the mortgage and the security that it affords, unless it is otherwise agreed between the parties, although there is no formal assignment of the mortgage or any part of it.[2048]

The Uniform Commercial Code—Negotiable Instruments does not permit the transfer of part of an individual negotiable instrument to which the code applies.[2049]

§ 815.   Effect of Transfer of Mortgage Without Debt

A mortgage may not be transferred apart from the debt it secures.

A mortgage may not be transferred apart from the debt it secures, and an attempt to do so is a mere nullity.[2050]

Thus, after a debt secured by a mortgage is discharged, an assignment of the

---

2045. M.L.P.2d Negotiable Instruments.

Rib Roof Metal Sys. v. Nat'l Storage Ctrs. of Redford, Inc., 2009 U.S. Dist. LEXIS 29586 (E.D. Mich. Apr. 8, 2009) (instrument valid).

Fair v. Moody, 2008 Mich. App. LEXIS 2542 (Mich. Ct. App. Dec. 23, 2008) (purchaser with full knowledge of forgery claims).

Johnson-Wilson v. Styburski, 2000 Mich. App. LEXIS 1271 (Mich. Ct. App. June 27, 2000) (defenses do not apply to bona fide purchasers).

Mox v. Jordan, 186 Mich. App. 42, 463 N.W.2d 114 (1990) (assignee had no actual or constructive knowledge of mortgagee's fraud in relation to mortgage assigned).

Barbour v. Handlos Real Estate & Bldg. Corp., 152 Mich. App. 174, 393 N.W.2d 581 (1986) (assignees had no constructive notice of lack of builder's license by mortgagee-contractor).

2046. Mox v. Jordan, 186 Mich. App. 42, 463 N.W.2d 114 (1990).

2047. M.L.P.2d Negotiable Instruments.

Barbour v. Handlos Real Estate & Bldg. Corp., 152 Mich. App. 174, 393 N.W.2d 581 (1986) (assignees had no constructive notice of lack of builder's license by mortgagee-contractor).

Determination of holder in due course

A holder in due course is defined as a holder who takes a negotiable instrument "for value; . . . in good faith; and . . . without notice . . . of any defense against or claim to it on the part of any person." It is apparent that a holder in due course is essentially the equivalent of a good faith purchaser for value. Defendant accepted the paychecks in good faith and without knowledge of the fraud. As a result, a determination of whether Defendant was a holder in due course hinges on the issue of value.—In re Peet Packing Co., 233 B.R. 387, 1999 Bankr. LEXIS 725, 34 Bankr. Ct. Dec. (LRP) 287, 42 Collier Bankr. Cas. 2d (MB) 399 (Bankr. E.D. Mich. 1999).

2048. Equitable Trust Co. v. Milton Realty Co., 263 Mich. 673, 249 N.W. 30 (1933).

Cooper v. Ulmann, Walk. Ch. 251 (Mich. 1843).

2049. M.L.P.2d Negotiable Instruments.

MCLS § 440.3203.

2050. Ginsberg v. Capitol City Wrecking Co., 300 Mich. 712, 2 N.W.2d 892, 1942 Mich. LEXIS 669 (1942).

mortgage without the debt is a mere nullity.[2051] Similarly, an assignment of a mortgage by the mortgagee to one person after transferring the mortgage note to another is a nullity.[2052]

§ 816.   Operation and Effect

A valid assignment of a mortgage generally transfers all rights and interests of the assignor.

A valid assignment of a mortgage generally transfers all rights and interests of the assignor.[2053] Thus, if the holder of a mortgage instrument has no lien upon the property, the holder can assign none.[2054]

On the other hand, in the absence of statute or a special agreement between the parties, the assignee of a mortgage cannot pay the taxes or incur expenses to clear the land covered by the mortgage from tax liens that have accrued prior to the execution of the assignment, and add the amounts so paid to the amount due under the mortgage, and make them a lien on the land.[2055]

Where a party purchases a mortgage with knowledge that the mortgagee in selling it is acting as the agent of the mortgagors, the purchaser in effect loans to the mortgagors, on the mortgage, the amount actually paid for it.[2056]

§ 817.   —Merger

Generally, in the absence of an intention to the contrary, a transfer of the mortgage or mortgage debt to the owner or other person having an interest may result in a merger of the two estates.

Generally, in the absence of an intention to the contrary, a transfer of the mortgage or mortgage debt to the owner or other person having an interest in the mortgaged premises may result in a merger of the two estates and preclude the

2051. Payment in full of mortgage note

Where it was established that note secured by mortgage was paid in full by debtors, subsequent assignment of note and mortgage was a nullity precluding recovery by assignee on it.—Plasger v. Leonard, 312 Mich. 561, 20 N.W.2d 296 (1945).

2052. McKeighan v. Citizens Commercial & Sav. Bank, 302 Mich. 666, 5 N.W.2d 524 (1942) (conveyance by quitclaim deed).

2053. Hilton v. Woodman's Estate, 124 Mich. 326, 82 N.W. 1056 (1900).

Briggs v. Hannowald, 35 Mich. 474 (1877).

Pease v. Warren, 29 Mich. 9 (1874).

Collateral rights

An assignment of a mortgage that appoints the assignee attorney, with full authority in assignor's name or otherwise to have, use, and take all lawful ways and means for the recovery of the money due on it, transfers to assignee all collateral rights of the assignor, including a claim against the latter's assignor for breach of the covenant that he had lawful authority to transfer.—Byles v. Lawrence, 35 Mich. 458 (1877).

Holder of remainder interest in mortgage

A purchaser of the interests of holders of remainder in a mortgage executed to them jointly with the owner of the life estate is entitled to no other or greater right, legal or equitable, than they possessed, which was to receive the principal after the termination of the life estate.—Horton v. Howard, 95 Mich. 134, 54 N.W. 636 (1893).

2054. Ginsberg v. Capitol City Wrecking Co., 300 Mich. 712, 2 N.W.2d 892, 1942 Mich. LEXIS 669 (1942).

2055. Macomb v. Prentis, 78 Mich. 255, 44 N.W. 324 (1889).

2056. Smithers v. Heather, 25 Mich. 447 (1872).

mortgage from being kept alive as a subsisting lien,[2057] unless that owner or other person is under no obligation to pay the debt.[2058] Thus, where mortgaged premises are sold, and the grantee assumes all indebtedness, an assignment of the mortgage to the grantee extinguishes the debt.[2059] A person generally cannot remain mortgagee of lands after acquiring the fee in the absence of any showing that the mortgage is to be kept alive to protect the rights under it against the claims of others.[2060] The grantee cannot, by assigning the mortgage to a third person, give him- or herself a right to foreclose.[2061]

On the other hand, the owner of lands who treats a mortgage on the lands that has been assigned to the owner as a valid instrument, and transfers it as such, is estopped from insisting, as against the assignee or any one claiming under the owner, that in the owner's hands, it had merged and disappeared in the fee.[2062]

§ 818.　—Assignment as Security

The assignment of a mortgage as collateral security for a debt amounts to a mortgage of a mortgage, and the relation between the parties becomes that of pledgor and pledgee.

Where a mortgage is assigned as collateral security for a debt, it amounts to a mortgage of a mortgage.[2063] The relation between the parties becomes that of pledgor and pledgee.[2064] Where a mortgage is transferred for much less than its real value, slight circumstances will be sufficient to determine the transaction to be a transfer as collateral security, and not a sale.[2065]

The Uniform Commercial Code—Secured Transactions applies to the assignment of a security interest in a mortgage, except a mortgage on a land contract.[2066] The assignment becomes enforceable upon the payment of value in exchange for a delivered security agreement transferring the interest. As soon as a security interest in a mortgage note secured by a lien on real property is enforceable, it gives an enforceable security interest in the mortgage on the real property.[2067]

2057. Vollmer v. Coenis, 309 Mich. 319, 15 N.W.2d 654 (1944).

First Nat'l Bank v. Ramm, 256 Mich. 573, 240 N.W. 32 (1932).

Olcott v. Crittenden, 68 Mich. 230, 36 N.W. 41 (1888).

Byles v. Kellogg, 67 Mich. 318, 34 N.W. 671 (1887).

2058. Scribner v. Malinowski, 148 Mich. 446, 111 N.W. 1032 (1907).

2059. Winans v. Wilkie, 41 Mich. 264, 1 N.W. 1049 (1879).

Conveyance to assignee of mortgage

The conveyance of the equity of redemption to the assignee of a mortgage creates a merger so as to satisfy the mortgage.—Snyder v. Snyder, 6 Mich. 470 (1859).

2060. Vollmer v. Coenis, 309 Mich. 319, 15 N.W.2d 654 (1944).

Jackson v. Evans, 44 Mich. 510, 7 N.W. 79 (1880).

2061. Winans v. Wilkie, 41 Mich. 264, 1 N.W. 1049 (1879).

2062. Powell v. Smith, 30 Mich. 451 (1874).

See, also, Dolese v. Bellows-Claude Neon Co., 261 Mich. 57, 245 N.W. 569 (1932).

2063. Graydon v. Church, 7 Mich. 36 (1859).

2064. Frey v. Farmers' & Mechanics' Bank, 273 Mich. 284, 262 N.W. 911 (1935).

2065. McKinney v. Miller, 19 Mich. 142 (1869).

2066. M.L.P.2d Personal Property, Chapter 3, Secured Transactions.

MCLS § 440.9109.

2067. M.L.P.2d Personal Property, Chapter 3, Secured Transactions.

A mortgagor of a mortgage may at any time require a retransfer upon satisfying the secured debt.[2068]

Generally, when a pledgee holding as collateral security a note secured by a mortgage forecloses the mortgage under a power of sale granted therein, or by a suit of foreclosure to which the pledgor is not made a party, without authority to purchase being expressly granted, the pledgee has converted the secured property. But the pledgor waives any claim of conversion by subsequently entering into a new security agreement with the pledgee secured by the pledgee's interest in the property derived from its purchase at foreclosure.[2069]

§ 819. Priorities

Generally, the assignee of a mortgage takes any priority of lien the assignor may have had by virtue of the mortgage assigned.

An unrecorded assignment of a mortgage is ineffective as to subsequent purchasers or assignees for value without notice.[2070] The same applies to an unperfected assignment of a security interest in a mortgage note secured by a mortgage under the Uniform Commercial Code—Secured Transactions.[2071]

A person who purchases mortgaged property is chargeable with notice that the mortgage is a lien in the hands of any person to whom it might legally have been transferred, and that such transfer need not be recorded to be valid.[2072] Thus, the purchaser of a mortgage is bound by such notice as the registry afforded of another mortgage of the same date, but subsequently recorded, of which the vendor had actual knowledge.[2073] Where both the senior and junior mortgages are of record when the junior mortgage is assigned, the fact that the junior mortgage is recorded first was immaterial, if the record shows that the senior mortgage is prior in time, and the junior mortgagee knows of its existence.[2074] Where a purchase-money mortgage is executed and acknowledged on the day the assignee's mortgage is acknowledged, and it covers the same property, the assignee is put upon inquiry as to the character of the purchase-money mortgage and has no greater rights than the assignor.[2075]

By acquiring a perfected security interest in a mortgage note under the Uniform Commercial Code—Secured Transactions,[2076] the secured party acquires a security interest in the mortgage that is senior to the rights of a person who becomes

MCLS § 440.9203.

2068. MCLS §§ 440.9209; MCLS §§ 440.9513.

Accord Cooper v. Smith, 75 Mich. 247, 42 N.W. 815 (1889).

2069. Crowley v. Atkinson's Estate, 297 Mich. 15, 296 N.W. 864 (1941).

2070. MCLS §§ 565.29, 565.34, 565.35.

2071. MCLS § 440.9317.

2072. Babcock v. Young, 117 Mich. 155, 75 N.W. 302 (1898).

2073. Van Aken v. Gleason, 34 Mich. 477 (1876).

2074. Matosh v. Metropolitan Trust Co., 262 Mich. 201, 247 N.W. 156 (1933).

2075. Fecteau v. Fries, 253 Mich. 51, 234 N.W. 113 (1931).

2076. M.L.P.2d Personal Property, Chapter 3, Secured Transactions.

MCLS § 440.9308.

a lien creditor of the mortgagee.[2077] Perfected security interests on the same mortgage generally receive priority according to time of perfection.[2078] Perfection of an assignment securing an interest in a mortgage note occurs upon the completion of the payment of consideration for the assignment and delivery of the assignment agreement,[2079] as well as the filing of a financing statement.[2080] The perfection of the assignment perfects a security interest in the mortgage instrument.[2081]

An assignment that gives an interest in fixtures on the property may also require a fixture filing to perfect the interest.[2082]

An assignment of a mortgage must be recorded in order for the assignee to foreclose the mortgage by advertisement.[2083] An assignee of an assignment of a security interest in a mortgage may record a copy of the security agreement and an affidavit alleging default with the register of deeds in whose office the mortgage is recorded, in order to institute foreclosure by advertisement.[2084]

The assignee of a refinancing mortgage securing nonnegotiable paper cannot claim any right under the recording laws superior to the holder of the original mortgage by reason of the failure of the latter to record his or her assignment, at least where the sole consideration for the transfer of the renewal mortgage is the satisfaction of a preexisting debt, because that fact does not entitle the assignee to be regarded as a bona fide purchaser for value.[2085] Where a mortgage is transferred by the mortgagee, though no assignment has been placed on record, the purchaser of a subsequent mortgage on the property, although buying it from the mortgagee in the original mortgage, is charged by the record with notice of the prior mortgage and to take subject to it, at least where the purchaser is not a bona fide purchaser for value.[2086]

Where a mortgagee, after assigning a mortgage and secured notes, forges a like mortgage and notes, and assigns them, the party taking the forged assignment in good faith acquires no right as against the assignee of the genuine instrument, although the assignment of the genuine mortgage is not recorded until after the

2077. M.L.P.2d Personal Property, Chapter 3, Secured Transactions.

MCLS § 440.9317.

2078. M.L.P.2d Personal Property, Chapter 3, Secured Transactions.

MCLS § 440.9322.

2079. M.L.P.2d Personal Property, Chapter 3, Secured Transactions.

MCLS §§ 440.9203, 440.9308.

2080. M.L.P.2d Personal Property, Chapter 3, Secured Transactions.

MCLS § 440.9310.

2081. M.L.P.2d Personal Property, Chapter 3, Secured Transactions.

MCLS § 440.9308.

2082. Fixtures, *see, supra*, Chapter 3.

MCLS § 440.9334.

2083. Rose v. Fed. Home Loan Mortg. Corp., 2010 U.S. Dist. LEXIS 98955 (W.D. Mich. Sept. 21, 2010).

Arnold v. DMR Fin. Servs., 448 Mich. 671, 532 N.W.2d 852 (1995).

Feldman v. Equitable Trust Co., 278 Mich. 619, 270 N.W. 809 (1937).

Davenport v. HSBC Bank USA, 275 Mich. App. 344, 739 N.W.2d 383, 2007 Mich. App. LEXIS 1078 (2007).

2084. MCLS § 440.9607.

2085. Brooke v. Struthers, 110 Mich. 562, 68 N.W. 272 (1896).

2086. Wilson v. Campbell, 110 Mich. 580, 68 N.W. 278 (1896).

assignment of the forged instruments.[2087]

§ 820.   Rights and Liabilities of Parties

The assignee of a mortgage obtains no greater rights than the assignor possessed. With certain exceptions, the general rule is that the assignee takes the mortgage subject to all equities and defenses between the original parties that arose out of the mortgage transaction prior to the assignment.

Generally, the assignee of a mortgage can obtain no greater rights by the assignment of the mortgage than are possessed by the mortgagee him- or herself.[2088] The fact that the assignee is a remote one in the chain of title, rather than a purchaser from the original mortgagee, does not alter or affect the assignee's rights.[2089]

Except in a case where the mortgage debt is evidenced by a negotiable instrument,[2090] and except insofar as the rule may be changed where the assignee is a bona fide purchaser, the general rule is that the assignee of a mortgage takes it subject to all equities and defenses between the original parties that arose out of the mortgage transaction prior to the assignment.[2091] No purchaser can safely rely on the inquiry made of his or her assignor alone, but if an inquiry becomes necessary, resort must usually be had to the debtor also.[2092] On the other hand, equities and defenses between the original parties arising after the assignment do not affect the rights of an assignee of the mortgage.[2093]

Where the assignee of a mortgage has actual notice of an equity or defense that was available against his or her assignor, the assignee may not claim immunity from the equity or defense under the doctrine of bona fide purchase.[2094] The same is generally true where the assignee has constructive notice from the public

2087. Lee v. Kellogg, 108 Mich. 535, 66 N.W. 380 (1896).

2088. Plasger v. Leonard, 312 Mich. 561, 20 N.W.2d 296 (1945).

Fecteau v. Fries, 253 Mich. 51, 234 N.W. 113 (1931).

2089. Ginsberg v. Capitol City Wrecking Co., 300 Mich. 712, 2 N.W.2d 892, 1942 Mich. LEXIS 669 (1942).

2090. Dutton v. Ives, 5 Mich. 515 (1858).

2091. Brooke v. Struthers, 110 Mich. 562, 68 N.W. 272 (1896).

Walker v. Thompson, 108 Mich. 686, 66 N.W. 584 (1896).

Goodale v. Patterson, 51 Mich. 532, 16 N.W. 890 (1883).

Humphrey v. Beckwith, 48 Mich. 151, 12 N.W. 28 (1882).

Bankers' Trust Co. v. Weber, 244 Mich. 697, 222 N.W. 81 (1928) (misrepresentation).

Cooley v. Harris, 92 Mich. 126, 52 N.W. 997 (1892) (prior mortgages).

Terry v. Tuttle, 24 Mich. 206 (1872) (assignee of mortgage given to secure a nonnegotiable bond is chargeable with notice of all defenses to the mortgage while in the hands of the mortgagee).

2092. Cooper v. Smith, 75 Mich. 247, 42 N.W. 815 (1889).

2093. Manning v. Rosenfield, 239 Mich. 459, 214 N.W. 424 (1927) (partial failure of consideration).

2094. Gottesman v. Rheinfrank, 303 Mich. 153, 5 N.W.2d 701 (1942).

Terzian v. Wadham, 236 Mich. 164, 210 N.W. 215 (1926).

Albion State Bank v. Knickerbocker, 125 Mich. 311, 84 N.W. 311 (1900).

Anderson v. Northern Nat'l Bank, 98 Mich. 543, 57 N.W. 808 (1894).

Knowledge of release

Deed to mortgagee of part of property mortgaged released such parcel from mortgage against assignee of mortgage knowing of release.—Cen-

records.[2095] The holder of a mortgage assigned to him or her by a mortgagee, as collateral security for a prior debt of the latter, is not a bona fide holder.[2096] A broker who makes fraudulent representations in negotiating an exchange of property cannot be an innocent purchaser of a mortgage given by the defrauded parties as a part of the transaction.[2097]

The common law rule that a bona fide purchaser in due course of a negotiable instrument takes the mortgage securing it free from all equities and defenses that the mortgagor may have against the mortgage[2098] is limited by an exception in the Uniform Commercial Code—Negotiable Instruments for the mortgagor's claims concerning the validity of the underlying mortgage.[2099] However, the mortgagor may join the mortgagee or other person to the action in order to have other claims heard.[2100] An assignee of a mortgage given to secure the payment of a negotiable note is entitled to the same protection that he or she would have as an assignee of the note without the mortgage.[2101] On the other hand, a party cannot execute a negotiable note and a mortgage collateral to it, and make the security good in the hands of a purchaser of the negotiable paper before due, when the mortgagor had no title at the time in the land, and an examination of the record would have disclosed that fact.[2102]

The plain meaning of a covenant, in an assignment of a mortgage, that the assignor has a good right and lawful authority to grant, bargain, and sell the same, gives the assignor the authority to convey it as a valid existing lien on the land according to its terms. That covenant is broken where the validity and force of the mortgage at the time of the sale was destroyed or impaired by a previous release secretly given of much of the security. The good faith of the assignor in making the assignment is not a defense.[2103]

If an assignor covenants that a certain sum is due on a mortgage that the assignor sells, but the mortgage debt was in fact fully paid at the time of the assignment, the assignee has two options. The assignee may sue upon the warranty, in which action the assignee can recover actual damages measured by the real value of the security purchased if nothing has been paid on it. Or the assignee can sue to recover back the money paid on the ground of a total failure of consideration.[2104]

A mortgagee who assigns a mortgage by way of collateral security is liable for

tral Land & Inv. Co. v. Stevenson, 250 Mich. 382, 230 N.W. 150 (1930).

2095. Schanhite v. Plymouth United Sav. Bank, 277 Mich. 33, 268 N.W. 801 (1936) (assignment as security).

Researching online real estate records in Michigan, 80 Mich. B.J. 22 (2001).

2096. Waterbury v. Andrews, 67 Mich. 281, 34 N.W. 575 (1887).

2097. Vanek v. Soumar, 218 Mich. 282, 187 N.W. 396 (1922).

2098. Bronson v. Stetson, 252 Mich. 6, 232 N.W. 741 (1930).

Newall v. Bridges, 251 Mich. 384, 232 N.W. 245 (1930).

Barnum v. Phenix, 60 Mich. 388, 27 N.W. 577 (1886).

2099. M.L.P.2d Negotiable Instruments.

MCLS § 440.3305.

2100. M.L.P.2d Negotiable Instruments.

MCLS § 440.3305.

2101. Helmer v. Krolick, 36 Mich. 371 (1877).

2102. Lockwood v. Noble, 113 Mich. 418, 71 N.W. 856 (1897).

2103. Byles v. Lawrence, 35 Mich. 458 (1877).

2104. Eaton v. Knowles, 61 Mich. 625, 28 N.W. 740 (1886).

any deficiency as obligor on his or her own debt to the assignee.[2105] The assignee generally may not add to the amount due under the mortgage expenses that the assignee incurs in clearing the mortgaged land from tax liens that accrued prior to the execution of the assignment.[2106]

In the case of an assignment as collateral security, the assignee has the duty to use proper diligence and care in the management of the security, in order that the assignor may have the benefit of its avails.[2107]

§ 821. —Payment of Debt.

The recording of an assignment does not give notice to the mortgagor with respect to payment on the debt. The person entitled to payment on an assigned mortgage securing negotiable instruments is usually the holder in due course alone.

A statute provides that the recording of an assignment of the mortgage does not, in itself, notify the mortgagor, or the mortgagor's heirs or personal representatives, of such assignment so as to invalidate any payment that they may make the mortgagee.[2108] Thus, the mortgagor is not required to search the records before making payment to one prima facie entitled to receive it.[2109] However, notwithstanding the fact that a mortgagor has no actual knowledge of the transfer of the mortgage, payment of the mortgage will not be good when made to a person not in possession of the securities, unless there is an agency in fact to receive the payment, or such facts as estop the assignee from denying the authority of such person to receive the payment.[2110] Where the assignee of a mortgage fails to give notice of the assignment, and so acts as to authorize the mortgagor and his or her grantees to believe that the assignor is the owner of the mortgage, and they deal with the assignor on that basis, the assignee is estopped from denying the right or authority of the assignor whether the money for which the mortgage was originally given was the assignor's or not.[2111]

2105. Wilcox v. Allen, 36 Mich. 160 (1877).

2106. Macomb v. Prentis, 78 Mich. 255, 44 N.W. 324 (1889).

2107. Right may be waived

Where the assignee of a real estate mortgage, assigned by the mortgagees as security, was made a party to condemnation proceedings under former condemnation procedures against mortgaged realty, the assignee, as pledgee of the mortgage, had the duty to protect the rights of the mortgagees and to notify them of pending proceedings, but the knowledge of the mortgagees of the pendency of the proceedings and their action in permitting the share received by the assignee in proceedings to be applied on their debts to the assignee and in executing a note for the balance due was a waiver of any failure of the assignee to protect their rights in the condemnation proceedings.—Frey v. Farmers' & Mechanics' Bank, 273 Mich. 284, 262 N.W. 911 (1935).

2108. MCLS § 565.33.

Recording does not prove lack of agency

The recording of an assignment of a mortgage does not prove that assignee of a mortgage did not give actual or apparent authority to assignor to receive payments on mortgage, including payment in full.—Meretta v. Peach, 195 Mich. App. 695, 491 N.W.2d 278 (1992).

2109. Williams v. Keyes, 90 Mich. 290, 51 N.W. 520 (1892).

2110. Bromley v. Lathrop, 105 Mich. 492, 63 N.W. 510 (1895).

Joy v. Vance, 104 Mich. 97, 62 N.W. 140 (1895).

Meretta v. Peach, 195 Mich. App. 695, 491 N.W.2d 278 (1992).

2111. McCabe v. Farnsworth, 27 Mich. 52 (1873).

The person entitled to payment on an assigned mortgage securing negotiable instruments is usually the holder in due course alone.[2112] More generally, any person with the right to enforce the negotiable instrument is entitled to payment, even if the mortgagor knows that another person has an unadjudicated claim to the instrument.[2113]

The mortgagor of a mortgage assigned for securing an interest in the mortgagee's interest in the mortgage is generally entitled to pay the mortgagor until the mortgagee receives adequate notification authenticated by either party to the assignment informing the mortgagor of the assignment and the need to pay the assignee. Upon receiving that notification, the mortgagor may only pay the assignee of the security interest.[2114]

A person who holds an assignment of a mortgage as collateral security has authority to receive payment and discharge it, and especially so when the assignment empowers that person to do so.[2115]

Agency is question of fact

Whether an assignee of a mortgage gave actual or apparent authority to assignor to receive payments on mortgage, including payment in full, is a question of fact for the factfinder to determine, especially given claims that servicing companies customarily accept even payment in full from mortgagors, so long as there is any evidence to support the claim of agency, and because plaintiff had educed testimony to that effect, summary judgment was improper.—Meretta v. Peach, 195 Mich. App. 695, 491 N.W.2d 278 (1992).

2112. Brooke v. Struthers, 110 Mich. 562, 68 N.W. 272 (1896) (a mortgagor in a mortgage securing negotiable paper is not justified in dealing with the mortgagee upon the assumption that he is still the owner of the securities, unless he produces them).

Rule stated

The maker of negotiable paper secured by mortgage is justified in paying only to the holder, and cannot assume that the paper has not been transferred; as to the mortgagor, a transferee is not required to place an assignment of the mortgage on record.—Wilson v. Campbell, 110 Mich. 580, 68 N.W. 278 (1896).

2113. M.L.P.2d Negotiable Instruments. MCLS § 440.3602.

2114. M.L.P.2d Personal Property. MCLS § 440.9406.

2115. Lowry v. Bennett, 119 Mich. 301, 77 N.W. 935 (1899).

Chapter 29

TRANSFER OF MORTGAGED PROPERTY OR OF EQUITY OF REDEMPTION

§ 831. In General

The mortgagor has the right to transfer the mortgaged premises subject to the lien of the mortgage. A party who has purchased lands, and as a part of the price, has covenanted to pay a mortgage given by the grantor, cannot avoid that liability by showing that the mortgage is not enforceable against the grantor.

Library References

Michigan Digest
John G. Cameron, Jr., Michigan Real Estate Forms
Midwest Transaction Guide
Thompson on Real Property, Thomas Edition (David A. Thomas, ed.)
Powell on Real Property® (Michael Allan Wolf, ed.)
Real Estate Financing

Law Reviews

Bruce D. Fisher, A Simple Explanation of Some Legal And Economic Aspects Of The Financial Meltdowns of Banks, 89 MI Bar Jnl. 38 (2010); Joel M. Ngugi, Re-Examining The Role Of Private Property In Market Democracies: Problematic Ideological Issues Raised By Land Registration, 25 Mich. J. Int'l L. 467 (2004).

An interest in mortgaged premises that the mortgagor grants without the mortgagee's consent is taken subject to the mortgage lien.[2116] While illegal restraints on the alienation of real property that are contained in a mortgage are generally not enforceable,[2117] the statute authorizing assignments of rents and profits under a trust mortgage or deed[2118] and the statute precluding the mortgagee from recovering possession of the mortgaged premises until after foreclosure and expiration of the equity of redemption[2119] do not constitute illegal restraints on alienation, and are enforceable.[2120] Similarly, due-on-sale clauses in combination with prepayment clauses, even if they substantially restrain alienation of the property,[2121] are enforceable mortgage covenants that can require the payment of the mortgage in full upon the sale of the property.[2122]

2116. Easement

Property owners did not acquire a perpetual and unobstructed easement over adjoining land by virtue of grant by original owner thereof, where grant was made subsequent to owner's execution of a mortgage and without the mortgagee's consent, and where mortgage was foreclosed, placing in mortgagee, who was grantor of owners of adjoining land, all right and title that existed in mortgagor at time of execution of mortgage.— Hanson v. Huetter, 339 Mich. 130, 62 N.W.2d 663 (1954).

2117. *See* M.L.P.2d Estates (restraints on alienation).

2118. MCLS § 554.211.

2119. MCLS § 600.2932.

2120. Pines v. Equitable Trust Co., 263 Mich. 458, 249 N.W. 32 (1933).

2121. Eyde Bros. Dev. Co. v. Equitable Life Assurance Soc'y, 697 F. Supp. 1431 (W.D. Mich. 1988), aff'd without op., 888 F.2d 127 (6th Cir. Mich. 1989).

Atlantic Partnership-XI v. John Hancock Mut. Life Ins. Co., 95 F. Supp. 2d 678, 2000 U.S. Dist. LEXIS 6294 (E.D. Mich. 2000).

2122. MCLS §§ 445.1621 et seq.

Where both parties to a conveyance of land that is mortgaged suppose that a title in fee is being transferred, although, in fact, it is not, and the grantor afterwards purchases the land at the foreclosure sale, the grantor is bound in chancery to recognize the grantee's right to a perfected title. If the grantor further becomes a party to an arrangement whereby a third person takes a fee from the grantee, and gives back a mortgage that grantor disposes of for his or her own purposes, the grantor is then estopped from disputing that the grantor's original deed conveyed title and that the grantor's foreclosure purchase related back to it.[2123] A provision of a mortgage on realty that the parties consider the furniture, fixtures, and equipment to be a part of the realty and covered by the mortgage is binding on the mortgagors' assignee who assumes payment of the mortgage and has knowledge of the provision relating to the furniture, fixtures, and equipment.[2124]

Right of purchaser or grantee to contest mortgage. A party who has purchased lands, and as a part of the price, has covenanted to pay a mortgage given by the grantor, cannot avoid that liability by showing that the mortgage is not enforceable against the grantor.[2125] Likewise, a grantee who buys under an agreement to pay a mortgage on the property cannot show as a defense against the mortgage that it was without consideration, inasmuch as the original mortgagor had a right, if he or she chose, to waive any defense the mortgagor might have had to the mortgage.[2126] The defense of usury in a mortgage is not available to one who has purchased the land and assumed the mortgage.[2127]

Personal liability of purchaser in general. A grantee of mortgaged land does not incur a personal liability for the payment of the mortgage debt, enforceable by the mortgagee, merely because the deed recites that it is made subject to the mortgage. Personal liability of the grantee to pay the mortgage debt is created only by the grantee's distinct assumption of the mortgage debt.[2128] Under statutes providing in part that "no covenant shall be implied in any conveyance of real estate," and that "no mortgage shall be construed as implying a covenant for the payment of the sum thereby . . . secured,"[2129] a person who takes a quitclaim deed of mortgaged premises that does not contain any covenant or agreement by the person to assume or pay the mortgage, or who does not agree to pay the same as a

---

LaFond v. Rumler, 226 Mich. App. 447, 574 N.W.2d 40, 1997 Mich. App. LEXIS 386 (1997).

Exception in mortgage did not lift application of due-on-sale clause to land contract

A provision in a due-on-sale clause of a mortgage instrument that liens or encumbrances subordinate to the mortgage would not amount to a sale or transfer of the security property, and thus not trigger acceleration provisions of the clause, was not intended to apply to liens created only as a result of the execution by the mortgagor of a land contract which had as its primary purpose the transfer or sale of the property.—Darr v. First Federal Sav. & Loan Ass'n, 426 Mich. 11, 393 N.W.2d 152 (1986).

2123. La Coss v. Wadsworth, 56 Mich. 421, 23 N.W. 75 (1885).

2124. Guardian Depositors' Corp. v. Keller, 286 Mich. 403, 282 N.W. 194 (1938).

2125. Comstock v. Smith, 26 Mich. 306 (1873).

2126. Crawford v. Edwards, 33 Mich. 354 (1876).

2127. Sellers v. Botsford, 11 Mich. 59 (1862).

2128. Petz v. Gaines, 286 Mich. 450, 282 N.W. 212 (1938).

Booth v. Connecticut Life Ins. Co., 43 Mich. 299, 5 N.W. 381 (1880).

Winans v. Wilkie, 41 Mich. 264, 1 N.W. 1049 (1879).

2129. MCLS §§ 565.5, 565.6.

part of the consideration, cannot be made personally liable on the mortgage.[2130]

Sale or transfer subject to mortgage. A purchaser of land subject to a mortgage takes merely the equity of redemption. The purchaser may be presumed to have bought the land at its value, less the amount of the debt secured by the mortgage.[2131]

Thus, where the owner deeds his or her homestead to the spouse but reserves a life estate, and the grant is expressly subject to a mortgage on the premises, the entire estate is charged with the mortgage debt, for the discharge of which the premises are the primary fund. The grantee may not maintain a claim against the estate of the grantor for disbursements in payment of the mortgage after the grantor's death.[2132]

Grantors, compelled to pay a mortgage on the premises, cannot recover a personal judgment against the grantees who took subject to but did not assume the mortgage.[2133]

§ 832.   Assumption of Mortgage Debt By Purchaser or Grantee

A personal liability on the part of the purchaser of mortgaged property to pay the mortgage debt is created only by a distinct assumption of the debt.

A mortgage assumption clause in a deed is not a covenant running with the land, but is a collateral undertaking personal in nature and relates to the consideration.[2134]

A personal liability on the part of the purchaser of mortgaged property to pay the mortgage debt is created only by distinct assumption of the debt. A mere recital that the premises are subject to a certain mortgage, or that the mortgage is excepted from the grantor's covenant or warranty, is not an assumption of the debt by the purchaser, unless the intention to assume the payment otherwise appears in the deed.[2135] Accordingly, where an agreement to assume a mortgage is incorporated by

---

2130. Gage v. Jenkinson, 58 Mich. 169, 24 N.W. 815 (1885).

2131. Agreement to convey subject to mortgage

A conveyance of land subject to mortgage is simple deed of whatever interest, estate, or equity grantor has after satisfaction of mortgage debt out of property sold, so that agreement to convey realty for specified sum subject to mortgage means that price payable is that sum without deduction because of mortgage.—Clark v. Thompson, 83 F. Supp. 133 (D. Mich. 1949).

2132. In re Appeal of Wisner, 20 Mich. 442 (1870).

2133. Ranke v. Sloan, 262 Mich. 231, 247 N.W. 165 (1933).

2134. Schram v. Coyne, 127 F.2d 205 (6th Cir. Mich. 1942).

Federal Bond & Mortg. Co. v. Shapiro, 219 Mich. 13, 188 N.W. 465 (1922) (consideration was sufficient).

2135. Petz v. Gaines, 286 Mich. 450, 282 N.W. 212 (1938).

Agreement to secure release insufficient

Where realty on which corporation business was conducted was owned by corporation's two stockholders subject to mortgage, and purchaser of realty and of corporation's stock agreed to secure release of the mortgage, purchaser undertook merely to procure release of the realty but not to undertake obligation under the mortgage.—Wiseman v. United Dairies, 324 Mich. 473, 37 N.W.2d 174 (1949).

Under quitclaim deed and assignment

Land purchasers, obtaining title by quitclaim deed and assignment of vendor's interest in sale

mistake or fraud in a deed without the knowledge of the grantee, and is promptly disaffirmed by the grantee, the grantee cannot be held to the undertaking by the mortgagee.[2136]

On the other hand, a grantee who, with knowledge of its contents, accepts a conveyance that requires the grantee to assume the payment of an existing mortgage becomes personally liable for it in equity even though the grantee does not sign the deed.[2137] Plainly, a person who accepts a deed subject to a mortgage that he or she agrees to pay becomes personally liable for its payment.[2138] A subsequent conveyance by that person to a third person does not relieve the person of the obligation.[2139] An assumption clause inserted in a deed is inconsistent with a pretended oral agreement that the grantor is to furnish the grantee with the funds with which the grantee is to make the payment.[2140] Similarly, a party who purchases land and takes a deduction from the purchase price of the amount of certain mortgages, as well as a deed providing that the party assume payment on the mortgages, is personally liable to the mortgagee to pay them.[2141] In turn, a mortgagee under a mortgage assumed by a purchaser from the mortgagor as a part of the purchase money and identified in the conveyance may be so far subrogated to the mortgagor's rights in a suit to foreclose the mortgage as to have the benefit of the obligation to pay assumed by the grantee.[2142]

An assumption agreement may rest wholly in parol.[2143]

Evidence as to assumption of debts. The assumption clause in a deed of mortgaged premises, like any other contract charging liability, must be proved. Whether an assumption of the mortgage has occurred is a question of fact to be established by the evidence, because it is competent for the purchaser under the deed with an assumption clause to deny an assumption.[2144] Where it is doubtful whether

contract from one to whom vendor had conveyed property and assigned that interest, were not bound by agreement in contract to assume and pay mortgage on land.—Gleaner Life Ins. Soc'y v. Roberts, 282 Mich. 67, 275 N.W. 769 (1937).

2136. Schram v. Marion, 44 F. Supp. 760 (D. Mich. 1942).

Bogart v. Noble, 112 Mich. 697, 71 N.W. 320 (1897).

Not guilty of laches

A grantee under a deed of mortgaged premises who had no knowledge that a clause assuming the mortgage was inserted in the deed and no possession of the deed until about the time the mortgagees first sought to hold him liable as a garnishee defendant on the mortgage, the grantee was not guilty of laches in retaining the deed, where the mortgagees knew that the grantee denied any liability, and no rights of third persons had intervened.—Marks v. Muir, 281 Mich. 262, 274 N.W. 786 (1937).

2137. Barnard v. Huff, 252 Mich. 258, 233 N.W. 213 (1930) (overruled in part on other grounds by People's Sav. Bank v. Geistert, 253 Mich. 694, 235 N.W. 888 (1931)).

Crawford v. Edwards, 33 Mich. 354 (1876).

2138. Jehle v. Brooks, 112 Mich. 131, 70 N.W. 440 (1897).

Carley v. Fox, 38 Mich. 387 (1878).

Crawford v. Edwards, 33 Mich. 354 (1876).

2139. Kollen v. Sooy, 172 Mich. 214, 137 N.W. 808 (1912).

2140. Smith v. Unger, 44 Mich. 22, 5 N.W. 1069 (1880).

2141. Miller v. Thompson, 34 Mich. 10 (1876).

2142. Hicks v. McGarry, 38 Mich. 667 (1878).

2143. Keeler v. Richards Storage Corp., 260 Mich. 23, 244 N.W. 215 (1932).

2144. Marks v. Muir, 281 Mich. 262, 274 N.W. 786 (1937).

Petz v. Gaines, 286 Mich. 450, 282 N.W. 212 (1938) (evidence was insufficient).

Grover v. Bishop, 138 Mich. 505, 101 N.W. 627 (1904) (evidence was sufficient).

Keeler v. Richards Storage Corp., 260 Mich. 23, 244 N.W. 215 (1932) (evidence supported finding of oral assumption).

a deed of mortgaged premises binds the grantee to pay existing encumbrances, evidence of the value of the premises or of the agreed consideration for them, and as to whether the grantee retained any of the consideration to pay the debt is admissible to aid in construing the deed.[2145]

§ 833.   Operation and Effect of Agreement

The assumption of a mortgage debt by the purchaser of mortgaged premises renders the purchaser personally liable to pay it. The purchaser's personal liability may be enforced in a suit to foreclose the mortgage brought by the holder of the mortgage.

A grantee of mortgaged premises assuming the mortgage indebtedness is bound by all the terms and provisions of the mortgage.[2146]

The assumption of a mortgage debt by the purchaser of mortgaged premises renders the purchaser personally liable to pay it.[2147] A provision in a warranty deed that the deed is subject to a mortgage that the grantees assume and agree to pay means that the grantees must pay the parties holding the mortgage and entitled to payment.[2148]

The purchaser's personal liability may be enforced in a suit to foreclose the mortgage brought by the holder of the mortgage.[2149] The mortgagee may treat both the mortgagor and the mortgagor's grantee as principal debtors, although as between the mortgagor and the grantee, the mortgagor becomes a surety for the debt.[2150] Where a grantee accepts a deed binding the grantee to pay a mortgage on the premises conveyed, the grantor can compel the grantee to pay the mortgage.[2151]

The defense of illegality of the mortgage is not available to a party who assumes the obligation to pay a mortgage.[2152]

Where the purchaser retains from the purchase price of land the amount of a mortgage on the land for the express purpose of paying it, the land becomes a fund in the purchaser's hands for that purpose. The purchaser is not at liberty to deal with it in a manner inconsistent with that obligation.[2153]

Purchasers of land who assume a mortgage as part of a contract of purchase

2145. Winans v. Wilkie, 41 Mich. 264, 1 N.W. 1049 (1879).

2146. Union Guardian Trust Co. v. Marquette Park Co., 300 Mich. 89, 1 N.W.2d 464 (1942).

2147. Winans v. Wilkie, 41 Mich. 264, 1 N.W. 1049 (1879).

2148. Guardian Depositors Corp. v. Brown, 290 Mich. 433, 287 N.W. 798 (1939).

2149. Kollen v. Sooy, 172 Mich. 214, 137 N.W. 808 (1912).

Miller v. Thompson, 34 Mich. 10 (1876).

2150. Crawford v. Edwards, 33 Mich. 354 (1876).

2151. Smith v. Unger, 44 Mich. 22, 5 N.W. 1069 (1880).

2152. Michigan Wineries, Inc. v. Johnson, 402 Mich. 306, 262 N.W.2d 651 (1978).

2153. No avoiding assumed mortgage

Purchaser may not attempt to avoid mortgage by buying in the land at the foreclosure sale under a prior mortgage and then claiming that the lien of the second mortgage, which the purchaser previously assumed, is discharged by the acquisition.— Manwaring v. Powell, 40 Mich. 371 (1879).

are not liable on the mortgage after the contract of purchase is rescinded.[2154]

§ 834.   —Enforcement of Liability by Mortgagee

A mortgagee may proceed against a grantee assuming the mortgage debt for a deficiency remaining after foreclosure sale.

A mortgagee was permitted in chancery to proceed directly against grantees assuming a mortgage debt for any deficiency remaining after the sale of the premises.[2155] In addition, a general statute[2156] empowering third party beneficiaries to sue as promisees authorizes the holder of a mortgage to maintain an action at law against a grantee assuming the mortgage for a deficiency remaining after foreclosure sale.[2157] The mortgagee's rights under this provision are subject to the validity of the clause in the conveyance calling for assumption.[2158]

Acquiescence of the grantee in the conduct of the mortgagee may preclude the grantee from asserting that the conduct constitutes laches.[2159]

In an action by the mortgagees against the mortgagor, as principal defendant, and against the grantees of a deed of the mortgaged premises, in which a clause assuming the mortgage had been inserted, as garnishee defendant, the mortgagees are subject to any defenses that the garnishee defendant might make in an action against that party by the principal defendant, because the mortgagees are strangers to the alleged contracts in the deed clause assuming the mortgage.[2160] On the other hand, as against an assignee of the mortgage, the grantee cannot defend on the ground of a want of consideration for the assignment.[2161]

Assignment. The obligation of the purchaser arising from a covenant to assume or indemnify the mortgagor against the mortgage debt may be assigned by the mortgagor to the mortgagee, and that assignment gives the mortgagee a direct right of action against the purchaser without the necessity of first bringing

2154. Capac State Sav. Bank v. McKnight, 34 Mich. App. 390, 191 N.W.2d 55 (1971).

2155. MCLS § 600.3160.

Marks v. Kindel, 41 F.2d 584 (6th Cir. Mich. 1930).

Barnard v. Huff, 252 Mich. 258, 233 N.W. 213 (1930) (overruled in part on other grounds by People's Sav. Bank v. Geistert, 253 Mich. 694, 235 N.W. 888 (1931)).

Anderson v. Thompson, 225 Mich. 155, 195 N.W. 689 (1923).

2156. MCLS § 600.1405.

2157. Guardian Depositors Corp. v. Brown, 290 Mich. 433, 287 N.W. 798 (1939).

2158. Schram v. Marion, 44 F. Supp. 760 (D. Mich. 1942).

2159. Failure to invoke acceleration clause or to notify of default

The trustee's failure to invoke acceleration clause and begin foreclosure and to notify assuming grantee of default of subsequent non-assuming grantee, did not constitute "laches" that "estopped" trustee from asserting that assuming grantee was liable for mortgage debt or any deficiency on foreclosure, where acceleration clause gave trustee option to declare the whole indebtedness due, and assuming grantee did not object to methods employed by trustee to collect indebtedness but impliedly acquiesced in those methods.—Union Guardian Trust Co. v. Marquette Park Co., 300 Mich. 89, 1 N.W.2d 464 (1942).

2160. Marks v. Muir, 281 Mich. 262, 274 N.W. 786 (1937).

2161. Terry v. Durand Land Co., 112 Mich. 665, 71 N.W. 525 (1897).

foreclosure proceedings.[2162]

Successive grantees. Where the mortgagor conveys the mortgaged premises to a company that assumes the mortgage indebtedness, and the company conveys to an individual who takes the property subject to but does not assume the mortgage indebtedness, the company must establish that a valid and binding extension agreement exists between the mortgagee and the individual in order to be discharged from its assumed liability for the mortgage indebtedness.[2163]

§ 835. Transfer of Part of Mortgaged Property

Transfer of part of the property covered by a mortgage does not reduce the security of the mortgagee or withdraw that portion from the lien, unless the assignment provides otherwise.

A portion of the mortgaged premises that the mortgagor sells remains subject to the mortgage unless the mortgagee consents to the sale or releases the portion sold from the mortgage lien on it.[2164]

Generally, if lands subject to a mortgage are alienated in parcels, the parcels are chargeable for the satisfaction of the mortgage in the inverse order of alienation.[2165] The rule is inapplicable if the mortgagee will be prejudiced by having the property sold in parcels, and this rule cannot depend upon the existence or nonexistence of covenants of warranty.[2166] However, where a mortgagor of land sells and conveys part of it, the part retained generally must first be applied to payment of the mortgage as between the mortgagor and the grantee.[2167] On the other hand, a grantee of land may agree, as part of the consideration, to pay a mortgage on the land conveyed and other land retained by the grantor, in which case the grantor is entitled to sue to have the mortgage foreclosed and the land conveyed sold first, because the grantor's remedy at law is not adequate.[2168]

Under the statute[2169] providing that every conveyance of real estate that is not recorded is void as against any subsequent bona fide purchaser whose deed is first recorded, a tract conveyed by a mortgagor by a deed not recorded is liable for the payment of the mortgage before another tract covered by the same mortgage and subsequently conveyed to a bona fide purchaser by a deed first placed on record.[2170]

The doctrine of liability in inverse order of alienation may apply as between

2162. Federal Bond & Mortg. Co. v. Shapiro, 219 Mich. 13, 188 N.W. 465 (1922).

2163. Union Guardian Trust Co. v. Marquette Park Co., 300 Mich. 89, 1 N.W.2d 464 (1942) (request to deposit rents held not an extension).

2164. Montague v. Haviland, 101 Mich. 80, 59 N.W. 404 (1894).

2165. Gray v. H.M. Loud & Sons Lumber Co., 128 Mich. 427, 87 N.W. 376 (1901).

McVeigh v. Sherwood, 47 Mich. 545, 11 N.W. 379 (1882).

Gilbert v. Haire, 43 Mich. 283, 5 N.W. 321 (1880).

McKinney v. Miller, 19 Mich. 142 (1869).

Payne v. Avery, 21 Mich. 524 (1870) (rule applies where owner has given several mortgages of different dates).

2166. Cooper v. Bigly, 13 Mich. 463 (1865).

2167. Gantz v. Toles, 40 Mich. 725 (1879).

2168. Mowry v. Mowry, 137 Mich. 277, 100 N.W. 388 (1904).

2169. MCLS § 565.29.

2170. Gray v. H.M. Loud & Sons Lumber Co., 128 Mich. 427, 87 N.W. 376 (1901).

a purchaser of one portion and a person taking a junior mortgage on another part. This is true even though the prior grantee is the debtor's spouse and has joined with the debtor in mortgaging the unsold residue to a stranger with notice.[2171]

A mortgagee who has notice that, since the mortgage was given, a portion of the land has been sold, cannot release any part of the land to the prejudice of the purchasers; hence, the rule is that where mortgaged property has been wrongfully released, to the prejudice of subsequent purchasers of a part of the property, and the value of the parcel paid to the mortgagor, the purchasers are equitably entitled, on foreclosure, to have the amount for which the parcel was released deducted from the mortgage debt before their parcel is sold.[2172]

§ 836. Acquisition of Property by Mortgagee

The mortgagor may convey the equity of redemption to the mortgagee for a sufficient consideration on fair terms, but such a transaction will be closely scrutinized for fraud, oppression, or the like.

While a mortgagor may convey the equity of redemption to the mortgagee for a good and valuable consideration, when done voluntarily, without fraud or undue influence, it cannot be done by a contemporaneous or subsequent executory contract according to which the forfeiture is absolute if the debt is unpaid at the stated day.[2173]

When a mortgagee has taken possession of the mortgaged premises under a deed from the mortgagor, the mortgagee is not at liberty to repudiate the mortgagor's title afterwards. All releases obtained to cover the defects in the title are by law obtained for the support of the mortgagor's title.[2174]

§ 837. —Merger and Extinguishment of Debt

Generally, the acquisition by the mortgagee of the equity of redemption results in a merger of the two estates and an extinguishment of the mortgage debt; however, the question of merger is primarily one of intention, and particularly of the intention of the mortgagee.

Generally, the purchase or acquisition of the equity of redemption in mortgaged premises by the mortgagee results in a merger of the two estates, vesting the mortgagee with the complete title, and putting an end to the mortgagor's rights

---

2171. J.I. Case Threshing Machine Co. v. Mitchell, 74 Mich. 679, 42 N.W. 151 (1889).

2172. Hall v. Barnes, 43 Mich. 473, 5 N.W. 652 (1880).

Dewey v. Ingersoll, 42 Mich. 17, 3 N.W. 235 (1879) (constructive notice).

2173. Batty v. Snook, 5 Mich. 231 (1858).

Deed was without consideration

Mortgagor's quitclaim deed before expiration of redemption period with 60-day option to repurchase was without consideration.—Hogan v. Hester Inv. Co., 257 Mich. 627, 241 N.W. 881 (1932).

2174. Farmers & Mechanics' Bank v. Bronson, 14 Mich. 361 (1866).

or title under the mortgage.[2175]

However, in the law of mortgages, merger is not a rigid rule to be enforced regardless of the just rights of third persons.[2176] It is a rule in equity that a mortgage is not merged by a purchase by the mortgagee of the equity of redemption where the interest of the mortgagee requires the title to be kept separate.[2177]

In that respect, the question whether a conveyance of the equity to the mortgagee results in a merger of the mortgage and fee is primarily one of intention of the parties, and particularly of the intention of the mortgagee.[2178] An intent not to effect a merger is indicated where the mortgagee takes a conveyance for other purposes than the extinguishment of the mortgage debt.[2179]

However, even when it is to the mortgagee's interest and it is the mortgagee's intention to keep the mortgage alive, there will still be merger if the rights of the

---

2175. United States Leather, Inc. v. Mitchell Mfg. Group, Inc., 276 F.3d 782 (6th Cir. Mich. 2002).

Vollmer v. Coenis, 309 Mich. 319, 15 N.W.2d 654 (1944).

Jackson v. Evans, 44 Mich. 510, 7 N.W. 79 (1880).

Nelson v. Ferris, 30 Mich. 497 (1874).

Acquisition from grantee

Mortgage once extinguished by acceptance of quitclaim deed by holder of mortgage from grantee of property assuming mortgage could not be revived subsequently against mortgagor.—First Nat'l Bank v. Ramm, 256 Mich. 573, 240 N.W. 32 (1932).

2176. Maxwell v. Hammond, 234 Mich. 461, 208 N.W. 443 (1926).

2177. United States Leather, Inc. v. Mitchell Mfg. Group, Inc., 276 F.3d 782 (6th Cir. Mich. 2002).

Quick v. Raymond, 116 Mich. 15, 74 N.W. 189 (1898).

Cooper v. Bigly, 13 Mich. 463 (1865).

See, also, Dolese v. Bellows-Claude Neon Co., 261 Mich. 57, 245 N.W. 569 (1932).

2178. Ponstein v. Van Dyk, 282 Mich. 350, 276 N.W. 475 (1937).

First Nat'l Bank v. Ramm, 256 Mich. 573, 240 N.W. 32 (1932).

Ann Arbor Sav. Bank v. Webb, 56 Mich. 377, 23 N.W. 51 (1885).

Sylvania Sav. Bank Co. v. Turner, 27 Mich. App. 640, 183 N.W.2d 894 (1970).

Tower v. Divine, 37 Mich. 443 (1877) (a mortgage will not be deemed merged in a deed between the same parties against their intention and the mortgagee's interest).

Mortgagee's foreclosure of one of two mortgages it held on property

Where bank, which held first and second mortgages on debtor's office, did not intend merger of its mortgage interests when it foreclosed its second mortgage on debtor's office, mortgages did not merge under Michigan law.—In re Price, 50 B.R. 226 (Bankr. E.D. Mich. 1985).

Second mortgage

Where it was not in interest of mortgagee for its first mortgage on restaurant to merge into fee acquired when mortgagee purchased restaurant at mechanic's lien foreclosure sale because at time that mortgagee acquired fee restaurant was encumbered by second mortgage, mortgage and fee interests of mortgagee had not merged.—Sylvania Sav. Bank Co. v. Turner, 27 Mich. App. 640, 183 N.W.2d 894 (1970).

2179. Avoidance of foreclosure

Where conveyance of mortgaged premises by quitclaim deed to mortgagees under agreement for reconveyance, if mortgagors paid unpaid taxes and accrued interest during following year, was for purpose of avoiding a foreclosure and it did not appear that any of parties intended that mortgage was to be discharged, mortgage was not discharged by conveyance to mortgagees, and they were subsequently entitled to foreclose upon further default by mortgagors after reconveyance to them by quitclaim deed.—Ponstein v. Van Dyk, 282 Mich. 350, 276 N.W. 475 (1937).

Lack of knowledge of other lien

Acceptance by first mortgagee of quitclaim deed to mortgaged premises without actual knowledge of existence of second mortgage, where first mortgage and note were not canceled or surrendered, did not extinguish first mortgage so as to subordinate it to second mortgage.—Beal v. Alschuler, 277 Mich. 66, 268 N.W. 813 (1936).

mortgagor or third persons are affected.[2180]

Absolute deed as mortgage. A transfer of the mortgaged property by the mortgagor to the mortgagee may constitute an absolute sale or a mere change in the form of security, depending on the intention of the parties as revealed by their conduct, the instruments executed by them, and all the surrounding circumstances.[2181] If the relation of debtor and creditor continues to exist after the conveyance, and the debt still subsists, the transaction will be treated as a mortgage.[2182] But if the debt is treated by the parties as extinguished by the transaction, the instrument is a deed rather than a mortgage.[2183]

2180. Bugden v. Bailey, 279 Mich. 12, 271 N.W. 534 (1937).

Titus v. Cavalier, 276 Mich. 117, 267 N.W. 799 (1936).

Anderson v. Thompson, 225 Mich. 155, 195 N.W. 689 (1923).

Injury to third party holder of lien against mortgagee

Where a quitclaim deed in lieu of foreclosure given to a corporation meant that the corporation held both title to and the mortgage on the property, the merger rule applied to extinguish the mortgage; even though the quitclaim deed expressly stated that the instrument would not constitute a merger with or extinguishment of the mortgage, the exception to the merger rule was inapplicable because the corporation was not seeking to protect its own interests from the creditors of the mortgage, but was rather seeking to prefer the debt it owed to its parent corporation over the debt it owed to a third party who had a judgment lien against the corporation; thus, the third party was permitted to levy on the real property owned by the corporation to enforce its judgment lien.—United States Leather, Inc. v. Mitchell Mfg. Group, Inc., 276 F.3d 782 (6th Cir. Mich. 2002).

2181. Hurst v. Beaver, 50 Mich. 612, 16 N.W. 165 (1883).

Simington v. Goldstein, 330 Mich. 536, 48 N.W.2d 116 (1951) (evidence supported finding that quitclaim deed by grantors in default on mortgage was given as security only).

Abbott v. Gruner, 121 Mich. 140, 79 N.W. 1065 (1899) (deed was absolute conveyance).

2182. Ferris v. Wilcox, 51 Mich. 105, 16 N.W. 252 (1883).

Estoppel

Where mortgage had been foreclosed but suit under mortgage moratorium act was pending and mortgagee was given a quitclaim deed and in return gave mortgagors a lease containing option to purchase and thereafter parties treated arrangement as still existing notwithstanding option to purchase was not exercised at time provided in lease, parties by their conduct treated the arrangement as a mortgage, and the mortgagee was estopped from claiming that the deed was not a mortgage.—Alber v. Bradley, 321 Mich. 255, 32 N.W.2d 454 (1948).

2183. Parol testimony admissible

In action on mortgage notes, parol testimony was admissible to show intention that delivery of mortgagors' deed to mortgagee out of escrow upon mortgagors' failure to make agreed payments was to extinguish mortgage debt.—Vollmer v. Coenis, 309 Mich. 319, 15 N.W.2d 654 (1944).

Chapter 30

PAYMENT OR PERFORMANCE OF CONDITION, RELEASE, AND SATISFACTION

§ 851. Payment of Debt Secured

The mortgage debt may be satisfied by payment in full by the person primarily liable. A mortgagee or the mortgagee's successor must record a discharge of a mortgage within 90 days after it is paid or otherwise satisfied.

Library References

Michigan Digest
John G. Cameron, Jr., Michigan Real Estate Forms
Midwest Transaction Guide
Thompson on Real Property, Thomas Edition (David A. Thomas, ed.)
Powell on Real Property® (Michael Allan Wolf, ed.)
Real Estate Financing

Law Reviews

Kevin Scott, Contracts And Commercial Law, 56 Wayne L. Rev. 171 (2010); Stephen R. Estey and Danielle Graceffa, Real Property, 54 Wayne L. Rev. 387 (2008); Lawrence R. Shoffner, Real Property Law: Real Evidence: Special Rules for Real Estate Disputes, 80 Mich. B.J. 28 (2001).

The debt secured by a mortgage may be satisfied by payment of the amount due in full by the person primarily liable.[2184] In the absence of a contrary intent, the general rule is that payment of the mortgage debt discharges the mortgage.[2185] Payment by one of several persons liable for payment of a mortgage discharges the liability of all on the mortgage.[2186]

A mortgagee or the mortgagee's successor must record a discharge of a mortgage within the applicable time period after the mortgage is paid or otherwise satisfied.[2187] A mortgage is discharged upon the recording of the mortgagee's

2184. Dutton v. Merritt, 41 Mich. 537, 2 N.W. 806 (1879).

2185. Fox v. Mitchell, 302 Mich. 201, 4 N.W.2d 518 (1942).

Scribner v. Malinowski, 148 Mich. 446, 111 N.W. 1032 (1907).

2186. Dye v. Mann, 10 Mich. 291 (1862).

2187. MCLS §§ 565.41, MCLS § 545.44(2).

Old Republic Nat'l Title Ins. Co. v. Escrow & Title Servs., 2010 U.S. Dist. LEXIS 66573 (W.D. Mich. June 30, 2010).

Deutsche Bank Trust Co. Ams. v. Spot Realty, Inc., 269 Mich. App. 607, 714 N.W.2d 409 (2005).

1993 Op. Atty. Gen. 6757 (financial institution may discharge more than one mortgage in a common recorded document involving more than one mortgagor).

Future advance mortgages

MCLS § 565.41 is applicable to future advance mortgages, but the statute only requires the mortgagee to prepare and file a discharge of the mortgage within 90 days after the mortgage "has been paid or otherwise satisfied" (MCLS § 565.41).—Deutsche Bank Trust Co. Ams. v. Spot Realty, Inc., 269 Mich. App. 607, 714 N.W.2d 409 (2005).

Statute not preempted by federal statutes

Plaintiffs' claims that a bank violated state law by charging its borrowers a recording fee to reimburse it for the fee charged by the register of deeds to record a discharge of a mortgage were not preempted by the federal Home Owners' Loan Act or the Depository Institutions Deregulation and Monetary Control Act of 1980.—Konynenbelt v. Flagstar Bank, F.S.B., 242 Mich. App. 21, 617 N.W.2d 706 (2000).

discharge or of a circuit court order to the effect that the mortgage has been paid.[2188]

Under the Uniform Commercial Code—Negotiable Instruments, to discharge a debt consisting of a negotiable instrument secured by a mortgage, the payment must be by or on behalf of the mortgagor and to a person entitled to enforce the instrument, even if the mortgagor knows that another person has an unadjudicated claim to the instrument.[2189]

Whether a given transaction constitutes payment and a resulting discharge of the mortgage depends upon the intention of the parties, which is to be determined by a consideration of the circumstances of the case.[2190]

Payment, in order to be effective to discharge the mortgage, must be made to the mortgagee or to some one authorized by the mortgagee to receive payment for the mortgagee.[2191] However, the fact that interest on a mortgage is collected from time to time by a person not in possession of the security is not sufficient in itself to justify an inference of authority to receive payment of the mortgage.[2192] Voluntary payment of a mortgage to a person not lawfully entitled to collect it, after notice from the real owner not to do so, does not constitute payment that discharges the mortgage.[2193] When a mortgage is assigned, the party entitled to payment generally changes.[2194]

Any means of satisfaction upon which the parties agree and that actually reaches the creditor constitutes payment of a mortgage.[2195] Pursuant to an agreement, the collection by the mortgagee of insurance benefits payable on the mortgaged premises may properly satisfy payment upon the mortgage.[2196] Similarly, the assignment of the mortgage and subsequent payment of another mortgage,[2197] and offsetting the mortgage debt against a counterclaim,[2198] can constitute sufficient payment to discharge a mortgage under an agreement of the parties to that effect.

Conversely, a bondholder under a trust mortgage may not be compelled to accept anything in satisfaction of the bond except that which he or she is required to take under the terms of the trust agreement embodied in the bond.[2199]

In the absence of specific direction by the mortgagor or an agreement between

2188. MCLS § 565.42.

2189. M.L.P.2d Negotiable Instruments. MCLS § 440.3602.

2190. Ormsby v. Barr, 21 Mich. 474 (1870).

2191. Herbert v. East Lansing Bldg. & Loan Ass'n, 331 Mich. 132, 49 N.W.2d 96 (1951).

Miller v. Seeley, 90 Mich. 218, 51 N.W. 366 (1892).

Donaldson v. Wilson, 79 Mich. 181, 44 N.W. 429 (1890).

Abbott v. Godfroy's Heirs, 1 Mich. 178 (1849).

2192. Bromley v. Lathrop, 105 Mich. 492, 63 N.W. 510 (1895).

2193. Chase v. Brown, 32 Mich. 225 (1875).

2194. Assignments of mortgages, *see, supra,* Chapter 28.

2195. Werner v. Werner, 357 Mich. 671, 99 N.W.2d 359 (1959).

Gallup v. Jackson, 47 Mich. 475, 11 N.W. 277 (1882).

Jones v. Smith, 22 Mich. 360 (1871).

2196. Wilcox v. Allen, 36 Mich. 160 (1877).

2197. Barnard v. McReynolds, 28 Mich. 411 (1874).

2198. Green v. Engelmann, 39 Mich. 460 (1878).

2199. Rudell v. Union Guardian Trust Co., 295 Mich. 157, 294 N.W. 132 (1940).

the parties, a creditor who holds a mortgage and an unsecured account may apply the mortgagor's payment to either.[2200] But where the debt secured by the mortgage is incurred prior to the unsecured debt, the mortgagee may have to apply payments in a general account by the mortgagor first to the secured debt.[2201]

Where a mortgage is payable at a day certain, the mortgagor cannot compel the mortgagee to accept payment until it falls due, unless the privilege of paying sooner is accorded by the terms of the mortgage.[2202]

§ 852.   Tender

Under common law, a tender of the full amount due on a mortgage will operate to discharge it where the tender is not refused in good faith. For a negotiable instrument, a tender discharges the amount of tender even if it is refused.

The general rule is that a sufficient tender by the mortgagor discharges the lien of a mortgage.[2203] A tender of the full amount due on a mortgage discharges the lien only if the tender is refused without adequate excuse.[2204] Conversely, a proper tender that is refused in good faith does not discharge a mortgage lien.[2205]

Under the Uniform Commercial Code—Negotiable Instruments, if a tender of payment on a debt consisting of a negotiable instrument secured by a mortgage is made by or on behalf of the mortgagor and to a person entitled to enforce the instrument, and the tender is refused, the payment obligation is discharged in the amount of the tender.[2206]

In general, a tender of the amount due on a mortgage must be open, fair, and reasonable, and must be made at the right time and place and to the proper person.[2207] The holder of a mortgage to whom a tender is proposed to be made is

---

2200. Payne v. Avery, 21 Mich. 524 (1870).

2201. Mauro v. Davie, 236 Mich. 309, 210 N.W. 308 (1926).

2202. Post v. Springsted, 49 Mich. 90, 13 N.W. 370 (1882).

2203. McKenna v. Wilson, 280 Mich. 227, 273 N.W. 457 (1937).

Potts v. Plaisted, 30 Mich. 149 (1874).

McLelland v. A.P. Cook Co., 94 Mich. 528, 54 N.W. 298 (1893) (tender not established).

Parks v. Allen, 42 Mich. 482, 4 N.W. 227 (1880) (insufficient tender).

2204. Federal Discount Corp. v. Rush, 269 Mich. 612, 257 N.W. 897 (1934).

Renard v. Clink, 91 Mich. 1, 51 N.W. 692 (1892).

Tender by second mortgagee

A tender by a second mortgagee of the amount secured by a prior mortgage, if accompanied by a demand for an assignment not only of the mortgage, but of certain notes of the mortgagor on which the owner of the first mortgage is endorser, and to which the second mortgagee has no right, will not discharge the lien of the first mortgage.— Schmittdiel v. Moore, 101 Mich. 590, 60 N.W. 279 (1894).

Tender coupled with claim of allowance

An absolute tender by a subsequent mortgagee will discharge the lien of a prior mortgage; but a tender coupled with a claim of an allowance not lawfully demandable will not have that effect.— Sager v. Tupper, 35 Mich. 134 (1876).

2205. Hayward v. Chase, 181 Mich. 614, 148 N.W. 214 (1914).

Canfield v. Conkling, 41 Mich. 371, 2 N.W. 191 (1879).

Waldron v. Murphy, 40 Mich. 668 (1879).

Dodge v. Brewer, 31 Mich. 227 (1875) (conditional tender).

2206. M.L.P.2d Negotiable Instruments. MCLS § 440.3603.

2207. Post v. Springsted, 49 Mich. 90, 13 N.W. 370 (1882).

entitled to a reasonable opportunity to look over the mortgage papers to calculate the amount due. For a mortgageholder is not bound, under the penalty or at the hazard of losing the entire debt, to know the precise amount due on any particular day.[2208]

Where the discharge of a mortgage is sought to be established on the ground of a tender, the evidence of the tender must be clear and satisfactory.[2209] The tender must be kept good for a reasonable time,[2210] and it must in fact be a tender in full.[2211] In that respect, a tender on a mortgage that is usurious may not have to include interest.[2212] The courts will hesitate to enforce the forfeiture of a mortgage security for the refusal of a tender when its apparent purpose is to force the mortgagee to accept it at once with no opportunity to determine whether it is in the proper amount.[2213]

Although a tender stops the accrual of interest, it does not discharge the debt itself.[2214]

Tender after default. A mortgagor's tender of the amount due at maturity of the mortgage and before foreclosure discharges the mortgage.[2215] Proper tender after foreclosure but before redemption also discharges the mortgage.[2216] However, in each case, the discharge of the lien results only from a tender that is refused without

---

Potts v. Plaisted, 30 Mich. 149 (1874).

Delay of one day by sick mortgagor was within mortgagor's right

Where a tender on a mortgage is made to the owner, who was known to be sick and nearly blind, and who declined to transact the business until the following morning, and next morning offered to receive the money, but reliance was then had on the tender, but it was not paid, the tender did not discharge the lien of the mortgage.—Waldron v. Murphy, 40 Mich. 668 (1879).

2208. Potts v. Plaisted, 30 Mich. 149 (1874).

Insufficient tender on the spot

A mortgagor offered to a mortgagee, a woman, while engaged in her ordinary occupations, a specific sum of money, demanding a discharge of the mortgage, which was refused, upon the ground that the amount was insufficient; this was an insufficient tender, since the mortgagee was not bound to know at all times what is due, or to be ready to determine forthwith whether she will accept a particular sum tendered.—Root v. Bradley, 49 Mich. 27, 12 N.W. 896 (1882).

2209. Hayward v. Chase, 181 Mich. 614, 148 N.W. 214 (1914).

Engle v. Hall, 45 Mich. 57, 7 N.W. 239 (1880).

Proctor v. Robinson, 35 Mich. 284 (1877).

Potts v. Plaisted, 30 Mich. 149 (1874).

2210. Ferguson v. Popp, 42 Mich. 115, 3 N.W. 287 (1879) (tender not kept good).

2211. Insufficient tender

Alleged tender of everything due upon notes and mortgage, both interest and principal, was too

small, and did not preclude foreclosure.—First State Bank v. Day, 188 Mich. 228, 154 N.W. 101 (1915).

2212. McKenna v. Wilson, 280 Mich. 227, 273 N.W. 457 (1937).

2213. Post v. Springsted, 49 Mich. 90, 13 N.W. 370 (1882).

2214. Eberle v. Sambab, 248 Mich. 508, 227 N.W. 690 (1929).

Cowles v. Marble, 37 Mich. 158 (1877).

2215. Federal Discount Corp. v. Rush, 269 Mich. 612, 257 N.W. 897 (1934).

Van Husan v. Kanouse, 13 Mich. 303 (1865).

Caruthers v. Humphrey, 12 Mich. 270 (1864).

No actual tender made

Where a mortgagor offered to pay and the mortgagee offered to receive the amount due on the mortgage, but before the money was produced other dealings were brought into the conversation in which a quarrel ensued, and they parted without further offer of the amount due on the mortgage alone, and afterwards the mortgagee left the mortgage with an attorney for foreclosure who sent word to the mortgagor to pay it before a certain time if he wished to save costs and no payment was made, no tender had been made that would discharge the mortgage lien.—Parks v. Allen, 42 Mich. 482, 4 N.W. 227 (1880).

2216. Eberle v. Sambab, 248 Mich. 508, 227 N.W. 690 (1929).

Zlotoecizski v. Smith, 117 Mich. 202, 75 N.W. 470 (1898) (technical default).

adequate excuse.[2217]

§ 853.   Discharge by New Agreement

A mortgage may be discharged by a new contractual agreement between the parties if the new agreement evidences that intention.

A discharge of a mortgage may be effected by a compromise and settlement between the parties.[2218]

As a general rule, however, the execution of a new mortgage to secure the same debt covered by the old mortgage does not discharge the old mortgage in the absence of clear intention to that effect.[2219]

Change in form of debt or terms of payment. A change in the form of the debt does not discharge the mortgage securing the debt in the absence of an agreement to that effect.[2220] Thus, when a note secured by a mortgage is taken up at or before maturity and a new note substituted for it, the mortgage continues as security for the debt in its new form and there is no change in the rights or remedies of the mortgagee.[2221] Similarly, the parties to a mortgage may extend the time for payment of the debt.[2222] An extension agreement continues the lien of the mortgage.[2223] But it must be supported by a sufficient consideration.[2224]

§ 854.   Release

A mortgage may be released by an agreement of the parties. Even a portion of the debt secured by a mortgage may be released.

A mortgage may be released or discharged by an agreement of the parties.[2225]

2217. Renard v. Clink, 91 Mich. 1, 51 N.W. 692 (1892).

No good cause for refusal

Where the purchaser of certain lots of a mortgaged tract tendered payment on such lots in accordance with a partial release clause of the mortgage, mortgagee's refusal to accept tender without good cause discharged the lien on those lots though mortgage was in default when the demand for release was made.—Federal Discount Corp. v. Rush, 269 Mich. 612, 257 N.W. 897 (1934).

2218. Ruloff v. Hazen, 124 Mich. 570, 83 N.W. 370 (1900).

King v. Brewer, 121 Mich. 339, 80 N.W. 238 (1899).

2219. One of two mortgagors

Where one of two brothers, to whom land was devised subject to a mortgage, failed to execute a mortgage for his share, the mortgage given by the other pursuant to an agreement was not an independent security and did not release the property devised to him from the original mortgage.—Clark v. Sheldon, 223 Mich. 323, 193 N.W. 876 (1923).

2220. Tucker v. Alger, 30 Mich. 67 (1874).

Boxheimer v. Gunn, 24 Mich. 372 (1872).

2221. Oakman v. Hurd Lumber & Woodwork Co., 250 Mich. 672, 230 N.W. 921 (1930).

2222. Havens v. Jones, 45 Mich. 253, 7 N.W. 818 (1881).

2223. Burt v. Gamble, 98 Mich. 402, 57 N.W. 261 (1894).

Griffin v. Walter, 74 Mich. 1, 41 N.W. 843 (1889) (timber lands).

2224. Urban v. McNinch, 265 Mich. 415, 251 N.W. 537, 1933 Mich. LEXIS 697 (1933).

2225. Ginsberg v. Capitol City Wrecking Co., 300 Mich. 712, 2 N.W.2d 892, 1942 Mich. LEXIS 669 (1942).

Benton Harbor State Bank v. Bubanovich, 259 Mich. 150, 242 N.W. 870 (1932).

A release by agreement may only be made by the owner of the obligation or someone that the owner authorizes.[2226] A release must be given for a valid consideration.[2227]

Partial release. A provision in a mortgage for the release of separate parcels of the mortgaged property, on the demand of the mortgagor, and on paying for each lot released a fixed sum or proportional part of the whole debt, is valid.[2228] The willful and absolute refusal by the mortgagee, without just cause, to accept a tender made for the purpose of securing such a partial release in accordance with the partial release clause in the mortgage, discharges the lien in respect to the lots covered by the tender.[2229]

The extent of the right to partial release depends on the construction of the release clause in each particular case.[2230] An agreement for partial release upon the payment of a sum equal to the value of a parcel must be construed as referring to the value of the parcel at the time of the release.[2231] The mortgagee who releases or purchases a portion of mortgaged realty has a duty to act in good faith to credit the full value of the portion released in favor of the purchasers of other portions in order that they may be charged only with the remainder of the mortgage debt.[2232]

McCarn v. Wilcox, 106 Mich. 64, 63 N.W. 978 (1895).

Bush v. Freer, 91 Mich. 315, 51 N.W. 1002 (1892).

Flynn v. Flynn, 68 Mich. 20, 35 N.W. 817 (1888).

Reynolds v. Smith, 57 Mich. 194, 23 N.W. 727 (1885).

2226. McIntire v. Conrad, 93 Mich. 526, 53 N.W. 829 (1892).

2227. Benton Harbor State Bank v. Bubanovich, 259 Mich. 150, 242 N.W. 870 (1932).

2228. Fowler v. Sapre, 243 Mich. 266, 220 N.W. 733 (1928).

Taylor v. Carter, 211 Mich. 365, 178 N.W. 712 (1920).

Commercial Bank v. Hiller, 106 Mich. 118, 63 N.W. 1012 (1895).

McVicar v. Denison, 81 Mich. 348, 45 N.W. 659 (1890).

Bankruptcy

In foreclosure suit on mortgage containing partial release clause, where mortgagee had, without just cause, refused tender under release clause by purchaser from mortgagor, fact that mortgagor, since institution of suit, had been released from debt by bankruptcy discharge, did not prevent discharge of mortgage lien regarding lots covered by the tender, though mortgagee would thereby

suffer hardship.—Federal Discount Corp. v. Rush, 269 Mich. 612, 257 N.W. 897 (1934).

2229. Federal Discount Corp. v. Rush, 269 Mich. 612, 257 N.W. 897 (1934).

2230. Federal Discount Corp. v. Rush, 269 Mich. 612, 257 N.W. 897 (1934).

Fowler v. Sapre, 243 Mich. 266, 220 N.W. 733 (1928).

Release on payment

Where mortgage contained a covenant for partial releases on payment of $1 per acre, and in partial releases given under it language was quite uniformly used preserving the mortgagee's lien upon the remaining land, such language is not construed to relieve the mortgagee from the covenant to give partial releases; the mortgage lien thus preserved being subject to partial release covenant.—Taylor v. Carter, 211 Mich. 365, 178 N.W. 712 (1920).

2231. People's Sav. Bank v. Nebel, 92 Mich. 348, 52 N.W. 727 (1892).

2232. Credit for full value of land at release

Where mortgagee knew that mortgagors had been divorced, that mortgaged land had been divided and apportioned between them, and that husband had agreed to assume mortgage, but accepted $2,500 to release husband's portion of land at time when value of that land was $4,500, $4,500 would be credited against interest and principal of mortgage.—Dusseau v. Roscommon State Bank, 80 Mich. App. 531, 264 N.W.2d 350 (1978).

A covenant for partial release may run with the land.[2233] It inures to the benefit of one claiming under the mortgagor,[2234] especially where the mortgage so provides.[2235]

A mortgagor's right under a covenant in a mortgage for a partial release is not lost by the institution of foreclosure proceedings.[2236]

§ 855.   Proceedings to Compel Release or Satisfaction

A circuit court may compel the release of a mortgage.

A court with equity jurisdiction may entertain a proceeding to compel the release or satisfaction of a mortgage.[2237]

Under the Revised Judicature Act of 1961, when a recorded mortgage on lands or property has been paid or satisfied or when 15 years have elapsed since the debt or lien secured by such mortgage became due or payable or since the last payment thereon, and no suit or proceedings have been commenced to collect the same, the owner of such land may present a petition to the circuit court for the county in which the land is situated for an order discharging the mortgage. Where it satisfactorily appears to the court that the debt or lien secured by such mortgage has been fully paid or that the debt has been past due for 15 years or that 15 years have elapsed since the last payment and that no suit or proceeding has been commenced to foreclose the mortgage, the court must deliver an attested judgment to the mortgagor that may be recorded in the office of the register of deeds for the county in which the mortgage is of record. The effect of the recording of the judgment is to formally discharge the mortgage.[2238] The purpose of this statute is to provide means whereby

2233. Kerschensteiner v. Northern Michigan Land Co., 244 Mich. 403, 221 N.W. 322 (1928).

2234. Kerschensteiner v. Northern Michigan Land Co., 244 Mich. 403, 221 N.W. 322 (1928).

Fowler v. Sapre, 243 Mich. 266, 220 N.W. 733 (1928).

Assign of original mortgagor

A mortgagee of a purchaser from the original mortgagors was an assign of the mortgagors, within the covenants of the mortgage to release any part of the land on payment by the mortgagor or his assigns of $1 an acre.—Taylor v. Carter, 211 Mich. 365, 178 N.W. 712 (1920).

2235. Federal Discount Corp. v. Rush, 269 Mich. 612, 257 N.W. 897 (1934).

2236. Taylor v. Carter, 211 Mich. 365, 178 N.W. 712 (1920).

2237. Eaton v. Eaton, 68 Mich. 158, 36 N.W. 50 (1888).

Flynn v. Flynn, 68 Mich. 20, 35 N.W. 817 (1888).

Canfield v. Conkling, 41 Mich. 371, 2 N.W. 191 (1879).

Rickle v. Dow, 39 Mich. 91 (1878).

Claim for damages

In connection with suit in equity to compel reconveyance, court has jurisdiction to determine claim for damages for refusal to reconvey.—Dunitz v. Satovsky, 243 Mich. 423, 220 N.W. 717 (1928).

Evidence supported discharge

Order discharging mortgage would be affirmed on review where it was supported by evidence that appellant was paid all that was due him under instrument in question, notwithstanding his contention that payments were pursuant to commission arrangement rather than a mortgage.—Pine Ridge Coal Co. v. Cronin, 41 Mich. App. 255, 199 N.W.2d 876 (1972).

2238. MCLS §§ 600.3175, 600.5803.

Computation of time for installment mortgage

Under statute of limitations for foreclosure of mortgage and discharge of mortgage statute, both containing language in alternative, greatest period of time to run is proper one to apply, i.e., correct time to commence to run is from due date provided in mortgage, and not date of last payment.—Degen v. Estate of Degen, 80 Mich. App. 573, 264 N.W.2d 64 (1978).

the owner of encumbered property, after the limitations period for foreclosure of the mortgage has run, can formally remove the encumbrance and clear title to the land.[2239]

A proceeding to compel the release or satisfaction of a mortgage may only be commenced by one having an interest in the land.[2240] All persons interested in the mortgage must be made parties to the proceeding.[2241] A right of action to obtain satisfaction of a mortgage arises only on full performance of the conditions included in it plus a demand on the mortgagee for satisfaction or release and his or her refusal.[2242]

§ 856.　Penalties or Damages Relating to Release or Satisfaction

One who refuses to release a mortgage that has been fully paid or as to which all legal conditions have been complied with is subject to a statutory penalty in addition to liability for actual damages.

A mortgagee or the mortgagee's successor who refuses or neglects to discharge the mortgage or execute a certificate of discharge or release of the mortgage as provided after being requested and after full performance of the conditions of a mortgage before or after breach, or if the same is entirely due and payable, after a tender of the whole amount due and payable, may be liable to the mortgagor in the sum of $1,000.[2243] However, this statutory penalty for the refusal

Installment mortgage

On an installment mortgage, the fifteen-year statute of limitation begins to run from the time each installment is due. Mortgage installments that are not foreclosed fifteen years after they are due are barred from collection.—Zachary v. Emmer, 1996 Mich. App. LEXIS 669 (Mich. Ct. App. Nov. 22, 1996).

2239. Degen v. Estate of Degen, 80 Mich. App. 573, 264 N.W.2d 64 (1978).

2240. Ormsby v. Barr, 22 Mich. 80 (1870).

Entire ownership

Where a son promised his father to pay off certain mortgages on his parents' property, and the mother's subsequent death vested the entire ownership in the father, the father alone can enforce agreement.—Swartz v. Swartz, 194 Mich. 617, 161 N.W. 827 (1917).

2241. Eaton v. Eaton, 68 Mich. 158, 36 N.W. 50 (1888).

2242. Trombley v. Cannon, 134 Mich. 417, 96 N.W. 516 (1903).

Mortgagee's liability for wrongfully disbursing funds on mortgage

In mortgagor's suit against mortgagee, a building and loan association, for accounting and dis-

charge of mortgage on ground of breach of duty by mortgagee, as mortgagor's financial agent, in making unauthorized payment of mortgagor's funds to contractor who became bankrupt and failed to finish mortgagor's house, evidence required conclusion that mortgagee knew that arrangement with mortgagor authorized payments to be made to contractor only when due and that payment in question was made before it was due; hence decree dismissing bill was reversed on mortgagor's appeal.—Herbert v. East Lansing Bldg. & Loan Ass'n, 331 Mich. 132, 49 N.W.2d 96 (1951).

2243. MCLS § 565.44.

Demand for attorney's fee

A mortgagee, after an irregular attempt to foreclose by advertisement, where his notice was imperfect, and was withdrawn after a single publication, is not entitled to demand the attorney fee provided for in the mortgage in case of foreclosure; and where he declined a tender of the full amount due because attorney fee was not paid in addition, and refused to execute a discharge of the mortgage, he was properly liable to statutory penalty.—Collar v. Harrison, 30 Mich. 66 (1874).

Statute applicable to all mortgages

Statute authorizing the recovery of $100 upon a bill filed to procure a discharge of a mortgage, in case of a refusal by a mortgagee, after a proper

to discharge a mortgage will generally not be enforced where the refusal of the mortgagee is made in good faith.[2244] Given that the penalty imposed for refusing to discharge a mortgage on tender of the amount due is intended, not only to indemnify the mortgagor, but to act as a punishment, where the discharge is demanded on the ground of tender, the evidence of tender must clearly show that the equities are against the defendant mortgagee.[2245] Similarly, the penalty provided under this statute cannot be recovered of a mortgagee who has no interest in the mortgage debt and who has no means of knowing him- or herself to be in default for not giving a discharge.[2246] The statute is also not applicable to a person who innocently takes a forged mortgage.[2247]

As a condition precedent to the maintenance of a cause of action for the statutory penalty, the mortgagor must show that the mortgagor has paid the debt secured by the mortgage in full or has tendered the full amount.[2248] The complainant must also show that all other legal conditions imposed have been fulfilled.[2249] The fact that a mortgage is invalid because it covers the mortgagor's homestead and is not signed by the mortgagor's spouse will not prevent a recovery where the mortgage has in fact been paid.[2250]

In addition to the statutory grounds for the recovery of penalty and damages, a right of action exists independently of statute for damages for refusal, after payment, to reconvey property deeded as security.[2251] The measure of damages in such an action where a sale has been lost is the excess of the sale price over the market value.[2252]

§ 857.   Effect of Release or Satisfaction

The release of a mortgage operates to put an end to any proceedings to foreclose it in the absence of accident, fraud, or mistake.

tender and request, to discharge the same, applies to all mortgages, whether large or small.—Collar v. Harrison, 28 Mich. 518 (1874).

2244. Shelton v. Wilson, 274 Mich. 433, 264 N.W. 854 (1936).

Continental Bank v. Kowalsky, 247 Mich. 348, 225 N.W. 496 (1929).

Parkes v. Parker, 57 Mich. 57, 23 N.W. 458 (1885).

Honest belief that larger sum due

That a mortgagee refused a tender of all that there was really due on the mortgage is no ground for imposing the statutory penalty for a willful and knowing refusal to discharge the mortgage, where the mortgagee acted in good faith, under the belief that a larger sum than the amount tendered was due him.—Canfield v. Conkling, 41 Mich. 371, 2 N.W. 191 (1879).

Honest difference of opinion

Where there has been an honest difference between the parties regarding their respective rights, the statutory penalty will not be imposed on the defendant for refusing to discharge a mortgage

after it was satisfied.—Burrows v. Bangs, 34 Mich. 304 (1876).

2245. Engle v. Hall, 45 Mich. 57, 7 N.W. 239 (1880).

2246. Murphy v. Fleming, 69 Mich. 185, 36 N.W. 787 (1888).

2247. Graham v. Sinderman, 238 Mich. 210, 213 N.W. 200 (1927).

2248. Shelton v. Wilson, 274 Mich. 433, 264 N.W. 854 (1936).

Barnard v. Harrison, 30 Mich. 8 (1874).

2249. Wilber v. Pierce, 56 Mich. 169, 22 N.W. 316 (1885).

2250. Wilber v. Pierce, 56 Mich. 169, 22 N.W. 316 (1885).

2251. Dunitz v. Satovsky, 243 Mich. 423, 220 N.W. 717 (1928).

2252. Dunitz v. Satovsky, 243 Mich. 423, 220 N.W. 717 (1928).

The delivery by a mortgagee of a discharge and its acceptance by the mortgagor operates as a recognition by the latter of the mortgagee's right to the amount of the debt.[2253] It also puts an end to foreclosure proceedings by the mortgagee.[2254]

However, such a discharge is not an absolute bar to foreclosure, unless there has been actual satisfaction. The discharge is sufficient evidence to sustain the rights of all persons interested only in the absence of accident, mistake, or fraud.[2255]

The payment of the mortgage debt by the mortgagor revests the legal title in the mortgagor without the necessity of a reconveyance. But where a reconveyance is necessary to clear the mortgagor's record title, the mortgagor is entitled to require an actual reconveyance.[2256]

A release of a parcel of land from a mortgage does not defeat the right of the mortgagee to sell the rest of the mortgaged premises under a power of sale.[2257]

§ 858.   Reinstatement of Mortgage

A mortgage may be reinstated under proper conditions. The reinstatement may entail the abrogation of a release.

A release or satisfaction of a mortgage may, under proper circumstances, be set aside, and the mortgage reinstated.[2258] But the party seeking reinstatement will be required to return what has been received in payment.[2259]

The abrogation of a release and the reinstatement of a mortgage are available if there is a failure of the consideration on which the release is given.[2260] Where a mortgagee releases mortgages on certain lands in consideration of a deed to a portion of them that is to be otherwise unencumbered, but on which, in fact, other encumbrances exist, the mortgagee may maintain an equitable action for the cancellation of the release on the ground of failure of consideration.[2261] The abrogation of a release or discharge and the reinstatement of a mortgage may also

---

2253. Waldron v. Murphy, 40 Mich. 668, 1879 Mich. LEXIS 659 (1879).

Fry v. Russell, 35 Mich. 229 (1876).

2254. McBride v. Wright, 46 Mich. 265, 9 N.W. 275 (1881).

2255. Ferguson v. Glassford, 68 Mich. 36, 35 N.W. 820 (1888).

Real Property Law: Real Evidence: Special Rules For Real Estate Disputes, 80 Mich. B.J. 28 (2001).

2256. Fletcher v. Morlock, 251 Mich. 96, 231 N.W. 59 (1930).

2257. Balen v. Lewis, 130 Mich. 567, 90 N.W. 416 (1902).

Botsford v. Botsford, 49 Mich. 29, 12 N.W. 897 (1882).

Dunn v. Fish, 46 Mich. 312, 9 N.W. 429 (1881).

2258. Plasger v. Leonard, 316 Mich. 174, 25 N.W.2d 156 (1946).

Reinstatement by son

Where a father bequeathed a mortgage to his son, the son, being an equitable assignee, properly filed his bill to set aside a satisfaction of the mortgage individually and not as executor.— Densmore v. Savage, 110 Mich. 27, 67 N.W. 1103 (1896).

2259. Brown v. Kelly, 252 Mich. 540, 233 N.W. 408 (1930).

2260. Plasger v. Leonard, 316 Mich. 174, 25 N.W.2d 156 (1946).

Wood v. De Pew, 250 Mich. 375, 230 N.W. 175 (1930).

Linn v. Linn, 122 Mich. 130, 80 N.W. 1000 (1899) (forgery).

2261. French v. De Bow, 38 Mich. 708 (1878).

be available on the ground of mistake,[2262] fraud,[2263] or because the lien of the mortgage has failed due to the fact that the title held by the mortgagor is adjudged invalid and the mortgagor afterwards secures a confirmation of it.[2264]

On the other hand, where a mortgagor of land conveys a part of it to a municipality to be used as a public park, and the mortgagee, for a valuable consideration, releases the mortgage on the part so conveyed, the fact the land conveyed is not used as a public park but is converted into a depot grounds does not entitle the mortgagee to have the land resubjected to the mortgage, where the mortgagee made no objection to the change in the use of the land.[2265]

§ 859.   Evidence as to Payment, Release, or Satisfaction

The party seeking to assert the payment, release, or satisfaction of a mortgage has the burden of establishing the claim.

The burden of proving payment of a mortgage debt is on the party asserting it,[2266] whether in defense to a foreclosure suit,[2267] or as a ground of relief in a suit to enjoin the enforcement of the mortgage.[2268] The burden of proving that a particular application was to be made of a certain payment is also upon the party asserting it.[2269]

Where the person seeking to enforce a mortgage does not produce the mortgage or note or bond secured by it, the debt is presumed to have been paid.[2270] This presumption can be overcome only by proof of the loss of the instrument or a sufficient explanation of its absence.[2271] Similarly, a mortgagor's possession of the note and mortgage raises a presumption of payment and discharge,[2272] which again is rebuttable only by very clear proof.[2273] This presumption of payment and discharge is also raised by possession of the mortgaged premises by the mortgagor beyond the maturity date of the debt.[2274] Thus, possession by a mortgagor of the mortgaged premises for more than 15 years without any recognition of the mortgage

2262. Ferguson v. Glassford, 68 Mich. 36, 35 N.W. 820 (1888).

2263. Brown v. Kelly, 252 Mich. 540, 233 N.W. 408 (1930).

Fraternal officer

An officer of a fraternal society, who wrongfully loaned funds of the society to a third person, obtaining a mortgage in his own name as security for the funds, will not be denied relief in equity, to protect the mortgage and secure the cancellation of a discharge obtained by the third person's fraud, as against the objection of the third person.—Downing v. Hill, 165 Mich. 559, 130 N.W. 1115 (1911).

2264. Toms v. Boyes, 50 Mich. 352, 15 N.W. 506 (1883).

2265. Morgan v. Michigan Cent. R. Co., 57 Mich. 430, 25 N.W. 161 (1885).

2266. Timm v. Parker, 316 Mich. 269, 25 N.W.2d 194 (1946).

2267. Oesterle v. Kinne, 243 Mich. 615, 220 N.W. 660 (1928).

2268. Andres v. National Loan & Inv. Co., 283 Mich. 663, 278 N.W. 726 (1938).

2269. Gerasimos v. Wartell's Estate, 237 Mich. 1, 211 N.W. 29 (1926).

2270. Ward v. Munson, 105 Mich. 647, 63 N.W. 498 (1895).

Bassett v. Hathaway, 9 Mich. 28 (1860).

2271. Ward v. Munson, 105 Mich. 647, 63 N.W. 498 (1895).

2272. Ormsby v. Barr, 21 Mich. 474 (1870).

2273. Rorke v. La Duke, 260 Mich. 105, 244 N.W. 247 (1932).

2274. Detroit & Mich. Bldg. & Loan Ass'n v. Oram, 200 Mich. 485, 167 N.W. 50 (1918).

or the debt is presumptive proof of payment.[2275]

Under the Uniform Commercial Code—Negotiable Instruments, the mortgagee may discharge a debt consisting of a negotiable instrument secured by a mortgage by surrendering the instrument to the mortgagee or marking it with words of discharge or cancelling or destroying it, or by a separate writing releasing the mortgagor.[2276] Where an instrument secured by a mortgage appears on its face to have been cancelled, the burden of proof is on the party alleging that the cancellation was made unintentionally or under a mistake or without authority.[2277]

The fact of payment, when disputed, must be established by a preponderance of the evidence.[2278] The failure to furnish that proof results in the refusal of the court to apply the alleged payments in satisfaction of a mortgage debt.[2279] In the same manner, it is also true that such matters as the alleged release[2280] or discharge[2281] of the mortgage in question must be established by a preponderance of the evidence.

2275. Michigan Ins. Co. v. Brown, 11 Mich. 265 (1863).

2276. M.L.P.2d Negotiable Instruments.

MCLS § 440.3604.

2277. Fox v. Mitchell, 302 Mich. 201, 4 N.W.2d 518 (1942).

2278. Niggeman v. McNair, 298 Mich. 357, 299 N.W. 106 (1941).

Rorke v. La Duke, 260 Mich. 105, 244 N.W. 247 (1932).

Shimp v. Sturgis Nat'l Bank, 256 Mich. 481, 239 N.W. 871 (1932).

Oesterle v. Kinne, 243 Mich. 615, 220 N.W. 660 (1928).

Pine Ridge Coal Co. v. Cronin, 41 Mich. App. 255, 199 N.W.2d 876 (1972).

Korf v. Korf, 125 Mich. 259, 84 N.W. 130 (1900) (payment by turning over note of third person).

Credit item

In suit by mortgagors' grantee against loan company to enjoin foreclosure of mortgage by advertisement, credit item appearing on mortgagors' passbook but not found on company's books showed payment of that item by mortgagors where neither party called them as witnesses and did not explain their absence.—Andres v. National Loan & Inv. Co., 283 Mich. 663, 278 N.W. 726 (1938).

2279. Simington v. Goldstein, 330 Mich. 536, 48 N.W.2d 116 (1951).

Goodman v. Rott, 242 Mich. 198, 218 N.W. 761 (1928).

Commercial State Sav. Bank v. Stevens, 180 Mich. 35, 146 N.W. 226 (1914).

York v. West, 147 Mich. 549, 111 N.W. 164 (1907).

Payment construed as down payment

In suit to set aside a mortgage release executed by elderly mortgagee before death, as being without consideration, evidence supported finding that payments made to mortgagee by her granddaughter and husband, the mortgagors, constituted down payments on the purchase price of the land that they acquired from mortgagee and not payments on the debt secured by the mortgage.—Timm v. Parker, 316 Mich. 269, 25 N.W.2d 194 (1946).

2280. Benton Harbor State Bank v. Bubanovich, 259 Mich. 150, 242 N.W. 870 (1932).

Herrick v. Odell, 29 Mich. 47 (1874).

No consideration for release

Evidence warranted a decree setting aside as without consideration a mortgage release executed by elderly mortgagee prior to her death, which purported to discharge mortgage executed by mortgagee's granddaughter and husband, and left mortgagee without security for the payment of debt owing to her.—Timm v. Parker, 316 Mich. 269, 25 N.W.2d 194 (1946).

Release by quitclaim deed

Evidence established that warranty deed to realty executed by husband and wife as owners by the entireties was in fact merely a mortgage to secure grantee against loss by reason of signing bail bond for grantor husband and hence subsequent quitclaim deed by grantee to grantor wife merely operated to release the mortgage or lien against the realty.—Frankowich v. Frankowich, 323 Mich. 516, 35 N.W.2d 478 (1949).

Validity of signature on release

Trial court's finding of material fact issue concerning authenticity of decedent's signature purporting to forgive mortgage debt so as to foreclose summary judgment in action to discharge mort-

Chapter 31

FORECLOSURE BY EXERCISE OF POWER OF SALE

§ 871.   Nature of Remedy

A foreclosure by virtue of a power of sale contained in a mortgage is an ex parte proceeding. A mortgage foreclosure by advertisement is an act of the party and not a judicial proceeding, and is possible only when the mortgage authorizes it.

Library References

> Michigan Digest
> John G. Cameron, Jr., Michigan Real Estate Forms
> Midwest Transaction Guide
> Thompson on Real Property, Thomas Edition (David A. Thomas, ed.)
> Powell on Real Property® (Michael Allan Wolf, ed.)
> Real Estate Financing

Law Reviews

> Frederick L. Miller, Bait and Switch in the Mortgage Market: Coping with High-Rate Sleight of Hand, 85 MI Bar Jnl. 21 (2006); Kevin W. Kevelighan, Consumer Mortgage Defense: Challenging Non-Judicial Foreclosures in District Court Summary Proceedings, 85 MI Bar Jnl. 32 (2006); Nicole Stelle Garnett, The Neglected Political Economy of Eminent Domain, 105 Mich. L. Rev. 101 (2006); Joel M. Ngugi, Re-Examining the Role of Private Property in Market Democracies: Problematic Ideological Issues Raised by Land Registration, 25 Mich. J. Int'l L. 467 (2004).

A power of sale in a mortgage enables the party in interest to effect a complete foreclosure of the mortgage by entirely ex parte proceedings, without submitting his or her rights to or invoking the aid of a court.[2282] The relevant provisions of the Revised Judicature Act of 1961[2283] are the sole basis for the right to effect a complete foreclosure of a mortgage by virtue of a power of sale.[2284] Foreclosure of a mortgage containing a power of sale may be instituted for the mortgagor's default

---

gage was proper on summary judgment transcript disclosing plaintiff's claim that debt was forgiven by memorandum signed by decedent, defendants' denial of authenticity of signature, and documents introduced for purpose of comparing signatures.— Degen v. Estate of Degen, 80 Mich. App. 573, 264 N.W.2d 64 (1978).

2281. Merriman v. Westlawn Cemetery Ass'n, 304 Mich. 12, 7 N.W.2d 126 (1942).

Fox v. Mitchell, 302 Mich. 201, 4 N.W.2d 518 (1942) (evidence sufficient to show discharge).

2282. Power of sale as to trust deed

Trust deed or mortgage with power of sale under foreclosure as provided by law, and without retention of beneficial interest by mortgagors beyond that of ordinary mortgagors, was in its legal effect mortgage and subject to foreclosure by advertisement.—Reid v. Rylander, 270 Mich. 263, 258 N.W. 630 (1935).

2283. MCLS §§ 600.3201 et seq.

No state action subject to constitutional scrutiny

Statute permitting mortgagee to foreclose by advertisement rather than by judicial process would be held to involve no state action as would raise question of due process in regard to mortgagee's exercise of foreclosure option in mortgage permitting such foreclosure by advertisement.— Cramer v. Metropolitan Sav. & Loan Ass'n, 401 Mich. 252, 258 N.W.2d 20 (1977).

Existence of Michigan statute which regulates foreclosure by advertisement is not state encouragement of foreclosure but rather reduces creditor's risk in making repossessions and is therefore not state action for purposes of Fourteenth Amendment.—Northrip v. Federal Nat'l Mortg. Ass'n, 527 F.2d 23 (6th Cir. Mich. 1975).

2284. Guardian Depositors Corp. v. Powers, 296 Mich. 553, 296 N.W. 675 (1941).

on any condition of the mortgage to which the power of sale applies.[2285]

A mortgage is not extinguished by foreclosure by advertisement until sale,[2286] at which point it is extinguished[2287] so long as the sale is valid.[2288]

A mortgage foreclosure by advertisement is an act of the party and not a judicial proceeding, and is possible only when the mortgage authorizes it.[2289] The foreclosure of a mortgage in this manner is valid only where the mortgage contains a power of sale,[2290] although it need not be coextensive with the conditions of the mortgage.[2291]

The statutory provisions for foreclosure by exercise of a power of sale are to be treated as a part of every mortgage with a power of sale.[2292] They must be construed reasonably.[2293] A foreclosure by sale cannot be enlarged beyond the terms of the power of sale and the incorporated relevant statutes.[2294] While statutory requirements pertaining to foreclosure by power of sale[2295] must be complied with,[2296] compliance need be only substantial.[2297] For mortgage foreclosures by sale are matters of contract, authorized by the mortgagor, which are not hampered by an

2285. MCLS § 600.3201.

Dan-Kai Tus v. Hurt, 2009 Mich. App. LEXIS 1440 (Mich. Ct. App. June 25, 2009).

Breach of duty to pay into escrow is grounds for foreclosure by advertisement

Mortgagor who refused to pay moneys into escrow account for property taxes and insurance required under provision of mortgage agreement would be held to have defaulted on condition of performance of mortgage agreement and not on mere covenant for breach of which mortgagee could sue for damages only, thereby justifying mortgagee's exercise of option in agreement authorizing foreclosure of mortgage by advertisement in accord with statute providing for such foreclosure in lieu of judicial process.—Cramer v. Metropolitan Sav. & Loan Ass'n, 401 Mich. 252, 258 N.W.2d 20 (1977).

2286. New York Life Ins. Co. v. Erb, 276 Mich. 610, 268 N.W. 754 (1936).

2287. Mortgage & Contract Co. v. First Mortg. Bond Co., 256 Mich. 451, 240 N.W. 39 (1932).

2288. Masella v. Bisson, 359 Mich. 512, 102 N.W.2d 468 (1960).

2289. Guardian Depositors Corp. v. Powers, 296 Mich. 553, 296 N.W. 675 (1941).

Stewart v. Eaton, 287 Mich. 466, 283 N.W. 651 (1939).

Jackson v. Laker Group, 2005 Mich. App. LEXIS 2736 (Mich. Ct. App. Nov. 3, 2005).

Manufacturers Hanover Mortg. Corp. v. Snell, 142 Mich. App. 548, 370 N.W.2d 401 (1985).

Gehrke v. Janowitz, 55 Mich. App. 643, 223 N.W.2d 107 (1974).

2290. Bradway v. Miller, 200 Mich. 648, 167 N.W. 15 (1918).

Bryan v. Straus Bros. & Co., 157 Mich. 49, 121 N.W. 301 (1909).

2291. Butler v. Ladue, 12 Mich. 173 (1863).

2292. Bass v. Federal Land Bank, 300 Mich. 418, 2 N.W.2d 447 (1942).

Hoffman v. Harrington, 33 Mich. 392 (1876).

2293. Bass v. Federal Land Bank, 300 Mich. 418, 2 N.W.2d 447 (1942).

2294. Arnold v. DMR Fin. Servs., 448 Mich. 671, 532 N.W.2d 852, 1995 Mich. LEXIS 838 (1995).

Senters v. Ottawa Sav. Bank, FSB, 443 Mich. 45, 503 N.W.2d 639 (1993).

Oades v. Standard Sav. & Loan Ass'n, 257 Mich. 469, 241 N.W. 262 (1932).

Spartan Distribs. v. Golf Coast Int'l, 2011 Mich. App. LEXIS 912 (Mich. Ct. App. May 17, 2011).

Jackson v. Laker Group, 2005 Mich. App. LEXIS 2736 (Mich. Ct. App. Nov. 3, 2005).

2295. Masella v. Bisson, 359 Mich. 512, 102 N.W.2d 468 (1960) (procedures for equitable foreclosure are inapplicable).

2296. Senters v. Ottawa Sav. Bank, FSB, 443 Mich. 45, 503 N.W.2d 639 (1993).

Masella v. Bisson, 359 Mich. 512, 102 N.W.2d 468 (1960).

2297. Peterson v. Jacobs, 303 Mich. 329, 6 N.W.2d 533 (1942).

unreasonable construction of the law.[2298]

However, foreclosure of a mortgage by advertisement is a legal remedy, which precludes the application of equitable principles between the parties.[2299] Purchasers at a sale for foreclosure by advertisement should conduct a title search not only at the time of the notice of the sale, but again just before the sale. If construction liens appear, the priority of which cannot be adjudicated in a foreclosure by advertisement, the merits of proceeding with a foreclosure by advertisement are highly questionable as a result.[2300]

A statute regulating the power of sale in a mortgage may constitutionally apply to mortgages previously made in so far as it merely regulates the manner or conditions of the exercise of the power.[2301]

Limitations. The Revised Judicature Act of 1961 provides that no action may be maintained to foreclose a mortgage on real estate by advertisement unless it is commenced within 15 years after the mortgage becomes due and payable or after the last payment is made on the mortgage.[2302]

Land contract mortgages. Mortgages on an interest in a land contract may be foreclosed by advertisement.[2303]

§ 872.   Existence of or Resort to Other Remedy

In order to foreclose a mortgage under a power of sale, it is necessary that no prior action shall have been instituted to recover the debt, or, if instituted, it must have been discontinued or resulted in an execution returned unsatisfied.

The provisions of the Revised Judicature Act of 1961 governing the foreclosure of mortgages by advertisement under a power of sale provide that to entitle a party to make this type of foreclosure, proceedings at law to recover the debt remaining secured by the mortgage must not be pending, and if a proceeding

2298. White v. Burkhardt, 338 Mich. 235, 60 N.W.2d 925 (1953).

Peterson v. Jacobs, 303 Mich. 329, 6 N.W.2d 533 (1942).

2299. Bakian v. Nat'l City Bank (In re Estate of Moukalled), 478 Mich. 854, 731 N.W.2d 87, 2007 Mich. LEXIS 996 (2007).

Senters v. Ottawa Sav. Bank, FSB, 443 Mich. 45, 503 N.W.2d 639 (1993) (redemption statute does not require payment of redemption on lien sale paid by mortgagee during redemption period after mortgagee purchased at foreclosure sale).

Eastern Sav. Bank v. Monroe Bank & Trust & Nationscredit Fin. Servs. Corp., 2002 Mich. App. LEXIS 1843 (Mich. Ct. App. Nov. 26, 2002).

Freeman v. Wozniak, 241 Mich. App. 633, 617 N.W.2d 46, 2000 Mich. App. LEXIS 162 (2000).

2300. Senters v. Ottawa Sav. Bank, FSB, 443 Mich. 45, 503 N.W.2d 639 (1993).

Duty to investigate title

It is the duty of a purchaser of real estate to investigate the title of his vendor, and to take notice of any adverse rights or equities of third persons which he has the means of discovering, and as to which he is put on inquiry. If he makes all the inquiry which due diligence requires, and still fails to discover the outstanding right, he is excused, but, if he fails to use due diligence, he is chargeable, as a matter of law, with notice of the facts which the inquiry would have disclosed.— First Nat'l Bank Of St. Ignace v. Frankovich, 1996 Mich. App. LEXIS 1690 (Mich. Ct. App. Dec. 20, 1996).

2301. Grand River Ave. Christian Church v. Berkshire Life Ins. Co., 254 Mich. 480, 236 N.W. 881 (1931).

2302. MCLS § 600.5803.

2303. MCLS § 565.359.

to that effect has been instituted, the proceeding has to have been discontinued or the execution upon the judgment rendered has to have been returned unsatisfied.[2304] "Proceedings at law" within the scope of this provision refers only to those proceedings in which judgment may be rendered and execution issued against the debtor's property.[2305] It does not include previous foreclosure proceedings,[2306] or a proceeding to have a receiver appointed during the pendency of the advertisement to foreclose the mortgage,[2307] or an action against a separate guarantor of the mortgage.[2308]

The purpose of this limitation that requires the mortgagee to forego an action for personal liability on the mortgage debt in order to maintain a foreclosure by advertisement is to force an election of remedies against the mortgagor.[2309]

The fact that the mortgage creditor had a remedy for the collection of the debt or the enforcement of the mortgage would compel that party to forego the exercise of the power of sale given by the mortgage where the rights of the parties were of such a nature that they could be properly ascertained and adjusted only through the aid of a court of chancery in a judicial foreclosure.[2310] Thus, a mortgagee under a judicially imposed mortgage lien had to foreclose under the provisions for judicial foreclosure of a mortgage.[2311]

2304. MCLS § 600.3204.

Flagstar Bank F.S.B. v. Estate Props., 2010 Mich. App. LEXIS 672 (Mich. Ct. App. Apr. 20, 2010).

No surprise or unfairness

Where plaintiff acknowledged that a record chain of title existed evidencing transfers from the original mortgage holder (Lehman Brothers) to the Trust, and from the Trust to the current lender (defendant). There are no unaccounted for or broken "links" in this chain. And, the foreclosure by advertisement in the case was not initiated by someone outside the chain of title. Plaintiff, however, was unsatisfied with the record chain of title; instead it purported to challenge whether other assignment documents do or should exist, and if so, whether they must be recorded. There is no evidence that other assignments were executed, rather than that the original assignment was executed in blank, transferred in blank to each subsequent assignee (whomever those entities may be), and ultimately (approximately one month later) that the Trust affixed its name as the assignee and recorded the assignment to place all the world (including Plaintiff) on notice of its claim. Because defendant has established a record chain of title from the original lender to it, it had substantially – if not completely – complied with the statutory requirements. Whether some interim assignee held an assignment in blank or any other unrecorded document does not alter or otherwise cloud the unbroken record chain of title in this case. In these circumstances, Plaintiff cannot credibly argue that it (or anyone else) will suffer "surprise or unfairness" if the foreclosure by advertisement proceeds.—Livonia Prop. Holdings, L.L.C. v. 12840-

12976 Farmington Rd. Holdings, L.L.C., 717 F. Supp. 2d 724, 2010 U.S. Dist. LEXIS 47595 (E.D. Mich. 2010).

2305. Larzelere v. Starkweather, 38 Mich. 96 (1878).

2306. Lee v. Clary, 38 Mich. 223 (1878).

2307. Calvert Associates v. Harris, 469 F. Supp. 922 (E.D. Mich. 1979).

2308. United States v. Leslie, 421 F.2d 763 (6th Cir. Mich. 1970).

2309. United States v. Leslie, 421 F.2d 763 (6th Cir. Mich. 1970).

2310. Drayton v. Chandler, 93 Mich. 383, 53 N.W. 558 (1892).

Three mortgages of cotenant

Where a tenant in common held three separate mortgages on a cotenant's interest, all of which were past due, he could not foreclose them by three separate advertisements, but was compelled to foreclose in chancery, where all the rights of the parties would be determined and protected.— Dohm v. Haskin, 88 Mich. 144, 50 N.W. 108 (1891).

2311. Court decree

Where notes and mortgages executed by an incompetent person are declared void by a court but one mortgage is permitted to stand as security for benefits actually received by the mortgagor, the mortgagee's lien exists by virtue of a court decree, rather than by the mortgage itself, and the case was not a proper one for statutory foreclosure by

§ 873.   Necessity for Recording

To entitle a party to foreclose a mortgage by advertisement, it is essential for the mortgage itself, and all assignments under which the foreclosing party claims, to have been recorded.

To entitle a party to foreclose a mortgage by advertisement under a power of sale, the mortgage containing the power of sale and all assignments of the mortgage must be duly recorded.[2312] The failure to keep the mortgage recorded in compliance with the statutory requirements precludes a foreclosure of this type.[2313]

However, a mortgagee's failure to record his or her assignment of the mortgage to a third party as security does not render the mortgagee's foreclosure by advertisement void. The record holder of the mortgage is the holder of the right to the cause of action.[2314]

Securities in a mortgagee's interest in a mortgage are not necessarily assignments subject to the recording requirement.[2315]

§ 874.   Restraining Exercise of Power

A court will enjoin the sale of mortgaged premises under a power of sale where to allow the foreclosure would work irreparable injury.

A court will not interfere with the foreclosure of mortgages in the absence of fraud or irregularity.[2316] The court will only enjoin the sale of mortgaged premises

---

advertisement, the only method of foreclosure being by a proceeding in chancery.—Strong v. Tomlinson, 88 Mich. 112, 50 N.W. 106 (1891).

2312. MCLS § 600.3204.

Michigan Fire & Marine Ins. Co. v. Hamilton, 284 Mich. 417, 279 N.W. 884 (1938).

Reynolds v. McMullen, 55 Mich. 568, 22 N.W. 41 (1885).

Dohm v. Haskin, 88 Mich. 144, 50 N.W. 108 (1891) (assignment not recordable).

2313. Austin v. Anderson, 279 Mich. 424, 272 N.W. 730 (1937).

2314. Livonia Props. Holdings, LLC v. 12840-12976 Farmington Rd. Holdings, LLC, 399 Fed. Appx. 97, 2010 U.S. App. LEXIS 22764, 2010 FED App. 662N (6th Cir.) (6th Cir. Mich. 2010).

Jarbo v. BAC Home Loan Servicing, 2010 U.S. Dist. LEXIS 132570 (E.D. Mich. Dec. 15, 2010).

Arnold v. DMR Fin. Servs., 448 Mich. 671, 532 N.W.2d 852 (1995) (validity of foreclosure was not affected by any unrecorded assignment of interest held for security only).

2315. Reservation of right to foreclose

Certificates of participation in a mortgage that were made payable to the bearer and provided that the mortgagee pay the principal when collected or within 18 months after demand subsequent to the due date, and that the mortgagee reserved the right of foreclosure, were not assignments within the recording statutes so as to make a foreclosure invalid because of the mortgagee's failure to record the certificates.—Canvasser v. Bankers Trust Co., 284 Mich. 634, 280 N.W. 71 (1938).

2316. Calaveras Timber Co. v. Michigan Trust Co., 278 Mich. 445, 270 N.W. 743 (1936).

M.L.P. 2d Mortgages cited in Manufacturers Hanover Mortg. Corp. v. Snell, 142 Mich. App. 548, 370 N.W.2d 401 (1985).

Newton v. Freeman, 213 Mich. 673, 182 N.W. 25 (1921) (action for injunction properly dismissed).

Mortgage upheld

Where redemption period had expired prior to trial of suit to set mortgage aside, provision of decree, upholding validity of mortgage, giving plaintiff 60 days to redeem from foreclosure sale, held in violation of injunction, was justified, and plaintiff was given additional 60 days, from date of filing of opinion affirming decree, within which he could redeem.—Scef v. Scef, 292 Mich. 354, 290 N.W. 826 (1940).

under a power of sale where it is shown that the sale would be against good conscience or that particular circumstances, extrinsic to the instrument, would render its enforcement in this manner inequitable and work irreparable injury.[2317]

A former chancery court would therefore not restrain a creditor from exercising his or her right of sale merely because it would result in a hardship to the mortgagor.[2318] A court of chancery would not interfere to prevent the sale by the mortgagee, under a power of sale contained in a mortgage, of the whole of the mortgaged premises for a single installment, where it appeared that they could not be sold in parcels without injury to the whole.[2319]

In a suit to restrain foreclosure, the court has jurisdiction to decide the question of the priority of mortgages.[2320]

In a suit to restrain the foreclosure of a mortgage under a power of sale, neither party is entitled to costs on denial of the injunction, where the defendant seeks to foreclose for a sum larger than that due, and plaintiff's tender of the amount due is not kept good by payment into court.[2321]

§ 875. Persons Who May Exercise Power

Only the person having legal title to the mortgage at the date of foreclosure is entitled to exercise the power of sale.

Generally, only the person having legal title to the mortgage at the date of foreclosure is entitled to exercise the power of sale contained in it.[2322] The executor or administrator of the owner of a mortgage containing a power of sale can, as the owner of the legal title, execute the power and foreclose the mortgage by

No ground for injunction shown

Evidence justified refusal to enjoin mortgage foreclosure on ground that mortgage was for amount greatly in excess of debt.—Miller v. Ashton, 241 Mich. 46, 216 N.W. 448 (1927).

2317. Calaveras Timber Co. v. Michigan Trust Co., 278 Mich. 445, 270 N.W. 743 (1936).

Larson v. Guaranty Trust Co., 248 Mich. 211, 226 N.W. 819 (1929).

2318. Crow v. Conant, 90 Mich. 247, 51 N.W. 450 (1892).

Case v. O'Brien, 66 Mich. 289, 33 N.W. 405 (1887).

Competitive bidding useless during depression

Harsh results of a mortgage foreclosure sale under a power in a mortgage at a time when real competitive bidding could not be effective because of a financial depression was not sufficient to warrant an injunction against the foreclosure.—Calaveras Timber Co. v. Michigan Trust Co., 278 Mich. 445, 270 N.W. 743 (1936).

2319. Disbrow v. Jones, Harrington Ch. 48 (Mich. 1842).

2320. Patterson v. Miller, 249 Mich. 89, 227 N.W. 674 (1929).

2321. Norris v. Ryno, 169 Mich. 193, 135 N.W. 463 (1912).

2322. Canvasser v. Bankers Trust Co., 284 Mich. 634, 280 N.W. 71 (1938).

Olcott v. Crittenden, 68 Mich. 230, 36 N.W. 41 (1888).

Assignee of mortgage

An assignee of a mortgage could not publish its first notice of foreclosure before it actually acquired its interest in the indebtedness, because the statute plainly requires that a party own the indebtedness or an interest in the indebtedness before undertaking to foreclose a mortgage by advertisement (MCLS § 600.3204(1)(d)).—Davenport v. HSBC Bank USA, 275 Mich. App. 344, 739 N.W.2d 383 (2007).

Nominee of mortgagee

A nominee of the mortgagee had standing to pursue relief from the bankruptcy automatic stay to institute foreclosure proceedings because under Michigan law governing foreclosure by advertisement, the mortgagor expressly gave the right to foreclose to the nominee of the mortgagee (MCLS §§ 600.3201, 600.3204).—In re Mentag (Mentag v. GMAC Mortgage), 430 B.R. 439, 2010 U.S. Dist. LEXIS 62266 (E.D. Mich. 2010).

advertisement.[2323]

A mortgagee who holds record title to a mortgage, but who executes an unrecorded assignment of it as security, is the sole party entitled to foreclose the mortgage by advertisement.[2324] The record holder of the mortgage is the holder of the right to the cause of action.[2325] An assignment of a mortgage must be recorded in order for the assignee to foreclose the mortgage by advertisement.[2326]

A trustee has no power to sell the debtor's property except as might be found in the deed of trust.[2327]

§ 876.   Notice of Sale

The party exercising the power of sale must comply with statutory provisions as to notice. A defect in the notice of foreclosure renders the foreclosure sale voidable, not void.

By statute, a notice of foreclosure under a power of sale contained in a mortgage is required to contain only the names of the parties to the mortgage and their assignees, the date of the mortgage and the date it was recorded, the amount claimed to be due, a description of the premises, and the length of the redemption period.[2328] These requirements are intended to prevent surprise or unfairness and

2323. Miller v. Clark, 56 Mich. 337, 23 N.W. 35 (1885).

2324. Rose v. Fed. Home Loan Mortg. Corp., 2010 U.S. Dist. LEXIS 98955 (W.D. Mich. Sept. 21, 2010).

Arnold v. DMR Fin. Servs., 448 Mich. 671, 532 N.W.2d 852 (1995).

Davenport v. HSBC Bank USA, 275 Mich. App. 344, 739 N.W.2d 383, 2007 Mich. App. LEXIS 1078 (2007).

2325. Arnold v. DMR Fin. Servs., 448 Mich. 671, 532 N.W.2d 852 (1995) (validity of foreclosure was not affected by any unrecorded assignment of interest held for security only).

2326. Jarbo v. BAC Home Loan Servicing, 2010 U.S. Dist. LEXIS 132570 (E.D. Mich. Dec. 15, 2010).

Feldman v. Equitable Trust Co., 278 Mich. 619, 270 N.W. 809 (1937).

Arnold v. DMR Fin. Servs., 448 Mich. 671, 532 N.W.2d 852 (1995).

Davenport v. HSBC Bank USA, 275 Mich. App. 344, 739 N.W.2d 383, 2007 Mich. App. LEXIS 1078 (2007).

2327. Deed clause did not require instruction from noteholder

A provision in a trust mortgage that upon default the trustees or their successors "shall, at the direction of the holder of the principal note herein described, proceed with the foreclosure," did not prevent the successor trustee from taking action on

his own initiative without explicit instruction from the holder of the principal note.—Reid v. Rylander, 270 Mich. 263, 258 N.W. 630 (1935).

2328. MCLS § 600.3212.

Deutsche Bank Nat'l Trust Co. v. Perfetto, 2010 Mich. App. LEXIS 348 (Mich. Ct. App. Feb. 18, 2010) (defendants alleged that the provision that foreclosure proceedings "may proceed unabated without further notice" waived their statutory right to notice of foreclosure).

Gehrke v. Janowitz, 55 Mich. App. 643, 223 N.W.2d 107 (1974) (mortgagors under purported mortgage, which had been foreclosed, could not maintain action for abuse of process against mortgagee on basis of fact that mortgage contained power of sale which was invalid due to lack of any requirement that notice be given).

Notice to condominium association

The statute requiring a foreclosing mortgagee to give a condominium owners association notice of the foreclosure sale of a condominium unit permits "legal recourse" for its violation, and this can include the filing of a civil action that seeks an award of monetary damages; to recover damages under the statute, a plaintiff must prove its actual damages with reasonable certainty, and remote, contingent, or speculative damages cannot be recovered. If actual damage is not sufficiently proved, an award of nominal damages is proper (MCLS § 559.2008(9)).—49 W. Maple Condominium Ass'n v. Countrywide Home Loans, Inc., 282 Mich. App. 452, 768 N.W.2d 88, 2009 Mich. App. LEXIS 303 (Mich. App. 2009).

must be enforced in everything substantial, but the provisions may not be enlarged or unreasonably construed so as to render mortgage sales unsafe or make bidding hazardous.[2329] Therefore, slight and inconsequential irregularities in the notice will not be allowed to vitiate the sale.[2330]

A defect in the notice of foreclosure renders the foreclosure sale voidable, not void. The sale will be voided only if the defect harmed a party.[2331]

The provision of the statute requiring the names of the mortgagor and the mortgagee and the assignee of the mortgage, if any, to be specified in the notice of foreclosure sale is mandatory.[2332] Likewise, a foreclosure sale will be considered invalid where the notice of sale fails to name the mortgagor,[2333] or states his or her name incorrectly.[2334]

But inconsequential errors and irregularities in the naming of the parties that do not affect the substantial rights of the parties will not render the notice invalid.[2335] Thus, the failure of a notice of mortgage foreclosure to indicate that an

2329. Guardian Depositors' Corp. v. Keller, 286 Mich. 403, 282 N.W. 194 (1938).

Purpose of posted notice

Purpose of posted notice of foreclosure sale is to inform mortgagor so that he may see that a price adequate to protect his interests is obtained at sale.—Schulthies v. Barron, 16 Mich. App. 246, 167 N.W.2d 784 (1969).

2330. Guardian Depositors' Corp. v. Keller, 286 Mich. 403, 282 N.W. 194 (1938).

Oades v. Standard Sav. & Loan Ass'n, 257 Mich. 469, 241 N.W. 262 (1932).

Reading v. Waterman, 46 Mich. 107, 8 N.W. 691 (1881).

Lee v. Clary, 38 Mich. 223 (1878).

Title not defeated by irregularities

Bacon v. Northwestern Mut. Life Ins. Co., 131 U.S. 258, 9 S. Ct. 787, 33 L. Ed. 128 (1889).

Unrecorded interim assignments

Unrecorded interim assignments of a mortgage do not create a defect in the record chain of title that would prevent foreclosure by advertisement; a failure by the foreclosing mortgagee to mention assignments to and from an interim assignee who held the mortgage is not a substantial irregularity as to render the foreclosure by advertisement void pursuant to the substantial-compliance rule. A rule that every assignment of a mortgage must occur pursuant to an executed and recorded assignment agreement would effectively prohibit all assignments in blank.—Livonia Property Holdings, L.L.C. v. 12840-Livonia Prop. Holdings, L.L.C., 717 F. Supp. 2d 724, 2010 U.S. Dist. LEXIS 47595 (E.D. Mich. 2010).

2331. Jaboro v. Wells Fargo Bank, N.A., 2010 U.S. Dist. LEXIS 134672 (E.D. Mich. Dec. 20, 2010).

Rose v. Fed. Home Loan Mortg. Corp., 2010 U.S. Dist. LEXIS 98955 (W.D. Mich. Sept. 21, 2010).

Arnold v. DMR Fin. Servs., 448 Mich. 671, 532 N.W.2d 852 (1995).

Us Bank, N.A. v. Whittier, 2010 Mich. App. LEXIS 2175 (Mich. Ct. App. Nov. 16, 2010).

Wells Fargo Bank Mn Na v. English Colony Condo. Ass'n, 2007 Mich. App. LEXIS 2098 (Mich. Ct. App. Sept. 11, 2007).

Homestead Sav. Bank v. Norman Nealey Builders, Inc., 2005 Mich. App. LEXIS 2647 (Mich. Ct. App. Oct. 25, 2005).

Jackson Inv. Corp. v. Pittsfield Products, Inc., 162 Mich. App. 750, 413 N.W.2d 99 (1987).

2332. Guardian Depositors' Corp. v. Keller, 286 Mich. 403, 282 N.W. 194 (1938).

Feldman v. Equitable Trust Co., 278 Mich. 619, 270 N.W. 809 (1937).

Oades v. Standard Sav. & Loan Ass'n, 257 Mich. 469, 241 N.W. 262 (1932).

2333. Oades v. Standard Sav. & Loan Ass'n, 257 Mich. 469, 241 N.W. 262 (1932).

2334. Lee v. Clary, 38 Mich. 223 (1878).

Fatal defect

A statutory notice of the foreclosure of a mortgage, which described one of the mortgagors as Julia, when in fact the name was Tofila, was fatally defective.—Zlotoecizski v. Smith, 117 Mich. 202, 75 N.W. 470 (1898).

2335. Reading v. Waterman, 46 Mich. 107, 8 N.W. 691 (1881).

Date of complaint

Plaintiffs filed their Complaint on March 29, 2010. According to the allegations in the Com-

assignee of the mortgage is a corporation constitutes an inconsequential irregularity that does not render the foreclosure and sale void, where the assignee is not the assignee who foreclosed the mortgage.[2336] Similarly, where a husband and wife execute a mortgage on land that is not a homestead, a notice of sale describing the mortgage as executed by the husband and wife and not specifying that her interest is to be sold will not render the foreclosure invalid.[2337] The failure to mention the assignment of the mortgage to a third party and its reassignment to the assignee of the mortgagee in the notice of sale in a statutory foreclosure is not such a substantial irregularity as to vitiate the sale.[2338]

The notice of foreclosure by sale need not be dated,[2339] or signed by the party foreclosing,[2340] and need not set out the place of sale with any particularity.[2341] It will not be considered invalid because of a failure to set out the fact that no proceeding has been instituted at law to recover the debt then remaining secured by the mortgage.[2342]

The statutory notice of foreclosure sale must also contain the date of the mortgage and the date on which it was recorded, but that notice need not state the hour and minute at which the recording took place.[2343] It also does not have to contain the volume and page number where the mortgage is recorded.[2344] A notice of foreclosure sale that identifies the mortgage by date and parties, and that

---

plaint, at that time the Sheriff's Sale already had been adjourned to March 30, 2010. This distinction, however, did not cause the Court to find that harm was suffered by the alleged defect. To the contrary, it tells the Court that plaintiffs had notice of the foreclosure proceedings and some delay in the foreclosure sale and therefore "lost no potential opportunity to preserve some or any portion of [their] interest in the property. . ." During the redemption period, plaintiffs never tendered any money to redeem the property and they have never stated their interest in doing so.—Jaboro v. Wells Fargo Bank, N.A., 2010 U.S. Dist. LEXIS 134672 (E.D. Mich. Dec. 20, 2010).

Incorrect gender of mortgagor

A published notice of foreclosure incorrectly describing the mortgagor as a "single woman," instead of a "single man," was an "inconsequential mistake" that did not warrant setting aside the foreclosure, because Michigan law does not require that the foreclosure notice include a mortgagor's gender (MCLS § 600.3212).—Worthy v. World Wide Fin. Servs., 347 F. Supp. 2d 502 (E.D. Mich. 2004), aff'd, 192 Fed. Appx. 369, 2006 U.S. App. LEXIS 19458 (6th Cir. Mich. July 28, 2006).

2336. Guardian Depositors' Corp. v. Keller, 286 Mich. 403, 282 N.W. 194 (1938).

2337. Yale v. Stevenson, 58 Mich. 537, 25 N.W. 488 (1885).

2338. Peterson v. Jacobs, 303 Mich. 329, 6 N.W.2d 533 (1942).

2339. Cook v. Foster, 96 Mich. 610, 55 N.W. 1019 (1893).

Date of creation of amended mortgage

Advertisement of foreclosure of mortgage was not insufficient for lack of date of creation of amended mortgage where missing date could not confuse anyone since advertisement contained adequate detailed information regarding property and mortgagor.—Calvert Associates v. Harris, 469 F. Supp. 922 (E.D. Mich. 1979).

2340. Michigan State Ins. Co. v. Soule, 51 Mich. 312, 16 N.W. 662 (1883).

2341. McCammon v. Detroit, Lansing & N. R. Co., 103 Mich. 104, 61 N.W. 273 (1894).

Sale at courthouse

A notice of mortgage foreclosure sale stating that sale would be held at the front door of courthouse without specifying which of two doors identical in appearance and construction was the front door of the courthouse was not violative of the statute prescribing what notice must contain, since the place of sale need not be stated with any particularity.—Bass v. Federal Land Bank, 300 Mich. 418, 2 N.W.2d 447 (1942).

2342. Guardian Depositors' Corp. v. Keller, 286 Mich. 403, 282 N.W. 194 (1938).

2343. Woodruff v. Coffman, 139 Mich. 634, 103 N.W. 166 (1905).

Lee v. Clary, 38 Mich. 223 (1878).

2344. McCammon v. Detroit, Lansing & N. R. Co., 103 Mich. 104, 61 N.W. 273 (1894).

accurately describes the time and place of its recording, is not rendered invalid by having the date of the mortgage given once incorrectly and once correctly.[2345] A notice giving the date of the mortgage, the names of the parties, and the volume and page where the mortgage is recorded is sufficient and valid even though the date of recording is not given.[2346] In like manner, a notice of foreclosure of a mortgage that states the correct date of the recording of the instrument and the volume and page of the record in which it is recorded is sufficient even though it does not state the correct date of the instrument.[2347]

The notice must also contain the amount claimed to be due on the mortgage at the date of the notice,[2348] but the mere fact that the notice claims a larger amount than is actually due will not render the foreclosure proceedings void, where no actual injury or fraudulent purpose is shown.[2349]

A foreclosure of a mortgage on a single parcel of realty for a delinquency in several installments of the secured indebtedness is not void because the notice of sale does not specify the amount of each installment and the sale is for a gross sum claimed to be due under the mortgage.[2350]

The description of the mortgaged premises in the notice of mortgage foreclosure sale is required only to agree with that in the mortgage substantially[2351] so as to prevent surprise or unfairness.[2352] Whether mistakes in a description of the mortgaged premises defeat the foreclosure sale depends upon the effect they are likely to have upon the persons interested.[2353] In this respect, a foreclosure under a power of sale is void if one advertisement is made to cover two mortgages in which the descriptions are not identical.[2354]

2345. Reading v. Waterman, 46 Mich. 107, 8 N.W. 691 (1881).

2346. Lau v. Scribner, 197 Mich. 414, 163 N.W. 914 (1917).

2347. Brown v. Burney, 128 Mich. 205, 87 N.W. 221 (1901).

2348. MCLS § 600.3212.

Wollet v. Wolf, 2009 Mich. App. LEXIS 477 (Mich. Ct. App. Mar. 3, 2009).

2349. Huyck v. Graham, 82 Mich. 353, 46 N.W. 781 (1890).

Amount due after date of notice

Under statute, providing that notice of foreclosure sale shall state the amount claimed to be due at the date thereof, the sale will not be void, where the amount stated included a sum due on the day after its date, but it was not published until several days thereafter, and it does not appear that there was bad faith, or that any one was misled.—Cook v. Foster, 96 Mich. 610, 55 N.W. 1019 (1893).

Claim of attorney's fee

A statutory foreclosure is not invalid because the notice of sale claimed an attorney's fee to which the mortgagee was not entitled.—Millard v. Truax, 47 Mich. 251, 10 N.W. 358 (1881).

2350. Canvasser v. Bankers Trust Co., 284 Mich. 634, 280 N.W. 71 (1938).

2351. MCLS § 600.3212.

Wollet v. Wolf, 2009 Mich. App. LEXIS 477 (Mich. Ct. App. Mar. 3, 2009).

2352. Snyder v. Hemmingway, 47 Mich. 549, 11 N.W. 381 (1882) (no designation of precise parcels to be sold).

Location ascertainable

Mortgage foreclosure and sale were not rendered void because of fact that the mortgaged property was erroneously described in the notice of foreclosure sale as the northwest instead of the northeast corner of West Vernor highway and Twenty-third avenues, since the notice described the mortgaged premises with such certainty that a prospective purchaser was directed to the record and plat from which he could ascertain the exact location of the premises.—Guardian Depositors' Corp. v. Keller, 286 Mich. 403, 282 N.W. 194 (1938).

2353. Guardian Depositors' Corp. v. Keller, 286 Mich. 403, 282 N.W. 194 (1938).

2354. Morse v. Byam, 55 Mich. 594, 22 N.W. 54 (1885).

Personal notice. Foreclosure by advertisement under a power of sale requires only constructive notice, not actual notice, to the mortgagor.[2355] For that reason, if the statutes authorizing the foreclosure are strictly followed, the fact that the mortgagor is not personally served with notice of the foreclosure proceedings does not require setting the proceedings aside.[2356]

§ 877.   —Publication and Posting

The notice of foreclosure must be published, and a copy of it must be posted on the premises to be sold.

Notice that the mortgage will be foreclosed by a sale of the mortgaged premises must be given by publishing the same for four successive weeks at least once each week in a newspaper. The newspaper has to be published in the county in which the premises included in the mortgage and intended to be sold are situated or, if no newspaper is published in that county, in an adjacent county.[2357] The publication is sufficient even if the newspaper is a village paper with small circulation,[2358] an obscure village paper,[2359] or the newspaper's location and name changes during the period of publication.[2360]

An interval having the duration of the number of weeks of publication must be maintained between the time of the first publication and the sale.[2361] A foreclosure is thus invalid where the notice, even though published once a week for the requisite number of weeks, provides for the sale on a day less than the statutory number of weeks from the first publication.[2362]

2355. Windisch v. Mortgage Sec. Corp., 254 Mich. 492, 236 N.W. 880 (1931).

2356. Robulus v. American State Bank, 258 Mich. 21, 241 N.W. 831 (1932).

Moss v. Keary, 231 Mich. 295, 204 N.W. 93 (1925).

2357. MCLS § 600.3208.

Mortgage provision contrary to statute is unenforceable

Mortgage provision that mortgagee may without notice to any persons take possession and sell property was directly contrary to this section, which provides for publication and posting by way of notice to the mortgagor that the foreclosure is under way, and while such power of sale may be valid in some states, under statutes which do not contain notice provisions of Michigan law, such a power of sale is not the power of sale contemplated by MCLS § 600.3201, and is foreign to Michigan jurisprudence and ineffectual as a basis for foreclosure by advertisement.—Gehrke v. Janowitz, 55 Mich. App. 643, 223 N.W.2d 107 (1974).

Publication constitutionally sufficient notice to secondary mortgagor

Statutory notice by publication was constitutionally sufficient as against junior mortgagor, without need for personal service to support valid foreclosure by advertisement.—Cheff v. Edwards, 203 Mich. App. 557, 513 N.W.2d 439 (1994).

Standing

Plaintiff asserted that he had standing because there is a actual dispute as to whether notice of the foreclosure was posted at the property as required. And that the foreclosure was invalid because defendant did not provide him with proper notice of his right to request a modification meeting. Implicit in this argument is the notion that these alleged defect are sufficient irregularities to void the foreclosure sale. Once the redemption period expired, plaintiff lost standing to assert defects in the foreclosure proceedings and/or the sheriff's sale.—Mazur v. Wash. Mut. Bank, F.A., 2011 U.S. Dist. LEXIS 1911 (E.D. Mich. Jan. 10, 2011).

2358. Moss v. Keary, 231 Mich. 295, 204 N.W. 93 (1925).

2359. Lau v. Scribner, 197 Mich. 414, 163 N.W. 914 (1917).

2360. Perkins v. Keller, 43 Mich. 53, 4 N.W. 559 (1880).

2361. Gantz v. Toles, 40 Mich. 725 (1879) (decided under prior statute).

2362. Bacon v. Kennedy, 56 Mich. 329, 22 N.W. 824 (1885) (decided under prior statute).

Posting on premises. In every case, within 15 days after the first publication of notice, a true copy of the notice must be posted in a conspicuous place on the premises described in the notice.[2363] In this regard, a notice of foreclosure may be posted on a stake or post close enough to a highway so that the notice is visible for inspection.[2364]

The purpose of the posted notice is to inform the mortgagor so that the mortgagor may see that a price adequate to protect his or her interests is obtained at sale, and not understanding the nature of the posted notice is not a defense to the mortgagor's failure to do so.[2365]

A party contending that a posting is insufficient has the burden of proof to that effect.[2366]

A mortgagee has a statutory right to enter the mortgaged premises to post notices necessary for an action for foreclosure by advertisement.[2367]

§ 878. Sale

The foreclosure sale must be executed in strict compliance with statutory provisions, and good faith will not excuse a

---

2363. MCLS § 600.3208.

Nafso v. Wells Fargo Bank, NA., 2011 U.S. Dist. LEXIS 44654 (E.D. Mich. Apr. 26, 2011) (assertion that party has standing because there is a actual dispute as to whether notice of the foreclosure was posted at the property as required).

Cox v. Townsend, 90 Mich. App. 12, 282 N.W.2d 223 (1979).

Conspicuous place

Where plaintiff supplied his affidavit stating that he did not see a notice of notice of a lien foreclosure sale on the condominium prior to the sheriff's sale, the defendant provided a copy of the Sheriff's Deed on lien foreclosure that states, "pursuant to the statute of the State of Michigan in such case made and provided, a notice was duly published and a copy thereof was duly posted in a conspicuous place upon the premises described in said lien. . ." The affidavit attached to the Sheriff's Deed reflected the posting on the left side of the door. Such an affidavit is presumptive evidence of the facts contained therein. The fact that plaintiff did not see the notice is insufficient to create a genuine issue of material fact in light of documentary evidence that the notice was duly posted in a conspicuous place.—Matteson v. Stonehenge Condo. Ass'n, 2002 Mich. App. LEXIS 1290 (Mich. Ct. App. Sept. 10, 2002).

Showing of proper posting

Where it appeared that the only contested issue was whether notice of foreclosure sale had been posted pursuant to statute and that affidavit setting forth time, manner and place of posting had been executed and recorded, and District Court found as a fact, on substantial evidence, that copy of notice was posted in conspicuous place on premises described, and that this constituted a proper posting in accordance with statutes, and that no defect was shown in connection with foreclosure proceedings, judgment was affirmed.—Goodell v. Provident Mut. Life Ins. Co., 129 F.2d 468 (6th Cir. Mich. 1942).

2364. Fence post

Requirement in mortgage foreclosure statute that notice of foreclosure sale be posted in conspicuous place on any part of premises described in notice was satisfied under circumstances by affixing notice to fence post at corner of subject 1,100-acre parcel near shoulder of highway allowing vehicles to safely stop for inspection, where post had been used in past for affixing sales and other notices and mortgagors did not reside on parcel.—Cox v. Townsend, 90 Mich. App. 12, 282 N.W.2d 223 (1979).

Stake

Notice of foreclosure posted on a stake driven into the ground on a knoll 300 feet from the mortgaged house and 30 feet from a highway from which the notice is visible, constitutes sufficient posting.—Jennings v. Arnold, 272 Mich. 599, 262 N.W. 419 (1935).

2365. Schulthies v. Barron, 16 Mich. App. 246, 167 N.W.2d 784 (1969).

2366. Cox v. Townsend, 90 Mich. App. 12, 282 N.W.2d 223 (1979).

2367. MCLS § 600.3276.

substantial defect. The person making the foreclosure sale may adjourn it from time to time at the request of the mortgagee.

The Revised Judicature Act of 1961 provides that a sale pursuant to a foreclosure by advertisement must be public, occur between the hours of 9 A.M. and 4 P.M. at the location of the circuit court in the county in which the premises to be sold are situated, and be made by the person appointed for that purpose in the mortgage, or by the sheriff, undersheriff, or deputy sheriff of the county, to the highest bidder.[2368] Upon the instructions of the mortgagee, the sale may thus be validly made by the sheriff,[2369] or by a deputy sheriff.[2370]

Proceedings to foreclose and sell under the statutes governing foreclosure by advertisement must comply with statutory directions in all particulars.[2371] Good faith on the part of the one making the sale is also required, but any misstep or defect in matters of substance cannot be cured merely by showing that it was not induced by bad faith or that it occurred by mistake.[2372]

A foreclosure by advertisement requires reasonable certainty that there will be no confusion on the part of prospective purchasers regarding the property offered for sale.[2373] Irregularities in the proceedings that may lead to confusion regarding the property offered will require the setting aside of the sale.[2374]

The validity of the mortgage is not affected by a foreclosure sale that is conducted in violation of the statutes for foreclosure by sale of the mortgaged property.[2375] A decree voiding a mortgage foreclosure sale for procedural defects does not preclude a subsequent foreclosure and sale in accordance with the statute, nor bar a suit in which a matter not embraced within the scope of the defective action can properly be raised and determined.[2376]

A sale under a power in a mortgage is not rendered invalid by the fact that it is made to satisfy an excessive claim.[2377] Nonetheless, a mortgagee may not execute the power of sale to compel the mortgagor to pay more than the mortgagor owes, on

2368. MCLS § 600.3216.

2369. Watson v. Lynch, 127 Mich. 365, 86 N.W. 807 (1901).

Snyder v. Hemmingway, 47 Mich. 549, 11 N.W. 381 (1882).

2370. Heinmiller v. Hatheway, 60 Mich. 391, 27 N.W. 558 (1886).

2371. Masella v. Bisson, 359 Mich. 512, 102 N.W.2d 468 (1960).

Feldman v. Equitable Trust Co., 278 Mich. 619, 270 N.W. 809 (1937).

Pierce v. Grimley, 77 Mich. 273, 43 N.W. 932 (1889).

Miller v. Clark, 56 Mich. 337, 23 N.W. 35 (1885).

2372. Grover v. Fox, 36 Mich. 461 (1877).

2373. Hogan v. Hester Inv. Co., 257 Mich. 627, 241 N.W. 881 (1932).

Mistake of installments versus gross sum does not invalidate sale

Foreclosure of a mortgage on a single parcel of realty for a delinquency in several installments of the secured indebtedness was not invalid because the sale was for the gross sum claimed to be due under the mortgage.—Canvasser v. Bankers Trust Co., 284 Mich. 634, 280 N.W. 71 (1938).

2374. Hogan v. Hester Inv. Co., 257 Mich. 627, 241 N.W. 881 (1932).

2375. Masella v. Bisson, 359 Mich. 512, 102 N.W.2d 468 (1960).

2376. Masella v. Bisson, 359 Mich. 512, 102 N.W.2d 468 (1960).

2377. Emmons v. Sowden, 78 Mich. 171, 43 N.W. 1100 (1889) (attorney's fees and unpaid taxes).

pain of forfeiting the entire estate.[2378]

The person making the foreclosure sale may adjourn it from time to time at the request of the mortgagee, but may have to give notice of the adjournment.[2379]

Who may purchase. The mortgagee, the mortgagee's assignees, or the mortgagee's or assignees' legal representatives may purchase all or part of the premises fairly and in good faith at the foreclosure sale.[2380] As a result, it is perfectly competent for the parties to a mortgage to insert a provision authorizing the mortgagee to bid and become the purchaser at his or her own sale under the mortgage, and such a purchase will be considered valid where the sale is honestly and fairly conducted.[2381]

With regard to the question of who may purchase at such a foreclosure sale, a purchaser at a sale who contracts to convey the land two years after the sale to the mortgagor's administrator in his or her own right, who uses the funds of the estate in making a part payment on the contract, does not show fraud and collusion at the

---

2378. Sandford v. Flint, 24 Mich. 26 (1871).

Interest properly includible

Interest accruing after institution of proceedings to foreclose mortgage becomes part of amount of lien for which land may be sold.—New York Life Ins. Co. v. Erb, 276 Mich. 610, 268 N.W. 754 (1936).

2379. MCLS § 600.3220.

Prudential Ins. Co. v. Dworkin, 266 Mich. 105, 253 N.W. 233 (1934).

Grand Rapids Trust Co. v. Von Zellen, 260 Mich. 341, 244 N.W. 496 (1932).

Absence of injury in lack of notice of adjournment

Where an injunction restraining a foreclosure sale by advertisement, which was served less than an hour before the time for sale, made no provision for adjournment and left no time to obtain an order for an adjournment and the sale was not held and no adjournment had or announcement made relative thereto but, later, the attorneys consented to modification of the injunction to permit a postponement and the advertisement appeared the next week and thereafter with a notice appended that there had been an adjournment to a certain date, and at a sale held on that date the mortgagee bid in the property, a suit by second mortgagees to enjoin conveyance by the purchaser after expiration of the redemption period on the ground that the sale was invalid under former section was properly dismissed in the absence of any showing of injury occasioned by the adjournment or reason for not redeeming from the sale or for not adopting adequate means of protection open to them as second mortgagees.—Ginsburg v. McBride, 248 Mich. 221, 226 N.W. 873 (1929).

Notice

Mortgagee may adjourn sale before or at time of and at place where sale is to be made, and posting notice of adjournment 25 minutes after sale time is within law.—Gottlieb v. McArdle, 580 F. Supp. 1523 (E.D. Mich. 1984).

Notice provided on a weekly basis

Valid weekly notices of the adjournment of a foreclosure sale are conclusive proof of compliance. Where notice of adjournment is provided on a weekly basis, the notice is required only to be posted in the place where the sale was to occur.—Bramlage v. Wells Fargo Home Mortg., Inc., 144 Fed. Appx. 489, 2005 U.S. App. LEXIS 15990, 2005 FED App. 648N (6th Cir.), 2005 FED App. 0648N (6th Cir.) (6th Cir. Mich. 2005).

2380. MCLS § 600.3228.

2381. Gage v. Sanborn, 106 Mich. 269, 64 N.W. 32 (1895).

Mortgage provision not in bonds

Where there was nothing on face of bonds indicating that holder of them would be compelled, in case of foreclosure of trust mortgage by which bonds were secured, to take a pro rata share in real estate held by trustee, and bonds contained provisions purporting to give them all attributes of a negotiable instrument, mortgage provision to which no reference was made in bonds, but which allegedly authorized trustee to bid at foreclosure sale for all bondholders without presenting the bonds or obtaining consent of all the bondholders, and to satisfy its bid by crediting the mortgage debt thereon, was unenforceable.—Equitable Trust Co. v. Barlum Realty Co., 294 Mich. 167, 292 N.W. 691 (1940).

foreclosure sale between the administrator and the purchaser.[2382]

§ 879.   —Sale in Parcels

Where the mortgaged premises consist of separate farms, tracts, or lots capable of separate use and enjoyment, they must be sold as parcels and not in gross.

Under the Revised Judicature Act of 1961, if the mortgaged premises consist of distinct farms, tracts, or lots not occupied as one parcel, they must be sold separately. But no more farms, tracts, or lots may be sold than are necessary to satisfy the amount due on the mortgage at the date of the notice of sale. If distinct lots are occupied as one parcel, they may in that case be sold together.[2383] This provision is for the benefit of the mortgagor's redemption rights[2384] and for obviating the sale of more property than is required to satisfy the mortgagee's claim.[2385]

The question whether the mortgaged premises are in one parcel, authorizing foreclosure in gross, is generally dependent on whether the premises are used or intended to be used as one tract.[2386] Thus, where the premises, as used or occupied,

---

2382. Harris v. Creveling, 80 Mich. 249, 45 N.W. 85 (1890).

2383. MCLS § 600.3224.

Imperial Constr. Co. v. Indep. Bank, 2011 Mich. App. LEXIS 514 (Mich. Ct. App. Mar. 17, 2011) (MCLS § 600.3224 is mandatory rather than discretionary).

"Distinct"

Under mortgage foreclosure statute requiring sale only of such tracts as necessary to satisfy mortgage debt where mortgaged premises consist of distinct farm, tracts, or lots not occupied as one parcel, term "distinct" means separate or different, as opposed to same in sense of being occupied and treated by owner as whole of one farm, even though it is cut by highway or section lines.—Cox v. Townsend, 90 Mich. App. 12, 282 N.W.2d 223 (1979).

Proper inquiry for determination

The proper inquiry in determining if the property consists of one parcel is whether, at the time of the foreclosure sale, the property was held, treated, occupied, or used as one continuous parcel. MCLS § 600.3224 does not require that the parcels be sold separately when doing so would be arbitrary or impractical. When land is mortgaged as a single parcel, it may be sold as such. Finally, the mortgagor has the burden of proof in establishing that the lots where not occupied as one parcel.—Sweet Air Inv., Inc. v. Kenney, 275 Mich. App. 492, 739 N.W.2d 656, 2007 Mich. App. LEXIS 1259 (2007).

2384. Masella v. Bisson, 359 Mich. 512, 102 N.W.2d 468 (1960).

Petoskey v. Home Owners' Loan Corp., 300 Mich. 391, 1 N.W.2d 584 (1942).

Cox v. Townsend, 90 Mich. App. 12, 282 N.W.2d 223 (1979).

Protection of redemption rights

The statutory provision requiring a sale in parcels on statutory foreclosure by advertisement, is not merely directory, but is for the benefit of the mortgagor and purchasers from him, and is intended to protect important rights in the redemption of the premises, as well as being best calculated to bring a better price at the sale.—Keyes v. Sherwood, 71 Mich. 516, 39 N.W. 740 (1888).

2385. Purposes

Purposes of statute providing that if mortgaged premises consist of distinct farms, tracts, or lots not occupied as one parcel, they should be sold separately is to protect parties having interests in mortgaged premises by insuring a right of redemption where occupancy and ownership are other than as one parcel, and to obviate sale of more of such interests than required to satisfy mortgage and incidental costs and expenses.—Masella v. Bisson, 359 Mich. 512, 102 N.W.2d 468 (1960).

2386. Masella v. Bisson, 359 Mich. 512, 102 N.W.2d 468 (1960).

Baratto v. Pitcher, 263 Mich. 307, 248 N.W. 631 (1933).

constitutes but one farm, lot, or parcel, the property must be offered as a whole.[2387] An owner's constructive occupancy of the whole of the mortgaged premises as one parcel justifies foreclosure in gross.[2388]

The sale of parcels in bulk that the mortgagor is entitled to have sold in parcels is invalid under the Revised Judicature Act of 1961.[2389]

On the other hand, although mortgaged premises may be sold under a power of sale in the mortgage as a single parcel where they are so mortgaged, even though they have been since subdivided by the mortgagor, but without the mortgagee's concurrence, where the parties have joined in obtaining the release of a parcel so situated as to leave the rest in distinct parcels, and thus affect the security, the sale is void if not made in parcels.[2390] Similarly, where the property covered by the mortgage is separated into several distinct tracts or lots either by natural boundaries or by the fact that the parcels are not contiguous so that the separate tracts or parcels are susceptible of separate and distinct enjoyment, the property should not be put up for sale as a whole, but the separate parcels must first be offered singly.[2391] In this

---

2387. Gage v. Sanborn, 106 Mich. 269, 64 N.W. 32 (1895).

Cox v. Townsend, 90 Mich. App. 12, 282 N.W.2d 223 (1979).

Harris v. Creveling, 80 Mich. 249, 45 N.W. 85 (1890) (two adjoining farm lots).

Yale v. Stevenson, 58 Mich. 537, 25 N.W. 488 (1885) (two lots enclosed by fence).

Burden on plaintiff

Where it was plaintiff's burden to establish that the lots were not occupied as one parcel, the trial court did not err in concluding that MCLS § 600.3224 did not require the sale of the lots as separate parcels.—Imperial Constr. Co. v. Indep. Bank, 2011 Mich. App. LEXIS 514 (Mich. Ct. App. Mar. 17, 2011).

Connected and interrelated parcels

The sale of individual parcels of property covered under a single mortgage is required only when those parcels are in fact physically separated and not connected or interrelated in their use or occupancy; parcels did not have to be sold separately where they were connected and physically accessible to each other by a bridge and the parcel occupied by the caretaker was integral to the main parcel because it was used to maintain the main parcel and for the primary function of the property, which was to raise show dogs (MCLS § 600.3224).—Sweet Air Inv., Inc. v. Kenney, 275 Mich. App. 492, 739 N.W.2d 656 (2007).

"Distinct"

Under mortgage foreclosure statute requiring sale only of such tracts as necessary to satisfy mortgage debt where mortgaged premises consist of distinct farm, tracts, or lots not occupied as one parcel, term "distinct" means separate or different, as opposed to same in sense of being occupied and treated by owner as whole of one farm, even

though it is cut by highway or section lines.—Cox v. Townsend, 90 Mich. App. 12, 282 N.W.2d 223 (1979).

Impossibility of separation

Mortgaged land improved by property overlapping lot lines, rendering it impossible to sell lots or parts of lots separately without impairing value of property, was properly sold as entirety.—Grand River Ave. Christian Church v. Berkshire Life Ins. Co., 254 Mich. 480, 236 N.W. 881 (1931).

240-acre farm

Under statute requiring that mortgaged tracts not occupied as one parcel must be sold separately, a 240-acre farm that for many years was occupied as an entirety by mortgagor's family was properly sold as a unit and not in separate parcels.—Postal v. Home State Bank for Sav., 284 Mich. 220, 279 N.W. 488 (1938).

2388. Baratto v. Pitcher, 263 Mich. 307, 248 N.W. 631 (1933).

2389. Masella v. Bisson, 359 Mich. 512, 102 N.W.2d 468 (1960).

2390. Keyes v. Sherwood, 71 Mich. 516, 39 N.W. 740 (1888).

Dunn v. Fish, 46 Mich. 312, 9 N.W. 429 (1881).

Long v. Kaiser, 81 Mich. 518, 46 N.W. 19 (1890) (no opposition to sale as one parcel).

2391. Northwestern Loan & Discount Corp. v. Scully, 256 Mich. 202, 239 N.W. 352 (1931).

Morse v. Byam, 55 Mich. 594, 22 N.W. 54 (1885).

Flax v. Mutual Bldg. & Loan Ass'n, 198 Mich. 676, 165 N.W. 835 (1917) (separate uses).

connection, although plat lines are not conclusive,[2392] on the sale of a large tract under foreclosure by advertisement, the rights of the purchasers of lots under contracts having at least constructive occupancy must be recognized.[2393] Where the mortgaged property is platted and different parcels sold to different purchasers, a statutory foreclosure sale of the property as an entirety is void.[2394] The separate occupancy of parcels of mortgaged premises precluding foreclosure in gross does not require actual residence, but may consist of possession and use that under common law would give title by adverse possession, or may be a constructive occupancy of part of the premises.[2395]

Where a foreclosure sale is made in parcels, the power of sale is exhausted and affords no authority to make further sales of remaining parcels when enough parcels have been sold to satisfy the mortgage debt and all costs and expenses.[2396]

A sale on statutory foreclosure of a mortgage made in parcels, if invalid as a sale in parcels, cannot be sustained as a sale in bulk, even though the sale might have been made in bulk.[2397]

The party asserting that the property consists of distinct parcels that warrant separate sales has the burden of proof.[2398]

§ 880.   —Bids

The property must be sold to the highest bidder. The sale may be set aside under state foreclosure law if the price is so low as to shock the conscience or raise a presumption of fraud or unfairness.

The statutes governing the foreclosure of mortgages by advertisement provide that the property must be sold to the highest bidder.[2399] Such a sale implies a sale to the highest bidder, and it will be presumed that a sale on foreclosure of a

---

Violation of statutory requirement

Where two lots were originally occupied as one parcel for residential purposes and for carrying on a landscaping business, and there was a house on one lot and the other lot was vacant and was used for storage of equipment in connection with landscaping business, but before mortgage foreclosure sale, landscaping business and equipment were sold, and no such business was thereafter conducted on either lot, lots were not occupied as one parcel at time of mortgage foreclosure sale and sale was invalid for failure to comply with statute providing that if mortgaged premises consist of distinct farms, tracts or lots not occupied as one parcel, they shall be sold separately.—Masella v. Bisson, 359 Mich. 512, 102 N.W.2d 468 (1960).

2392. Baratto v. Pitcher, 263 Mich. 307, 248 N.W. 631 (1933).

2393. Northwestern Loan & Discount Corp. v. Scully, 256 Mich. 202, 239 N.W. 352 (1931).

Cox v. Townsend, 90 Mich. App. 12, 282 N.W.2d 223 (1979) (no proof of constructive occupancy).

2394. Walker v. Schultz, 175 Mich. 280, 141 N.W. 543 (1913).

2395. Baratto v. Pitcher, 263 Mich. 307, 248 N.W. 631 (1933).

2396. Grover v. Fox, 36 Mich. 461 (1877).

2397. Grover v. Fox, 36 Mich. 461 (1877).

2398. Imperial Constr. Co. v. Indep. Bank, 2011 Mich. App. LEXIS 514 (Mich. Ct. App. Mar. 17, 2011).

Sweet Air Inv., Inc. v. Kenney, 275 Mich. App. 492, 739 N.W.2d 656, 2007 Mich. App. LEXIS 1259 (2007).

Cox v. Townsend, 90 Mich. App. 12, 282 N.W.2d 223 (1979).

2399. MCLS § 600.3216.

mortgage by advertisement was made to the highest bidder.[2400] Therefore, the inadequacy of the bid price in relation to the value of the realty generally will not alone vitiate an otherwise fair and regular statutory mortgage foreclosure sale where foreclosure is by statutory advertisement rather than by decree.[2401] Thus, a fair price at a mortgage foreclosure sale may reflect a decreased value due to the forced sale of the property.[2402] Even when state-law mortgage foreclosure procedures have been followed, the sale may be set aside under state foreclosure law if the price is so low as to shock the conscience or raise a presumption of fraud or unfairness.[2403]

Where a sale on foreclosure of a mortgage is made to the mortgagee for a grossly inadequate price, without notice to the mortgagor, and the latter files a bond conditioned to raise the bid to an amount considerably in excess of that for which it is sold, the court may, in its discretion, set aside the sale and order a new one.[2404]

The foreclosure sale is not legally complete or binding until the purchaser has actually paid the amount of his or her bid.[2405] Of course, where the mortgagee purchases at the foreclosure sale, failure to pay the amount bid to the sheriff does not render the sale invalid.[2406] The mortgagee is not required to pay the amount of the bid except where it is in excess of the unpaid balance on the mortgage.[2407]

Where a foreclosure occurs by virtue of a power of sale contained in a

---

2400. McCammon v. Detroit, Lansing & N. R. Co., 103 Mich. 104, 61 N.W. 273 (1894).

Farmers' Bank of Grass Lake v. Quick, 71 Mich. 534, 39 N.W. 752 (1888).

2401. BFP v. Resolution Trust Corp., 511 U.S. 531, 114 S. Ct. 1757, 128 L. Ed. 2d 556 (1994).

Macklem v. Warren Constr. Co., 343 Mich. 334, 72 N.W.2d 60 (1955).

Jackson v. Laker Group, 2005 Mich. App. LEXIS 2736 (Mich. Ct. App. Nov. 3, 2005).

Chase Manhattan Bank v. Bos, 2004 Mich. App. LEXIS 2756 (Mich. Ct. App. Oct. 19, 2004).

Intervening condemnation award

Mortgagee's acceptance of condemnation award moneys during period of redemption would not invalidate prior foreclosure proceedings of mortgage, that contained provision allowing mortgagee to apply condemnation award to payment of mortgage debt, where evidence disclosed that total amount of defendant mortgagee's bids at foreclosure sales and amount received as condemnation award were less than mortgage debt.—Petoskey v. Home Owners' Loan Corp., 300 Mich. 391, 1 N.W.2d 584 (1942).

No evidence of potential higher price

Foreclosure sale will not be set aside on the ground of inadequacy of the price bid in the absence of a showing that a larger price could have been obtained, or on the ground that no other bid was made than that of the mortgagee to whom the property was sold where all statutory requirements are observed and there is no stifling of bidding.— Detroit Trust Co. v. Agozzinio, 280 Mich. 402, 273 N.W. 747 (1937).

2402. Removal of business

In action by United States, holder of defaulted mortgage note, against defendant note guarantors for balance due on note after application of foreclosure sale proceeds, evidence, including consideration of loss of automobile dealership formerly operated on premises and depressing effect that forced sale has on value of property, sustained finding that $55,969 bid at foreclosure sale was fair.—United States v. Leslie, 421 F.2d 763 (6th Cir. Mich. 1970).

2403. BFP v. Resolution Trust Corp., 511 U.S. 531, 114 S. Ct. 1757, 128 L. Ed. 2d 556 (1994).

Grossly inadequate price

Where the owner of a mortgage agreed to buy the land on foreclosure sale, but, instead of doing so, sold the land for a grossly inadequate price, which was suffered in reliance upon his agreement, the sale was set aside regardless of the validity of the agreement.—Mix v. Loranger, 50 Mich. 199, 15 N.W. 81 (1883).

2404. Nugent v. Nugent, 54 Mich. 557, 20 N.W. 584 (1884).

2405. C.P.A. Co. v. First Mortg. Bond Co., 287 Mich. 255, 283 N.W. 574 (1939).

2406. Griffin v. Union Guardian Trust Co., 261 Mich. 67, 245 N.W. 572 (1933).

2407. Feldman v. Equitable Trust Co., 278 Mich. 619, 270 N.W. 809 (1937).

Full credit bid rule

The "full credit bid rule" provides that if a mortgage lender makes a "full credit bid" at a

mortgage and the land is struck off for the amount claimed to be due, which includes a considerable sum not allowable as costs, and the owner of the mortgage has become the purchaser, without paying to the officer making the sale the amount of the bid, less what is legally demandable, the sale is incomplete, and the purchaser cannot claim title under it.[2408] However, it will generally not be presumed that a mortgagee who purchases at a statutory foreclosure retains any illegal allowance that the mortgagee claims.[2409] Accordingly, a sale to a mortgagee on statutory foreclosure for an amount in excess of that legally demandable, but claimed by the mortgagee to be due, is not invalid, in the absence of proof that the surplus was not in fact paid to the officer.[2410]

foreclosure sale, the mortgage debt is satisfied, the mortgage is extinguished, and the lender is precluded from making a claim based on an assertion that the property was worth less than the bid; to allow a mortgagee, after effectively cutting off or discouraging lower bidders, to take the property—and then establish that it was worth less than the bid—encourages fraud, creates uncertainty as to the mortgagor's rights, and most unfairly deprives the sale of whatever leaven comes from other bidders. A "full credit bid" is when a lender is permitted to make a credit bid at a foreclosure sale in an amount equal to the unpaid principal and interest on the mortgage plus the cost of foreclosure, and is not required to pay cash because any cash tendered would be returned to it.—New Freedom Mortgage Corp. v. Globe Mortgage Corp., 281 Mich. App. 63, 761 N.W.2d 832 (2008).

Full credit bid rule

A mortgage lender's claims against a mortgage broker, title insurer, appraiser, and others alleging fraud that caused the lender to issue loans on mortgaged property that were worth less than the loan amounts were precluded by the "full credit bid rule"; because the mortgage lender made a full credit bid at the foreclosure sale and was able to assign the mortgages for valuable consideration, the mortgage lender suffered no damages.—New Freedom Mortgage Corp. v. Globe Mortgage Corp., 281 Mich. App. 63, 761 N.W.2d 832 (2008).

The full credit bid rule overrode an indemnity provision in a loan purchase agreement because a mortgagee bidding at a foreclosure sale purchases subject to the conditions of the property, and a lender who makes a full credit bid stands in the same position as any other purchaser.—New Freedom Mortgage Corp. v. Globe Mortgage Corp., 281 Mich. App. 63, 761 N.W.2d 832 (2008).

The full credit bid rule prevented a mortgage lender's recovery under closing protection letters issued by a title insurer.—New Freedom Mortgage Corp. v. Globe Mortgage Corp., 281 Mich. App. 63, 761 N.W.2d 832 (2008).

The full credit bid rule precluded a mortgage lender's claims of negligence and fraud against the

appraiser of the mortgaged property; under the full credit bid rule, the mortgage lender did not suffer any damages.—New Freedom Mortgage Corp. v. Globe Mortgage Corp., 281 Mich. App. 63, 761 N.W.2d 832 (2008).

Mortgagee as purchaser

As a purchaser at a foreclosure sale, a mortgagee stands in the same position as any other purchaser. And if a third party had bought the foreclosed property for the same amount, specifically the unpaid principal and interest on the mortgage, no "delinquent indebtedness" would have remained for defendants to have to pay under guarantee. Consequently, plaintiff's identity as the full credit bidder, rather than a third party, does not expand defendants' obligations under the guarantee. "With [plaintiff's] bid at the foreclosure sale of the entire amount of the indebtedness, no deficiency existed and the absence of a deficiency removed any potential claim of [plaintiff] under the guarantee." In summary, because plaintiff made a full credit bid, no deficiency, i.e., no "amount of delinquent indebtedness," existed that defendants were obligated to pay.—Pines Inv. Co. v. Steuer, 2010 Mich. App. LEXIS 1589 (Mich. Ct. App. Aug. 19, 2010).

2408. Louder v. Burch, 47 Mich. 109, 10 N.W. 129 (1881).

2409. Damon v. Deeves, 62 Mich. 465, 29 N.W. 42 (1886).

Millard v. Truax, 47 Mich. 251, 10 N.W. 358 (1881).

Interest

The inclusion in amount of bid at foreclosure sale of amount of interest installment falling due between date of commencement of foreclosure and date of sale of mortgaged premises did not invalidate foreclosure.—Canvasser v. Bankers Trust Co., 284 Mich. 634, 280 N.W. 71 (1938).

2410. Gage v. Sanborn, 106 Mich. 269, 64 N.W. 32 (1895).

Damon v. Deeves, 62 Mich. 465, 29 N.W. 42 (1886).

§ 881. —Affidavits and Record of Sale

Evidence of a mortgage foreclosure sale may be perpetuated by recorded affidavit.

The Revised Judicature Act of 1961 provides for proving the proceedings in the exercise of the power of foreclosure by sale by recording certified affidavits of the facts and circumstances of the sale with the register of deeds of the county in which the premises are situated as presumptive evidence of the facts that they contain.[2411]

A sheriff's affidavit of postponement of a foreclosure sale is entitled to record. It is admissible in a proceeding to recover possession of lands purchased at the foreclosure sale to establish the facts that it contains, notwithstanding the fact that it was not recorded until after the sheriff's deed and other papers were recorded.[2412]

However, the statutes do not require the proof of the sale to be perpetuated in the records so as to prevent proof of notice by testimony.[2413]

§ 882. Conveyance to Purchaser

The person making the mortgage foreclosure sale must execute a deed to each purchaser. A delay in recording the deed given to the foreclosure purchaser does not invalidate the foreclosure.

The Revised Judicature Act of 1961 provides that the officer or person making a foreclosure sale under power of sale must execute, acknowledge, and deliver to each purchaser a deed of the premises that he or she sells that must be deposited with the register of deeds of the county in which the land is situated as soon as practicable, and within 20 days after the sale.[2414] This statutory provision that the deed be deposited within 20 days after the sale is directory.[2415] A delay in recording the deed given to the foreclosure purchaser does not invalidate the foreclosure.[2416]

2411. MCLS §§ 600.3256, 600.3260, 600.3264.

Purpose of statutes

The statutes relating to foreclosure of mortgage by advertisement authorize affidavits for the purpose of preserving evidence of the sale only, and they are not evidence of the mortgage or conditions therein contained.—Hebert v. Bulte, 42 Mich. 489, 4 N.W. 215 (1880).

2412. Prudential Ins. Co. v. Dworkin, 266 Mich. 105, 253 N.W. 233 (1934).

2413. Lee v. Clary, 38 Mich. 223 (1878).

Testimony did not invalidate affidavit of publication

In proceeding to determine validity of statutory mortgage foreclosure, testimony of witness that she had no present recollection of publication of notice of foreclosure sale, although she identified her signature to affidavit of publication and testi-

fied that statements made therein were true, did not overcome presumption that affidavit was accurate, but was merely to effect that at time of trial she did not remember publication of particular notice, as, under prior similar statute, present recollection was not necessary.—Guardian Depositors' Corp. v. Keller, 286 Mich. 403, 282 N.W. 194 (1938).

2414. MCLS § 600.3232.

2415. Mills v. Jirasek, 267 Mich. 609, 255 N.W. 402 (1934).

2416. Perkins v. Keller, 43 Mich. 53, 4 N.W. 559 (1880).

12-year delay

Neglecting for more than 12 years to record a sheriff's deed of property sold under mortgage foreclosure does not invalidate the foreclosure; for, if redemption is not made within one year from the date of sale, all rights become barred.—

Furthermore, the mortgagor may be estopped to question the sale and the validity of the deed for failure to comply with the statutory provision.[2417]

The officer conducting a statutory foreclosure sale pursuant to a power of sale contained in the mortgage stands in the shoes of the mortgagee, but represents both parties.[2418] Although the presumption that an officer performs his or her duty is applicable to the immediate filing by the sheriff of the requisite deed,[2419] the sheriff's deed is not of itself proof that the foreclosure proceedings were regular and legal.[2420]

The validity of a sheriff's deed executed pursuant to a foreclosure sale is not affected by the fact that no showing is furnished the sheriff prior to or at the time of sale that the notice of sale has been published.[2421] Nor is a sheriff's deed on foreclosure rendered invalid by an error in setting forth the date of a mortgage, that is so described otherwise as to be clearly identified.[2422] Although it is contemplated that the sheriff's deed must be acknowledged,[2423] the fact that a deed on a mortgage foreclosure sale is not acknowledged by the sheriff until five days after it is filed in the register's office does not affect the rights of the grantee of the deed.[2424]

The officer or person making the sale must execute a deed of the premises bid off by each purchaser, and where the lands are situated in several counties, must make separate deeds of the lands in each county.[2425]

A deed that represents a sale as one made in bulk for a single bid is not proper where the sale is in fact in separate parcels and for several bids.[2426]

§ 883.   Title and Rights of Purchaser

The purchaser at a mortgage foreclosure sale acquires all the right, title, and interest of the mortgagor. A purchaser of foreclosed property at a sheriff's sale takes the property subject to all prior liens.

The purchaser at a foreclosure sale executed pursuant to a power of sale, at the

Sanford v. Cahoon, 63 Mich. 223, 29 N.W. 840 (1886).

But see Doyle v. Howard, 16 Mich. 261 (1867).

2417. Mills v. Jirasek, 267 Mich. 609, 255 N.W. 402 (1934).

2418. Hoffman v. Harrington, 33 Mich. 392 (1876).

2419. Sinclair v. Learned, 51 Mich. 335, 16 N.W. 672 (1883).

2420. Bryan v. Straus Bros. & Co., 157 Mich. 49, 121 N.W. 301 (1909).

Hebert v. Bulte, 42 Mich. 489, 4 N.W. 215 (1880).

Barman v. Carhartt, 10 Mich. 338 (1862).

2421. McCammon v. Detroit, Lansing & N. R. Co., 103 Mich. 104, 61 N.W. 273 (1894).

2422. Reading v. Waterman, 46 Mich. 107, 8 N.W. 691 (1881).

2423. MCLS § 600.3232.

Grover v. Fox, 36 Mich. 461 (1877).

2424. McCammon v. Detroit, Lansing & N. R. Co., 103 Mich. 104, 61 N.W. 273 (1894).

2425. MCLS § 600.3232.

Specification of amount

Under statute relating to foreclosure of real estate mortgages by advertisement, an officer making a foreclosure sale under a foreclosure by advertisement of a mortgage on land located in adjoining counties was bound to make a separate deed for land sold in each county and to specify amount for which each parcel was sold.— Heimerdinger v. Heimerdinger, 299 Mich. 149, 299 N.W. 844 (1941).

2426. Grover v. Fox, 36 Mich. 461 (1877).

time of the expiration of the period of redemption, acquires all the right, title, and interest in the premises that the mortgagor has at the time of the execution of the mortgage or at any time thereafter.[2427] Legal title does not vest in the purchaser at the foreclosure sale until after the expiration of the period for redemption.[2428] During this period, the purchaser does have an equitable estate in the property that he or she may assign or transfer.[2429] The assignee or grantee, if there is no redemption, takes the legal title when it matures as the original purchaser would take it.[2430] Under early decisions, such a purchaser could resort to a court of chancery to obtain an injunction to prevent the removal of chattels covered by the mortgage,[2431] and could maintain an action for injury done to the premises by the cutting of timber.[2432] Although the interest of a good faith purchaser at a mortgage foreclosure sale is not subject to prior unrecorded liens,[2433] a sale under foreclosure of a mortgage payable in installments, made subject to such installments, leaves the installments a lien on the land as against both the mortgagor and purchaser at the sale.[2434] However, a foreclosure sale that is not made subject to subsequent installments, after the time for redemption has expired, vests in the purchaser full title to the premises, discharged from all liens of the subsequent installments.[2435]

Where, in order to keep good his or her lien during the period of redemption, the purchaser pays taxes and insurance that the mortgagor is bound to pay under the mortgage, the purchaser cannot, when further installments fall due, again resort to the power of sale for the purpose of securing repayment.[2436]

The purchaser at a sale in foreclosure by advertisement who does not take possession of the property is not liable for premises liability during the redemption

2427. MCLS § 600.3236.

Hanson v. Huetter, 339 Mich. 130, 62 N.W.2d 663 (1954).

Schwartz v. Irons, 4 Mich. App. 628, 145 N.W.2d 357 (1966).

2428. In re Bennett, 29 B.R. 380, 1981 U.S. Dist. LEXIS 10188 (W.D. Mich. 1981).

Bankers Trust Co. v. Rose, 322 Mich. 256, 33 N.W.2d 783 (1948).

2429. Roff v. Miller, 189 Mich. 558, 155 N.W. 517 (1915).

Deed to junior mortgagees

Mortgagee holding sheriff's deed after purchase at foreclosure sale transferred inchoate title by quitclaim deed to second mortgagees while right to redeem was open.—Chauvin v. American State Bank, 242 Mich. 269, 218 N.W. 788 (1928).

2430. Chauvin v. American State Bank, 242 Mich. 269, 218 N.W. 788 (1928).

Roff v. Miller, 189 Mich. 558, 155 N.W. 517 (1915).

Second mortgagee

Second mortgagee, purchasing interest of first mortgagee, who acquired premises at foreclosure,

obtained legal title after statutory redemption period.—Gerasimos v. Continental Bank, 237 Mich. 513, 212 N.W. 71 (1927).

Where mortgagee foreclosed and purchased the property, and after the period of redemption expired second mortgagees acquired the property from the mortgagee, legal title vested in them; the fact that they were second mortgagees not preventing them from acquiring title.—Sanderson v. Ressler, 223 Mich. 232, 193 N.W. 829 (1923).

2431. Guardian Depositors' Corp. v. Keller, 286 Mich. 403, 282 N.W. 194 (1938).

2432. Stout v. Keyes, 2 Doug. 184 (Mich. 1845).

2433. Martin v. Pardee, 223 Mich. 63, 193 N.W. 836 (1923).

2434. Miles v. Kinner, 42 Mich. 181, 3 N.W. 918 (1879).

McCurdy v. Clark, 27 Mich. 445 (1873).

2435. Miles v. Kinner, 42 Mich. 181, 3 N.W. 918 (1879).

McCurdy v. Clark, 27 Mich. 445 (1873).

2436. Walton v. Bagley, 47 Mich. 385, 11 N.W. 209 (1882).

period.[2437]

Land contract mortgages. The purchaser at a sale in foreclosure by advertisement of a mortgage on an interest in a land contract thereby obtains all interests of the foreclosed land-contract vendor or vendee, as the case may be.[2438]

§ 884.   —Possession of Property

A purchaser at a mortgage foreclosure sale may maintain a summary proceeding for possession of the premises involved after expiration of the redemption period.

Mortgagors have the risks and benefits of the mortgaged premises against the mortgagee until the expiration of the redemption period.[2439] During that time, the mortgagee can obtain possession only for consideration and by agreement with the mortgagor.[2440]

Under the Revised Judicature Act of 1961, a proceeding by the purchaser at a foreclosure sale under a power of sale generally will lie to obtain possession of the premises after expiration of the redemption period.[2441] Such a proceeding is a summary one,[2442] and is legal rather than equitable.[2443] Given that the Michigan Court Rules of 1985 allow only the real party in interest to bring an action,[2444] the purchaser is not entitled to prosecute a summary proceeding to recover possession if the purchaser has deeded or assigned the property to another.[2445] In the absence of the purchaser's conveyance, or obligation to convey, there is a presumption that the purchaser is the real party in interest and is entitled to prosecute such a proceeding.[2446]

The purchaser of the property must serve[2447] the requisite demand for

---

2437. Kubczak v. Chemical Bank & Trust Co., 456 Mich. 653, 575 N.W.2d 745 (1998).

Kiley v. Chase Manhattan Mortg. Co., 2008 Mich. App. LEXIS 1441 (Mich. Ct. App. July 15, 2008).

2438. MCLS § 565.359.

2439. Kubczak v. Chemical Bank & Trust Co., 456 Mich. 653, 575 N.W.2d 745 (1998).

Am. Home Mortg. Acceptance v. City of Detroit, 2008 Mich. App. LEXIS 1794 (Mich. Ct. App. Sept. 11, 2008).

Kiley v. Chase Manhattan Mortg. Co., 2008 Mich. App. LEXIS 1441 (Mich. Ct. App. July 15, 2008).

Bennos v. Waderlow, 291 Mich. 595, 289 N.W. 267 (1939).

Russo v. Wolbers, 116 Mich. App. 327, 323 N.W.2d 385 (1982).

2440. Kubczak v. Chemical Bank & Trust Co., 456 Mich. 653, 575 N.W.2d 745 (1998).

Kiley v. Chase Manhattan Mortg. Co., 2008 Mich. App. LEXIS 1441 (Mich. Ct. App. July 15, 2008).

2441. MCLS § 600.5714.

See, also, Guardian Depositors' Corp. v. Keller, 286 Mich. 403, 282 N.W. 194 (1938); Penn Mut. Life Ins. Co. v. Burge, 272 Mich. 350, 262 N.W. 265 (1935); Reid v. Rylander, 270 Mich. 263, 258 N.W. 630 (1935); Prudential Ins. Co. v. Dworkin, 266 Mich. 105, 253 N.W. 233 (1934); and Gage v. Sanborn, 106 Mich. 269, 64 N.W. 32 (1895) (all decided under prior similar statutes).

2442. MCLS § 600.5714.

2443. Shelby Co. v. Dickinson, 259 Mich. 197, 242 N.W. 885 (1932) (decided under a prior similar statute).

2444. MCR 2.201.

2445. Guardian Depositors' Corp. v. Keller, 286 Mich. 403, 282 N.W. 194 (1938).

2446. Guardian Depositors' Corp. v. Keller, 286 Mich. 403, 282 N.W. 194 (1938).

Gage v. Sanborn, 106 Mich. 269, 64 N.W. 32 (1895).

2447. MCLS § 600.5718.

possession prior to initiating the summary process action.[2448]

The burden is on the purchaser or a person claiming under the purchaser in a summary proceeding to obtain possession of the premises to establish the right to possession,[2449] including the burden of proving the regularity of the foreclosure proceeding.[2450]

A summary proceeding against a mortgagor holding over after a foreclosure sale may try the questions of the validity of the foreclosure,[2451] and the sale.[2452] But the purchaser in such a proceeding cannot obtain an injunction to prevent the removal of chattels subject to the mortgage.[2453]

An agreement to extend the time for redemption does not deprive the purchaser of the right to acquire possession by summary means at the expiration of the extended time.[2454]

The mortgagor has the right to rely on fatal defects in the foreclosure proceedings to defeat recovery of possession.[2455] The mortgagor's defenses do not include the right to challenge the validity or effectiveness of the mortgage,[2456] or the capacity of the mortgagee or trustee.[2457] The mortgagor also may not raise matters wholly irrelevant to the record, such as a demand for an accounting to determine the

---

2448. MCLS § 600.5716.

2449. Reid v. Rylander, 270 Mich. 263, 258 N.W. 630 (1935).

2450. Caswell v. Ward, 2 Doug. 374 (Mich. 1846).

Sale as one parcel

In suit to restrain mortgagee from taking possession after claimed invalid foreclosure by advertisement, mortgagor had burden to prove claim that at time of sale of property as one parcel premises consisted of distinct lots not occupied as one parcel.—New England Mut. Life Ins. Co. v. Lindenbaum, 276 Mich. 111, 267 N.W. 797 (1936).

2451. Gage v. Sanborn, 106 Mich. 269, 64 N.W. 32 (1895).

Sale as one parcel

Evidence supported judgment awarding mortgagee possession of mortgaged premises after foreclosure by advertisement on ground that lots covered by mortgage were occupied as one parcel, and hence sale of premises as one parcel in foreclosure proceeding was not invalid.—New England Mut. Life Ins. Co. v. Lindenbaum, 276 Mich. 111, 267 N.W. 797 (1936).

2452. Reid v. Rylander, 270 Mich. 263, 258 N.W. 630 (1935).

Gayles v. Deutsche Bank Nat'l Trust Co., 2010 Mich. App. LEXIS 2040 (Mich. Ct. App. Oct. 21, 2010).

Jackson v. Laker Group, 2005 Mich. App. LEXIS 2736 (Mich. Ct. App. Nov. 3, 2005).

Zachary v. Emmer, 1996 Mich. App. LEXIS 669 (Mich. Ct. App. Nov. 22, 1996).

Defense of invalid sale is available to mortgagor

A mortgagor may hold over after foreclosure by advertisement and may test the validity of the foreclosure sale by raising the question of the validity of the foreclosure sale as a defense to a summary proceeding to recover possession of the property.—Manufacturers Hanover Mortg. Corp. v. Snell, 142 Mich. App. 548, 370 N.W.2d 401 (1985).

2453. Guardian Depositors' Corp. v. Keller, 286 Mich. 403, 282 N.W. 194 (1938).

2454. Audretsch v. Hurst, 126 Mich. 301, 85 N.W. 746 (1901).

See, also, Dodge v. Brewer, 31 Mich. 227 (1875).

2455. Guardian Depositors' Corp. v. Keller, 286 Mich. 403, 282 N.W. 194 (1938).

Gage v. Sanborn, 106 Mich. 269, 64 N.W. 32 (1895).

2456. Reid v. Rylander, 270 Mich. 263, 258 N.W. 630 (1935).

2457. Reid v. Rylander, 270 Mich. 263, 258 N.W. 630 (1935).

amount due.[2458]

But it is not necessary to the maintenance of a summary proceeding against a mortgagor holding over that the mortgagee exhibit the sheriff's deed to the mortgagor.[2459]

§ 885.   —Effect of Defects in Proceedings

Minor irregularities in foreclosure proceedings will not vitiate the title acquired by the purchaser. A decree voiding a mortgage foreclosure sale for procedural defects does not preclude a subsequent foreclosure and sale in accordance with the statute.

The validity of the mortgage is not affected by a foreclosure sale that is conducted in violation of the statutes for foreclosure by sale of the mortgaged property.[2460] An irregular sale is not necessarily a nullity.[2461] Where the right to foreclose exists, the mere improper execution of the power will render the sale at most voidable.[2462] Where the defect is so substantial as to render the sale void, the purchaser generally acquires all the rights previously held by the mortgagee.[2463]

A decree voiding a mortgage foreclosure sale for procedural defects does not preclude a subsequent foreclosure and sale in accordance with the statute, nor bar a suit in which a matter not embraced within scope of defective action can properly be raised and determined.[2464]

Where the parties interested adversely to a mortgage foreclosure allow a considerable period of time to elapse without taking steps to contest the sale, their delay will constitute sufficient assent to the proceedings to entitle the purchaser at the foreclosure sale to hold the land as mortgagee at least, if not as owner.[2465]

Subsequent purchaser as assignee or mortgagee in possession. A subsequent grantee of a purchaser at a void foreclosure sale may become an equitable assignee of the mortgage.[2466] Such a grantee may acquire the status of a mortgagee in possession where the grantee enters with the knowledge and acquiescence or consent of the mortgagor or other person claiming under the mortgagor.[2467]

§ 886.   Proceeds and Surplus

Any surplus after a mortgage foreclosure sale generally belongs to the mortgagor. That the mortgagee fails to pay

---

2458. Reid v. Rylander, 270 Mich. 263, 258 N.W. 630 (1935).

2459. Shelby Co. v. Dickinson, 259 Mich. 197, 242 N.W. 885 (1932).

2460. Masella v. Bisson, 359 Mich. 512, 102 N.W.2d 468 (1960).

2461. Kuschinski v. Equitable & Central Trust Co., 277 Mich. 23, 268 N.W. 797 (1936).

Failure to pay surplus

That the surplus arising at a mortgage foreclosure sale was not paid over to the mortgagor does not render the sale incomplete, and prevent title passing under sale deed.—Sinclair v. Learned, 51 Mich. 335, 16 N.W. 672 (1883).

2462. Fox v. Jacobs, 289 Mich. 619, 286 N.W. 854 (1939).

2463. Lariverre v. Rains, 112 Mich. 276, 70 N.W. 583 (1897).

Hoffman v. Harrington, 33 Mich. 392 (1876).

2464. Masella v. Bisson, 359 Mich. 512, 102 N.W.2d 468 (1960).

2465. Sinclair v. Learned, 51 Mich. 335, 16 N.W. 672 (1883).

2466. Walker v. Schultz, 175 Mich. 280, 141 N.W. 543 (1913).

2467. Morse v. Byam, 55 Mich. 594, 22 N.W. 54 (1885).

over the surplus does not prevent the title from vesting in the mortgagee.

The disposition of any surplus resulting from a mortgage foreclosure sale may be provided for in the instrument itself.[2468] In the absence of stipulations in the mortgage, the surplus remaining, after paying the mortgage debt and proper expenses, belongs to the mortgagor or to a party who has acquired the equity of redemption.[2469] This provision is intended to apply for the protection of subsequent mortgage claimants or lienholders.[2470]

Thus, a mortgagee who bids in the premises on foreclosure at a sum exceeding the debt and legal charges is liable for the excess to the owner of the equity of redemption.[2471] That the mortgagee fails to pay over the surplus does not prevent the title from vesting in the mortgagee.[2472]

With regard to the question of who is entitled to such a surplus, it has been held that a junior judgment creditor, who levies on the debtor's land, subject to a mortgage, but who permits title acquired by the purchaser at a foreclosure sale under the mortgage to become perfect and then purchases such title in hostility to the title of the mortgagor, is not the owner of the equity of redemption so as to enable him to sue the mortgagee for a surplus in his hands arising from the foreclosure sale.[2473]

In addition to the provision that any surplus remaining in the hands of the

---

2468. Wales v. Gray, 109 Mich. 346, 67 N.W. 334 (1896).

Hayes v. Stockwell, 73 Mich. 366, 41 N.W. 324 (1889).

2469. MCLS § 600.3252.

Kennedy v. Brown, 50 Mich. 336, 15 N.W. 498 (1883).

Schwartz v. Irons, 4 Mich. App. 628, 145 N.W.2d 357 (1966).

Effect of mortgagee's bid of entire debt at one foreclosure sale

Where a debtor's bank loan was secured by mortgages on property located in Wisconsin and Michigan, and the bank instituted a judicial foreclosure on the Wisconsin property and a foreclosure by advertisement on the Michigan property, but made "a terrible unilateral mistake" and bid the entire amount of the debt in the Michigan foreclosure, the debtor's debt to the bank was fully satisfied by the Michigan foreclosure and he took the Wisconsin property free and clear of the bank's prior mortgage; the Michigan statute provides that if after the sale of real estate there remains any surplus money after satisfying the mortgage the surplus must be paid to the mortgagor (MCLS § 600.3252).—In re Miller, 442 B.R. 621 (W.D. Mich. 2011).

Interest on surplus

If the interest earned on the overbid surpluses from the county's deposit of the funds in its interest-bearing bank account is greater than the fees properly attributed to those surpluses, the resulting net interest is the property of the individual who owns the principal; the county's retention of such interest, if any exists, without any compensation constitutes a taking of property in violation of the Fifth Amendment (MCLS § 600.3252).—HRSS, Inc. v. Wayne County Treasurer, 279 F. Supp. 2d 846 (E.D. Mich. 2003).

Surplus not claimable by purchaser

The excess paid by a purchaser at a statutory foreclosure sale above the amount due by reason of the addition of attorney's fees belongs to whoever is entitled to the surplus arising in such sale, and cannot be claimed by the purchaser.—Macomb v. Wilkinson, 83 Mich. 486, 47 N.W. 336 (1890).

Value of insurance

Assignees of mortgagors were entitled to cash surrender value of insurance which was not sold with premises, there being no deficiency.—Guaranty Trust Co. v. Shapero, 257 Mich. 608, 242 N.W. 234 (1932).

2470. Schwartz v. Irons, 4 Mich. App. 628, 145 N.W.2d 357 (1966).

2471. Millard v. Truax, 50 Mich. 343, 15 N.W. 501 (1883).

Kennedy v. Brown, 50 Mich. 336, 15 N.W. 498 (1883).

2472. Damon v. Deeves, 62 Mich. 465, 29 N.W. 42 (1886).

2473. Baxter's Estate v. Wilkinson, 97 Mich. 536, 56 N.W. 931 (1893).

person making a foreclosure sale must be paid to the mortgagor or the one entitled to the equity of redemption, the statute governing the distribution of surplus proceeds of a foreclosure by sale provides that a party having a claim against this surplus may file the claim with the person making the sale, who must then pay the surplus to the register of the circuit court of the county in which the sale is made. The court then directs the disposition of the surplus in accordance with statutory procedures.[2474] A claimant's failure to file his or her claim with the person conducting the sale precludes the availability of this remedy to that claimant. That party must seek relief from the party to whom the person conducting the sale properly paid the surplus.[2475]

§ 887.   Fees and Costs

The mortgagee may retain out of the proceeds of a mortgage foreclosure sale the necessary costs and expenses of the sale. A limited attorney's fee on foreclosure of a mortgage by advertisement is allowed.

The expenses of foreclosing a mortgage by advertisement may generally be taxed in the circuit court as in civil actions[2476] upon the request of a party.[2477] The mortgagee may retain out of the proceeds of a mortgage foreclosure sale the necessary costs and expenses of the sale, including advertising costs.[2478] But costs for the sale of property that is withheld from sale because the mortgagor redeems are not taxable to the mortgagor.[2479]

A limited attorney's fee on foreclosure of a mortgage by advertisement is allowed.[2480] But if a redemption payment is made after foreclosure proceedings are commenced but before sale, one half of the allowed attorney's fee may be collected.[2481]

A foreclosure is not rendered invalid because the mortgagee, in the notice of sale, claims an attorney's fee to which the mortgagee is not entitled and makes the purchase for a sum including this fee.[2482] Rather, the illegal attorney's fee must be regarded as a part of the surplus, belonging to the owner of the equity of

2474. MCLS § 600.3252.

Allen v. Wayne Circuit Judges, 57 Mich. 198, 23 N.W. 728 (1885).

Schwartz v. Irons, 4 Mich. App. 628, 145 N.W.2d 357 (1966) (holder of equitable title has claim for surplus).

2475. Schwartz v. Irons, 4 Mich. App. 628, 145 N.W.2d 357 (1966).

2476. *See* M.L.P. 2d Civil Procedure and MCR 2.625.

2477. MCLS § 600.2431.

2478. MCLS § 600.3252.

J.I. Case Threshing Machine Co. v. Mitchell, 74 Mich. 679, 42 N.W. 151 (1889).

Detroit Trust Co. v. Detroit City Service Co., 262 Mich. 14, 247 N.W. 76 (1933) (audit expenses under trust mortgage).

2479. Myer v. Hart, 40 Mich. 517 (1879) (printers' fees cannot be charged if the advertisement is withheld from publication, and payment is meanwhile tendered on the mortgage).

2480. MCLS § 600.2431.

In re Schafer's Bakeries, 155 F. Supp. 902 (D. Mich. 1957).

2481. MCLS § 600.2431.

In re Schafer's Bakeries, 155 F. Supp. 902 (D. Mich. 1957).

2482. Millard v. Truax, 47 Mich. 251, 10 N.W. 358 (1881).

redemption.[2483]

§ 888. Deficiency and Personal Liability

A deficiency remaining after a mortgage foreclosure sale may be recovered from the mortgagor.

The mortgagor is liable for any deficiency arising if a valid sale of the property under the power of sale does not bring enough to satisfy the proper claims of the mortgagee.[2484] The mortgagee may initiate an action at law in order to recover a deficiency to which he or she may be entitled.[2485] A recoverable deficiency may be recovered from a grantee of the mortgaged realty who assumes the mortgage debt.[2486] In such an action, taxes paid by the mortgagee after the commencement of the foreclosure proceedings and before a sale may be added to the mortgage debt of principal and interest in order to compute the entire amount of the mortgage lien and resulting deficiency.[2487]

If a foreclosure sale by advertisement of a real estate mortgage is made and the mortgagee purchases the premises for less than the amount due, and within the allotted time the mortgagors redeem, the recovery of a deficiency is not precluded.[2488]

Generally, a mortgagee is not barred by waiver or estoppel from seeking a deficiency judgment if the mortgagee does not make any admission or statement, or do any act, inconsistent with his or her claim, and the mortgagor is not induced to take any position to the mortgagor's injury.[2489] But the acts of the mortgagee in delaying an unreasonable length of time before the sale that operate to the detriment of the mortgagor may estop the mortgagee from seeking a deficiency judgment.[2490]

The Revised Judicature Act of 1961 provides a defense to a deficiency action resulting from a foreclosure of a mortgage by advertisement. If the mortgagee, payee or other holder of the obligation secured becomes the purchaser at the foreclosure sale, and thereafter sues for a deficiency judgment against the mortgagor, it is competent for the defendant to show, to the extent only of the amount of the plaintiff's claim, that the property sold was fairly worth the amount of the debt secured by it at the time and place of sale or that the amount bid was substantially less than its true value. A showing of those facts act as a defense to the action and

2483. Baxter's Estate v. Wilkinson, 97 Mich. 536, 56 N.W. 931 (1893).

2484. Schram v. Pillon, 45 F. Supp. 942 (D. Mich. 1942).

Postal v. Home State Bank for Sav., 284 Mich. 220, 279 N.W. 488 (1938).

2485. Schram v. Coyne, 45 F. Supp. 1021 (D. Mich. 1940), aff'd, 127 F.2d 205 (6th Cir. Mich. 1942).

Gruskin v. Fisher, 405 Mich. 51, 273 N.W.2d 893 (1979).

Harrow v. Metropolitan Life Ins. Co., 285 Mich. 349, 280 N.W. 785 (1938).

New York Life Ins. Co. v. Erb, 276 Mich. 610, 268 N.W. 754 (1936).

2486. Schram v. Coyne, 45 F. Supp. 1021 (D. Mich. 1940), aff'd, 127 F.2d 205 (6th Cir. Mich. 1942).

2487. New York Life Ins. Co. v. Erb, 276 Mich. 610, 268 N.W. 754 (1936).

2488. Bankers Trust Co. v. Rose, 322 Mich. 256, 33 N.W.2d 783 (1948).

2489. Bankers Trust Co. v. Rose, 322 Mich. 256, 33 N.W.2d 783 (1948).

2490. Eldridge v. Bliss, 20 Mich. 269 (1870).

to defeat the deficiency judgment, either in whole or in part.[2491] Thus, the mortgagor may not obtain a deficiency judgment if the property value exceeds the amount that the property secures for the mortgagor.[2492]

The principal purpose of the statute giving the mortgagor a defense against a deficiency judgment is to prevent a mortgagee from obtaining a judgment for a deficiency where the mortgagee has obtained, by way of foreclosure, the actual title to premises that are of greater value than the amount of the debt secured by the mortgage.[2493] The statute is primarily designed for the protection of mortgagors owning property within the state and not for the protection of mortgagors owning property outside the state.[2494]

Under the statutory defense, the mortgagor is entitled to be credited with the value of the property only if the mortgagee, payee, or other holder of the obligation thereby secured buys the land at the foreclosure sale.[2495] It does not affect any of the other rights of the mortgagee.[2496]

No deficiency judgment may be recovered where there has been foreclosure by advertisement except after an action has been brought against the defendant and

---

2491. MCLS § 600.3280.

Bayview Loan Servicing, L.L.C. v. Batch, 2010 U.S. Dist. LEXIS 108961 (E.D. Mich. Oct. 13, 2010).

Crown Life Ins. Co. v. Hicks, 1994 U.S. Dist. LEXIS 5562 (E.D. Mich. Jan. 7, 1994).

Guardian Depositors Corp. v. Powers, 296 Mich. 553, 296 N.W. 675 (1941).

Chase Manhattan Bank v. Bos, 2004 Mich. App. LEXIS 2756 (Mich. Ct. App. Oct. 19, 2004).

Add amount of all mortgages for determining debt secured by property

Amount of senior mortgage on property was properly considered in determining for deficiency judgment purposes whether second mortgagee paid "true value" of property at foreclosure sale where second mortgagee would have had to pay off senior mortgage or lose land.—First of America Bank-Oakland Macomb, NA v. Brown, 158 Mich. App. 76, 404 N.W.2d 706 (1987).

Evidence supported finding of fair price compared to property's value

Trial court's failure to frame its decision regarding market value of property in dispute in language borrowed from statute governing amounts bid on real property at foreclosure sales did not obscure its finding as the court referred to expert testimony offered by both parties as to market value of property and held that based upon evidence, bid-in price was reasonable.—Kansas City Life Ins. Co. v. Durant, 99 Mich. App. 754, 298 N.W.2d 630 (1980).

Sum paid to prevent satisfaction of deficiency from collateral is not covered by defense

Statute providing that mortgagor may show as defense and setoff to deficiency judgment that property sold at foreclosure sale was worth amount of debt secured by it or that bid was substantially less than true value of property does not apply to provide mortgagor with claim against mortgagee for sum that mortgagor paid to mortgagee to prevent latter from satisfying deficiency out of available additional collateral.—Chabut v. Chabut, 66 Mich. App. 440, 239 N.W.2d 401 (1976).

2492. Two mortgages

One who holds both the first and second mortgages on a property, who forecloses by advertisement the second mortgage, and who purchases the property at the foreclosure sale may not recover the amount owed on the note secured by the first mortgage where it is undisputed that the fair market value of the property exceeds the amount secured by both the first and second mortgages.—Board of Trustees v. Ren-Cen Indoor Tennis & Racquet Club, 145 Mich. App. 318, 377 N.W.2d 432 (1985).

2493. Bankers Trust Co. v. Rose, 322 Mich. 256, 33 N.W.2d 783 (1948).

2494. Reconstruction Finance Corp. v. Mercury Realty Co., 97 F. Supp. 491 (D. Mich. 1951).

2495. Stewart v. Eaton, 287 Mich. 466, 283 N.W. 651 (1939).

2496. Guardian Depositors Corp. v. Powers, 296 Mich. 553, 296 N.W. 675 (1941).

jurisdiction acquired by personal service or by appearance.[2497]

§ 889.   Setting Aside Sale

A mortgagor may maintain a bill to set aside a foreclosure sale in which irregularities of a prejudicial nature occurred. Mere inadequacy of price is not in itself a sufficient ground for setting aside a foreclosure sale.

The mortgagor, on a showing of sufficient grounds, may maintain an action to set aside a foreclosure sale.[2498] This type of action is considered as a bill to redeem.[2499] The decree must provide for redemption on payment of the amount due within a specified time.[2500]

The mortgagee may also have the sale set aside if the mortgagee can show proper grounds, such as excusable mistake.[2501]

A foreclosure will not be set aside without some good reason.[2502] Mere irregularities not affecting the substantial rights of the parties will not warrant the setting aside of a foreclosure sale.[2503] But a sale may be set aside for material and prejudicial errors in the exercise of the power of sale.[2504]

Mere inadequacy of price is not in itself a sufficient ground for setting aside a foreclosure sale.[2505] One reason for that rule is that the owner of the equity of redemption cannot be prejudiced thereby, since he or she may always redeem within the prescribed period by refunding the amount paid.[2506] Furthermore, to set aside a sale for inadequacy of price, there must be either actual or constructive fraud.[2507] Even when state-law mortgage foreclosure procedures have been followed, the sale

---

2497. Stewart v. Eaton, 287 Mich. 466, 283 N.W. 651 (1939).

2498. Kuschinski v. Equitable & Central Trust Co., 277 Mich. 23, 268 N.W. 797 (1936).

Reid v. Nusholtz, 264 Mich. 220, 249 N.W. 831 (1933).

2499. Huyck v. Graham, 82 Mich. 353, 46 N.W. 781 (1890).

2500. Huyck v. Graham, 82 Mich. 353, 46 N.W. 781 (1890).

Schwarz v. Sears, Harrington Ch. 440 (Mich. 1842).

2501. Destruction by fire

Mortgagee bidding in property at amount of mortgage, not knowing buildings were destroyed by fire on day before sale, was entitled to have foreclosure set aside and mortgage restored because of loss through mistake of fact.—Federal Land Bank v. Edwards, 262 Mich. 180, 247 N.W. 147 (1933).

2502. White v. Burkhardt, 338 Mich. 235, 60 N.W.2d 925 (1953).

2503. White v. Burkhardt, 338 Mich. 235, 60 N.W.2d 925 (1953).

Detroit Trust Co. v. Agozzinio, 280 Mich. 402, 273 N.W. 747 (1937).

Griffin v. Union Guardian Trust Co., 261 Mich. 67, 245 N.W. 572 (1933).

Peterson v. Jacobs, 303 Mich. 329, 6 N.W.2d 533 (1942) (irregular notice).

Bass v. Federal Land Bank, 300 Mich. 418, 2 N.W.2d 447 (1942) (irregular notice).

2504. Masella v. Bisson, 359 Mich. 512, 102 N.W.2d 468 (1960).

Louder v. Burch, 47 Mich. 109, 10 N.W. 129 (1881).

2505. Macklem v. Warren Constr. Co., 343 Mich. 334, 72 N.W.2d 60 (1955).

Moss v. Keary, 231 Mich. 295, 204 N.W. 93 (1925).

Blackwood v. Sakwinski, 221 Mich. 464, 191 N.W. 207 (1922).

Chabut v. Chabut, 66 Mich. App. 440, 239 N.W.2d 401 (1976).

2506. Cameron v. Adams, 31 Mich. 426 (1875).

2507. Postal v. Home State Bank for Sav., 284 Mich. 220, 279 N.W. 488 (1938).

may be set aside under state foreclosure law if the price is so low as to shock the conscience or raise a presumption of fraud or unfairness.[2508] Whether a sale may be set aside on this ground generally depends on the particular facts of each case.[2509]

Violation of the requirement that if mortgaged premises consist of distinct farms, tracts, or lots not occupied as one parcel, they must be sold separately is grounds in a proper proceeding for the setting aside of the sale.[2510]

A mortgagor seeking relief from an irregularity in the sale of mortgaged premises by the mortgagee under a power of sale must act promptly.[2511] An unreasonable delay may warrant the denial of relief on the ground of laches.[2512] However, the right of the owner of legal title to contest a voidable sale under a mortgage foreclosure will not be barred by laches where the delay does not materially alter the situation of either party to his or her prejudice.[2513]

A mortgagor may hold over after foreclosure by advertisement and test the

Root v. King, 91 Mich. 488, 51 N.W. 1118 (1892) (mistake).

2508. BFP v. Resolution Trust Corp., 511 U.S. 531, 114 S. Ct. 1757, 128 L. Ed. 2d 556 (1994).

Grossly inadequate price

Where the owner of a mortgage agreed to buy the land on foreclosure sale, but, instead of doing so, sold the land for a grossly inadequate price, which was suffered in reliance upon his agreement, the sale was set aside regardless of the validity of the agreement.—Mix v. Loranger, 50 Mich. 199, 15 N.W. 81 (1883).

2509. Petoskey v. Home Owners' Loan Corp., 300 Mich. 391, 1 N.W.2d 584 (1942).

Guardian Depositors' Corp. v. Keller, 286 Mich. 403, 282 N.W. 194 (1938) (sale price not grossly inadequate).

Postal v. Home State Bank for Sav., 284 Mich. 220, 279 N.W. 488 (1938) (fair and adequate price).

Possibility of higher bid

Where mortgaged property, the fair value of which is shown not to exceed $900, is sold on foreclosure for $890, the fact that one who was present at the first sale is willing to pay $1,000 for the property is no ground for ordering a resale.—Page v. Kress, 80 Mich. 85, 44 N.W. 1052 (1890).

2510. Masella v. Bisson, 359 Mich. 512, 102 N.W.2d 468 (1960).

2511. Fox v. Jacobs, 289 Mich. 619, 286 N.W. 854 (1939).

Kuschinski v. Equitable & Central Trust Co., 277 Mich. 23, 268 N.W. 797 (1936).

Adequate remedy at law

Where mortgagors' property had been foreclosed, period of redemption had expired, circuit court commissioner had entered judgment of pos-session against them and purchaser at sale had taken possession, mortgagors could not maintain bill in equity to require purchasers to restore mortgagors to statu quo enjoyed previous to foreclosure, and mortgagors attacking validity of sheriff's deed had to pursue remedy at law, if any.—Ruda v. American Sav. & Loan Ass'n, 371 Mich. 675, 124 N.W.2d 739 (1963).

2512. Bacon v. Northwestern Mut. Life Ins. Co., 131 U.S. 258, 9 S. Ct. 787, 33 L. Ed. 128 (1889) (13 years' delay).

Rose v. Fed. Home Loan Mortg. Corp., 2010 U.S. Dist. LEXIS 98955 (W.D. Mich. Sept. 21, 2010).

Fox v. Jacobs, 289 Mich. 619, 286 N.W. 854 (1939) (19 months' delay).

Kuschinski v. Equitable & Central Trust Co., 277 Mich. 23, 268 N.W. 797 (1936) (13 months' delay).

Hogan v. Hester Inv. Co., 257 Mich. 627, 241 N.W. 881 (1932).

Jackson Inv. Corp. v. Pittsfield Products, Inc., 162 Mich. App. 750, 413 N.W.2d 99 (1987) (challenging adequacy of notice).

Challenging acceleration

By requesting a reversal of the acceleration, foreclosure, sale and sheriff's deed, plaintiff seeks specific performance of an alleged oral agreement to reinstate the mortgage. Specific performance is an equitable remedy. But because plaintiff did not assert his challenge to the acceleration, foreclosure, sale and sheriff's deed until very late– after the six-month redemption period expired (at which time title vested in defendant) – plaintiff is guilty of laches.—Ursery v. Option One Mortg. Corp., 2007 Mich. App. LEXIS 1861 (Mich. Ct. App. July 31, 2007).

2513. Walker v. Schultz, 175 Mich. 280, 141 N.W. 543 (1913).

validity of the foreclosure sale by raising the question of the validity of the foreclosure sale as a defense to a summary proceeding to recover possession of the property.[2514]

Pleading and proof. A complaint seeking to set aside a foreclosure sale must distinctly allege the particular facts or equities on which relief is asked.[2515] The party who asserts that the foreclosure sale has not been properly conducted must allege that he or she has suffered damage by reason of the manner of sale.[2516] But a pleading that does not demand affirmative relief may be amended so that the defendant can recover possession.[2517]

The plaintiff has the burden of proving the facts relied upon to set aside the sale.[2518] The plaintiff has the burden to prove allegations that the sale was not properly conducted.[2519] The facts alleged as a ground for setting aside the sale must be proved by clear and satisfactory evidence.[2520]

2514. Gayles v. Deutsche Bank Nat'l Trust Co., 2010 Mich. App. LEXIS 2040 (Mich. Ct. App. Oct. 21, 2010).

Jackson v. Laker Group, 2005 Mich. App. LEXIS 2736 (Mich. Ct. App. Nov. 3, 2005).

Zachary v. Emmer, 1996 Mich. App. LEXIS 669 (Mich. Ct. App. Nov. 22, 1996).

Manufacturers Hanover Mortg. Corp. v. Snell, 142 Mich. App. 548, 370 N.W.2d 401 (1985).

2515. Petoskey v. Home Owners' Loan Corp., 300 Mich. 391, 1 N.W.2d 584 (1942).

2516. Petoskey v. Home Owners' Loan Corp., 300 Mich. 391, 1 N.W.2d 584 (1942).

2517. Griffin v. Union Guardian Trust Co., 261 Mich. 67, 245 N.W. 572 (1933).

2518. Moss v. Keary, 231 Mich. 295, 204 N.W. 93 (1925).

Markoff v. Tournier, 229 Mich. 571, 201 N.W. 888 (1925).

Fraud in mortgage itself

In a suit for a restoration of property sold under a mortgage foreclosure, where it was alleged that the mortgage was void because of fraud, the burden of proof is upon the one alleging fraud to prove it.—Jobert v. Wagner, 147 Mich. 409, 110 N.W. 942 (1907).

Posting of notice

A party contending that a posting is insufficient has the burden of proof to that effect.—Cox v. Townsend, 90 Mich. App. 12, 282 N.W.2d 223 (1979).

2519. Baratto v. Pitcher, 263 Mich. 307, 248 N.W. 631 (1933).

Jerome v. Coffin, 243 Mich. 324, 220 N.W. 675 (1928).

Gage v. Sanborn, 106 Mich. 269, 64 N.W. 32 (1895).

Harris v. Creveling, 80 Mich. 249, 45 N.W. 85 (1890).

2520. Baratto v. Pitcher, 263 Mich. 307, 248 N.W. 631 (1933).

Jerome v. Coffin, 243 Mich. 324, 220 N.W. 675 (1928).

Moss v. Keary, 231 Mich. 295, 204 N.W. 93 (1925).

Jobert v. Wagner, 147 Mich. 409, 110 N.W. 942 (1907).

Frickee v. Donner, 35 Mich. 151 (1876).

Evidence supported finding of fair price compared to property's value

Trial court's failure to frame its decision regarding market value of property in dispute in language borrowed from statute governing amounts bid on real property at foreclosure sales did not obscure its finding as the court referred to expert testimony offered by both parties as to market value of property and held that based upon evidence, bid-in price was reasonable.—Kansas City Life Ins. Co. v. Durant, 99 Mich. App. 754, 298 N.W.2d 630 (1980).

Fair price at sale

In action by United States, holder of defaulted mortgage note, against defendant note guarantors for balance due on note after application of foreclosure sale proceeds, evidence, including consideration of loss of automobile dealership formerly operated on premises and depressing effect that forced sale has on value of property, sustained finding that $55,969 bid at foreclosure sale was fair.—United States v. Leslie, 421 F.2d 763 (6th Cir. Mich. 1970).

Notice of sale

In suit to set aside mortgage foreclosure, on ground that notice of foreclosure was allegedly not posted on house on mortgaged realty, mortgagor's evidence was insufficient to sustain burden of

Resale. The vacation or setting aside of a mortgage foreclosure restores the mortgage.[2521] If a foreclosure sale by advertisement is invalid and has been set aside, the parties may proceed to a new foreclosure and resale.[2522]

proving that notice was not posted as required by statute.—White v. Burkhardt, 338 Mich. 235, 60 N.W.2d 925 (1953).

2521. Masella v. Bisson, 359 Mich. 512, 102 N.W.2d 468 (1960).

Northwestern Loan & Discount Corp. v. Scully, 256 Mich. 202, 239 N.W. 352 (1931).

2522. Masella v. Bisson, 359 Mich. 512, 102 N.W.2d 468 (1960).

Huyck v. Graham, 82 Mich. 353, 46 N.W. 781 (1890).

Vary v. Chatterton, 50 Mich. 541, 15 N.W. 896 (1883).

Atwater v. Kinman, Harrington Ch. 243 (Mich. 1842).

Chapter 32

FORECLOSURE OF MORTGAGES AND LAND CONTRACTS BY SUIT

A. IN GENERAL

§ 901. Nature and Form of Remedy

Foreclosure proceedings are special and statutory.

Library References

> Michigan Digest
>
> John G. Cameron, Jr., Michigan Real Estate Forms
>
> Midwest Transaction Guide
>
> Thompson on Real Property, Thomas Edition (David A. Thomas, ed.)
>
> Powell on Real Property® (Michael Allan Wolf, ed.)
>
> Real Estate Financing

Law Reviews

> Rita Subhedar, A Proposed State Response To The Michigan Housing Crisis, 11 J.L. Soc'y 173 (2009); Stephen R. Estey and Danielle Graceffa, Real Property, 54 Wayne L. Rev. 387 (2008); Thomas Gunton, Coping with the Specter of Urban Malaise in a Postmodern Landscape: The Need for a Detroit Land Bank Authority, 84 U. Det. Mercy L. Rev. 521 (2007); Daniel J. Schairbaum, Annual Survey of Michigan Law: June 1, 2003 - May 31, 2004: Real Property, 51 Wayne L. Rev. 881 (2005); Lawrence R. Shoffner, Real Property Law: Real Evidence: Special Rules For Real Estate Disputes, 80 Mich. B.J. 28 (2001).

A party who holds a real estate mortgage may have recourse to one of several remedies, in the event of nonpayment on the part of the mortgagor. The party may bring an action at law on the note secured by the mortgage, or an action at law on the covenant in the mortgage, or may foreclose the mortgage by advertisement with a subsequent right to an action for any deficiency, or may foreclose the mortgage in suit, with a right to a deficiency judgment in an amount fixed by the court's decree.[2523] However, the legal title of the mortgagor can be divested only by statutory foreclosure by advertisement or by foreclosure by suit.[2524] Foreclosure by advertisement is discussed elsewhere.[2525]

A former suit in chancery for the foreclosure of a mortgage or land contract was a judicial proceeding.[2526] A court had jurisdiction without showing any other ground for its action than a breach of the condition.[2527] Foreclosure proceedings are

---

2523. Guardian Depositors Corp. v. Powers, 296 Mich. 553, 296 N.W. 675 (1941).

Up Front: Pro Bono Attorneys Tackle Increasing Load Of Foreclosure Cases, 88 MI Bar Jnl. 9 (2009).

President's Page: No Foreclosure of Access to Justice, 87 MI Bar Jnl. 14 (2008).

2524. Union Guardian Trust Co. v. Rood, 261 Mich. 188, 246 N.W. 74 (1933).

Kollen v. Sooy, 172 Mich. 214, 137 N.W. 808 (1912).

Buck v. Sherman, 2 Doug. 176 (Mich. 1845).

Lashbrook v. Ferguson, 202 Mich. 307, 168 N.W. 415 (1918) (foreclosure in chancery necessary).

2525. See, supra, Chapter 31.

2526. Butters v. Butters, 153 Mich. 153, 117 N.W. 203 (1908).

Real Property And Consumer Law Sections Team Up On "Ask The Lawyer" To Discuss Mortgage Foreclosures, 87 MI Bar Jnl. 8 (2008).

2527. Battle v. Battjes, 274 Mich. 267, 264 N.W. 367 (1936).

special and statutory, and do not involve the exercise of the court's inherent equitable powers.[2528] The jurisdiction of the court in proceedings to foreclose a mortgage or land contract is wholly dependent upon the statutory provisions.[2529] Nonetheless, they are equitable in nature.[2530]

A party who invoked the aid of a former court of chancery in mortgage foreclosure proceedings thereby subjected him- or herself to the exercise of the equitable powers inherent in the chancery court, and hence could not justly complain of an effort on the part of the court to ultimately accomplish what was equitable between the parties.[2531]

Rules against the splitting of claims and requiring joinder do not bar successive foreclosures upon separate mortgage instruments.[2532]

Strict foreclosure. "Strict foreclosure" is a proceeding designed to foreclose the equity of redemption, rather than to collect the proceeds of a loan secured by a mortgage. Its object is to cut off the debtor's equity of redemption absolutely and finally, unless the debtor pays the amount ascertained as due within a fixed time, and to vest absolute title to the property in the mortgagee without any sale.[2533]

Strict foreclosure may be resorted to only in a very limited class of cases and under exceptional circumstances.[2534]

§ 902. Prior or Concurrent Proceedings

During the pendency of foreclosure proceedings, no proceedings may be had at law for recovery of the mortgage debt, unless by leave of court. The court may consolidate any other actions filed after the foreclosure complaint by holders of the indebtedness.

2528. Wurzer v. Geraldine, 268 Mich. 286, 256 N.W. 439 (1934).

United Growth Corp. v. Kelly Mortg. & Inv. Co., 86 Mich. App. 82, 272 N.W.2d 340 (1978) (mortgage foreclosure proceedings are strictly statutory and courts are bound by statutory provisions).

2529. Rea v. Wells Fargo Home Mortg., Inc., 2009 U.S. Dist. LEXIS 76315 (E.D. Mich. Aug. 7, 2009).

Franklin Bank v. Tindall, 2008 U.S. Dist. LEXIS 27765, 66 U.C.C. Rep. Serv. 2d (CBC) 133 (E.D. Mich. 2008).

Wurzer v. Geraldine, 268 Mich. 286, 256 N.W. 439 (1934).

Bleakley v. Oakwayne Farms Co., 265 Mich. 268, 251 N.W. 354 (1933).

Union Trust Co. v. Detroit Trust Co., 243 Mich. 451, 220 N.W. 728 (1928).

Kollen v. Sooy, 172 Mich. 214, 137 N.W. 808 (1912).

MBW Investors v. Circles Assocs., 1996 Mich. App. LEXIS 1021 (Mich. Ct. App. Oct. 18, 1996).

Stewart v. Isbell, 155 Mich. App. 65, 399 N.W.2d 440 (1986) (proceeding to foreclose a land contract is purely statutory in nature).

2530. MCLS § 600.3180.

Minchella v. Fredericks, 138 Mich. App. 462, 360 N.W.2d 896 (1984).

Superior Products Co. v. Merucci Bros., Inc., 107 Mich. App. 153, 309 N.W.2d 188 (1981).

2531. Michigan Trust Co. v. Cody, 264 Mich. 258, 249 N.W. 844 (1933).

2532. Successive foreclosures

So long as mortgagors' indebtedness remained unsatisfied, mortgagee's foreclosure in Benzie County action did not preclude subsequent foreclosure upon additional mortgages in Kent County litigation, where each mortgage instrument constituted a separate and distinct contract.—Michigan Nat'l Bank v. Martin, 19 Mich. App. 458, 172 N.W.2d 920 (1969).

2533. Detroit Trust Co. v. Detroit City Service Co., 262 Mich. 14, 247 N.W. 76 (1933).

2534. Detroit Trust Co. v. Detroit City Service Co., 262 Mich. 14, 247 N.W. 76 (1933) (allowance of strict foreclosure error).

If a mortgagee obtains a judgment for any portion of the money demanded in a complaint for foreclosure, the foreclosure action may not proceed until the execution of the money judgment is returned unsatisfied.[2535]

Under the Revised Judicature Act of 1961, after a complaint for foreclosure of a mortgage or land contract is filed in the circuit court, while it is pending, and after the claim is reduced to judgment, no proceedings whatever may be had at law for the recovery of any part of the debt secured by the mortgage unless the other action is authorized by the court.[2536] To proceed at law without leave while a foreclosure in a former court of chancery is pending is an abuse of practice. Furthermore, leave to proceed at law should not be granted ex parte, where the defendant is within reach.[2537]

The statute put foreclosure suits on the same footing with other suits in chancery, where an election of remedies was enforced subject to discretion.[2538] The statutory prohibition did not render the pendency of the foreclosure suit in chancery pleadable in abatement of an action at law.[2539]

Under another statute, at any time after a complaint to foreclose a trust mortgage or deed of trust securing indebtedness, the court may consolidate any other actions filed after the foreclosure complaint by holders of the indebtedness.[2540]

Neither the vendor's notice of forfeiture of a land contract nor a judgment in a summary process action under forfeiture of a land contract automatically dissolves the contract. The vendor may refuse to take possession and commence an action

---

2535. MCLS § 600.3105.

Shields v. Riopelle, 63 Mich. 458, 30 N.W. 90 (1886).

Affirmative duty

There is an affirmative duty upon a mortgagee who has secured a judgment to seek satisfaction out of the other property of the mortgagor prior to attempting foreclosure.—Southern Floridabanc, S.A. v. Feldman, 703 F. Supp. 627, 1989 U.S. Dist. LEXIS 652 (E.D. Mich. 1989).

Not yet unsatisfied

Under Michigan statute precluding mortgage foreclosure proceedings on money judgment until execution on judgment has been returned unsatisfied, plaintiff mortgagee obtained sister state judgment on note secured by properties both in another state and in Michigan, without stating amount of judgment, could not obtain foreclosure in Michigan until such time as court in other state determined amount of liability so as to permit defendant to satisfy debt and enable defendant to satisfy requirement for return of unsatisfied charges.— Southern Floridabanc, S.A. v. Feldman, 703 F. Supp. 627 (E.D. Mich. 1989).

Unsatisfied

Fact that plaintiff, who held assignment of a land contract vendees' interest as security for promissory note given for improvements, had first attempted to collect note by proceeding against principal debtors, defendants' predecessors in interest, did not estop him from attempting to foreclose mortgage, his efforts to collect from principal debtors having failed.—Boraks v. Siegel, 366 Mich. 308, 115 N.W.2d 126 (1962).

2536. MCLS § 600.3105.

Pending action on same property for different mortgage

Michigan law does not preclude a mortgagee from proceeding by foreclosure by advertisement if a judicial foreclosure on the same property is pending by a different mortgagee; the statute only prohibits a separate proceeding for recovery of a debt secured by a mortgage if a proceeding has already been initiated to recover the same debt secured by the same mortgage (MCLS § 600.3105(2)).—Church & Church, Inc. v. A-1 Carpentry, 766 N.W.2d 30 (Mich. App. 2008), affirmed in part and vacated in part on other grounds by, affirmed on other grounds by, in part by, 483 Mich. 885, 759 N.W.2d 877, 2009 Mich. LEXIS 110 (2009).

2537. Goodrich v. White, 39 Mich. 489 (1878).

2538. Joslin v. Millspaugh, 27 Mich. 517 (1873).

2539. Joslin v. Millspaugh, 27 Mich. 517 (1873).

2540. MCLS § 600.3105.

either for foreclosure or for money damages.[2541]

§ 903.   Jurisdiction and Venue

A foreclosure suit must be brought in the circuit court of the county in which the mortgaged premises, or a part thereof, are situated. The general rules of procedure in Michigan courts apply to actions for foreclosure of mortgages and land contracts.

The general rules of procedure in Michigan courts apply to actions for foreclosure of mortgages and land contracts.[2542] All complaints for the foreclosure or satisfaction of mortgages must be filed in the circuit court.[2543] The circuit court for a county other than that where the land is situated has no power to foreclose a mortgage or to compel its discharge.[2544]

The trustee under a bond mortgage, by invoking the aid of equity in foreclosing under a statute, submits itself to the exercise of the equitable powers inherent in the court.[2545]

A complaint seeking foreclosure of an interest in lands in another state cannot be maintained in Michigan.[2546]

A mortgage of property in the state that is payable outside of the state is enforceable by Michigan courts.[2547]

§ 904.   Persons Entitled to Foreclosure and as to Whom Foreclosure May be Had

A mortgage may be enforced by the legal holder of the mortgage against the owner of the land or anyone whose rights are subordinate to the mortgage.

2541. Gruskin v. Fisher, 405 Mich. 51, 273 N.W.2d 893 (1979).

Ames v. Maxson, 157 Mich. App. 75, 403 N.W.2d 501, 1987 Mich. App. LEXIS 2283 (1987).

2542. MCR 3.410.

Kent v. Pipia, 185 Mich. App. 599, 462 N.W.2d 800, 1990 Mich. App. LEXIS 403 (1990).

Stewart v. Isbell, 155 Mich. App. 65, 399 N.W.2d 440, 1986 Mich. App. LEXIS 2943 (1986).

Bishop v. Brown, 118 Mich. App. 819, 325 N.W.2d 594 (1982) (circuit courts have jurisdiction to foreclose land contracts).

Union Trust Co. v. Detroit Trust Co., 243 Mich. 451, 220 N.W. 728 (1928).

Kollen v. Sooy, 172 Mich. 214, 137 N.W. 808 (1912).

2543. MCLS § 600.3101.

2544. Wipfler v. Warren, 163 Mich. 189, 128 N.W. 178 (1910).

2545. Michigan Trust Co. v. Cody, 264 Mich. 258, 249 N.W. 844 (1933).

2546. Richard v. Boyd, 124 Mich. 396, 83 N.W. 106 (1900).

2547. Foreclosure under Michigan law proper

A mortgage was executed and recorded in Michigan on land in such state, and it provided that the mortgage should be paid at the mortgagee's residence in New York with a rate of interest that was illegal in the latter state, but that was valid in Michigan; mortgagee had the right to elect to proceed with the foreclosure of his mortgage under the laws of Michigan, where the whole contract was valid.—Fitch v. Remer, 9 F. Cas. 181, 1860 U.S. App. LEXIS 453, 1860 U.S. Dist. LEXIS 54 (C.C.D. Mich. 1860) (No. 4,836).

The legal holder of a mortgage is entitled to enforce it, because he or she has an interest in the property.[2548] A complaint to foreclose may also be filed by a party having only an equitable right to the mortgage.[2549]

The right to foreclose a mortgage for support and maintenance belongs to the mortgagee, and not to a third person who has supplied the support at the request of the mortgagor.[2550]

The right to sue is not lost when the trustee takes over the management of the mortgaged premises under a trust mortgage or deed of trust.[2551] On the removal or disqualification of the trustee, the right to institute foreclosure proceedings is in the trustee appointed in the trustee's place by the court or by the bondholders,[2552] or in one who is otherwise a successor in office.[2553]

Although, generally, the beneficiary of a trust deed may, in the beneficiary's own name, sue to foreclose when the trustee unreasonably refuses to do so, a bondholder has no right to file a complaint where the court has directed the receiver of a trust company, the trustee under the mortgage, to foreclose.[2554]

Generally, the assignee of a mortgage has the right to foreclose it.[2555] The fact that a mortgagee does not elect to declare the whole amount of a mortgage due on default in the payment of an installment does not estop the mortgagee's assignee from electing to declare it due on default in the payment of a subsequent installment.[2556]

2548. Lee v. Clary, 38 Mich. 223 (1878).

2549. Martin v. McReynolds, 6 Mich. 70 (1858).

2550. Daniels v. Eisenlord, 10 Mich. 454 (1862).

2551. Union Guardian Trust Co. v. Stillman, 300 Mich. 27, 1 N.W.2d 439 (1942).

2552. Detroit Trust Co. v. Manilow, 272 Mich. 211, 261 N.W. 303 (1935) (bondholders).

2553. Gray v. Waldron, 101 Mich. 612, 60 N.W. 288 (1894).

2554. Wallace v. Guaranty Trust Co., 259 Mich. 342, 243 N.W. 49 (1932).

Bondholder's objection to suspension of foreclosure

A holder of outstanding bonds issued under trust mortgage, in filing objection to trustee's petition for an order adjourning foreclosure proceeding for five years or during time building covered by mortgage was occupied under lease by certain company, was asserting a right of action on part of trustee in behalf of all bondholders, and was not seeking to take action in his individual right, so as to be precluded from doing so under provision in trust instrument that no one or more of holders of the bonds has any right to enforce

it.—Detroit Trust Co. v. Rivard, 315 Mich. 62, 23 N.W.2d 206 (1946).

2555. Bendey v. Townsend, 109 U.S. 665, 3 S. Ct. 482, 27 L. Ed. 1065 (1884).

Continental Nat'l Bank v. Gustin, 297 Mich. 134, 297 N.W. 214 (1941).

Youmans v. Loxley, 56 Mich. 197, 22 N.W. 282 (1885).

Fisher v. Meister, 24 Mich. 447 (1872).

Multiple interests including under assignment

Plaintiff, who had held both vendor's interest under a land contract, and vendees' interest under assignment for security for promissory note for improvement, was not estopped from enforcing security against defendants, as purchasers of vendees' interest, where defendants acquired vendees' interest at time plaintiff's lien claim was on record, plaintiff promptly asserted claim against defendants, and plaintiff's subsequent conveyance of vendor's interest reserved that debt so secured, in absence of showing that defendants were led to believe that plaintiff's several interests had merged.—Boraks v. Siegel, 366 Mich. 308, 115 N.W.2d 126 (1962).

2556. Brand v. Smith, 99 Mich. 395, 58 N.W. 363 (1894).

The assignee of a mortgage taken as collateral security may foreclose it.[2557]

A debt secured by a mortgage, when assigned, carried with it in a former court of chancery the mortgage as an incident to the debt, and the assignee could file a complaint to foreclose the mortgage.[2558] Even though a written assignment of a mortgage is insufficient at law to authorize the assignees to foreclose it, a delivery of the mortgage is sufficient to transfer the title to it and will entitle the assignees to maintain foreclosure by judicial sale.[2559] A transferee of a note to whom the mortgage securing it is transferred by endorsement and delivery is at least an equitable holder of the mortgage and is entitled to foreclose it.[2560]

On the death of the mortgagee or other person legally entitled, the right to foreclose can be exercised by the executors or administrators only.[2561]

Generally, a mortgage may be foreclosed against the owner of the land or any person whose rights are subordinate to the mortgage,[2562] but not against a person to whose rights the mortgage is subject.[2563]

§ 905.   Right to Foreclose

Generally, a right to foreclose arises upon the breach of the condition of a valid mortgage that secures a debt wholly or partly unpaid.

The general prerequisites to the right of foreclosure of a mortgage are that there be a valid mortgage that secures a debt or duty that remains wholly or in part unpaid or unperformed, and by which some kind of estate or title has been conveyed to the mortgagee as security, and that there is a breach of the condition of the mortgage.[2564] To enforce a mortgage, the mortgagee must prove that debt, and the mortgagee can recover only to the extent of the debt that he or she proves.[2565] But the mortgagee does not have to prove nor does the court have to determine who must pay the secured debt in default.[2566]

Generally, a default in the payment of the debt secured by the mortgage, at its

---

2557. Death of assignor

Where holder of two notes, which together with two other notes were secured by two mortgages which ran to holder as trustee for himself and another, delivered his two notes and mortgages to bank as security for an indebtedness, and later legal title of other two notes secured by mortgages was assigned to bank, bank was a "real party in interest" and entitled to bring action to foreclose mortgages, notwithstanding that holder who had assigned notes and mortgages to bank as security had died since commencement of suit.—Continental Nat'l Bank v. Gustin, 297 Mich. 134, 297 N.W. 214 (1941).

2558. Martin v. McReynolds, 6 Mich. 70 (1858).

2559. Moreland v. Houghton, 94 Mich. 548, 54 N.W. 285 (1893).

2560. John Schweyer & Co. v. Mellon, 196 Mich. 590, 162 N.W. 1006 (1917).

2561. Haines v. Perkins, 155 Mich. 417, 119 N.W. 439 (1909).

2562. Provident Mut. Life Ins. Co. v. Vinton Co., 282 Mich. 84, 275 N.W. 776 (1937).

Dorenberg v. Ockerman, 130 Mich. 23, 89 N.W. 579 (1902).

2563. Poole v. Horton, 45 Mich. 404, 8 N.W. 59 (1881).

2564. Frost v. Cockerham, 164 Mich. App. 759, 417 N.W.2d 599 (1987).

2565. Wood v. Weimar, 104 U.S. 786, 26 L. Ed. 779 (1881).

2566. Frost v. Cockerham, 164 Mich. App. 759, 417 N.W.2d 599 (1987).

maturity, is ground for immediate foreclosure.[2567] A default, to justify foreclosure, must relate to the debt secured.[2568] The separate mortgages on several properties securing the same indebtedness may all be foreclosed in order to satisfy that debt.[2569]

If the secured debt is payable in installments, default in the payment of any installment gives the mortgagee or land-contract vendor the right to foreclose as to that installment without waiting for the maturity of the whole debt, unless there is a stipulation to the contrary.[2570] This provision does not apply to installment mortgages containing an acceleration clause.[2571] Where a mortgage is foreclosed for an installment only, it remains in force with respect to notes secured by subsequent installments. Endorsers of those notes may look to the security for indemnity if called upon to pay them.[2572]

A default in the payment of interest may constitute a default justifying a foreclosure of the mortgage.[2573] However, the practice of foreclosing for small installments of interest has been condemned by the Michigan Supreme Court as oppressive.[2574] Thus, a forfeiture under an interest clause in a mortgage might not be enforced where the cause of delay of payment is that the mortgagor, in good faith but erroneously, denied his or her liability.[2575]

If, after a decree of sale is entered against defendant, he or she brings into court the principal and interest due, with costs, the proceedings in the suit must be stayed; however, the court must enter a decree of foreclosure and sale, to be enforced by further order of the court, upon a subsequent default in the payment of

---

2567. Wheeler v. Martin, 364 Mich. 41, 110 N.W.2d 635 (1961).

Stuart v. Worden, 42 Mich. 154, 3 N.W. 876 (1879).

Pease v. Warren, 29 Mich. 9 (1874).

2568. Open end mortgage did not secure advances in excess of mortgage limit

Where original loan from bank to debtor was for $4,000 and the open-end mortgage given as security limited any further loans on that mortgage to an amount that would bring the total debt to no more than $4,000 and where debtors were not in default on original loan, subsequent third and fourth loans that were in default had nothing to do with the original loan despite the open-end mortgage, so that bank was not entitled to foreclosure.—Macomb County Sav. Bank v. Kohlhoff, 5 Mich. App. 531, 147 N.W.2d 418 (1967).

2569. Michigan Nat'l Bank v. Martin, 19 Mich. App. 458, 172 N.W.2d 920 (1969).

2570. MCLS § 600.3110.

Kent v. Pipia, 185 Mich. App. 599, 462 N.W.2d 800 (1990).

Wurzer v. Geraldine, 268 Mich. 286, 256 N.W. 439 (1934).

Brown v. Thompson, 29 Mich. 72 (1874).

No payments

Court properly ordered foreclosure of a land contract covering real estate on which lumber business stood and mortgage on other real estate given to secure promissory note given for down payment, when no payments had been made on either, and only payments made were those on chattel mortgage covering inventory.—Wheeler v. Martin, 364 Mich. 41, 110 N.W.2d 635 (1961).

2571. Dumas v. Helm, 15 Mich. App. 148, 166 N.W.2d 306 (1968).

2572. Bacon v. Johnson, 44 Mich. 491, 7 N.W. 83 (1880).

No surplus available for second mortgage

Where a receiver for mortgaged property was appointed on petition of the second mortgagee after the trustee had foreclosed for an installment and purchased, leaving the property still subject to the first mortgage, there was no surplus to which the second mortgage was entitled.—Krolik v. Bankers' Trust Co., 264 Mich. 376, 249 N.W. 878 (1933).

2573. MCLS § 600.3110.

Dederick v. Barber, 44 Mich. 19, 5 N.W. 1064 (1880).

2574. Mabie v. Hatinger, 48 Mich. 341, 12 N.W. 198 (1882).

2575. Wilcox v. Allen, 36 Mich. 160 (1877).

any portion or installment of the principal, or of any interest due.[2576]

§ 906.   —Breach of Condition Other Than Payment of Debt

Foreclosure may be instituted for the nonperformance of any act the performance of which is stipulated for or secured by the mortgage.

Where a mortgage is conditioned for the support and maintenance of the mortgagee, a breach of the support condition will justify a foreclosure.[2577] Partial performance, however, may prevent foreclosure for the full penalty of the obligation secured.[2578]

If authorized by the mortgage, foreclosure may be had for default in the payment of taxes, or for default as to a covenant to insure.[2579] Where, subsequent to sale on foreclosure and purchase by the mortgagee, the mortgagee pays taxes and insurance premiums on the premises, the mortgagee is not entitled, after redemption is made from the mortgage sale, to again foreclose the mortgage for the amount of those expenditures.[2580]

When liability under a mortgage is conditioned on some future and contingent event, the right to foreclose accrues immediately on the occurrence of the event. The mortgagee must show the happening of the contingency with sufficient evidence.[2581]

If a mortgage is conditioned not only to indemnify the mortgagee after damage but to pay debts described, a right of foreclosure in chancery arises at once on a breach of the condition to pay, notwithstanding that the power of sale contained in the mortgage is limited to the case of the mortgagee being damaged by paying debts that the mortgagor fails to pay.[2582] Where the mortgagor, in a mortgage given to secure the mortgagee against liabilities on endorsements, executes to the mortgagee a note for all the notes that the mortgagee has endorsed, which is endorsed by the mortgagee and used by the mortgagor in taking up the other notes, a right of action on the mortgage does not accrue until the mortgagee is called upon to pay the consolidated note. Until that time, the mortgagee is not a creditor of the mortgagor.[2583]

§ 907.   —Maturity of Debt, In General

Generally, a mortgage may not be foreclosed until the debt secured has matured.

A mortgage may not be foreclosed prior to the maturity of the debt secured.

2576. Redemption, *see, infra,* Chapter 33. MCLS § 600.3120.

2577. Tucker v. Tucker, 24 Mich. 426 (1872). Hawkins v. Clermont, 15 Mich. 511 (1867).

2578. Wright v. Wright, 49 Mich. 624, 14 N.W. 571 (1883).

2579. Cramer v. Metropolitan Sav. & Loan Ass'n, 401 Mich. 252, 258 N.W.2d 20 (1977).

2580. Walton v. Bagley, 47 Mich. 385, 11 N.W. 209 (1882).

2581. Ligare v. Semple, 32 Mich. 438 (1875).

2582. Butler v. Ladue, 12 Mich. 173 (1863). Thurston v. Prentiss, 1 Mich. 193 (1849) (mortgage to indemnify sureties for payment of a judgment).

2583. Burt v. Gamble, 98 Mich. 402, 57 N.W. 261 (1894).

The right of foreclosure of a mortgage in which the time for payment of the mortgage debt is made to depend on the happening of some event or contingency, or on the performance of a condition subsequent, arises only on the happening of that event or contingency, or on that performance.[2584]

A new agreement extending the time for payment of the debt secured by a mortgage has the effect of modifying the original condition of the mortgage to the same extent as though it were incorporated in the original condition, and suspends the right to foreclose until the expiration of the extended time.[2585] In construing an agreement for the extension of a mortgage, all provisions concerning maturity and default should be given some meaning, if at all possible.[2586]

§ 908.   —Acceleration of Maturity

A clause accelerating the maturity of the entire debt secured by a mortgage or land contract is valid and enforceable in foreclosure by suit. An acceleration clause may be contractually triggered by the sale of the mortgaged property.

Provisions for the acceleration of the maturity of the entire debt are common in mortgages and land contracts, and are valid.[2587] A mortgagee ordinarily is entitled to enforce an acceleration clause according to its terms.[2588] Acceleration clauses constitute a severe remedy and may not be implied if the instrument does not provide for it.[2589]

An acceleration clause may be conditioned on the default of the mortgagor or land-contract vendee and give the mortgagee or vendor the right to declare the entire

---

2584. Trust

Where, at the time of the execution of a mortgage, the mortgagor deeded to the mortgagee certain lands in trust, to be sold and the proceeds applied on the mortgage, the mortgage did not become due until the mortgagee had discharged the obligation cast upon him by the agreement, which became a part of the mortgage.—A. P. Cook Co. v. Bell, 114 Mich. 283, 72 N.W. 174 (1897).

2585. Agreement separately recorded

Some time after a mortgaging of land an agreement was separately recorded between the mortgagor and mortgagee, purporting to be an extension of "the within mortgage"; given that registry of the agreement was not connected with the mortgage, and contained no reference to it, it was the same as if the agreement were on a separate piece of paper, and that its record was not evidence that would connect it with any particular instrument as an endorsement.—Bassett v. Hathaway, 9 Mich. 28 (1860).

2586. Equitable Trust Co. v. Simpson, 286 Mich. 460, 282 N.W. 215 (1938).

2587. Sindlinger v. Paul, 428 Mich. 161, 404 N.W.2d 212 (1987).

Young v. Zavitz, 365 Mich. 354, 112 N.W.2d 493 (1961).

Bedford v. Tetzlaff, 338 Mich. 102, 61 N.W.2d 60 (1953).

Benincasa v. Mihailovich, 31 Mich. App. 473, 188 N.W.2d 136 (1971) (land contract).

2588. 66 Sindlinger v. Paul, 428 Mich. 161, 404 N.W.2d 212 (1987) (land contract).

Jaarda v. Van Ommen, 265 Mich. 673, 252 N.W. 485 (1934).

Rathje v. Siegel, 243 Mich. 376, 220 N.W. 658 (1928).

First State Bank v. Day, 188 Mich. 228, 154 N.W. 101 (1915).

Crosby v. Crosby, 2000 Mich. App. LEXIS 2737 (Mich. Ct. App. Feb. 11, 2000).

Gorham v. Denha, 77 Mich. App. 264, 258 N.W.2d 196 (1977).

2589. Benincasa v. Mihailovich, 31 Mich. App. 473, 188 N.W.2d 136 (1971) (land contract).

unpaid balance due and payable.[2590]

An acceleration clause may be contractually triggered by the sale of the mortgaged property, in which case the clause is referred to as a "due-on-sale" clause.[2591]

Where the parties so agree, the entire debt may become due, with a consequent right of foreclosure, on default in the payment of interest,[2592] or on default in the payment of taxes.[2593]

A provision for acceleration is generally construed as permissive only, so as to make the whole debt due and collectible only if the mortgagee so elects. Such a clause imposes no obligation upon the mortgagee to elect to accelerate the maturity of the debt.[2594] Accordingly, the words "option of the trustee," in a trust mortgage that provides that on default of payment of any of the principal or interest the whole mortgage indebtedness, at the option of the trustee, becomes due, contemplates the exercise of some discretion by the trustee.[2595]

Some affirmative action by the mortgagee is generally necessary to exercise effectively an option to accelerate the maturity of the debt secured. The institution of foreclosure proceedings sufficiently indicates such an election, previous notice in that case being unnecessary.[2596]

A mortgagor may be relieved from the effect of an operative acceleration

2590. Young v. Zavitz, 365 Mich. 354, 112 N.W.2d 493 (1961).

2591. Darr v. First Federal Sav. & Loan Ass'n, 426 Mich. 11, 393 N.W.2d 152 (1986).

Real Property, 54 Wayne L. Rev. 387 (2008).

2592. Jaarda v. Van Ommen, 265 Mich. 673, 252 N.W. 485 (1934).

Rathje v. Siegel, 243 Mich. 376, 220 N.W. 658 (1928).

First State Bank v. Day, 188 Mich. 228, 154 N.W. 101 (1915).

Brand v. Smith, 99 Mich. 395, 58 N.W. 363 (1894).

2593. Jaarda v. Van Ommen, 265 Mich. 673, 252 N.W. 485 (1934).

Acceleration clause construed

By the terms of a mortgage, the mortgagor covenanted to pay the taxes within 40 days after they became due. If he defaulted, however, the mortgagee might pay the taxes due, and in that case the sum so paid became a further lien on the premises and payable forthwith with interest; if the principal, interest, or taxes were not paid "when the same become payable," and remained unpaid for 30 days, then the option was given the mortgagee to declare the whole sum due; expression "when the same become payable," as it related to taxes, meant when payable to the mortgagee as provided in the mortgage; that is, forthwith, after payment by the mortgagee as authorized by the mortgage, and not when payable to the tax collec-

tor.—Union Trust Co. v. Grant, 148 Mich. 501, 111 N.W. 1039 (1907).

2594. Union Guardian Trust Co. v. Marquette Park Co., 300 Mich. 89, 1 N.W.2d 464 (1942).

2595. Union Guardian Trust Co. v. Marquette Park Co., 300 Mich. 89, 1 N.W.2d 464 (1942).

2596. Sindlinger v. Paul, 428 Mich. 161, 404 N.W.2d 212 (1987).

Hawes v. Detroit Fire & Marine Ins. Co., 109 Mich. 324, 67 N.W. 329 (1896).

Bowen v. Bradley, 2009 Mich. App. LEXIS 1107 (Mich. Ct. App. May 21, 2009).

Crosby v. Crosby, 2000 Mich. App. LEXIS 2737 (Mich. Ct. App. Feb. 11, 2000).

Kent v. Pipia, 185 Mich. App. 599, 462 N.W.2d 800, 1990 Mich. App. LEXIS 403 (1990).

Knowledge on part of assignee to a land contract

Vendor did not have to give a vendee's assignee notice of the vendor's election to declare the whole amount under a land contract due by virtue of an acceleration clause before bringing suit to foreclose, where the assignee knew of an existing default by the assignor.—Bedford v. Tetzlaff, 338 Mich. 102, 61 N.W.2d 60 (1953).

Notice not required

Notice of vendors' intention to accelerate and foreclose land sale contract and security agreement was not required following purchasers' de-

clause when the default results from some unconscionable or inequitable conduct on the part of the mortgagee.[2597]

Similarly, an acceleration clause in a land contract would not be enforced against a defendant whose default is attributable to a good faith dispute as to factual representations by the vendors concerning the condition of the premises.[2598]

A payment or tender of the sum in arrears may bar the acceleration of the maturity of the debt secured by the mortgage because of such default, where the payment or tender is made before an election to accelerate.[2599] However, where the mortgagee, upon default on the part of the mortgagor, demands full payment under the acceleration clause, the mortgagee cannot be compelled to accept a payment of interest, costs of suit, and an installment on the principal, because he or she is entitled to foreclosure of all future payments due.[2600]

Land-contract vendors who defer asserting their rights under the acceleration clause in a defaulted land contract until the filing of their complaint for foreclosure do not thereby prejudice their acceleration rights or become estopped from foreclosing.[2601]

§ 909.   —Conditions Precedent

A mortgagee, to gain the right to foreclose, must perform any conditions requisite to complete his or her right of action or to fix liability on the mortgagor.

Where a mortgage is not to become operative or enforceable until the mortgagee has complied with certain conditions, no right to foreclose arises until performance on the mortgagee's part.[2602] A mortgage made conditional on the removal of certain specified defects of title is enforceable on performance of the condition. It cannot be defeated by a showing of other defects not specified in the condition.[2603]

A demand for performance may be required as a matter of fair dealing under peculiar circumstances.[2604] Demand is not made necessary by the fact that the debt

---

fault in payment.—Minchella v. Fredericks, 138 Mich. App. 462, 360 N.W.2d 896 (1984).

2597. Jaarda v. Van Ommen, 265 Mich. 673, 252 N.W. 485 (1934).

2598. Moore v. Bunch, 29 Mich. App. 498, 185 N.W.2d 565 (1971).

Acceleration clause

Enforcement of acceleration clause was held inequitable, in view of honest dispute as to purchaser's right to deduct rent due.—Hygelund v. Atlas, 247 Mich. 605, 226 N.W. 217 (1929).

2599. Sindlinger v. Paul, 428 Mich. 161, 404 N.W.2d 212 (1987).

2600. Jaarda v. Van Ommen, 265 Mich. 673, 252 N.W. 485 (1934).

2601. Russell v. Glantz, 57 Mich. App. 44, 225 N.W.2d 191 (1974).

2602. No condition precedent

A mortgagee may, on breach of a mortgage, foreclose a mortgage executed to secure the payment of a mortgage encumbrance on land conveyed to him, without first paying off the encumbrance.—Raffel v. Epworth, 107 Mich. 143, 64 N.W. 1052 (1895).

2603. Goodenow v. Curtis, 33 Mich. 505 (1876).

2604. De minimus delinquency

At a foreclosure for less than $10 interest, without calling on the mortgagor for payment, whereby costs are made to many times the amount of the interest, is oppressive and entitled to no

or interest is expressly made payable at a particular place.[2605]

By statute, if it appears that any judgment has been obtained in an action at law for any of the moneys demanded by a bill for foreclosure, no proceedings may be had with respect to foreclosure unless an execution against the property of the defendant in that judgment is returned unsatisfied, and unless it is made to appear by the return that defendant has no property to satisfy the execution, except the mortgaged premises.[2606] This provision requires affirmative action on the part of the mortgagee as a condition to bringing foreclosure proceedings.[2607]

§ 910.   —Postponement of Right To Foreclose

The parties to a mortgage, either by a stipulation in the mortgage or by an extrinsic agreement, may postpone the right to foreclose.

A stipulation in the mortgage postponing foreclosure until a period subsequent to the maturity of the debt secured is valid and will be given effect, and the parties to a mortgage may postpone the right to foreclose it by a separate agreement to that effect.[2608]

A conditional agreement will become effective only on the fulfillment of the condition, unless performance of the condition is obstructed by the mortgagor.[2609]

§ 911.   Defenses to Foreclosure

Generally, the same defenses may be made in a foreclosure suit as might be made in an action on the debt secured by the mortgage.

The validity of a mortgage may be attacked in foreclosure proceedings for fraud that undermines the very foundation of the mortgage.[2610] However, a purchaser who does not undertake ordinary care against fraud cannot raise it as a

---

favor.—Louder v. Burch, 47 Mich. 109, 10 N.W. 129 (1881).

2605. Norton v. Ohrns, 67 Mich. 612, 35 N.W. 175 (1887).

2606. MCLS § 600.3105.

Southern Floridabanc, S.A. v. Feldman, 703 F. Supp. 627 (E.D. Mich. 1989) (foreign state judgment).

Stegeman v. Fraser, 161 Mich. 35, 125 N.W. 769 (1910) (prior similar statute).

Dennis v. Hemingway, Walk. Ch. 387 (Mich. 1844) (prior similar statute).

Residential Funding Co., LLC v. Saurman, 2011 Mich. App. LEXIS 719 (Mich. Ct. App. Apr. 21, 2011) (limiting foreclosure by advertisement to those parties that were entitled to enforce the debt instrument, resulting in an automatic credit toward payment on the instrument on the event of foreclosure).

2607. Stegeman v. Fraser, 161 Mich. 35, 125 N.W. 769 (1910).

2608. Dutton v. Merritt, 41 Mich. 537, 2 N.W. 806 (1879) (enforcement not suspended).

Byers v. Byers, 65 Mich. 598, 32 N.W. 831 (1887) (foreclosure not a breach of agreement).

2609. Haney v. Roy, 54 Mich. 635, 20 N.W. 621 (1884).

2610. Abner A. Wolf, Inc. v. Walch, 385 Mich. 253, 188 N.W.2d 544 (1971) (question of fact).

Interest in business

Where a defendant was induced by fraud to purchase an interest in a business, and gave a mortgage to secure the purchase price, the fraud was available, in a subsequent foreclosure suit, to defeat the mortgage, even though the defendant might have made a more careful investigation, and might have been less credulous.—John Schweyer

defense in a foreclosure action.[2611]

Where a note and mortgage are executed in consideration of the mortgagee's agreement to transfer property to the mortgagor, or to perform some other act for the mortgagor's benefit, a foreclosure can be prevented by showing a failure of consideration on the part of the mortgagee.[2612] The defendant may show the extinguishment of the mortgage,[2613] or the abatement of the amount claimed.[2614] Where not all of the defendants answer, an affirmative showing made by those who do that the mortgage constituting the only ground of relief set up in the complaint is extinguished inures equally to the benefit of all the defendants.[2615]

On the other hand, a grantee cannot defeat the foreclosure of a purchase-money mortgage on the ground of want or defect of title in the grantor, where the grantee has remained in possession and has not been evicted by a paramount title, and where no fraud was practiced on the grantee.[2616] Similarly, a mortgagor may not challenge a foreclosure suit due to the harshness or hardship that the foreclosure might cause alone.[2617] A mortgagor may not prevent foreclosure by attacking the validity of a prior mortgage, paid off out of the proceeds of the one being foreclosed,

---

& Co. v. Mellon, 196 Mich. 590, 162 N.W. 1006 (1917).

No fraud shown as matter of law

Statement of president of bank to mortgagor, that her son would be subject to criticism because of his conduct of the business of the bank, of which he was formerly president, which might lead to his arrest and imprisonment, but that all would be forgiven if she would make security and take up her unsecured notes and those of her son and daughter, did not, under the circumstances, sustain mortgagor's contentions, in suit to foreclose mortgages so given, regarding duress, coercion and fraud in bringing about their execution, where considerable time was afforded for reflection, investigation, consultation and consideration of the matter by mortgagor, an experienced business woman.—Payne v. Cavanaugh, 292 Mich. 305, 290 N.W. 807 (1940).

2611. False representations not discovered

Vendee of lands, who went into possession immediately after the purchase and should at once have discovered any false representations of the vendor regarding the lands and the crops thereon, but who gave a purchase-money mortgage without making any complaint on that account, could not reduce the amount of the mortgage on the ground of such false representations.—Wright v. Peet, 36 Mich. 213 (1877).

2612. Walker v. Thompson, 108 Mich. 686, 66 N.W. 584 (1896).

Evidence showed lack of consideration

In suit to foreclose real estate mortgage executed by defendants to secure promissory note given plaintiff by defendant corporation for assignment of plaintiff's interest in gravel pit lease,

wherein defendants sought cancellation of note and mortgage on ground of failure of consideration, evidence sustained determination that plaintiff failed to prove that assets allegedly transferred by such assignment to defendant corporation were of any value, warranting decree for defendants.—Cummings v. Continental Machine Tool Corp., 371 Mich. 177, 123 N.W.2d 165 (1963).

Prior judgment validated consideration

Where plaintiff, who held vendor's interest in a land contract, and assignor's interest under assignment of vendees' interest given as security for promissory note for improvements, obtained justice court judgment or note against those vendees, defendants, who had previously acquired vendees' interest in a land contract, could not defend, in plaintiff's proceedings to foreclose security, on ground of failure of consideration for note, since judgment was not subject to collateral attack in such proceedings.—Boraks v. Siegel, 366 Mich. 308, 115 N.W.2d 126 (1962).

2613. McCabe v. Farnsworth, 27 Mich. 52 (1873).

2614. Hull v. Swarthout, 29 Mich. 249 (1874).

2615. McCabe v. Farnsworth, 27 Mich. 52 (1873).

2616. Smith v. Fiting, 37 Mich. 148 (1877) (adverse tax title).

Pungs v. Hilgendorf, 289 Mich. 46, 286 N.W. 152 (1939) (foreclosure under a land contract).

2617. Cramer v. Metropolitan Sav. & Loan Ass'n, 401 Mich. 252, 258 N.W.2d 20 (1977).

Dumas v. Helm, 15 Mich. App. 148, 166 N.W.2d 306 (1968).

on the ground of the illegality of its consideration.[2618] The fact that a mortgage contains a palpable clerical error in the figures of the sum due does not constitute a defense, and the mortgagee is not precluded by the error from foreclosing, after default, and selling the property to satisfy the amount really due.[2619] The fact that a mortgagee of real property may at the same time hold additional or cumulative security for the same debt ordinarily does not interfere with the mortgagee's right to foreclose the mortgage or compel the mortgagee to exhaust the other security before foreclosing, in the absence of equitable circumstances.[2620]

A party who assumes a mortgage may not defend against foreclosure of it with an attack on the validity of the mortgage.[2621] The question of the mortgage's negotiability is not material where defendants had no defense against the mortgage at the time of the assignment.[2622]

Various other matters have not constituted a valid defense to a foreclosure suit.[2623]

The right to defend against a foreclosure belongs to the spouse of a mortgagor who has joined in the execution of the mortgage.[2624]

A defense to foreclosure may be waived if it is entered too late in the proceeding.[2625]

2618. Quigley v. Wolf, 177 Mich. 467, 143 N.W. 882 (1913).

2619. Damon v. Deeves, 62 Mich. 465, 29 N.W. 42 (1886).

2620. Dobson v. Dobson, 212 Mich. 669, 180 N.W. 365 (1920) (nonapplication of other collateral no defense).

Davis v. Rider, 5 Mich. 423 (1858) (mortgagee could not be compelled to resort to collaterals).

Several mortgages to secure single debt

Party who holds several mortgages to secure a single debt may foreclose any of them at his or her option separately until the mortgagor's debt is satisfied.—McKinney v. Miller, 19 Mich. 142 (1869).

2621. Michigan Wineries, Inc. v. Johnson, 68 Mich. App. 310, 242 N.W.2d 568 (1976), aff'd, 402 Mich. 306, 262 N.W.2d 651 (1978) (illegality of consideration).

2622. Manning v. Rosenfield, 239 Mich. 459, 214 N.W. 424 (1927).

2623. Harris v. Brown, 172 Mich. 164, 137 N.W. 681 (1912) (quarrels between brother and sister who were vend).

Allegedly unauthorized assignment in trust

When a mortgage held by a citizen of New York was assigned in trust to the treasurer of New Jersey for the benefit of holders of policies in a certain New Jersey insurance company, the mortgagor cannot, in a suit to foreclose, set up that no statute of New Jersey authorizes the treasurer to hold such

security.—Gray v. Waldron, 101 Mich. 612, 60 N.W. 288 (1894).

Debtor's improvement of property is no defense

Improvement of property is not sufficient ground to invoke equitable powers of court to defeat seller's right under a land contract to exercise acceleration clause and foreclose.—Dumas v. Helm, 15 Mich. App. 148, 166 N.W.2d 306 (1968).

Notice of prior security

Foreclosure of a mortgage is not barred by the notice of another mortgage as prior security.—Connerton v. Oakman, 41 Mich. 608, 2 N.W. 932 (1879).

Plaintiff's action in borrowing money on the mortgage

The fact that a plaintiff who is seeking to foreclose a mortgage has, pending the suit, borrowed money of a third person on the mortgage on the understanding that she should continue the prosecution of the cause, and in the event of her success should repay the money so borrowed, with interest, is no defense to the foreclosure.—Chase v. Brown, 32 Mich. 225 (1875).

2624. Butters v. Butters, 153 Mich. 153, 117 N.W. 203 (1908).

2625. Defense not timely raised in action

An objection that leave should not be given to file the bill of foreclosure—the mortgaged premises being at the time in the possession of a receiver appointed in a former suit in the same

Estoppel and waiver. There can, of course, be no waiver of the right to foreclose without knowledge of what is being waived.[2626]

A mortgagee, by conduct inducing others to believe and act on the belief that the mortgagee will not enforce the mortgage, may be estopped from so doing.[2627]

§ 912.   —Tender

A mortgagor's tender of the overdue amount on a mortgage or a land contract prior to judgment in an action to foreclose bars foreclosure of the mortgage or land contract by suit.

Tender by a land contract vendee of an overdue payment prior to receipt of the vendor's notice of intent to foreclose prevents the exercise of the foreclosure option brought pursuant to an acceleration clause; however, such foreclosure action requires no preliminary notice to the vendee and can be instituted by simply bringing the foreclosure action for the full amount.[2628]

After the filing of an action in foreclosure, the mortgagor may obtain dismissal of the action upon his or her payment of principal and interest due with costs prior to judgment in the action.[2629] The mortgagor must pay the money into the court after the tender is made in open court.[2630] Upon meeting those conditions, the mortgagor

court—if, under any circumstances, available, will not be sustained, if made a year and a half after the bill was filed, and when the party objecting had in the meantime appeared, answered it, and cross-examined the witnesses of the complainant.—Jerome v. McCarter, 94 U.S. 734, 24 L. Ed. 136 (1877).

2626. Waldron v. Murphy, 40 Mich. 668 (1879).

2627. Faxton v. Faxon, 28 Mich. 159 (1873).

No estoppel

No estoppel due to prior action for performance that did not yield amount due.—Boraks v. Siegel, 366 Mich. 308, 115 N.W.2d 126 (1962).

First State Bank v. Day, 188 Mich. 228, 154 N.W. 101 (1915).

Bloomer v. Dau, 122 Mich. 522, 81 N.W. 331 (1899).

No evidence of knowledge on which to base estoppel

Plaintiffs' claim that defendant mortgagee's failure to assert his rights under mortgage during administration of deceased mortgagor's estate prejudiced plaintiffs so that defendant was estopped from foreclosing mortgage was without merit, where there were no contacts between defendant and plaintiffs respecting sale of property by administrator, record did not show that defendant knew of impending sale, and plaintiffs had constructive notice of existence of mortgage that

had been on record for 26 months prior to execution of deed of conveyance.—Lewis v. Hook, 18 Mich. App. 405, 171 N.W.2d 221 (1969).

2628. Sindlinger v. Paul, 428 Mich. 161, 404 N.W.2d 212 (1987).

Agency to accept tender

In foreclosure action following mortgagor-assignor's prepayment of mortgage in full to mortgage servicing company which became bankrupt before it could forward proceeds to plaintiff assignee, summary disposition for plaintiff was inappropriate where genuine material fact issue of agency existed regarding plaintiff's control over company, as well as to alleged custom of servicing companies to accept mortgage prepayments and plaintiff's knowledge of it, question of apparent authority traceable to plaintiff, and whether plaintiff, by placing company in position of authority, was estopped from denying existence of such authority.—Meretta v. Peach, 195 Mich. App. 695, 491 N.W.2d 278 (1992).

Inability to tender under a land contract

Purchasers would not be granted equitable relief from foreclosure of a land contract where they made no showing that by any date not depending on sanguinary expectancy they would be able to make substantial payment.—Gassel v. Franjac, 362 Mich. 477, 107 N.W.2d 833 (1961).

2629. MCLS § 600.3110.

2630. Manzeta v. Heidloff, 371 Mich. 248, 123 N.W.2d 779 (1963).

is entitled to dismissal of the action.[2631] The mortgagee may not refuse the tender of the amount owed.[2632]

In the case of a mortgage allowing the mortgagor to accelerate some or all amounts due upon default and fulfillment of specified conditions, the amount that the mortgagor must tender consists of all accelerated payments as provided by the mortgage.[2633]

However, acceptance of payments by a land contract vendor from a court-appointed receiver for the vendee during the pendency of a foreclosure action does not waive the foreclosure and reinstate the land contract.[2634]

§ 913.   Limitations and Laches

Limitations or laches may bar the right to foreclose a mortgage.

The Revised Judicature Act of 1961 provides that no suit or proceeding may be maintained to foreclose a mortgage on real estate unless it is commenced within 15 years from and after such mortgage becomes due and payable, or within 15 years after the last payment is made on the mortgage. Where it satisfactorily appears to the court that the debt or lien secured by such mortgage has been fully paid or that the debt has been past due for 15 years or that 15 years have elapsed since the last payment and that no suit or proceeding has been commenced to foreclose the mortgage, the court must deliver an attested judgment to the mortgagor that may be recorded in the office of the register of deeds for the county in which the mortgage is of record. The effect of the recording of the judgment is to formally discharge the mortgage.[2635] A suit to cancel the discharge of a mortgage, and to foreclose the mortgage as reinstated, is a suit for foreclosure of the mortgage, and is not barred by limitations when it is instituted within 15 years after the mortgage becomes due.[2636] A payment by one of two joint mortgagors or by the principal mortgagor is sufficient to toll the statute.[2637]

The defense of laches, the lapse of time in connection with the nonpayment of interest and the continued possession of the mortgagor during which the mortgagee makes no effort to enforce payments, is not a legal but an equitable or presumptive

---

2631. Kent v. Pipia, 185 Mich. App. 599, 462 N.W.2d 800 (1990).

2632. Manzeta v. Heidloff, 371 Mich. 248, 123 N.W.2d 779 (1963).

2633. Dumas v. Helm, 15 Mich. App. 148, 166 N.W.2d 306 (1968) (purchasers paid into court missed monthly payments and costs).

2634. Colby v. Tobba, Inc., 146 Mich. App. 592, 381 N.W.2d 411 (1985).

2635. MCLS §§ 600.3175, 600.5803.

Computation of time for installment mortgage

Under statute of limitations for foreclosure of mortgage and discharge of mortgage statute, both containing language in alternative, greatest period of time to run is proper one to apply, i.e., correct time to commence to run is from due date provided in mortgage, and not date of last payment.—Degen v. Estate of Degen, 80 Mich. App. 573, 264 N.W.2d 64 (1978).

Delay until after foreclosure of other mortgage

Delay in foreclosure of second mortgage until after mortgagor had redeemed from foreclosure of first mortgage did not estop second mortgagee from foreclosing his mortgage, if within statutory period.—Piech v. Beaty, 298 Mich. 535, 299 N.W. 705 (1941).

2636. Plasger v. Leonard, 316 Mich. 174, 25 N.W.2d 156 (1946).

2637. Brown v. Hayes, 146 Mich. 474, 109 N.W. 845 (1906) (decided under prior similar statute).

bar. The presumption may be rebutted by circumstances dependent on the facts of each particular case.[2638] Laches is an affirmative defense, and a mere lapse of time in the bringing of a foreclosure suit, without a showing of prejudice, does not constitute laches.[2639]

While evidence of lapse of time must be considered with other facts and circumstances of a case in determining laches, laches will not be permitted to defeat recovery in equity if it would be inequitable to do so.[2640]

§ 914. Setoff and Counterclaim

In a proper case, defendant may counterclaim or setoff a claim or demand against plaintiff that is connected with the mortgage transaction and affects the consideration between the parties.

Generally, where the foreclosure proceeding is, in effect, one to recover money on a contract, and the amount of the mortgage debt is in issue and plaintiff seeks to enforce defendant's personal liability by a deficiency judgment, defendant may counterclaim or setoff a claim or demand against the plaintiff that is connected with the mortgage transaction and affects the consideration of it.[2641]

Counterclaims or setoffs that are not meritorious will, of course, be refused.[2642]

A complaint to redeem may take the form of a counterclaim to have a sale and lease-back arrangement declared a mortgage with a right of redemption.[2643]

§ 915. Restraining Foreclosure

In a proper case, a court may restrain a proceeding to foreclose a mortgage.

A court may, within its sound discretion, restrain foreclosure proceedings. The

2638. Abbott v. Godfroy's Heirs, 1 Mich. 178 (1849).

2639. Plasger v. Leonard, 316 Mich. 174, 25 N.W.2d 156 (1946).

Kelley v. Hoogerhyde, 314 Mich. 37, 22 N.W.2d 63 (1946).

Laches shown

Cook v. Rounds, 60 Mich. 310, 27 N.W. 517 (1886).

Thompson v. Jarvis, 39 Mich. 689 (1878).

Burrow v. Debo, 47 Mich. 242, 10 N.W. 469 (1881).

2640. Plasger v. Leonard, 316 Mich. 174, 25 N.W.2d 156 (1946).

Kelley v. Hoogerhyde, 314 Mich. 37, 22 N.W.2d 63 (1946).

Laches not shown

Olmstead v. Taylor, 126 Mich. 316, 85 N.W. 740 (1901).

Shelden v. Warner, 45 Mich. 638, 8 N.W. 529 (1881).

Fletcher v. Carpenter, 37 Mich. 412 (1877).

2641. Conwisher v. Schimmel, 271 Mich. 446, 260 N.W. 904 (1935).

2642. Conwisher v. Schimmel, 271 Mich. 446, 260 N.W. 904 (1935) (setoff of certain sums refused).

Kertson v. Liberty Park Amusement Co., 244 Mich. 177, 221 N.W. 143 (1928).

Pfirrman v. Wattles, 86 Mich. 254, 49 N.W. 40 (1891) (counterclaim not allowed).

Adams v. Bradley, 12 Mich. 346 (1864).

Griggs v. Detroit & M. R. Co., 10 Mich. 117 (1862).

2643. Ferd L. Alpert Industries, Inc. v. Oakland Metal Stamping Co., 379 Mich. 272, 150 N.W.2d 765 (1967).

restraint of foreclosure proceedings may be based on any ground sufficient to justify the interposition of equity for that purpose.[2644] Some equity must be shown before the court will enjoin or restrain a proceeding to foreclose a mortgage, and matters that do not show it to be illegal or unconscionable for the suit to proceed are not sufficient grounds for the granting of injunctive relief.[2645]

A mortgagor and the mortgagor's vendee with warranty have a common interest in removing the mortgage lien enabling them to unite in a suit to enjoin its enforcement.[2646]

In an action seeking the restraint of a foreclosure, either party may request the appointment of a receiver of the property.[2647]

All persons claiming ownership of the mortgage debt or portions of it, or the notes or other obligations evidencing it, are necessary parties and must be joined.[2648] A mortgagor and the mortgagor's spouse are necessary parties to a suit by a judgment creditor to enjoin foreclosure.[2649]

The party seeking to restrain foreclosure proceedings must set forth in his or her complaint, with certainty and precision, the matters relied on as ground for equitable relief.[2650] The complainant must also sustain the burden of proof

---

2644. Barck v. Grant State Bank, 137 Mich. App. 440, 357 N.W.2d 872 (1984) (no grounds shown).

Foreclosure enjoined

A husband gave to his wife a mortgage on land purchased by him to secure money advanced by her; afterwards they made an agreement for a separation, under which the property was divided between them, but no satisfaction of the mortgage was entered; under such circumstances, a suit to foreclose the mortgage, begun several years later, without rescinding the separation agreement, would be enjoined.—Brown v. Miller, 63 Mich. 413, 29 N.W. 879 (1886).

A mortgagee turned over to his wife a mortgage and note in satisfaction of claims held by her against him, and afterwards formally assigned the same to a third person without delivery; mortgagor made payment to the wife and took up the mortgage; consequently, he can obtain injunction restraining the subsequent assignee from proceeding to foreclose the mortgage.—Haescig v. Brown, 34 Mich. 503 (1876).

No power to order adjournment of foreclosure proceedings

Where holders of majority of outstanding bonds issued under trust mortgage did not have right to direct trustee to waive payment of principal or interest on bonds for more than six months after they became due and payable, trial court, in absence of an applicable moratorium statute, did not have power to order adjournment of foreclosure proceeding over objection of a minority bondholder, so as to thereby in effect extend maturity date of the outstanding bonds, notwith-

standing that a majority of holders of outstanding bonds had consented to it.—Detroit Trust Co. v. Rivard, 315 Mich. 62, 23 N.W.2d 206 (1946).

2645. Schaffer v. Eighty-One Hundred Jefferson Ave. East Corp., 267 Mich. 437, 255 N.W. 324 (1934).

2646. Dedrick v. Den Bleyker, 85 Mich. 475, 48 N.W. 633 (1891).

2647. Discretion of court

In view of mortgagor's prior failure to meet financial obligations, and fact that mortgagor would have lost all rights to building had judge not tolled redemption statute in foreclosure, there was no abuse of discretion in ordering receivership.—Francis Martin, Inc. v. Lomas, 62 Mich. App. 706, 233 N.W.2d 702 (1975).

2648. Trustees

In suit by creditor of owner of mortgaged hotel to enjoin trustees from foreclosing mortgage and for accounting, both trustees were necessary parties.—Albert Pick & Co. v. Cass-Putnam Hotel Co., 41 F.2d 74 (D. Mich. 1930).

2649. Melze-Alderton Shoe Co. v. First State Sav. Bank, 171 Mich. 26, 137 N.W. 208 (1912).

2650. Lowe v. Schuyler, 187 Mich. 526, 153 N.W. 786 (1915) (bill sufficient to warrant relief granted).

Complaint insufficient

A bill to enjoin defendant from foreclosing mortgages on land that plaintiff bought at its own execution sale under judgment against the mort-

concerning all facts on which the equity of the case depends.[2651] The complainant must submit sufficient pertinent evidence to warrant the relief sought.[2652]

In a proceeding to restrain a suit for the foreclosure of a mortgage, the relief must be confined to the issues raised by the pleadings and must not be allowed in broader terms than prayed for in it.[2653] But the court in exercising its equitable jurisdiction may exact equity between the parties.[2654] Costs may be allowed to the prevailing party.[2655]

An injunction restraining a mortgagee from foreclosing by advertisement does not necessarily preclude the mortgagee from initiating an action for foreclosure by judicial sale.[2656]

An injunction *pendente lite* need not continue for the full redemption period after the issuance of judgment for the mortgagee.[2657]

§ 916. Costs and Fees

The expenses of foreclosing a mortgage by suit may generally be taxed against the losing party in the circuit court as in civil actions upon the request of a party. Costs that are merely incidental to foreclosure should be paid out of the proceeds of the sale.

The expenses of foreclosing a mortgage by suit may generally be taxed against

gagor is insufficient where it fails to show that the land is not worth enough to take care of both the judgment and mortgage claims.—Melze-Alderton Shoe Co. v. First State Sav. Bank, 171 Mich. 26, 137 N.W. 208 (1912).

2651. Gordon v. Frischkorn Real Estate Co., 257 Mich. 285, 241 N.W. 198 (1932).

2652. Real property law: Real evidence: Special rules for real estate disputes, 80 Mich. B.J. 28 (2001).

Injunction denied

In a suit to restrain the foreclosure of a mortgage on the ground that the vendor's assignees realized secret profits from the transfer, the evidence justified a decree permitting foreclosure.—Gordon v. Frischkorn Real Estate Co., 257 Mich. 285, 241 N.W. 198 (1932).

Crow v. Conant, 90 Mich. 247, 51 N.W. 450 (1892).

2653. Lowe v. Schuyler, 187 Mich. 526, 153 N.W. 786 (1915).

2654. Dissolution of restraining order after redemption did not preclude damages

Where circuit judge dissolved temporary restraining order against mortgage foreclosure after finding that plaintiff mortgagor was in default on mortgage in action grounded on alleged wrongful

foreclosure and other improprieties by mortgagee in connection with mortgage charges, plaintiff, following exercise of right of redemption from foreclosure, and in light of resulting change in factual setting from circuit judge's order year and one-half earlier, was entitled to file amended complaint alleging redemption and any damages incurred as result of improper foreclosure and wrongful mortgage charges.—Cramer v. Metropolitan Federal Sav. & Loan Ass'n, 34 Mich. App. 638, 192 N.W.2d 50 (1971).

2655. Costigan v. Howard, 100 Mich. 335, 58 N.W. 1116 (1894).

2656. Federal restraining order

A suit in federal court begun by original mortgagors, the guarantor and a subsequent purchaser under which a temporary injunction was issued restraining a mortgage company from foreclosure by publication, presented no conflict of jurisdiction with a suit by the mortgage trustee to foreclose in chancery under former statute, when no counterclaim asking foreclosure was filed in the federal suit and the relief asked for in the chancery suit was not sought in the federal action.—Detroit Trust Co. v. Manilow, 272 Mich. 211, 261 N.W. 303 (1935).

2657. Barck v. Grant State Bank, 137 Mich. App. 440, 357 N.W.2d 872 (1984) (ten days after judgment where entire six months' redemption period ran during pendency of litigation).

the losing party in the circuit court as in civil actions upon the request of a party.[2658]

Costs that are merely incidental to foreclosure must be paid out of the proceeds of the sale[2659] and not taxed personally against a party, such as a junior mortgagee,[2660] unless a party contests the foreclosure, in which event costs can be taxed against the contesting party, at least if the proceeds are insufficient to discharge them.[2661]

The matter of costs may be affected by agreement, including a consent decree.[2662] But an agreement may not require payment of unreasonable stipulated fees.[2663]

Also, a mortgagee making a new foreclosure for the purpose of correcting errors or irregularities in his or her own proceedings in a prior defective proceeding cannot, either legally or equitably, charge the mortgagor with the expense of the new proceedings.[2664]

Attorney's fees. A mortgagor generally may not be charged attorney's fees of the mortgagee in a mortgage foreclosure action in the absence of a relevant statutory provision or contractual stipulation between the parties.[2665]

The court is under a duty to protect debtors against exaction of extortionate forfeitures, even by means of stipulation as to attorney's fees.[2666] Accordingly, a provision in the note or mortgage stipulating for an attorney's fee in a fixed sum will not be sustained without regard to its reasonableness.[2667]

On the other hand, a provision for the payment of reasonable fees will be enforced.[2668] A reasonable fee is measured by the fair value of services rendered.[2669]

2658. M.L.P.2d Civil Procedure.

MCR 2.625.

2659. Botsford v. Botsford, 49 Mich. 29, 12 N.W. 897 (1882).

United Growth Corp. v. Kelly Mortg. & Inv. Co., 86 Mich. App. 82, 272 N.W.2d 340 (1978).

Cost of audit

Where mortgage gave bondholders right to audit, cost of audit made during foreclosure must be added to mortgage debt, where that cost had no tendency to make transaction usurious.—Detroit Trust Co. v. Detroit City Service Co., 262 Mich. 14, 247 N.W. 76 (1933).

2660. Michigan Mut. Life Ins. Co. v. Conant, 40 Mich. 530 (1879).

2661. Ireland v. Woolman, 15 Mich. 253 (1867).

2662. Vokes & Schaeffer v. Bollin-McKinney Hotel Co., 238 Mich. 1, 212 N.W. 953 (1927).

2663. United Growth Corp. v. Kelly Mortg. & Inv. Co., 86 Mich. App. 82, 272 N.W.2d 340 (1978).

2664. Clark v. Stilson, 36 Mich. 482 (1877).

2665. United Growth Corp. v. Kelly Mortg. & Inv. Co., 86 Mich. App. 82, 272 N.W.2d 340 (1978).

2666. Millard v. Truax, 50 Mich. 343, 15 N.W. 501 (1883).

2667. Bendey v. Townsend, 109 U.S. 665, 3 S. Ct. 482, 27 L. Ed. 1065 (1884).

Butzel v. Webster Apartments Co., 112 F.2d 362 (6th Cir. Mich. 1940).

Botsford v. Botsford, 49 Mich. 29, 12 N.W. 897 (1882).

Van Marter v. McMillan, 39 Mich. 304 (1878).

United Growth Corp. v. Kelly Mortg. & Inv. Co., 86 Mich. App. 82, 272 N.W.2d 340 (1978).

2668. In re Schafer's Bakeries, 155 F. Supp. 902 (D. Mich. 1957).

Attorney for bondholders under trust mortgage

Allowance of attorney fees to attorney who appeared upon hearing of petition of trustee under leasehold trust mortgage, for advice of court relative to proposed settlement of foreclosure suit, actively participated therein, and represented himself and all bondholders other than those present or

A provision in a power of sale, having reference to a foreclosure under the power of sale, will not authorize the allowance of an attorney's fee in case of foreclosure by suit.[2670]

A second mortgagee has no ground for complaint regarding a reasonable allowance for attorney's fees if the fees are authorized by the mortgage.[2671]

§ 917.   Operation and Effect

Ordinarily, foreclosure by suit extinguishes the mortgage or land contract, but extinguishes the debt only to the extent of the proceeds realized from the sale.

The effect of foreclosure is ordinarily to extinguish the mortgage or land contract,[2672] at least where the purchaser conveys by warranty deed.[2673] The foreclosing party obtains title to the extent of his or her mortgagor's title.[2674] A foreclosure for a delinquent installment, however, does not extinguish the mortgage unless the parties so intend.[2675] The foreclosure ordinarily satisfies the debt only to the extent of the amount realized from the sale of the premises.[2676]

When the right of redemption expires, the mortgagor loses his or her interest in the property.[2677] The same is true of junior encumbrancers if they are parties to the foreclosure suit and fail to redeem the property.[2678] In this connection, a junior mortgagee who has already been impleaded by a prior mortgagee cannot file a complaint of foreclosure.[2679]

---

represented in court, was affirmed.—In re Detroit Metropolitan Corp., 289 Mich. 358, 286 N.W. 646 (1939).

2669. Butzel v. Webster Apartments Co., 112 F.2d 362 (6th Cir. Mich. 1940).

Boston Safe-Deposit & Trust Co. v. Adrian, Mich., Waterworks, 47 F. 8 (C.C.D. Mich. 1891).

Union Trust Co. v. Tonquish Temple Ass'n, 247 Mich. 36, 225 N.W. 572 (1929).

United Growth Corp. v. Kelly Mortg. & Inv. Co., 86 Mich. App. 82, 272 N.W.2d 340 (1978).

2670. Hardwick v. Bassett, 29 Mich. 17 (1874).

2671. Security Trust Co. v. Solomon, 241 Mich. 52, 216 N.W. 405 (1927).

2672. Wallace v. Field, 56 Mich. 3, 22 N.W. 91 (1885).

Hazen v. Reed, 30 Mich. 331 (1874).

2673. Bacon v. Johnson, 44 Mich. 491, 7 N.W. 83 (1880).

2674. Title to mortgaged remainder interest under trust

Mortgagee who took mortgage on remainder interest of mortgagor in corpus of trust would, on completion of foreclosure, be vested only with

defeasible interest of mortgagor in trust estate.— Glaser's Elevator & Lumber Co. v. Lee Homes, Inc., 65 Mich. App. 328, 237 N.W.2d 312 (1975).

2675. Krolik v. Bankers' Trust Co., 264 Mich. 376, 249 N.W. 878 (1933).

2676. Additional security

Mortgagees who are in possession of premises under a lease given to them for additional security can, even as against the mortgagor's assignee of the rentals, hold the premises and apply the amount due for rentals upon an amount still due under the decree of foreclosure.—Storey v. Dutton, 46 Mich. 539, 9 N.W. 844 (1881).

2677. Detroit Fidelity & Surety Co. v. Donaldson, 255 Mich. 129, 237 N.W. 380 (1931).

2678. Graydon v. Hurd, 55 F. 724 (6th Cir. Mich. 1893).

Swarthout v. Shields, 185 Mich. 427, 152 N.W. 202 (1915).

Connecticut Mut. Life Ins. Co. v. Bulte, 45 Mich. 113, 7 N.W. 707 (1881).

Tower v. Divine, 37 Mich. 443 (1877).

2679. Sutherland v. Lake Superior Ship Canal, R. & Iron Co., 23 F. Cas. 459 (C.C.E.D. Mich. 1874) (No. 13,643).

On the other hand, junior encumbrancers[2680] or vendees who have succeeded to the interests of the mortgagor after the delivery of the mortgage but before the commencement of the suit to foreclose it[2681] are not affected in their rights if they are not made parties. Conversely, the mere fact that a senior mortgagee is made a party to a suit for foreclosure of a junior mortgage does not affect the rights of the senior mortgagee in the absence of an allegation of some facts that would entitle the junior mortgagee to preference.[2682]

Where the same party holds both a first and second mortgage on property and forecloses on the second mortgage, the debt secured by the first mortgage is discharged and the holder may not proceed for any deficiency on it.[2683]

As to tax liens or tax titles arising from tax foreclosures on taxes levied prior to January 1, 1999,[2684] a title acquired by the mortgagor or on the mortgagor's behalf is cut off by foreclosure.[2685] But a tax lien acquired by a junior mortgagee survives.[2686]

The effect of a default in a suit to foreclose for an installment due on a mortgage is only to admit the securities as alleged and the amount then due. It cannot operate as an admission in the future of the nonpayment of an installment not yet due.[2687]

B. PARTIES AND PROCESS

§ 931. Parties in General

All persons interested in the controversy must be made parties to a foreclosure proceeding.

The general rules of procedure in Michigan courts apply to determining necessary and proper parties to actions for foreclosure of mortgages and land contracts.[2688] All persons who are interested in the controversy must be made parties to a foreclosure proceeding, in order that there may be an end of litigation.[2689] All persons directly affected by the decree must be made parties.[2690]

If the proper and necessary parties are not before the court, it may refuse to proceed with foreclosure of a contract for the sale of land.[2691]

2680. Sherman v. Fisher, 138 Mich. 391, 101 N.W. 572 (1904).

2681. Thompson v. Smith, 96 Mich. 258, 55 N.W. 886 (1893).

2682. Dawson v. Danbury Bank, 15 Mich. 489 (1867).

2683. Board of Trustees v. Ren-Cen Indoor Tennis & Racquet Club, 145 Mich. App. 318, 377 N.W.2d 432 (1985).

2684. MCLS § 211.72, repealed by 1999 Pub. Act 123, effective December 31, 2003.

2685. Vreeland v. Monnier, 127 Mich. 304, 86 N.W. 819 (1901).

2686. Connecticut Mut. Life Ins. Co. v. Bulte, 45 Mich. 113, 7 N.W. 707 (1881).

2687. Brown v. Thompson, 29 Mich. 72 (1874).

2688. MCR 3.410.

2689. MCR 2.205.

Frank v. Applebaum, 270 Mich. 402, 259 N.W. 302 (1935).

2690. Martin v. McReynolds, 6 Mich. 70 (1858).

2691. Miskinis v. Bement, 301 Mich. 365, 3 N.W.2d 307 (1942).

Proper parties are those who are so connected with the subject matter that their presence on the record cannot be objected to as a misjoinder,[2692] while, on the other hand, if they are not included, a full and complete decree can still be made without considering or affecting their rights.[2693] Strictly speaking, probably the only necessary parties are the mortgagor and the mortgagee and those who have acquired rights or interests in the premises subsequent to the mortgage.[2694]

Improper or unnecessary parties need not be joined to an action foreclosing a land contract.[2695] The lack of joinder of proper but unnecessary parties does not forestall a foreclosure proceeding on a land contract.[2696]

Prior lienholders, or those claiming under a title paramount to the mortgage, are not proper parties to a suit for its foreclosure, nor can their claims be litigated in that suit.[2697] Prior mortgagees are not necessary parties to the complaint of a junior mortgagee that seeks only the foreclosure or the sale of the equity of redemption.[2698] However, prior encumbrancers are necessary parties to such a bill where the effort of the junior mortgagee is to obtain a sale of the entire property or estate, and not merely the sale of the equity of redemption, or where there is substantial doubt respecting the amount of the debts due the prior encumbrancers.[2699]

The Michigan Court Rules of 1985 provide that all persons having an interest in the subject matter of a suit and in obtaining the some or all of the relief demanded may join as plaintiffs. Persons having a united interest must be joined on the same side as plaintiffs or defendants, but when any one refuses to join, he or she may for such reason be made a defendant.[2700]

§ 932.   Plaintiffs

A foreclosure suit must generally be brought by the real and beneficial owner of the debt secured.

2692. MCR 2.207.

2693. Proper party

One tenant in common sold the land under the agreement of the cotenant to release his interest to the purchaser. Before the release was given the purchaser sold the land and took a purchase-money mortgage from his grantee. The cotenant, in pursuance of his agreement for a release, and by agreement with said grantee, executed a deed of the land to the grantee's brother. In a suit for foreclosure of the purchase-money mortgage, the brother was a proper party, for the purpose of having the deed to him decreed to be a release.—Adams v. Bradley, 12 Mich. 346 (1864).

2694. Wineman v. Phillips, 93 Mich. 223, 53 N.W. 168 (1892).

Chamberlain v. Lyell, 3 Mich. 448 (1855).

2695. Brock v. Sobole, 285 Mich. 14, 280 N.W. 91 (1938) (auditor general).

Mortgage & Contract Co. v. Linenberg, 260 Mich. 142, 244 N.W. 428 (1932) (spouses not parties to contract).

2696. Proper but not necessary

Third person purchasing realty from vendor after execution of a land contract was proper but not necessary party to suit for foreclosure of a land contract.—Smith v. Heppner, 276 Mich. 463, 267 N.W. 882 (1936).

2697. Dickerson v. Uhl, 71 Mich. 398, 39 N.W. 472 (1888).

2698. Jerome v. McCarter, 94 U.S. 734, 24 L. Ed. 136 (1877).

2699. Jerome v. McCarter, 94 U.S. 734, 24 L. Ed. 136 (1877).

Sutherland v. Lake Superior Ship Canal, R. & Iron Co., 23 F. Cas. 459 (C.C.E.D. Mich. 1874) (No. 13,643).

2700. M.L.P.2d Civil Procedure. MCR 2.206.

Generally, the plaintiff in a foreclosure suit must be the real party in interest in the debt secured, such as the person named in the mortgage note, mortgage, or land contract or assignment of the note, mortgage, or land contract.[2701] Suit may be brought by a person who is legally empowered to collect the debt for the owner.[2702]

Where a person holds the equitable title alone, the complainant must join as a party to the foreclosure action that person holding the legal title to the mortgage.[2703]

Generally, an assignee of a mortgage may sue to foreclose in his or her own name, and the assignor is not a necessary party.[2704] Likewise, in a proper case the land contract may be foreclosed by the vendor's transferee.[2705] Where a mortgage is assigned as security to an officer of an entity, the officer is not a necessary party in an action by the entity to foreclose the mortgage.[2706] Where a mortgage has been assigned in trust for several individuals, it is not necessary to make the beneficiaries parties to an action to foreclose it.[2707]

§ 933.   Defendants

All parties who, on the face of the instrument, appear to be liable or claim an interest adverse to the plaintiff may be made defendants in a foreclosure suit.

In a mortgage foreclosure suit, the court will permit the bringing in of all parties who, on the face of the instrument, appear to be liable, so that their rights may be adjusted in a single suit.[2708]

The mortgagor is a necessary party to a foreclosure suit. This is true

---

2701. MCR 2.201.

2702. Norton v. Ohrns, 67 Mich. 612, 35 N.W. 175 (1887) (guardian).

2703. Martin v. McReynolds, 6 Mich. 70 (1858).

2704. Briggs v. Hannowald, 35 Mich. 474 (1877).

Assignor guardian of minors

Minors, whose guardian had assigned a mortgage that he held for them, were not necessary parties to a bill by the assignee to foreclose such mortgage.—Livingston v. Jones, Harrington Ch. 165 (Mich. 1842).

Death of one of several assignees

Where one of several assignees of a mortgage dies, his personal representative is not a necessary party to a bill for the foreclosure of the mortgage.—Martin v. McReynolds, 6 Mich. 70 (1858).

2705. Foreclosure of mortgage on vendor's interest

Vendees who defaulted in payment of taxes and monthly installments under a land contract, before vendor defaulted in mortgage payments, were not entitled to prevent foreclosure of mortgage by mortgagee, as transferee of vendor's interest, where vendees' prior default caused vendor to default and necessitated transfer of his interest to mortgagee.—Stryker v. Marschner, 274 Mich. 205, 264 N.W. 344 (1936).

2706. Michigan State Bank v. Trowbridge, 92 Mich. 217, 52 N.W. 632 (1892).

MCR 2.201.

2707. Sill v. Ketchum, Harrington Ch. 423 (Mich. 1842).

Mortgagee in capacity of trustee

Under a mortgage authorizing the mortgagee to sell participating certificates and act in the capacity of a trustee, with reservation of the right of foreclosure, where the mortgagee sold certificates, a foreclosure sale at suit of mortgagee was not void because holders of the certificates did not join in foreclosure.—Canvasser v. Bankers Trust Co., 284 Mich. 634, 280 N.W. 71 (1938).

MCR 2.201.

2708. Frank v. Applebaum, 270 Mich. 402, 259 N.W. 302 (1935).

Dederick v. Barber, 44 Mich. 19, 5 N.W. 1064 (1880) (all makers of joint and several note).

notwithstanding the fact that the remedy against the mortgagor personally is barred by the statute of limitations.[2709] The mortgagee has the right to foreclose all of the interests derived from the mortgagor subsequent to the mortgagor's own mortgage.[2710] A mortgagee of a land-contract vendor's or vendee's interest is a necessary party to any action by the other party to the land contract that would terminate the mortgagee's lien.[2711]

Where the mortgagor dies before the institution of foreclosure proceedings, the action must be brought against the heirs of the deceased.[2712] The personal representative of the deceased is not a necessary party,[2713] unless by reason of a deficiency in the mortgaged premises the personal estate is sought to be charged.[2714]

A mortgagee can make judgment creditors of the mortgagor's grantor parties to a foreclosure suit, when those creditors assert a claim on the ground that the transfer to the mortgagor is in fraud of their rights and that, therefore, their executions, levied after the execution of the mortgage, are prior liens on the land.[2715]

In accordance with the joinder rules of the Michigan Court Rules of 1985,[2716] a person having an interest in the subject matter as to make the person a necessary party who has been omitted in the first instance may be brought in pending the proceedings.[2717]

The assignee in bankruptcy of a bankrupt mortgagor is not a necessary party defendant to foreclosure proceedings instituted prior to the adjudication in bankruptcy.[2718]

It is not necessary to make defendants of those against whom nothing is alleged and from whom no relief is asked.[2719] Further, if the complaint fails to show any connection between a person named as a defendant and the mortgage or the equity of redemption, that person is not a proper party, the action against that person will be dismissed.[2720]

A person who had no interest in the mortgaged realty at the time the complaint was filed, and who buys an interest in the realty, knowing at the time that he or she is buying an interest in real property in litigation, is not a proper party defendant in

---

2709. Michigan Ins. Co. v. Brown, 11 Mich. 265 (1863).

2710. Provident Mut. Life Ins. Co. v. Vinton Co., 282 Mich. 84, 275 N.W. 776 (1937).

2711. MCLS § 565.360.

2712. Abbott v. Godfroy's Heirs, 1 Mich. 178 (1849).

2713. Abbott v. Godfroy's Heirs, 1 Mich. 178 (1849).

MCR 2.202.

2714. Abbott v. Godfroy's Heirs, 1 Mich. 178 (1849).

2715. Converse v. Michigan Dairy Co., 45 F. 18 (C.C.D. Mich. 1891).

2716. MCR 2.205.

2717. Pearce v. Ware, 94 Mich. 321, 53 N.W. 1106 (1892) (bringing in parties a prerequisite to decree).

2718. Oliver v. Cunningham, 6 F. 60 (C.C.D. Mich. 1880).

2719. Jerome v. McCarter, 94 U.S. 734, 24 L. Ed. 136 (1877).

2720. Havens v. Jones, 45 Mich. 253, 7 N.W. 818 (1881).

Ramsdell v. Eaton, 12 Mich. 117 (1863).

Grand Rapids Sav. Bank v. Denison, 92 Mich. 418, 52 N.W. 733 (1892) (chattel mortgagee not necessary party defendant).

Defendant relieved from liability

Where the complainant's own showing in a suit to foreclose a mortgage proves that a person impleaded as defendant is not a proper party, he will be relieved from liability, even though he did not appear and defend.—Poole v. Horton, 45 Mich. 404, 8 N.W. 59 (1881).

a foreclosure suit.[2721]

§ 934.   —Adverse Claimants of Title

Generally, the claimant of an adverse and paramount title to the mortgaged premises is not a proper party to a foreclosure suit.

As a general rule, a person setting up a claim of title to the mortgaged premises adverse and paramount to that of the mortgagor and not derived from the mortgagor is not a proper party to the foreclosure suit.[2722] However, a plaintiff, in order to foreclose all interests derived from the mortgagor subsequent to his or her own mortgage, as is the right of a mortgagee,[2723] may name as a defendant a person claiming under a paramount title, when the latter is also owner of an interest in the equity of redemption.[2724]

With respect to tax title claimants arising from tax foreclosures on taxes levied prior to January 1, 1999,[2725] there is no reason for making the holder of a tax title on mortgaged premises a defendant in a suit for the foreclosure of the mortgage. If the plaintiff fails to show any other claim on that person's part, the complaint will be dismissed as to that defendant.[2726]

§ 935.   —Encumbrancers

Generally, neither prior nor junior encumbrancers are necessary parties to a foreclosure suit, although prior encumbrancers may be, and junior encumbrancers always are, proper parties.

As a general rule, a prior encumbrancer is not a necessary party to a suit to foreclose a mortgage.[2727] However, the holder of a prior encumbrance may be a proper party if relief is sought against that person, or the validity or priority of the lien or the amount due is disputed.[2728]

A subsequent lienholder is a proper party defendant in a suit to foreclose a mortgage if the mortgagee claims that the lienholder had actual notice of the existence of the mortgage before the lien attached, even though the mortgage is not recorded until afterwards.[2729]

§ 936.   —Purchasers and Vendors of Mortgaged Property

Purchasers of mortgaged property are proper parties to a foreclosure suit. In that case, the mortgagor-vendor is not a

2721. Provident Mut. Life Ins. Co. v. Vinton Co., 282 Mich. 84, 275 N.W. 776 (1937).

2722. Chamberlain v. Lyell, 3 Mich. 448 (1855).

2723. Provident Mut. Life Ins. Co. v. Vinton Co., 282 Mich. 84, 275 N.W. 776 (1937).
Horton v. Ingersoll, 13 Mich. 409 (1865).

2724. Horton v. Ingersoll, 13 Mich. 409 (1865).

2725. *Former* MCLS § 211.72, repealed by 1999 Pub. Act 123, effective December 31, 2003.

2726. Hayward v. Kinney, 84 Mich. 591, 48 N.W. 170 (1891).

2727. Jerome v. McCarter, 94 U.S. 734, 24 L. Ed. 136 (1877).

2728. Jerome v. McCarter, 94 U.S. 734, 24 L. Ed. 136 (1877).

2729. Campbell v. Bane, 119 Mich. 40, 77 N.W. 322 (1898).

necessary party if no relief against that person personally is sought.

Purchasers of mortgaged property are proper parties in a proceeding to foreclose the mortgage.[2730] The purchasers of land after the abatement of a suit to foreclose a mortgage on the land, although with notice, must be made parties upon the revival of the action.[2731]

In a proceeding to foreclose a land contract, the purchaser's assignee may be joined as a defendant.[2732]

After a conveyance of lands subject to a mortgage that the grantee assumes to pay, the mortgagor-grantor is not a necessary party to a suit to foreclose if no relief against the mortgagor-grantor personally is sought.[2733] However, if the foreclosure suit seeks a personal decree for any deficiency that may result, a mortgagor who has sold his or her interest in the mortgaged property subject to the mortgage debt, which the purchaser has assumed, is a necessary party.[2734]

§ 937.   —Persons Liable on Debt Secured

If the mortgage debt is secured by the obligation of another besides the mortgagor, plaintiff may make that person a party to the foreclosure action.

Under the Revised Judicature Act of 1961, if the mortgage debt is secured by the obligation or other evidence of debt of any other person besides the mortgagor, the plaintiff may make that person a party to the proceeding. The court may decree payment of the balance of the debt remaining unsatisfied, after a sale of the mortgaged premises, against the other securing person as well as against the mortgagor. The court may enforce the decree against that person as in other cases.[2735] This type of provision is permissive only, and not mandatory.[2736]

Although a guarantor of the payment of bonds secured by a mortgage is not a necessary party to a suit to foreclose the mortgage,[2737] under the aforementioned statute,[2738] relief may be had against those guarantors in a foreclosure suit.[2739]

Sureties only for the provision by the mortgagor of a sinking fund to be invested in a specified manner for the payment of the mortgage are not proper

2730. Hayward v. Kinney, 84 Mich. 591, 48 N.W. 170 (1891).

2731. Haines v. Perkins, 155 Mich. 417, 119 N.W. 439 (1909).

2732. Krueger v. Campbell, 264 Mich. 449, 250 N.W. 285 (1933).

2733. Miller v. Thompson, 34 Mich. 10 (1876).

2734. Ayres v. Wiswall, 112 U.S. 187, 5 S. Ct. 90, 28 L. Ed. 693 (1884).

2735. MCLS § 600.3160.

Guardian Depositors Corp. v. Wagner, 287 Mich. 202, 283 N.W. 29 (1938)

Miller v. McLaughlin, 132 Mich. 234, 93 N.W. 435 (1903).

Michigan State Bank v. Trowbridge, 92 Mich. 217, 52 N.W. 632 (1892).

2736. Steele v. Grove, 109 Mich. 647, 67 N.W. 963 (1896).

2737. Owen v. Potter, 115 Mich. 556, 73 N.W. 977 (1898).

2738. MCLS § 600.3160.

Mazur v. Young, 507 F.3d 1013 (6th Cir. Mich. 2007).

2739. Union Trust Co. v. Detroit Motor Co., 117 Mich. 631, 76 N.W. 112 (1898).

defendants in a foreclosure suit.[2740] However, a person who may be chargeable with the balance in case the proceeds of the mortgaged premises do not satisfy the debt is an indispensable party to the proceeding.[2741]

§ 938.   Intervention and Substitution

Anyone claiming such an interest in the mortgaged premises, or in the debt secured, that his or her rights might be compromised by the rendition of a judgment in that person's absence from the action has the right to intervene in foreclosure proceedings.

The Michigan Court Rules of 1985 provide that any one claiming an interest in the litigation may, at any time, assert his or her right to intervene upon meeting the criteria.[2742]

A person without interest generally will not be permitted to intervene,[2743] except as permitted by the court. A party may also seek permissive intervention.[2744] If, however, a person has such an interest in the mortgaged premises, or in the debt secured, that the person's rights might be compromised by the rendition of a decree in his or her absence, that person is allowed to intervene in foreclosure proceedings as of right.[2745]

In accordance with the joinder rules of the Michigan Court Rules of 1985,[2746] a person having an interest in the subject matter as to give the person a right to intervene who has been omitted in the first instance may be brought in pending the proceedings.[2747]

A person who acquires an interest in mortgaged realty after the filing of a complaint in a foreclosure suit may make application for intervention in the suit, if he or she desires to be heard.[2748] But a person who becomes a junior encumbrancer after the institution of the mortgage foreclosure proceedings has no right to intervene.[2749]

Substitution of parties. In accordance with the substitution rules of the Michigan Court Rules of 1985,[2750] the cause of action in a mortgage foreclosure action survives to the personal representative of a plaintiff in a mortgage foreclosure

2740. Joy v. Jackson & Michigan Plank Road Co., 11 Mich. 155 (1863).

2741. Matcalm v. Smith, 16 F. Cas. 1091 (C.C.D. Mich. 1855) (No. 9,272).

2742. M.L.P.2d Civil Procedure.

MCR 2.209.

2743. Detroit Trust Co. v. Sosensky, 300 Mich. 353, 1 N.W.2d 570 (1942).

2744. M.L.P.2d Civil Procedure.

MCR 2.209.

2745. MCR 2.209.

Accord Oliver v. Cunningham, 6 F. 60 (C.C.D. Mich. 1880) (assignee in bankruptcy of bankrupt mortgagor).

2746. MCR 2.206.

2747. Pearce v. Ware, 94 Mich. 321, 53 N.W. 1106 (1892) (bringing in parties a prerequisite to decree).

2748. Provident Mut. Life Ins. Co. v. Vinton Co., 282 Mich. 84, 275 N.W. 776 (1937).

2749. Union Trust Co. v. C.H. Miles Adams Ave. Corp., 247 Mich. 341, 225 N.W. 594 (1929).

2750. MCR 2.202.

Codd v. Carpenter, 109 Mich. 120, 67 N.W. 819 (1896).

suit who dies while the suit is pending.[2751] The personal representative must file a proper motion to proceed with the action.[2752]

§ 939. Defects and Objections as to Parties

Defects as to parties may be obviated by amendment of the pleadings.

Under the Michigan Court Rules of 1985, the misjoinder of parties is not cause for dismissal of the action. New parties may be added and parties misjoined may be dropped, by order of the court, at any stage of the proceedings, as the ends of justice may require for granting complete relief.[2753] Defects with respect to parties to a mortgage or land-contract foreclosure may be obviated by an exercise of the power of amendment.[2754]

The maker of a note and mortgage cannot complain because the payee of the note is not made a party to a suit to foreclose brought by a subsequent assignee of the mortgage.[2755]

§ 940. Process

Process in a foreclosure suit must substantially comply with the Constitution, statutes, and court rules.

The general rules of procedure in Michigan courts apply to determining necessity of service and adequacy of process in actions for foreclosure of mortgages and land contracts.[2756]

A valid decree foreclosing a mortgage or a land contract cannot be rendered if the process fails substantially to comply with constitutional or statutory requirements.[2757] Mere irregularities, however, do not vitiate the decree.[2758]

New notice or service of process may be necessary on a petition for a supplemental decree to order a sale for an additional installment of the mortgage debt,[2759] or to ascertain and determine a deficiency.[2760]

It is the duty of plaintiffs in foreclosure proceedings to see to it that the defendants are not misled, and plaintiffs are responsible for the correctness of their

---

2751. MCR 2.201.

Haines v. Perkins, 155 Mich. 417, 119 N.W. 439 (1909).

2752. MCR 2.201.

Haines v. Perkins, 155 Mich. 417, 119 N.W. 439 (1909).

2753. M.L.P.2d Civil Procedure.
MCR 2.207.

2754. Swight v. Humphreys, 8 F. Cas. 187, 1842 U.S. App. LEXIS 521 (C.C.D. Mich. 1842) (No. 4,216) (party improperly joined).

2755. Michigan State Bank v. Trowbridge, 92 Mich. 217, 52 N.W. 632 (1892).

2756. MCR 3.410.

2757. Forbes v. Darling, 94 Mich. 621, 54 N.W. 385 (1893).

2758. Kerr v. Weeks, 191 Mich. 652, 158 N.W. 131 (1916).

2759. Brown v. Thompson, 29 Mich. 72 (1874).

MCR 2.106.

2760. Field v. Snow, 124 Mich. 68, 82 N.W. 798 (1900).

MCR 2.106.

process.[2761]

Under the Michigan Court Rules of 1985, a defendant in a foreclosure action who is not a resident of the state may be served by substitute service of process.[2762] If substitute service is shown to be ineffectual,[2763] the court may order notice by publication or posting,[2764] or other means.[2765]

A mortgagee of a land-contract vendor's or vendee's interest is entitled to the same notices that the vendor or vendee is entitled to from the other party to the land contract.[2766]

C. PLEADING AND PROOF

§ 951. Complaint

A foreclosure suit is begun by the filing of a complaint, which must contain a proper statement of all facts essential to plaintiff's cause of action.

An action for foreclosure of a mortgage or a land contract is commenced by the filing of a complaint in accordance with the rules of court.[2767] The complaint must conform to the usual rules of pleading and contain a proper statement of all the facts essential to the plaintiff's cause of action.[2768]

The plaintiff must state in a complaint for foreclosure of a mortgage or a land contract whether any proceedings have been had at law for the recovery of any part of the debt secured by the mortgage, and whether any part of the debt has been collected or paid.[2769] The complaint for foreclosure must allege nonpayment or other breach of condition entitling the plaintiff to maintain the suit.[2770] A complaint that fails to state that anything is due on the note, or whether any proceedings have been had at law for the recovery of the debt, is subject to attack.[2771]

Under the Revised Judicature Act of 1961, if a judgment has been obtained for the moneys demanded in a complaint for foreclosure, the complainant may not maintain a proceeding unless an execution against the property of the defendant on that judgment has been returned unsatisfied, in whole or in part.[2772] Accordingly,

2761. Vaughan v. Black, 63 Mich. 215, 29 N.W. 523 (1886).

2762. MCR 2.105.

2763. MCR 2.105.

2764. MCR 2.106.

Unconstitutionality of provision for notice by publication where person to be notified and his place of residence are known, *see* 10 Wayne L. Rev. 13, 15 (1963).

2765. MCR 2.105.

2766. MCLS § 565.360.

2767. MCR 3.410.

2768. McCabe v. Farnsworth, 27 Mich. 52 (1873).

Griggs v. Detroit & M. R. Co., 10 Mich. 117 (1862) (bill sufficient to foreclose mortgage).

Proctor v. Plumer, 112 Mich. 393, 70 N.W. 1028 (1897) (bill sufficient to foreclose a land contract).

2769. MCR 3.410.

2770. Bennett v. Clark, 181 Mich. 690, 148 N.W. 372 (1914) (allegation of nonpayment).

Martin v. McReynolds, 6 Mich. 70 (1858) (allegation of nonpayment sufficient).

2771. Bailey v. Gould, Walk. Ch. 478 (Mich. 1844).

2772. MCLS § 600.3105.

Foreign judgment

Under Michigan statute precluding mortgage foreclosure proceedings on money judgment until

where proceedings at law have been had, the bill seeking foreclosure must allege the return of an execution unsatisfied in whole or in part.[2773]

The description of the note in the mortgage and that in the pleadings must correspond, but trifling or unimportant differences are not to be treated as a fatal variance.[2774] A foreclosure complaint filed by an assignee who claims to be the owner of one of four mortgage notes must account for the remaining notes.[2775]

Where a mortgage is given to secure the sureties on an official bond, it is immaterial that the complaint to foreclose it does not correctly state the date of the officer's appointment, if it correctly recites the mortgage and the breach, and the testimony makes out full ground for the suit.[2776]

If a bill charges that an instrument is a mortgage, seeks a foreclosure on it as a mortgage, and contains a prayer for other and further relief, the court may declare it a mortgage in the proceeding, even though there is no special prayer for that purpose in the pleadings.[2777]

Where the mortgage requires the mortgagee to perform certain conditions precedent to the right to foreclose, or makes the debt payable only on a certain contingency, the pleadings must contain proper averments to show the performance of the one or the happening of the other, or it will not sustain a decree.[2778]

§ 952.   —Description of Property

The mortgaged property must be described in the complaint for foreclosure with reasonable certainty and particularity.

Generally, the premises subject to the foreclosure of a mortgage or a land contract are sufficiently described when the description follows that given in the instrument.[2779]

Where the mortgage is inaccurate in its description of the premises, and has some elements that have to be rejected as surplusage, but the description is nevertheless sufficient in light of the extrinsic facts to identify the property intended,

---

execution on judgment has been returned unsatisfied, plaintiff mortgagee which obtained judgment in another state on note secured by properties in Michigan and the other state without stating amount awarded, could not obtain foreclosure in Michigan until such time as court in other state determined amount of liability so as to permit defendant to satisfy debt and enable defendant to satisfy requirement for return of unsatisfied charges.—Southern Floridabanc, S.A. v. Feldman, 703 F. Supp. 627 (E.D. Mich. 1989).

2773. Cooper v. Bresler, 9 Mich. 534 (1862).

2774. Variance not fatal

An objection that the bill in a foreclosure suit describes the note secured by the mortgage as being given by one of two persons, while the mortgage describes it as being given by both

persons, is not a fatal variance, and is of no importance except as to personal liability.—Botsford v. Botsford, 49 Mich. 29, 12 N.W. 897 (1882).

2775. Cooper v. Smith, 75 Mich. 247, 42 N.W. 815 (1889).

2776. Shelden v. Warner, 45 Mich. 638, 8 N.W. 529 (1881).

2777. Abbott v. Godfroy's Heirs, 1 Mich. 178 (1849).

2778. Curtis v. Goodenow, 24 Mich. 18 (1871) (complaint insufficient).

Dye v. Mann, 10 Mich. 291 (1862) (complaint sufficient).

2779. Cook v. Wiles, 42 Mich. 439, 4 N.W. 169 (1880).

it is proper, in a complaint to foreclose the mortgage, to describe the property actually mortgaged by a description that is accurate. A variance in terms from the description in the mortgage is unimportant.[2780]

An error as to the block in describing land in a bill to foreclose a mortgage is no ground for setting aside the decree, where the property is fully identified otherwise and an amended bill is filed by consent of the parties correctly describing the land.[2781]

§ 953.   —Interests of the Parties

Plaintiff, in the complaint for foreclosure, must sufficiently allege his or her ownership of the mortgage and the mortgage debt. A complaint for foreclosure of a mortgage or a land contract does not have to specify in detail the nature and basis of the defendant's interest in the property.

The plaintiff in an action to foreclose a mortgage or a land contract must set forth his or her own interest in the property in the complaint.[2782]

The plaintiff's ownership of the mortgage and the mortgage debt must be sufficiently alleged.[2783] The failure of the plaintiff in a foreclosure suit to make out a complete title to the mortgage as a valid security will bar relief.[2784]

Where a foreclosure suit is instituted by an assignee of the mortgage and debt, the pleadings must show a prima facie title in plaintiff as assignee.[2785] While it is not necessary to set out the instrument of assignment in full, the complaint must at least allege facts from which it can be inferred that a valid assignment was made to plaintiff.[2786] A foreclosure bill filed by an assignee whose assignment shows upon its face that it is not absolute should set forth the existence and amount of the notes secured, and the assignor should be made a party to the suit.[2787]

2780. Slater v. Breese, 36 Mich. 77 (1877).

No misdescription

A note given by two persons was secured by a mortgage from only one of them; foreclosure bill described the note as given by the mortgagor, but no objection was made for nonjoinder, and the bill made profert of the note and mortgage, and described the mortgage by its record; this was not a case of misdescription, and therefore not one of fatal variance; and the nonjoinder was unimportant unless as bearing upon personal responsibility.—Botsford v. Botsford, 49 Mich. 29, 12 N.W. 897 (1882).

2781. Stevenson v. Kurtz, 98 Mich. 493, 57 N.W. 580 (1894).

2782. MCR 3.410.

2783. Cooper v. Smith, 75 Mich. 247, 42 N.W. 815 (1889).

Spear v. Hadden, 31 Mich. 265 (1875).

Proctor v. Robinson, 35 Mich. 284 (1877) (complaint sufficient).

Absolute deed as mortgage

An allegation that a deed absolute in form was given the complainant as security for a debt due a copartnership, the members of which were made parties to the proceeding, that the suit was authorized by them, but the debt had not been paid nor any proceeding at law taken to collect it, was sufficient as a bill by a trustee to foreclose a mortgage.—Bennett v. Clark, 181 Mich. 690, 148 N.W. 372 (1914).

2784. Cooper v. Smith, 75 Mich. 247, 42 N.W. 815 (1889).

2785. Spear v. Hadden, 31 Mich. 265 (1875).

2786. Allegation sufficient

An allegation, in a bill for foreclosure by an assignee, that the bond and mortgage were "duly sold, assigned, and set over by said mortgagees" to said complainants, by an assignment under seal, is a sufficient allegation of a legal assignment.—Martin v. McReynolds, 6 Mich. 70 (1858).

2787. Cooper v. Smith, 75 Mich. 247, 42 N.W. 815 (1889).

An allegation that the plaintiff received an absolute deed as a mortgage is generally sufficient statement of interest in the complaint for foreclosure.[2788]

Interests of defendants. A complaint for foreclosure of a mortgage or a land contract does not have to specify in detail the nature and basis of the defendant's interest in the property, so long as it states that the defendant claims some interest in the premises.[2789]

Where a purchaser from the mortgagor is a defendant, the complaint must allege that person's claim as the subsequent purchaser of the property.[2790] A foreclosure complaint that makes persons defendants as subsequent purchasers or encumbrancers is not multifarious because it alleges that the defendants claim some adverse interest.[2791]

Where the mortgagor is dead, the interest of defendants is sufficiently alleged by describing them as the mortgagor's surviving children.[2792]

§ 954.   Answer

The general rules of procedure in Michigan courts apply to the defendant's answer in actions for foreclosure of mortgages and land contracts.

The general rules of procedure in Michigan courts apply to the defendant's answer in actions for foreclosure of mortgages and land contracts.[2793]

In answering a foreclosure complaint containing the general allegation that a person has or claims to have rights in the mortgaged premises "as a subsequent purchaser or encumbrancer or otherwise," defendant need not set up a claim of title paramount to the mortgage. A mere disclaimer is sufficient to protect the defendant's rights.[2794]

Where the defense to the foreclosure depends on new matter by way of avoidance, defendant must allege it circumstantially, and prove it as alleged.[2795] If the defendant relies on a discharge of the mortgage, it is for the defendant to allege and prove the discharge.[2796] If the mortgagor relies upon an election to pay before maturity and a tender in pursuance of it, the mortgagor must allege it in the

---

2788. Bennett v. Clark, 181 Mich. 690, 148 N.W. 372 (1914).

2789. MCR 3.410.

2790. MCR 3.410.

Accord Wurcherer v. Hewitt, 10 Mich. 453 (1862) (averment insufficient).

2791. Wilkinson v. Green, 34 Mich. 221 (1876).

Summers v. Bromley, 28 Mich. 125 (1873).

2792. Gray v. Franks, 86 Mich. 382, 49 N.W. 130 (1891).

2793. MCR 3.410.

2794. Comstock v. Comstock, 24 Mich. 39 (1871).

2795. Post v. Springsted, 49 Mich. 90, 13 N.W. 370 (1882).

2796. Spear v. Hadden, 31 Mich. 265 (1875).

Agreement for partial release

A defense to a bill to foreclose a mortgage, that an arrangement was made between a subsequent purchaser made a defendant and complainant's assignor that the portion so purchased was to be released from the mortgage on conditions which were complied with, must clearly show the agreement.—Suhr v. Ellsworth, 29 Mich. 57 (1874).

answer.[2797]

§ 955.   Counterclaims and Cross-Claims

The general rules of procedure in Michigan courts apply to the parties' counterclaims and cross-claims in actions for foreclosure of mortgages and land contracts.

The general rules of procedure in Michigan courts apply to the parties' counterclaims and cross-claims in actions for foreclosure of mortgages and land contracts.[2798]

In a mortgage foreclosure suit, a counterclaim may be filed by the mortgagor under appropriate circumstances.[2799]

Parties with interests in the mortgaged property that are at odds with the interest of the foreclosing mortgagee may file cross-claims to preserve their interests in the property.[2800] Furthermore, if a complaint is filed to foreclose an invalid mortgage, and a subsequent mortgagee of the same property is made a party defendant, the subsequent mortgagee may take advantage of the invalidity of the first mortgage by answer, without filing a cross-claim.[2801] Where a portion of the land covered by a mortgage is conveyed subject to the payment of the entire mortgage by the grantee, and a complaint is filed to foreclose the mortgage, the subsequent purchaser need not file a cross-claim in order to protect his or her rights, but may set out the facts in the answer.[2802]

§ 956.   Amended and Supplemental Pleadings

Under most circumstances, the pleadings in a foreclosure suit may be amended, or supplemental pleadings may be filed.

In harmony with the provisions of the Michigan Court Rules providing for liberal amendment of pleadings,[2803] a suit for foreclosure by the mortgagee may be continued by the assignee of the mortgagee, who may file supplemental pleadings to set up the change of title and to obtain the same relief that the mortgagee could have under the original bill.[2804]

2797. Post v. Springsted, 49 Mich. 90, 13 N.W. 370 (1882).

2798. MCR 3.410.

2799. Wilcox v. Allen, 36 Mich. 160 (1877).

Statute of limitation applies

A claim for damages for fraud in obtaining a mortgage cannot be setoff in a suit to foreclose the mortgage more than seven years after the fraud occurred.—Houle v. Camp, 247 Mich. 457, 226 N.W. 240 (1929).

2800. Assignee of collateral mortgage

Assignee of one of several notes secured by a mortgage as collateral for an indebtedness of the assignor whose equities may turn out to be different from those of the mortgagee has the right to file a cross-claim in a suit to foreclose the mortgage, and is not deprived of that right where, although his rights would be fully protected as a defendant in the original case if the plaintiffs should prevail therein, he would, in case of a dismissal of the original bill, be deprived of the means of obtaining the relief to which he might be entitled.—Wilcox v. Allen, 36 Mich. 160 (1877).

2801. Dye v. Mann, 10 Mich. 291 (1862).

2802. Caruthers v. Hall, 10 Mich. 40 (1862).

2803. MCR 2.118.

2804. Cooper v. Bigly, 13 Mich. 463 (1865).

A supplemental pleading in an action to foreclose a mortgage need not be filed merely to show that, after the commencement of the suit, the mortgagor made a payment and the mortgagee executed a discharge of a part of the premises. It is only necessary that the decree of foreclosure omit the description covered by the discharge.[2805] Further, where a mortgage provides for the payment of taxes, it is not necessary to file a supplemental bill alleging the payment of taxes after the filing of the original bill in order to have those taxes included in the decree.[2806]

In foreclosure proceedings, the right to grant amendments at the hearing in the court of first resort is broad, where the amendment sought to be made is germane to the controversy and is calculated to help produce a better or more complete result.[2807] While in the end the proof must correspond to the allegations of the complaint,[2808] in mortgage and land contract foreclosure suits, any variance between the averments of the pleadings and the cause of action on which the proceeding is based may generally be corrected by amendment.[2809]

Conditions may justify the granting of leave to defendant to amend an answer.[2810] Thus, the court can permit a defendant who purchased part of the mortgaged premises to amend the answer by alleging that the defendant had no notice of plaintiff's mortgage, because that amendment is in furtherance of justice.[2811]

On the other hand, the circumstances may be such as to justify a denial of leave to defendant to amend the pleadings in a particular manner.[2812]

2805. Commercial Nat'l Bank v. Gaukler, 165 Mich. 403, 130 N.W. 655 (1911).

2806. Commercial Nat'l Bank v. Gaukler, 165 Mich. 403, 130 N.W. 655 (1911).

2807. Slater v. Breese, 36 Mich. 77 (1877).

MCR 2.118.

2808. Schmidt v. Gaukler, 156 Mich. 243, 120 N.W. 746 (1909) (variance not shown).

Waterfield v. Wilber, 64 Mich. 642, 31 N.W. 553 (1887) (land contract foreclosure).

2809. MCR 2.118.

Amendments authorized

Where mortgagor brought action against mortgagee who allegedly demanded excessive escrow deposits and, after dissolution of temporary restraining order, mortgagee foreclosed and mortgagor exercised right of redemption, mortgagor was entitled to file amended complaint restating and amending her allegations.—Cramer v. Metropolitan Federal Sav. & Loan Ass'n, 34 Mich. App. 638, 192 N.W.2d 50 (1971).

Description in corrected mortgage

A mortgage containing an erroneous description was replaced by one describing the premises correctly; complaint to foreclose was based on the original mortgage; amended complaint set up the new mortgage; new mortgage could be construed as being given to correct the mistake in the original

without destroying the identity of the debt and to bring out the real equity, authorizing the court to allow the amendment.—McMann v. Westcott, 47 Mich. 177, 10 N.W. 190 (1881).

Reply to defense

Where complaint to foreclose a mortgage was not framed originally so as to afford the proper reply to a defense of estoppel, the estoppel should be introduced by an amendment to the bill.— Connerton v. Oakman, 41 Mich. 608, 2 N.W. 932 (1879).

Subsequent mortgages held by mortgagee

Where plaintiff in a foreclosure bill held subsequent mortgages not referred to in his bill, and the answer of a defendant, brought in as a subsequent encumbrancer, referred to such intervening mortgages and based asserted equities on their existence, it is proper to permit plaintiff to so amend his bill at the hearing as to make it aver the facts as to these mortgages.—Slater v. Breese, 36 Mich. 77 (1877).

2810. MCR 2.118.

2811. Balen v. Mercier, 75 Mich. 42, 42 N.W. 666 (1889).

2812. Counterclaim to injunction

Where a mortgagor sues to restrain foreclosure by advertisement of a real estate mortgage given as part of a usurious transaction, and the mortgagee files a counterclaim asking foreclosure in chan-

§ 957. Issues, Proof, and Variance

In a mortgage foreclosure suit, only those claims, defenses, and questions may be litigated that the pleadings have put in issue.

In a mortgage foreclosure suit, only those claims, defenses, and questions may be litigated that the pleadings have put in issue.[2813]

A title that is adverse and paramount to that of both the mortgagor and the mortgagee cannot be litigated in a foreclosure action. But the question whether an asserted claim is such an adverse one as to come within the rule depends, not upon what is set up in the answer in regard to it, but rather upon what the complaint charges and the proofs show to be its real character.[2814]

A defendant who claims that the mortgage is void or that he or she is not liable on the mortgage must support that answer by pertinent evidence.[2815]

If either party to a complaint that describes the premises in different terms than are used in the mortgage itself desires a judicial settlement regarding what precise parcels the description attaches, a proper request for that relief must be made and followed by proper proof.[2816]

Evidence in a mortgage foreclosure suit is limited to the issues raised by the pleadings, and evidence outside those issues is inadmissible.[2817] In an equitable action to foreclose an open-ended mortgage that allegedly secures certain notes, the court's proper admission of testimony to construe the intent of parties does not constitute allowance of testimony to change the terms of the mortgage instrument.[2818] Any variance between the averments of the pleadings and the cause of action on which the proceeding is based may generally be corrected by amendment.[2819]

§ 958. Evidence

In a foreclosure suit, plaintiff must establish the facts necessary to entitle him or her to the relief sought, while

cery, court might not permit the mortgagee to amend pleadings so as to withdraw the counterclaim, in view of the fact that the amendment would prejudice the mortgagor by reviving his or her liability for legal interest.—Sultan v. Central Life Ins. Co., 302 Mich. 425, 4 N.W.2d 713 (1942).

2813. Matteson v. Morris, 40 Mich. 52 (1879) (existence of note and mortgage put in issue).

Higman v. Stewart, 38 Mich. 513 (1878) (defense not raised by issues joined is unavailable).

Smith v. Fiting, 37 Mich. 148 (1877) (equitable setoff).

Hess v. Final, 32 Mich. 515 (1875) (equitable setoff).

2814. Wilkinson v. Green, 34 Mich. 221 (1876).

2815. Smith v. Fiting, 37 Mich. 148 (1877).

2816. Shepard v. Shepard, 36 Mich. 173 (1877).

2817. Proof within issues

Where the answer to a complaint to foreclose a mortgage asserts a want of consideration, proof that the mortgage was supported by an illegal consideration is within the issues.—Dierkes v. Wideman, 143 Mich. 181, 106 N.W. 735 (1906).

Hall v. Nash, 10 Mich. 303, 1862 Mich. LEXIS 52 (1862).

2818. Macomb County Sav. Bank v. Kohlhoff, 5 Mich. App. 531, 147 N.W.2d 418 (1967).

2819. MCR 2.118.

defendant has the burden of establishing affirmative or special defenses.

Although the plaintiff is not required to prove unnecessary facts or immaterial allegations, the plaintiff must establish the facts necessary to entitle him or her to the relief sought in a foreclosure action.[2820] Summary judgment is inappropriate against a plaintiff who submits evidence that could meet the plaintiff's burden if it is credible.[2821]

The introduction of the note and mortgage may be sufficient to cast upon defendant the burden of showing payment of them, if nothing is claimed but the sums shown upon the instruments and the accumulations provided in them to be determined from computation as provided in them.[2822] However, if the plaintiff makes a further claim for taxes and insurance premiums, the defendant must prove their payment, as well as the amount paid.[2823]

Where it is shown that the title of any person who has negotiated the instrument is defective, plaintiff has the burden of showing that he or she is a holder in due course.[2824]

Defendant in a suit to foreclose a mortgage has the burden of establishing affirmative or special defenses.[2825] Thus, the burden is on the mortgagor to prove mental incapacity to execute the mortgage as a defense.[2826] The burden of showing that the amount due on the mortgage sought to be foreclosed is less than what the plaintiff claims it to be rests on the defendant.[2827] If the giving of a note and mortgage, and the correctness of the amount, are admitted, and defendant does not allege that they were ever surrendered and cancelled, but alleges payments sufficient

2820. Behrens v. Apessos, 39 Mich. App. 426, 197 N.W.2d 886 (1972).

Bishop v. Felch, 7 Mich. 371 (1859) (consideration for mortgage).

Real property Law: Real Evidence: Special Rules for Real Estate Disputes, 80 Mich. B.J. 28 (2001).

Facts conceded for purposes of motion for summary judgment do not necessarily bar that party's right to contest them at trial

Defendant's motion for accelerated or summary judgment in action for foreclosure under a land contract, although in effect conceding facts in complaint for purposes of motion, did not finally and completely concede such facts as would preclude defendant from raising factual issues concerning timely performance, default status of contract, and mistake as defenses on remand following reviewing court's reversal of trial court's order dismissing complaint pursuant to defendant's motion.—Cooper v. Jefferson Inv. Co., 402 Mich. 294, 262 N.W.2d 650 (1978).

2821. Agency to accept tender

In foreclosure action following mortgagor-assignor's prepayment of mortgage in full to mortgage servicing company which became bankrupt before it could forward proceeds to plaintiff as-

signee, summary disposition for plaintiff was inappropriate where genuine material fact issue of agency existed regarding plaintiff's control over company, as well as to alleged custom of servicing companies to accept mortgage prepayments and plaintiff's knowledge of it, question of apparent authority traceable to plaintiff, and whether plaintiff, by placing company in position of authority, was estopped from denying existence of such authority.—Meretta v. Peach, 195 Mich. App. 695, 491 N.W.2d 278 (1992).

2822. Collateral Liquidation, Inc. v. Lippman, 273 Mich. 586, 263 N.W. 747 (1935).

2823. Collateral Liquidation, Inc. v. Lippman, 273 Mich. 586, 263 N.W. 747 (1935).

2824. Larsen v. Muehl, 276 Mich. 267, 267 N.W. 829 (1936).

2825. Baker v. Clark, 52 Mich. 22, 17 N.W. 225 (1883).

2826. Baker v. Clark, 52 Mich. 22, 17 N.W. 225 (1883).

2827. Lyon v. McDonald, 51 Mich. 435, 16 N.W. 800 (1883).

Johnson v. Van Velsor, 43 Mich. 208, 5 N.W. 265 (1880).

to cancel them, the defendant has the burden of proving the payments.[2828]

In a suit to foreclose a mortgage on lands in the hands of a subsequent purchaser, the purchaser may make a prima facie case of want of notice of the mortgage by showing that the mortgage has not been recorded. The burden is then thrown on plaintiff to show that the purchaser either had actual notice of the mortgage, or that the circumstances should have put the purchaser on inquiry respecting its existence.[2829]

There is a presumption that the representation of the amount of the debt expressed in the mortgage by the parties to it is correct, and nothing short of clear and cogent evidence will establish the contrary.[2830]

If the mortgage or note is lost or destroyed, the fact may be established by evidence, and secondary proof of its contents may be admitted.[2831] In this connection, where a note and mortgage are destroyed by a fire, and their contents are proved without contradiction, it is immaterial on foreclosure that the mortgage is not entitled to record, and that some evidence of it is made or offered by the certified copy of the record.[2832]

§ 959.   —Weight and Sufficiency of Evidence

Plaintiff must prove his or her right to foreclose by a preponderance of the evidence.

In an action to foreclose a mortgage or a land contract, the plaintiff must sufficiently prove his or her right to foreclose by a preponderance of the evidence.[2833] If plaintiff wishes to recover for taxes and insurance premiums paid, the plaintiff must sufficiently establish that claim.[2834]

The existence and identity of the mortgage and the amount of the mortgage

---

2828. Coon v. Bouchard, 74 Mich. 486, 42 N.W. 72 (1889).

Burden cast on mortgagee by claim of payment by services

Where, on foreclosure, the mortgagor claims to have paid the mortgage by his services and proves the services, the burden of proof is on the mortgagee to show that the mortgagor has been paid for his services otherwise than by credit on the mortgage debt.—Webber v. Ryan, 54 Mich. 70, 19 N.W. 751 (1884).

2829. White v. McGarry, 47 F. 420 (C.C.D. Mich. 1880).

2830. Wiswall v. Ayres, 51 Mich. 324, 16 N.W. 667 (1883).

No presumption from memorandum on mortgage

A memorandum on the back of a mortgage as printed in the record was: "No. 131. January 2. Quincy. $4,719.50," which was not called to the court's or counsel's attention at the trial, and no proof was offered in reference to it; it raised no presumption of being in the mortgagee's handwriting, or made in the year the mortgage matured, and intended to represent the amount due at that time.—Rose v. Lockerby, 116 Mich. 277, 74 N.W. 476 (1898).

2831. Coon v. Bouchard, 74 Mich. 486, 42 N.W. 72 (1889).

2832. Coon v. Bouchard, 74 Mich. 486, 42 N.W. 72 (1889).

2833. Larsen v. Muehl, 276 Mich. 267, 267 N.W. 829 (1936).

Breach not in dispute

Record supported court's grant of summary judgment upholding vendor's foreclosure and acceleration of a land contract upon finding that breach thereof was not in dispute and parties had, by terms of contract, provided for acceleration on purchasers' default.—Larson v. Pittman, 3 Mich. App. 348, 142 N.W.2d 479 (1966).

2834. Collateral Liquidation, Inc. v. Lippman, 278 Mich. 508, 270 N.W. 767 (1936) (evidence sufficient).

debt must be proved by sufficient evidence.[2835] When a foreclosure bill is brought against an alleged subsequent purchaser, after the death of the mortgagor, and nearly 20 years after the maturity of the mortgage, a very satisfactory showing of a continuing obligation is required, in the absence of the securities themselves.[2836]

The production by plaintiff of a regular and formal written assignment to the plaintiff of the note and mortgage is ample proof of plaintiff's title to them and of the right to bring the suit, provided the assignment identifies plaintiff as the assignee,[2837] and clearly shows that it applies to or includes the mortgage in suit.[2838]

Questions of notice to a subsequent purchaser are determinable on extraneous evidence that must be clear and satisfactory.[2839]

Defenses interposed in a suit to foreclose a mortgage must be established by a preponderance of the evidence.[2840] The same rule generally applies to counter-claims or setoffs.[2841]

Subject to some exceptions, in proceedings to foreclose a mortgage securing a note or bond, it is imperatively necessary for plaintiff to produce the note or bond or to account satisfactorily for the failure to do so.[2842] The fact that the execution of the note is admitted does not relieve plaintiff from the necessity of producing it.[2843]

2835. Grossbart v. Gilbert, 364 Mich. 96, 110 N.W.2d 812 (1961) (finding of balance due sustained).

Stiglitz v. Weingstein, 227 Mich. 691, 199 N.W. 621 (1924) (lesser amount shown due than that claimed).

George v. Ludlow, 66 Mich. 176, 33 N.W. 169 (1887) (claim of discharge sustained).

2836. Hungerford v. Smith, 34 Mich. 300 (1876).

Shattuck v. Foster, 32 Mich. 427 (1875) (evidence contradicting claim of valid and subsisting lien).

2837. Cooper v. Smith, 75 Mich. 247, 42 N.W. 815 (1889) (assignment insufficiently proved).

2838. Lashbrooks v. Hatheway, 52 Mich. 124, 17 N.W. 723 (1883) (bill dismissed).

2839. Grosvenor v. Harrison, 54 Mich. 194, 19 N.W. 951 (1884) (evidence insufficient to prove notice).

2840. Webber v. Ryan, 54 Mich. 70, 19 N.W. 751 (1884) (payment by services sustained).

Cameron v. Culkins, 44 Mich. 531, 7 N.W. 157 (1880) (forgery not sustained).

Hart v. Carpenter, 36 Mich. 402 (1877) (that parcel was twice described in deed was not shown).

Wakeman v. Akey, 29 Mich. 308 (1874) (payment not sustained).

Gift of principal of mortgage not in evidence

Evidence, in suit against daughter-in-law of mortgagee, as survivor of herself and her husband, to foreclose mortgage and for deficiency decree was not found sufficient to show a gift of the principal of the mortgage either inter vivos or causa mortis.—Clemens v. Gibbs, 303 Mich. 417, 6 N.W.2d 730 (1942).

2841. Stevens v. Stevens, 181 Mich. 438, 148 N.W. 225 (1914) (accounting asked by defendant).

2842. George v. Ludlow, 66 Mich. 176, 33 N.W. 169 (1887).

Mickle v. Gould, 42 Mich. 304, 3 N.W. 961 (1879).

Hungerford v. Smith, 34 Mich. 300 (1876).

Young v. McKee, 13 Mich. 552 (1865).

Moreland v. Houghton, 94 Mich. 548, 54 N.W. 285 (1893) (assignor not entitled to object).

2843. Young v. McKee, 13 Mich. 552 (1865).

D.   RECEIVERSHIP

§ 971.   Receivers in Foreclosures of Mortgages and Land Contracts

With certain exceptions, a receiver will not be appointed to take charge of mortgaged premises during foreclosure proceedings.

Under a provision of the Revised Judicature Act of 1961 that limits actions for possession of property by a mortgagee until after the mortgagee receives absolute title in fee,[2844] a mortgagor generally cannot be deprived of any possessory rights, nor of the income or profits from the mortgaged premises, until after perfection of the foreclosure.[2845] That right precludes the appointment of a receiver of mortgaged property prior to foreclosure sale of the property, unless otherwise provided by statute.[2846]

Accordingly, a receiver generally will not be appointed to take charge of mortgaged premises during foreclosure proceedings.[2847] Even the agreement of the parties in the mortgage cannot authorize the appointment of a receiver not otherwise authorized by law.[2848] A mortgage generally cannot be enforced in equity in a manner that deprives the mortgagor of possession until title upon foreclosure becomes absolute.[2849]

However, a receiver may be appointed to protect bondholders under a trust mortgage because taxes and insurance premiums are unpaid. The Court characterized the nonpayment of taxes and insurance premiums as a form of waste.[2850] This rule has reference to a trust mortgage solely, and is based upon the fact that under a trust mortgage the plaintiff, being a naked trustee, cannot otherwise protect the rights of the bondholders whose interests are dependent upon their security being held intact. The rule does not authorize a mortgagee under a straight mortgage to secure the appointment of a receiver because of the mortgagor's failure to pay

2844. MCLS § 600.2932.

2845. Wagar v. Stone, 36 Mich. 364 (1877).

2846. Wagar v. Stone, 36 Mich. 364 (1877).

Receiver appointed after foreclosure

In plaintiff mortgagor's action against mortgagee bank in which plaintiff, *inter alia*, requested nullification of foreclosure sale of apartment building, trial court's grant of bank's petition to set up receivership for apartment, even though bank had filed no cross-claim, was not abuse of discretion on record disclosing that plaintiff filed cause only week before expiration of statutory right to redeem and would have lost all rights to apartment had not trial judge tolled statute two days before expiration, that plaintiff had failed to meet its financial obligation to bank and failed to pay real estate taxes or procure insurance on apartment even though plaintiff was receiving rents from tenants, and that receivership was set up only after court had allowed plaintiff ten days to meet its

obligations and plaintiff had failed to do so.— Francis Martin, Inc. v. Lomas, 62 Mich. App. 706, 233 N.W.2d 702 (1975).

2847. Fifth Nat'l Bank v. Pierce, 117 Mich. 376, 75 N.W. 1058 (1898).

2848. Hazeltine v. Granger, 44 Mich. 503, 7 N.W. 74 (1880).

Discretion of court

Under statute excluding a mortgagee from possession until he acquires absolute title, a clause in the mortgage giving him possession in case of default cannot be carried into effect by appointing a receiver in foreclosure until after default; and even then it would be a matter of discretion.— Beecher v. Marquette & Pacific Rolling Mill Co., 40 Mich. 307 (1879).

2849. White v. Fulton, 260 Mich. 346, 244 N.W. 498 (1932).

2850. Nusbaum v. Shapero, 249 Mich. 252, 228 N.W. 785 (1930).

taxes.[2851]

Nonetheless, the courts have also allowed the appointment of a receiver if there is a possibility of unpaid taxes ripening into a tax title,[2852] which rule is reflected also in the Revised Judicature Act of 1961.[2853]

In addition, statutes authorizing the assignments of rents and profits are valid in all trust mortgages,[2854] which allows receivers to be appointed to collect rents and profits with respect to such mortgages.[2855] Other statutes authorize similar assignment of rents and profits of certain commercial and industrial properties subject to a mortgage.[2856]

When authorized, the appointment of a receiver is merely ancillary to the main purpose of the suit to effect a foreclosure.[2857] Generally, the appointment will not be made unless the mortgagee has a maintainable cause of action for foreclosure.[2858] The appointment of a receiver to reach the rents and profits of the premises pending foreclosure may be secured only in the foreclosure suit.[2859]

Land contract foreclosures. The common law concerning appointment of receivers in foreclosures of land contracts allows the court to be governed by equitable considerations in determining whether or not to appoint a receiver.[2860] Noteworthy, however, is the amendment of the aforementioned provision of the Revised Judicature Act of 1961 that the courts have interpreted to preclude receiverships in mortgage foreclosures unless otherwise authorized by law. That amendment precludes actions for possession of property sold under a land contract by a party with the right to declare a forfeiture and obtain possession of the property in summary process[2861] under the terms of the land contract.[2862]

2851. Union Guardian Trust Co. v. Rau, 255 Mich. 324, 238 N.W. 166 (1931).

2852. Detroit Trust Co. v. Lipsitz, 264 Mich. 404, 249 N.W. 892 (1933).

Union Guardian Trust Co. v. Rau, 255 Mich. 324, 238 N.W. 166 (1931).

2853. MCLS § 600.2927.

2854. MCLS §§ 554.211 et seq.

2855. Union Guardian Trust Co. v. McBride, 281 Mich. 680, 275 N.W. 731 (1937) (mortgage a "trust mortgage").

2856. MCLS §§ 554.231 et seq.

2857. Freedman v. Massachusetts Mut. Life Ins. Co., 81 F.2d 698 (6th Cir. Mich. 1936).

Massachusetts Mut. Life Ins. Co. v. Ruetter, 268 Mich. 175, 255 N.W. 754 (1934).

2858. Equitable Trust Co. v. Simpson, 286 Mich. 460, 282 N.W. 215 (1938) (default was shown with respect to right to have receiver appointed).

2859. Agreement for extension

Appointment of receiver for rents and profits from mortgaged premises pursuant to agreement for extension of time for payment of mortgage indebtedness, where foreclosure proceeding had not been instituted and appointment of receiver was not ancillary to other relief, was not authorized.—Massachusetts Mut. Life Ins. Co. v. Ruetter, 268 Mich. 175, 255 N.W. 754 (1934).

2860. Burton v. May, 297 Mich. 571, 298 N.W. 286 (1941) (competent basis for determination of vendors' petition for appointment of receiver shown under court rule).

Leibrand v. Curtright, 268 Mich. 98, 255 N.W. 283 (1934) (statute as not providing for appointment of receiver).

Smith v. Sherman, 265 Mich. 590, 251 N.W. 920 (1933).

Appointment of receiver

Action seeking foreclosure on a land contract was an action in equity and trial court acted properly in appointing a receiver.—Collins v. Kerstiens, 30 Mich. App. 633, 186 N.W.2d 847 (1971).

2861. *Supra*, Chapter 20.

2862. MCLS § 600.2932.

Collins v. Kerstiens, 30 Mich. App. 633, 186 N.W.2d 847 (1971) (appointment after default).

§ 972. Who May Apply

An application for appointment of a receiver must be made by a party having the requisite interest in the subject matter of the foreclosure suit.

Generally, an application for the appointment of a receiver in a foreclosure suit must be made by a party having the requisite interest in the subject matter.[2863]

The trustee of the trust may seek the assignment of rents from a property in a trust mortgage.[2864] The rule is designed for the benefit of bondholders and must be given effect to that end. The purpose of the rule is to put the trustee in the mortgagor's shoes until the debt is paid.[2865] The remedy is statutory and not allowed at common law, and must be construed in light of the rule that the mortgagee may not divest the mortgagor of possession until title becomes absolute on foreclosure.[2866]

The appointment of a receiver at the request of the mortgagor who has sold the land to protect the mortgagor against a deficiency decree is without authority of law.[2867]

§ 973. Grounds

To obtain receivership in foreclosure proceedings, the applicant must make a clear showing of strong grounds. Usually, there must be a danger of ultimate loss of the property or the waste of it.

A receivership in foreclosure is an extraordinary remedy and is not a matter of legal right. In other words, it is an equitable remedy that will not be granted except on equitable grounds and for substantial reasons, when reasonably necessary for the protection of the mortgagee. In order to obtain it, the applicant must make a clear showing of strong grounds.[2868]

Where the property is being wasted, depreciated, or materially injured, or is in imminent danger thereof, while it is in the possession of the mortgagor or the

2863. Mortgagor's wife

Mortgagor's wife was not entitled to appointment of receiver to take possession of and operate husband's mortgaged hotel property after foreclosure, especially where mortgage gave trustee those rights on mortgagor's default.—Tuller v. Detroit Trust Co., 259 Mich. 670, 244 N.W. 197 (1932).

2864. Equitable Trust Co. v. Simpson, 286 Mich. 460, 282 N.W. 215 (1938).

Union Guardian Trust Co. v. Lipsitz, 268 Mich. 209, 255 N.W. 766 (1934).

Equitable Trust Co. v. Milton Realty Co., 263 Mich. 673, 249 N.W. 30 (1933).

2865. Security Trust Co. v. Sloman, 252 Mich. 266, 233 N.W. 216 (1930).

2866. Detroit Trust Co. v. Detroit City Service Co., 262 Mich. 14, 247 N.W. 76 (1933).

2867. American Life Ins. Co. v. Bee, 260 Mich. 489, 245 N.W. 503 (1932).

2868. Equitable Trust Co. v. Wetsman, 264 Mich. 26, 249 N.W. 480 (1933) (order refusing appointment affirmed by divided court).

Detroit Fidelity & Surety Co. v. King, 264 Mich. 91, 249 N.W. 477 (1933) (appointment improper or unjustified).

White v. Fulton, 260 Mich. 346, 244 N.W. 498 (1932) (appointment improper or unjustified).

Tuller v. Detroit Trust Co., 259 Mich. 670, 244 N.W. 197 (1932) (appointment improper or unjustified).

Beardslee v. Citizens' Commercial & Sav. Bank, 112 Mich. 377, 70 N.W. 1027 (1897) (appointment improper or unjustified).

mortgagor's grantee, the court may properly grant relief by the appointment of a receiver.[2869] To justify such appointment, there must be a danger of ultimate loss of the property or the waste of it.[2870] The mere disuse of a manufacturing plant under an agreement with other manufacturers to restrict production, although attended with the decay and dilapidation inseparable from disuse, is not destruction or waste entitling the mortgagee to a receiver.[2871]

The appointment of a receiver for mortgaged premises can be provided for in an agreement extending the time for payment of the mortgage, by reference to a provision in the mortgage.[2872] Where such a stipulation is valid, it is binding on a purchaser of the premises with notice of it.[2873]

A receivership clause in a mortgage, even if valid, does not alone entitle the mortgagee to the appointment of a receiver. The appointment must not be made if there is no danger of ultimate loss or waste of the property.[2874]

Land contract foreclosures. Generally, it is essential to show threatened or actual waste or impairment of the property together with insolvency in order to secure the appointment of a receiver in an action for foreclosure of a land contract.[2875] However, the vendee's default in payment of money due the vendor affords ground for appointment of a receiver.[2876]

§ 974.   —Assignment of Rents and Profits

Receivers may be appointed with respect to trust mortgages or commercial or industrial mortgages containing provisions for the assignment of rents and profits.

Under the statute permitting the rents and profits of property mortgaged to the trustees under a trust mortgage or deed of trust to be assigned to the benefit of bondholders or holders of other obligations issued or to be issued by the trustees,[2877] receivers may be appointed with respect to trust mortgages or deeds containing provisions for the assignment of rents or profits.[2878] This remedy applies equally to

2869. Detroit Trust Co. v. Lipsitz, 264 Mich. 404, 249 N.W. 892 (1933).

Nusbaum v. Shapero, 249 Mich. 252, 228 N.W. 785 (1930).

2870. Union Trust Co. v. Charlotte General Electric Co., 152 Mich. 568, 116 N.W. 379 (1908).

2871. Union Mut. Life Ins. Co. v. Union Mills Plaster Co., 37 F. 286 (C.C.D. Mich. 1889).

2872. After commencement of foreclosure

Written agreement between the owner of mortgaged premises and the holder of the mortgage, providing for the amendment of the terms of payment of the unpaid and then due indebtedness, and for an extension of time for payment of the balance and the appointment of a receiver after the commencement of a foreclosure proceeding, was valid and enforceable after the commencement of the foreclosure suit.—Hathaway v. Miller Inv. Corp., 281 Mich. 621, 275 N.W. 653 (1937).

2873. Hathaway v. Miller Inv. Corp., 281 Mich. 621, 275 N.W. 653 (1937).

2874. Union Trust Co. v. Charlotte General Electric Co., 152 Mich. 568, 116 N.W. 379 (1908).

2875. Denby v. Ozeran, 255 Mich. 477, 238 N.W. 218 (1931).

2876. Burton v. May, 297 Mich. 571, 298 N.W. 286 (1941).

2877. MCLS § 554.211.

2878. Central Trust Co. v. Wolf, 262 Mich. 209, 247 N.W. 159 (1933).

Guaranty Trust Co. v. Feldman, 247 Mich. 524, 226 N.W. 233 (1929).

No allowance for assignment in mortgage prevented appointment of receiver

On bill by plaintiffs for specific performance of defendants' oral contract to enter into a land

land contract mortgages.[2879] The appointment is usually made where the party seeking the appointment shows that the security is inadequate to cover the debt,[2880] that waste has been committed,[2881] or that the security is endangered by nonpayment of taxes.[2882]

Under a statute permitting the rents from any commercial or industrial property other than family residences or buildings containing five or fewer apartments to be assigned as security in addition to the property described in a mortgage,[2883] the court may appoint a receiver to enforce a provision of a mortgage to that effect upon the default of the mortgagor.[2884] This remedy applies equally to a land contract mortgage.[2885]

Under common law, a court may appoint a receiver if a contract for assignment of rents is given after a default in payment under the terms of the mortgage and for a valuable consideration.[2886]

§ 975.   —Failure to Pay Taxes or to Insure

The mortgagor's failure to pay taxes or to insure as required by most mortgages may be a ground for the appointment of a receiver.

Under the Revised Judicature Act of 1961, a mortgagee or assignee of a mortgagee may obtain from the circuit court the appointment of a receiver to collect rents or profit from most mortgaged real property whose mortgagor fails to pay taxes or insurance premiums on the property.[2887] This remedy applies equally to a land contract mortgage.[2888] It does not apply to a dwelling or farm occupied by the owner as his or her home, nor to a business property having an assessed valuation of $7,500 or less.[2889]

Under common law, in the case of a trust mortgage, the failure of the

contract, where defendants filed cross-bill averring that deed by which they had obtained title to property was taken as security for moneys loaned plaintiffs and asked that deed be decreed mortgage and prayed foreclosure of it, and later petitioned for appointment of temporary receiver to collect monthly rentals and control property pending determination of suit on merits, trial court's order appointing receiver, which deprived plaintiffs of possession, income, and control of property was error, in absence of agreement in mortgage allowing defendants in case of default, to income or possession pending foreclosure and averment of emergency to justify trial court's appointment of receiver.—Lendzion v. Senstock, 300 Mich. 346, 1 N.W.2d 567 (1942).

2879. MCLS § 565.359.

2880. Equitable Trust Co. v. Simpson, 286 Mich. 460, 282 N.W. 215 (1938).

2881. Nusbaum v. Shapero, 249 Mich. 252, 228 N.W. 785 (1930).

2882. Union Guardian Trust Co. v. McBride, 281 Mich. 680, 275 N.W. 731 (1937).

2883. MCLS § 554.231.

2884. Smith v. Mutual Ben. Life Ins. Co., 362 Mich. 114, 106 N.W.2d 515 (1960) (receiver to collect rents and apply them to accrued interests, maintenance costs, insurance, taxes, and a deficiency until expiration of redemption period).

2885. MCLS § 565.359.

2886. Freedman v. Massachusetts Mut. Life Ins. Co., 81 F.2d 698 (6th Cir. Mich. 1936).

Massachusetts Mut. Life Ins. Co. v. Ruetter, 268 Mich. 175, 255 N.W. 754 (1934).

Pines v. Equitable Trust Co., 263 Mich. 458, 249 N.W. 32 (1933).

McVicar v. Denison, 81 Mich. 348, 45 N.W. 659 (1890).

2887. MCLS § 600.2927.

2888. MCLS § 565.359.

2889. MCLS § 600.2927.

mortgagor to pay taxes or to insure as required by the provisions of the trust mortgage may furnish a ground for the appointment of a receiver.[2890] Where the trust mortgagor has corrected the default, the trustee loses his or her right to obtain receivership over the property.[2891]

Also under common law, a situation where the delinquent taxes might ripen into a tax title before the sale or before the expiration of the redemption period warrants the appointment of a receiver in the case of a nontrust mortgage,[2892] with no stated limitation as for the provision of the statute regarding owner-occupied dwellings and small business properties.[2893]

The holder of a first mortgage is not entitled to have a receiver appointed to collect rents for application to the payment of delinquent taxes if the second mortgagee is collecting the rents under an assignment contained in the second mortgagee's mortgage.[2894]

§ 976. Procedure

An application for a receiver must fully and specifically allege facts entitling the mortgagee to the remedy.

Generally, before a receiver may be appointed, the mortgage debt must have been already due and there must have been such a default as to entitle the mortgagee to commence a foreclosure suit, and the mortgagee must have already filed the complaint for foreclosure.[2895] Under the provision of the Revised Judicature Act of 1961, the circuit court has jurisdiction to hear a complaint or motion for receivership for failure to pay taxes or insurance premiums, for the purpose of preventing the waste of the property.[2896]

An application for the appointment of a receiver in foreclosure proceedings must contain full and specific allegations of the facts entitling the mortgagee to the remedy.[2897]

A provision in a mortgage that the mortgagee has the right, after default, to have a receiver appointed without notice is invalid. An order appointing a receiver on an ex parte application must be set aside.[2898]

The court must examine the request for appointment of a receiver to ascertain

2890. Union Guardian Trust Co. v. McBride, 281 Mich. 680, 275 N.W. 731 (1937).

Nusbaum v. Shapero, 249 Mich. 252, 228 N.W. 785 (1930).

2891. Security not impaired

Nonpayment of taxes did not justify transfer of possession of mortgaged property to trustee of bond issue secured by mortgage, where trustee had redeemed from sale for taxes, thereby avoiding impairment of security by tax title.—Union Guardian Trust Co. v. Commercial Realty Co., 265 Mich. 604, 251 N.W. 786 (1933).

2892. Union Guardian Trust Co. v. Rau, 255 Mich. 324, 238 N.W. 166 (1931).

2893. MCLS § 600.2927.

2894. Reserve Loan Life Ins. Co. v. Witt, 264 Mich. 536, 250 N.W. 301 (1933).

2895. Equitable Trust Co. v. Simpson, 286 Mich. 460, 282 N.W. 215 (1938) (default shown).

Massachusetts Mut. Life Ins. Co. v. Ruetter, 268 Mich. 175, 255 N.W. 754 (1934) (proceeding not instituted).

2896. MCLS § 600.2927.

2897. Lendzion v. Senstock, 300 Mich. 346, 1 N.W.2d 567 (1942) (allegations insufficient).

2898. Hazeltine v. Granger, 44 Mich. 503, 7 N.W. 74 (1880).

whether a proper showing for the appointment is made. But the right to the appointment is not determined solely on allegations and denials in the pleadings.[2899]

The burden of proof is on the mortgagee to establish the grounds on which the receivership is asked.[2900]

Under the general provisions of the Revised Judicature Act of 1961 concerning appointment of receivers, where otherwise authorized, the court may exercise its authority to appoint a receiver in vacation, in chambers, and during sessions of the court. The court must provide for bond and define the receiver's duties as provided by law.[2901]

If the default of a mortgagor is not admitted, the court cannot determine that fact on a motion to appoint a receiver in the foreclosure suit.[2902]

Where the court passes on conflicts in the evidence in determining the question of whether or not a receiver should be appointed, the findings of the court must be sufficient to sustain the order.[2903]

Under the general provisions of the Revised Judicature Act of 1961 concerning appointment of receivers, where otherwise authorized, the court may terminate a receivership if doing so is in the best interest of all interested parties.[2904]

§ 977.   Operation and Effect of Appointment of Receiver

The appointment of a receiver in foreclosure proceedings places the mortgaged property in the receiver's custody, for the benefit of the parties ultimately proved to be entitled to it.

By invoking the power of the court to appoint a receiver, a mortgagee thereby submits the management and control of the property to the reasonable discretion of the court, through its receiver, and the action of the court in that respect binds the mortgagee.[2905] After thus generally submitting the property to the discretion of the court, the mortgagee may not say that the court had no power to do any act in the conservation and management of the property that lessens the lien of the mortgage, without the mortgagee's special consent.[2906]

The receiver's possession is not necessary to maintain the court's jurisdiction

---

2899. Lambrecht v. Lee, 264 Mich. 56, 249 N.W. 490 (1933).

2900. Brown v. Chase, Walk. Ch. 43 (Mich. 1842).

Union Guardian Trust Co. v. Commercial Realty Co., 265 Mich. 604, 251 N.W. 786 (1933) (burden of showing waste not met).

Union Trust Co. v. Charlotte General Electric Co., 152 Mich. 568, 116 N.W. 379 (1908) (burden of showing waste not met).

2901. M.L.P.2d Receivers.

MCLS § 600.2926.

2902. Beecher v. Marquette & Pacific Rolling Mill Co., 40 Mich. 307 (1879).

2903. Equitable Trust Co. v. Simpson, 286 Mich. 460, 282 N.W. 215 (1938) (findings sufficient).

2904. M.L.P.2d Receivers.

MCLS § 600.2926.

2905. Fidelity Trust Co. v. Saginaw Hotels Co., 259 Mich. 254, 242 N.W. 906 (1932).

2906. Fidelity Trust Co. v. Saginaw Hotels Co., 259 Mich. 254, 242 N.W. 906 (1932).

over the property, because the doctrine of notice by lis pendens is sufficient.[2907]

The court may require rents, collected by a trustee under the mortgage during the pendency of foreclosure proceedings and prior to the appointment of a receiver to be turned over to the receiver to be applied to the preservation of the property.[2908]

§ 978.   Rights, Powers, and Duties of Receiver

A receiver has the powers that the court grants him or her and generally must act for the benefit of all interested parties.

Under the general provisions of the Revised Judicature Act of 1961 concerning appointment of receivers, where otherwise authorized, the receiver is charged with all of the "estate, real and personal debts of the debtor as trustee for the benefit" of all interested parties. The powers of the receivership may of course be limited by law or order of the court.[2909] A receiver appointed in foreclosure proceedings is an officer of the court.[2910]

Under the Revised Judicature Act of 1961, the receiver may collect rents and income from the property in receivership for payment of taxes or insurance premiums and exercise other control over the property that the court authorizes.[2911]

The appointment of a receiver for mortgaged property does not generally alter the rule that the mortgagor is entitled to possession and to the rents and profits until the foreclosure sale and the expiration of the equity of redemption.[2912] In the absence of statutory authority, the court has no power to order a receiver appointed by the court to take possession of and collect proceeds arising from the rents, income, and profits of the real estate mortgaged, and to apply the proceeds to the payment of taxes.[2913] A receiver who was improperly appointed in a foreclosure suit brought by a first mortgagee and collecting rents and income rightfully belonging to the trustee of a second mortgage is not entitled to use the funds collected to purchase an outstanding tax title, where the properties are not assessed for taxation to the trustee or to anyone having a beneficial interest in the second mortgage.[2914]

The receiver may pay out of the funds collected from the property the expenses of collecting the rents, managing the property, and otherwise administering the trust.[2915] A receiver who was wrongfully appointed may take credit only for moneys expended for the benefit of the premises.[2916]

In addition, the receiver may be allowed proper compensation for his or her

2907. Gardner v. Grand Beach Co., 48 F.2d 491 (6th Cir. Mich. 1931).

2908. Fidelity Trust Co. v. Saginaw Hotels Co., 259 Mich. 254, 242 N.W. 906 (1932).

2909. M.L.P.2d Receivers.

MCLS § 600.2926.

2910. Fidelity Trust Co. v. Saginaw Hotels Co., 259 Mich. 254, 242 N.W. 906 (1932).

2911. MCLS § 600.2927.

2912. Straus v. Barbee, 262 Mich. 113, 247 N.W. 125 (1933).

2913. Straus v. Barbee, 262 Mich. 113, 247 N.W. 125 (1933).

2914. Bankers' Trust Co. v. Russell, 270 Mich. 568, 259 N.W. 328 (1935).

2915. Lalley v. Tuller Hotel Co., 256 Mich. 105, 239 N.W. 258 (1931).

2916. Detroit Fidelity & Surety Co. v. King, 264 Mich. 91, 249 N.W. 477 (1933).

own services, and the amount of the receiver's compensation is a proper subject for attack by the parties on the hearing of the receiver's final account.[2917] A receiver who was wrongfully appointed for mortgaged premises is not entitled to compensation from the estate of the mortgagor for his or her services.[2918]

§ 979.   Distribution of Proceeds

A receiver in possession must distribute moneys received, as directed by the court.

A receiver in possession of mortgaged premises has the duty of making distribution of moneys received, as directed by the court.[2919]

The charges and expenses of the receivership must be paid, and a decree directing a receiver to pay the "surplus" to the trust mortgagee refers to the amount remaining in the receiver's hands after payment of the administrative expenses.[2920]

The charges and expenses of the receivership may include, in a proper case, a fee for plaintiff's attorney.[2921]

Where the appointment is general in nature, and for the benefit of all parties in interest, the respective rights to money received from rents are controlled by the priority of the parties' liens.[2922]

The proceeds of a receivership belong primarily to the senior mortgagee if the receiver was appointed at his or her instance, or if the senior mortgagee has joined in the foreclosure proceedings, as against junior mortgagees or other creditors. However, the law protects a junior mortgagee who, by superior diligence in suing for foreclosure and obtaining the appointment of a receiver for his or her own benefit alone, has acquired a specific lien on the rents and profits, superior to the equities of the prior mortgagee. The law prefers the junior mortgagee over a first mortgagee as to money coming into the receiver's hands only when the appointment is limited in its benefits to the junior mortgagee.[2923]

E.   TRIAL, DECREE, AND REVIEW

§ 991.   Dismissal or Nonsuit

Plaintiff, ordinarily, may dismiss a foreclosure suit at any time, and defendant, on motion, may obtain a dismissal or nonsuit for an apparent defect.

2917. Lalley v. Tuller Hotel Co., 256 Mich. 105, 239 N.W. 258 (1931).

2918. Detroit Fidelity & Surety Co. v. King, 264 Mich. 91, 249 N.W. 477 (1933).

2919. Detroit Properties Corp. v. Detroit Hotel Co., 258 Mich. 156, 242 N.W. 213 (1932).

2920. Lalley v. Tuller Hotel Co., 256 Mich. 105, 239 N.W. 258 (1931).

2921. Other compensation
An attorney's fee for plaintiff would not be allowed as a claim against the receiver, in a suit for foreclosure of a third mortgage, subsequent to a consent decree that provided compensation for the receiver's attorney, and in which compensation plaintiff's attorney shared.—Vokes & Schaeffer v. Bollin-McKinney Hotel Co., 238 Mich. 1, 212 N.W. 953 (1927).

2922. Krolik v. Bankers' Trust Co., 264 Mich. 376, 249 N.W. 878 (1933).

2923. Krolik v. Bankers' Trust Co., 264 Mich. 376, 249 N.W. 878 (1933).

A foreclosure suit ordinarily may be dismissed by the plaintiff at any time, or a dismissal or nonsuit may be granted, on the motion of defendant, for some defect apparent on the face of the proceedings.[2924]

By statute, a complaint for the foreclosure of a mortgage or a land contract because of default in the payment of interest or an installment of principal, there being other installments to become due subsequently, must be dismissed upon defendant's bringing into court the principal and interest due with costs at any time before the decree of sale.[2925] The mortgagor must pay the money into the court after the tender is made in open court.[2926] Upon meeting those conditions, the mortgagor is entitled to dismissal of the action.[2927] The mortgagee may not refuse the tender of the amount owed.[2928]

A plaintiff in a foreclosure suit who is confident that a defendant has no interest in the property is not prevented from discharging that defendant from the suit.[2929]

§ 992. Trial or Hearing

In a foreclosure suit, both parties are entitled to a hearing on the merits. A third person's title, adverse and paramount to that of both the mortgagor and mortgagee, may not be litigated.

Both the plaintiff[2930] and the defendant[2931] in a foreclosure suit are entitled to a fair and impartial trial or hearing on the merits. The court, as a general rule, may entertain all questions in issue that are necessary to be determined in order that justice may be done and complete relief be granted as between all the parties before it.[2932] In a proper case, the court may, in its discretion, permit the reopening of the

---

2924. Sultan v. Central Life Ins. Co., 302 Mich. 425, 4 N.W.2d 713 (1942) (dismissal refused).

Leach v. Dolese, 186 Mich. 695, 153 N.W. 47 (1915) (dismissal refused).

2925. MCLS § 600.3110.

Kent v. Pipia, 185 Mich. App. 599, 462 N.W.2d 800 (1990).

2926. Manzeta v. Heidloff, 371 Mich. 248, 123 N.W.2d 779 (1963).

2927. Kent v. Pipia, 185 Mich. App. 599, 462 N.W.2d 800 (1990).

2928. Manzeta v. Heidloff, 371 Mich. 248, 123 N.W.2d 779 (1963).

2929. McDonald v. McDonald, 45 Mich. 44, 7 N.W. 230 (1880).

2930. Right to hearing before a judge

Plaintiff, in action to foreclose real estate and chattel mortgages, wherein defendant mortgagor counterclaimed for fraud, breach of contract and wrongful interference with business, was entitled to that which, but for defendants' demand for jury trial, it would have obtained as a matter of course,

namely, an opportunity to argue facts independently before trial judge in an effort to persuade him that, irrespective of jury's general and advisory verdict of no cause of action as to both claim and counterclaim, proof did not preponderate in favor of defendants' affirmative defenses.—Abner A. Wolf, Inc. v. Walch, 385 Mich. 253, 188 N.W.2d 544 (1971).

2931. McDonald v. McDonald, 45 Mich. 44, 7 N.W. 230 (1880).

2932. Ligare v. Semple, 32 Mich. 438 (1875) (question of dower right).

Amount due on mortgage

The determination of the exact amount due on the mortgage, which involves the determination of the precise amount of a payment, is imperatively involved in a foreclosure suit.—Hazen v. Reed, 30 Mich. 331 (1874).

Defendant's title put in issue required hearing

A foreclosure bill containing averments showing the title of the lands to have become regularly vested in defendant by record conveyances puts defendant's title into controversy, and the court

case for further evidence.[2933]

It is not competent, in a foreclosure suit, to litigate the right of a party who sets up a legal title which, if valid, is adverse and paramount to the title of both the mortgagor and the mortgagee.[2934]

§ 993.   New Trial or Rehearing

The general rules of procedure in Michigan courts apply to the parties' requests for a new trial or rehearing in actions for foreclosure of mortgages and land contracts.

The general rules of procedure in Michigan courts apply to the parties' requests for a new trial or rehearing in actions for foreclosure of mortgages and land contracts.[2935]

Subject to the relevant provisions of the Michigan Court Rules of 1985,[2936] a motion for a rehearing or new trial may be granted in a foreclosure suit if the motion is based on sufficient grounds and is presented within due time.[2937] In the absence of fraud, an extension of time within which to move for a rehearing may not be granted.[2938]

Where the applicant has an intimation that the "newly discovered" evidence might have been obtained on the trial, and yet does not compel its production, a rehearing will not be granted in an action to foreclose a mortgage or a land contract.[2939]

§ 994.   Judgment

A foreclosure decree may grant all appropriate relief to which the parties are entitled and that will insure justice between them.

has no power to decide his equities in any way except a hearing of the merits.—McDonald v. McDonald, 45 Mich. 44, 7 N.W. 230 (1880).

Scope of issues

Circuit court, in receivership proceedings by plaintiff, as assignor under assignment of vendees' land contract interest as security for promissory note for improvements, to foreclose security, did not and could not adjudicate rights in property of defendants, who had previously acquired vendees' interest; issue was merely whether there was any interest of defendants' predecessors in interest which could be reached by plaintiff.—Boraks v. Siegel, 366 Mich. 308, 115 N.W.2d 126 (1962).

2933. Continental Nat'l Bank v. Gustin, 297 Mich. 134, 297 N.W. 214 (1941) (refusal to reopen case not abuse of discretion).

2934. Bell v. Pate, 47 Mich. 468, 11 N.W. 275 (1882).

Summers v. Bromley, 28 Mich. 125 (1873).

Partridge v. Hemenway, 89 Mich. 454, 50 N.W. 1084 (1891) (determination of right to lien on removed buildings not objectionable).

Wilkinson v. Green, 34 Mich. 221 (1876) (alleged adverse title declared void).

2935. MCR 3.410.

2936. MCR 2.611.

2937. Central Trust Co. v. Breitenwischer, 259 Mich. 532, 244 N.W. 153 (1932) (application untimely).

Denby v. Ellis, 245 Mich. 124, 222 N.W. 118 (1928) (application untimely).

Union Trust Co. v. Detroit Trust Co., 240 Mich. 646, 216 N.W. 442 (1927) (application untimely).

2938. Denby v. Ellis, 245 Mich. 124, 222 N.W. 118 (1928).

2939. Detroit Sav. Bank v. Truesdail, 38 Mich. 430 (1878).

A foreclosure judgment, within the pleadings and proof, ordinarily may settle and determine all questions and claims raised between the different parties, and grant all the appropriate relief to which the parties are entitled and that will insure justice between them.[2940] The character of the judgment to be rendered in an action to foreclose a land contract must be determined by the facts and circumstances involved, and with regard to equitable principles and the rights of the parties in the particular case,[2941] and this principle governs with respect to the amount of the judgment or decree.[2942]

In a proper case, a decree foreclosing a mortgage may be entered *nunc pro tunc.*[2943]

In an action to foreclose a mortgage, an interlocutory decree may be made directing the cause to stand continued until the coming in of a report. A decree expressly reserving and retaining jurisdiction for entertaining a petition for the entry of a foreclosure decree and sale after an accounting is had cannot be attacked as a refusal to decree foreclosure.[2944]

The decree in foreclosure of a land contract must dispose of all matters involved in the case.[2945] As long as the decree in a foreclosure suit contains all of the essential elements of the relief asked for, the form in which it is made is generally immaterial.[2946]

Unsubstantial errors in a decree of foreclosure do not invalidate the proceedings with respect to a sale under the judgment.[2947]

2940. Timber rights

Where it appeared that timber rights claimed by one of defendants originated in a quitclaim deed executed by mortgagors subsequent to executing two mortgages on realty, timber rights of such defendant were properly included in decree foreclosing mortgages.—Continental Nat'l Bank v. Gustin, 297 Mich. 134, 297 N.W. 214 (1941).

2941. Gordon Grossman Bldg. Co. v. Elliott, 11 Mich. App. 620, 162 N.W.2d 107 (1968), rev'd on other grounds, 382 Mich. 596, 171 N.W.2d 441 (1969) (foreclosure).

Pungs v. Hilgendorf, 289 Mich. 46, 286 N.W. 152 (1939).

Amster v. Stratton, 259 Mich. 683, 244 N.W. 201 (1932).

Chanler v. Venetian Properties Corp., 254 Mich. 468, 236 N.W. 838 (1931).

Affirmative relief against subpurchaser denied

Boening v. Schaefer, 284 Mich. 621, 279 N.W. 917 (1938).

Second decree

Second decree after confirmation of commissioner's report, in suit to foreclose a land contract, was not necessary, where first decree fixed personal liability.—Grimore v. Beauch, 247 Mich. 439, 225 N.W. 930 (1929).

2942. Brown v. Mudge, 242 Mich. 324, 218 N.W. 687 (1928) (decreeing entire purchase price due on purchaser's default was held erroneous as to installments not yet due, where contract failed to so provide).

2943. Powell v. Pierce, 168 Mich. 427, 134 N.W. 447 (1912).

2944. Gardner v. Grand Beach Co., 29 F.2d 481 (6th Cir. Mich. 1928).

2945. Pungs v. Hilgendorf, 289 Mich. 46, 286 N.W. 152 (1939) (duty to adjudge claimed defects in title).

Amster v. Stratton, 259 Mich. 683, 244 N.W. 201 (1932).

No provision for sale

A land contract foreclosure that failed to provide for sale of premises was valid but would be modified on appeal to allow purchasers time within which to redeem after sale conducted as provided by statutory provisions for mortgage foreclosures.—Young v. Zavitz, 365 Mich. 354, 112 N.W.2d 493 (1961).

2946. Union Trust Co. v. Electric Park Amusement Co., 168 Mich. 574, 135 N.W. 115 (1912).

2947. Union Trust Co. v. Electric Park Amusement Co., 168 Mich. 574, 135 N.W. 115 (1912).

Subject to the relevant provisions of the Michigan Court Rules of 1985,[2948] a decree foreclosing a mortgage may be entered on default of the defendant.[2949] A default decree is not rendered erroneous because it recites that defendant was personally served with notice, when in fact he or she was brought in by publication as a nonresident. The misrecital may be treated as surplusage, as no recital of the kind is essential.[2950]

§ 995.   —Ascertainment of Indebtedness

A foreclosure decree must find and adjudge the amount of indebtedness for which the mortgaged property is answerable. That amount may include certain disbursements by the mortgagee to the benefit of the property and certain credits to the mortgagor.

Under the Revised Judicature Act of 1961, the court must in the original judgment in foreclosing a mortgage or a land contract determine which defendants, if any, are personally liable for the mortgage debt. The court must provide in the judgment that upon the confirmation of the report of sale, if there is any part of the money decreed to be due left unpaid after applying the amount received on the sale, the clerk of the court must, on application of the plaintiff and without notice to the defendant or the defendant's attorney, issue execution for the amount of the deficiency.[2951]

Thus, the foreclosure decree ordinarily must find and adjudge the exact amount of indebtedness due to the plaintiff, for which the mortgaged property is answerable. To this end the court must hear evidence upon which to base its finding.[2952] The decree of foreclosure must be for the true amount of the debt secured,[2953] even though it is less than the amount specified in an accompanying bond,[2954] or the mortgage is mistakenly drawn for a larger amount.[2955] A foreclosure decree may grant the amount of a proposed compromise, which never amounted to more than an offer on either side, so long as the court considers the amount a sufficient approximation of the debt to fairly represent it at the time the compromise was proposed.[2956]

A foreclosure decree is given for everything due when it is granted, including installments that have become due since the commencement of the suit, even though

Ireland v. Woolman, 15 Mich. 253 (1867) (erroneous but unnecessary recital treated as surplusage).

2948. MCR 2.603.

2949. Ireland v. Woolman, 15 Mich. 253 (1867).

2950. Ireland v. Woolman, 15 Mich. 253 (1867).

2951. MCLS § 600.3150.

Stewart v. Isbell, 155 Mich. App. 65, 399 N.W.2d 440 (1986).

2952. MCLS § 600.3150.

Tucker v. Tucker, 24 Mich. 426 (1872) (fixing amount without evidence error).

2953. Laylin v. Knox, 41 Mich. 40, 1 N.W. 913 (1879).

Scriven v. Hursh, 39 Mich. 98 (1878).

2954. Scriven v. Hursh, 39 Mich. 98 (1878).

2955. Laylin v. Knox, 41 Mich. 40, 1 N.W. 913 (1879).

2956. Lyon v. McDonald, 51 Mich. 435, 16 N.W. 800 (1883).

the suit may have been filed when fewer installments of the debt had matured.[2957]

The judgment must allocate costs that the mortgagor must pay on the foreclosed mortgage or land contract.[2958] Successful plaintiffs in mortgage or land-contract foreclosure actions are entitled to reasonable attorney's fees if the mortgage or land contract provides for them.[2959] Written provisions of the mortgage of a stipulated amount are not controlling.[2960]

The determination of personal liability in a foreclosure decree is contingent or provisional and, until a deficiency arises and the mortgagors are required to answer for it, the mortgagors are not bound to pay it even if responsible.[2961]

Interest. The foreclosure decree must include interest on the amount of the mortgage indebtedness.[2962] In the foreclosure of a mortgage given to secure the purchase money of public land, the title to which was not in the vendor at the time of the sale, interest is allowed only from the time the title vests in the grantee.[2963]

Disbursements by mortgagee. The court is authorized by statute to provide, in any foreclosure decree, for adding to the amount therein determined to be due any sum paid, at any time thereafter and prior to the expiration of the period of redemption, as taxes assessed against the property or the premium upon any insurance policy covering buildings located on the property as is required to keep the policy in force until the expiration of the period of redemption, provided that under the terms of the mortgage it would have been the duty of the defendants, determined to be personally liable, to have paid such taxes or insurance premium, had the mortgage not been foreclosed.[2964]

2957. Johnson v. Van Velsor, 43 Mich. 208, 5 N.W. 265 (1880).

Howe v. Lemon, 37 Mich. 164 (1877).

Vaughn v. Nims, 36 Mich. 297 (1877).

Mortgage securing two notes

Where a mortgage securing two notes is foreclosed before one of them has fallen due, its amount may nevertheless be included in the decree if it falls due before the decree is rendered.—Hanford v. Robertson, 47 Mich. 100, 10 N.W. 125 (1881).

2958. MCLS § 600.3110.

Foreclosure after fire

Plaintiff mortgagees would be held not to be required to pay foreclosure costs and attorney fees in addition to amount outstanding on mortgage at time of total fire loss on mortgaged premises where mortgagee after fire foreclosed mortgage and purchased property at foreclosure for amount of debt owing thereon, following which it claimed right to proceeds of fire policy covering premises.—Smith v. General Mortg. Corp., 402 Mich. 125, 261 N.W.2d 710 (1978).

2959. Farwell v. Bigelow, 112 Mich. 285, 70 N.W. 579 (1897).

United Growth Corp. v. Kelly Mortg. & Inv. Co., 86 Mich. App. 82, 272 N.W.2d 340 (1978).

Butzel v. Webster Apartments Co., 112 F.2d 362 (6th Cir. Mich. 1940) (trustees' attorney).

2960. United Growth Corp. v. Kelly Mortg. & Inv. Co., 86 Mich. App. 82, 272 N.W.2d 340 (1978).

Butzel v. Webster Apartments Co., 112 F.2d 362 (6th Cir. Mich. 1940) (reasonableness is measured by value of services rendered).

2961. Powers v. Golden Lumber Co., 43 Mich. 468, 5 N.W. 656 (1880).

Stewart v. Isbell, 155 Mich. App. 65, 399 N.W.2d 440 (1986).

2962. MCLS § 600.3110.

Toms v. Boyes, 59 Mich. 386, 26 N.W. 646 (1886).

Fifth Nat'l Bank v. Pierce, 117 Mich. 376, 75 N.W. 1058 (1898) (clerical error respecting rate).

Stewart v. Isbell, 155 Mich. App. 65, 399 N.W.2d 440 (1986) (interest rate from contract, not from statute allowing interest on judgment).

2963. Toms v. Boyes, 59 Mich. 386, 26 N.W. 646 (1886).

2964. MCLS § 600.3145.

Accordingly, payments of taxes[2965] or insurance premiums[2966] covering the mortgaged property and properly made by the mortgagee generally may be allowed as a part of the indebtedness decreed.[2967] If the mortgage provides for the payment of taxes, the taxes paid after the filing of the bill and before the decree of foreclosure are properly included in the decree.[2968]

When a mortgage provides that the mortgagee be reimbursed the cost of repairs, as well as his or her disbursements for taxes and insurance, that amount is properly included in the decree of foreclosure.[2969]

On the other hand, a mortgagee who bids in the land at tax sale on default by the mortgagor in the payment of taxes cannot on subsequent foreclosure have the sums so paid included in the decree, because payments in bidding in the property at tax sale are not the payment of taxes.[2970]

Credits to defendant. The foreclosure decree must give credit to the mortgagor or other defendant for partial payments made, for anything transferred and accepted in part satisfaction of the mortgage, or for any legitimate offset or claim against the mortgagee.[2971] The mortgagor, however, is not entitled to a deduction or credit from a transaction by which the mortgagor did not suffer a loss or the mortgagee gain a

---

2965. Commercial Nat'l Bank v. Gaukler, 165 Mich. 403, 130 N.W. 655 (1911).

Walsh v. Robinson, 135 Mich. 16, 97 N.W. 55 (1903) (taxes paid by junior encumbrancer).

Vaughn v. Nims, 36 Mich. 297 (1877).

2966. City Lumber Co. v. Hollands, 181 Mich. 531, 148 N.W. 361 (1914).

Walton v. Bagley, 47 Mich. 385, 11 N.W. 209 (1882).

2967. Prybeski v. Piechoviak, 170 Mich. 572, 136 N.W. 371 (1912).

Jehle v. Brooks, 112 Mich. 131, 70 N.W. 440 (1897).

2968. Commercial Nat'l Bank v. Gaukler, 165 Mich. 403, 130 N.W. 655 (1911).

Jehle v. Brooks, 112 Mich. 131, 70 N.W. 440 (1897) (taxes and insurance).

2969. Prybeski v. Piechoviak, 170 Mich. 572, 136 N.W. 371 (1912).

2970. Maxfield v. Willey, 46 Mich. 252, 9 N.W. 271 (1881).

2971. Additional collateral to mortgage

Claim of defendant, in suit to foreclose mortgages, that certain collateral pledged as security for other notes was sold at less than fair market value, and that she was entitled to credit therefor on indebtedness in instant case, was allowed where before final disposition of controversy in trial court, collateral in dispute was turned over to nominees of defendant at price plaintiff paid for it with interest at five percent and plaintiff released

all claim to it.—Payne v. Cavanaugh, 292 Mich. 305, 290 N.W. 807 (1940).

Value of released portion of property

On determining that trial court's finding of value was clearly erroneous on de novo review of equitable action to restrain defendant from foreclosing mortgage until value of portion of mortgaged premises released by defendant was duly ascertained and credited against mortgage, Court of Appeals would adopt value disclosed by proofs on record and order that valuation amount be credited against mortgage principal and interest for appropriate time period, with foreclosure on remaining amount of interest and principal.—Dusseau v. Roscommon State Bank, 80 Mich. App. 531, 264 N.W.2d 350 (1978).

Value of timber cut, and of use of land

The value of timber cut from the mortgaged land and sold by the mortgagee, and of the use and occupation of the land by him, should be deducted from the amount due on the notes.—Abele v. McGuigan, 78 Mich. 415, 44 N.W. 393 (1889).

Wife's services

In former husband's suit to foreclose mortgage given by wife incident to prior divorce decree under which she obtained parties' home, wherein wife sought compensation for board, room and services furnished husband after divorce, evidence warranted decree involving finding that mortgage indebtedness had been paid by virtue of wife's services, but that wife did not establish right to amount over and above amount of note plus interest.—Werner v. Werner, 357 Mich. 671, 99 N.W.2d 359 (1959).

profit.[2972]

§ 996.   —Provision For Sale of Mortgaged Premises

A foreclosure judgment that orders a sale must designate the property or interest to be sold. The court may also set a minimum bid at which each parcel must be sold.

Under the Revised Judicature Act of 1961, whenever a complaint is filed for the foreclosure or satisfaction of a mortgage or a land contract, the court has power to decree a sale of the mortgaged premises, or a part of it that is sufficient to discharge the amount due on the mortgage and the costs of suit. The court may not, by such decree, order any mortgaged lands to be sold within 6 months or any lands sold under an executory land contract within 3 months after the filing of a complaint of foreclosure.[2973] If the complaint is amended, the judgment must not authorize the sale before the expiration of the prescribed period following the filing of the amended bill.[2974]

A judgment that directs a sale of undivided interests in land mortgaged as a whole is erroneous.[2975]

Where the mortgage covers both real and personal property, the court may decree the sale of the personal property separate from that of the realty.[2976]

The decree of foreclosure may not order the sale on less than 42 days' notice.[2977]

The foreclosure decree must direct the manner in which the proceeds of the sale of the mortgaged property are to be applied.[2978] In a suit to foreclose a mortgage given to secure a large number of creditors, some of whom do not appear, though all are notified by service or publication, a decree ordering the proceeds of the sale to be held in court until proof of the interests of the other parties is taken is improper.[2979]

Minimum bid or "upset price." Under common law[2980] and statute,[2981] the court may set a minimum bid or "upset price" at which the foreclosed property must

2972. Bean v. Granger, 275 Mich. 603, 267 N.W. 746 (1936).

2973. MCLS § 600.3115.

No provision for sale

A land contract foreclosure that failed to provide for sale of premises was valid but would be modified by Supreme Court to allow purchasers 90 days within which to redeem after sale conducted as provided by statutory provisions for mortgage foreclosures.—Young v. Zavitz, 365 Mich. 354, 112 N.W.2d 493 (1961).

2974. Gray v. Federal Bank of Canada, 83 Mich. 365, 47 N.W. 221 (1890).

2975. Spear v. Hadden, 31 Mich. 265 (1875).

2976. Anderson v. Smith, 108 Mich. 69, 65 N.W. 615 (1895).

2977. MCR 3.410.

2978. Van Aken v. Gleason, 34 Mich. 477 (1876) (two mortgages; ratable application of proceeds).

2979. Shelden v. Erskine, 78 Mich. 627, 44 N.W. 146 (1889).

2980. Michigan Trust Co. v. Dutmers, 265 Mich. 651, 252 N.W. 478 (1934).

2981. MCLS § 600.3155.

Manufacturers Nat'l Bank v. Pink, 128 Mich. App. 696, 341 N.W.2d 181 (1983).

Not unconstitutional impairment of contract

Statute under which trial court in a land contract foreclosure suit properly fixed upset price for foreclosure sale, in advance of sale, as applied in

be sold. The court has discretion whether to do so.[2982]

The minimum bid must be based on the actual value of the premises, not on the remaining indebtedness.[2983] The determination of the actual value of the property may consist of a forced-sale valuation given that the authorizing statute manifests no legislative intent to view the sale as an arm's length, private transaction or preclude consideration of the compulsion attending mortgage foreclosure sales.[2984] Rather than set a minimum bid in the absence of proof of actual value, the court should order the sale and grant an execution for any deficiency.[2985]

Generally, the minimum price must be set at the time of judgment of foreclosure.[2986] Indeed, a court may fix an upset price for the foreclosure sale on a land contract, proceed to fix the deficiency before the sale takes place, and specify in its judgment that if no bid equal to the upset price is made, title to the property then vests in the vendors as if they had made the minimum bid.[2987] But fixing the minimum or upset price at the time of confirmation of the sale, at defendant's request, is not subject to complaint by the defendant, although the applicable statute contemplates that the minimum price must be fixed prior to the sale.[2988]

§ 997.   —Sale of Part or in Parcels

The judgment must specify which parcels or portion of a parcel of the entire mortgaged real estate must be sold to satisfy the mortgage or land-contract debt if it is less than the whole, and if more than one parcel is involved, the order in which they are to be sold to satisfy the debt.

The judgment in foreclosure by suit of a mortgage or a land contract must

instant case, was not unconstitutional, as impairment of obligation of contract, which statute antedated.—Kramer v. Davis, 371 Mich. 464, 124 N.W.2d 292 (1963).

2982. Mutual Benefit Life Ins. Co. v. Wetsman, 277 Mich. 322, 269 N.W. 189 (1936).

James S. Holden Co. v. Applebaum, 267 Mich. 632, 255 N.W. 601 (1934).

Michigan Trust Co. v. Dutmers, 265 Mich. 651, 252 N.W. 478 (1934).

Manufacturers Nat'l Bank v. Pink, 128 Mich. App. 696, 341 N.W.2d 181 (1983).

2983. Michigan Trust Co. v. Dutmers, 265 Mich. 651, 252 N.W. 478 (1934).

2984. United Growth Corp. v. Kelly Mortg. & Inv. Co., 86 Mich. App. 82, 272 N.W.2d 340 (1978).

2985. Fuoss v. Soellner, 267 Mich. 186, 255 N.W. 189 (1934).

Sufficient evidence to set upset price

Evidence, in a land contract foreclosure suit, warranted finding fixing $5,000 as upset price for foreclosure sale, as against rejected contention that there was no evidence as to fair value of property

upon which to make such determination.—Kramer v. Davis, 371 Mich. 464, 124 N.W.2d 292 (1963).

2986. Kramer v. Davis, 371 Mich. 464, 124 N.W.2d 292 (1963).

No change for increase in value between judgment and second sale

In mortgage foreclosure proceedings wherein trial court entered foreclosure judgment and set foreclosure sale upset price, following which first sale was set aside for deficiency in notice and second sale held and confirmed by court, defendant's subsequent motion to increase upset price on ground that value of property had increased between setting of price and second sale was properly denied by court where authorizing statute conferred no authority to set upset price other than prior to sale, and where defendant's allegation of increased volume was neither supported on record nor by affidavit as required by general court rule.—United Growth Corp. v. Kelly Mortg. & Inv. Co., 86 Mich. App. 82, 272 N.W.2d 340 (1978).

2987. Kramer v. Davis, 371 Mich. 464, 124 N.W.2d 292 (1963).

2988. Schmeltz v. Rowen, 287 Mich. 657, 284 N.W. 597 (1938).

designate the property or interest to be sold.[2989] The judgment must specify which parcels or portion of a parcel of the entire mortgaged real estate must be sold to satisfy the mortgage or land-contract debt if it is less than the whole.[2990] So long as it does not injure the interests of the parties, the judgment must not order the sale of the entire mortgaged property, but only so much as may be necessary to satisfy the mortgage debt.[2991] This rule is mandatory in nature, so as to protect the mortgagor's or land-contract vendee's right of redemption.[2992] The judgment remains as security for any subsequent default, for which the court may order the sale of another part of the real property.[2993]

On the other hand, if the sale of the whole property would be most beneficial to the parties, the judgment may provide for the sale of the whole premises in the first foreclosure action.[2994] A foreclosure decree permitting a sale of the mortgaged premises as an entirety will not be disturbed in the absence of a showing that the property ought to have been sold in parcels.[2995] The parties to a mortgage or a land contract may contract for the sale of the premises whole in the event of foreclosure.[2996]

In a case in which circumstances do not clearly dictate the choice, the court has a measure of discretion.[2997]

Where the foreclosure decree orders the sale of the mortgaged premises by

---

2989. Damm v. Damm, 91 Mich. 424, 51 N.W. 1069 (1892).

2990. MCLS § 600.3165.

2991. MCLS § 600.3165.

Damm v. Damm, 91 Mich. 424, 51 N.W. 1069 (1892) (decreeing sale of entire mortgaged interest error).

Satisfaction from one parcel

Where one of several mortgaged properties, if sold upon foreclosure, would yield funds sufficient to satisfy the principal debt, requiring foreclosure upon all of the properties would needlessly involve the additional properties in litigation.—Michigan Nat'l Bank v. Martin, 19 Mich. App. 458, 172 N.W.2d 920 (1969).

Waiver of right to sale by parcels

Property in a foreclosure sale is required to be sold in parcels in order to protect right of redemption, but where party waives his right to redeem in advance and for valuable consideration, he cannot object to fact that sale was not made in parcels.—Metropolitan Life Ins. Co. v. Foote, 95 Mich. App. 399, 290 N.W.2d 158 (1980).

2992. Metropolitan Life Ins. Co. v. Foote, 95 Mich. App. 399, 290 N.W.2d 158 (1980).

2993. MCLS § 600.3165.

2994. MCLS § 600.3165.

2995. Vaughn v. Nims, 36 Mich. 297 (1877).

2996. Metropolitan Life Ins. Co. v. Foote, 95 Mich. App. 399, 290 N.W.2d 158 (1980).

2997. Macomb v. Prentis, 57 Mich. 225, 23 N.W. 788 (1885).

Several parcels, one mortgage

Where a mortgagor sold one of several tracts subject to a described mortgage that vendee agreed to assume, and the vendee conveyed to another by deed reciting the payment of interest and containing a similar covenant, that subsequent purchaser had no right to rely on the description of the mortgage or representation or covenant made by the mortgagor in the latter's deed, the covenant being one that did not run with the land, and hence was not entitled to have the other tracts of land sold first to pay the mortgage debt, though the mortgagor's deed misrepresented the terms of the mortgage.—Pease v. Warner, 153 Mich. 140, 116 N.W. 994 (1908).

Three parcels, three mortgages

If a first mortgage covering three parcels of land was foreclosed, and on the first and second parcels a second mortgage had been given, and on the second and third a third mortgage had been given, the second mortgage having been earlier foreclosed and both the first and second parcels sold subject to the first mortgage, and the second parcel, at the instance of the third mortgagee, sold last on such prior foreclosure, the third mortgagee has no right to demand that the parcel not covered by his mortgage should be sold first, and the purchaser under prior foreclosure had a right to insist that the third parcel should be first sold.—Sibley v. Baker, 23 Mich. 312 (1871).

parcels, it should give specific directions as to the order in which the parcels are to be sold, decreeing a sale in the inverse order of the alienation of the parcels, where such order will best serve the interests of all the parties.[2998] On a bill to foreclose a land contract against lots not released because of a default in payment under the contract, the rule requiring sale in the inverse order of alienation is inapplicable.[2999]

Several parcels may be sold as a unit if the mortgage covers part of certain lots that constitute one contiguous parcel,[3000] or if, by reason of the nature of the use of the property, it constitutes a unit.[3001] As to what constitutes separate parcels, the mere fact that land is divided by a highway or section lines is not controlling, at least where the premises as a whole are used as a unit.[3002] Nor does the fact that the mortgaged premises are described in the mortgage and decree as three parcels constitute a controlling factor if the property, by reason of use, constitutes a parcel.[3003] Nonetheless, the manner of description is a factor to be considered.[3004]

Conversely, of course, if land covered by a mortgage is divided into two separate farms, the land should be sold in two separate parcels.[3005] If separate parcels are not used as a unit, the mere fact that they are enclosed by one fence is not controlling.[3006]

A claim of right or choice to have certain property sold first must be timely asserted in the foreclosure suit.[3007]

§ 998.   —Provision for Relief to Defendants

The foreclosure decree must provide for any relief to which the mortgagor or other defendant is entitled.

The decree of foreclosure may give directions respecting any relief to which the mortgagor or other defendant may be entitled.[3008]

If the notes secured by a mortgage are missing, and a foreclosure decree is allowed on the theory that they are still in existence, the plaintiff is required to

2998. Ireland v. Woolman, 15 Mich. 253 (1867).

2999. McClure v. Edward J. Meyer Southfield Woods Corp., 254 Mich. 686, 236 N.W. 907 (1931).

3000. Stolte v. Krentel, 271 Mich. 98, 260 N.W. 127 (1935).

3001. Detroit Trust Co. v. Detroit City Service Co., 262 Mich. 14, 247 N.W. 76 (1933).

Cox v. Townsend, 90 Mich. App. 12, 282 N.W.2d 223 (1979).

House on two lots

Where a house stands on two lots and a portion of one lot has been otherwise used with the other, it seems clear that both lots should be sold as a unit, at least in the absence of a request for division.—Butters v. Butters, 153 Mich. 153, 117 N.W. 203 (1908).

3002. Larzelere v. Starkweather, 38 Mich. 96 (1878) (farm).

3003. Security Trust Co. v. Sloman, 252 Mich. 266, 233 N.W. 216 (1930).

3004. McIntyre v. Wyckoff, 119 Mich. 557, 78 N.W. 654 (1899).

3005. McIntyre v. Wyckoff, 119 Mich. 557, 78 N.W. 654 (1899).

3006. O'Connor v. Keenan, 132 Mich. 646, 94 N.W. 186 (1903).

3007. Butters v. Butters, 153 Mich. 153, 117 N.W. 203 (1908).

3008. Continental Nat'l Bank v. Gustin, 297 Mich. 134, 297 N.W. 214 (1941).

City Lumber Co. v. Hollands, 181 Mich. 531, 148 N.W. 361 (1914) (defendant's rights sufficiently protected).

Terry v. Terry, 170 Mich. 330, 136 N.W. 448 (1912) (mortgagor's claim recognized).

indemnify defendant against their enforcement, in case they reappear in the hands of strangers.[3009]

The Revised Judicature Act of 1961 provides for a right of redemption after foreclosure sale under a mortgage or a land contract.[3010] The judgment must give effect to that provision by an appropriate direction.[3011]

A defendant is entitled to equitable relief on his or her counterclaims.[3012]

A junior lienor has an interest that entitles the junior lienor to insist that plaintiff's recovery be kept down to that to which the plaintiff is strictly entitled, and that there be a marshaling of securities sufficient to leave for the junior lienor the best possible residuum.[3013]

Where a junior mortgage is set aside as unenforceable, the junior mortgagee is entitled to credit for payments that he or she made on the first mortgage after the mortgagor's default, and for sums expended for taxes, repairs, insurance, and other lawful charges, less the amount of payments made on the second mortgage, and rents received from the property.[3014] Even though the second mortgagee may be entitled to a lien on the property, subject to the first mortgage, for the balance due for payments made on the first mortgage and the sums expended for lawful charges, the second mortgagee may be required to repay to the mortgagor the amounts that the second mortgagee receives on the second mortgage in excess of the credit and sums expended.[3015]

§ 999.   —Modification or Vacation

The court may modify or vacate its foreclosure judgment.

Under proper circumstances, the court may amend or modify its decree

3009. Walker v. Gillett, 98 Mich. 59, 56 N.W. 1052 (1893).

Yerkes v. Blodgett, 48 Mich. 211, 12 N.W. 218 (1882).

3010. Redemption, *see, infra*, Chapter 33.

MCLS § 600.3140.

3011. Teal v. Hayes, 309 Mich. 221, 15 N.W.2d 139 (1944).

3012. Wrongful foreclosure

Where mortgagor sought injunctive relief and money damages in action against mortgagee that allegedly required excessive escrow deposits and that commenced foreclosure proceedings, dissolution of temporary restraining order after summary hearing did not end mortgagor's action and mortgagor was entitled to full trial hearing on her claim of wrongful foreclosure in consequence of which she was entitled to money damages.—Cramer v. Metropolitan Federal Sav. & Loan Ass'n, 34 Mich. App. 638, 192 N.W.2d 50 (1971).

3013. Slater v. Breese, 36 Mich. 77 (1877) (third mortgagee not entitled to complain).

Lien claimant

Where trial court's order in mortgage foreclosure action providing for sale of subject property by receiver and transfer of all lien rights to sale proceeds terminated rights of all litigants to proceed further against property, including corporate mechanic's lien claimant which was joined as defendant in action after filing its mechanic's lien enforcement less than year earlier, summary judgment could not be entered against defendant lien claimant in favor of plaintiff mortgagee on ground that limitations period on enforcement of lien had expired, since defendant's enforcement of lien prior to expiration would have violated court's order, and as of date of order lien rights were transferred in accord with order to proceeds of sale and were to be determined by court according to attachment and priority provisions of statute, with further pleadings to be controlled by statute and court rule relating to civil actions generally.— American Sav. Ass'n v. I.C.I. Development Corp., 400 Mich. 74, 252 N.W.2d 806 (1977).

3014. Meek v. Wilson, 283 Mich. 679, 278 N.W. 731 (1938).

3015. Meek v. Wilson, 283 Mich. 679, 278 N.W. 731 (1938).

foreclosing a mortgage.[3016] An error in the computation of interest on a mortgage may be corrected after a decree of foreclosure, in the discretion of the trial court.[3017]

A foreclosure must not be set aside without some very good reasons for doing so.[3018] The burden of proving good cause to set aside the judgment is on the party who seeks to have the decree set aside.[3019]

Generally, a mere error or irregularity in the foreclosure decree, not going to the court's jurisdiction of the cause, does not warrant vacation.[3020]

A default judgment of foreclosure may be opened on proper grounds, such as mistake, accident, surprise, or fraud.[3021] A defendant seeking relief from a default judgment on the basis of fraud who alleges no substantial defect or irregularity in the proceedings, a reasonable excuse for not appearing, manifest injustice resulting from the enforcement of the judgment, or meritorious defense will not receive relief from the judgment.[3022]

If a decree of foreclosure is opened to let in a defense on the petition of a defendant, after a sale is made under the decree, no one will be bound by the proceedings on that petition but the parties to it and those who have subsequently acquired interests under them. Anyone who, before the decree is opened, becomes a purchaser under the plaintiff, is not affected by those proceedings unless that person is made a party to them and allowed an opportunity to be heard.[3023]

§ 1000.   —Conclusiveness

A foreclosure decree is conclusive as to all matters in issue or necessarily involved in the adjudication, and on all persons who were properly made parties to the suit.

3016. Montague v. Haviland, 101 Mich. 80, 59 N.W. 404 (1894).

Lachman v. Ottawa Circuit Judge, 125 Mich. 27, 83 N.W. 1025 (1900) (amendment denied).

3017. Montague v. Haviland, 101 Mich. 80, 59 N.W. 404 (1894).

3018. Madill v. Michigan Nat'l Bank, 302 Mich. 251, 4 N.W.2d 538 (1942).

Markoff v. Tournier, 229 Mich. 571, 201 N.W. 888 (1925).

Opening or modifying decree unnecessary

Michigan Trust Co. v. Grand Rapids Democrat, 113 Mich. 615, 71 N.W. 1102 (1897).

3019. Markoff v. Tournier, 229 Mich. 571, 201 N.W. 888 (1925).

3020. Union Trust Co. v. Detroit Trust Co., 240 Mich. 646, 216 N.W. 442 (1927).

3021. Montague v. Haviland, 101 Mich. 80, 59 N.W. 404 (1894) (claim inconsistent with facts).

Stone v. Welling, 14 Mich. 514 (1866) (order allowing defense).

3022. Sylvania Sav. Bank Co. v. Turner, 27 Mich. App. 640, 183 N.W.2d 894 (1970) (denial of motion was not abuse of discretion).

Denial after unexplained delay

Trial court did not abuse its discretion in refusing to set aside default decree of mortgage foreclosure upon defendants' motion alleging that bill of complaint was never filed at outset of foreclosure proceedings, where record indicated that defendants were served with copies of original bill of complaint which was thereafter mislaid by court clerk, and where defendants' motion contained no offer to do equity but was filed after unexplained 18-month delay following mortgagee's change in position by payment of prior first mortgage on premises.—Presque Isle Bank v. Kowalski, 6 Mich. App. 266, 148 N.W.2d 880 (1967).

Rehearing on motion after granted new hearing without good cause and showing of defense

Testimonial hearing conducted by trial court on remand from appellate court for purpose of determining factual and legal basis for trial court's setting aside default judgment in action involving foreclosure of security agreement would be held to have no direct bearing on invalidity of original order which record disclosed was product of abuse of discretion as granted without requisite showing of good cause and existence of meritorious defense.—Badalow v. Evenson, 62 Mich. App. 750, 233 N.W.2d 708 (1975).

3023. Stone v. Welling, 14 Mich. 514 (1866).

The judgment in a foreclosure suit is conclusive on all persons who were properly made parties to the suit.[3024] A judgment foreclosing a mortgage is res judicata with respect to an action by the owners of the realty, who were parties to the foreclosure suit, to declare the mortgage void.[3025]

The judgment in an action to foreclose a mortgage[3026] or a land contract[3027] is a final adjudication of the rights of the parties, imports verity, and is conclusive, so long as it is in full force and effect and not modified, vacated, or set aside. It cannot be attacked collaterally for mere irregularities that do not go to the jurisdiction.[3028] It is res judicata as to all matters in issue or necessarily involved in the adjudication,[3029] including the validity of the mortgage,[3030] the existence and amount of the mortgage debt, and the fact that it remains unpaid.[3031]

The judgment of the court, in a suit to foreclose a mortgage, is not res judicata as to any matter that the defendant is not entitled, as a matter of right, to have litigated in the suit.[3032] Nor is the decree conclusive as to matters not in issue or not necessarily involved in the adjudication.[3033]

3024. City Rescue Mission v. First State Bank, 280 Mich. 264, 273 N.W. 563 (1937).

Walsh v. Robinson, 135 Mich. 16, 97 N.W. 55 (1903) (trustee bound individually).

Kelly v. Bowerman, 113 Mich. 446, 71 N.W. 836 (1897) (mortgagor's administrator bound).

Lien claimant not precluded from relief

Where trial court's order in mortgage foreclosure action providing for sale of subject property by receiver and transfer of all lien rights to sale proceeds terminated rights of all litigants to proceed further against property, including corporate mechanic's lien claimant which was joined as defendant in action after filing its mechanic's lien enforcement less than year earlier, summary judgment could not be entered against defendant lien claimant in favor of plaintiff mortgagee on ground that limitations period on enforcement of lien had expired, since defendant's enforcement of lien prior to expiration would have violated court's order, and as of date of order lien rights were transferred in accord with order to proceeds of sale and were to be determined by court according to attachment and priority provisions of statute, with further pleadings to be controlled by statute and court rule relating to civil actions generally.—American Sav. Ass'n v. I.C.I. Development Corp., 400 Mich. 74, 252 N.W.2d 806 (1977).

3025. City Rescue Mission v. First State Bank, 280 Mich. 264, 273 N.W. 563 (1937).

3026. Smith v. Heppner, 276 Mich. 463, 267 N.W. 882 (1936).

3027. Smith v. Heppner, 276 Mich. 463, 267 N.W. 882 (1936).

Modification on appeal

Where, though decree in mortgage foreclosure suit between former spouses did not provide affir-

matively that mortgage indebtedness had been paid in full and that mortgage should be cancelled and discharged, case had been heard in trial court primarily on that issue, decree would be modified in the Supreme Court accordingly.—Werner v. Werner, 357 Mich. 671, 99 N.W.2d 359 (1959).

Setting aside sale conducted in violation of order of remand

Circuit court was authorized to set aside sale and deed after affirmance of decree foreclosing a land contract, because sale was "further proceeding" necessary to carry Supreme Court's decree into effect within statute authorizing such proceedings to be taken; and where decree foreclosing a land contract gave purchasers' assignee 60 days from filing of decree to redeem and proceedings were commenced immediately after filing in lower court of Supreme Court's decree of affirmance on vendors' appeal, sale was properly vacated as premature.—Garwood v. Burton, 274 Mich. 219, 264 N.W. 349 (1936).

3028. Torrans v. Hicks, 32 Mich. 307 (1875).

3029. Smith v. Heppner, 276 Mich. 463, 267 N.W. 882 (1936).

3030. Horbal v. St. John's Greek Catholic Church, 260 Mich. 331, 244 N.W. 493 (1932).

3031. Smith v. Heppner, 276 Mich. 463, 267 N.W. 882 (1936).

Hazen v. Reed, 30 Mich. 331 (1874).

3032. Oliver v. Cunningham, 7 F. 689 (C.C.D. Mich. 1881).

3033. Carrier v. Caplan, 247 Mich. 38, 225 N.W. 581 (1929).

§ 1001.   —Assignment

A foreclosure judgment may be assigned. The assignee must present a petition setting forth the assignment, and ask for a sale under the judgment.

A judgment in a mortgage foreclosure suit may be assigned. The assignee succeeds to all the rights under the decree possessed by the assignor.[3034] The assignment of an invalid judgment does not transfer any valid decree, but it does transfer the mortgage debt, with the authority to enforce it and the note by all appropriate remedies.[3035]

After a plaintiff has voluntarily assigned a judgment in his or her favor foreclosing a mortgage, the assignee must resort to the court to obtain the benefit of the assignment.[3036] The assignee must present a petition setting forth the assignment, and ask for a sale under the judgment, a foreclosure sale in the name of the assignor being void.[3037]

§ 1002.   Review

A mortgagor who is personally liable can appeal from a foreclosure judgment even though the mortgagor has parted with his or her title to the mortgaged premises.

A mortgagor who is personally liable for any deficiency may appeal from an adverse foreclosure judgment notwithstanding that the mortgagor has parted with title to the mortgaged premises to a party who has allowed the decree to be taken by default and who has failed to appeal.[3038] Similarly, a party who has conveyed to a third party after purchasing at a foreclosure sale has an interest in the subject matter that supports that person's appeal from an order setting aside the sale.[3039]

An issue may be addressed for the first time on appeal of the judgment in the case if the record is complete so that no further evidence is necessary for the determination of any question of public policy, and where both parties have argued the question in briefs and oral arguments.[3040]

3034. Moore v. Smith, 103 Mich. 387, 61 N.W. 538 (1894).

Brand v. Smith, 99 Mich. 395, 58 N.W. 363 (1894).

Terry v. McClintock, 41 Mich. 492, 2 N.W. 787 (1879).

3035. Lillibridge v. Tregent, 30 Mich. 105 (1874).

3036. Moore v. Smith, 103 Mich. 387, 61 N.W. 538 (1894).

Terry v. McClintock, 41 Mich. 492, 2 N.W. 787 (1879).

3037. Moore v. Smith, 103 Mich. 387, 61 N.W. 538 (1894).

3038. McCabe v. Farnsworth, 27 Mich. 52 (1873).

3039. Lawrence v. Jarvis, 36 Mich. 281 (1877).

3040. Meek v. Wilson, 283 Mich. 679, 278 N.W. 731 (1938) (unenforceability of second mortgage on ground of public policy).

Modification on appeal

Where, though decree in mortgage foreclosure suit between former spouses did not provide affirmatively that mortgage indebtedness had been paid in full and that mortgage should be cancelled and discharged, case had been heard in trial court primarily on that issue, decree would be modified in the Supreme Court accordingly.—Werner v. Werner, 357 Mich. 671, 99 N.W.2d 359 (1959).

Value of released portion of property

On determining that trial court's finding of value was clearly erroneous on de novo review of equitable action to restrain defendant from fore-

An appeal of a mortgage foreclosure nearly one year earlier would be addressed by the Court of Appeals on the merits, if leave is granted for delayed appeal where appellants were not negligent in filing the appeal.[3041] On the other hand, if there is a failure to take proper action to appeal for a year after the judgment becomes final and for six months after the last extension of time expires, the foreclosure judgment becomes absolute and an appeal from an order nisi confirming a second sale by a stranger to the case cannot be considered.[3042]

The appeal in a former court of chancery from a trust mortgage foreclosure decree was de novo,[3043] as was the review of an action to compel a proper offset for released property in the court's determination of the amount due.[3044]

The trial court must rule on any request for an appeal bond from either party.[3045]

Grounds for reversal. An appellate court will not reverse the trial court because the trial court determined the value of the mortgaged property without a jury if the parties acquiesced in the procedure and no harm resulted;[3046] because the judgment directed the foreclosure sale "at any time" after a specified date, in view of the parties' failure to present any facts relevant to the proper time of sale;[3047] because the sale price at the foreclosure sale is inadequate;[3048] because the trial court ordered a resale, in the absence of a clear showing of abuse of discretion;[3049] because of an alleged failure, complained of by the assignor of the mortgage, to produce the original notes or account for their non-production;[3050] because of any errors in the complaint for foreclosure, or in the judgment or proceedings culminating in the judgment, the appeal being from the order confirming the

closing mortgage until value of portion of mortgaged premises released by defendant was duly ascertained and credited against mortgage, Court of Appeals would adopt value disclosed by proofs on record and order that valuation amount be credited against mortgage principal and interest for appropriate time period, with foreclosure on remaining amount of interest and principal.—Dusseau v. Roscommon State Bank, 80 Mich. App. 531, 264 N.W.2d 350 (1978).

3041. United Growth Corp. v. Kelly Mortg. & Inv. Co., 86 Mich. App. 82, 272 N.W.2d 340 (1978) (upset price set by trial court).

3042. Grand Rapids Trust Co. v. Von Zellen, 267 Mich. 533, 255 N.W. 424 (1934).

3043. Union Guardian Trust Co. v. Building Sec. Corp., 280 Mich. 144, 273 N.W. 424 (1937).

3044. Dusseau v. Roscommon State Bank, 80 Mich. App. 531, 264 N.W.2d 350 (1978).

3045. MCR 7.209.

Amount of bond

Common pleas court rule requiring that appeal bond be set on "reasonable conditions" where appellants cannot obtain sureties following judgment of summary possession pursuant to mortgage foreclosure, although not defining quoted terms, would be construed in accord with definition in district court rule limiting bond to include only those amounts due from appellants after time of appeal, thereby precluding court from conditioning appellants appeals on bonds requiring them to pay mortgage payments that became due prior to time of appeals and that could not be said to be within proper scope of appeal bond to provide appellees indemnity against further trouble, expense, and costs while cause is undergoing review.—Federal Nat'l Mortg. Ass'n v. Wingate, 404 Mich. 661, 273 N.W.2d 456 (1979).

3046. Kramar v. Hackett, 316 Mich. 31, 24 N.W.2d 544 (1946).

3047. Union Guardian Trust Co. v. Building Sec. Corp., 280 Mich. 144, 273 N.W. 424 (1937).

3048. Chabut v. Chabut, 66 Mich. App. 440, 239 N.W.2d 401 (1976).

Sylvania Sav. Bank Co. v. Turner, 27 Mich. App. 640, 183 N.W.2d 894 (1970).

3049. Michigan Trust Co. v. Cody, 264 Mich. 258, 249 N.W. 844 (1933).

3050. Moreland v. Houghton, 94 Mich. 548, 54 N.W. 285 (1893).

sale;[3051] or because the complaint failed to allege that the appellant-widow's children, who are made defendants, are the mortgagor's heirs at law.[3052]

Determination and disposition. Even if an action in foreclosure is heard by a jury on account of the counterclaims, the trial court must still enter a judgment containing findings of fact and conclusions of law sufficient for an appellate court to review the trial court's decision.[3053]

If a case is remanded to the circuit court for rehearing, the circuit court's refusal to permit an amendment of the answer to permit a defense that is not propounded until the rehearing is not an abuse of discretion.[3054]

A party who is interested only as a subsequent encumbrancer, and who alone appeals, has a right to have the foreclosure judgment altered by striking out the amount of an attorney's fee improperly allowed, even though it will operate incidentally to the benefit of other parties who have not appealed, and notwithstanding the value of the property exceeds the amount of liens on it.[3055]

Effect of disposition on review. In a case in which the judgment was reversed, the sale of the mortgaged premises pursuant to the judgment and pending the appeal taken without giving bond is void.[3056]

F.   SALE

§ 1011.   In General

> **The sale of real property due to foreclosure by suit of a mortgage or a land contract on the real estate must be made by the county clerk or the person otherwise authorized by the circuit court in its judgment.**

Under the Revised Judicature Act of 1961, the sale of real property due to foreclosure by suit of a mortgage or a land contract on the real estate must be made by the county clerk or the person otherwise authorized by the circuit court in its judgment.[3057] The sale is subject to the procedures[3058] for judicially ordered sales,[3059] which make it subject to the procedures applicable to the sale of property

---

3051. Farmers' Bank of Grass Lake v. Quick, 71 Mich. 534, 39 N.W. 752 (1888).

3052. Gray v. Franks, 86 Mich. 382, 49 N.W. 130 (1891).

3053. Remand for opinion on merits

Although, because of common issue as to foreclosure and counterclaim, entire case was tried to a jury, which rendered verdict of no cause of action as to both claim and counterclaim, where trial judge, in adopting jury's advisory verdict and in entering judgment thereon, did not render opinion wherein he found facts and dealt with such legal questions as were requisite to determination of case, it was unwise for Supreme Court to undertake decisional review of decretal judgment without such opinion, and record would be remanded for reargument of case before trial judge,

for preparation by him of independent opinion, and for entry of new decretal judgment deciding merits of plaintiff mortgagee's claimed right of foreclosure and defendants' denial of it.—Abner A. Wolf, Inc. v. Walch, 385 Mich. 253, 188 N.W.2d 544 (1971).

3054. Collateral Liquidation, Inc. v. Lippman, 278 Mich. 508, 270 N.W. 767 (1936).

3055. Hardwick v. Bassett, 29 Mich. 17 (1874).

3056. Horbal v. St. John's Greek Catholic Church, 264 Mich. 372, 249 N.W. 891 (1933).

3057. MCLS § 600.3125.

3058. MCLS § 600.6091.

3059. MCLS § 600.3125.

by execution.[3060]

Equitable jurisdiction to foreclose mortgages is statutory.[3061] In the absence of a moratorium statute, the court has no power to prevent the sale or to change the terms of the contract by directing that the appraised value of the property be credited upon the mortgage debt.[3062] In a proper case, nevertheless, the court may enjoin a sale, such as where the mortgage, though unsatisfied of record, has in fact been paid,[3063] or where the foreclosure decree is for a grossly excessive sum.[3064]

The subsequent dealings of the parties after the entry of a foreclosure judgment generally will not affect the order for sale unless the manifest intent of the parties is otherwise.[3065]

The mortgagor of real property cannot compel the mortgagee to sell it under a foreclosure decree.[3066]

Sale of trust properties. The statute relating to trust mortgages and authorizing the court, under certain circumstances, to order the sale of the property to the trustee for the benefit of holders of the obligations secured by the mortgage[3067] does not improperly affect substantial constitutional rights of the mortgagor.[3068] It also is not invalid as contravening public policy against the stifling of bidding.[3069]

§ 1012.   Time for Sale

Within the limitations of statutes and court rules, the time for the sale is primarily within the trial court's discretion. The person holding the sale may adjourn or postpone it under specified conditions.

3060. MCLS §§ 600.6052 et seq.

3061. Bleakley v. Oakwayne Farms Co., 265 Mich. 268, 251 N.W. 354 (1933).

Stewart v. Isbell, 155 Mich. App. 65, 399 N.W.2d 440 (1986).

3062. Bleakley v. Oakwayne Farms Co., 265 Mich. 268, 251 N.W. 354 (1933).

3063. Eaton v. Eaton, 68 Mich. 158, 36 N.W. 50 (1888).

3064. Scriven v. Hursh, 39 Mich. 98 (1878).

3065. No new mortgage

In a case where the mortgagor borrowed money to pay the mortgagee after the foreclosure judgment was rendered, and the lender took an assignment from the mortgagee of the mortgage and the mortgagee's rights under the decree, and there being no understanding as to when the load was to be repaid and no understanding for an extension of time before sale, loan did not amount to the making of a new mortgage and a new judgment before sale was not required.—Walker v. Lillibridge, 112 Mich. 384, 70 N.W. 1031 (1897).

3066. No necessity for sale to determine mortgagor's deficiency

Where a mortgagor sought to compel the mortgagee to sell under a foreclosure decree, the sale could not be compelled even though the mortgagor urged, *inter alia*, that he could not ascertain his liability for deficiency unless and until the sale was made.—Leonard v. Frazer, 126 Mich. 377, 85 N.W. 959 (1901).

3067. MCLS § 600.3170.

Resignation and no wrongful acts

It was not per se improper for a trustee under a trust indenture agreement by which nonnegotiable subordinated debentures were issued to also become mortgagee of property owned by the issuer of the debentures and relied upon by the issuer to provide income for payments on the mortgage indebtedness and to pay amounts owed on the debentures to foreclose the mortgages, resulting in the issuer being unable to satisfy its indebtedness to the debenture holders, where the trustee filed notice of its intention to resign its position as such prior to commencing its action to foreclose the mortgage and where no fraud, bad faith, or other willful misconduct was alleged.—Mintener v. Michigan Nat'l Bank, 117 Mich. App. 633, 324 N.W.2d 110 (1982).

3068. Detroit Trust Co. v. Stormfeltz-Lovley Co., 257 Mich. 655, 242 N.W. 227 (1932).

3069. Detroit Trust Co. v. Stormfeltz-Lovley Co., 257 Mich. 655, 242 N.W. 227 (1932).

Under the Revised Judicature Act of 1961, the court may not order any mortgaged lands to be sold within 6months or any lands sold under an executory land contract within 3months after the filing of a complaint of foreclosure.[3070] If it is sought by an amended complaint to impose personal liability on the mortgagor, the statutory time period runs from the date of filing of the amended complaint.[3071]

Under the Michigan Court Rules of 1985, the sale may only be conducted after at least 42 days' publication of notice. Publication may not begin until after the period of time specified as aforementioned in the Revised Judicature Act of 1961 and after the expiration of the redemption period.[3072]

The Revised Judicature Act of 1961 also limits the time of day at which a foreclosure sale by suit may be held.[3073]

Within the constraints of the statutes and court rules, the time for the sale is primarily within the trial court's sound discretion.[3074]

On the other hand, where the judgment allows a mortgagor a specified time before sale, and a sale has been prematurely made without notice to the mortgagor, a waiver of the time allowed by the judgment will not be presumed.[3075] A sale under those circumstances is void.[3076]

Adjournment. The person selling real property pursuant to a judgment must conduct the sale as for a sale of real property on execution, or as the court otherwise provides.[3077] The provisions for an execution sale allow the party conducting the sale to adjourn the sale under certain conditions.[3078]

Postponement. The person selling real property pursuant to a judgment must conduct the sale as for a sale of real property on execution, or as the court otherwise provides.[3079] The provisions for an execution sale allow the party conducting the sale to postpone the sale under certain conditions.[3080]

A violation of an agreement for postponement may be sufficient ground for a resale.[3081]

3070. MCLS § 600.3115.

3071. Canfield v. Shear, 49 Mich. 313, 13 N.W. 605 (1882).

Burt v. Thomas, 49 Mich. 462, 12 N.W. 911 (1882).

3072. MCR 3.410.

Carpenter v. Smith, 147 Mich. App. 560, 383 N.W.2d 248 (1985) (publication sufficient if it occurs one time in each of the six weeks prior to sale even if 42 days do not elapse between the first publication and the date of sale).

Improper trustee sale before expiration of redemption period

Trustee under trust mortgage providing that trustee would do any and all things required of him by majority vote of noteholders had no implied power to sell trust land before natural expiration of equity of redemption where trustee had no duties

which required him to sell land prior to expiration of equity of redemption.—Sadow v. Losh, 38 Mich. App. 404, 196 N.W.2d 350 (1972).

3073. MCLS § 600.3125.

3074. Union Guardian Trust Co. v. Building Sec. Corp., 280 Mich. 144, 273 N.W. 424 (1937).

3075. Shier v. Prentis, 55 Mich. 175, 20 N.W. 892 (1884).

3076. Shier v. Prentis, 55 Mich. 175, 20 N.W. 892 (1884).

3077. MCLS § 600.6091.

3078. MCLS § 600.6053.

3079. MCLS § 600.6091.

3080. MCLS § 600.6042.

3081. Demaray v. Little, 19 Mich. 244 (1869).

§ 1013.   Notice of Sale

A sale of real property pursuant to a judgment must give notice of the sale as for the sale of real property on execution, or as the court otherwise provides.

A sale of real property pursuant to a judgment must give notice of the sale as for the sale of real property on execution, or as the court otherwise provides.[3082] Statutory notice of a sale as under the provisions for a sale of property on execution[3083] is indispensable to the validity of the sale.[3084] Personal notice is not required, however.[3085]

With respect to the usual foreclosure sale authorized by trust mortgages, no notice to bondholders is necessary. But the Revised Judicature Act of 1961[3086] requires notice[3087] under the special type of proceeding provided by the act for administration of mortgage trusts[3088]

No particular form of notice is specifically prescribed or required,[3089] and it is unnecessary to disclose in the notice the existence of prior mortgages.[3090]

An officer who sells real property without adequate notice has specified liability to any party injured by that action.[3091]

Adjournment. The holder of the sale must provide the required notice of any adjournment.[3092] Notice of an adjournment cannot be given effectively by posting an adjournment notice prior to the day of sale.[3093]

Postponement. The holder of the sale must provide the required notice of any

3082. MCLS § 600.6091.

3083. MCLS § 600.6052.

3084. New York Baptist Union v. Atwell, 95 Mich. 239, 54 N.W. 760 (1893).

Perrien v. Fetters, 35 Mich. 233 (1876).

3085. Sanford v. Haines, 71 Mich. 116, 38 N.W. 777 (1888).

3086. MCLS § 600.3170.

Detroit Trust Co. v. Stormfeltz-Lovley Co., 257 Mich. 655, 242 N.W. 227 (1932).

3087. MCR 3.410.

3088. MCLS §§ 451.401 et seq.

3089. Provident Mut. Life Ins. Co. v. Vinton Co., 282 Mich. 84, 275 N.W. 776 (1937).

3090. Flax v. Mutual Bldg. & Loan Ass'n, 198 Mich. 676, 165 N.W. 835 (1917).

3091. MCLS § 600.6054.

3092. MCLS § 600.6052.

Remedy for improper adjournment
Even if the mortgagor was correct in asserting that the mortgagee did not properly adjourn the foreclosure sale, there were insufficient grounds for the court to invalidate the foreclosure sale given that (1) the mortgagor let several months pass after the foreclosure sale before filing a complaint, and (2) the mortgagor never tendered any money to redeem the property.—Worthy v. World Wide Fin. Servs., 347 F. Supp. 2d 502 (E.D. Mich. 2004), aff'd, 192 Fed. Appx. 369, 2006 U.S. App. LEXIS 19458 (6th Cir. Mich. July 28, 2006).

Mortgagors were not prejudiced by any alleged defect in the notice of adjournment of the foreclosure sale and, therefore, were not entitled to set aside the sale; the mortgagors were not timely in challenging the validity of the foreclosure sale, made no effort to redeem or take any action until after the redemption period expired, and waited until proceedings were instituted to evict them before challenging the adequacy of the notice.— Sweet Air Inv., Inc. v. Kenney, 275 Mich. App. 492, 739 N.W.2d 656 (2007).

3093. Grand Rapids Trust Co. v. Von Zellen, 260 Mich. 341, 244 N.W. 496 (1932).

postponement.[3094]

Description of property. Within the limits of the statutory provision on the notice,[3095] the property to be sold must be described in the notice with such a reasonable degree of certainty that the public, by the exercise of ordinary intelligence, may be enabled to identify it, and may be directed to the means of obtaining an exact description if desired.[3096] The notice must describe the property with substantial accuracy and in such a manner as to identify it clearly, and inform intending purchasers of its situation, character and extent. It is generally sufficient to follow the description contained in the mortgage.[3097] A description in accordance with the statute providing for the sale of realty on execution is ordinarily sufficient.[3098]

Publication and posting. Publication once in each week, for six successive weeks, is required in a newspaper meeting statutory requirements.[3099] A notice first published December 12th for a sale on January 18th following is not sufficient.[3100]

Publication in a daily newspaper of general circulation is not required, however, and the notice may be published in a weekly newspaper that has been published for years as a medium for the publication of legal advertisements.[3101]

The notice must also be posted in at least three public places in the town or city in which the property is to be sold and, if different, in which the property is located.[3102]

Effect of irregularities. The fact that the sum claimed in the notice is slightly excessive may be disregarded under the de minimis rule.[3103]

Where the notice fails to state that only an undivided portion of the land will be sold, that irregularity is not a jurisdictional defect subject to collateral attack.[3104]

In the case of a discrepancy between the day of the week and the day of the month, the latter controls.[3105]

Where a foreclosure decree is a final decree, and no appeal is taken from it,

3094. MCLS §§ 600.6042, 600.6052.

3095. MCLS § 600.6052.

3096. Provident Mut. Life Ins. Co. v. Vinton Co., 282 Mich. 84, 275 N.W. 776 (1937).

3097. Provident Mut. Life Ins. Co. v. Vinton Co., 282 Mich. 84, 275 N.W. 776 (1937).

3098. Provident Mut. Life Ins. Co. v. Vinton Co., 282 Mich. 84, 275 N.W. 776 (1937).

3099. MCLS § 600.6052.

3100. Goodwin v. Burns, 1 Mich. N.P. 228 (1870).

3101. Hoock v. Sloman, 155 Mich. 1, 118 N.W. 489 (1908).

3102. MCLS § 600.6052.

3103. Flax v. Mutual Bldg. & Loan Ass'n, 198 Mich. 676, 165 N.W. 835 (1917).

De minimis rule

Michigan courts apply the principle of *de minimis non curat lex* in deciding whether an overstatement of the amount due is large enough to necessitate setting aside the foreclosure sale; an excessive claim for the amount due warrants setting aside a foreclosure sale only if it is significantly excessive or in bad faith and an attempt was made to redeem the property.—Sweet Air Inv., Inc. v. Kenney, 275 Mich. App. 492, 739 N.W.2d 656 (2007).

3104. Brown v. Phillips, 40 Mich. 264 (1879).

3105. Resolution of conflict

Where a notice fixed the day of the sale as Friday, August 9th, it was held that the notice was not fatally defective merely because August 9th fell on Saturday, the day of the month controlling.—First State Bank v. Day, 188 Mich. 228, 154 N.W. 101 (1915).

objections to confirmation of the sale based upon the fact that a claimed easement had not been specifically mentioned in the notice of sale may be properly overruled, the claimed easement being mentioned in the decree and the right to its enjoyment being unaffected by the sale.[3106]

§ 1014.   Sale in Separate Parcels

Parcels may be sold as a unit if no offers are received for any separate parcels, or if the nature of the use is such that the parcels constitute a unit, as provided by the foreclosure judgment.

The judgment in a foreclosure by suit must specify which parcels or portion of a parcel of the entire mortgage real estate must be sold to satisfy the mortgage or land-contract debt if it is less than the whole.[3107]

A party who has, for a valuable consideration, agreed to waive his right to redeem cannot object if the sale is not made in parcels.[3108] In this connection it must be kept in mind that the mortgagor's right of redemption is not deemed superior to the mortgagee's right to collect the debt.[3109] Accordingly, the parcels may be sold as one unit if no offers are received for any separate parcels at the sale[3110] and if the sale is in conformity with a decree that in turn conforms to the statute.[3111]

There is a presumption that a sale has been made in accordance with a decree drawn in compliance with the statutory requirement as to sale in parcels.[3112]

§ 1015.   Who May Purchase

The fact that the notice of sale contained no notice of prior mortgages does not preclude the mortgagee from purchasing.

A trust mortgage provision requiring that the purchaser present bonds or coupons for credit may preclude a decretal provision to the contrary.[3113] With further reference to trust mortgage foreclosures, a bondholder may insist upon his or her contract, and cannot be forced to become an owner in common in a trust created by other bondholders.[3114]

3106. Provident Mut. Life Ins. Co. v. Vinton Co., 282 Mich. 84, 275 N.W. 776 (1937).

3107. MCLS § 600.3165.

3108. Clark v. Stilson, 36 Mich. 482 (1877).

Purpose of statute

Statute providing for foreclosure sale of mortgaged property by parcels, rather than en masse, is designed to protect redemption rights of parties where no other provision for foreclosure sale is specified.—Metropolitan Life Ins. Co. v. Foote, 95 Mich. App. 399, 290 N.W.2d 158 (1980).

3109. Security Trust Co. v. Sloman, 252 Mich. 266, 233 N.W. 216 (1930).

3110. Burroughs v. Teitelbaum, 309 Mich. 251, 15 N.W.2d 151 (1944).

3111. Walsh v. Colby, 153 Mich. 602, 117 N.W. 207 (1908).

3112. Walsh v. Colby, 153 Mich. 602, 117 N.W. 207 (1908).

3113. Union Guardian Trust Co. v. Building Sec. Corp., 280 Mich. 717, 276 N.W. 697 (1937).

3114. Detroit Trust Co. v. Stormfeltz-Lovley Co., 257 Mich. 655, 242 N.W. 227, 1932 Mich. LEXIS 890 (1932).

See, also, Bradley v. Tyson, 33 Mich. 337 (1876).

The fact that the notice of sale contains no notice of prior mortgages does not preclude the mortgagee from purchasing.[3115]

Where a plaintiff in an action seeking possession mortgaged the premises, the defendant may buy in at the foreclosure sale, and thus obtain a title that inures to the defendant's benefit.[3116]

Anyone, even a mortgagee, can, unless estopped, buy a foreclosed property at the foreclosure of a junior mortgage.[3117]

A second mortgagee, so long as there is enough land left from the sale under the first mortgage, can refrain from bidding on the sale of the property under the first mortgage, and rely for his or her security on the unsold land. Or the second mortgagee may bid in enough of the land to discharge the first mortgage, and enforce his or her security on the remainder, if the second mortgagee is guilty of no deception or fraud in the purchase, especially when the owner of the remainder of the land is present and fully apprised and is in a position to protect him- or herself by also bidding on the parcel or parcels sold.[3118]

The statutes concerning execution sales applicable to sales by judicial order[3119] provide that the officer making the sale and his or her deputies must not directly or indirectly purchase or take a legal interest in the purchase of foreclosed real estate.[3120]

§ 1016.   Bids

It is the duty of the official conducting the sale to realize the largest amount possible from the sale on foreclosure of a land contract or mortgage. The highest bidder's refusal to increase his or her bid to the minimum bid gives the court the discretion to order a resale of the foreclosed real estate.

It is the duty of the official conducting the sale to realize the largest amount possible from the sale on foreclosure of a land contract or mortgage.[3121]

If the court has set a minimum bid on the property, the court may require the highest bidder if the highest bid is below the minimum to raise his or her bid to the amount of the minimum bid in order to purchase the property.[3122] The bidder's refusal to do so gives the court the discretion to order a resale of the foreclosed real estate.[3123]

The transfer of a bid works no prejudice to the mortgagor, and is not a ground

3115. Flax v. Mutual Bldg. & Loan Ass'n, 198 Mich. 676, 165 N.W. 835 (1917).

3116. Snyder v. Hemmingway, 47 Mich. 549, 11 N.W. 381 (1882).

3117. Moote v. Scriven, 33 Mich. 500 (1876).

3118. Watson v. Grand Rapids & I. R. Co., 91 Mich. 198, 51 N.W. 990 (1892).

3119. MCLS § 600.6091.

3120. MCLS § 600.6046.

3121. Huck v. Stormfeltz-Loveley Co., 261 Mich. 79, 245 N.W. 808 (1933).

3122. Schmeltz v. Rowen, 287 Mich. 657, 284 N.W. 597 (1938).

3123. Ample opportunity to increase bid

Where defendant in foreclosure of a land contract refused to increase the bid on a resale and also refused plaintiff's offer of a six-months' option to purchase the property at the amount of the sale bid, or to take a deed conditioned upon

for ordering a new sale.[3124] On the other hand, interference that prevents a fair and usual sale, as by deterring persons who intended to bid, may furnish grounds for estoppel precluding a deficiency judgment.[3125]

Payment and enforcement. The statutes concerning execution sales applicable to sales by judicial order[3126] provide that the sale of the foreclosed real estate must go to the highest bidder. If the highest bidder does not take it, the officer may sell the property again if the sale is in progress, or sell it at a new sale with notice. The officer may bring an action against highest bidders who refuse to take the property at the bid price.[3127]

These statutes contemplate that every opportunity will be afforded to intending purchasers so that the premises may be sold at the best price obtainable.[3128] Accordingly, subsequent purchasers cannot resist the reopening of a mortgage sale if the successful bidder takes back the offer immediately after acceptance, and while competing bidders are still present.[3129]

A bidder who has made a bid in excess of the debts and legal charges is not ordinarily in a position to be relieved of the excess amount of the bid.[3130] Nor can a holder of a junior execution lien, who has bought in at a mortgage foreclosure sale to protect his or her interests, reduce the recovery on his or her note for the purchase price by the amount of illegal attorney's fees included in the price.[3131]

Where a prior encumbrancer announces at the sale that the purchaser would take subject to prior encumbrances held by the encumbrancer, the encumbrancer cannot ask to be relieved from his or her own highest bid on the assertion that he or she was misled and acted under the misapprehension that he or she would be entitled to have any surplus money that there might be applied to the payment of the encumbrances.[3132]

Where the terms of a trust mortgage permit the use of first mortgage bonds and coupons toward payment on foreclosure, the decree may properly permit the same,

making payment of the unpaid balance, the court did not abuse its discretion in refusing to order a resale.—James S. Holden Co. v. Applebaum, 267 Mich. 632, 255 N.W. 601 (1934).

3124. Culver v. McKeown, 43 Mich. 322, 5 N.W. 422 (1880).

3125. Innes v. Stewart, 36 Mich. 285 (1877).

Evidence of purposeful and unreasonable underbidding

In action by plaintiffs to recover sum paid to redeem additional security from defendant mortgagee who allegedly purposely and unreasonably underbid value of subject property at mortgage foreclosure sale, appraisals on subject property by qualified appraisal expert, on one of which defendant had relied in authorizing mortgage, were properly introduced as substantive evidence of value of mortgage.—Chabut v. Chabut, 66 Mich. App. 440, 239 N.W.2d 401 (1976).

3126. MCLS § 600.6091.

3127. MCLS § 600.6045.

Other sanctions on highest bidder refusing property not permitted

It was improper to impose, as a condition of resale, that the first bidder deposit a sum equal to the amount of his two bids and a bond conditioned that the premises on the resale would bring the amount of the prior sale, together with the costs of the cause and of the resale.—Converse v. Clay, 86 Mich. 375, 49 N.W. 473 (1891).

3128. Miller v. Miller, 48 Mich. 311, 12 N.W. 209 (1882).

3129. Miller v. Miller, 48 Mich. 311, 12 N.W. 209 (1882).

3130. Kennedy v. Brown, 50 Mich. 336, 15 N.W. 498 (1883).

Buchoz v. Walker, 19 Mich. 224 (1869).

3131. Macomb v. Wilkinson, 83 Mich. 486, 47 N.W. 336 (1890).

3132. Ledyard v. Phillips, 32 Mich. 13 (1875).

if the decree also requires the deposit of sufficient cash to pay expenses of the sale and to make pro rata distribution among nondepositing bondholders.[3133]

§ 1017.   Report or Return

The court may, on petition of the purchaser and on notice to all interested persons, correct a clerical error in the report in describing the premises, if the error is apparent from the face of the record.

A court rendering a foreclosure judgment has authority on the petition of the purchaser and on notice to all persons interested to correct a clerical error in the report in describing the premises sold, if the error is apparent from the face of the record.[3134] Similarly, an error in reciting the date of the judgment in the report of sale is immaterial where the record furnishes the means of correcting it.[3135]

Where exceptions to a report have been abandoned, and the objecting parties have defaulted, they must show cause in order to be relieved of the default and to be heard.[3136]

§ 1018.   Confirmation

Ordinarily, only interested parties may resist confirmation of a foreclosure sale, but if those parties resist, the sale cannot be made absolute until the objections have been passed upon.

The trial court's practice of requiring confirmation of a foreclosure sale in a foreclosure by suit antedates the statutes, and the latter have been construed in light of the preexisting practice.[3137]

Generally, no one may file objections to confirmation except parties having an interest in the subject matter.[3138] But if interested parties object, then the sale cannot be made absolute so long as the objections have not been passed upon.[3139]

The court is vested with a large measure of discretion in confirming a sale or in refusing confirmation.[3140] Although the court must consider all circumstances pertinent to each individual case,[3141] an order made in the exercise of discretion

---

3133. Detroit Trust Co. v. Detroit City Service Co., 262 Mich. 14, 247 N.W. 76 (1933).

3134. Walsh v. Colby, 153 Mich. 602, 117 N.W. 207 (1908).

3135. Ruggles v. First Nat'l Bank, 43 Mich. 192, 5 N.W. 257 (1880).

3136. Spike v. Washtenaw Circuit Judge, 248 Mich. 101, 226 N.W. 822 (1929).

3137. Demaray v. Little, 17 Mich. 386 (1868).

3138. Provident Mut. Life Ins. Co. v. Vinton Co., 282 Mich. 84, 275 N.W. 776 (1937).

3139. Howard v. Bond, 42 Mich. 131, 3 N.W. 289 (1879).

3140. Provident Mut. Life Ins. Co. v. Vinton Co., 282 Mich. 84, 275 N.W. 776 (1937).

Union Guardian Trust Co. v. Rood, 267 Mich. 343, 255 N.W. 347 (1934).

Michigan Trust Co. v. Cody, 264 Mich. 258, 249 N.W. 844 (1933).

Carpenter v. Smith, 147 Mich. App. 560, 383 N.W.2d 248 (1985).

3141. Michigan Trust Co. v. Cody, 264 Mich. 258, 249 N.W. 844 (1933).

does not violate the contract rights of either mortgagors or mortgagees.[3142]

Grounds of objection. Confirmation may be properly refused, or improperly granted, in cases where the amount of the bid is so inadequate as to shock the conscience of the court,[3143] or where the sale was made in violation of court order and after tender of payment of the amount due.[3144]

On the other hand, mere irregularities are not necessarily a sufficient ground of objection, particularly where the irregularities are in the decree and the mortgagors have knowledge of them,[3145] or where the irregularities are, by reason of the circumstances, harmless.[3146] Further, no objection will ordinarily be considered if it should have been interposed before rendition of the judgment.[3147] In that case, a sale in conformity with the judgment will ordinarily be confirmed.[3148]

An objection that the price is inequitable may be insufficient in the absence of a showing that the property is worth more or that more may be obtained on resale.[3149] In this connection, the test in determining the adequacy of the bid is not merely whether the value of the property exceeds the bid, and good faith is an important factor to be considered.[3150] A foreclosure price that reflects the decrease in value due to the forced sale is not grossly inadequate.[3151]

Mere lapse of time after rendition of the judgment, even though the plaintiff and one of the solicitors has died during the intervening time, is an insufficient

3142. Michigan Trust Co. v. Cody, 264 Mich. 258, 249 N.W. 844 (1933).

3143. Guardian Depositors Corp. v. Powers, 296 Mich. 553, 296 N.W. 675 (1941).

Detroit Trust Co. v. Hart, 274 Mich. 144, 264 N.W. 321 (1936).

Carpenter v. Smith, 147 Mich. App. 560, 383 N.W.2d 248 (1985) (price was not grossly inadequate).

Large deficiency, depression

Order denying confirmation of mortgage sale in equitable foreclosure during depression and at price far below assessed valuation, which would result in large deficiency decree, was not abuse of discretion.—Michigan Trust Co. v. Cody, 264 Mich. 258, 249 N.W. 844 (1933).

3144. French v. Grand Beach Co., 239 Mich. 575, 215 N.W. 13 (1927).

3145. Union Trust Co. v. Electric Park Amusement Co., 168 Mich. 574, 135 N.W. 115 (1912).

3146. Actual notice

Court properly overruled objection to order confirming report of foreclosure sale, where no injury resulted from lack of service of notice of filing report, the defendants having had actual notice.—Wesbrook Lane Realty Corp. v. Pokorny, 250 Mich. 548, 231 N.W. 66 (1930).

3147. Reason for rule

Judgment of foreclosure sale of real estate mortgage is final adjudication of rights of parties, imports verity, and is conclusive so long as it is in full force and effect and unmodified, vacated, or set aside, so that, on objection to confirmation of sale, no question adjudicated thereby may be considered, and ordinarily no objection will be considered that should have been interposed before judgment.—Smith v. Heppner, 276 Mich. 463, 267 N.W. 882 (1936).

3148. Provident Mut. Life Ins. Co. v. Vinton Co., 282 Mich. 84, 275 N.W. 776 (1937).

3149. Union Guardian Trust Co. v. Rood, 267 Mich. 343, 255 N.W. 347 (1934).

Hoock v. Sloman, 155 Mich. 1, 118 N.W. 489 (1908).

United Growth Corp. v. Kelly Mortg. & Inv. Co., 86 Mich. App. 82, 272 N.W.2d 340 (1978).

Carpenter v. Smith, 147 Mich. App. 560, 383 N.W.2d 248 (1985) (state equalized value does not reflect forced nature of foreclosure sale).

3150. Detroit Trust Co. v. Hart, 277 Mich. 561, 269 N.W. 598 (1936).

Demaray v. Little, 19 Mich. 244 (1869).

3151. Carpenter v. Smith, 147 Mich. App. 560, 383 N.W.2d 248 (1985).

ground on which to resist confirmation.[3152]

Procedure. The confirmation of a sale by the court is not a mere ministerial act, but a judicial function involving consideration of the circumstances and the exercise of sound discretion.[3153]

The judgment generally cannot be modified incidentally to the application for confirmation.[3154]

Where the sale is invalid by reason of an invalid adjournment, evidence concerning the circumstances of the sale and of the claims of parties claiming under it may be properly excluded.[3155]

Setting aside confirmation. A much stronger case must be made to warrant the setting aside of a sale after confirmation of the report than would have been necessary before confirmation.[3156]

§ 1019.   Waiver and Estoppel to Attack Validity

One who receives and retains the proceeds of the sale may be estopped to attack the regularity of that sale.

If the mortgagor receives and accepts from the proceeds of the sale the surplus due him or her, and takes no steps to have the proceedings set aside within the time allowed by law, the mortgagor waives all irregularities, and sanctions the validity of the proceedings.[3157] Consistently, if the holder of rights under the foreclosure decree not only allows the sale to proceed but receives and retains the proceeds of the sale, that person is estopped to question the regularity of it.[3158]

Similarly, a party for whose convenience a mere irregularity has been permitted to occur will not be granted a resale as matter of right.[3159]

Where a party who purchases the rights of the purchaser at a sale does not assert any rights under that purchase but instead enters into possession under a later purchase at a subsequent foreclosure sale, the party is not estopped from questioning the validity of a void decree under which the first sale was made.[3160]

§ 1020.   Vacation

If the mortgagee bids in the mortgaged property at foreclosure, giving an opportunity for redemption, and the

3152. Powell v. Pierce, 168 Mich. 427, 134 N.W. 447 (1912).

3153. Detroit Trust Co. v. Hart, 277 Mich. 561, 269 N.W. 598 (1936).

3154. Michigan Trust Co. v. Cody, 264 Mich. 258, 249 N.W. 844 (1933).

3155. Grand Rapids Trust Co. v. Von Zellen, 260 Mich. 341, 244 N.W. 496 (1932).

3156. Bullard v. Green, 10 Mich. 268 (1862).

3157. Colton v. Rupert, 60 Mich. 318, 27 N.W. 520 (1886).

3158. Farr v. Lachman, 130 Mich. 40, 89 N.W. 688 (1902).

3159. Irregular postponement
Where sale was postponed at request of mortgagor, sale, made at time to which postponed, would not be set aside at the instance of defendant as matter of strict right, and in the absence of any showing of equities, on the ground that it was made after the time when by the published notice the sale was advertised to take place.—Isbell v. Kenyon, 33 Mich. 63 (1875).

3160. Horton v. Howard, 79 Mich. 642, 44 N.W. 1112 (1890).

mortgagor abandons an attempt to redeem, the court will not thereafter order a resale.

If the mortgagee bids in the mortgaged property at foreclosure, giving an opportunity for redemption, and the mortgagor abandons an attempt to redeem, the court will not thereafter order a resale.[3161]

In a case where the deed from purchasers at the sale is invalid, the mortgagor's election to recover damages sustained by reason of the invalid deed by an action in trespass precludes the mortgagors from seeking to set aside a second sale and to have an accounting rendered.[3162]

The fact that the rights of third parties have intervened does not, of itself, necessarily preclude a setting aside of the sale.[3163]

§ 1021.   —Grounds

Neither irregularity nor surprise is necessarily a sufficient ground for vacating a sale. Fraud, accident, or mistake as well as a grossly inadequate sale price may be grounds for vacating a foreclosure sale.

A mere irregularity is not, as such, necessarily a sufficient ground for vacating a foreclosure sale.[3164] Absent a showing that there was fraud, accident, or mistake, the trial court lacks authority to set aside a foreclosure sale where the mortgagee complies with all the statutory requirements for foreclosing the mortgage.[3165]

A refusal to vacate has been upheld: where the death of a mortgagor-copartner

---

3161. Stebbins v. Heath, 115 Mich. 661, 74 N.W. 205 (1898).

3162. Grand Rapids Trust Co. v. Von Zellen, 267 Mich. 533, 255 N.W. 424 (1934).

3163. Brewer v. Landis, 111 Mich. 217, 69 N.W. 493 (1896).

3164. Smith v. General Mortg. Corp., 402 Mich. 125, 261 N.W.2d 710 (1978) (sufficient grounds shown).

Deed not filed

The court could not set aside a sale in a chancery foreclosure of mortgage, because the deed to the purchaser was not filed in the office of the register of deeds, as required by statute.—Butters v. Butters, 153 Mich. 153, 117 N.W. 203 (1908).

3165. Freeman v. Wozniak, 241 Mich. App. 633, 617 N.W.2d 46 (2000).

Fraud

Where a tenant in common of a mill, in foreclosing a mortgage on his cotenant's half of the realty, insisted at the sale on the validity of the chattel mortgage which he held on his cotenant's interest in the machinery, and threatened to foreclose it, and bought in the property, his cotenant

might avoid the sale, though she might have had reason to believe, as was the fact, that the chattel mortgage was invalid.—Dohm v. Haskin, 88 Mich. 144, 50 N.W. 108 (1891).

Where one who had a lien on land was not apprised of a foreclosure affecting that land as well as several other parcels, nor of a sale thereunder, and the sale was conducted in such a manner that the other parcels which were first charged were bid in for comparatively insignificant sums, while that constituting the lienor's security was bid in for all it was worth, chancery would set aside the sale and order another, the lienor giving security to bid for the parcels first charged a sum equal to the amount of the decree, and to pay to the purchaser at the former sales all sums expended by him, less a reasonable rent.—Gilbert v. Haire, 43 Mich. 283, 5 N.W. 321 (1880).

Mistake

Where a trustee in whose name a mortgage had been taken to secure the payment of several creditors purchased at the foreclosure sale for the joint benefit of all the creditors, and made the purchase in good faith in pursuance of what he deemed to be his authority and his duty to the beneficiaries of the trust, he was entitled to have the property resold at the option of creditors who objected to the purchase.—Bradley v. Tyson, 33 Mich. 337 (1876).

was not brought to the attention of the court until ten years after its occurrence, the surviving partner having meanwhile looked after the interests of the partnership;[3166] where the trustee of a mortgagee's assignee bid in the property eight minutes after the opening of the sale, there being no showing that any bids were prevented or that any other bidders were present at the sale;[3167] where a person from whom the mortgagors had expected to get money to cover the amount due had disappointed the mortgagors;[3168] and where the mortgagee, seeking to set aside the foreclosure, had bid in each of two lots for one-half the debt, on the erroneous assumption that valuable buildings stood on both lots, whereas in fact they stood on one lot that was redeemed.[3169]

Surprise is not necessarily a sufficient ground for vacation, and cannot be sufficient where it has arisen from negligence and inattention on the part of the complaining party.[3170] Similarly, the trial court cannot setting aside the foreclosure sale on the grounds that the mortgagor was incompetent during the foreclosure proceedings.[3171] Along the same lines, the mortgagors cannot object to the relations between the purchaser and the purchaser's ward in the taking of the property in the sale.[3172]

Inadequacy of price. The highest bidder's refusal to pay at least the minimum price set in the foreclosure judgment gives the court the discretion to order a resale of the foreclosed real estate.[3173]

Mere inadequacy of price, however, unless it is so gross as of itself to justify a suspicion of fraud, surprise, or mistake, is not ground for the interference of the court to set aside the sale.[3174] In any event, inadequacy of price, to a degree warranting relief vacating a completed foreclosure sale, is not lightly established.[3175]

A claim of inadequacy of price may be more seriously considered in cases

3166. Grand Rapids Trust Co. v. Von Zellen, 267 Mich. 533, 255 N.W. 424, 1934 Mich. LEXIS 585 (1934).

3167. Grand Rapids Trust Co. v. Von Zellen, 267 Mich. 533, 255 N.W. 424, 1934 Mich. LEXIS 585 (1934).

3168. Bope v. Ferris, 77 Mich. 299, 43 N.W. 874 (1889).

3169. Marx v. Smith, 111 Mich. 125, 69 N.W. 150 (1896).

3170. Bullard v. Green, 10 Mich. 268 (1862).

3171. Freeman v. Wozniak, 241 Mich. App. 633, 617 N.W.2d 46 (2000) (error).

3172. Moore v. Smith, 103 Mich. 387, 61 N.W. 538 (1894) (purchaser to whom the deed ran personally had bought the property at the sale in the interests of her infant ward).

3173. Ample opportunity to increase bid

Where defendant in foreclosure of a land contract refused to increase the bid on a resale and also refused plaintiff's offer of a six-months' option to purchase the property at the amount of the sale bid, or to take a deed conditioned upon making payment of the unpaid balance, the court did not abuse its discretion in refusing to order a resale.—James S. Holden Co. v. Applebaum, 267 Mich. 632, 255 N.W. 601 (1934).

3174. West v. Davis, 29 F. Cas. 714 (C.C.D. Mich. 1847) (No. 17,422).

Carlisle v. Dunlap, 203 Mich. 602, 169 N.W. 936 (1918).

Carpenter v. Smith, 147 Mich. App. 560, 383 N.W.2d 248 (1985) (inadequacy of price was not gross).

3175. Detroit & Sec. Trust Co. v. Tuller Hotel Co., 253 Mich. 415, 235 N.W. 203 (1931).

Degree of inadequacy

That mortgaged premises sold under a decree of foreclosure brought $350, though appearing to be worth $400 in cash, and $700 on long time, did not warrant a setting aside of the sale.—Bullard v. Green, 10 Mich. 268 (1862).

where the mortgagee is the purchaser.[3176]

§ 1022.   —Laches and Limitations

Laches will bar the vacation of a foreclosure sale. Even a delay of six months, under some circumstances, may preclude the granting of relief.

A party who seeks to have a sale vacated must move promptly, at least after the party becomes aware of the facts that furnish the ground for complaint.[3177] Unreasonable delay,[3178] such as until after the period of redemption has expired,[3179] will warrant refusal of relief, at least if merely technical irregularities are urged as grounds for relief,[3180] and in the absence of excuse for the delay.[3181]

Intervening rights of third parties are also a factor for consideration in determining whether delay has been unreasonable.[3182]

The purchaser's title may, of course, become indefeasible through adverse possession for the requisite length of time.[3183] Even a delay of six months, under some circumstances, may preclude relief.[3184]

§ 1023.   —Procedure and Relief

Where the sale is to one other than the mortgagee, or when the rights of a third party have subsequently arisen, the sale will not be vacated without notice to the third party.

Where the sale is to a third party other than the mortgagee, or when the rights of a third party have subsequently arisen, the sale will not be vacated without giving notice to that third party and giving that party an opportunity to be heard.[3185]

A petition to vacate the sale must contain an offer of payment to the plaintiff, or to increase the sum bid at the sale if a new sale is ordered.[3186] A petition may have to be accompanied by adequate security and contain an offer to redeem or procure a higher bidder.[3187]

The validity of the foreclosure proceedings or the judgment cannot be assailed on an application for a writ of execution for a deficiency.[3188]

3176. Nugent v. Nugent, 54 Mich. 557, 20 N.W. 584 (1884).

3177. Lyon v. Brunson, 48 Mich. 194, 12 N.W. 32 (1882).

3178. Goodwin v. Burns, 21 Mich. 211 (1870).

3179. Madill v. Michigan Nat'l Bank, 302 Mich. 251, 4 N.W.2d 538 (1942).

3180. Madill v. Michigan Nat'l Bank, 302 Mich. 251, 4 N.W.2d 538 (1942).

Goodwin v. Burns, 21 Mich. 211 (1870).

3181. Bullard v. Green, 10 Mich. 268 (1862).

3182. Leonard v. Taylor, 12 Mich. 398 (1864).

3183. Chesebro v. Powers, 70 Mich. 370, 38 N.W. 283 (1888).

3184. Bullard v. Green, 10 Mich. 268 (1862).

3185. Jewett v. Morris, 41 Mich. 689, 3 N.W. 186 (1879).

Lawrence v. Jarvis, 36 Mich. 281 (1877).

3186. Leonard v. Taylor, 12 Mich. 398 (1864).

3187. Thomas v. Burt, 52 Mich. 489, 18 N.W. 231 (1884).

3188. Corning v. Burton, 102 Mich. 96, 62 N.W. 1040 (1894).

Wallace v. Field, 56 Mich. 3, 22 N.W. 91 (1885).

Relief. Aside from jurisdictional questions, "on an application of this kind, the Court cannot inquire into the regularity of the foreclosure proceedings, or whether the decree was for a greater or less sum than it should have been."[3189] Thus, it is error to modify the judgment in an action to vacate a foreclosure sale.[3190]

Consistently, if the sale is found void, the foreclosure proceedings as a whole need not be set aside, but the mortgagor is given a fixed time in which to pay the amount due. In default of payment of that amount, a resale should be permitted.[3191]

A complaint to set aside the foreclosure may be considered as a complaint to redeem, though it contains no specific prayer for that relief and no express offer to pay the mortgage debt.[3192] Conversely, in a case where the mortgagor, in a suit to set aside the foreclosure, seeks exercise of the court's power to restrain the purchaser from interfering with the mortgagor's possession, the court may then give the purchaser possession, notwithstanding the absence of any demand by the purchaser for affirmative relief.[3193]

In the end, the court may always apply its equitable powers to resolve the issues presented by the parties in an effort to vacate a foreclosure sale.[3194]

§ 1024.   Rights of Purchaser

Generally, the mortgagee, by the sale and deed, gets all the right, title, and interest in and to the mortgaged premises that the mortgagor possessed at the time of execution of the mortgage, or that the mortgagor subsequently acquired.

Generally, the purchaser gets all the right, title, and interest in and to the mortgaged premises that the mortgagor possessed at the time of execution of the mortgage, or that the mortgagor subsequently acquired.[3195] But that title is inchoate

---

3189. Bullard v. Green, 10 Mich. 268 (1862).

3190. Michigan Trust Co. v. Cody, 264 Mich. 258, 249 N.W. 844 (1933).

3191. O'Connor v. Keenan, 132 Mich. 646, 94 N.W. 186 (1903).

3192. Brown v. Burney, 128 Mich. 205, 87 N.W. 221 (1901).

3193. Mason v. American Trust Co., 275 Mich. 651, 267 N.W. 757 (1936).

3194. Not set aside

In a case where a mortgagee took a new mortgage from the purchaser at a foreclosure sale for part of the purchase price, the balance being paid by one of the heirs of the original mortgagor, who allowed the title to be taken by such purchaser, chancery would not set aside the sale at the instance of the heirs, without reviving the original mortgage.—De May v. Defer, 103 Mich. 239, 61 N.W. 524 (1894).

3195. Hanson v. Huetter, 339 Mich. 130, 62 N.W.2d 663 (1954).

Von Meding v. Strahl, 319 Mich. 598, 30 N.W.2d 363 (1948) (overruled on other grounds as stated in Schmidt v. Eger, 94 Mich. App. 728, 289 N.W.2d 851 (1980)).

Stolte v. Krentel, 271 Mich. 98, 260 N.W. 127 (1935).

Cooley v. Marx, 17 Mich. App. 470, 169 N.W.2d 655 (1969).

One cotenant purchasing at foreclosure obtains rights of all cotenants

A cotenant of property owned in tenant-in-common relationship could purchase the property at mortgage foreclosure sale so that title vested in such cotenant as sole owner, where there was no agreement that he would bid in the property for mutual benefit of himself and other heirs, it did not appear that he did anything to cause anyone else to believe he was acting for anyone else in bidding in the property at sale, all heirs knew, or with exercise of reasonable diligence would have known, that someone would bid in the property at sale, and none of heirs had made any kind of tender to him either before or after commencement

in that it is subject to be defeated by redemption.[3196]

The mortgagor is presumed to have been the owner of the inheritance, and the purchaser gets the benefit of this presumption.[3197]

Accordingly, appurtenances, such as an appurtenant easement for a right of way in favor of the mortgaged premises, pass to the purchaser at the sale.[3198] They pass even if they are not specifically mentioned in the foreclosure deed.[3199] Similarly, good will, if mortgaged, will pass with the property to the purchaser.[3200]

On the other hand, a purchaser cannot acquire by foreclosure any greater right than the mortgagor had.[3201]

A mortgagee who purchases has the same rights as any other person purchasing at the sale.[3202]

The rights acquired by the purchaser do not merge into a quitclaim deed from the mortgagors, and are not affected by any restrictions entered into by the mortgagors after the giving of the mortgage.[3203]

The purchaser has no right to have a receiver appointed in the absence of a showing that conditions have changed since the time of his or her purchase at the sale.[3204]

A mortgagor's spouse may buy the property from the purchaser after the foreclosure has become absolute and, upon doing so, acquires a good title as against a second mortgagee.[3205]

A purchaser at a foreclosure sale who has not taken possession is not subject to premises liability prior to the expiration of the redemption period.[3206]

§ 1025. —Relief Against Title Defects

Though, to some extent at least, the rule of caveat emptor applies to mortgage foreclosure sales, the purchaser, if he or she buys in good faith and without notice, has rights as a bona fide purchaser.

Generally, the rule of caveat emptor applies to mortgage foreclosure sales.[3207]

of suit to have the property declared to be held in trust for decedent's estate.—Fick v. Fick, 38 Mich. App. 226, 196 N.W.2d 18 (1972).

3196. Hanson v. Huetter, 339 Mich. 130, 62 N.W.2d 663 (1954).

Stout v. Keyes, 2 Doug. 184 (Mich. 1845).

3197. Wyman v. Baer, 46 Mich. 418, 9 N.W. 455 (1881).

3198. First Nat'l Trust & Sav. Bank v. Smith, 284 Mich. 579, 280 N.W. 57 (1938).

3199. First Nat'l Trust & Sav. Bank v. Smith, 284 Mich. 579, 280 N.W. 57 (1938).

3200. Detroit Trust Co. v. Detroit City Service Co., 262 Mich. 14, 247 N.W. 76 (1933).

3201. Kirchen v. Remenga, 291 Mich. 94, 288 N.W. 344 (1939).

3202. Ledyard v. Phillips, 47 Mich. 305, 11 N.W. 170 (1882).

3203. Shedd v. Krushinski, 298 Mich. 160, 298 N.W. 490 (1941).

3204. Janower v. F.M. Sibley Lumber Co., 245 Mich. 571, 222 N.W. 736 (1929).

3205. Gantz v. Toles, 40 Mich. 725 (1879).

3206. Kubczak v. Chemical Bank & Trust Co., 456 Mich. 653, 575 N.W.2d 745 (1998).

3207. Stolte v. Krentel, 271 Mich. 98, 260 N.W. 127 (1935).

At the same time, the purchaser, to the extent that he or she acts in good faith and without notice, has rights as a bona fide purchaser.[3208] The purchaser can maintain a suit to quiet title or for reformation.[3209] Or the purchaser may attempt to bolster his or her title with a conveyance from the mortgagor.[3210]

A foreclosure purchaser under a mortgage given by a mortgagor who has no right to the land described is not entitled to relief against a third person, on the ground that the latter has fraudulently obtained the title to the land of the actual owner, notwithstanding that the owner may have intended, without consideration, to put the title where it would have inured to the benefit of the purchaser, but was deceived into giving it to the third person.[3211]

§ 1026.   Conveyance to Purchaser

The officer making the sale must execute a sale deed and endorse upon the deed the time when it becomes operative in case the premises are not redeemed according to law.

Filing for record. The officer making the sale must execute a sale deed and endorse upon the deed the time when it becomes operative in case the premises are not redeemed according to law. The officer must record the deed as soon as practicable, and within 20 days after the sale, with the register of deeds.[3212] There is a presumption that the deed has been filed as required, and the presumption prevails far enough at least to throw the burden of proof on the party questioning the performance of this duty.[3213]

The filing of the deed for record before confirmation does not make the recording irregular.[3214]

Execution and delivery. An officer who has knowledge of the reopening and postponement of a sale has no right to execute or deliver a deed to the first purchasers.[3215]

Clerical errors. The court rendering the decree has authority, on the petition of the purchaser and on notice to all persons interested, to correct a clerical error in the description of the property in the deed, if the error is apparent from the face of

Janower v. F.M. Sibley Lumber Co., 245 Mich. 571, 222 N.W. 736 (1929).

3208. Smith, Hinchman & Grylls v. Campau Holbrook Co., 168 F. 2d 326 (6th Cir. Mich. 1948).

Miller v. Clark, 56 Mich. 337, 23 N.W. 35 (1885).

Christensen v. Christensen, 126 Mich. App. 640, 337 N.W.2d 611 (1983) (mere occupancy not notice to purchasers).

Bona fides

A foreclosure purchaser is not to be charged as a purchaser in bad faith merely because he buys with notice of an outstanding title derived from the mortgagor himself.—Miller v. Clark, 56 Mich. 337, 23 N.W. 35 (1885).

3209. Banks v. Allen, 127 Mich. 80, 86 N.W. 383 (1901).

Merrifield v. Ingersoll, 61 Mich. 4, 27 N.W. 714 (1886).

3210. Norris v. Michigan State Ins. Co., 51 Mich. 621, 17 N.W. 207 (1883).

3211. Waterman v. Seeley, 28 Mich. 77 (1873).

3212. MCLS § 600.3130.

3213. Sinclair v. Learned, 51 Mich. 335, 16 N.W. 672 (1883).

3214. Miller v. McLaughlin, 141 Mich. 433, 104 N.W. 780 (1905).

3215. Miller v. Miller, 48 Mich. 311, 12 N.W. 209 (1882).

the record.[3216] The correction may be made by the execution and delivery, pursuant to an order of the court, of a second deed, reciting that it is given for the purpose of correcting the first deed.[3217]

Appurtenances. As already noted, an appurtenance such as a right of way that has been created in favor of the mortgaged premises passes to the purchaser, though it is not specifically sold or described in the deed. Accordingly, a transfer not specifically mentioning the right of way is not void.[3218]

§ 1027. Liens, Encumbrances, and Taxes

The title of a purchaser on valid foreclosure of a mortgage regularly recorded relates back to the delivery of the mortgage, as against all intervening purchasers and encumbrancers who are made parties or who become interested *pendente lite*.

The title of a purchaser on valid foreclosure of a mortgage regularly recorded relates back to the delivery of the mortgage, as against all intervening purchasers and encumbrancers who are made parties or who become interested *pendente lite*.[3219] Accordingly, when a junior mortgage is foreclosed, nothing more than the equity of redemption can be sold without the consent of prior mortgagees, under any judgment made in the case.[3220] Nevertheless, the junior mortgagee on foreclosure and purchase at the sale succeeds to the mortgagor's rights, and can make any defense against other mortgagees that the mortgagor could have made.[3221]

Where there are taxes due under such circumstances that a failure to pay them within a short time would determine the right of redemption, the taxes may be specifically provided for in the judgment and the amount thereof included in the sale price.[3222]

A foreclosure sale for installments due on a mortgage is not presumed to have been made subject to other installments.[3223]

The mortgagee of a subdivision, subsequent to the platting of the land, acquires title upon foreclosure of the mortgage subject to the irrevocable dedication

---

3216. Walsh v. Colby, 153 Mich. 602, 117 N.W. 207 (1908).

Survey line

Line established by survey in conformity to calls and distances of plaintiff's record title, absent claim by defendants to anything more than they owned, was proper line between plaintiff's and defendants' properties despite error in description in sheriff's deed under mortgage foreclosure by which defendants' predecessor in title obtained title to land creating overlap along plaintiff's boundary.—Cooley v. Marx, 17 Mich. App. 470, 169 N.W.2d 655 (1969).

3217. Walsh v. Colby, 153 Mich. 602, 117 N.W. 207 (1908).

3218. Flax v. Mutual Bldg. & Loan Ass'n, 198 Mich. 676, 165 N.W. 835 (1917).

3219. Ruggles v. First Nat'l Bank, 43 Mich. 192, 5 N.W. 257 (1880).

Gamble v. Horr, 40 Mich. 561 (1879).

3220. Jerome v. McCarter, 94 U.S. 734, 24 L. Ed. 136 (1877).

3221. Thompson v. Jarvis, 39 Mich. 689 (1878).

3222. Union Trust Co. v. Electric Park Amusement Co., 168 Mich. 574, 135 N.W. 115 (1912).

3223. Millard v. Truax, 50 Mich. 343, 15 N.W. 501 (1883).

of the lands designated in the plat as parks.[3224]

A deed of mortgaged premises following a foreclosure sale does not convey a claimed easement of way appurtenant the property if the mortgagor had no such easement or other interest in the alleged servient estate when the mortgagor executed the mortgage purporting to mortgage and convey the easement.[3225]

§ 1028.   Effect of Irregularities in Decree or Sale

A sale is not necessarily invalid for being made for more than was in fact due, but if nothing in fact was due at the time of foreclosure, the deed passes no title.

If a defect in the decree or proceedings is not jurisdictional,[3226] and at least if the irregularity is harmless,[3227] the sale is not void, and a collateral attack will not be sustained.[3228]

A purchaser under a fatally defective foreclosure is only in the position of a mortgagee and can only recover possession by new foreclosure proceedings.[3229]

On that point, a mortgage foreclosure sale is not necessarily invalid for being made for more than was in fact due. The excessive claim becomes important only when the mortgagor attempts to redeem from the sale, its importance depending on its magnitude or apparent want of good faith.[3230] However, if no money is actually due on the mortgage at the time of foreclosure, the officer's deed passes no title.[3231]

An unnecessary attempt to perfect foreclosure proceedings by securing an order for the enrollment of the decree *nunc pro tunc* does not affect the rights of the purchaser.[3232]

If a purchaser at a sale under an invalid foreclosure afterwards acquires the equity of redemption, it will operate to perfect the purchaser's own previous conveyance of the land, and to discharge the purchaser from liability on the

3224. Kirchen v. Remenga, 291 Mich. 94, 288 N.W. 344 (1939).

3225. Von Meding v. Strahl, 319 Mich. 598, 30 N.W.2d 363 (1948) (overruled as stated in Schmidt v. Eger, 94 Mich. App. 728, 289 N.W.2d 851 (1980)) (right of way to which mortgagor had no right could not pass to foreclosure purchaser).

3226. Absence of order confirming

Absence of order confirming sale under decree of foreclosure of mortgage on insane person's property does not render sale a nullity.—McPherson v. Waters, 228 Mich. 410, 200 N.W. 146 (1924).

3227. Erroneous date of adjournment

That commissioner's report and deed gave erroneous date for adjournment of foreclosure sale was harmless irregularity, and court properly allowed correction.—Central Trust Co. v. Breitenwischer, 259 Mich. 532, 244 N.W. 153 (1932).

3228. Death of mortgagor before confirmation

Where a judgment in mortgage foreclosure proceedings is entered, and sale is made under the judgment during the lifetime of the mortgagor, a confirmation of the sale after his death, without making his legal representatives parties, is not an irregularity that exposes the proceedings to attack by an action for possession.—Hochgraf v. Hendrie, 66 Mich. 556, 34 N.W. 15 (1887).

3229. Nims v. Sherman, 43 Mich. 45, 4 N.W. 434 (1880).

3230. Millard v. Truax, 50 Mich. 343, 15 N.W. 501 (1883).

3231. Bowen v. Brogan, 119 Mich. 218, 77 N.W. 942 (1899).

3232. Gerasimos v. Wartell, 244 Mich. 588, 222 N.W. 211 (1928).

covenants of warranty, if that is the purpose of the parties.[3233]

§ 1029.   Possession By Purchaser

Delay does not generally operate to defeat the purchaser's right to possession, unless the delay is for the statutory period of limitation, but the right may nevertheless be qualified by delay, depending upon the circumstances. Summary proceedings allow the purchaser to obtain possession from an occupant holding over.

The purchaser's right to possession is, of course, unaffected by any equities that may exist between the defendant in possession and any codefendants in the foreclosure suit.[3234] A right of possession may accrue to the purchaser under a foreclosure of a mortgage on the property of an incompetent before the order confirming the sale is made.[3235]

Delay does not generally operate to defeat the mortgagee's right to possession, unless the delay is for the statutory period of limitation.[3236] Also, if any new arrangement is expressly made between the parties, the original decree may not be controlling, and in those circumstances, the parties cannot be required to try their rights upon affidavits, and the possession must be sought in some way in which the nature and extent of the rights under the new contract can be litigated.[3237]

Statutory summary proceeding. A statutory summary proceeding is provided in cases, inter alia, when any person continues in possession of any premises sold by virtue of a mortgage after the expiration of the time limited by law for the redemption of the premises.[3238]

If the occupant asserts claims that have not been foreclosed by the decree, a summary possessory proceeding will not lie.[3239]

Facts that might warrant the granting of equitable relief to the occupant are not a defense as such to the summary proceeding.[3240]

Action for title, interest, or possession. No action for title to, interest in, or possession of mortgaged real property may be maintained by a mortgagee or a mortgagee's assigns or representatives for the recovery of the mortgaged premises until the title has become absolute upon foreclosure.[3241] Thus, a prior mortgagee who has obtained possession from the mortgagor during a foreclosure suit of a

---

3233. Michigan State Ins. Co. v. Soule, 51 Mich. 312, 16 N.W. 662 (1883).

3234. Ketchum v. Robinson, 48 Mich. 618, 12 N.W. 877 (1882).

3235. McPherson v. Waters, 228 Mich. 410, 200 N.W. 146 (1924).

3236. Pere Marquette R. Co. v. Graham, 136 Mich. 444, 99 N.W. 408 (1904).

3237. Ramsdell v. Maxwell, 32 Mich. 285 (1875).

3238. MCLS § 600.5714.

3239. Martin v. Brown, 49 Mich. 565, 14 N.W. 497 (1883).

3240. Deceit

Any deceit on the part of the mortgagee that would still authorize the redemption by the mortgagor in equity was ground for application to a court of equity, but no defense to a summary proceeding for possession of the land after expiration of the redemption period.—Roff v. Miller, 189 Mich. 558, 155 N.W. 517 (1915).

3241. MCLS § 600.2932.

subsequent mortgage cannot retain possession after a sale on the foreclosure of that subsequent mortgage.[3242]

If an action for possession is brought by the mortgagee after the running of the five-year limitation statute pertaining to judicial sales,[3243] the mortgagor may not affirmatively defend by attacking the foreclosure proceedings or asserting claims of fraud arising prior to foreclosure.[3244]

Writ of assistance. A writ of assistance is a regular process for carrying out a decree of possession, and it lies on foreclosure sales.[3245]

Generally, the applicant must show a demand for possession and a refusal.[3246] The demand is regularly made by showing the deed and a certified copy of the order of confirmation to the occupant.[3247] Formal service of a copy of the order of confirmation is not required under all circumstances, however.[3248]

The writ will ordinarily lie against anyone who was bound by the decree, such as a party who claims under a defendant.[3249] But if the defendant asserts claims under things like tax titles, which have not been litigated, the writ will not lie,[3250] nor will the writ lie against a mortgagor who claims under an arrangement made subsequent to the sale.[3251]

Conversely, however, the defendant cannot set up as a defense any equities existing prior to the sale.[3252] Any matter set up in opposition to the issuance of the writ cannot affect the foreclosure decree.[3253]

The objections to the issuance of the writ must be made formally. A mere verbal statement will not suffice.[3254]

§ 1030.   Crops

The mortgagor probably is entitled to crops harvested during the redemption period.

Before the statutory allowance of the right of redemption, there was a

3242. Crippen v. Morrison, 13 Mich. 23 (1864).

3243. MCLS § 600.5801.

3244. Olmstead v. Johnson, 313 Mich. 57, 20 N.W.2d 809 (1945).

3245. Ramsdell v. Maxwell, 32 Mich. 285 (1875).

3246. Howard v. Bond, 42 Mich. 131, 3 N.W. 289 (1879).

3247. Hart v. Lindsay, Walk. Ch. 144 (Mich. 1843).

3248. Detroit Trust Co. v. Dunitz, 59 F.2d 905 (6th Cir. Mich. 1932).

3249. Benhard v. Darrow, Walk. Ch. 519 (Mich. 1844) (service of order upon one not party to suit).

3250. Hayward v. Kinney, 84 Mich. 591, 48 N.W. 170 (1891).

3251. Ramsdell v. Maxwell, 32 Mich. 285 (1875).

3252. Ketchum v. Robinson, 48 Mich. 618, 12 N.W. 877 (1882).

3253. Howe v. Lemon, 47 Mich. 544, 11 N.W. 379 (1882).

3254. Aldrich v. Donovan, 111 Mich. 525, 69 N.W. 1108 (1897).

presumption that the bid included any unharvested crops on the premises.[3255]
Accordingly, they ordinarily passed with the land to the purchaser at the sale.[3256]
The rule was subject, of course, to any contractual arrangement to the contrary,[3257]
at least if the purchaser's promise was supported by consideration,[3258] and if the
mortgagor's or occupant's equities under the arrangement were not cut off by the
sale.[3259]

In a proper case, and on proper application, the court could perhaps provide
for the preservation of the growing crops until possession was given to the
purchaser.[3260]

Since the advent[3261] of the statutory right to redeem,[3262] the appellate courts
made a ruling that might be construed as indicating that crops growing on the land
at the time of the sale pass to the purchaser, notwithstanding the mortgagor's
subsequent period of redemption.[3263]

§ 1031.   Rents and Profits

**Generally, the mortgagor is entitled to rents and profits
from the mortgaged premises during the redemption
period, unless they are properly assigned.**

As a general rule, the mortgagor is entitled to rents and profits from the
mortgaged premises during the redemption period.[3264] The mortgagor's general
creditors may claim an interest in the rents and profits for that period.[3265]

The statutory limitation on actions for possession by a mortgagee until after
the mortgagee obtains absolute title[3266] prevents the mortgagor from bargaining
away his or her right to rents and profits accruing before expiration of the
redemption period.[3267] At least, the mortgagor may not do so unless the assignment

3255. Ledyard v. Phillips, 47 Mich. 305, 11 N.W. 170 (1882).

3256. Dayton v. Dakin's Estate, 103 Mich. 65, 61 N.W. 349 (1894).

Ledyard v. Phillips, 47 Mich. 305, 11 N.W. 170 (1882).

Ruggles v. First Nat'l Bank, 43 Mich. 192, 5 N.W. 257 (1880).

Scriven v. Moote, 36 Mich. 64 (1877).

3257. Dayton v. Dakin's Estate, 103 Mich. 65, 61 N.W. 349 (1894).

3258. Dayton v. Dakin's Estate, 103 Mich. 65, 61 N.W. 349 (1894).

3259. Scriven v. Moote, 36 Mich. 64 (1877).

3260. Ruggles v. First Nat'l Bank, 43 Mich. 192, 5 N.W. 257 (1880).

3261. 1899 Pub. Acts 200.

Mutual Benefit Life Ins. Co. v. Wetsman, 277 Mich. 322, 269 N.W. 189 (1936).

3262. MCLS § 600.3140.

3263. Diefenbaker v. Post, 276 Mich. 514, 267 N.W. 652 (1936).

3264. Meyers v. Ermolik, 301 Mich. 284, 3 N.W.2d 276 (1942).

3265. Detroit Trust Co. v. Detroit City Service Co., 262 Mich. 14, 247 N.W. 76 (1933).

3266. MCLS § 600.2932.

3267. Detroit Trust Co. v. Lipsitz, 264 Mich. 404, 249 N.W. 892 (1933).

Hazeltine v. Granger, 44 Mich. 503, 7 N.W. 74 (1880).

Wagar v. Stone, 36 Mich. 364 (1877).

Contract void; estoppel

Purported mortgaging of rents and profits in first mortgage was void, and second mortgagee, which first foreclosed, was not estopped to claim rents and profits, as against the first mortgagee, merely by reason of having taken the second mortgage "subject to" the first.—American Trust Co. v. Michigan Trust Co., 263 Mich. 337, 248 N.W. 829 (1933).

is executed subsequent to the date of the mortgage.[3268]

By separate statutes, a mortgage or a land contract may authorize the assignment of rents and profits of property mortgaged under a trust mortgage or deed of trust,[3269] or a mortgage of commercial or industrial property.[3270] These statutes do not require the taking of possession or the appointment of a receiver as a condition precedent to the collection of rents. Where necessary, the mortgagee may obtain the aid of the court, by appointment of receiver, to make collections. The collection of rents or profits is not merely an incident to the right of possession of the land, but is a distinct remedy and additional security. Without the court's aid, the mortgagee is in the shoes of the mortgagor until the debt is paid, with all the mortgagor's rights to the rents and profits.[3271]

Given that the jurisdiction of the chancery court to foreclose mortgages was statutory, it did not include the power to determine the mortgagor's liability for rents collected after the sale became absolute.[3272]

Interest payments on a land contract entered into by the mortgagor as vendor are comparable to rents and profits. Accordingly, the payments accruing during the period of redemption belong to the mortgagor-vendor's estate in the absence of assignment.[3273]

§ 1032.   Disposition of Proceeds

The proceeds of a foreclosure sale ordinarily go to pay the mortgage debt, with the balance going to the mortgagor.

Under the Revised Judicature Act of 1961, the proceeds of the sale of real property under a mortgage or a land contract foreclosed by suit must be applied to the discharge of the debt adjudged by the court to be due, and of the costs awarded. If there is any surplus, it must be brought into court for the use of the persons entitled to it, subject to the order of the court.[3274] The mortgagor and mortgagee may, nevertheless, effectively agree to a special disposition, subject to the rights of third parties.[3275]

Any party to the action may move for the disposition of the surplus in accordance with the rights of those entitled to it.[3276] Parties interested in the equity of redemption and junior encumbrancers are entitled to be heard on the matter of the

---

3268. First Nat'l Bank v. Gillam, 123 Mich. 112, 81 N.W. 979 (1900).

After default for consideration

In a case in which the assignment had been made after default and in consideration of forbearance from threatened foreclosure, the assignment was enforced.—Mutual Benefit Life Ins. Co. v. Wetsman, 277 Mich. 322, 269 N.W. 189 (1936).

3269. MCLS §§ 554.211 et seq.

3270. MCLS § 554.231.

3271. Security Trust Co. v. Sloman, 252 Mich. 266, 233 N.W. 216 (1930).

3272. Dunitz v. Braver, 252 Mich. 111, 233 N.W. 347 (1930).

Union Trust Co. v. Detroit Trust Co., 243 Mich. 451, 220 N.W. 728 (1928).

3273. Meyers v. Ermolik, 301 Mich. 284, 3 N.W.2d 276 (1942).

3274. MCLS § 600.3135.

3275. Perrin v. Kellogg, 38 Mich. 720 (1878).

3276. MCR 3.410.

Stewart v. Isbell, 155 Mich. App. 65, 399 N.W.2d 440 (1986).

surplus proceeds.[3277] The surplus is personalty, and in event of the death of the owner of the equity of redemption, his or her personal representatives are entitled to be heard.[3278]

Generally, the surplus over and above what the judgment has set forth as what the mortgagor is required to pay for the lien of the mortgage, interest, costs, and the amounts paid by the mortgagee to protect his or her rights as against, for example, liens for delinquent taxes,[3279] will be paid to the mortgagor or the mortgagor's successor.[3280] In connection with the matter of succession to rights by assignment, it must be kept in mind that the assignee can ordinarily claim no greater rights by virtue of the assignment than his or her assignor had.[3281]

The rule that the assignee can acquire no greater rights than the assignor is, however, subject to qualification in so far as the assignee may be able to claim rights as a bona fide purchaser for value and without notice.[3282]

A junior mortgagee who pays the residue of the purchase money due on the land as part of the consideration for the mortgage is entitled pro tanto to a preference over the holder of a senior mortgage.[3283]

Where a mortgage is given to secure two notes and the mortgage and notes are assigned, one note being endorsed in blank and the other without recourse, the proceeds of the sale of the premises must be applied pro rata in reduction of both notes, leaving the endorser liable only for the proportionate share of the deficiency according to the amount of the respective notes.[3284]

Where the assignee of a mortgage assigns it as security for a debt that is less than the amount due on the mortgage, the assignee is entitled to the excess.[3285]

Where one of two joint makers of a mortgage sells land to the mortgagee and takes in payment an assignment of an interest in the mortgage, the mortgagor is entitled, on foreclosure, to have that interest in the mortgage first satisfied.[3286]

3277. Smith v. Smith, 13 Mich. 258 (1865).

3278. Smith v. Smith, 13 Mich. 258 (1865).

3279. MCLS § 600.3145.

Taxes paid after foreclosure

A mortgagee paying taxes due after foreclosure was entitled to reimbursement out of the surplus on foreclosure sale.—Union Trust Co. v. Electric Park Amusement Co., 168 Mich. 574, 135 N.W. 115 (1912).

3280. Junior mortgagee

A junior mortgagee acquiring the title of the mortgagors by foreclosure of second mortgage and by deeds from mortgagors was entitled to a surplus from a foreclosure of the first mortgage.—Union Trust Co. v. Electric Park Amusement Co., 168 Mich. 574, 135 N.W. 115 (1912).

3281. Nonexistent excess

Where the amount of a mortgage was, for the mortgagor's benefit, recited to be $11,500 when in fact the debt was only $6,000, and the mortgagee bid in the property for a price exceeding $13,000 but did not pay the excess to the sheriff, the mortgagor could not recover the nonexistent "excess," and his assignee could not do so either.—First State Bank v. Grossman, 243 Mich. 369, 220 N.W. 726 (1928).

3282. Kent v. Mellus, 69 Mich. 71, 37 N.W. 48 (1888).

3283. Balen v. Mercier, 75 Mich. 42, 42 N.W. 666 (1889).

3284. English v. Carney, 25 Mich. 178 (1872).

3285. Moreland v. Houghton, 96 Mich. 346, 55 N.W. 979 (1893).

3286. Quinnin v. Brown, 72 Mich. 304, 40 N.W. 336 (1888).

G. DEFICIENCY DECREE AND PERSONAL LIABILITY

§ 1041. Contingent Personal Liability

The determination of personal liability in a foreclosure decree is contingent or provisional and, until a deficiency arises and the mortgagors or land-contract vendees are required to answer for it, the mortgagors or vendees are not bound to pay it even if responsible.

Under the Revised Judicature Act of 1961, the court must in the original decree in foreclosing a mortgage or a land contract determine which defendants, if any, are personally liable for the mortgage debt.[3287] Indeed, a court may proceed to fix the deficiency before the sale takes place, and specify in its judgment that if no bid equal to the upset price is made, title to property then vests in the vendors as if they had made the minimum bid.[3288]

The determination of personal liability in a foreclosure decree is contingent or provisional and, until a deficiency arises and the mortgagors or land-contract vendees are required to answer for it, the mortgagors or vendees are not bound to pay it even if responsible.[3289]

There is no implied covenant of personal liability on a mortgage.[3290] In the absence of an express promise in the mortgage or separate instrument, the mortgagee is limited to the mortgaged property.[3291]

The mortgage or note may by its terms preclude a deficiency decree, and those terms will be given effect even if the results indicate that the mortgagee has made a bad bargain.[3292] Also, a mortgagee may be estopped to claim a deficiency.[3293]

A deficiency decree on a land contract will not be entered that would result in a forfeiture contrary to equitable principles.[3294] Moreover, where the vendor

3287. MCLS § 600.3150.

Stewart v. Isbell, 155 Mich. App. 65, 399 N.W.2d 440 (1986).

3288. Kramer v. Davis, 371 Mich. 464, 124 N.W.2d 292 (1963).

3289. Kelly v. Gaukler, 164 Mich. 519, 129 N.W. 703 (1911).

Powers v. Golden Lumber Co., 43 Mich. 468, 5 N.W. 656 (1880).

Stewart v. Isbell, 155 Mich. App. 65, 399 N.W.2d 440 (1986).

3290. MCLS § 565.6.

3291. Heberling v. Palmer's Mobile Feed Service, Inc., 119 Mich. App. 150, 326 N.W.2d 404 (1982).

3292. Words of preclusion

Statement: "This note is secured by a real estate mortgage of even date and is without recourse only as to the mortgage," in a mortgage note precludes a deficiency decree.—Grover v. Gratiot Macomb Development Co., 257 Mich. 26, 240 N.W. 66 (1932).

3293. Smith v. Smith, 46 Mich. 301, 9 N.W. 425 (1881).

Innes v. Stewart, 36 Mich. 285 (1877).

3294. Forfeiture of land contracts, *see, supra,* Chapter 20.

Foreclosure of a land contract in accordance with contract

Where there was no provision in a land contract permitting vendors to declare whole sum due on default, interest to be sold on foreclosure is equitable title of vendee, and deficiency judgment against vendee for part of purchase price not due is improper, since to require sale to satisfy payments to become due in future would be to declare forfeiture, which court of equity may not do.— Cady v. Taggart, 223 Mich. 191, 193 N.W. 848 (1923).

declares the contract forfeited and takes immediate possession of the land, the vendor is without right to recover a deficiency.[3295]

Where a defendant is brought into the foreclosure suit merely by publication, and has not been personally served and has not appeared, no personal decree, such as a provision directing payment of a deficiency, can be rendered against that defendant.[3296] However, if the trial court finds that a particular defendant had no notice or knowledge of the foreclosure proceedings until served with a petition for execution for a deficiency, but the defendant has an opportunity for defense in a later proceeding and is unable to produce any defense, the resulting deficiency decree is binding.[3297]

§ 1042. Persons Liable

The court may decree payment of the balance of the debt remaining unsatisfied, after a sale of the mortgaged premises, against any other securing person as well as against the mortgagor.

Under the Revised Judicature Act of 1961, if the mortgage debt is secured by the obligation or other evidence of debt of any other person besides the mortgagor, the plaintiff may make that person a party to the proceeding. The court may decree payment of the balance of the debt remaining unsatisfied, after a sale of the mortgaged premises, against the other securing person as well as against the mortgagor. The court may enforce the decree against that person as in other cases.[3298] This type of provision is permissive only, and not mandatory.[3299] This remedy can only be enforced in cases clearly within the statute.[3300] To bring a third party within the application of this statute, the contract or promise must be shown to have been to pay the mortgage debt.[3301]

3295. Forfeiture of land contracts, *see, supra,* Chapter 20.

Dedmon v. Sarkesion, 252 Mich. 613, 233 N.W. 434 (1930).

Durda v. Chembar Development Corp., 95 Mich. App. 706, 291 N.W.2d 179 (1980).

3296. Stewart v. Eaton, 287 Mich. 466, 283 N.W. 651 (1939).

Innes v. Stewart, 36 Mich. 285 (1877).

3297. Dickerson v. Corning, 122 Mich. 631, 81 N.W. 575 (1900).

3298. MCLS § 600.3160.

Miller v. McLaughlin, 132 Mich. 234, 93 N.W. 435 (1903).

Michigan State Bank v. Trowbridge, 92 Mich. 217, 52 N.W. 632 (1892).

Guarantor of a land contract

In action for claim and delivery of property that was subject of conditional sales contract, in which original debtor filed no responsive pleading in cause, plaintiffs, after foreclosure sale of property,

could properly add guarantors of debt as parties liable for deficiency by way of amendment to complaint without court order.—Brunswick Corp. v. Starlite Lanes, Inc., 33 Mich. App. 490, 190 N.W.2d 302 (1971).

Personal liability of trustee

Under the circumstances of the case, a personal decree against a mortgagor individually on foreclosure was proper, though the mortgage had been executed by him in the capacity of trustee.—Hannah v. Carnahan, 65 Mich. 601, 32 N.W. 835 (1887).

3299. Steele v. Grove, 109 Mich. 647, 67 N.W. 963 (1896).

3300. Winsor v. Ludington, 77 Mich. 215, 43 N.W. 866 (1889).

Vaughan v. Black, 63 Mich. 215, 29 N.W. 523 (1886).

McCrickett v. Wilson, 50 Mich. 513, 15 N.W. 885 (1883).

3301. Winsor v. Ludington, 77 Mich. 215, 43 N.W. 866 (1889).

A grantee of the mortgagor, if the grantee assumes the mortgage and agrees to pay the same, may be held liable for a deficiency.[3302]

The fact that a mortgagor's grantee has in turn conveyed to another, who in turn has agreed to pay the mortgage, does not relieve the first grantee from the potential liability.[3303]

On the other hand, a party may not be held for a mere promise to buy the mortgage, as opposed to a promise to pay the same, a breach of the former promise rendering the promisor liable only for damages in some proceeding other than the foreclosure suit.[3304] Similarly, the rescission of the purchase contract relieves the purchasers of land who assume a mortgage as part of the contract of purchase from liability for a deficiency on the mortgage.[3305] The grantee of a mortgagor's interest under a void mortgage who assumes liability under the mortgage generally cannot be held liable under the mortgage.[3306] Of course, a grantee of a mortgagor who does not assume liability for the mortgage does not have to pay a deficiency upon foreclosure.[3307]

The assignees of a mortgagor or land-contract vendee is only liable under the mortgage if he or she expressly assumes that liability.[3308]

In a trust arrangement whereby contributions are taken from beneficiaries to make payments, but those contributions cannot be enforced, the beneficiaries are not

Vaughan v. Black, 63 Mich. 215, 29 N.W. 523 (1886).

3302. MCLS § 600.1405.

Frank v. Applebaum, 270 Mich. 402, 259 N.W. 302 (1935).

Keeler v. Richards Storage Corp., 260 Mich. 23, 244 N.W. 215 (1932).

Corning v. Burton, 102 Mich. 96, 62 N.W. 1040 (1894).

Smith v. Unger, 44 Mich. 22, 5 N.W. 1069 (1880).

Grantee of trust mortgagor

In suit to foreclose mortgage, where evidence disclosed that there was no valid agreement between trustee of trust mortgage and nonassuming grantee of mortgagor's grantee, extending mortgage indebtedness and suspending trustee's right to foreclose, the obligation of defendant mortgagor's grantee for mortgage debt, as either surety or quasi surety was not altered, hence defendant remained liable to pay the mortgage debt, which it had assumed and agreed to pay, as well as, any deficiency arising from sale of property at mortgage sale.—Union Guardian Trust Co. v. Marquette Park Co., 300 Mich. 89, 1 N.W.2d 464 (1942).

3303. Corning v. Burton, 102 Mich. 96, 62 N.W. 1040 (1894).

3304. Winsor v. Ludington, 77 Mich. 215, 43 N.W. 866 (1889).

3305. Capac State Sav. Bank v. McKnight, 34 Mich. App. 390, 191 N.W.2d 55 (1971).

3306. Schram v. Marion, 44 F. Supp. 760 (D. Mich. 1942).

3307. Mistaken assumption clause

In suit against mortgagors' grantee to recover amount due on certain notes and mortgages, assumption of mortgage clause in deed to grantee never became valid or enforceable as between grantors and grantee because inserted by mistake, without intent that liability should attach to grantee, and without any consideration, and that there was nothing to estop grantee from so contending.—Schram v. Marion, 44 F. Supp. 760 (D. Mich. 1942).

3308. Roberts v. Rubin, 13 Mich. App. 652, 164 N.W.2d 740 (1968).

Vendee's estate was liable

Where vendee's interest in a land contract had been assigned, but assignee had not assumed and agreed to pay the contract and there was no novation releasing vendee from liability, vendee's estate, and not assignee's estate, was liable for deficiency, if any, upon foreclosure sale, even though vendor failed to notify vendee of assignee's default in payments.—Taylor v. Groll, 288 Mich. 590, 286 N.W. 88 (1939).

liable for a deficiency.[3309]

§ 1043. Forum, Jurisdiction, and Time for Adjudication of Deficiency

Jurisdiction to render deficiency decrees is wholly statutory. Under the circuit court's power to determine liability in the original foreclosure judgment, a separate deficiency action is ordinarily unnecessary.

The jurisdiction of a former court of chancery to render deficiency decrees was wholly statutory.[3310] In a case in which no lien validly attached to be foreclosed, the court could not decree payment of a deficiency.[3311] On the other hand, in a default case, the court can grant a personal decree even where the mortgage lien is extinguished by the foreclosure of a senior mortgage.[3312]

The court may gain personal jurisdiction over a party liable for a deficiency under a land contract even after the report of sale, upon the plaintiff's amendment of the complaint to include that party.[3313]

Under the circuit court's power to determine liability in the original foreclosure judgment,[3314] a separate deficiency action is ordinarily unnecessary.[3315]

§ 1044. —Actions at Law

Generally, after the complaint for foreclosure has been filed, no proceeding can be maintained at law for the deficiency, but the rule does not apply to an action based solely upon a deficiency decree.

Under the Revised Judicature Act of 1961, after the complaint for foreclosure is filed, while the foreclosure action is pending, and after a decree is rendered on the complaint, no proceeding whatever may be had at law for the recovery of any part of the debt secured by the mortgage, unless authorized by the court.[3316] On the one hand, no subsequent deficiency proceeding may be had in an action at law without

---

3309. Frank v. Applebaum, 270 Mich. 402, 259 N.W. 302 (1935).

No assumption by trust beneficiaries

In action to foreclose mortgage on real estate subdivision, denial of deficiency decree against members of syndicate, who were beneficiaries of trust agreement covering property but who did not assume or agree to pay mortgage, was affirmed by equally divided court.—Rossman v. Marsh, 287 Mich. 580, 283 N.W. 696 (1939).

3310. Lutz v. Dutmer, 286 Mich. 467, 282 N.W. 431 (1938).

Harrow v. Metropolitan Life Ins. Co., 285 Mich. 349, 280 N.W. 785 (1938).

Shelden v. Erskine, 78 Mich. 627, 44 N.W. 146 (1889).

Vaughan v. Black, 63 Mich. 215, 29 N.W. 523 (1886).

Johnson v. Shepard, 35 Mich. 115 (1876).

3311. Moore v. Probst, 220 Mich. 497, 190 N.W. 188 (1922).

3312. Bartnik v. Samonek, 313 Mich. 464, 21 N.W.2d 817 (1946).

3313. Brunswick Corp. v. Starlite Lanes, Inc., 33 Mich. App. 490, 190 N.W.2d 302 (1971) (guarantor).

3314. MCLS § 600.3150.

3315. National Bank of Commerce v. Corliss, 225 Mich. 441, 196 N.W. 423 (1923).

3316. MCLS § 600.3105.

leave of court.[3317] But on the other hand, the statute properly applies only to remedies on the personal securities given with the mortgage, or that are intended to be secured by it, and only to the parties to those instruments, and those who are liable on them or properly made parties to the proceedings in foreclosure suit,[3318] so that the statute does not apply to an action based solely upon a deficiency decree.[3319] Further, it does not apply to an action begun by leave of the probate court upon the bond of an executor, conditioned upon the payment of the debts of the decedent, including the mortgage indebtedness in question, or to a case where proceedings for the foreclosure and for deficiency on the bond are ineffective.[3320]

If leave was required, a former court of chancery could not authorize an action at law for the deficiency until execution had been issued in chancery and returned unsatisfied. The statutory mode for collection of the deficiency by execution in chancery had to be resorted to before an action at law could be maintained.[3321] Furthermore, if the application to the chancery court for a deficiency decree was refused, no action at law could be maintained.[3322] But the required leave was not jurisdictional, and the omission to obtain leave was an irregularity that could be waived.[3323]

In an action of assumpsit on the mortgage note, following foreclosure proceedings in another state, culminating in a foreclosure judgment without personal service on the defendant or the defendant's appearance, the defendant may litigate the issue and extent of his or her liability on the mortgage note in the assumpsit action.[3324]

§ 1045.   Calculation of and Execution for Deficiency

The clerk of the court must, on application of the plaintiff and without notice to the defendant or the defendant's attorney, issue execution for the amount of the deficiency. Execution for a deficiency cannot be issued after the statutory time limitation has run against the decree.

3317. Stewart v. Eaton, 287 Mich. 466, 283 N.W. 651 (1939).

Innes v. Stewart, 36 Mich. 285 (1877).

3318. Culver v. Detroit Superior Court Judge, 57 Mich. 25, 23 N.W. 469 (1885).

3319. Union Guardian Trust Co. v. Rood, 308 Mich. 168, 13 N.W.2d 248 (1944).

Trust

Where a deed of trust contained a promise to pay the debts specified, with power of sale in the trustee, and the trustee sued to realize upon the security, without demanding any personal decree in case of a deficiency, and a decree was entered for the relief prayed, the cestuis que trust could, after sale under judgment resulting in a deficiency, maintain an action at law for the deficiency.— National City Bank v. Torrent, 130 Mich. 259, 89 N.W. 938 (1902).

3320. Culver v. Detroit Superior Court Judge, 57 Mich. 25, 23 N.W. 469 (1885).

3321. Shields v. Riopelle, 63 Mich. 458, 30 N.W. 90 (1886).

3322. Shields v. Riopelle, 63 Mich. 458, 30 N.W. 90 (1886).

3323. Stewart v. Eaton, 287 Mich. 466, 283 N.W. 651 (1939).

Culver v. Detroit Superior Court Judge, 57 Mich. 25, 23 N.W. 469 (1885).

3324. Low sale price

Where assumpsit is brought for the deficiency, and where circumstances are such that the defendant may defend on the ground that the property should have brought more than was bid by the purchaser, the burden of proving such fact is upon the defendant, the issue being, upon sufficient evidence, a question of fact.—Stewart v. Eaton, 287 Mich. 466, 283 N.W. 651 (1939).

The circuit court must provide in the judgment that upon the confirmation of the report of sale, if there is any part of the money decreed to be due left unpaid after applying the amount received on the sale, the clerk of the court must, on application of the plaintiff and without notice to the defendant or the defendant's attorney, issue execution for the amount of the deficiency.[3325]

The inadequacy of the price paid at the foreclosure sale does not justify the refusal to confirm the mortgage foreclosure sale and, likewise, cannot flaw the deficiency judgment resulting from that sale.[3326]

Execution for a deficiency cannot be issued after the statutory time limitation has run against the decree.[3327] But delay for a lesser period of time does not constitute laches.[3328]

In any proceeding in which it is sought to resist the issuance of an execution, the resistance must be made upon grounds consistent with the foreclosure decree.[3329] The burden of proving a ground for resistance, such as satisfaction of the decree, is upon the defendant so resisting.[3330]

3325. MCLS § 600.3150.

Stewart v. Isbell, 155 Mich. App. 65, 399 N.W.2d 440 (1986).

Release under trust deed

Trustee in a trust deed securing payment of bonds, acting on behalf of 93% of the bondholders, could release the mortgagor and his successor in interest from liability for deficiency in order to obtain confirmation of a foreclosure sale of property, but that the remaining and nonassenting seven percent of the bondholders were entitled to a deficiency decree.—Michigan Trust Co. v. Howe, Snow & Bertles Realty Co., 267 Mich. 1, 254 N.W. 826 (1934).

3326. United Growth Corp. v. Kelly Mortg. & Inv. Co., 86 Mich. App. 82, 272 N.W.2d 340 (1978).

3327. Albert v. Patterson, 167 Mich. 162, 132 N.W. 548 (1911).

Quinnin v. Quinnin, 144 Mich. 232, 107 N.W. 906 (1906).

3328. Wallace v. Field, 56 Mich. 3, 22 N.W. 91 (1885).

3329. Corning v. Burton, 102 Mich. 96, 62 N.W. 1040 (1894).

Haldane v. Sweet, 58 Mich. 429, 25 N.W. 383 (1885).

Ransom v. Sutherland, 46 Mich. 489, 9 N.W. 530 (1881).

3330. Ransom v. Sutherland, 46 Mich. 489, 9 N.W. 530 (1881).

Chapter 33

REDEMPTION OF MORTGAGE OR LAND CONTRACT

§ 1061. The Right of Redemption

A right of redemption is the right granted by statute to redeem property after it has been sold in foreclosure by suit or by advertisement. The mortgagor's equity of redemption is lost after a foreclosure, and only the right of redemption during the statutory period remains.

Law Reviews

Rita Subhedar, Comment: A Proposed State Response to the Michigan Housing Crisis, 11 J.L. Soc'y 173 (2009); Naseem Stecker and Mike Eidelbes, Up Front: Real Property and Consumer Law Sections Team up on "Ask The Lawyer" to Discuss Mortgage Foreclosures, 87 MI Bar Jnl. 8 (2008); Gregg A. Nathanson, Feature: Real Property Law: What's New in Residential Transactions?, 86 MI Bar Jnl. 16 (2007); Lawrence R. Shoffner, Real Property Law: Real Evidence: Special Rules for Real Estate Disputes, 80 MI Bar Jnl. 28 (2001).

The term "right of redemption" is a legal term of art used to define the right granted by statute to redeem property after it has been sold in foreclosure by suit or by advertisement.[3331]

Redemption is a transaction through which the mortgagor, by means of a payment or the performance of a condition, reacquires the title that may have passed under the mortgage or land contract, or divests the premises of the lien created by the mortgage or land contract.[3332]

The mortgagor's equity of redemption is lost after a foreclosure, and only the right of redemption during the statutory period remains.[3333] This right can neither be enlarged nor restricted by the courts.[3334] Absent some unusual circumstances or additional considerations not within the ambit of the statute pertaining to redemption from foreclosure, the court must follow the clear and plain meaning of the redemption statutes.[3335] In case of doubt as to the continued existence of the right of a mortgagor to redeem, the law will resolve the doubt in favor of the mortgagor,

3331. Russo v. Wolbers, 116 Mich. App. 327, 323 N.W.2d 385 (1982).

3332. Provision not mandatory

Provision in foreclosure decree authorizing lessee to redeem to protect its interests if lessor-mortgagor did not do so was not mandatory, and lessor was deprived of no legal right by lessee's failure to redeem.—Teal v. Hayes, 309 Mich. 221, 15 N.W.2d 139 (1944).

3333. Gerasimos v. Continental Bank, 237 Mich. 513, 212 N.W. 71 (1927).

3334. Gordon Grossman Bldg. Co. v. Elliott, 382 Mich. 596, 171 N.W.2d 441 (1969).

Detroit Trust Co. v. Detroit City Service Co., 262 Mich. 14, 247 N.W. 76 (1933).

Wood v. Button, 205 Mich. 692, 172 N.W. 422 (1919).

3335. No power to order conveyance

Where vendee was fully aware at least one week before expiration of redemption period that unless she followed one of statutory methods of redemption her property would be lost, yet she did nothing to preserve her right of redemption until after it had expired, it was improper to require vendor who had brought proceeding to foreclose a land contract and had purchased property at foreclosure sale to execute warranty deed in compliance with a land contract.—Gordon Grossman Bldg. Co. v. Elliott, 382 Mich. 596, 171 N.W.2d 441 (1969).

and permit redemption.[3336]

Under foreclosure by advertisement[3337] and foreclosure by suit,[3338] a redemption is complete when a party having the right to redeem pays within the proper time, to a proper person, the sum that was bid at the foreclosure sale, with interest from the time of the sale, and in case such payment is made to a register of deeds, the necessary fee.[3339]

Generally, the mortgagor cannot waive the equitable right to redeem by a stipulation in the mortgage itself, by any separate contemporaneous agreement, or by giving a deed intended as a mortgage.[3340] The courts have consistently given careful scrutiny to any transaction in which a mortgagor waives any alleged equitable or statutory right of redemption.[3341]

Nonetheless, in the absence of a contrary statutory provision, a mortgagor may sell and convey his or her equity of redemption to the mortgagee by a separate and distinct contract entered into in good faith and for good consideration.[3342] Likewise,

---

3336. Williams v. Bolt, 170 Mich. 517, 136 N.W. 472 (1912).

Right of grantor to redeem

Whether a deed to a trustee for the purpose of satisfying the claims of creditors be treated as an irrevocable power to convey and dispose of the land for the purposes of the trust, or as a mortgage, requiring foreclosure proceedings before sale, the grantor and those claiming under him have the right to redeem and to a reconveyance before the execution of the trust upon payment of said claims.—Webster v. Peet, 97 Mich. 326, 56 N.W. 558 (1893).

Right of mortgagor to redeem

Where a mortgagor refrains from making a redemption on promise of a third person to furnish him funds with which to make it, and such person thereafter fraudulently buys up the mortgage and cuts off redemption, the mortgagor will not be allowed specific performance of the contract to loan, but will be allowed to redeem.—Wilson v. Eggleston, 27 Mich. 257 (1873).

3337. MCLS § 600.3240.

3338. MCLS § 600.3140.

3339. Heimerdinger v. Heimerdinger, 299 Mich. 149, 299 N.W. 844 (1941).

Eberle v. Sambab, 248 Mich. 508, 227 N.W. 690 (1929) (mortgagor, having tendered amount due before expiration of redemption period, was entitled to redeem).

Acceptance of redemption money under one of two mortgages

Where a foreclosure has become absolute and the purchaser holds a second mortgage that the purchaser forecloses, and then accepts tender of redemption money, though the purchaser claims absolute title to the land, and retains not only the excess received on the first foreclosure but also the redemption money accepted on the second, the mortgagor's assignee is allowed to maintain an action to redeem from the first foreclosure.— Millard v. Truax, 50 Mich. 343, 15 N.W. 501 (1883).

Chattels and realty sold together

Where mortgaged chattels and realty of ice company may be sold to best advantage together, right of redemption must extend to both upon condition that receivers pay purchasers fair rental for period that possession of chattels is withheld plus amount to cover depreciation and loss of chattels so sold.—Detroit Trust Co. v. Detroit City Service Co., 262 Mich. 14, 247 N.W. 76 (1933).

Purchase of title not redemption

Where defendant was made a party to mortgage foreclosure proceedings simply because he was holder of second mortgage, his purchase of title from mortgagee after purchase by it at foreclosure sale before equity of redemption expired would not amount to redemption.—Steel v. Steel, 201 Mich. 424, 167 N.W. 1019 (1918).

3340. Hazeltine v. Granger, 44 Mich. 503, 7 N.W. 74 (1880).

Executory contract is not allowed

Mortgagor's release of equity of redemption cannot be done by a contemporaneous or subsequent executory contract by which the equity of redemption is to be forfeited if the mortgage debt is not paid on the day stated in such contract.— Russo v. Wolbers, 116 Mich. App. 327, 323 N.W.2d 385 (1982).

3341. Russo v. Wolbers, 116 Mich. App. 327, 323 N.W.2d 385 (1982).

3342. Requisites for sale of equity of redemption

Michigan adheres to the doctrine against clogging a mortgagor's equity of redemption; a mort-

all rights to redeem mortgaged real estate may be sold on execution in the manner prescribed for the sale of other real estate on execution. The sold equity of redemption may be redeemed, and the rights of any purchaser may be acquired in the same manner and upon the same terms and conditions as other real estate sold on execution.[3343]

A court's construction of an instrument in the form of an absolute deed or conveyance as security for the payment of a debt[3344] allows the equitable mortgagor to maintain an equitable action to redeem an instrument constituting a mortgage.[3345]

While a mortgagor's right of redemption is to be safeguarded, it is not superior to the mortgagee's right to collect the debt secured by the mortgage or land contract.[3346]

§ 1062.   Persons Entitled to Redeem

Generally, the mortgagor or, where applicable, the land-contract vendee; the mortgagor's or, where applicable, the land-contract vendee's heirs, executors, or administrators; or any person lawfully claiming under any of those persons; may redeem the premises sold.

Under foreclosure by advertisement[3347] and foreclosure by suit;[3348] the mortgagor or, where applicable, the land-contract vendee; the mortgagor's or, where applicable, the land-contract vendee's heirs, executors, or administrators; or any person lawfully claiming under any of those persons; may redeem the premises sold.[3349] The mortgagee of the interest of a land-contract vendee in a land contract is entitled to the same redemption rights to which the vendee is entitled.[3350] The

gagor may release his equity of redemption to the mortgagee for a good and valuable consideration when done voluntarily and there is no fraud and no undue influence brought to bear upon the mortgagor for that purpose by the mortgagee.—Russo v. Wolbers, 116 Mich. App. 327, 323 N.W.2d 385 (1982).

3343. MCLS §§ 600.6018, 600.6023, 600.6062.

3344. Wilson v. Potter, 339 Mich. 247, 63 N.W.2d 413 (1954).

Weise v. Anderson, 134 Mich. 502, 96 N.W. 575 (1903).

3345. Crawford v. Osmun, 70 Mich. 561, 38 N.W. 573 (1888).

Knowledge that deed is mortgage

In suit to enjoin party knowing deed in chain of title was mortgage from exercising dominion over property, defendant cannot be reimbursed for taxes in absence of evidence of amount.—Goodman v. Rott, 242 Mich. 198, 218 N.W. 761 (1928).

3346. Cox v. Townsend, 90 Mich. App. 12, 282 N.W.2d 223 (1979).

3347. MCLS § 600.3240.

3348. MCLS § 600.3140.

3349. Dodge v. Kennedy, 93 Mich. 547, 53 N.W. 795 (1892).

Powers v. Golden Lumber Co., 43 Mich. 468, 5 N.W. 656 (1880).

Administrator claiming fraud against creditors

The principal of a mortgage securing a debt from the mortgagor to his sister-in-law was made payable to the mortgagor's children; the interest being payable to the sister-in-law for life; mortgagor conveyed the equity of redemption to his son, and the sister-in-law foreclosed for default in payment of interest; administrator of the mortgagor, suing to set aside the conveyance to the son as fraudulent against creditors, was not entitled to redeem, except on the ground that the conveyance of the equity of redemption was fraudulent.—Palmer v. Bray, 136 Mich. 85, 98 N.W. 849 (1904).

3350. MCLS § 565.360.

grantee of a missing mortgagor's heir has a right to redeem,[3351] as does the holder of a remainder in the property under the mortgagor.[3352]

A wife having a dower and homestead interest in the land mortgaged by her husband and sold under a foreclosure sale has a right to redeem from the mortgage foreclosure against the husband's property, though she was not a party to the foreclosure proceedings.[3353]

A junior mortgagee has the right to redeem from a foreclosure sale by paying the amount due on the senior mortgage.[3354] The junior mortgagee's right to redeem is not subject to enlargement or abridgement by the courts.[3355]

A junior mortgagee's right to redeem cannot be cut off, prejudiced, or enlarged by an agreement between the mortgagor and the first mortgagee for an extension of time within which to pay off the first mortgage, unless enlargement of the right to redeem is stipulated.[3356] Nor is a junior mortgagee's right affected by a foreclosure judgment and sale under a prior mortgage, where at the time of the judgment and sale no party to the foreclosure suit in any way represented, or had any right or interest in, the junior mortgage.[3357]

But a mortgagee has a right to refuse any tender of the amount due on the mortgage if made by one who, as between the mortgagor and the mortgagee, is a stranger to their dealings, and therefore has no right of redemption.[3358]

Priority among eligible redeemers. The statutes on redemption after a land contract foreclosure are silent on the problem of priority between parties entitled to redeem; therefore, absent any overriding equitable considerations, priority must be granted to the first party to exercise the right of redemption.[3359]

§ 1063.   Time for Redemption and Loss of Right to Redeem

Generally, one redeeming from a foreclosure by advertisement has anywhere from one month to one year from the time of the sale in which to redeem, while one redeeming from a foreclosure by suit has six months in which to redeem.

3351. Squire v. Wright, 85 Mich. 76, 48 N.W. 286 (1891).

3352. Engel v. Ladewig, 153 Mich. 8, 116 N.W. 550 (1908).

3353. Tuller v. Detroit Trust Co., 259 Mich. 670, 244 N.W. 197 (1932).

Moore v. Smith, 95 Mich. 71, 54 N.W. 701 (1893).

3354. Titus v. Cavalier, 276 Mich. 117, 267 N.W. 799 (1936).

Chauvin v. American State Bank, 242 Mich. 269, 218 N.W. 788 (1928).

J.I. Case Threshing Machine Co. v. Mitchell, 74 Mich. 679, 42 N.W. 151 (1889).

Carter v. Lewis, 27 Mich. 241 (1873).

3355. Herman Hughes Lumber Co. v. Wood, 288 Mich. 684, 286 N.W. 126 (1939).

See, also, Jennings v. Moore, 83 Mich. 231, 47 N.W. 127 (1890).

3356. Herman Hughes Lumber Co. v. Wood, 288 Mich. 684, 286 N.W. 126 (1939).

Sager v. Tupper, 35 Mich. 134 (1876).

3357. Avery v. Ryerson, 34 Mich. 362 (1876).

3358. Sinclair v. Learned, 51 Mich. 335, 16 N.W. 672 (1883).

Huxley v. Rice, 40 Mich. 73 (1879).

Harwood v. Underwood, 28 Mich. 427 (1874).

3359. Feldman v. M.J. Associates, 117 Mich. App. 770, 324 N.W.2d 496 (1982).

A party redeeming mortgaged premises sold under foreclosure by advertisement has anywhere from 30 days to one year from the time of the sale in which to redeem, depending on the nature and possession of the property.[3360] A party redeeming premises has six months from the time of the sale if the foreclosure of the mortgage or land contract is by suit.[3361]

The statutory period runs from the day on which the property is sold, not from the date of recording the sheriff's deed.[3362] In computing the time, the day from which the period begins to run is excluded and the day of performance included.[3363]

The parties to a foreclosure may extend the redemption period by agree-

---

3360. MCLS § 600.3240.

Abandoned property redeemable only within 30 days

Though property was apparently not occupied before or after mortgagors' notices of intent to occupy, foreclosure purchaser failed to satisfy statutory requirements for presumptive abandonment of foreclosed property, so as to invoke 30-day redemption period rather than one-year period, where mortgagors' written notices of intent to occupy were given within 15 days of purchaser's affidavit of vacancy.—Gitler v. Oakland County Register of Deeds, 181 Mich. App. 173, 449 N.W.2d 122 (1989).

Mistake in certificate

Where the statute itself fixes the time of redemption on foreclosure of a mortgage, a sheriff's certificate endorsed on it that fixes an impossible time does not destroy the validity of the foreclosure.—Reading v. Waterman, 46 Mich. 107, 8 N.W. 691 (1881).

3361. MCLS § 600.3140.

Holland v. Michigan Nat'l Bank-West, 166 Mich. App. 245, 420 N.W.2d 173 (1988).

Redemption from foreclosure, *see* 17 Wayne L. Rev. 641 (1971).

Bankruptcy

Where Chapter 11 debtor and creditor bank failed to obtain stay of order permitting liquidating and disbursing agent to sell debtor's single asset, an office building, pursuant to liquidation plan submitted by creditor-insurance company, appeal of order by debtor and bank was rendered moot and no exception to bankruptcy's mootness rule under state law was applicable since six-month window permitted by state statute for redemption of commercial property lawfully sold had long since closed.—255 Park Plaza Assocs. Ltd. P'ship v. Connecticut Gen. Life Ins. Co., 100 F.3d 1214 (6th Cir. Mich. 1996).

The 6-month period for redeeming property from a foreclosure sale is extended by 60 days under the bankruptcy code; a junior mortgage holder's rights were not extinguished where it

redeemed the property before the expiration of the extended redemption period.—In re Parlovecchio, 315 B.R. 694 (Bankr. E.D. Mich. 2004).

Loss of right to rescind transaction

Because a mortgagor's failure to redeem the property within six months after the foreclosure sale terminated his right to rescind the mortgage transaction, the mortgagor's claims that the mortgagee violated the federal Truth in Lending Act and the state Secondary Mortgage Loan Act failed; completion of the foreclosure action terminated any right to rescind the transaction under federal or state law.—Worthy v. World Wide Fin. Servs., 347 F. Supp. 2d 502 (E.D. Mich. 2004), aff'd, 192 Fed. Appx. 369, 2006 U.S. App. LEXIS 19458 (6th Cir. Mich. July 28, 2006).

Redemption after quitclaim

In lieu of granting leave to appeal, the Supreme Court vacated the portion of the Court of Appeals decision holding that a lis pendens was invalid, and affirmed the trial court's conclusion that, regardless of the validity of the lis pendens, any rights the plaintiff held under the lis pendens were merged into and extinguished by the quitclaim deed; thus, because plaintiff failed to exercise its right of redemption, plaintiff's rights to the property were extinguished when the redemption period expired and the foreclosure became final.—Ruby & Associates v. Shore Fin. Servs., 480 Mich. 1107, 745 N.W.2d 752 (2008).

Rights to property acquired through a quitclaim were extinguished when the grantee failed to redeem the property during the redemption period following foreclosure; the redemption period began running before the quitclaim and expired the day following the quitclaim.—Ruby & Assocs. v. Shore Financial Servs., 276 Mich. App. 110, 741 N.W.2d 72 (2007), vacated on other grounds, 480 Mich. 1107, 745 N.W.2d 752 (2008).

3362. Young v. Union Joint Stock Land Bank, 266 Mich. 83, 253 N.W. 225 (1934).

Trombly v. Klersy, 147 Mich. 370, 110 N.W. 940 (1907).

1928–1930 Op. Atty. Gen. 884.

3363. Perkins v. Century Ins. Co., 303 Mich. 679, 7 N.W.2d 106 (1942).

ment.[3364] Even a verbal agreement is not within the statute of frauds and is enforceable.[3365]

The court may extend the period for redeeming in case of fraud, accident, or mistake.[3366] But before a court is justified in extending the time of redemption, equitable grounds must clearly appear.[3367] A pending condemnation that would give mortgagor award to apply to redemption is not grounds for an extension of the period of redemption.[3368]

The failure to redeem within the redemption period after a foreclosure of a first mortgage passes title to the purchaser at the foreclosure.[3369] It precludes redemption by a second mortgagee or the second mortgagee's successor.[3370]

The maxim, "Once a mortgage always a mortgage," does not mean that a right

3364. Proof of agreement

Failure of defendant in suit for specific performance of verbal agreement for extension of redemption period of one year after foreclosure of mortgage on realty, to produce available evidence in corroboration of defendant's testimony that defendant was away from his office for a week at time plaintiff claimed extension was agreed upon during telephone call plaintiff allegedly made to defendant at defendant's office, merely gave rise to inference of fact in favor of plaintiff and did not justify reversal of finding that plaintiff failed to meet burden of proof as to making of such agreement for extension.—Macklem v. Warren Constr. Co., 343 Mich. 334, 72 N.W.2d 60 (1955).

3365. Macklem v. Warren Constr. Co., 343 Mich. 334, 72 N.W.2d 60 (1955).

3366. Detroit Trust Co. v. George, 262 Mich. 362, 247 N.W. 697 (1933).

Mortgage & Contract Co. v. Kupalian, 249 Mich. 577, 229 N.W. 416 (1930).

McIntyre v. Wyckoff, 119 Mich. 557, 78 N.W. 654 (1899) (an allowance of 20 days in which to pay the amount found due was not unreasonable).

Equitable extension of redemption period

When a statute specifies the requirements for redemption, there is no room for an equitable extension of the redemption period absent fraud, accident, or mistake.—Deutsche Bank Trust Co. Ams. v. Spot Realty, Inc., 269 Mich. App. 607, 714 N.W.2d 409 (2005).

Mistake as to length of redemption period is not grounds for extension

Mortgagor's mistake in believing that period of redemption was one year rather than six months would not permit an equitable extension of period to redeem from statutory foreclosure sale by advertisement and posting of notice.—Schulthies v. Barron, 16 Mich. App. 246, 167 N.W.2d 784 (1969).

3367. Palmer v. Palmer, 194 Mich. 79, 160 N.W. 404 (1916).

Schulthies v. Barron, 16 Mich. App. 246, 167 N.W.2d 784 (1969).

Violation of injunction

A record showing that mortgage foreclosure sale was held in violation of injunction against such foreclosure authorized granting mortgagor the right to redeem after expiration of redemption period, notwithstanding determination that mortgage was valid.—Scef v. Scef, 292 Mich. 354, 290 N.W. 826 (1940).

3368. Detroit Trust Co. v. George, 262 Mich. 362, 247 N.W. 697 (1933).

3369. Flax v. Mutual Bldg. & Loan Ass'n, 198 Mich. 676, 165 N.W. 835 (1917).

Tender within redemption period

Where a dispute existed between mortgagor and mortgagee as to amount necessary for mortgagor to pay to redeem premises from foreclosure sale, a tender by a mortgagor of an amount claimed sufficient to redeem property, after expiration of statutory redemption period, came too late, since, if mortgagor desired to preserve his rights, a tender had to have been made while statutory redemption period was still running, because thereafter absolute title vested in mortgagee.—Strempek v. First Nat'l Bank, 293 Mich. 435, 292 N.W. 358 (1940).

3370. Dunitz v. Braver, 252 Mich. 111, 233 N.W. 347 (1930).

Gantz v. Toles, 40 Mich. 725 (1879).

Action to redeem allowed

Where a second mortgagee demands the right to redeem after the foreclosure of a first mortgage by the payment of the first mortgage debt and interest after a foreclosure of it, which is claimed to be invalid, and the first mortgagee fails to give a positive answer to offer until after the expiration of the time of redemption, though frequently urged to do so, the conduct of the latter will authorize a bill to redeem by the second mortgagee after the expiration of redemption period, on payment of

of redemption cannot be lost except under foreclosure.[3371] Thus, a deed given as a mortgage may subsequently be changed by the parties to an absolute deed.[3372]

Foreclosure by suit[3373] being equitable in nature, the right to redeem may also be barred by laches.[3374]

Where the assignee of a mortgagee succeeds in foreclosing without the knowledge of a half owner of the land, the latter may redeem; but, if, with knowledge of the fraud, the half owner purchases the equity of redemption and accepts half of the surplus money paid at the sale, that owner is not entitled to redeem.[3375]

§ 1064. Amount Required to Redeem

The redemption amount is the amount that the purchaser at the foreclosure paid plus allowable costs and advances.

The amount to be paid by a party redeeming property sold under foreclosure of a mortgage or a land contract is the sum bid for the property at the sale, plus interest from the time of the sale at the rate borne by the mortgage or land contract.[3376]

If the purchaser, following the sale on foreclosure by suit, has paid a sum as taxes assessed against the property or premiums upon the insurance policies covering any buildings located on the property which, under the terms of the mortgage, it would have been the duty of the mortgagor to have paid had the mortgage not been foreclosed, and which premiums are necessary to keep the policy in force until the expiration of the period of redemption, the taxes and premiums may also be included in the amount due.[3377] The same is true on foreclosure by

---

debt and costs of foreclosure.—Brown v. Burney, 128 Mich. 205, 87 N.W. 221 (1901).

3371. Sauer v. Fischer, 247 Mich. 283, 225 N.W. 518 (1929).

3372. Hoffman v. Harrington, 33 Mich. 392 (1876).

3373. MCLS § 600.3180.

3374. Hoffman v. Harrington, 33 Mich. 392 (1876).

Smith v. O'Dell, 240 Mich. 185, 215 N.W. 408 (1927) (laches of purchaser defaulting under unrecorded a land contract divested his claim to property of any equitable standing against one foreclosing mortgage).

Right not barred

Where in a suit to redeem, defendants recognized plaintiff's ownership of the property up to a short time before suit was brought, but withheld from her the true facts as regarded payments made, and, knowing her claims, acted in defiance of her rights, knowing that she did not acquiesce in defendants' position, plaintiff's right to redeem was not barred by laches, the delay having worked

no injury to defendants which could not be redressed.—Cusick v. Spencer, 149 Mich. 434, 112 N.W. 1111 (1907).

3375. Norton v. Tharp, 53 Mich. 146, 18 N.W. 601, 1884 Mich. LEXIS 653 (1884).

3376. MCLS §§ 600.3140, 600.3240.

Heimerdinger v. Heimerdinger, 299 Mich. 149, 299 N.W. 844 (1941).

Dryden State Bank v. Fisher, 256 Mich. 314, 239 N.W. 330 (1931) (amount need not be paid to register of deeds).

Stewart v. Isbell, 155 Mich. App. 65, 399 N.W.2d 440 (1986) (interest from the time of the sale at the rate borne by a land contract).

Payment of interest

On the redemption of a mortgage securing notes bearing interest payable semiannually, interest on the unpaid interest should be allowed.—Millard v. Truax, 73 Mich. 381, 41 N.W. 328 (1889).

3377. MCLS § 600.3145.

Buchta v. Lehmann, 263 Mich. 41, 248 N.W. 542 (1933).

advertisement, except that in addition to taxes and insurance premiums paid, the redemption amount can be made to include amounts necessary to redeem senior liens from foreclosure, condo fees, and homeowner or community association assessments.[3378]

Similarly, where the purchaser makes necessary and reasonable repairs and improvements on the premises after foreclosure of a mortgage, the purchaser is entitled to a reasonable allowance for their cost in a suit to redeem.[3379]

If desired by the mortgagors, an accounting may be had at the end of the period of redemption.[3380] A mortgagee or purchaser in actual possession of the premises is chargeable with the rents from the time of taking possession up to the final settlement.[3381]

A redemption from a statutory foreclosure cannot be conditioned on the payment of any allowances in the nature of fees beyond those authorized by statute.[3382]

A redemptioner may redeem a distinct lot or parcel sold separately, leaving a portion of the premises unredeemed. The foreclosure sale deed becomes inoperative relative to the redeemed parcel or lot and remains valid concerning the rest.[3383]

If the amount necessary to redeem the premises is in dispute, the mortgagor may obtain relief and protection of his or her rights by tendering the amount necessary to redeem during the redemption period, although the mortgagee refuses to accept the tender.[3384] Where the failure to tender the amount due is caused by the mortgagee's own fraudulent conduct in hindering the mortgagor from raising the money necessary, the mortgagee is estopped from setting up that fact as a defense in a suit by the mortgagor to compel an assignment of the mortgage.[3385]

§ 1065. Suits to Redeem

A suit may be instituted under certain circumstances to enforce the right of redemption or set aside a deed given on a statutory foreclosure.

Millard v. Truax, 73 Mich. 381, 41 N.W. 328 (1889).

3378. MCLS § 600.3240.

3379. Cusick v. Spencer, 149 Mich. 434, 112 N.W. 1111 (1907).

Taines v. Munson, 42 Mich. App. 256, 201 N.W.2d 685 (1972).

3380. Palazzini v. Vanasco, 292 Mich. 317, 290 N.W. 811 (1940).

Shuler v. Bonander, 80 Mich. 531, 45 N.W. 487 (1890).

Resolution of doubtful questions

In determining the amount due on mortgages assigned to mortgagee's agent, who had been exceedingly careless in looking after mortgagee's interest in property during a period of years so long as to render the memory of witnesses unreliable, doubtful questions will be resolved in favor of subsequent purchasers of the mortgaged premises in their suit for an accounting for the amount due.—Clark v. Sheldon, 223 Mich. 323, 193 N.W. 876 (1923).

3381. Miller v. Peter, 158 Mich. 336, 122 N.W. 780 (1909).

Kunz v. Torcellini, 51 Mich. App. 742, 216 N.W.2d 479 (1974).

3382. Vosburgh v. Lay, 45 Mich. 455, 8 N.W. 91 (1881).

Liability for attorney fees

Millard v. Truax, 50 Mich. 343, 15 N.W. 501 (1883).

Kennedy v. Brown, 50 Mich. 336, 15 N.W. 498 (1883).

3383. MCLS §§ 600.3140, 600.3240.

3384. Strempek v. First Nat'l Bank, 293 Mich. 435, 292 N.W. 358 (1940).

3385. Moore v. Smith, 95 Mich. 71, 54 N.W. 701 (1893).

A suit may be instituted to enforce the right of redemption or to set aside a deed given on a statutory foreclosure.[3386] Accordingly, a party may bring an action seeking redemption on the basis that the purchaser at the foreclosure sale purchased the property in order to allow the redemptioner a further time for redemption.[3387] All persons materially interested in a suit or in the subject matter, such as the spouse of the mortgagor, must be made parties to the suit.[3388]

A complaint to redeem must show that the plaintiff has an interest in the equity of redemption,[3389] and is entitled to relief.[3390] Reliance cannot be put upon an assignment to the plaintiff of an equity of redemption that is not alleged in the complaint.[3391]

The plaintiff has the burden of proving an alleged extension of time for redemption from a mortgage foreclosure.[3392] An verbal agreement to extend the redemption period must be established by a preponderance of the evidence.[3393] A defendant to an action to redeem will not be allowed to increase the amount due upon the mortgage by proving an agreement to pay a higher rate of interest than

3386. Hawes v. Detroit Fire & Marine Ins. Co., 109 Mich. 324, 67 N.W. 329 (1896).

3387. Decree for redemption allowed

Where the equity of redemption from a foreclosure sale is of considerable value, and it appears that defendant in the foreclosure understood that one who purchased it from the vendee at the sale took the title to allow him to redeem, and therefore gave up efforts to obtain money from other sources for that purpose, he is entitled to a decree for redemption and an accounting.—Newman v. Locke, 66 Mich. 27, 36 N.W. 166 (1887).

3388. Hawes v. Detroit Fire & Marine Ins. Co., 109 Mich. 324, 67 N.W. 329 (1896).

Sanborn v. Sanborn, 104 Mich. 180, 62 N.W. 371 (1895).

Glass v. Glass, 50 Mich. 289, 15 N.W. 460 (1883).

3389. Smith v. Austin, 9 Mich. 465 (1862).

Subsequent mortgagee

If complaint to redeem from a mortgage averred that plaintiff owned a certain mortgage, subsequent to that of defendant, and was not demurred to, it could be sustained, notwithstanding it failed to set forth facts showing that plaintiff's mortgage and that from which he sought to redeem were mortgages in the same chain of title.—Lamb v. Jeffrey, 47 Mich. 28, 10 N.W. 65 (1881).

3390. Drayton v. Chandler, 93 Mich. 383, 53 N.W. 558 (1892) (complaint to set aside the sheriff's deed, and have the foreclosure proceed-

ings declared void, and praying general relief, was sufficient as a complaint to redeem).

Cause of action not stated

Complaint alleging execution of mortgage securing $65,000 and payment by plaintiffs to defendant of $15,000 cash, that on a specified date, plaintiffs were coerced into acknowledging an indebtedness of some $54,000 and executed a lease of the premises with option to purchase, when considered with the undisputed answer that mortgage had been foreclosed and property sold for some $51,000 and on the last day of the period of redemption, the lease and option was delivered, did not state a cause of action for accounting and reconveyance of mortgaged premises on theory that plaintiffs had been coerced into signing the agreement.—Grevnin v. Collateral Liquidation, 302 Mich. 274, 4 N.W.2d 547 (1942).

3391. Glass v. Glass, 50 Mich. 289, 15 N.W. 460 (1883).

3392. Chauvin v. American State Bank, 242 Mich. 269, 218 N.W. 788 (1928) (evidence was insufficient to show extension of time for redemption from mortgage foreclosure).

Right to redeem not established

In action to extend time of redemption from statutory foreclosure, evidence of negotiations between plaintiff and defendant for purchase of plaintiff's equity, not showing misleading representations, did not establish plaintiff's right to redeem.—Palmer v. Palmer, 194 Mich. 79, 160 N.W. 404 (1916).

3393. Macklem v. Warren Constr. Co., 343 Mich. 334, 72 N.W.2d 60 (1955).

called for in the mortgage and not mentioned in the pleadings.[3394]

Judgment. Generally, a judgment in an action to redeem mortgaged land may not be for a strict foreclosure, but should direct a sale on the failure to pay the redemption money.[3395] However, resale will not be ordered when to do so is obviously inequitable or an idle ceremony because of the confessed inability of the complaining party to redeem even if opportunity to do so is afforded.[3396] If the mortgagee has conveyed his or her interest to another defendant before the filing of the bill, the judgment must require the amount due from the plaintiff to be paid to the assignee, and not the mortgagee.[3397]

Where redemption is allowed and the case referred for an accounting with leave to take further testimony, the decree may be affirmed without a full examination of the transactions involved until a later stage of the case, if it is clearly apparent from the record that the plaintiff is entitled to the particular relief asked for.[3398]

Costs. Costs must ordinarily be paid by the plaintiff,[3399] unless the defendant unreasonably refuses to receive money when it is tendered to the defendant,[3400] or refuses to notify the plaintiff of the amount due.[3401]

§ 1066. Operation and Effect

A redemption has the effect of rendering a deed obtained on a foreclosure sale void and of no effect to the extent of the property redeemed. A valid redemption of property after foreclosure of a land contract generally operates to cut off the redemption rights of other parties entitled to redeem.

Under foreclosure by advertisement[3402] and foreclosure by suit,[3403] a redemption has the effect of rendering a deed obtained on a foreclosure sale void and of no effect to the extent of the property redeemed.[3404] The redemption satisfies the

3394. Fosdick v. Van Husan, 21 Mich. 567 (1870).

3395. Leach v. Grube, 147 Mich. 348, 110 N.W. 1076 (1907).

Meigs v. McFarlan, 72 Mich. 194, 40 N.W. 246 (1888).

Newkirk v. Newkirk, 56 Mich. 525, 23 N.W. 206 (1885).

Grover v. Fox, 36 Mich. 461 (1877).

Fosdick v. Van Husan, 21 Mich. 567 (1870).

Removal of cloud on title

Judgment granting mortgagor's wife right to redeem from foreclosure on equitable conditions should also have decreed foreclosure of right and removal of it as cloud on mortgagee's title, if she failed to redeem, as prayed in mortgagee's counterclaim.—Tuller v. Detroit Trust Co., 259 Mich. 670, 244 N.W. 197 (1932).

3396. Tuller v. Detroit Trust Co., 259 Mich. 670, 244 N.W. 197 (1932).

3397. Emerson v. Atwater, 12 Mich. 314 (1864).

3398. Curtis v. Sheldon, 47 Mich. 262, 11 N.W. 151, 1882 Mich. LEXIS 626 (1882).

3399. Lamb v. Jeffrey, 47 Mich. 28, 10 N.W. 65 (1881).

3400. Lamb v. Jeffrey, 47 Mich. 28, 10 N.W. 65 (1881).

Lamb v. Jeffrey, 41 Mich. 719, 3 N.W. 204 (1879).

3401. Meigs v. McFarlan, 72 Mich. 194, 40 N.W. 246 (1888).

3402. MCLS § 600.3240.

3403. MCLS § 600.3140.

3404. Steinhauser v. Kuhn, 50 Mich. 367, 15 N.W. 513 (1883).

Feldman v. M.J. Associates, 117 Mich. App. 770, 324 N.W.2d 496 (1982).

mortgage lien and is not an assignment of the mortgage.[3405] Thus, the mortgagee or a purchaser cannot assert title to the property after having received payment for his or her interest in it.[3406]

It is the duty of the person receiving the redemption money to have the mortgage discharged from the record of the register of deeds after a foreclosure by suit.[3407]

A valid redemption of property after foreclosure of a land contract generally operates to cut off the redemption rights of other parties entitled to redeem.[3408]

Nonetheless, a party redeeming from a sale secures such an interest in the land as is necessary to protect that party.[3409] Where a conveyance of mortgaged lands is set aside, except as to a homestead interest, at the suit of an execution creditor, the grantee, on redeeming from the mortgage foreclosure, is entitled, in the absence of special circumstances, to be subrogated to the full extent of the mortgage lien against a purchaser at the execution sale.[3410] Liens junior to the mortgage that is redeemed are not cut off when the redemption is made by the mortgagor or by one to whom the mortgagor has conveyed before foreclosure.[3411]

A purchaser of property at a tax sale of that property merely restores the chain of title and equity should enforce all contracts that existed prior to the tax sale where the sale is necessitated by a breach of a covenant to pay taxes. Although the statute on redemption after foreclosure by suit of a land contract does not contain an analogous provision, equitable considerations justify application of similar enforcement of prior contracts where the sale and redemption of the property is necessitated by the vendee's failure to make the payments on the land contract.[3412]

Redemption from partial foreclosure

A quitclaim obtained by the mortgagor from the mortgagee of premises for the purpose of perfecting title by redeeming from a sale on partial foreclosure cannot be construed as discharging the entire mortgage.—Mabie v. Hatinger, 48 Mich. 341, 12 N.W. 198 (1882).

3405. Lieblien v. Hansen, 178 Mich. 11, 144 N.W. 496 (1913).

3406. Dryden State Bank v. Fisher, 256 Mich. 314, 239 N.W. 330 (1931).

3407. MCLS §§ 600.3140, 600.3244, 600.6070

3408. Feldman v. M.J. Associates, 117 Mich. App. 770, 324 N.W.2d 496 (1982).

3409. Moore v. Smith, 95 Mich. 71, 54 N.W. 701 (1893).

Equitable right to lien for redemption money on first mortgage

Where a second mortgagee who had redeemed from a prior mortgage failed to receive reimbursement when his own mortgage was discharged by redemption, redemption from the first mortgage created no merger of the liens, but rather the claims were separate and distinct, and paying one could not release the other, in which case an action to enforce the lien for the redemption money was allowed.—Powers v. Golden Lumber Co., 43 Mich. 468, 5 N.W. 656 (1880).

3410. Wolcott v. Tweddle, 133 Mich. 389, 95 N.W. 419 (1903).

3411. Piech v. Beaty, 298 Mich. 535, 299 N.W. 705 (1941).

Walsh v. Robinson, 135 Mich. 16, 97 N.W. 55 (1903).

3412. Feldman v. M.J. Associates, 117 Mich. App. 770, 324 N.W.2d 496 (1982).